Applied Topics in Health

Applied Topics in Health Psychology

Edited by

Marie L. Caltabiano and Lina A. Ricciardelli

A John Wiley & Sons, Ltd., Publication

Library of Congress Cataloging-in-Publication Data

Applied topics in health psychology / edited by Marie Louise Caltabiano and Lina Ricciardelli.
    p. ; cm.
  Includes index.
  ISBN 978-1-119-97193-1 (pbk.)
  I. Caltabiano, Marie L., 1959–   II. Ricciardelli, Lina.
  [DNLM: 1. Health Behavior–Australia.   2. Attitude to Health–Australia.   3. Behavioral
Medicine–Australia.   4. Evidence-Based Medicine–Australia.   W 85]
  616.8900994–dc23

                                                                                      2012017996

A catalogue record for this book is available from the British Library.

Cover image: Mountain Biker © Imre Forgo / Fotolia
                Couple Walking Dog Along Pavement © moodboard Premium / Fotolia
                Family Football Game © ClickPop / Fotolia
Cover design by Nicki Averill Design.

Set in 9/12pt Minion by Aptara Inc., New Delhi, India

1   2013

Contents

Contents

Contents

About the Editors

Associate Professor Marie L. Caltabiano teaches in the Department of Psychology in the School of Arts and Social Sciences at James Cook University Cairns campus. She is a Member of the Australian Psychological Society (APS), the American Psychological Association, the Public Health Association of Australia, and the College of Health Psychologists. She is the Membership Secretary on the national executive of the APS College of Health Psychologists. Marie has 20 years of teaching experience in clinical health psychology and is a recipient of both an Australian Learning & Teaching Citation (ALTC) and a James Cook University Faculty Teaching Citation 2010 for Outstanding Contribution to Student Learning. Marie is coauthor of *Health Psychology: Biopsychosocial Interactions* now in its second Australasian edition. Her principal areas of research are psychosocial aspects of health, stress, and coping; health promotion and disease prevention; women's health in particular the climateric; Type 2 diabetes and self-regulation; adult attachment and health processes; social self-efficacy within the doctor–patient relationship; caregiving in dementia; and resilient aging. Marie has published five books and close to 100 papers in refereed conference proceedings and journals, both nationally and internationally.

Associate Professor Lina A. Ricciardelli completed her postgraduate training at the University of Adelaide, Australia, in 1990. She is currently an Associate Professor in the School of Psychology at Deakin University, and the Chair of the College of Health Psychologists in the Australian Psychological Society. Lina has published over 100 papers in the fields of health psychology, developmental psychology, and substance use. A large focus of her research has been on the role that sociocultural factors play in the development of body image, and other health risk behaviors among children, adolescents, and adults. These have included gender-role stereotypes, sport, the media, peers, social comparisons, acculturation, and the family. In the last 5 years she has also focused on the body image and related health behaviors among males from a range of cultural backgrounds which include Indigenous Australians, Indigenous and Indian Fijians, Tongans, and Chinese men living in Australia.

About the Contributors

Felicity C. Allen is an adjunct Associate Professor at Monash University and works as a consultant. Having recently completed a second book on health psychology in Australia, Felicity is interested in both health psychology and equal opportunity. Some of her research, for example, a recent evaluation of the needs of people with disabilities in Victoria combines both areas. Felicity has a strong commitment to promoting positive health behaviors (e.g., exercise). She has considerable experience in evaluating the intervention strategies of major public and private sector employers and service providers. Felicity has written three books and coauthored two novels, numerous articles, chapters, and monographs, and presented at 25 conferences. She is the Chair of the Melbourne Branch of the Australian Psychological Society.

Delwyn Bartlett is an Associate Professor in the Central Clinical School of Medicine at the University of Sydney; a registered psychologist who has been predominantly working in the area of sleep health and psychology since 1993. She is a member of the College of Health Psychologists. Delwyn is a Coordinator of Medical Psychology at the Woolcock Institute of Medical Research and is involved in a number of sleep research projects relating to treatment interventions for insomnia (adolescents, adults, and older adults with mild cognitive impairment), the neurobehavioral effects of untreated obstructive sleep apnea (OSA), and interventions to increase adherence to continuous positive airway pressure (CPAP) with cognitive behavior therapy, motivational interviewing, and health coaching.

Lee Beames is a Clinical Psychologist and has completed postgraduate Master's training at the University of Queensland. He has 25 years' experience in public sector health services predominantly in mental health, alcohol and drug, and health psychology at the Prince Charles Hospital. He has 10 years' experience in a drug and alcohol community clinic. As well as significant clinical experience, he has over 20 years' experience supervising postgraduate psychology students, GPs, psychiatrists in training, and clinical psychologists. On top of clinical and supervision roles he has been Director of Psychology at the Prince Charles Hospital since 1995 and also has a small private practice.

Lisa Beatty works at Flinders University and Flinders Medical Centre in Adelaide, South Australia, as a Clinical Psychologist and Postdoctoral Research Fellow. She has considerable research and clinical experience in providing psychological therapy for individuals affected by cancer, including developing accessible psychological interventions. Her PhD dissertation focused on developing and evaluating self-help workbooks for women with breast cancer, and current research directions include evaluating an Internet self-help coping program for patients and partners. Lisa also has extensive experience in providing individual and group psychological therapy, using cognitive behavior therapy as a primary therapeutic framework. She has a number of publications in the area of adjustment to cancer, and is a regular presenter at psycho-oncology conferences.

Ann Bonner is a registered nurse with extensive clinical experience which enables her to bring a dual perspective on research and practice. She is Professor of Nursing in the School of Nursing, Queensland University of Technology and Visiting Research Fellow, Royal Brisbane and Women's Hospital. She has established collaborative multidisciplinary research related to chronic conditions, supervises doctoral students, and coordinates postgraduate nursing courses. Ann is recognized nationally and internationally as an expert renal nurse, and is the invited Chair of the Scientific Committee for the Renal Society of Australasia and is the Associate Editor of the society's international peer-reviewed journal. Since 2006 she has published 19 book chapters and 50 journal articles in the nursing literature.

Leah Brennan is a Clinical, Health, and Educational and Developmental Psychologist. Leah's research interests involve the application of psychological approaches to understand, prevent, and treat obesity, eating disorders, and their psychosocial comorbidities in children, adolescents, and adults. She is particularly interested in the development, evaluation, and dissemination of evidence-based interventions for the treatment of obesity, eating disorders, and their psychosocial comorbidities across the lifespan. Leah had worked in a range of clinical settings targeting the treatment of eating and weight disorders within inpatient, outpatient, and community-based services.

Colette Browning is a Professor and Co-Director of the Melbourne Longitudinal Studies on Healthy Ageing Program, an ongoing longitudinal study of older people living in Melbourne that commenced in 1994. Colette Browning holds the position of Research Professor in Healthy Ageing at Monash University. She is recognized as a national and international leader in psychology and health with a special focus on healthy aging and chronic illness. She is a Fellow of the Australian Psychological Society. She has edited books including *Behavioural Change: An Evidence-Based Handbook for Social and Public Health* and is the series editor, with Professor Shane Thomas, of the forthcoming book series *Healthy Ageing* for Springer Publications.

Sue Burney is an Adjunct Senior Lecturer, School of Psychology and Psychiatry, Faculty of Medicine, Nursing and Health Sciences, Monash University and Head, Cabrini Monash Psycho-oncology Research Unit. She is also a practicing Health Psychologist with a particular interest in the identification and management of the distress associated with a diagnosis of cancer and family-focused grief therapy. She is a member of the Victorian Cooperative Oncology Psycho-Oncology committee and is actively involved in supervising postgraduate research and clinical students and running seminars on psycho-oncology issues for health professionals. She is currently the lead investigator on a range of research projects concerned with the treatment side effects of cancer and the supportive care needs of patients, their carers, and families.

Mitchell K. Byrne is a Clinical and Forensic psychologist with 25 years' experience in the provision of applied psychological services. He has worked in both government and private services across several states in Australia and in the UK. Since 1997 he has also held full-time academic positions and is currently a Senior Lecturer on the Clinical Training program at the University of Wollongong.

Mitchell completed his PhD in 2009 in the area of medication adherence, receiving the Australian Psychological Society's 2009 Award for Excellent PhD Thesis in Psychology. He routinely delivers training to healthcare providers on the enhancement of adherence across multiple chronic illnesses.

Nerina J. Caltabiano is a Senior Lecturer in the Department of Psychology, James Cook University. Both her Honours degree and PhD were in social psychology, namely nonverbal behavior in children and attitudes towards compulsive casino gamblers. She is a member of the Australian and the American Psychological Societies. She publishes within the area of social and development psychology and also supervises higher degree research students in these areas. Together with her collaborators she has been the recipient of several grants including some internal faculty grants, an Australian Rotary Health Research Fund, a Cairns Campus, James Cook University Student Association Grant, Education Queensland grant, and an ARC Discovery Grant.

Jennifer Chamberlain-Salaun completed a Bachelor of Arts degree and a Certificate of Business before gaining extensive experience in the primary healthcare sector. In 2009 and 2010 she was a recipient of Primary Health Care Research, Evaluation and Development grants. For the past 2 years she has worked as a research assistant in the James Cook University (JCU) School of Nursing, Midwifery and Nutrition. Jennifer has been a research team member in qualitative research studies covering topics such as disaster management, community rehabilitation, simulation in nursing education, cervical screening, and mentoring circles. She has completed a Certificate in Research Methods and is a current PhD candidate in the JCU School of Nursing, Midwifery and Nutrition.

Anna Chur-Hansen is a Professor and registered Health Psychologist and a Fellow of the Australian Psychological Society. She is a long-standing member of the College of Health Psychologists. Anna has written over 100 papers in the areas of health professional education and health psychology. In the latter area she has focused on patients' perceptions of their health and illness, and the role of companion animals in physical and psychological health. She is a member of the School of Medicine, Discipline of Psychiatry, at the University of Adelaide.

Jason P. Connor is an Associate Professor in Health and Clinical Psychology, Director of the Centre for Youth Substance Abuse Research, the University of Queensland and a National Health and Medical Research Council (NH&MRC) of Australia Career Development Fellow. He is a member of the Australian Psychological Society (APS) College of Health Psychologists and APS College of Clinical Psychologists. He has coordinated advanced postgraduate health psychology courses, as well as advanced courses in clinical psychopathology and disabilities and rehabilitation. Dr Connor's research in the field of addiction is characterized by cross-disciplinary fertilization of molecular biology, clinical pharmacology, epidemiology, and information technology. Specific research themes include understanding the psychological mechanisms that contribute to addiction, identification of genes associated with alcohol and nicotine dependence, and youth substance abuse.

Lyn G. Courtney a registered Psychologist, is nearing completion of a PhD in the Department of Psychology, James Cook University (JCU) investigating successful aging of Australian baby boom career women. She is a member of the Australian Psychological Society, the American Psychological Association, the International Society of Quality of Life Studies, Australia Research Council/National Health and Medical Research Council, and the International Wellbeing Group. Lyn is a senior research associate working on Australian Research Council Linkage Grants and part of the JCU Cairns Institute, utilizing her proficiencies in research protocols and statistical analysis. She has an extensive publication record and is the recipient of five publication awards. Additionally, Lyn has 6 years' teaching experience at JCU Australia and JCU Singapore.

Robert A. Cummins has held a Personal Chair in Psychology at Deakin University since 1997. He has published widely on the topic of quality of life and is regarded as an international authority in this area. He is a Fellow of the International Society for Quality-of-Life Studies and the Australian Psychological Society. He is on the editorial board of 11 journals and is an editor of the *Journal of Happiness Studies*. His research concerns quality-of-life theory and how such understanding can be used to improve the life experience of people who are disadvantaged.

Nichola Davis is a general practitioner in North Queensland and a Senior Lecturer and the Academic Coordinator of Year 4 MBBS at the Cairns Clinical School of James Cook University School of Medicine and Dentistry. Nichola is also a medicolegal advisor for the medical indemnity organization MIPS and has extensive experience in medicolegal issues and the delivery of risk management education to health professionals. A director and former chairperson of General Practice Cairns (Cairns Division of General Practice), Nichola has over 25 years experience in broad-based clinical practice and has played a leading role in advocacy and lobbying for primary healthcare in North Queensland.

Justine L. Ebenreuter is a Clinical Psychologist who graduated from Bond University as a Master of Psychology in 2010. During her studies she was a teaching fellow and completed an externship at the Gold Coast Hospital Neuropsychology Rehabilitation Ward. Justine currently works at the Department of Human Services, in their assessment team on the Gold Coast, conducting complex assessments for work capacity and also works with children and their families in a community clinic setting. Justine's research interests were initially on leadership styles and her current focus is on subclinical diagnostic criteria of eating disorders. She is working with Richard Hicks on further developments in the measurement and assessment of eating disorders and their health correlates.

Jane Fletcher is an Adjunct Lecturer, School of Psychology and Psychiatry, Faculty of Medicine, Nursing and Health Sciences, Monash University and Deputy Head, Cabrini Monash Psycho-oncology Research Unit. Jane also runs a private psycho-oncology clinical practice at Cabrini and has many years experience working in a range of cancer agencies. She is currently the Chair of the Victorian Cooperative Oncology Group Psycho-oncology Committee and was actively involved in the development and dissemination of the Australian Clinical Practice Guidelines for the Psychosocial Care of Adults with Cancer. She is also involved in a range of psycho-oncology research projects and student supervision at Cabrini Health.

Matthew Fuller-Tyszkiewicz completed his PhD on the relationship between dissociation and disordered eating symptomatology in 2008. He is currently a lecturer in the School of Psychology at Deakin University. Matthew's primary research interests include sociocultural determinants of body image dissatisfaction and the health implications of body image disturbances. He is currently exploring the extent to which contextual influences on body image satisfaction can be explained by traditionally recognized risk factors for body image disturbances and eating disorders.

Janette Gale is a Health Psychologist and founder and Managing Director of Health Change Australia (HCA). HCA is one of the major trainers of health practitioners in health behavior change techniques for chronic condition prevention, self-management, and rehabilitation in Australia. Janette consults to government and industry on the implementation and evaluation of health behavior change protocols in clinical practice and in health coaching-based programs.

Alan W. Gemmill is a Senior Research Fellow at the Parent-Infant Research Institute (PIRI). An ecologist by training, he has published across the evolutionary, medical, and psychological fields with an overarching interest in the pathologies associated with reproductive processes. Alan has focused on perinatal mental health research for 13 years, with a specific interest in the identification and prevention of maternal mental health problems and in the conduct of treatment randomized controlled trials. He has considerable experience in the implementation of screening programs for perinatal mood disorders.

J. Robert Grove is a Winthrop Professor in the School of Sport Science, Exercise and Health at the University of Western Australia. He is a member of the College of Health Psychologists and the College of Sport and Exercise Psychologists within the Australian Psychological Society. Bob has published more than 140 chapters, articles, or reviews in academic and professional outlets. His publications have focused on the anxiety-reducing effects of exercise, exercise as a component of cognitive behavior therapies for smoking cessation and weight loss, exercise as a treatment for chronic fatigue syndrome, the impact of exercise on self-perceptions and mental health, and the development of exercise habits.

Chyrisse Heine is a speech pathologist and audiologist. She is a Senior Research Fellow at Monash University, School of Primary Health Care and a lecturer at La Trobe University, School of Human Communication Sciences. Chyrisse is a Fellow of Speech Pathology Australia and has received the Audiology Australia Certificate of Outstanding Service. Her research focuses on healthy aging and the assessment and management of communication and quality-of-life issues in older adults with vision and/or hearing loss. Chyrisse also has a special interest in (central) auditory processing disorder and is recognized as a national and international expert in this area.

Richard E. Hicks is Professor of Psychology at Bond University; he has published more than 200 articles, books, chapters, psychological tests, surveys, and classroom simulations and exercises. He has also presented numerous conference papers. He supervises students in a range of organizational, clinical, counselling, health, and personality-related areas. Richard is a Fellow of the Australian and British Psychological Societies and of the Australian Institute of Management and a member of the Clinical, Counselling, and Organisational Colleges of the Australian Psychological Society. His current research interests are in identifying relationships among perfectionism, personality, stress, and psychological wellbeing. He has an extensive history in test and questionnaire development and in questionnaire analysis.

Evelyn L. C. Howe is Head of Behavioural Sciences in the Faculty of Dentistry, University of Sydney. As a Clinical and Health Psychologist, she is distinguished as the first woman in Australia to hold a PhD in Dentistry. Her research and teaching span behavioral dentistry, where she has developed treatment programs for a range of functional oral disorders, and medical professionalism. She is internationally recognized for her work in the development of communication skills programs for the health professions. Her published work includes films, videos, and training curricula to facilitate effective communication with patients and multidisciplinary health teams. She is active in clinical work, holding consultancies in rehabilitation and health psychology.

Ben Jackson received his PhD from the University of Leeds in the UK in June 2008, and is currently An Assistant Professor in the School of Sport Science, Exercise and Health at the University of Western Australia. With a research interest that spans social and health psychology, his work explores the formation and consequences of close relationships in various health settings (e.g., physical education, sport, rehabilitation). His research is supported by the Australian Research Council, and his work has been published in well-respected peer-reviewed journals including

Journal of Sport & Exercise Psychology, *Journal of Research in Personality*, *Journal of Social and Personal Relationships*, and *Applied Psychology: An International Review*.

Lester E. Jones is currently a Lecturer in the La Trobe University Faculty of Health Sciences and has postgraduate qualifications in teaching and learning and pain and pain management. He is a member of the Australian Physiotherapy Association, the Chartered Society of Physiotherapy (UK), the International Association for the Study of Pain, and the Australian Pain Society. He is the Australian Physiotherapy Association's representative for Pain Australia and has also been involved in guideline development for assessment of pain (British Pain Society/British Geriatric Society) and outcome measures (Australian Pain Society/Faculty of Pain Medicine). He has previously authored and coauthored chapters on pain topics for physiotherapy and interdisciplinary texts.

Moira Junge is a registered psychologist, having completed a doctorate in health psychology. She has over 20 years' experience in the healthcare sector and has worked in the sleep field since 1994. Moira uses cognitive behavior therapy techniques as well as drawing on hypnosis, mindfulness and acceptance and commitment therapy, imagery rehearsal therapy, and well-developed counselling skills. She is passionate about, and actively involved in, educating other psychologists about treating sleep disorders, and she supervises students in the field of sleep problems. She is a member of the Australian Psychological Society College of Health Psychologists and the Australasian Sleep Association.

Nadine Kasparian is Head of Psychological Research and Supportive Care at the Heart Centre for Children, the Children's Hospital at Westmead. She holds appointments at the University of NSW and University of Sydney. Nadine's research focuses on the psychological experiences of individuals and families affected by illness, with a particular emphasis on psychosocial aspects of genetic testing for disease risk. She has developed interventions in this area, as well as clinical programs for women suffering from postnatal depression and anxiety. Nadine's current work is dedicated to the psychological care of infants, children, and families affected by heart disease. She has received numerous awards, including the 2011 International Psycho-Oncology Society Hiroomi Kawano New Investigator Award for outstanding contributions to research.

David Kavanagh was educated at Sydney and Stanford Universities, and currently holds a Research Chair in the Institute of Health & Biomedical Innovation and School of Psychology and Counselling at Queensland University of Technology. He has an extensive record of research funding and publication, especially in addiction, comorbidity, Internet-based treatment, and service enhancement, and has contributed strongly to state and national policy development in those areas.

Adrian B. Kelly is a Principal Research Fellow at the Centre for Youth Substance Abuse Research, the University of Queensland. His primary research interests are in cost-effective family-oriented prevention programs for youth substance abuse, processes involving families and peers that contribute to the development of substance use and related problems, and community-based prevention strategies. A clinical psychologist by background, Adrian has developed and evaluated a variety of early intervention and treatment programs for families affected by alcohol and other drug use.

Christina A. Kolar is a Research Assistant in the School of Psychology at Deakin University. She completed her postgraduate diploma in 2010, with a thesis topic focusing on substance abuse and cognition. She plans to begin studying a Master of Industrial and Organisational Psychology in 2013.

Brigitte Laville completed her Graduate Diploma of Psychology in 2009 at Deakin University where her research project was based on the relationship between body image and social comparisons in children. Brigitte's primary research interests include the mental health implications of body image disturbance, with particular interest in age appropriate body image intervention programs. She is currently working in the organisational psychology field as a consultant.

Helen Lindner is a Health Psychologist and the Executive Manager, Member Groups and Resources at the Australian Psychological Society. Helen was an academic for 17 years in the School of Psychological Science at La Trobe University, where she was actively involved in the Master's and doctoral programs in health psychology. Her research interests are self-management of chronic illness such as diabetes, heart disease, and lupus. She has extensive experience in the training of health professionals in behavior change skills, including motivational interviewing techniques and goal setting within the readiness to change framework. This training has occurred in Australia and China. She was a scientist with the World Health Organization's global project on "Adherence to long-term therapies: Evidence for action."

Jay-Lee Longbottom holds an MA in psychology from Californian State University, Fullerton, and a PhD in sport and exercise psychology from the University of Western Australia. She is registered as a psychologist with the Psychology Board of Australia and currently works as a Sport Psychologist in Singapore. Her research interests include perfectionism, motivation regulation, and self-presentation processes in exercise.

Paul R. Martin is Professor and Head of the School of Applied Psychology at Griffith University in Queensland, Australia. He trained at the University of Oxford before migrating to Australia and taking up positions at Monash University, University of Western Australia, University of New England, and RMIT University. He has held a number of professional leadership positions including National President of the Australian Behaviour Modification Association, Director of Science, and then President of the Australian Psychological Society. He was also President of the 27th International Congress of Applied Psychology. He has published eight books and over 130 journal articles and chapters. He is a Fellow of the British Psychological Society and an Honorary Fellow of the Australian Psychological Society.

Jane L. Mathias completed undergraduate studies and a PhD in psychology at the University of Adelaide, after which she worked at the Women's and Children's Hospital. She is currently a Professor in the School of Psychology in the Faculty of Health Sciences and teaches clinical neuropsychology, psychological assessment, and quantitative meta-analytic techniques to undergraduate, Honours, and postgraduate coursework students, as well as supervising the research projects of Honours, Masters, and PhD students. She has conducted research in the areas of traumatic brain injury, craniofacial disorders, dementia, chronic fatigue syndrome, attention deficit disorder, cardiovascular disease, and aging.

Marita P. McCabe is a Professor of Psychology at Deakin University. Her areas of interest include psychological adjustment among older people and human sexuality, adolescent dating, childhood abuse, sexual dysfunction, sexual harassment, sexuality and disability, adolescent body image, dieting, bingeing, and excessive exercise among adolescent boys and girls. She has published over 300 papers in a range of international journals.

Nikola Medic is a Senior Lecturer in the School of Exercise and Health Sciences at Edith Cowan University. He is a member of the College of Sport and Exercise Psychologists within the Australian Psychological Society and is registered as a psychologist with the Psychology Board of Australia. His research interests include intrinsic motivation and self-determination, the development of sport commitment and expertise, and the impact of physical activity on aging processes.

David Mellor is a Professor of Psychology at Deakin University. His research interests are varied but fall within the areas of Clinical and Health Psychology. He has considerable experience and expertise in cross cultural research, and has published papers related to adolescent body disturbance with colleagues in Chile, China, and Malaysia. He has also worked in clinical practice and conducted research with Indigenous Australians.

Jeannette Milgrom is a Professor of Psychological Sciences at University of Melbourne and Director of Clinical and Health Psychology, Austin Health, Melbourne. She has established a psychology hospital department that integrates clinical services, research, and teaching. She was chair of the National Executive of the College of Health Psychologists, Australian Psychological Society, 2002–6 and convened the Doctor of Psychology (Health), University of Melbourne, 1999–2008. Jeannette established the Parent–Infant Research Institute in 2001 focusing on high-risk infants, postnatal depression, prematurity, and developing psychological treatments (mothers, fathers, and babies). Jeannette has had a major role in the Beyondblue National Perinatal Depression Initiative since 2001. She is recipient of 41 research grants and author of four books, 13 chapters, and 90 scientific articles.

Jane Mills is an expert grounded theorist with extensive experience in the field of primary health-care. Currently employed as an Associate Professor in the School of Nursing, Midwifery and Nutrition at James Cook University in Australia, Jane holds the position of Director of Research and Associate Dean Research in the Faculty of Medicine, Health and Molecular Sciences.

Kylie Murphy is a Psychologist working in Clinical Health Psychology. She has treated overweight adults in both hospital outpatient and community health settings. In addition to her clinical work, Kylie has a research interest in the area of obesity and weight management and is currently working at Monash University's Centre for Obesity Research and Education. Of particular interest is the relationship between psychological distress, motivations for weight loss, and weight-loss outcomes.

Alexander J. Mussap is an Associate Professor who completed his doctoral training at Deakin University, Australia, and his postdoctoral training at the University of Houston, USA. He is currently Deputy Head of School of Psychology at Deakin University. He has published over 50 papers in the areas of vision research, cognition, and health psychology. His most recent research focuses on sociocultural influences on body image and unhealthy body change behaviors.

Danielle C. Newton is a Research Fellow in the Centre for Women's Health, Gender and Society at the University of Melbourne. Her interest in Health Psychology began with her PhD investigation into the psychosocial impact of sexually transmitted infections. Since this time she has continued to focus her research primarily in sexual health and has published papers in journals such as *Sexually Transmitted Infections, International Journal of STD & AIDS, Sexual Health, Sexually Transmitted Diseases, Journal of Sex Research, Sexual and Relationship Therapy, Journal of Health Psychology, Annals of Family Medicine,* and *Sociology of Health & Illness.* Danielle also holds a Master of Psychology (Health) and has practiced clinically in the area of sexual and reproductive health.

Sarah Nowoweiski is a registered Psychologist who has been working in the field of infertility since 2005. Her doctorate research investigated parents' experiences of complicated childbirth, particularly focusing on males' perspectives which had been previously underreported. Since then, Sarah has worked on the management of mental health issues associated with parent-infant psychology and reproductive health. Sarah has also presented research findings at both national and international conferences, and has published her research in international and national peer-reviewed journals. Sarah is an approved infertility counsellor in Victoria and has experience working with complex cases including third-party reproduction and surrogacy. She is chair of the ANZICA Research Sub-Committee.

Paul O'Halloran is a Senior Lecturer in the School of Public Health at La Trobe University (Bundoora). His principal research interest relates to physical activity and health; his PhD examining mental health benefits of physical activity. He has published articles pertaining to physical activity in national and international refereed journals. Specifically, these have related to the mood enhancing effects of physical activity and on strategies and programs designed to increase physical activity in both the general population and in people with chronic illnesses in rehabilitation settings. He has been involved in professional practice of health/sport/general psychology for over 10 years working with individuals and organizations.

Melissa Oxlad is a Clinical and Health Psychologist who works in private practice where she consults to adults and children. She has had many years of research and clinical experience assisting people with cancer and life-threatening illness including working in the Royal Adelaide Hospital Cancer Centre and currently providing services to clients of the Leukaemia Foundation and the Little Heroes Foundation. Melissa is a Visiting Research Fellow at the University of Adelaide. Her health psychology research with cancer and cardiac populations has been published in peer-reviewed journals and presented at national and international conferences. In addition, Melissa has also undertaken a number of tertiary teaching roles.

Dawn Proctor is a Postdoctoral Research Fellow at the Institute of Health and Biomedical Innovation, Queensland University of Technology. As a Clinical Psychologist Dawn previously held a senior position working in the statewide alcohol and drug inpatient service. She completed her doctoral training at the University of Manchester, specializing in metacognitive therapy for anxiety disorders. Dawn is currently involved in the development of online interventions for a range of mental health concerns and the application of metacognitive techniques for dual diagnosis.

Julie Pryor is an Associate Professor and registered nurse with a particular interest in the processes of clinical service delivery. From the various clinical, management, education, and research positions she had held in rehabilitation over the past 25 years and the consultancy work she has done with around 20 rehabilitation service providers across Australia and New Zealand Julie has developed a deep appreciation of the centrality, complexity, and challenges of cross-disciplinary working in health. At the Royal Rehabilitation Centre Sydney, Julie is the Director of the Rehabilitation Nursing Research & Development Unit. As an Associate Professor at Flinders University she supervises research students enrolled in Australia's only postgraduate multidisciplinary clinical rehabilitation program.

Rachel M. Roberts has worked with children with craniofacial conditions at the Women's and Children's Hospital, Adelaide, for many years. She has conducted research in child and adolescent health psychology, including work in the areas of craniofacial disorders, metabolic conditions, prematurity, and sleep disorders. She is currently a Senior Lecturer in the School of Psychology at the University of Adelaide where she teaches in the Master of Psychology Health and Clinical programs and coordinates postgraduate training in clinical psychology. She continues to consult at the Women's and Children's Hospital.

Bosco C. Rowland is a registered Psychologist and Research Fellow with the School of Psychology in the Faculty of Health at Deakin University. He has been working in the area of community-based interventions for the last 10 years. He has been extensively involved with developing and piloting the Good Sports program, an alcohol-management program for community sports clubs. Bosco's interests include health behaviors around alcohol consumption, healthy eating, and mental health, especially from a health promotion, preventative, and public health perspective.

Laura Sciacchitano has an Honours degree in Psychology and has several publications related to her thesis. She has held the position of project officer at the Australian Psychological Society for the past 4 years, and as part of her role is involved in the development of practice resources and online training programs for psychologists and other allied health professionals, including social workers, mental health nurses, and occupational therapists. Laura's research interests include coping with chronic illness and perinatal mental health. Laura has also worked as a researcher in the alcohol and drug field where she conducted health services research and evaluations.

Kerry Sherman is a Senior Lecturer in the Centre for Emotional Health, Department of Psychology, at Macquarie University, Sydney, and a consultant health psychology researcher with the Westmead Breast Cancer Institute. She is the current President of the Australasian Society for Behavioural Health and Medicine. Since undertaking a postdoctoral fellowship at the Fox Chase Cancer Centre, Philadelphia, Kerry has worked extensively in health psychology, particularly in the area of psycho-oncology incorporating aspects of diagnosis, survivorship, and genetic risk. Kerry's research in clinical contexts includes the evaluation of psychosocial interventions that are designed to minimize distress, improve surgical decision making, and improve spousal support among individuals with a cancer diagnosis and those undergoing genetic testing for hereditary cancer susceptibility.

Helen Skouteris is an Associate Professor in developmental psychology in the Department of Psychology at Deakin University, Melbourne, Australia. Her research interests pertain to understanding factors that influence maternal and child health and wellbeing, including body image concerns, ante- and postnatal depression, excessive gestational weight gain, and postpartum weight retention.

Heather Soo is a practicing Psychologist and doctoral student at Macquarie University, Sydney. She has a particular interest in the psychological management of individuals with chronic illness. Her current research focuses on how styles of thinking, specifically ruminative processes, influence adjustment to chronic and acute illnesses, such as diabetes and cancer. Since completing a Master's degree at Monash University in health psychology, Heather has published in the area of ruminative processes in the context of diabetes.

Jacqui Stanford is currently a Director and Principal Psychologist of Empower Rehab, who specialize in providing interdisciplinary pain management as well as working with clients presenting with a range of psychological presentations. Jacqui provides training and supervision to health professionals and return to work professionals about the management of clients with persistent pain to help facilitate recovery and optimal function. She also lectures Master's and Doctor of Psychology students in pain management. She is a member of the Australian Psychological Society and the Health College, the International Association for the Study of Pain, and the Australian Pain Society. Jacqui was the Australian Psychological Society representative of the Australian National Pain Summit.

Esben Strodl is a Senior Lecturer at the Queensland University of Technology (QUT). He teaches health psychology and cognitive behavior therapy in the Master's and professional doctorate degrees in clinical psychology at QUT. Previously he worked for 10 years as a clinical health psychologist for the Queensland Health Department. Esben's research interests include psychotherapy and health psychology. He is currently serving as the Queensland Chair of the Australian Psychological Society College of Health Psychologists, as well as being on the college's national executive.

Shane Thomas is Professor and Director of Primary Care Research in the School of Primary Health Care, Faculty of Medicine and professor and Director of the Problem Gambling Research and Treatment Centre at Monash University. He is also an adjunct professor at Peking University and an honorary professor at University of Sydney. He is currently Honorary President and Chair of the Board of the Heart Research Centre. Professor Thomas has written over 200 refereed publications including four authored books, one of which is in its fifth edition. He has led the development of several high-profile measurement systems including the Australian Commonwealth Work Ability Tables, the Thomas Post Acute Care Risk Screen, and the Royal Australian College of General Practitioners' Patient Satisfaction Survey.

John W. Toumbourou is a Professor and Chair in Health Psychology at the School of Psychology and the Associate Dean (Partnerships and Workplace) in the Faculty of Health at Deakin University. He is an Honorary Senior Research Fellow in the Murdoch Children's Research Institute at the Centre for Adolescent Health (Royal Children's Hospital Melbourne). John's interests include evaluation, drug abuse prevention and the role of community, family, and peer groups in adolescent health promotion. He is recognized both in Australia and internationally for his research examining adolescent substance use and mental health. In 2010 he was appointed to the International Task Force for the Society for Prevention Research.

Robert J. Williams completed his postgraduate training in the Department of Psychology at the Auckland University and Kingseat Psychiatric Hospital in New Zealand. He has been researching and teaching in the field of substance abuse, health psychology, men and masculinity, and counselling for 25 years. A large focus of his work has been on the study of gender-role stereotypes in relation to both binge drinking and binge eating among adolescents, and he has published over 50 papers in the field. He is currently researching the embodiment of consciousness, body image, and mindfulness in the School of Letters, Arts and Media at the University of Sydney, Australia.

Helen R. Winefield is a Professor in the School of Psychology and the Discipline of Psychiatry at the University of Adelaide. A foundation member of the College of Health Psychologists, she has published widely on occupational and health psychology topics, and currently coordinates a Master of Psychology (Health).

Foreword

As President of the Australian Psychological Society, it is with great pleasure and pride that I commend to you this excellent volume. It is a pleasure, because it is clear that the evidence base and the theoretical rationale which underpins the crucial work of health psychology has now truly come of age with an entire new resource to inform its treatment and practice. Pride, because so much of this outstanding work arises from the many members of the College of Health Psychology of the Australian Psychological Society. The College is just over 10 years young and during that relatively brief time the specialty has proved beyond a shadow of a doubt the important contribution that health psychology can make to the theory, treatment, and management of the effects of psychological factors related to health and illness in the contemporary Australian context.

The book contains no fewer than 36 chapters by Australian researchers and practitioners in health psychology, and each of the two main practice areas of contemporary health psychology (i.e., health promotion and clinical health) are well represented in the volume. I feel sure that this comprehensive text will provide a powerful resource for the many health psychologists across the country and throughout the world who are engaged in the prevention of illness and the promotion of health-related behaviors, as well as to the integrated application of psychology to illness assessment, treatment, and rehabilitation.

Particular acknowledgement and respect are due to the editors of this wonderful volume, Associate Professors Marie Caltabiano and Lina Ricciardelli. First of all they are to be congratulated for their own powerful contributions to the volume but also for their indefatigable ability to be able to organize, cajole, and convince a virtual army of health psychologists to produce such a comprehensive and well-integrated text. Truly a *tour de force* and one I am sure that we will still be referring to over the many years to come. Enjoy this wonderful read!

Simon Crowe, PhD
President
Australian Psychological Society Ltd

Preface

Health psychology, with its emphasis on disease prevention, health promotion, and clinical applications, is a growing field within professional practice, research, and training. It is largely concerned with the enhancement of wellbeing through the application of psychological principles to prevent ill health and assist individuals with chronic conditions in their adjustment to, and management of, these conditions.

Given that many of the leading causes of mortality in Australia have substantial behavioral components, which are preventable, there is an increasing demand for the skills and expertise of health psychologists. In addition, health psychologists have become vital members of multidisciplinary clinical and research teams in rehabilitation, cardiology, pediatrics, oncology, endocrinology, anesthesiology, family practice, dentistry, community health, and other medical fields.

Applied Topics in Health Psychology comprises a selection of topical chapters by internationally recognized Australian researchers and/or clinicians working in the field and allied disciplines. The chapters provide an in-depth, critical, and comprehensive consideration of the particular health topic or issues, and address both the applied and academic (theoretical and methodological) aspects of that area, where appropriate. Other chapters focus on health psychology topics/issues with an emphasis on applied techniques to illustrate a particular evidence-based therapy/approach. The book provides a comprehensive, in-depth, state-of-the-art coverage of topics in clinical health psychology and health promotion.

The book is divided into eight sections. In Part 1 consideration is given to theories of health behavior change and the psychological techniques health psychologists use to bring about health change. In Chapter 1, Lindner and Sciacchitano discuss the health and illness management model as an approach to long-term behavior change, and advocate the inclusion of health behavior change specialists in interdisciplinary models of care. In Chapter 2, Gale and Skouteris present the Health Change Australia (HCA) model as a clinical practice framework for chronic disease prevention and illness self-management. Their health coaching approach bridges theory and practice by incorporating theoretical ideas regarding the development of a behavioral goal intention, how intentions are transformed into action and maintenance, and communication within the patient-centered therapeutic approach. Chapters 3 and 4 specifically focus on the health behavior of physical activity. Paul O'Halloran discusses the physiological health benefits of physical activity for the prevention of obesity, cardiovascular disease, cancer, and diabetes, and the mental health benefits for reduced depression. Guidelines for physical activity, potential risks of physical activity, and the evidence-based efficacy for individual and small-group approaches to achieve benefits are discussed. Grove, Jackson, Longbottom, and Medic outline four processes which they believe to be the basis of positive exercise habits (strengthening of stimulus-response bonds, automaticity, patterning of action, and negative consequences for nonperformance) and suggest some cognitive-behavioral strategies to increase habit strength.

Part 2 of the book considers factors which are important to our understanding of health-related behavior, health disadvantage, and variability in response to chronic illness. Gender, age, and culture are central to the health psychologist's understanding of the different health attitudes, beliefs, motivations, emotion, and behaviors of a multicultural clientele. The application of psychological theory to practice should be made with sensitivity to the background of the persons with whom we are working. With a trend towards an increasing older population across many countries, Browning, Heine, and Thomas in Chapter 5 consider how to best facilitate aging well. They provide the evidence base for interventions in six areas: physical activity to improve health, physical activity and sleep, self-management of chronic disease, psychological therapies and depression, cognitive training, and seniors as mentors. In Chapter 6, Robert Williams explores how stereotypical gender roles can be used to explain drinking behavior in males and disordered eating in females. In Chapter 7 Ricciardelli, Mellor, McCabe, Mussap, and Kolar present cultural differences in morbidity, mortality, lifestyle factors (diet, exercise), health service usage, and health screening. Participatory action research with Indigenous persons to understand risk and protective factors is also covered.

In Part 3 of the Handbook, the first two chapters examine conceptual and measurement issues in regard to subjective wellbeing and theoretical perspectives on the construct. Robert Cummins (Chapter 8) concludes from 24 surveys conducted as part of the Australian Unity Wellbeing Index since 2001 that subjective wellbeing of the population has remained relatively stable over time, a finding which is attributed to a homeostatic management system complete with internal and external buffers to return the individual to their set-point. Courtney, Caltabiano, and Caltabiano advocate the refinement of conceptual models of wellbeing to take into account life contexts, life histories, beliefs, values, and expectations of subpopulations for targeted interventions to address specific needs of these groups (Chapter 9). The last three chapters in this section focus on specific areas and their relationship to physical health and wellbeing. Chur-Hansen and Winefield in Chapter 10 explore the potential of companion animals in health promotion and clinical practice, and argue for interprofessional education and more rigorous systematic research into the health benefits of the human–animal companion bond. In Chapter 11, Howe explores the contribution of psychology to dentistry within the broad foci of oral health promotion and clinical oral health psychology. In the chapter the use of motivational interviewing and oral health coaching for oral hygiene, the treatment of dental anxiety and specific phobias, psychological management of orofacial pain, graded exposure techniques to prevent abnormal gagging during dental procedures, and behavioral techniques to eliminate parafunctional habits such as thumb sucking and fingernail biting are discussed. Chapter 12 by Helen Winefield considers the negative impact on health of work stress, how workplace wellness programs can benefit health, and the importance of work–life balance for optimal wellbeing.

In Part 4 a range of health conditions and health issues form the basis of the chapters. Kerry Sherman and Nadine Kasparian in Chapter 13 discusses genetic testing for disease susceptibility, the factors determining the decision to undergo testing, reactions to testing and disclosure of test results, and how families adjust to results disclosed. The contribution of psychology to the genetic testing process is also considered. In Chapter 14, Sarah Nowoweiski reviews the literature on the psychological impact of infertility and infertility treatment for the individual's and couple's sense of self-worth, sense of loss or failure, and strain on the sexual relationship. Theoretical models which underpin therapeutic approaches, both individual and group-based, are given consideration in the treatment of depression, and anxiety in infertile couples, and in facilitating coping with, and adjustment to infertility. In Chapter 15, Danielle Newton examines how psychological interventions can assist individuals at the initial diagnosis of a sexually transmitted disease or a diagnosis of HIV/AIDS, in managing depression and anxiety, in minimizing risk to sexual partners, and in the case of AIDS in medication adherence. In Chapter 16, Milgrom and Gemmill provide guidelines on screening and diagnostic assessment of perinatal depression, and evidence for the efficacy of treatments such as cognitive behavior therapy (CBT), interpersonal psychotherapy, psychodynamic therapy, antidepressant medication, and combination therapies. Quality sleep is essential to wellbeing and effective performance in the workplace. In Chapter 17, Bartlett and Junge examine the efficacy of cognitive-behavioral treatments over conventional drug treatment for insomnia, and explore the potential of mindfulness techniques, and acceptance and commitment therapy (ACT). In Chapter 18, Roberts and Mathias make some recommendations for interventions which target psychosocial functioning in persons with craniofacial conditions. They advocate social skills training with an emphasis on problem solving, coping, and skill development, with cognitive-behavioral interventions to address negative beliefs about appearance and body image.

Part 5 of the book focuses on recent advancements in body image, maladaptive eating practices, and obesity. Fuller-Tyszkiewicz, Ricciardelli, McCabe and Laville in Chapter 19 examine body image concerns among both women and men in relation to health behaviors, obesity, and mental health. In addition, the authors evaluate treatments for body image disturbances. Chapter 20 by Ebenreuter and Hicks examines maladaptive eating practices using an eating disorder framework. Specifically the authors have developed and evaluated a new instrument on eating practices, the Inner Thoughts on Eating Questionnaire, which consists of three main domains: cognitions, emotions, and behaviors. In Chapter 21 Skouteris reviews psychosocial determinants and the implications for childhood obesity. To date there has been very limited research on the determinants of maternal obesity during pregnancy and at postpartum, and a case is made for the need for observational research to examine the nature of interactions between mother and child, and how these may influence child weight gain. The final chapter in this section (Chapter 22) by Brennan and Murphy examines the efficacy of a range of treatment approaches including the key components of behavioral and cognitive-behavioral interventions for treating obesity among adults. A brief overview of the definition, prevalence, and biopsychosocial consequences of excess weight are also outlined.

The focus in Part 6 is on the prevention and treatment of substance use. Chapter 23 by Rowland, Toumbourou, and Allen examines the PRECEDE/PROCEED framework, for reducing the abuse and misuse of alcohol within the context of sporting clubs. Specifically this framework considers predisposing, enabling, and reinforcing factors. In Chapter 24 Kelly, Connor, and Toumbourou address substance-use disorders in young people with a focus on both prevention and treatment. The overarching conceptual framework for this chapter is ecology of human development theory. According to this theory individuals are viewed in the context of their environments (families, peers, school, communities), and a key assumption is that health risk behaviors such as substance abuse disorders are best treated with consideration of these multiple nested ecological systems. The final chapter in this section, Chapter 25 by Strodl, Proctor, Kavanagh, and Beames, examines a new intervention, metacognitive therapy, as a treatment for alcohol problems among adults. This involves working with individuals' maladaptive metacognitions, such as their attention towards disorder congruent information or unhelpful styles of coping that fail to challenge their negative beliefs. In addition, two brief case studies are provided to illustrate the application of this new intervention.

In Part 7 of the volume, the focus shifts to chronic illness, adjustment to different conditions, the management of pain, and issues of medication adherence. The section begins with two chapters on the contribution of psycho-oncology in facilitating adjustment to a diagnosis of cancer and in assisting individuals to maintain health-related quality of life. Chapter 26 by Burney and Fletcher addresses evidence-based interventions used in psycho-oncology such as supportive psychotherapy, cognitive and behavioral interventions, and existential therapy in the care of cancer patients and their families throughout the disease process. Chapter 27 by Beatty and Oxlad provides guidelines for the assessment of cancer patients, and presents evidence for the efficacy of CBT, mindfulness-based interventions, clinical hypnosis, and self-help interventions. Within the chapter, clinical case tasks are used to facilitate reader engagement and learning. In Chapter 28 Felicity Allen examines musculoskeletal disorders such as osteoarthritis, rheumatoid arthritis, and fibromyalgia, and how psychological interventions can help persons with these disorders better manage the conditions within a multimodal approach to treatment. The effectiveness of CBT for pain management, psychoeducation, drug treatment, surgical joint replacement or reconstruction, management of obesity, and encouragement of exercise are considered. In Chapter 29 rumination as a cognitive style and how it may impact on adjustment to chronic illness is explored by Soo and Sherman, along with the potential of mindfulness-based cognitive therapy and ACT in the management of rumination in illness. Chapter 30 takes a self-regulation perspective to examine the interplay of cognitive, emotional, and behavioral factors in diabetes. In the chapter, Caltabiano reports on the evidence base for a range of psychological interventions in diabetes management such as educational and self-management interventions, counselling and psychotherapeutic approaches, cognitive-behavioral approaches, behavioral family systems therapy, ACT, and multisystemic therapy. In Chapter 31 Felicity Allen considers psychological approaches in the management of asthma which facilitate patient adherence to medication and monitoring, treat comorbid psychological conditions such as panic disorder, or have behavioral, cognitive, or psychodynamic components. Adherence to medication is crucial for the management of chronic physical illness to prevent further progression and complications of the disease. In Chapter 32 Mitchell Byrne examines the causes of nonadherence and how psycho-education, behavioral, and cognitive interventions can be used to increase patient medical adherence. The last two chapters in the section focus on the experience of pain, which is central to many chronic conditions, especially in the later stages. In Chapter 33 Paul Martin provides a guide to the functional assessment and treatment of common primary headaches such as migraine and tension-type headache. The chapter considers the efficacy of approaches such as thermal and electromyographic biofeedback training, relaxation, and CBT. In Chapter 34 Jacqui Stanford and Lester Jones discuss pain management more generally as it relates to a number of conditions. In their chapter the authors focus on new developments in our understanding of the human pain experience as propounded by the neruomatrix theory of pain, multidimensional assessment, case formulation, and development of a treatment plan within interdisciplinary pain management, and present case studies as examples.

The last section, Part 8, acknowledges that health psychologists often work within multidisciplinary teams. As such it is important to have a basic understanding of other disciplines and their healthcare approach. In Chapter 35, Bonner and Pryor provide a perspective from the field of nursing, while in Chapter 36 Chamberlain-Salaun, Mills, and Davis provide a glimpse of how the general practitioner views their role in relation to that of nurses, psychologists, and other allied health workers.

Marie L. Caltabiano & Lina A. Ricciardelli
Editors

Acknowledgments

We would like to thank all of the contributing authors to this book, as each individual has brought a wealth of expertise and experience. Secondly, we would like to thank everyone at Wiley-Blackwell publishers: Andrew Peart (publisher), Karen Shield (senior project editor), and Victoria Halliday (editorial assistant). Our sincere appreciation is extended to Baljinder Kaur (project manager, Aptara Delhi), Nik Prowse (copy-editor) and Suchitra Srinivasan (production editor). In addition, we would like to thank Kate Morrison, and more recently Janne Morrison and Christina Kolar, for assisting us in corresponding with authors and in managing collation of submitted abstracts, biographies, chapters, reviews, chapter resubmissions, and finding missing references. We would also like to thank those academics who reviewed submitted chapters, all members of the National committee of the APS College of Health Psychologists (2009–2012) for their support, and especially, Donna Goodman, the Secretary in 2009–2010, who collated many of the initial emails and abstracts, we received when we first flagged this project. A special thanks is also extended to Yvonne Drazic who helped with formatting chapters and checking references and style guidelines. Each editor would also personally like to thank a number of other significant persons, as outlined below.

Marie Caltabiano: First and foremost I would like to thank Lina Ricciardelli for providing me with the opportunity to work alongside her on this project. Her unwavering support and commitment to the book are unsurpassed. It has been a truly rewarding experience being a co-editor with you. I would also like to thank my sister Nerina for her friendship, continued support, and belief in me; to my niece Amelia for providing stimulating debate; to the students whose enthusiasm for health psychology makes it all worthwhile; to my friends who have always been there for me; and lastly to my snow-dog Mischa who is accepting of my long working days and who waits patiently for her night walks.

Lina Ricciardelli: I would firstly like to thank Marie Caltabiano for her dedication and enthusiasm for this book, and her passion for health psychology. Her vision that anything is possible and her achievements in the field have been continual inspirations for me. I am so honoured to have worked with Marie on this exciting project we began in 2010, and I have enjoyed every minute. I would also like to thank members of the College of Health Psychologists, the health psychology students

I have taught since we began the Doctor of Psychology (Health) in 1999 at Deakin University, and all my colleagues both near and far. Finally, I want to thank my parents, Diodoro and Incoronata, for their never ending acceptance, support and who first gave me a thirst for knowledge; my sister and brother, and their partners for their encouragement and love; my three nieces and nephew for endless questions, fun, and laughter; and Amanda Kaczmarek, Robert Williams, Marita McCabe, Tess Knight, Lesley Hall, and Grace Sinclair for their long-term friendship.

Part 1

Health Behavior Change and Enhancing Health Behaviors

1

Health Behavior Change Techniques

Helen Lindner and Laura Sciacchitano

Health behavior change interventions are an essential component to the treatment of chronic medical conditions, illnesses, and injuries. The demand for health behavior change experts – that is, health psychologists – is rapidly growing, particularly with the world-wide phenomena of aging populations. Specifically, the World Health Organization (WHO; 2010) has referred to chronic illness as a "global epidemic" that will have the highest impact on deaths and disability across the world in coming years.

Health Behavior Change

While many individuals develop chronic illnesses due to genetic and biological factors (e.g., cystic fibrosis, systemic lupus, Type 1 diabetes), a significant proportion of the population develop diseases due to unhealthy behaviors, such as smoking, excess consumption of alcohol, or unhealthy eating (WHO, 2011). In order to manage and prevent the onset of chronic medical conditions which result from an individual's unhealthy behavior, health behavior change must occur on a number of different levels including, establishing new healthy behaviors, increasing existing healthy behaviors, and decreasing unhealthy behaviors. Examples of the types of health behavior changes that occur at each of these levels are presented in Figure 1.1.

Maintaining health behavior changes

The long-term maintenance of positive health behaviors has been found to be problematic for individuals. For example, a recent study has indicated that behavior change, in terms of increased levels of physical activity, was only evident in 27% of patients with coronary heart disease at 18 month follow-up (Hansen *et al.*, 2010). Therefore, in addition to the development of medical and pharmacological interventions, developing interventions that focus on changing poor health

Applied Topics in Health Psychology, First Edition. Edited by M. L. Caltabiano and L. Ricciardelli.
© 2013 John Wiley & Sons, Ltd. Published 2013 by John Wiley & Sons, Ltd.

Establish new healthy behaviors	Increase existing healthy behaviors	Decrease unhealthy behaviors
• Taking medication as prescribed • Participating in rugular physical activity • Consuming reduced-fat food products • Conducting regular health checks such as blood-glucose testing	• Scheduling more regular doctor appointments • Increasing consumption of fruit, vegetables, and proteins • Ensuring adequate amounts of sleep	• Decreasing amount of salt, sugar, and fat from diet • Quiting smoking • Reducing daily alcohol consumption

Figure 1.1 Examples of health behavior change.

behaviors is important in reducing the burden of illness. In fact, nutritional, pharmacological, and surgical interventions for a range of conditions, such as weight management, have been shown to have greater positive health outcomes when a behavioral component is included as part of the intervention. For example, a study by Papalazarou and colleagues (2010) investigated the effectiveness of a behavioral and lifestyle intervention following vertical banded gastroplasty in severely obese patients. It was found that patients who received the behavior-modification intervention (e.g., nutrition education, self-monitoring, goal setting, reinforcement, stimulus control) lost significantly more weight and recorded more positive health behavior changes (e.g., improved eating behavior) compared to controls at 12, 24, and 36 months post-surgery.

Models of Health Behavior Change

Health behavior change models of care have been implemented on a range of intervention levels, from primary care administered by medical, nursing, and allied health professionals, health coaches, and carers to higher levels of care which involve interventions administered by health psychologists. Health psychologists are trained in high-level skills to help patients and other health professionals better manage the behavioral, cognitive, and emotional factors of the development and management of medical conditions.

This chapter focuses on the higher-level knowledge of models and skills required for complex health behavior change. More specifically, it outlines a range of evidence-based health behavior change models and discusses a range of techniques used by health psychologists to achieve successful health behavior change outcomes using time- and cost-effective implementation approaches.

Underlying principles of health behavior change

The foundation knowledge and skills for health behavior change assessment and intervention approaches come from cognitive behavior theories and cognitive behavior therapies (CBTs).

Although health behavior change can appear to be straightforward and easily implemented, in reality individual or small-group interventions are rarely straightforward and best outcomes for a range of individual, medical, and social situations require a thorough grounding in the assumptions of CBT techniques. That is, positive patient outcomes in terms of medical, psychological, and social indicators is best achieved when: patient–psychologist communications are structured; health behavior change treatment is focused on overt symptoms and outcomes; the treatment identifies clearly defined goals; health behavior change interventions are adapted to the patient's health problem; the patient is seen as an essentially competent source of pertinent information; the intervention focuses on changes that can be made in the immediate future; and any treatment approach places value on empirical support for intervention techniques that work (Dobson & Dozois, 2001).

While health behavior change involves the application of these basic behavior change principles, health behavior change interventions also incorporate a biopsychosocial view where psychological and social factors, in addition to biological factors, are said to influence the severity and nature of an individual's illness and an individual's capacity to maintain or undertake health behavior change (Browning & Thomas, 2005). For example, negative emotions or low self-efficacy will predict unsuccessful attempts to implement health behavior changes (Luszczynska *et al.*, 2007). Additionally, social factors, such as relationship difficulties, cultural expectations, or financial problems can also have a negative impact on health behavior change (Abbott *et al.*, 2010; Abraham *et al.*, 2011; Blackburn *et al.*, 2005).

Health Psychology Models of Health Behavior Change

There are a large number of models of health and illness which outline factors related to health beliefs, health decisions, and behavioral intentions from both public health and clinical health perspectives. However, in terms of individual health behavior change, the decision-making and illness-perception-based models, known as the readiness to change model and the self-regulatory model, respectively, dominate the research literature (e.g., Kim *et al.*, 2004; Whitmarsh *et al.*, 2003).

Readiness to change model

The theoretical framework of the readiness to change model (Prochaska & Velicer, 1997) helps the health practitioner to understand that patients who have not internalized a need for change do not respond well to an immediate focus on goals for change. The constructs of the readiness to change model include five temporal stages of change. Each of the five stages of change are related to an individual's readiness to change, where a person in the *precontemplation* stage of change has no active intention to change. The *contemplation* stage of change describes a person with some awareness of a need to change but has no intention to change within the next 6 months, whereas a person in the *preparation* stage of change has an intention to change within the next 6 months, and is likely to be engaging in activities that could be identified as preparing for action. The *action* stage of change is when a person is undertaking the target behavior, such as quitting smoking, or daily blood glucose monitoring, and the *maintenance* stage of change is when an individual has successfully carried out the target behavior for at least the past 6 months.

The model proposes that interventions aimed at achieving health behavior change need to be appropriate to the patient's readiness to make the required change. This view has been supported by Mau and colleagues (2001) who suggested that "tailoring a lifestyle intervention to a person's stage of change may enhance its effectiveness in changing diet and exercise behaviors" (p. 1774). Furthermore, the development of stage-matched interventions has been shown to increase

Table 1.1 Suggested behavior change discussion points for healthy eating across the five stages of change

Stage of change	Suggested stage-relevant discussion points for the health professional
Pre-contemplation	Explore the cost of medicines and medical appointments over time versus the adoption of health behaviors
	Discuss with the patient the consequences of continued poor eating habits, even in terms of worst-case scenarios
	Ask the patient to consider the future impact of their illness on others
Contemplation	Evaluate and list the barriers to healthy eating: determine things that can be changed easily and those that will take time
Preparation	Suggest that the patient browse recipe books to assist in making healthy food choices
	Suggest that the patient involve a family member to assist them in making healthy food choices
Action	Work with the patient to plan on preparing smaller food portions
	Discuss with the patient the option of walking to the shops to establish a healthy mind-set before they buy food
	Help the patient plan regular reviews with health professionals
	Work with the patient to keep a diary of positive comments people make about the changes in their behavior and appearance
Maintenance	Help the patient to develop a system of visual reminders around their house/office

adherence behavior for patients with a chronic illness, including diabetes (Kim *et al.*, 2004; Mau *et al.*, 2001).

In a study involving 1029 participants, Jones *et al.* (2003) found a significant effect of a telephone-counselling intervention, developed from the readiness to change model, on multiple self-management behaviors for diabetes. Participants, randomly selected for the intervention group, were provided with a list of health behaviors requiring change. They were more likely to move from one of the pre-action stages of change to the action stage of change when one or two health behaviors were listed as requiring change compared to a "treatment as usual" group of diabetes sufferers.

Furthermore, Miller and colleagues identified numerous processes that facilitate cognitive and behavior change which are more evident in one stage compared to other stages (Miller *et al.*, 1997). As a result, it is of particular importance that health professionals engage in processes of discussion and exploration for health behavior change in a manner that is relevant to the patient's stage of change. Table 1.1 presents suggested discussion points between the health professional and patient across the stages of change using healthy eating as an example of the behavior change goal.

Self-regulatory model

Another model that has been used in the investigation of treatment adherence for chronic illness has been Leventhal's self-regulatory model (SRM; Leventhal *et al.*, 1992). This is an illness behavior model that treats the patient as an active self-manager of their illness. The SRM proposes that three stages are involved in an individual's health behavior change. In the first stage, the patient's cognitive (categorized into five components: identity, cause, consequences, time line, and cure/control) and emotional illness perceptions are interpreted (Hagger & Orbell, 2003; Leventhal *et al.*, 1992). These factors then influence the patient's second stage in which coping strategies, such as adherence to medication and behavior treatment recommendations, are used to manage the illness. The third stage involves the patient's appraisal of their coping strategy to achieve positive management of the illness. This appraisal is then fed back to the initial illness-perception stage.

The SRM has been a useful framework for understanding health behavior change (e.g., treatment adherence) for a range of chronic conditions. Of particular interest is the effect of illness representations in directing the coping strategy adopted by the patient. A study by Whitmarsh *et al.* (2003) investigated whether patients' illness representations of their myocardial infarctions were an important determinant of their coping response (i.e., attendance at a cardiac rehabilitation program). The study consisted of 71 males and 22 females who had received a confirmed diagnosis of myocardial infarction.

It was found that the patient's attendance at cardiac rehabilitation was significantly related to the patient's illness representations of identity as well as consequences. That is, those patients who attended cardiac rehabilitation perceived significantly greater symptoms and consequences of their illness compared to poor/non-attenders. Furthermore, in addition to fewer perceptions of symptoms, lower perceptions of controllability/curability of illness was also found to be a predictor of poor/non-attendance. Therefore, illness representations, specifically identity, consequences, and controllability of the disease, can have a significant effect on the coping and behavior change strategies adopted by the patient, such as treatment attendance/adherence.

Health and illness management model

Reviewing the literature on health behavior change (e.g., Browning & Thomas, 2003) provides support for a *three-phase approach* to long-term health behavior change. These phases are comprised of (1) health education, (2) health behavior change, and (3) health behavior maintenance (Australian Psychological Society, 2011). The authors of this chapter have termed this three-phase approach as the health and illness management model. The phases of this model are sequential, but overlap, across the period of health change. Both the readiness to change model and the SRM provide evidence-based interventions within all stages of this model.

There is also evidence that interventions which incorporate a three-phase approach are best undertaken within interdisciplinary teams in the public and clinical health domains. An example of such an intervention is the Good Life Club (GLC) project, which incorporated health education, health behavior change, and maintenance for chronic condition self-management. An evaluation by Browning and Thomas (2003) found a significant improvement in health outcomes for a sample of 85 individuals who were diagnosed with Type 2 diabetes and who received the GLC intervention. The GLC project was based on the readiness to change model (Prochaska *et al.*, 1992) and used motivational interviewing (MI; Rollnick *et al.*, 1992) and CBT frameworks. MI has been defined as a "directive, client-centered counselling style for eliciting behavior change by helping patients to explore and resolve ambivalence" (Rollnick & Miller, 1995, p. 325).

Specifically, the project was a community-based intervention in which sufferers of diabetes received telephone support (coaching) approximately once a month from health professionals, including psychologists, physiotherapists, dieticians, podiatrists, nurse practitioners, diabetes educators, and occupational therapists. The intervention focused on the patient's ambivalence to change specific health-related behaviors, such as daily monitoring of blood glucose levels, taking medications, increasing activity levels, and/or engaging in regular medical checks on feet and eyes. All health professionals who took part in the project had received specific training in MI skills, behavior change strategies, such as goal setting, and the stages and processes of change. The training also focused on health behavior change techniques to help patients achieve functional illness perceptions and emotions that ensured positive health changes, such as focusing on the patient's views on the importance of change, and their confidence in making the desired changes (Lindner *et al.*, 2003).

The three phases of the health and illness management model will now be outlined in further detail.

Health education phase   According to the WHO (2003), in order to produce significant changes to an individual's health behavior, patient education is an essential component of any behavior change intervention. The health education phase of the health and illness management model involves approaches to increase an individual's knowledge of the illness, but also an awareness of the negative consequences of unhealthy behavior(s) and lifestyles.

Examples of illness-related education programs include diabetes education classes and cardiac rehabilitation programs. The focus of these interventions is on educating patients about their condition, with an expectation that this will support an intention for behavior change. Topics often covered in such programs include the nature of the disease, the required medical and lifestyle changes, and the consequences of the disease if it is not controlled (Donato, 2006; Schechter & Walker, 2002).

While disease education has been identified as being beneficial in the health behavior change process, two studies which focused on diabetes self-management revealed that behavioral education would be a positive adaptation to traditional education programs (Vale *et al.*, 2003; Watson *et al.*, 2003). Furthermore, researchers have proposed that, although disease education programs are vital, they alone do not necessarily translate into successful self-management and behavior change and, as a result, would be well complemented by evidence-based health behavior change interventions (Deakin *et al.*, 2003; Watson *et al.*, 2003). Behavior change interventions are a focus of the health behavior change phase of the health and illness management model and will be discussed in detail in the following section.

Health behavior change phase   The health behavior change phase of the health and illness management model involves the implementation of strategies to reduce unhealthy behaviors (e.g., smoking, drinking) and increase healthy behaviors (e.g., filling prescriptions, taking medication, attending medical appointments, nutrition, physical activity, sleep). The key factor to health behavior change at this stage of the model is to support individuals to get ready for change as well as implement that change. Interventions which have been shown to be efficacious in changing health behaviors during this phase have been classified as CBT techniques and include motivational interviewing, goal setting, and action plans.

Motivational interviewing   MI involves a range of techniques which can be used by health professionals to help patients change unhealthy behaviors, maintain healthy behaviors, and assess and build motivation for change. These techniques include expressing empathy (i.e., acknowledge that ambivalence to change is normal), developing discrepancy (i.e., highlight and explore the discrepancy between the patient's present behavior and his/her goals for the future), avoiding argumentation (i.e., confrontation is seen as counterproductive to MI), rolling with resistance (i.e., avoid arguing for change), and supporting self-efficacy (i.e., help the patient feel confident that he/she is capable of change).

In order for MI to be utilized effectively, it is important for the health professional to first consider an individual's readiness to change. In fact, the interaction style of MI is often used concurrently with the readiness to change model, which was described earlier in this chapter. Furthermore, given its focus on the patient's intrinsic values and goals, MI has been identified as a

Table 1.2 MI techniques across the five stages of change

Stage of change	MI techniques
Pre-contemplation	Establish rapport with the patient and focus on building a sense of trust
	Listen to the patient's point of view
	Do not force behavior change upon the patient
	Create a supportive environment where the patient can consider, explore and appreciate the advantages and disadvantages of behavior change
	Encourage a more positive attitude towards behavior change
Contemplation	Normalize the patient's ambivalence
	Encourage patients to "go slow" on the actual change at this time
	Discuss the benefits of behavior change and the positive impact this will have on the patient's health
	Identify discrepancies between the patient's values and actions
Preparation	Acknowledge the significance of the patient's decision to change their behavior
	Assist the patient in making clear, specific, and unambiguous goals and help them choose treatment options/change strategies that are appropriate for them
	Suggest some strategies for change or treatment but remember that it is important that the patient chooses the strategies that they would like to use
	Discuss the support available for the patient as they prepare to change their behavior
Action	Reinforce the importance of behavior change to the patient; be a source of encouragement and support
	Acknowledge the patient's feelings and experiences as a normal part of behavior change
	Help the patient identify high-risk situations and develop coping strategies for overcoming these
Maintenance	Help the patient identify the challenges that may trigger a relapse
	Develop prevention plans with the patient to address the challenges identified
	Acknowledge and draw from the patient's previous successes
	Review long-term goals with the patient

particularly effective technique in helping individuals change their health behaviors and move into the action stage of change (Prochaska *et al.*, 2008). Table 1.2 outlines examples of MI techniques which can be used at the different stages of change identified by the readiness to change model.

Support for the use of MI techniques in enhancing an individual's health behavior change has come from a range of empirical investigations. For example, Clark and Hampson (2001) found that diabetes patients allocated to a MI intervention group reported greater recommended lifestyle changes than patients in the usual care group. Another study, by Brodie *et al.* (2008), investigated the effectiveness of a MI intervention which incorporated behavior change principles to promote physical activity among patients diagnosed with chronic heart failure. It was found that compared to standard care the MI intervention significantly improved patient's quality of life across a number of domains, including social functioning, physical functioning, and health status.

Goal setting   The use of goal setting techniques in the management of chronic illness has been identified as a vital component for promoting health behavior change. According to Langford *et al.* (2007), goal setting allows patients to become active participants in their own healthcare and enables them to feel a sense of responsibility over their own health behavior. As a result, goal setting can often be an effective technique for increasing a patient's self-efficacy and can also facilitate the patient's ability to learn about their illness, identify risk factors, and solve problems (Langford *et al.*, 2007).

Table 1.3 Process for developing a general goal for losing weight into more specific goals

Goal	General methods to achieve goal	Target behavior
Lose weight	Reduce quantity of food	Serve small portions of food
		Eat from smaller plates and bowls
		Avoid snacking during the day
	Remove certain food	No consumption of fried food
		No fatty meat
		No sweet food on weekdays
	Improve quality of food	At least two servings of vegetables every day
	Food substitution	Steamed rice instead of fried rice
		Piece of fruit instead of chocolate
	Exercise	Walk around the block four times a week
		Participate in a sporting activity (e.g., swimming) once a week

The use of brainstorming techniques can often help patients with the goal setting process as it can help them generate a number of solutions to the problems they are experiencing, direct discussions around problem areas, and help them evaluate the most appealing/appropriate option for them. When brainstorming, it is important that health practitioners encourage the patient to generate as many ideas as possible, without criticism, and help them review and rank these options in a supportive manner so that the patient is able to identify specific behavior change goals. Questions to use to help initiate brainstorming and evaluate potential solutions include: What is the problem to be solved? What options do you have? What might happen if you put these options into practice? How will you implement your decision?

Once the patient has brainstormed ideas to change a particular problem, it is important for health professionals to encourage the patient to develop clear, focused, and unambiguous behavior change goals that are relevant to the patient's health. An example of developing a general goal into specific goals is included in Table 1.3.

Action plans   In addition to goal setting, another strategy which has been identified as being efficacious in promoting health behavior change involves a collaborative process where the health professional and patient work together to develop an action plan specific to the patient's identified goal(s). An action plan has been described as an agreement between a health professional and a patient in which the patient commits to changing one or more behaviors which are negatively impacting upon their health (MacGregor *et al.*, 2006).

Action plans need to be concrete and specific and address key questions regarding the patient's desired health behavior such as: What? How much? When? How many? For example, if the patient's goal is to engage in increased amounts of physical activity, an initial action plan may be "This week I will walk (what) for at least 30 minutes (how much) in the morning (when) three times a week (how many)". In order to enhance a patient's likelihood that they will succeed with their established action plan, it is also important that health professionals help the patient develop a plan that they feel confident will have an effect and that they feel they are able to realistically accomplish.

Handley and colleagues (2006) investigated the effectiveness of action plans in promoting health behavior change among patients who presented to primary healthcare settings with coronary heart disease risk factors. It was found that the majority of patients who made an action plan (53%) also reported making a health behavior change in line with their action plan during the following

3 weeks. It was therefore concluded that collaborative goal setting and the subsequent development of action plans is a useful strategy to encourage health behavior change (Handley *et al.*, 2006).

Health behavior maintenance phase   The health behavior maintenance phase is an essential component for long-term health behavior change as relapse can be quite common. Relapse can be due to a range of factors, including environmental (e.g., change of job, relocation of house), social (e.g., marriage breakdown), psychological (e.g., grief due to death of parent/partner/child), and physical health factors (e.g., injury, disease progression). Interventions in this phase of the health and illness management model need to focus on reinforcing the lifestyle behaviors that have become automatic and embedded into daily life following the active decision-making processes of the action stage of change. Good practice to assure maintenance of health behavior change is to empower the individual in relapse-prevention strategies (Greaves *et al.*, 2011). This is emphasized by Abraham and Michie (2008), who state that relapse prevention can "help identify situations likely to result in readopting risk behaviors or failure to maintain new behaviors and help the person plan to avoid or manage these situations" (p. 382).

Some examples of relapse-prevention strategies that can be used with a patient during the health behavior maintenance phase include:

- actively teaching strategies for illness perception/attitude changes to others;
- reinforce success through health outcomes, such as weight or blood pressure measurements, on an intermittent schedule;
- build self-efficacy for sustained change by reflecting on successes and benefits of health behavior changes;
- develop lifestyle-mindfulness skills that maintain awareness of physical, cognitive, and emotion changes that support positive health outcomes;
- manage distress, such as depression and anxiety, which can undermine positive health behaviors; and
- review progress in the treatment plan and introduce new health behavior goals as the patient has improved efficacy for change.

Interdisciplinary Models of Care

Notwithstanding the importance of the role of the health psychologist in the health behavior change process, this work with the patient is best not undertaken in isolation of concurrent medical, nursing, and allied health interventions. Interdisciplinary care is increasingly recognized as being critical to improving health outcomes for people living with chronic conditions. Interdisciplinary care is defined as an integrated approach to healthcare, being in contrast to multidisciplinary care, which often involves "silo" and non-integrated services (McCallin, 2001; see also Chapters 35 and 36 in this volume).

Development of a skill training program in chronic disease management by the main author of this chapter and a colleague (Lindner & Fuller, 2010) involved construction of an interdisciplinary model of care that places the patient in the center of the healthcare team (refer to Figure 1.2). Therefore, an important role of the health psychologist is to help the patient develop skills to be the central source of communications between their team of health professionals.

It is also important for health professionals working in an interdisciplinary team to actively ask about the patient's full health-intervention program, looking for opportunities to

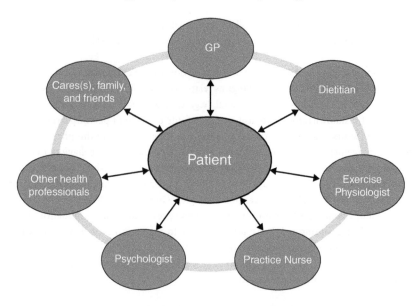

Figure 1.2 Patient-centered, interdisciplinary collaborative care model. From Lindner, H., & Fuller, T. (2010). Chronic Disease Self-Management and Lifestyle Risk Modification Training. Melbourne: The Australian Psychological Society.

reinforce the range of recommended treatments; for example, medications, testing procedures, and lifestyle changes.

Future Directions in the Study of Health Behavior Change

The growing acknowledgment of the importance of chronic illness management strategies emphasizes that professional support has an important role to play. However, the dominant model of chronic disease management still appears to focus on a medical model of healthcare, which does not actively support the important role of health behavior change in the prevention and treatment of illness. Furthermore, the role of health behavior change specialists, such as health psychologists, has not been routinely incorporated into interdisciplinary models of care. Therefore, it is important that future research investigates the health and healthcare system benefits of integrating health behavior change experts into routine healthcare.

References

Abbott, P., Davison, J., Moore, L., & Rubinstein, R. (2010). Barriers and enhancers to dietary behaviour change for Aboriginal people attending a diabetes cooking course. *Health Promotion Journal of Australia: Official Journal of Australian Association of Health Promotion Professionals, 21*, 33–38.

Abraham, C., & Michie, S. (2008). A taxonomy of behavior change techniques used in interventions. *Health Psychology, 27*, 379–387.

Abraham, C., Sheeran, P., & Henderson, M. (2011). Extending social cognition models of health behaviour. *Health Education Research, 26*, 624–637.

Australian Psychological Society. (2011). *Body Weight Management Interventions: Practice Guidelines.* Melbourne: Australian Psychological Society.

Blackburn, C., Bonas, S., Spencer, N., Dolan, A., Coe, C., & Moy, R. (2005). Smoking behaviour change among fathers of new infants. *Social Science & Medicine (1982), 61,* 517–526.

Brodie, D. A., Inoue, A., & Shaw, D. G. (2008). Motivational interviewing to change quality of life for people with chronic heart failure: A randomised controlled trial. *International Journal of Nursing Studies, 45,* 489–500.

Browning, C. J., & Thomas, S. A. (2003). Six-month outcome data for the Good Life Club project: An outcomes study of diabetes self-management. *Australian Journal of Primary Health, 9,* 192–198.

Browning, C. J., & Thomas, S. A. (2005). Models of behaviour change and health promotion. In C. Browning & S. A. Thomas (Eds.), *Behavioural Change: An Evidence-Based Handbook for Social and Public Health* (pp. 7–15). Edinburgh: Churchill Livingstone.

Clark, M., & Hampson, S. E. (2001). Implementing a psychological intervention to improve lifestyle self-management in patients with Type 2 diabetes. *Patient Education and Counseling, 42,* 247–256.

Deakin, T., Cade, J., & Williams, D. (2003). Group based self management strategies in people with type 2 diabetes mellitus. (Protocol for a Cochrane review). *The Cochrane Library, 1.*

Dobson, K. S., & Dozois, D. J. A. (2001). Historical and philosophical bases of the cognitive-behavioral therapies. In K. S. Dobson (Ed.), *Handbook of Cognitive-Behavioral Therapies* (pp. 3–39). New York: Guilford Press.

Donato, K. A. (2006). National health education programs to promote healthy eating and physical activity. *Nutrition Reviews, 64*(2 Pt 2), S65–S70.

Greaves, C. J., Sheppard, K. E., Abraham, C., Hardeman, W., Roden, M., Evans, P. H., IMAGE Study Group. (2011). Systematic review of reviews of intervention components associated with increased effectiveness in dietary and physical activity interventions. *BMC Public Health, 11,* 119.

Hagger, M. S., & Orbell, S. (2003). A meta-analytic review of the common-sense model of illness representations. *Psychology & Health, 18*(2), 141–184.

Handley, M., MacGregor, K., Schillinger, D., Sharifi, C., Wong, S., & Bodenheimer, T. (2006). Using action plans to help primary care patients adopt healthy behaviors: a descriptive study. *Journal of the American Board of Family Medicine: JABFM, 19,* 224–231.

Hansen, D., Dendale, P., Raskin, A., Schoonis, A., Berger, J., Vlassak, I., & Meeusen, R. (2010). Long-term effect of rehabilitation in coronary artery disease patients: randomized clinical trial of the impact of exercise volume. *Clinical Rehabilitation, 24,* 319–327.

Jones, H., Edwards, L., Vallis, T. M., Ruggiero, L., Rossi, S. R., Rossi, J. S. *et al.* (2003). Changes in diabetes self-care behaviors make a difference in glycemic control: The diabetes stages of change (DiSC) study. *Diabetes Care, 26,* 732–737.

Kim, C.-J., Hwang, A.-R., & Yoo, J.-S. (2004). The impact of a stage-matched intervention to promote exercise behavior in participants with Type 2 diabetes. *International Journal of Nursing Studies, 41,* 833–841.

Langford, A. T., Sawyer, D. R., Gioimo, S., Brownson, C. A., & O'Toole, M. L. (2007). Patient-centered goal setting as a tool to improve diabetes self-management. *The Diabetes Educator, 33*(Suppl. 6), 139S–144S.

Leventhal, H., Diefenbach, M., & Leventhal, E. A. (1992). Illness cognition: Using common sense to understand treatment adherence and affect cognition interactions. *Cognitive Therapy and Research, 16,* 143–163.

Lindner, H., & Fuller, T. (2010). *Chronic Disease Self-Management and Lifestyle Risk Modification Training.* Melbourne: The Australian Psychological Society.

Lindner, H., Menzies, D., & Kelly, J. (2003). Telephone coach training for health professionals in patient self-management strategies. *Australian Journal of Primary Health, 9,* 199–207.

Luszczynska, A., Gregajtys, A., & Abraham, C. (2007). Effects of a self-efficacy intervention on initiation of recommended exercises in patients with spondylosis. *Journal of Aging and Physical Activity, 15,* 26–40.

MacGregor, K., Handley, M., Wong, S., Sharifi, C., Gjeltema, K., Schillinger, D., & Bodenheimer, T. (2006). Behavior-change action plans in primary care: a feasibility study of clinicians. *Journal of the American Board of Family Medicine: JABFM, 19,* 215–223.

Mau, M. K., Glanz, K., Severino, R., Grove, J. S., Johnson, B., & Curb, J. D. (2001). Mediators of lifestyle behavior change in native Hawaiians. *Diabetes Care, 24,* 1770–1775.

McCallin, A. (2001). Interdisciplinary practice–a matter of teamwork: an integrated literature review. *Journal Of Clinical Nursing, 10,* 419–428.

Miller, N. H., Hill, M., Kottke, T., & Ockene, I. S. (1997). The multilevel compliance challenge: recommendations for a call to action. A statement for healthcare professionals. *Circulation, 95,* 1085–1090.

Papalazarou, A., Yannakoulia, M., Kavouras, S. A., Komesidou, V., Dimitriadis, G., Papakonstantinou, A., & Sidossis, L. S. (2010). Lifestyle intervention favorably affects weight loss and maintenance following obesity surgery. *Obesity (Silver Spring, Md.), 18,* 1348–1353.

Prochaska, J. O., & Velicer, W. F. (1997). The transtheoretical model of health behavior change. *American Journal of Health Promotion: AJHP, 12,* 38–48.

Prochaska, J. O., DiClemente, C. C., & Norcross, J. C. (1992). In search of how people change. Applications to addictive behaviors. *The American Psychologist, 47,* 1102–1114.

Prochaska, J. O., Butterworth, S., Redding, C. A., Burden, V., Perrin, N., Leo, M., & Prochaska, J. M. (2008). Initial efficacy of MI, TTM tailoring and HRI's with multiple behaviors for employee health promotion. *Preventive Medicine: An International Journal Devoted to Practice and Theory, 46,* 226–231.

Rollnick, S., & Miller, W. R. (1995). What is motivational interviewing? *Behavioural and Cognitive Psychotherapy, 23,* 325–334.

Rollnick, S., Heather, N., & Bell, A. (1992). Negotiating behaviour change in medical settings: The development of a brief motivational interviewing. *Journal of Mental Health, 1,* 25–37.

Schechter, C. B., & Walker, E. A. (2002). Improving adherence to diabetes self-management recommendations. *Diabetes Spectrum, 15,* 170–175.

Vale, M. J., Jelinek, M. V., Best, J. D., Dart, A. M., Grigg, L. E., Hare, D. L. *et al.* (2003). Coaching patients On Achieving Cardiovascular Health (COACH): A multicenter randomized trial in patients with coronary heart disease. *Archives of Internal Medicine, 163,* 2775–2783.

Watson, M., Briganti, E., Skinner, T., & Manning, C. (2003). Self-management strategies for adults with Type 1 diabetes mellitus (Protocol for a Cochrane Review). *The Cochrane Library, 1.*

Whitmarsh, A., Koutantji, M., & Sidell, K. (2003). Illness perceptions, mood and coping in predicting attendance at cardiac rehabilitation. *British Journal Of Health Psychology, 8,* 209–221.

WHO. (2003). *Adherence to Long-Term Therapies: Evidence for Action.* Geneva: World Health Organization.

WHO. (2010). *Global Status Report on Noncommunicable Diseases 2010.* Geneva: World Health Organization.

WHO. (2011). *Noncommunicable Diseases: Country Profiles 2011.* Geneva: World Health Organization.

2

Health Coaching

Facilitating Health Behavior Change for Chronic Condition Prevention and Self-Management

Janette Gale and Helen Skouteris

The increasing prevalence of chronic disease and chronic disease risk factors for conditions such as diabetes, stroke, heart, lung, kidney, and other so-called lifestyle diseases has been well documented [World Health Organization (WHO), 2005]. Chronic disease is estimated to account for 60% of deaths worldwide (WHO, 2008) and 50% of encounters with a general practitioner (medical doctor) involve management of a problem associated with chronic disease (Britt et al., 2004). Such chronic diseases can be prevented in many cases, or their impact reduced, by altering lifestyle behaviors and self-managing conditions more effectively [Centers for Disease Control and Prevention (CDC), 2009]. Yet adherence to recommendations for the management of chronic diseases has been estimated to be around only 50% and there is growing recognition that provision of information/education/advice alone is not sufficient to produce significant changes in health behavior (WHO, 2003). Adoption of new behaviors is more likely if patients are encouraged to form a behavioral intention at the time of being provided with health information (Boyce et al., 2008), and if they engage in volitional planning processes in order to convert that intention to action (Sniehotta et al., 2005). Hence there is a recognition that health behavior change interventions need to include strategies that directly target changes in cognition and behavior in addition to providing patient education. As a consequence, health coaching interventions are increasingly being used by private and public health organizations worldwide to increase adherence to recommendations and to facilitate health behavior change for chronic disease prevention and chronic condition self-management (e.g., Butterworth et al., 2007; Lindner et al., 2003). Health coaching techniques are also being integrated into everyday clinical practice by a growing number of health practitioners for the same reasons.

In this chapter, we review the theoretical and empirical evidence base for health coaching. The theoretical evidence is drawn from well-known health behavior change frameworks and psychological clinical practice models. The empirical evidence, while currently limited, is growing. We differentiate health coaching from other types of coaching and counselling interventions, and outline the commonalities between health coaching applications being used in various health and medical contexts. An integrated health behavior change model that has been developed in

Applied Topics in Health Psychology, First Edition. Edited by M. L. Caltabiano and L. Ricciardelli.
© 2013 John Wiley & Sons, Ltd. Published 2013 by John Wiley & Sons, Ltd.

Australia is presented as an example of how learning from the extensive theoretical literature can be incorporated into health coaching programs and clinical consultations in a parsimonious manner.

Health Coaching: What Is It?

The term "health coaching" implies that the role of the person delivering the intervention (usually a health practitioner) is to actively assist clients to change their health behaviors in a collaborative and individualized manner; that is, to coach, in contrast to educating, "telling," or counselling clients regarding which actions to take. In discussing the health coaching approach, Linden *et al.* (2010) note that:

> behavior change theories and models have evolved, moving health education interventions away from the traditional information-based and advice-giving model to one that embraces and addresses the complex interaction of motivations, cues to action, perception of benefits and consequences, environmental and cultural influences, expectancies, self-efficacy, state of readiness to change, ambivalence and implementation intentions. (p. 166)

The physiological and behavioral targets of health coaching interventions are usually risk factors and/or indicators of chronic disease. Examples of individual and program goals pursued in health coaching interventions are: self-managing chronic diseases or conditions such as diabetes, cardiovascular disease, obesity, arthritis, and chronic pain; managing weight; increasing activity; improving nutrition; managing stress; lowering blood glucose levels, lipid levels, and blood pressure; and engaging in specific treatment options for medical conditions, such as immunotherapy for multiple sclerosis.

Although there is no single agreed definition of health coaching, a constant theme among researchers and practitioners is that health coaching is a practice in which health practitioners apply evidence-based health behavior change principles and techniques to assist their clients to adhere to treatment and lifestyle recommendations, for the purpose of achieving better health outcomes or quality of life (Gale, 2012). For example, Palmer *et al.* (2003) defined health coaching as "the practice of health education and health promotion within a coaching context, to enhance the wellbeing of individuals and to facilitate the achievement of their health-related goals" (p. 92). Similarly, Butterworth *et al.* (2007) defined health coaching as "a behavioral health intervention that facilitates participants in establishing and attaining health-promoting goals in order to change lifestyle-related behaviors, with the intent of reducing health risks, improving self-management of chronic conditions and increasing health-related quality of life" (p. 300). Different definitions reflect greater relative emphasis on a subset of the various components most often included in health coaching interventions:

- provision of health education and information, e.g., disease-specific, treatment-specific, and general health and lifestyle recommendations;
- provision of health behavior change education and information, e.g., understanding change and change processes, tips on decision-making, how to set goals, track progress, and solve problems;
- behavior modification support, e.g., goal setting, action planning, environment modification, and contingency management/reward systems;
- motivation enhancement, e.g., moving clients through readiness-based states or stages of change, and decisional balance assistance;

- problem solving support, e.g., identifying and addressing behavioral, emotional, situational, and cognitive barriers to change, decision-support, and relapse prevention;
- psychosocial support, e.g., brief emotion-management strategies and/or referral to deal with psychosocial aspects of managing health conditions (acceptance, fear, distress, guilt, etc.).

Indeed, many industry-based health coaching interventions contain an education component, goal setting, and recognition of the need to acknowledge and address client readiness to change [Healthcare Intelligence Network (HIN), 2009]. These interventions are, therefore, cognitive-behavioral in intent (if not explicitly so). They aim to change cognitive variables such as beliefs, motivation, and self-efficacy in order to induce behavior change. However, cognitive behavior therapy (CBT) has been used primarily as an intervention to address emotional or psychosocial aspects of chronic disease, and infrequently applied to health behavior change impacting directly on lifestyle change and self-management of health conditions (Butler *et al.*, 2006). We propose that, given that common clinically observed barriers to health behavior change concern values, priorities, beliefs, expectations, attitudes, and everyday thinking patterns, it is essential to include techniques that actively identify and address cognitive as well as behavioral, emotional, and environmental barriers to change.

Health coaching contrasts with traditional medical provision of treatment and lifestyle advice, and also with general coaching and counselling modalities. Figure 2.1 shows graphically where health coaching-based clinical practice and health coaching-based chronic disease and lifestyle management programs are positioned along several continua in relation to these other modalities.

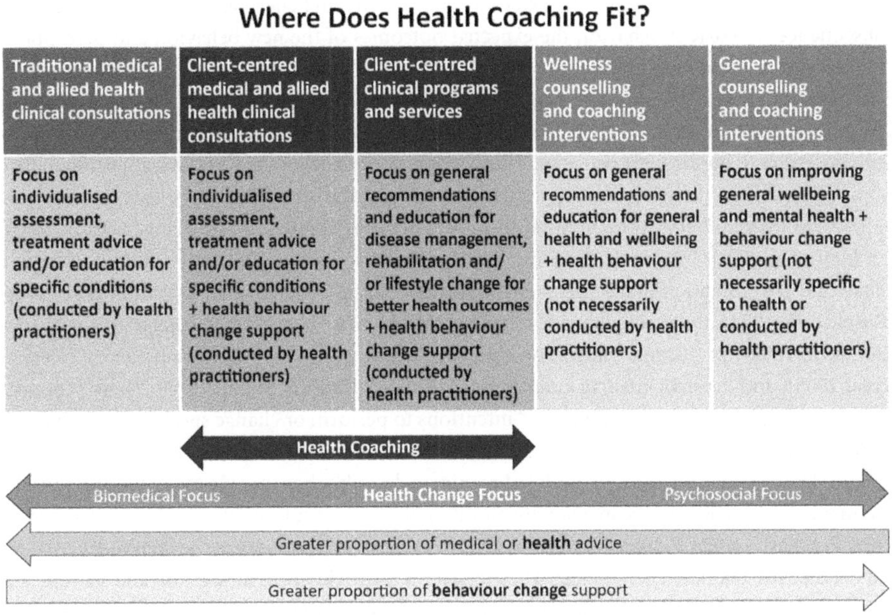

Where Does Health Coaching Fit?

Traditional medical and allied health clinical consultations	Client-centred medical and allied health clinical consultations	Client-centred clinical programs and services	Wellness counselling and coaching interventions	General counselling and coaching interventions
Focus on individualised assessment, treatment advice and/or education for specific conditions (conducted by health practitioners)	Focus on individualised assessment, treatment advice and/or education for specific conditions + health behaviour change support (conducted by health practitioners)	Focus on general recommendations and education for disease management, rehabilitation and/ or lifestyle change for better health outcomes + health behaviour change support (conducted by health practitioners)	Focus on general recommendations and education for general health and wellbeing + health behaviour change support (not necessarily conducted by health practitioners)	Focus on improving general wellbeing and mental health + behaviour change support (not necessarily specific to health or conducted by health practitioners)

Health Coaching ◄──────►

Biomedical Focus ◄──────── Health Change Focus ──────── Psychosocial Focus ►

Greater proportion of medical or **health** advice

Greater proportion of **behaviour change** support

Figure 2.1 The health change spectrum. *Source:* Gale (2012). *A Practical Guide to Health Behaviour Change Using the HCA Approach.* Sydney: Health Change Australia. Reproduced by permission of Health Change Australia Pty Ltd.

The Rationale for Health Coaching: The Theoretical Evidence

Health coaching interventions generally incorporate multiple complementary theoretical health behavior change models and concepts in their design. Organizations that reported utilizing health coaching in a HIN (2009) industry survey stated that they used the following well-known behavior change models (the percentage of organizations ($n=235$) using each model is presented in parentheses): stages of change (86%), a positive psychology model (48%), social cognitive theory/increasing confidence (36%), theory of planned behavior (26%), and the implementation intentions model (14%).

The many theoretical models, constructs, and principles that exist in the health behavior change literature provide insight into human behavior. They explain why only 50% of people (or less) adhere to treatment and lifestyle recommendations, and suggest what is required to facilitate and maintain change (Becker, 1985). There have been a number of attempts to distil essential concepts from the different theories (Abraham *et al.*, 2009; Dixon, 2008; Fishbein *et al.*, 2001; Michie *et al.*, 2005; Noar & Zimmerman, 2005; Webb *et al.*, 2010). From these there appear to be three main categories of processes required to optimally facilitate health behavior change: (1) processes required to form a behavioral goal intention, (2) processes required to convert the behavioral goal intention into action and maintenance, and (3) communication processes that are characteristic of a patient-centered therapeutic approach.

There is a general consensus in the literature that two fundamental cognitive drivers that affect intention to make a behavioral change are motivation (i.e., one's desire or will to engage in the behavior) and self-efficacy (i.e., belief in one's ability to perform the behavior) (Bandura, 2001; Dixon, 2008; Fishbein *et al.*, 2001; Mason & Butler, 2010; Rollnick *et al.*, 1999). A number of different factors are known to influence motivation, including conscious and subconscious processes, risk appraisal, internal and external drivers, different beliefs (and knowledge) about the consequences of current behavior, the expected outcomes of the new behavior, and perceptions of social norms including others' attitudes and behavioral approval (Dixon, 2008; Fishbein *et al.*, 2001; Martin *et al.*, 2010; Michie *et al.*, 2005). The second component, self-efficacy (Bandura, 1986), is related to one's confidence in or perception of behavioral control, and appraisal of one's skills necessary to perform the behavior. Thus, people need to believe that making a specific change is important, given their other competing priorities, and they need to believe that they are able to perform the required action, in order to form a behavioral intention to change (Dixon, 2008; Fishbein *et al.*, 2001; Michie *et al.*, 2005). What we refer to here as processes required to form a behavioral goal intention draws together the essential components from the health belief model (Rosenstock, 1974), theory of planned behaviour (Fishbein & Ajzen, 1975), social cognitive theory (Bandura, 2001), protection motivation theory (Rogers, 1983), self-regulation theory (Deci & Ryan, 2008), and decision-making and decisional balance (Janis & Mann, 1977). These processes are the driving forces behind individuals' intentions to perform or change specific behaviors.

Motivation and self-efficacy relate closely to the commonly used concept of readiness to change. The most widely utilised model of readiness describes how people move toward, initiate, and maintain behavior change in qualitatively different stages over time (Prochaska & DiClemente, 1984; Prochaska *et al.*, 2008b). Rollnick *et al.* (1999) describe readiness as the combined effect of importance and confidence to change. These concepts relate closely to motivation and self-efficacy respectively. Gale (2012) suggests that it is also clinically useful to conceptualize timing (of current situational factors in an individual's life) as a third factor that impacts on readiness to change. In essence, readiness is a useful concept due to the assumption that the clinical intervention and processes of change that will most effectively move a person toward the ultimate behavioral goal will vary depending on the individual's current stage (or level) of readiness (Prochaska & DiClemente, 1984).

Once an individual has made the decision to change his or her behavior and has formed a behavioral goal intention, processes such as those encapsulated in the notion of volitional planning are required to convert the goal intention into action and maintenance (Sheeran *et al.*, 2005). According to the model of action phases (Heckhausen & Gollwitzer, 1987), volitional processes are required because "whereas intention formation is guided by people's beliefs about the desirability and feasibility of particular courses of action, intention realization is guided by conscious and unconscious processes that promote the initiation and effective pursuit of the goal" (Sheeran *et al.*, 2005, pp. 279–80). The components of behavioral volition include goal setting and action planning (which incorporates a knowledge of both what to do and how); overcoming barriers (dealing with environmental or tangible constraints, coping planning, building hope and cognitive-behavioral therapy strategies to overcome psychological or emotional barriers); and forming implementation intentions (planning "if-then" strategies to identify when and how to act, and how to respond in a specific situation that may otherwise undermine intended behavior). These volitional processes draw together the essential theoretical components from goal setting theory (Locke *et al.*, 1981), the model of action phases (Heckhausen & Gollwitzer, 1987), implementation intentions model (Gollwitzer, 1993, 1999), coping Planning (Sniehotta *et al.*, 2005), and hope theory (Snyder, 2002). These processes are also reflected in clinical tools from CBT (Beck, 1993), solution-focused coaching (Grant & Greene, 2003), and relapse prevention (Marlatt & Gordon, 1980).

The third and final set of processes required for health systems and clinicians to optimally facilitate behavioral change is the "therapeutic approach" or the context and communication processes of the health consultation and patient–practitioner interaction. The literature in this area indicates that a patient-centered approach that encourages a positive therapeutic alliance, client choice and decision-making, respect for the needs and preferences of the client, a focus on client autonomy and intrinsic motivation (rather than extrinsic or controlled motivation), and communication that is non-confrontational and non-judgmental (rather than didactic, coercive or fear inducing) is positively associated with effective performance, maintained behavior change, and psychological wellbeing (Becker, 1985; Butler *et al.*, 1999; Moller *et al.*, 2006; Wagner *et al.*, 2005). These communication processes incorporate theory and intervention models from motivational interviewing (Miller & Rollnick, 2002), the patient-centered approach (as in Wagner *et al.*, 2005), therapeutic alliance (Bordin, 1975; Luborsky, 1976), self-determination theory (Deci & Ryan, 2008), and intrinsic motivation (Deci & Ryan, 2008; Vansteenkiste *et al.*, 2006).

In order to understand why health behavior change interventions work and how to design them to be optimally effective and efficient, we need to be able to measure the effectiveness of the interactions that occur between clinicians and patients or program participants (Dixon, 2008). This requires the systematic application of behavior change principles across clinicians in any one intervention, and the collection of behavior change process data that can shed light on which techniques and processes are responsible for changes in relevant psychological variables, behavior, and – ultimately – the physiological outcome measures targeted in health coaching interventions.

The Efficacy of Health Coaching: Empirical Evidence

Much of the evidence for the efficacy of health coaching interventions is to be found in the health management industry in the USA. Unfortunately, this evidence tends not to be published in the academic research literature and is not usually subjected to rigorous scientific research protocols due to commercial-in-confidence considerations, the costs involved in conducting large controlled clinical trials, and the need to include all clients in the intervention group. However, insights into this growing health coaching industry in corporate health services can be seen in reports such as those compiled by the HIN (e.g., HIN, 2009). This organization publishes industry surveys (self-selecting respondents) and provides input from senior managers of health coaching programs within large, reputable not-for-profit health service providers such as the Mayo Clinic and Duke University medical services, in addition to many commercial industry leaders.

The most commonly cited target health issues in the 2009 HIN survey were weight management, tobacco cessation, and stress management, followed by exercise, diabetes management, and nutrition. Among the surveyed organizations, telephone health coaching was the primary delivery mode (86%) followed by 58% online delivery, 40% by mail, and only 38% delivered in person. Being in the corporate domain, health risk assessments were the main referral method (76%). Other referral methods were self-referral (71%), health claims (47%), and physician referral (32%). Organizations responding to the survey reported return on investment of between 1/5:1 and 5:1 (HIN, 2009).

In the public health domain, a survey of public health organizations within the state of Victoria in Australia in 2007 mapped self-management training for health practitioners across 216 government and non-government agencies providing disease management services. The report concluded: "The responses suggest that health coaching, motivational interviewing and the Flinders model of care planning are the most common approaches being applied in practice, with 78%, 72% and 54% of practitioners trained in the approach using it in practice. This may indicate that health coaching is the most practical in terms of transferability into practice" [Victorian Government Department of Human Services (DHS), 2007, p. 6].

Health coaching in community health programs such as the Victorian Early Intervention in Chronic Disease (EICD) program and Hospital Admission Risk Program (HARP) included in the above report is mainly delivered face to face. However, it is becoming increasingly common for government health interventions to incorporate telephonic health coaching. Examples of these are the Get Healthy Information and Coaching Service® (www.gethealthynsw.com.au) being run in Australia by the NSW, ACT, and Tasmanian governments, and the WorkSafe Victoria WorkHealth Coach telephonic health coaching program (www.workhealth.vic.gov.au), both of which aim to reduce chronic disease risk factors in the population. Outcome evidence from these interventions is still pending as data collection continues at the time of writing this chapter.

Most of the evidence base that supports the use of health coaching principles comes directly from the peer-reviewed literature on health behavior change and chronic disease prevention and management programs that use evidence-based health behavior change protocols. This literature is extensive and continues to grow. However, the empirical evidence base for health coaching programs is still in its infancy and randomized controlled trials are few.

An integrative review of interventions aiming to improve healthy lifestyle behaviors via health coaching was recently published by Olsen and Nesbitt (2010); their search was limited to peer-reviewed research articles published between 1999 and 2008. The common elements of effective health coaching programs were the use of goal setting, motivational interviewing (to help clients both select and achieve their health behavior goals), collaboration with primary healthcare providers, and program durations of 6–12 months.

As an extension of Olsen and Nesbitt's review, we reviewed the literature for controlled studies published between 2000 and 2011 and found 15 studies that have evaluated the effectiveness of a health coaching intervention on physiological, behavioral, and psychological aspects of health and non-communicable disease; six of the studies we reviewed were also included in Olsen and Nesbitt's paper (Bennett *et al.*, 2005; Brodin *et al.*, 2008; Butterworth *et al.*, 2007; Holland *et al.*,

2005; Paineau *et al.*, 2008; Vale *et al.*, 2003). The type of health coaching offered differed between studies, and included the following behavior change strategies: identification of stress, problems, and barriers, and resolving these to achieve goals (Bennett *et al.*, 2005; Brodin *et al.*, 2008; Grey *et al.*, 2009; Hibbard *et al.*, 2007; Saelens *et al.*, 2002), goal setting (Bennett *et al.*, 2005; Brodin *et al.*, 2008; Edelman *et al.*, 2006; Spence *et al.*, 2008), enhancing self-efficacy (Campbell *et al.*, 2009; Grey *et al.*, 2009; Linden *et al.*, 2010), moving stage of readiness to change (Campbell *et al.*, 2009; Linden *et al.*, 2010; Prochaska *et al.*, 2008a), developing an individualized action plan (Chen *et al.*, 2010; Grey *et al.*, 2009; Holland *et al.*, 2005; Vale *et al.*, 2003), resolving conflict and improving communication (Grey *et al.*, 2009; Hibbard *et al.*, 2007), creating a risk overview and self-assessment (Chen *et al.*, 2010; Linden *et al.*, 2010), communication and assertiveness training (Hibbard *et al.*, 2007; Vale *et al.*, 2003), and increasing patient activation (Hibbard *et al.*, 2007; Linden *et al.*, 2010).

Findings from physiological outcomes of interest were generally positive. Health coaching interventions resulted in a decrease in hypertension (Chen *et al.*, 2010), improvements for sufferers of rheumatoid arthritis (Brodin *et al.*, 2008), greater reduction in total cholesterol and low-density-lipoprotein cholesterol (Vale *et al.*, 2003), and improved overall physical health (Butterworth *et al.*, 2007). However, four studies reported mixed or inconclusive results (Bennett *et al.*, 2005; Edelman *et al.*, 2006; Holland *et al.*, 2005; Prochaska *et al.*, 2008a). Of the six studies that measured body mass index (BMI) as an outcome only three studies reported significant improvements in BMI; two in adult BMI only (Paineau *et al.*, 2008; Vale *et al.*, 2003) and the other in adolescent BMI (Saelens *et al.*, 2002).

Findings were more consistent for behavioral outcome measures. For instance, all studies that reported on nutrition, goal attainment, and self-management plan formulation found improvements in these measures (Brodin *et al.*, 2008; Campbell *et al.*, 2009; Chen *et al.*, 2010; Hibbard *et al.*, 2007; Paineau *et al.*, 2008; Spence *et al.*, 2008; Vale *et al.*, 2003). Four studies examining changes in physical activity reported improvements in this outcome (Brodin *et al.*, 2008; Edelman *et al.*, 2006; Holland *et al.*, 2005; Prochaska *et al.*, 2008a), and Vale *et al.* (2003) reported that more intervention participants had taken up walking. However, two studies found no improvements in physical activity (Paineau *et al.*, 2008; Saelens *et al.*, 2002).

Similar to behavioral measures, findings regarding changes in psychological outcomes were generally positive in nature. As a result of their health coaching interventions, studies reported improvements in motivation to change (Edelman *et al.*, 2006; Linden *et al.*, 2010; Prochaska *et al.*, 2008a), stress (Prochaska *et al.*, 2008a; Spence *et al.*, 2008), general mental health (Butterworth *et al.*, 2007), perceived global health status (Linden *et al.*, 2010), anxiety (Spence *et al.*, 2008), and self-efficacy (Linden *et al.*, 2010). Findings were less consistent for patient activation (Hibbard *et al.*, 2007; Linden *et al.*, 2010) and depression (Grey *et al.*, 2009; Holland *et al.*, 2005; Spence *et al.*, 2008).

As described, health coaching has potential for application to reduce risk factors associated with preventable diseases such as high BMI, physical inactivity, and a poor diet, and to increase health change facilitators such as motivation and self-efficacy. There is, however, a need for studies to elaborate on the health behavior change processes and theories underlying their models of health coaching and to use consistent behavior change facilitators across studies to allow detailed comparison. This may shed some light on the reasons for the outcome inconsistencies reported above. More research evaluating specific outcomes tailored to reflect health behavior change process variables is also needed.

Whereas the evidence base in health behavior change informs practitioners regarding important concepts and techniques, the number of competing and overlapping models makes it difficult to apply the theory base in a coherent, integrated, and time-efficient manner in clinical and program-based interventions. In order to standardize these processes in an intervention, clinicians require clear, structured guidance regarding which principles to apply and how exactly to apply them. Hence, program designers need to clearly articulate which health behavior change models and processes will be used and how they will be operationalized, ensure that clinicians are supported to gain and develop the required knowledge and skill sets, and build in quality-assurance processes to verify appropriate use of the nominated processes by clinicians. These program design features are essential if evaluators are to fully assess the efficacy of interventions and to attribute any observed positive outcomes to the various intervention processes.

The HCA Model: a Theoretically Driven Health Coaching Model

The Health Change Australia (HCA) Model of Health Change™ (Gale, 2012) is a clinical practice framework for integrating client-centered communication and behavior change principles and processes into clinical practice and programs. It provides practitioners with an evidence-based health behavior change clinical pathway to complement usual clinical pathways for prevention and treatment of health conditions. Many public and corporate health organizations in Australia have trained their staff in health coaching skills using this model. These include the majority of organizations reporting uptake of health coaching in the Victorian DHS 2007 chronic disease self-management mapping survey cited above.

The HCA model is a cognitive-behavioral model that helps health practitioners to assess, build, and support client readiness, willingness, and ability to adhere to medical treatment and lifestyle recommendations. The aim of the model is to identify and address behavioral, emotional, situational, and cognitive barriers to health behavior change in a time-efficient manner. It systematically combines a diverse range of theoretical concepts and health behavior change processes into an integrated framework so that they can be applied consistently by health practitioners in clinical consultations and health coaching programs. The 10-step decision framework of the HCA model allows practitioners to assist clients to prioritise their health changes, increase their motivation, make appropriate decisions and increase their self-efficacy to engage in sustainable health behavior change. The 10 steps represent 10 different points in a health consultation when barriers to change can be expected to emerge for a client. Each step provides guidance regarding the methods to use to check for these potential barriers and the techniques to use to address them (Gale, 2012).

The model embraces and operationalizes a patient-centered approach. It includes the use of motivational, volitional, and problem solving processes from brief motivational interviewing (Rollnick *et al.*, 1999), solution-focused coaching (Grant & Greene, 2003), and CBT (Beck, 1993; British Association for Behavioural and Cognitive Psychotherapies, 2005) that have been adapted for use in medical and health consultations to increase adherence to treatment and lifestyle recommendations.

The HCA model bridges the gap between behavior change theory and practice for health practitioners. It guides and enables health practitioners to build client knowledge and understanding, motivation, and self-efficacy in the following ways.

- Provide clients with individualized treatment and/or lifestyle recommendations, education, and referral advice in a way that reduces resistance and increases comprehension and acceptance of this information.

- Assist clients to decide whether or not it is in their own interests to adopt treatment recommendations and/or healthy lifestyle changes, given the personal tradeoffs that they will have to make to do this. The aim is to build and support clients' autonomous motivation and engagement in pursuing health goals, with a deliberate emphasis on those goals with the most critical or beneficial health and/or quality-of-life outcomes.
- Develop clients' problem solving skills so that they are more systematic and successful in making decisions and planning, initiating, and sustaining behavior changes.

The main guiding principle of the HCA model is the RICk Principle™. It prompts practitioners to be mindful of the client's *readiness* to adopt new behaviors, perceived personal *importance* in making changes (relative to other priorities), *confidence* in carrying out the required actions, and *knowledge* and understanding of relevant health information. These factors have been adapted from the brief motivational interviewing of Rollnick *et al.* (1999). Depending on a client's RICk profile, a practitioner is guided to systematically employ techniques that target deficiencies in any of the client's RICk factors to facilitate the client's change processes. Using this model it is clinically common to see clients move from low readiness (or precontemplation) to high readiness (preparation) within a consultation, once their barriers to taking action have been identified and addressed.

The HCA model incorporates aspects of a number of well-regarded health behavior change models and concepts, including the three categories of processes identified in the previous section as critical to facilitating health behavior change. The theoretical flow chart depicted in Figure 2.2 shows the key links between theory and processes for the model. The various back arrows in the figure represent the often dynamic nature of the behavior change process when using the HCA decision framework. These dynamics reflect the changing levels of readiness experienced by clients depending upon the presence of barriers and facilitators for change and the subsequent responsiveness of practitioners to fluctuating levels of the client's readiness, importance, and confidence in taking action.

A defining feature of the model is a decision line that acts as a reminder to clinicians not to progress into goal setting and action planning until the client has made a conscious decision to pursue health behavior change goals for their own autonomously motivating reasons. Above the decision line, the clinician's task is primarily to support motivational and decision-making processes to guide the client toward forming a macrolevel behavioral intention to make health-enhancing changes. Below the decision line the main task is to engage the client in volitional processes such as implementation planning and coping planning, and to build and support the client's self-efficacy in relation to his or her chosen microlevel goal(s).

The systematic nature of the HCA model allows health behavior change process measures to be recorded for evaluation and quality-assurance purposes. These measures can be used to determine whether the health behavior change component of an intervention is effective, and whether or not individual clinicians are applying health behavior change protocols effectively and efficiently.

To effectively use models like the one described here, clinicians need to have preexisting knowledge and skill sets in:

- intervention-relevant medical and health knowledge;
- patient-centered communication (especially motivational interviewing and solution-focused approaches);

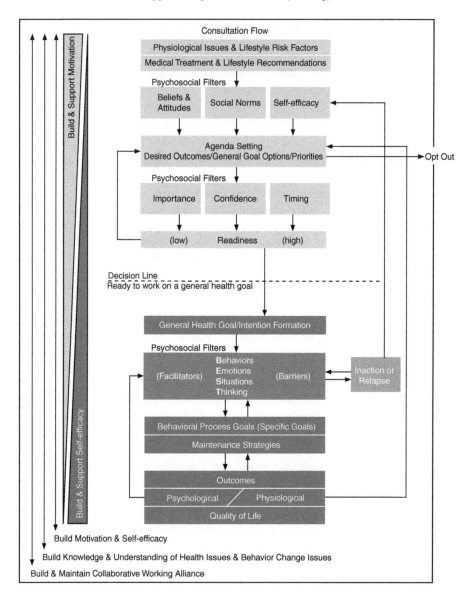

Figure 2.2 HCA theoretical model. *Source:* Gale (2010). Health Coaching Guide for Health Practitioners: Using the HCA Model of Health Coaching. Sydney: Health Coaching Australia. Reproduced by permission of Health Coaching Australia Pty Ltd.

- the health behavior change theory base underpinning the model; and
- identifying and addressing behavioral, emotional, situational, and cognitive barriers to health behavior change.

Figure 2.3 shows the HCA 10-step decision framework that operationalizes the theory base. It depicts the relationship of the 10 steps to readiness, the decision line, and the relative focus on building motivation and confidence above and below the decision line.

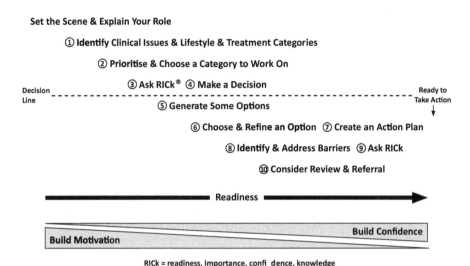

Set the Scene & Explain Your Role

① Identify Clinical Issues & Lifestyle & Treatment Categories

② Prioritise & Choose a Category to Work On

Decision Line ③ Ask RICk® ④ Make a Decision Ready to Take Action

⑤ Generate Some Options

⑥ Choose & Refine an Option ⑦ Create an Action Plan

⑧ Identify & Address Barriers ⑨ Ask RICk

⑩ Consider Review & Referral

Readiness

Build Confidence

Build Motivation

RICk = readiness, importance, confi dence, knowledge

Figure 2.3 The HCA model 10-step decision framework. *Source:* Gale (2012). *A Practical Guide to Health Behaviour Change Using the HCA Approach.* Sydney: Health Change Australia. Reproduced by permission of Health Change Australia Pty Ltd.

Conclusions

The development and promulgation of models such as the HCA Model of Health Change, which explicitly show the theoretical constructs and practical processes that can be included in chronic condition prevention and management interventions, offer the potential for greater transparency, accountability, and evaluation (and, thus, comparison) of programs. For this potential to be realized, however, there will need to be greater attention paid to articulating and recording the processes used in such interventions, and, ideally, a greater range of process measures used. Traditionally, most studies only report simple outcome measures of programs (mainly behavioral or physiological outcome variables), which does not allow an assessment of the relative effectiveness of the individual components of the intervention. There is clearly a much wider range of measures (including behavioral, emotional, and cognitive intervening variables and correlates) that could be included, and which should lead to a greater understanding of what is working and what is not in a given intervention. This may provide a better understanding of the wide range of results reported in the literature. In time, this may lead to the development of new models that will improve the effectiveness and efficiency of health interventions. These models should not only add to our understanding of the types of interventions that improve health outcomes, but also which health behavior change mechanisms are responsible for any positive results.

References

Abraham, C., Kelly, M. P., West, R., & Michie, S. (2009). The UK national institute for health and clinical excellence public health guidance on behaviour change: A brief introduction. *Psychology, Health & Medicine, 14,* 1–8.

Bandura, A. (1986). *Social foundations of thought and action: A social cognitive theory*. Englewood Cliffs, NJ: Prentice-Hall.

Bandura, A. (2001). Social cognitive theory: An agentic perspective. *Annual Review of Psychology, 52*, 1–26.

Beck, A. (1993). *Cognitive Therapy and the Emotional Disorders*. New York: Penguin.

Becker, M. H. (1985). Patient adherence to prescribed therapies. *Medical Care, 23*, 539–555.

Bennett, J. A., Perrin, N. A., Hanson, G., Bennett, D., Gaynor, W., Flaherty-Robb, M. *et al.* (2005). Healthy aging demonstration project: Nurse coaching for behavior change in older adults. *Research in Nursing & Health, 28*, 187–197.

Bordin, E. S. (1975). *The Working Alliance: Basis for a General Theory of Psychotherapy*. Paper presented at the Annual Meeting of the Society for Psychotherapy Research.

Boyce, T., Robertson, R., & Dixon, A. (2008). *Commissioning and Behaviour Change: Kicking Bad Habits Final Report*. www.kingsfund.org.uk/publications/kbh_final_report.html.

British Association for Behavioural and Cognitive Psychotherapies. (2005). *Mapping Psychotherapy – What is CBT? What are Cognitive and/or Behavioural Psychotherapies?* Paper prepared for a UKCP/BACP mapping psychotherapy exercise, K. Graesbrook, A. Garland, & the Board of BABCP. www.babcp.com/silo/files/what-is-cbt.pdf.

Britt, H., Miller, G. C., Knox, S., Charles, J., Valenti, L., Bayram, C. *et al.* (2004). *General Practice Activity in the States and Territories of Australia 1998–2003*. www.aihw.gov.au/publication-detail/?id=6442467636.

Brodin, N., Eurenius, E., Jensen, I., Nisell, R., & Opava, C. H. (2008). Coaching patients with early rheumatoid arthritis to healthy physical activity: A multicenter, randomized, controlled study. *Arthritis & Rheumatism, 59*, 325–331.

Butler, C. C., Rollnick, S., & Stott, N. C. H. (1999). The practitioner, the patient and resistance to change: Recent ideas on compliance. *Canadian Medical Association Journal, 154*, 1357–1362.

Butler, A. C., Chapman, J. E., Forman, E. M., & Beck, A. T. (2006). The empirical status of cognitive-behavioral therapy: A review of meta-analyses. *Clinical Psychology Review, 26*, 17–31.

Butterworth, S. W., Linden, A., & McClay, W. (2007). Health coaching as an intervention in health management programs. *Disease Management & Health Outcomes, 15*, 299–307.

Campbell, M. K., Carr, C., DeVellis, B., Switzer, B., Biddle, A., Amamoo, M. A. *et al.* (2009). A randomized trial of tailoring and motivational interviewing to promote fruit and vegetable consumption for cancer prevention and control. *Annals of Behavioral Medicine, 38*, 71–85.

CDC. (2009). *The Power of Prevention: Chronic Disease . . . the Public Health Challenge of the 21st Century*. Atlanta, GA: Centers for Disease Control and Prevention. www.cdc.gov/chronicdisease/pdf/2009-Power-of-Prevention.pdf.

Chen, E., Thom, D., Hessler, D., Phengrasamy, L., Hammer, H., Saba, G., & Bodenheimer, T. (2010). Using the teamlet model to improve chronic care in an academic primary care practice. *Journal of General Internal Medicine, 25*, 610–614.

Deci, E. L., & Ryan, R. M. (2008). Self-determination theory: A macrotheory of human motivation, development, and health. *Canadian Psychology, 49*, 182–185.

DHS. (2007). *Self-management Mapping State-Wide Report: Self-Management Support – a State-Wide View 2006–7*. Melbourne, Victoria: Department of Human Services.

Dixon, A. (2008). *Motivation and Confidence: What Does it Take to Change Behaviour?* www.kingsfund.org.uk/current_projects/kicking_bad_habits/.

Edelman, D., Oddone, E., Liebowitz, R., Yancy, W., Olsen, M., Jeffreys, A. *et al.* (2006). A multidimensional integrative medicine intervention to improve cardiovascular risk. *Journal of General Internal Medicine, 21*, 728–734.

Fishbein, M., & Ajzen, I. (1975). *Belief, Attitude, Intention, and Behavior: an Introduction to Theory and Research*. Reading, MA: Addison-Wesley.

Fishbein, M., Triandis, H. C., Kanfer, F. H., Becker, M. H., Middlestadt, S. E., & Eichler, A. (2001). Factors influencing behavior and behaviour change. In A. Baum, T. A. Revenson, & J. E. Singer (Eds.), *Handbook of Health Psychology* (pp. 3–17). Mahwah, NJ: Lawrence Elbaum.

Gale, J. (2010). Health Coaching Guide for Health Practitioners: Using the HCA Model of Health Coaching. Sydney: Health Coaching Australia

Gale, J. (2012). *A Practical Guide to Health Behaviour Change Using the HCA Approach.* Sydney: Health Change Australia.

Gollwitzer, P. (1993). Goal achievement: The role of intentions. *European Review of Social Psychology, 4,* 141–185.

Gollwitzer, P. (1999). Implementation intentions: Strong effects of simple plans. *American Psychologist, 54,* 493–503.

Grant, A., & Greene, J. (2003). *Solution-Focused Coaching.* Harlow: Pearson Education.

Grey, M., Jaser, S. S., Holl, M. G., Jefferson, V., Dziura, J., & Northrup, V. (2009). A multifaceted school-based intervention to reduce risk for type 2 diabetes in at-risk youth. *Preventive Medicine, 49,* 122–128.

Heckhausen, H., & Gollwitzer, P. M. (1987). Thought contents and cognitive functioning in motivational versus volitional states of mind. *Motivation and Emotion, 11,* 101–120.

Hibbard, J. H., Mahoney, E. R., Stock, R., & Tusler, M. (2007). Do increases in patient activation result in improved self-management behaviors? *Health Services Research, 42,* 1443–1463.

HIN. (2009). *Health Coaching Benchmarks: Operations and Performance Data for Optimal Program ROI and Participant Health Status.* Manasquan, NJ: Healthcare Intelligence Network.

Holland, S. K., Greenberg, J., Tidwell, L., Malone, J., Mullan, J., & Newcomer, R. (2005). Community-based health coaching, exercise, and health service utilization. *Journal of Aging and Health, 17,* 697–716.

Janis, I. L., & Mann, L. (1977). *Decision Making: a Psychological Analysis of Conflict, Choice and Commitment.* New York: Free Press.

Linden, A., Butterworth, S. W., & Prochaska, J. O. (2010). Motivational interviewing-based health coaching as a chronic care intervention. *Journal of Evaluation in Clinical Practice, 16,* 166–174.

Lindner, H., Menzies, D., Kelly, J., Taylor, S., & Shearer, M. (2003). Coaching for behaviour change in chronic disease: a review of the literature and the implications for coaching as a self-management intervention. *Australian Journal of Primary Health, 9,* 177–185.

Locke, E. A., Shaw, K. N., Saari, L. M., & Latham, G. P. (1981). Goal setting and task performance. *Psychological Bulletin, 90,* 125–152.

Luborsky, L. (1976). Helping alliances in psychotherapy. In J. L. Cleghhorn (Ed.), *Successful Psychotherapy* (pp. 92–116). New York: Brunner/Mazel.

Marlatt, G. A., & Gordon, J. R. (1980). Determinants of relapse: Implications for the maintenance of behaviour change. In P. O. Davidson & S. M. Davidson (Eds.), *Behavioural Medicine: Changing Health Lifestyles.* New York: Brunner/Mazel.

Martin, L. R., Haskard-Zolnierek, K. B., & DiMaetteo, M. R. (2010). *Health Behavior Change and Treatment Adherence.* New York: Oxford University Press.

Mason, P., & Butler, C. C. (2010). *Health Behavior Change: a Guide for Practitioners.* London: Churchill Livingstone Elsevier.

Michie, S., Johnston, M., Abraham, C., Lawton, R., Parker, D., & Walker, A. (2005). Making psychological theory useful for implementing evidence based practice: A consensus approach. *Quality & Safety in Health Care, 14,* 26–33.

Miller, W. R., & Rollnick, S. (2002). *Motivational Interviewing: Preparing People to Change.* New York: Guilford Press.

Moller, A. C., Ryan, R. M., & Deci, E. L. (2006). Self-determination theory and public policy: Improving the quality of consumer decisions without using coercion. *Journal of Public Policy & Marketing, 25,* 104–116.

Noar, S. M., & Zimmerman, R. S. (2005). Health behavior theory and cumulative knowledge regarding health behaviors: Are we moving in the right direction? *Health Education Research, 20,* 275–290.

Olsen, J. M., & Nesbitt, B. J. (2010). Health coaching to improve healthy lifestyle behaviors: an integrative review. *American Journal Of Health Promotion, 25*(1), e1–e12.

Paineau, D. L., Beaufils, F., Boulier, A., Cassuto, D.-A., Chwalow, J., Combris, P. *et al.* (2008). Family dietary coaching to improve nutritional intakes and body weight control: a randomized controlled trial. *Archives of Pediatrics & Adolescent Medicine, 162,* 34–43.

Palmer, S., Tubbs, I., & Whybrow, A. (2003). Health coaching to facilitate the promotion of healthy behaviour and achievement of health-related goals. *International Journal of Health Promotion & Education, d41,* 91–93.

Prochaska, J. O., & DiClemente, C. C. (Eds.). (1984). *The Transtheoretical Approach: Crossing the Traditional Boundaries of Change.* Homewood, IL: Irwin.

Prochaska, J. O., Butterworth, S., Redding, C. A., Burden, V., Perrin, N., Leo, M. *et al.* (2008a). Initial efficacy of MI, TTM tailoring and HRI's with multiple behaviors for employee health promotion. *Preventive Medicine, 46,* 226–231.

Prochaska, J. O., Redding, C., & Evers, K. (2008b). The transtheoretical model and stages of change. In K. Glanz, B. Rimer, & F. Lewis (Eds.), *Health Behavior and Health Education: Theory, Research, and Practice* (3rd edn.). San Francisco: Jossey-Bass.

Rogers, R. W. (1983). Cognitive and physiological processes in fear appeals and attitude change: A revised theory of protection motivation. In J. T. Cacioppo & R. E. Petty (Eds.), *Social Psychophysiology: a Sourcebook* (pp. 153–176). London: Guilford Press.

Rollnick, S., Mason, P., & Butler, C. (1999). *Health Behavior Change: a Guide for Practitioners.* London: Churchill Livingstone.

Rosenstock, I. M. (1974). Historical origins of the health belief model. *Health Education Monographs, 2,* 1–8.

Saelens, B. E., Sallis, J. F., Wilfley, D. E., Patrick, K., Cella, J. A., & Buchta, R. (2002). Behavioral weight control for verweight adolescents initiated in primary care. *Obesity, 10,* 22–32.

Sheeran, P., Milne, S., Webb, T. L., & Gollwitzer, P. M. (2005). Implementation intentions and health behaviors. In M. Conner & P. Norman (Eds.), *Research and Practice with Social Cognition Models* (pp. 276–323). Buckingham: Open University Press.

Sniehotta, F., Scholz, U., & Schwarzer, R. (2005). Bridging the intention–behaviour gap: Planning, self-efficacy, and action control in the adoption and maintenance of physical exercise. *Psychology & Health, 20,* 143–160.

Snyder, C. R. (2002). Hope theory: Rainbows in the mind. *Psychological Inquiry, 13,* 249–275.

Spence, G. B., Cavanagh, M. J., & Grant, A. M. (2008). The integration of mindfulness training and health coaching: An exploratory study. *Coaching: An International Journal of Theory, Research and Practice, 1,* 145–163.

Vale, M. J., Jelinek, M. V., Best, J. D., Dart, A. M., Grigg, L. E., Hare, D. L. *et al.* (2003). Coaching patients On Achieving Cardiovascular Health (COACH): A multicenter randomized trial in patients with coronary heart disease. *Archives of Internal Medicine, 163,* 2775–2783.

Vansteenkiste, M., Lens, W., & Deci, E. L. (2006). Intrinsic versus extrinsic goal contents in self-determination theory: Another look at the quality of academic motivation. *Educational Psychologist, 41,* 19–31.

Wagner, E. H., Bennett, S. M., Austin, B. T., Greene, S. M., Schaefer, J. K., & Vonkorff, M. (2005). Finding common ground: Patient-centeredness and evidence-based chronic illness care. *The Journal of Alternative and Complimentary Medicine, 11*(Suppl. 1), S7–S15.

Webb, T. L., Sniehotta, F. F., & Michie, S. (2010). Using theories of behavior change to inform interventions for addictive behaviors. *Addiction, 105,* 1879–1892.

WHO. (2003). *Adherence to Long-Term Therapies: Evidence for Action.* Geneva: World Health Organization.

WHO. (2005). *Chronic Diseases and their Common Risk Factors.* Geneva: World Health Organization.

WHO. (2008). *Action Plan for the Gobal Strategy for the Prevention and Control of Non-Communicable Diseases: Prevent and Control Cardiovascular Diseases, Cancers, Chronic Respiratory Diseases and Diabetes.* Geneva: World Health Organization.

3

Physical Activity

An Evidence-Based Examination of Why, How Much, and How to Increase It

Paul O'Halloran

Physical activity is a core determinant of health and wellbeing. Regular participation in physical activity can reduce the risk of coronary heart disease, some cancers, Type 2 diabetes, hypertension, stroke, and depression. Indeed, the World Health Organization (WHO; 2009) identified physical inactivity as a leading risk factor for global mortality that is responsible for more deaths per year (6%) than overweight and obesity (5%). In relation to morbidity, physical inactivity has been reported to account for 6.6% of the total disease burden in Australia (Begg *et al.*, 2007). To put this in perspective, the Australian Institute of Health and Welfare (AIHW) in their 2010 report on Australia's health, point out that the only modifiable risk factor that accounts for a greater proportion of the disease burden in Australia is tobacco usage (AIHW, 2010). Figures such as these led health promotion experts some 10 years ago to refer to physical activity as the new imperative for public health (Sparling *et al.*, 2000). Despite the considerable impact of physical activity on health and wellbeing, most people are not sufficiently active. The WHO (2004) estimates that some 60% of the world's population does not engage in sufficient physical activity. Thus, one critical consideration for any health-related professional is how to most effectively increase physical activity. In addition, there is emerging evidence that being active is not enough: we also need to reduce sedentary behaviors. That is, a person who meets recommended activity levels can still be at risk for health problems if they spend too much of their day sitting (e.g., constant hours watching TV or uninterrupted time in front of the computer).

The aim of this chapter is to provide the reader with an evidence-based discussion (supported by the most recent research findings) of physical activity and the core concepts related to this important health-related behavior. Major issues to be examined in this chapter include: (1) benefits and risks of physical activity to health and wellbeing; (2) how much physical activity is needed to achieve benefits in health and wellbeing [key government and organizational guidelines and research findings pertaining to obtaining specific benefits (e.g., how much is needed to improve mood and produce positive changes in body weight)]; (3) risks of sedentary behavior; and (4) how to increase physical activity (individual/small-group approaches).

Applied Topics in Health Psychology, First Edition. Edited by M. L. Caltabiano and L. Ricciardelli.
© 2013 John Wiley & Sons, Ltd. Published 2013 by John Wiley & Sons, Ltd.

Benefits of Physical Activity

The physiological and mental health benefits of physical activity are well documented. An overview of these benefits (including the magnitude where available) will be presented below. Information about minimum dosages of physical activity (such as duration, regularity, and intensity) to achieve these benefits will typically be presented in the section *How much is enough: Recommendations for general health and specific benefits.*

Physiological Benefits of Exercise

Weight loss

Notwithstanding the potential of physical activity to increase fitness [see American College of Sports Medicine (ACSM), 1998], strength, and muscular endurance (Haskell *et al.*, 2007) physical activity has been shown to alter several key dimensions of body weight (ACSM, 2009a). For instance, the ACSM, in their updated position pertaining to physical activity and weight loss (ACSM, 2009a), provide evidence which suggests that regular moderate physical activity performed at an appropriate duration and intensity (for specifics see Table 3.1) will prevent weight gain greater

Table 3.1   Recommended amounts of physical activity for some specific health benefits

Desired outcome	Recommended amount	Source
Reduced risk of cancer	30–60 min of moderate to vigorous activity per day to reduce risk of colon and breast cancer	Lee (2003)
Reduced risk of cardiovascular disease	Increasing the amount of activity per week from 150 to 300 min and by including 150 min or more of vigorous activity will provide additional protection	O'Donovan *et al.* (2010)
Reduced risk of depression	Some evidence for a protective effect from as little as 60 min per week but most studies suggest a minimum 150 min moderate intensity activity per week	Teychenne *et al.* (2008)
Reduction in minor and mild-to-moderate depression	Average of three sessions per week of moderate duration (45–60 min) over 10–14 weeks tailored to an individual to maximize adherence	National Institute for Health and Clinical Excellence (2009)
Mood benefits: acute (short-term)	7–60 min of low to moderate intensity activity: largest benefits 30–35 min low intensity	Reed & Ones (2006)
Mood benefits: long term	30–35 min of low intensity activity 3–5 days per week for 10–12 weeks	Reed & Buck (2009)
Prevention of weight gain	150–250 min per week with an energy equivalent of 1200–2200 kcal (5040–8400 kJ) per week	ACSM (2009a)
Weight loss	For modest weight loss (e.g. 2–3 kg) at least 150 min moderate activity per week with dose response (e.g. 225–420 min per week for weight loss range 5–7.5 kg)	ACSM (2009a)
Weight maintenance after weight loss	200–300 min of moderate activity per week: more is better	ACSM (2009a)

than 3% in most adults as they age, provide a 3% or greater weight loss from initial weight as an intervention, and typically be the best predictor of being able to maintain weight that is lost following an intervention involving physical activity or dietary changes. Despite the modest magnitude of the benefits of physical activity on weight, their positive impact on chronic disease risk factors suggests they are clinically significant (ACSM, 2009a).

Protection from specific disease states

Extensive evidence has accumulated which suggests that physically active individuals are far less likely to suffer from premature death and disability compared with their inactive counterparts (see AIHW, 2010; WHO, 2010). For instance, Myers *et al.* (2004) reported that being active was associated in a 50% reduction in death from any cause.

Cardiovascular disease The benefit of an active lifestyle on the prevention and treatment of cardiovascular disease has been well documented (see reviews by Hu *et al.*, 2004; Wannamethee & Shaper, 2001). As noted by Wannamethee and Shaper (2001) in an extensive review of the literature, "There is compelling epidemiological evidence from many different populations that leisure time physical activity is associated with a reduced risk of coronary heart disease (CHD) and cardiovascular disease in middle age" (p. 102). Further, Hu and colleagues (2004) report that inactive middle-aged women have double the risk of cardiovascular disease relative to their active counterparts.

Cancer Findings outlined in Thune and Furberg's (2001) systematic review of the literature pertaining to physical activity and cancer risk indicate that there is an association between physical activity and both overall and site-specific cancer risk. The strongest support for a positive effect of physical activity on site-specific cancers relates to colon and breast cancer (see reviews by Lee, 2003; Sternfeld, 1992; Thune & Furberg, 2001). The mechanisms through which physical activity might offer this protective effect include improved circulation, improved immune system function, reduction in bowel transit time (particularly in relation to colon cancer), and potentially DNA repair (Thune & Furberg, 2001).

Diabetes Physical activity, particularly aerobic or resistance-type activity, also offers protection against the development of Type 2 diabetes (see Warburton *et al.*, 2006). Physical activity offers this benefit through its potential for improving glucose tolerance in patients at risk for developing Type 2 diabetes (i.e. those with impaired glucose tolerance). Data from a large prospective study show that each increase in physical activity equivalent to burning an extra 500 kcal (2100 kJ) per week is associated with a further 6% reduction in the risk of Type 2 diabetes (Helmrich *et al.*, 1991).

Other positive physical health outcomes of physical activity

Notwithstanding the benefits of physical activity in terms of preventing chronic conditions there is strong evidence that physical activity is highly beneficial in the effective management of physical chronic disease states such as Type 2 diabetes and cardiovascular disease (see review by Warbuton *et al.*, 2006). Physical activity can also protect against the development of osteoporosis (Grove & Londeree, 1992) and reduce the risk of upper respiratory tract infections through positive changes in immune system functioning (Gleeson, 2007).

Mental Health Benefits of Physical Activity

Mood

There is extensive evidence from both population-based surveys and intervention studies that exercise is associated positively with mood, emotion, and other positive feeling states (see reviews by Biddle, 2000; Biddle & Mutrie, 2001; Reed & Buck, 2009; Reed & Ones, 2006). For instance, in a recent meta-analysis of 105 studies conducted between 1980 and 2008, Reed and Buck (2009) reported that long-term aerobic exercise, such as structured programs of jogging or aerobic dance, leads to significant improvements in positive affective states, such as energy, positive wellbeing, and vitality. Further, the overall corrected effect size of $d = 0.57$ suggested that the magnitude of this improvement was of a medium size.

A substantial number of studies have shown that a single session of aerobic exercise, such as running or cycling, can lead to improvements in both negative mood states (e.g., anxiety and depression) and positive mood states, such as feelings of revitalization and positive wellbeing (e.g., Barabasz, 1991; Berger & Owen, 1998; Blanchard *et al.*, 2001). In a recent meta-analysis of 158 studies (conducted between 1979 and 2005) that examined the relationship between single sessions of physical activity and alterations in positive mood, Reed and Ones (2006) reported that the magnitude of this improvement also approximated a medium effect size ($d = 0.47$).

Depression

Physical activity has been advocated as both a means of reducing the risk of depression (Teychenne *et al.*, 2008) and as a treatment (e.g., Craft & Perna, 2004; Lawlor & Hopker, 2001). With respect to reducing the risk of depression, in their recent review of 67 studies conducted between 1980 and 2007, Teychenne *et al.* (2008) reported that 93% of the observational studies reviewed (25 of 27) and 78% of the intervention studies (31 out of 40) reported an inverse relationship between the performance of physical activity and the likelihood of developing depression. Further, meta-analyses conducted since 1990 have consistently shown that physical activity can produce reductions in depression that have been of a reasonable magnitude. For instance, Lawlor and Hopker, (2001) in a meta-analysis of 14 randomized controlled studies that examined the effect of exercise programs of 4–12 weeks' duration, found that exercise had a significant anti-depressant effect with a large effect size (effect size of −1.1) relative to no treatment. Craft and Perna (2004) noted that the effect size of −1.1 reported by Lawlor and Hopker (2001) translated to a 74% increase in the success rate of treatment. Indeed, it is noteworthy that exercise has been reported to be as effective as cognitive therapy in reducing depressive symptoms (Lalwor & Hopker, 2001). A recent meta-analysis has revealed that physical activity can be effective in terms of reducing depressive symptoms in people without clinical depression (Conn, 2010).

Potential Risks of Physical Activity

Notwithstanding the potential benefits of physical activity outlined above, it is important to acknowledge that planned physical activity (i.e., exercise) can be detrimental to both physical and mental health. For instance, impaired immune system function and an increased risk of upper respiratory tract infection is often associated with intensified training over a week or more (Gleeson, 2007). A further potential negative consequence of physical activity is injury (Haskell *et al.*

2007). As pointed out by Haskell and colleagues (2007), the risk of musculoskeletal injuries can be particularly elevated in high-impact activities such as jogging. However, there is evidence that rates of musculoskeletal injuries do not differ much between active and inactive individuals (Carlson *et al.*, 2006): it is just the setting that differs. Active men and women tend to injure themselves during sport and leisure time activity while inactive individuals tend to injure themselves in activities not related to sport or physical activity (Haskell *et al.*, 2007). Physical activity can also have several potential negative psychological impacts (see Szabo, 2000). For instance overreaching and overtraining can result in increased anxiety, insomnia, fatigue, staleness, impaired immune system function, and even distress (see Halson & Jeukendrup, 2004). Of potentially greater concern are data that suggest engagement in regular physical activity can increase the risk of sudden cardiac death (see Thompson & Fahrenbach, 1994). However, it should be pointed out that this risk is modest and is typically confined to individuals with a preexisting condition. Additionally, it is important to note, as pointed out by Haskell *et al.*, that this increased risk is more than negated by the protective effect of physical activity on these adverse cardiovascular conditions.

How Much is Enough?: Recommendations for General Health and Specific Benefits

The answer to the question of how much activity is enough is often dependent on the population in question (children, adults aged 18–65, or older people) and the specific benefit in question. Guidelines adopted by governments and key agencies typically represent the minimum for achieving general health benefits. A large body of research has also accumulated evidence regarding the amount of physical activity that is required to achieve specific health benefits such as reductions in weight, depression, and mood benefits. Important issues that relate to the benefits of physical activity are potential dose–response relationships and whether the activity needs to be continuous.

How much activity is required to achieve general health benefits?

Basic guidelines for adults aged 18–65 recommend that the minimum amount of activity required to achieve general health benefits is 150 min per week in which 30 min of moderate-intensity physical activity is performed on most (typically defined as 5 days), preferably all days of the week. For instance, this basic recommendation has been used in the national physical activity guidelines for Australians [Australian Government Department of Health and Ageing (DoHA), 1999] and Americans [Department of Health and Human Services (DHHS), 2008], and adopted by the British Association of Sport and Exercise Sciences (O'Donovan *et al.*, 2010), the ACSM, and the American Heart Association (Haskell *et al.*, 2007). Moderate-intensity activity includes activities such as brisk walking, swimming, doubles tennis, and medium-paced cycling (AIHW, 2010). However, what is important to note is that this activity need not be planned exercise: movement and incidental activity (e.g., walking to a shopping centre, or housework) or leisure time activity (such as gardening) fits within the guidelines as long as it is of a moderate intensity. Evidence pertaining to the benefits of the accumulation of at least 150 min of moderate-intensity physical activity includes positive changes in blood pressure, lipid profiles, and insulin sensitivity, and a reduced risk of cardiovascular disease and Type 2 diabetes (see O'Donovan *et al.*, 2010).

In all of these guidelines it is recognized that this moderate-intensity activity need not be undertaken in a continuous 30 min bout. In fact, it is recommended that three 10 min sessions of moderate-intensity activity can produce equivalent health benefits as one 30 min session (e.g., Haskell *et al.*, 2007). Indeed, this contention has been partially supported in a recent review of 16 studies (involving 836 participants) comparing the effect of accumulated versus continuous physical activity, conducted by Murphy *et al.* (2009). These investigators concluded that accumulated and continuous activity of the same duration produce similar benefits for physical fitness. However, the evidence was inconclusive regarding other health outcomes such as body mass composition and fat distribution (Murphy *et al.*, 2009).

It is important to recognize that this recommendation of 150 min of activity per week is for adults aged 19–65, and is indeed a minimum. For instance it is recommended that children and adolescents aged 5–16 years should accumulate at least 60 min of moderate-intensity physical activity per day (e.g. O'Donovan *et al.*, 2010). For older adults, the 150 min criterion applies with the caveat that people who are impacted by chronic conditions should be as active as their abilities and conditions allow (ACSM, 2009b). Further, most guidelines recommend that further benefits for adults can be achieved by doing more activity and by incorporating muscle-strengthening activities (e.g. Ferney *et al.*, 2009; Haskell *et al.*, 2007; O'Donovan *et al.*, 2010). For instance, in the updated recommendations produced by the ACSM and American Heart Association it is recommended that adults should spend at least 2 days per week in activities that maintain or increase muscular strength (e.g. weight training) and endurance (e.g., more vigorous aerobic activity such as running) (Haskell *et al.*, 2007). In addition, based on the evidence of a dose–response relationship between physical activity and many health benefits, it has been recommended that people would achieve greater health benefits with respect to fitness, risk of chronic conditions, and weight by exceeding the minimum recommended amounts of physical activity (Haskell *et al.*, 2007; O'Donovan *et al.*, 2010).

How much activity is required to achieve specific health benefits?

The guidelines discussed above refer to minimum amounts of physical activity required to achieve benefits such as protection against common chronic diseases such as cardiovascular disease and increases in fitness. These recommendations do not necessarily hold true for other important benefits such as weight loss and maintenance, mood, and depression. Recent accumulated evidence regarding minimal and optimal physical activity dose (where available) for a range of important health benefits are presented in Table 3.1.

As noted in Table 3.1 there are several deviations from the general recommended physical activity guidelines with respect to both intensity and duration. For instance, the largest short-term benefits in mood have been found with low-intensity activity rather than moderate activity (Reed & Ones, 2007). With respect to weight loss there appears to be a relatively clear dose–response relationship with activity: more is better. Even the minimum recommended amount for weight maintenance after weight loss exceeds the general recommendation by between 50 and 150 min per week (ACSM, 2009a).

Prevalence of Physical Activity

Despite the substantial health benefits of physical activity only a minority of the population reaches the level of activity that is required to achieve these benefits. For instance, the AIHW in their 2010 report of Australia's health reported that only 37% of Australians exercised at a level that was required (at least 30 min per day on at least 5 days per week) to obtain health benefits. This was based on 2007–2008 data from the National Health Survey which asked participants about their physical activity levels in the week prior to the survey. Similarly, recent data collected from the National Health Interview Schedule from the USA, in which some 21 000 people were asked about their leisure time physical activity, reported that just 32.6% of the US population could be classified as aerobically active (Carlson *et al.*, 2010). However, a slightly more promising picture emerged in a recent international comparison of physical activity levels (Bauman *et al.*, 2009). These investigators used the short form of the International Physical Activity Questionnaire (IPAQ) to examine the physical activity levels of over 52 000 adults in 20 countries that included Australia, the USA, Canada, New Zealand, India, and Japan. In contrast to the large National Health Survey data reported above, it was reported that in all 20 countries more than half of the adult population could be classified as regularly active (e.g., 5 days of moderate intensity activity for at least 30 min on these days or 3 days of vigorous activity of at least 20 min per day). Indeed, in eight of the 20 countries, including Australia and the USA, more than 50% of the population met the criteria for high physical activity (e.g., vigorous activity on more than 3 days per week accumulating at least 1500 standard metabolic equivalent (MET)-min per week). There are several possible explanations for the discrepancy between these data and the National Health Survey data from Australia and the USA. Notwithstanding that definitions of physical activity differed across the surveys, Bauman and his colleagues acknowledge that there are some limitations with the IPAQ, including evidence that the IPAQ can overestimate levels of physical activity more than other self-report measures. It is noteworthy that estimates of physical activity prevalence are substantially lower when data are obtained using objective measures such as accelerometers. Data obtained from samples in both the USA (Troiano *et al.*, 2008) and Sweden (Hagströmer *et al.*, 2007) suggest that fewer than 5% of adults accumulate 30 min of activity (in at least 10 min bouts) or more on most days of the week. While these prevalence rates are substantially lower than those obtained using self-report data as acknowledged by Troiano *et al.* (2008), accelerometers do not record certain activities such as cycling and swimming. Thus, while the actual percentage of people who are sufficiently active depends on factors such as the method used to obtain prevalence data, physical activity rates are far too low. Evidence regarding the effectiveness of interventions for increasing physical activity will be examined shortly. However, prior to this it is important to examine the risks of sedentary behavior.

Risks of Sedentary Behavior: More than the Absence of Activity

Sedentary is a term that has typically been used to define people who are not sufficiently active; that is, individuals who do not perform the recommended amount of moderate to vigorous activity per week (i.e., 150 min). However, research that has emerged over the last decade has suggested that sedentary behavior should be conceptualized as the time spent sitting during a day rather than as the absence of moderate-intensity physical activity *per se* (Pate *et al.*, 2008). This is because too much sitting, in the context of behaviors such as TV viewing, computer use, workplace sitting, and travelling to work in a car, has been found to have health risks that are independent of too little exercise (Owen *et al.*, 2010; Pate *et al.*, 2008). As noted by Owen and colleagues (2010, p. 105) research has shown that ". . . adults can meet public health guidelines on physical activity, but if they sit for prolonged periods, their metabolic health is compromised."

Among physically active people self-reported TV time has been shown to have dose–response relationships with important indicators of poor physical health, such as waist circumference, blood pressure, and blood glucose in both men and women and cholesterol levels in women (Healy *et al.*, 2008a). Similar detrimental effects of sedentary behavior on metabolic health have been reported when sedentary time has been measured more objectively by low activity rates on an accelerometer

(Healy *et al.*, 2007). The overall impact of these sedentary behaviors can be increased risk of chronic health conditions such as Type 2 diabetes and cardiovascular conditions and even poorer mental health (Hamer *et al.*, 2010). Not surprisingly, high levels of sedentary behavior have been associated with poorer long-term mortality outcomes (see Owen *et al.*, 2010).

Given the potential impact of sedentary behaviors and that modern life is conducive to such behaviors in both work and leisure time, researchers such as Owen *et al.* (2010) have recommended that public health campaigns could consider emphasizing the importance of reducing sitting time as well as increasing physical activity. Sitting time, particularly at work, may be unavoidable if one's occupation dictates work on a computer in an office environment for the majority of the day. However, recent research has suggested that it may not be total sitting time that is the problem but rather uninterrupted sitting behavior (Healy *et al.*, 2008b). That is, accelerometer research has shown that taking regular breaks from the sitting behavior reduces the negative impact of sitting on metabolic indicators of health (Healy *et al.*, 2008b). Taking regular mini breaks at work, such as taking a walk to fill a water bottle at regular intervals, and the use of height-adjustable work desks (Owen *et al.*, 2010), are some simple strategies that could be used to reduce the impact of sitting. The recent review by Owen and his coworkers (2010) provides an excellent review of the population health risks of sedentary behavior and what can be done to reduce these risks.

How to Increase Physical Activity: Individual/Small Group Approaches

Given the benefits of physical activity and evidence which suggests that only a small proportion of the population are sufficiently active, an important goal at both a population and individual level is to increase physical activity. This section of the chapter will provide a brief overview of physical activity interventions that target individuals and/or small groups. Key issues include whether these interventions work and, if so, what kind of interventions are most effective. These issues will be discussed in relation to interventions that have been carried out with adults in healthcare- and community-based settings. Readers interested in other populations or settings may wish to examine a recent systematic review of the effectiveness of promoting physical activity in children and adolescents (van Sluijs *et al.*, 2008), a multidisciplinary review of the effectiveness of physical activity interventions specifically in older people (Taylor *et al.*, 2004), and a recent meta-analysis of workplace interventions to increase physical activity (Conn *et al.*, 2009).

Do interventions work?

One approach to increasing the physical activity that has been used quite widely has been for health professionals to offer advice and/or counselling to individuals or small groups. Hillsdon and colleagues undertook a review of eight reviews, conducted between 1997 and 2002, that examined the effectiveness of physical activity interventions carried out in healthcare settings such as general practice and hospital outpatient departments (Hillsdon *et al.*, 2005). The type of interventions in these reviews included: information and advice given by a nurse or general practitioner; written prescriptions for physical activity; self-help materials such as brochures; referral to an exercise specialist; and telephone follow-up. This review suggested that brief advice from a health professional, when supported by written materials, can be effective in producing a modest improvement in physical activity (Hillsdon *et al.*, 2005). This improvement, reported by five of the eight reviews, related to the promotion of moderate-intensity activity, typically walking, in previously inactive people. One important caveat with these findings is that this modest improvement was short-lived. That is, the change in activity level from interventions delivered in healthcare settings is most likely to last just 6–12 weeks (Hillsdon *et al.*, 2005). There is some evidence from this review that longer-term changes in physical activity of 8 months or more can be achieved if people, in addition to being offered advice and written materials, are also referred to an exercise specialist to create a personalized exercise plan. Notwithstanding that this review only examined reviews conducted up until 2002, it suggests that improvements in physical activity targeted to individuals in primary healthcare settings tend to be modest and short-lived. Support for this position comes from a more recent systematic review of studies conducted up until 2007 (Williams *et al.*, 2007). Williams *et al.* (2007) reviewed 18 studies (including six randomized controlled studies) that examined the effectiveness of exercise-referral schemes delivered by primary care clinicians. Results from a meta-analysis of five randomized controlled studies revealed that there was a significant increase in the number of individuals performing moderate-intensity activity; however, this increase was modest (relative risk of 1.20). Indeed, this was interpreted by the investigators as suggesting that 17 inactive individuals would need to be treated using these referral schemes for just one person to become active (Williams *et al.*, 2007).

Several large systematic reviews have also examined the effectiveness of community-based physical activity interventions (Foster *et al.*, 2005; Hillsdon *et al.*, 2005; Kahn *et al.*, 2002; Müller-Riemenschneider *et al.*, 2008). Kahn *et al.* (2002) conducted a systematic review of 10 studies that targeted individual time spent engaged in physical activity using community-based strategies such as peer support (e.g. phone calls) and formal discussion groups in which factors such as barriers to exercise were addressed. This analysis revealed that these interventions produced a median net increase of 35.4% in time spent in physical activity. This finding, and the median increase of 64.3% measured change in energy expenditure reported in a further four studies, was interpreted by the investigators (Kahn *et al.*, p. 85) as suggesting that "... this type of intervention is effective in increasing physical activity." Consistent with this, Hillsdon *et al.* (2005) concluded on the basis of data from 13 experimental studies that interventions targeting individuals in community settings are effective in the short term and are likely to be so in the medium- and long-term as well. These studies included interventions such as group exercise counselling, telephone education and support, stage-of-change written materials, and self-monitoring and reinforcement.

The long-term effectiveness of physical activity interventions was the specific focus of a recent systematic review by Müller-Riemenschneider *et al.* (2008). Results from 25 randomized control trials were interpreted as providing good evidence for the long-term effectiveness of physical activity interventions (Müller-Riemenschneider *et al.*, 2008). Specifically, high- and good-quality studies produced increases in energy expenditure of 975 kcal (4095 kJ) more than 12 months after the intervention, and the odds ratio to meet targets in the intervention compared to the no-intervention group was 3.31. A further finding of note to emerge from this review was that comprehensive interventions that included tailored advice or counselling and a booster session delivered by mail, phone, or Internet were more effective than general advice and strategies delivered by health professionals (Müller-Riemenschneider *et al.*, 2008).

What kinds of interventions are effective?

The issue of what kind of interventions are most effective can be addressed in several ways. For instance, the literature reviewed in the preceding section suggests that interventions delivered in community settings are more effective than those delivered in healthcare settings, particularly for longer-term change. This is likely to be due to the type of intervention rather than the setting *per se*. While advice and use of supportive written materials are commonly used in primary healthcare settings, interventions that rely on offering social support, tailored counselling, and advice and booster sessions are often utilized in community settings (Hillsdon *et al.*, 2005; Müller-Riemenschneider *et al.*, 2008). It is these later strategies that were identified by Müller-Riemenschneider *et al.* (2008) as being most effective in producing longer-term changes in physical activity.

A further way of approaching this issue is to examine theory-based mediators of physical activity behavior change (Rhodes & Pfaeffli, 2010). This approach examines the evidence that specific constructs, from key behavior change theories, such as the transtheoretical model (TTM; Prochaska & DiClemente, 1982), social cognitive theory (SCT; Bandura, 1997), theory of planned behavior (TPB; Ajzen, 1991), protection motivation theory (PMT; Rogers, 1983), or self-determination theory (SDT; Deci & Ryan, 1985), can be used to explain observed changes in physical activity interventions. Thus, this line of research could indicate which behavior change constructs, such as self-efficacy or processes of change, are most likely to be effective in producing changes in physical activity. Rhodes and Pfaeffli (2010) examined the role of constructs from the TTM, SCT, TPB, PMT, and SDT in explaining physical activity improvements in 22 high-quality studies between 1998 and 2008. The authors reported mixed support for constructs from all five behavior change theories and that further research is necessary before any definitive conclusions can be reached (Rhodes & Pfaeffli, 2010). However, the authors did recommend in the interim that physical activity interventions that focus on maximizing feeling states that are valued by an individual (such as feelings of pleasure and enjoyment) and behavioral control and self-efficacy are most likely to be effective (Rhodes & Pfaeffli, 2010).

What kinds of interventions are useful for increasing physical activity?

As noted above further research is required to elucidate the most useful and effective theoretical models for increasing physical activity. However, for illustration purposes a brief summary of the usefulness of two behavior change approaches that continue to generate considerable research and interest will be presented: the transtheoretical model (TTM: Prochaska & DiClemente, 1982) and motivational interviewing (MI; Miller & Rollnick, 2002). In order to illustrate the usefulness of the TTM and MI, I will give a brief summary of how these strategies may be applied to assist clients with increasing their physical activity. In keeping with the evidence-based approach of this chapter, this will be followed by an examination of the evidence pertaining to the effectiveness of interventions based on these strategies.

The TTM has been described as one of the most frequently applied frameworks for interventions designed to increase physical activity (Hutchinson *et al.*, 2009). The TTM posits there are five stages of change that represent how ready people are to change their behavior (Prochaska & DiClemente, 1982). When applied to physical activity these are as follows: *precontemplation*, not thinking about becoming more active in the next 6 months; *contemplation*, some thoughts of becoming more active in the next 6 months; *preparation*, beginning to make some more formal plans of becoming more active in the next month; *action*, has been active but for less than 6 months; *maintenance*, has been active for at least 6 months. Under a simple application of the TTM, strategies are tailored to a persons' readiness for change. For instance, if the person is at the contemplation stage it is recommended that interventions should aim to increase the importance of change for the person (Jordan & Nigg, 2002). For instance, it is recommended at this stage that you provide people with as much relevant information about the benefits of activity and to increase self-efficacy (Jordan & Nigg, 2002). At later stages of readiness for change such as preparation or action behavioral strategies that focus on assisting the person to commence or maintain their activity would be more effective. These strategies might include encouraging people to ask for support and encouragement from family and friends and displaying reminders to exercise (Jordan & Nigg, 2002). For a more in-depth analysis of how the TMM can be tailored to a person's readiness to change the interested reader is referred to Jordan and Nigg (2002). Whereas the TTM has been a popular theoretical framework for increasing physical activity, its efficacy in producing meaningful behavior change in physical activity has been queried (Adams & White, 2003; Bridle *et al.*, 2005). For instance, a systematic review by Adams and White (2003) suggested that interventions based on the TTM are reasonably effective for producing short-term changes in physical activity but are not particularly effective for longer-term changes. More recent reviews have suggested that one potential reason for this lack of effectiveness is that previous applications of the model have been too simplistic and have not applied all dimensions of the model (Bridle *et al.*, 2005; Hutchinson, *et al.*, 2009). Indeed, the recent systematic review by Hutchinson *et al.* (2009) provided some evidence for the long-term effect of the interventions based on more complete representations of the TTM.

Motivational Interviewing: MI (Miller & Rollnick, 2002) has generated considerable interest and application as a behavior change strategy in health settings (Martins & McNeil, 2009). According to MI people are often resistant to becoming more active due to feelings of ambivalence about this change. Individuals can experience their own internal conflict between their idiosyncratic pros (e.g., feel better, increase health) and cons (e.g., too much pain, not enough time) about becoming more active. The goal of MI is to enhance people's intrinsic motivation to exercise by resolving these feelings of ambivalence. Following some minimal training healthcare practitioners can utilize the following principles to increase their clients motivation to change: expression of empathy; developing a discrepancy between what they do now and what they would like to do; rolling with resistance (not directly arguing with a client who is resistant to change); and supporting self-efficacy (Miller & Rollnick, 2002). The goal is to assist clients to form their own arguments for change, thereby increasing importance of becoming more active and developing their self-efficacy that they can maintain the change. MI can be delivered in person (one on one), in groups, and via telephone. Although relatively few studies have systematically examined the effect of MI on physical activity, some promising results have been reported (Cummings *et al.*, 2009; Martins & McNeil, 2009; Rubak *et al.*, 2005). For instance, Rubak *et al.* (2005) reported that eight out of 10 randomized controlled trials examining the effectiveness of MI on weight loss/physical activity reported favourable results. Indeed, a meta-analysis of the effectiveness of four studies revealed that the magnitude of the effect size of MI on diet and exercise was medium to large ($d = 0.78$) (Hettema *et al.*, 2005).

Summary and Conclusion

The performance of physical activity at the minimum recommended guidelines of 150 min (5 × 30 minute sessions) of moderate activity per week is associated with considerable benefits to both physical and mental health. Evidence suggests that for many benefits this activity need not be continuous, provided the activity is performed in bouts of at least 10 min. As noted above, it is noteworthy that several health benefits, such as those pertaining to weight loss and mood, are associated with dosages of activity that deviate from the general guidelines. Despite the documented benefits of physical activity, data suggest that somewhere between just 5% (accelerometer studies) and 40% (most self-report surveys) of people are sufficiently active. Further, evidence that has accumulated over the last 10 years has suggested that being active may not be enough to avoid poor health outcomes: we also need to avoid prolonged periods of sitting (i.e. sedentary behavior).

Data reviewed in this chapter suggest that interventions targeting individuals or small groups that rely on advice with supplementary written materials will produce short-lived, modest changes in physical activity. However, interventions that use strategies such as offering social support, tailored counselling and advice, and booster sessions in community settings have the potential to produce meaningful medium- to long-term changes in physical activity. Further, high-quality research is required to ascertain which specific strategies and techniques produce the largest prolonged changes in physical activity. Given emerging evidence regarding health risks associated with prolonged sitting it seems that public awareness of this issue needs to be increased and research needs to continue regarding the most efficacious interventions to reduce uninterrupted sitting.

References

Adams, J., & White, M. (2003). Are activity promotion interventions based on the transtheoretical model effective? A critical review. *British Journal of Sports Medicine, 37,* 106–114.

ACSM. (1998). The recommended quantity and quality of exercise for developing and maintaining cardiorespiratory and muscular fitness, and flexibility in healthy adults. *Medicine and Science in Sports and Exercise, 22,* 265–274.

ACSM. (2009a). Position stand: Appropriate physical activity intervention strategies for weight loss and prevention of weight regain for adults. *Medicine & Science in Sports & Exercise, 41,* 459–471.

ACSM. (2009b). Position stand: Exercise and physical activity for older adults. *Medicine & Science in Sports & Exercise, 41,* 1510–1530.

AIHW. (2010). *Australia's Health 2010.* Australia's Health Series no.12, cat. no. Aus 122. Canberra: Australian Institute of Health and Welfare.

Ajzen, I. (1991). The theory of planned behavior. *Organizational Behavior and Human Decision Processes, 50,* 179–211.

Bandura, A. (1997). *Self-Efficacy, the Exercise of Control.* New York: Freeman.

Barabasz, M. (1991). Effects of aerobic exercise on transient mood state. *Perceptual and Motor Skills, 73,* 657–658.

Bauman, A., Bull, F., Chey, T., Craig, C. L., Ainsworth, B. E. *et al.* The IPS Group. (2009). The international prevalence study on physical activity: Results from 20 countries. *International Journal of Behavioral Nutrition and Physical Activity, 6,* 21.

Begg, S., Vos, T., Barker, B., Stevenson, C., Stanley, L., & Lopez, A. D. (2007). *The Burden of Disease and Injury in Australia 2003.* AIHW cat. no. PHE 82. Canberra: AIHW.

Berger, B. G., & Owen, D. R. (1998). Relation of low and moderate intensity exercise with acute mood change in college joggers. *Perceptual and Motor Skills, 87,* 611–621.

Biddle, S. J. H. (2000). Emotions, mood and physical activity. In S. J. H. Biddle, K. R. Fox, & S. H. Boutcher (Eds.), *Physical Activity and Psychological Well-Being* (pp. 63–87). London: Routledge.

Biddle, S. J. H., & Mutrie, N. (2001). *Psychology of Physical Activity. Determinants, Well-Being and Interventions.* London: Routledge.

Blanchard, C. M., Rodgers, W. M., Spence, J. C., & Courneya, K. S. (2001). Feeling state response to acute exercise of high and low intensity. *Journal of Science and Medicine, 4,* 30–38.

Bridle, C., Riemsma, R. P., Pattenden, J., Sowden, A. J., Mather, L., Watt, I. S., & Walker, A. (2005). Systematic review of the effectiveness of health behaviour interventions based on the transtheoretical model. *Psychology and Health, 20,* 283–301.

Carlson, S. A., Hootman, J. M., Powell, K. E., Marcera, C. A., Heath, G. W., Gilchrist, J. *et al.* (2006). Self-reported injury and physical activity levels: United States 2000–2002. *Annals of Epidemiology, 16,* 712–719.

Carlson, S. A., Fulton, J. E., Schoenborn, C. A., & Loustalot, F. (2010). Trend and prevalence estimates based on the 2008 physical activity guidelines for Americans. *American Journal of Preventative Medicine, 39,* 305–313.

Conn, V. S. (2010). Depressive symptom outcomes of physical activity interventions: Meta-analysis findings. *Annals of Behavioral Medicine, 39,* 128–138.

Conn, V. S., Hafdahl, A. R., Cooper, P. S., Brown, L. M., & Lusk, S. K. (2009). Meta-analysis of workplace physical activity interventions. *American Journal of Preventative Medicine, 37,* 330–339.

Craft, L. L., & Perna, F. M. (2004). The benefits of exercise for the clinically depressed. *Primary Care Companion Journal of Clinical Psychiatry, 6,* 104–113.

Cummings, S. M., Cooper, R. L., & Cassie, K. M. (2009). Motivational interviewing to affect behavioral change in older adults. *Research on Social Work Practice, 19,* 195–204.

Deci, E. L, & Ryan, R. M. (1985). *Intrinsic Motivation and Self-Determination in Human Behavior.* New York: Plenum Press.

DHHS. (2008). *Physical Activity Guidelines for Americans.* Washington DC: Department of Health and Human Services. www.health.gov/PAGuidelines/pdf/paguide.pdf.

DoHa. (1999). *National Physical Activity Guidelines for Australians.* Canberra: Department of Health and Ageing.

Ferney, S. L., Moorhead, G. E., Bauman, A. E., & Brown, W. J. (2009). Awareness of a changing perceptions of physical activity guidelines among delegates at the Australian conference of science and medicine in sport. *Journal of Science and Medicine in Sport, 12,* 642–646.

Foster, C., Hillsdon, M., & Thorogood, M. (2005). Interventions for promoting physical activity (Review), *Cochrane Database of Systematic Reviews, 1,* CD003180.

Gleeson, M. (2007). Immune function in sport and exercise. *Journal of Applied Physiology, 103,* 693–699.

Grove, K. A., & Londeree, B. R. (1992). Bone density in postmenopausal women: High impact vs low impact exercise. *Medicine and Science in Sports & Exercise, 24,* 1190–1194.

Hagströmer, M., Oja, P., & Sjöström, M. (2007). Physical activity and inactivity in an adult population assessed by accelerometry. *Medicine and Science in Sports & Exercise, 39,* 1502–1508.

Halson, S. L., & Jeukendrup, A. E. (2004). Does overtraining exist? An analysis of overreaching and overtraining research. *Sports Medicine, 34,* 967–981.

Hamer, M., Stamatakis, E., & Mirsha, G. A. (2010). Television-and screen-based activity and mental well-being in adults. *American Journal of Preventative Medicine, 38,* 375–380.

Haskell, W. L., Lee, I.-M., Pate, R. R., Powell, K. E., Blair, S. N. *et al.* (2007). Physical activity and public health. Updated recommendations for adults from the American College of Sports Medicine and the American Heart Association. *Circulation, 116,* 1081–1093.

Healy, G. N., Dunstan, D. W., Salmon, J., Cerin, E., Shaw, J. E., Zimmet, P. Z., & Owen, N. (2007). Objectively measured light-intensity physical activity is independently associated with 2-h plasma glucose. *Diabetes Care, 30,* 1384–1389.

Healy, G. N., Dunstan, D. W., Salmon, J., Shaw, J. E., Zimmet, P. Z., & Owen, N. (2008a). Television time and continuous metabolic risk in physically active adults. *Medicine & Science in Sports & Exercise, 40,* 639–645.

Healy, G. N., Dunstan, D. W., Salmon, J., Cerin, E., Shaw, J. E., Zimmet, P. Z., & Owen, N. (2008b). Breaks in sedentary time: Beneficial associations with metabolic risk. *Diabetes Care, 31,* 661–666.

Helmrich, S. P., Ragland, D. R., Leung, R. W., & Paffenberger, R. S. (1991). Physical activity and reduced occurrence of non-insulin dependent diabetes mellitus. *New England Journal of Medicine, 325,* 147–152.

Hettema, J., Steele, J., & Miller, W. R. (2005). Motivational Interviewing. *Annual Review of Clinical Psychology. 1,* 91–111.

Hillsdon, M., Foster, C., Cavill, N., Crombie, H., & Naidoo, B. (2005). *The Effectiveness of Public Health Interventions for Increasing Physical Activity Among Adults: a Review of Reviews* (Evidence briefing 2nd edn.). London: NHS, Health Development Agency.

Hu, F. B., Willett, W. C., Li, T., Stampfer, M. J., Colditz, G. A., & Manson, J. E. (2004). Adiposity as compared with physical activity in predicting mortality among women. *New England Journal of Medicine, 351,* 2694–2673.

Hutchinson, A. J., Breckon, J. D., & Johnston, L. H. (2009). Physical activity behavior change interventions based on the transtheoretical model. *Health Education & Behavior, 36,* 829–845.

Jordan, P. J., & Nigg, C. R. (2002). Applying the transtheoretical model: Tailoring interventions to stages of change. In P. M. Burbank & D. Riebe (Eds.), *Promoting Exercise and Behavior Change in Older Adults: Interventions with the Transtheoretical Model* (pp. 181–208). New York: Springer Publishing.

Kahn, E. B., Ramsey, L. T., Brownson, R. C., Heath, G. W., Howze, E. H., Powell, K. E. *et al.* Task Force on Community Preventative Services. (2002). The effectiveness of interventions to increase physical activity. A systematic review. *American Journal of Preventative Medicine, 22*(4S), 73–107.

Lawlor, D. A., & Hopker, S. W. (2001). The effectiveness of exercise as an intervention in the management of depression: Systematic review and meta-regression analysis of randomised controlled trials. *British Medical Journal, 322*, 1–8.

Lee, I. M. (2003). Physical activity and cancer prevention-data from epidemiological studies. *Medicine & Science in Sports & Exercise, 35*, 1823–1827.

Martins, R. K., & McNeil, D. W. (2009). Review of motivational interviewing in promoting health behaviors. *Clinical Psychology Review, 29*, 283–293.

Miller, W. R., & Rollnick, S. (2002) *Motivational Interviewing: Preparing People for Change* (2nd edn.). New York: Guilford Press.

Müller-Riemenschneider, F., Reinhold, T., Nocon, M., & Willich, S. N. (2008). Long-term effectiveness of interventions promoting physical activity: A systematic review. *Preventative Medicine, 47*, 354–368.

Murphy, M. H., Blair, S. N., & Murtagh, E. M. (2009). Accumulated versus continuous exercise for health benefits. A review of empirical studies. *Sports Medicine, 39*, 29–43.

Myers, J., Kaykha, A., George, S., Abella, J., Zaheer, N., Lear, S. *et al.* (2004). Fitness versus physical activity patterns in predicting mortality in men. *American Journal of Medicine, 117*, 912–918.

National Institute for Health and Clinical Excellence. (2004). *CG23 depression: Management of Depression in Primary Care – NICE Guidance*. London: National Health Service.

O'Donovan, G., Blazevich, A. J., Boreham, C., Cooper, A. R., Crank, H. *et al.* (2010). The ABC of physical activity for health: A consensus statement from the British Association of Sport and Exercise Sciences. *Journal of Sports Sciences, 28*, 573–591.

Owen, N., Healy, G. N., Matthews, C. E., & Dunstan, D. W. (2010). Too much sitting: The population health science of sedentary behavior. *Exercise and Sport Science Reviews, 38*, 105–113.

Pate, R. R., O'Neill, J. R., & Lobelo, F. (2008). The evolving definition of "sedentary". *Exercise and Sport Science Reviews, 36*, 173–178.

Prochaska, J. O., & DiClemente, C. C. (1982) Transtheoretical therapy: Toward a more integrative model of change. *Psychotherapy: Theory, Research & Practice, 19*, 276–288.

Reed, J., & Ones, D. S. (2006). The effect of acute aerobic exercise on positive-activated affect: A meta-analysis. *Psychology of Sport and Exercise, 7*, 477–514.

Reed, J., & Buck, S. (2009). The effect of regular aerobic exercise on positive-activated affect: A meta-analysis, *Psychology of Sport and Exercise, 10*, 581–594.

Rhodes, R. E., & Pfaeffli, L. A. (2010). Mediators of physical activity behavior change among adult non-clinical populations: A review update. *International Journal of Behavioral Nutrition and Physical Activity, 7*, 37–47.

Rogers, R.W. (1983). Cognitive and physiological processes in fear appeals and attitude change: A revised theory of protection motivation. In J. T. Cacioppo & R.E. Petty (Eds.), *Social Psychophysiology* (pp. 153–176). New York: Guilford Press.

Rubak, S., Sandaek, A., Lauritzen, T., & Christensen, B (2005). Motivational Interviewing: A systematic review and meta-analysis. *British Journal of General Practice, 55*, 305–312.

Sparling, P. B., Owen, N., Lambert, E. V., & Haskell, W. L. (2000). Promoting physical activity: The new imperative for public health. *Health Education Research Theory & Practice, 15*, 367–376.

Sternfeld, B. (1992). Cancer and the protective effects of physical activity: The epidemiological evidence. *Medicine and Science in Sports and Exercise, 24*, 1195–1209.

Szabo, A. (2000). Physical activity as a source of psychological dysfunction. In S. J. H. Biddle, K. Fox, & S. Boutcher (Eds.)*Physical Activity and Psychological Well-Being* (pp. 130–153). London: Routledge.

Taylor, A. H., Cable, N. T., Faulkner, G., Hillsdon, M., Narici, M., & VanDer Bij, A. K. (2004). Physical activity and older adults: A review of health benefits and the effectiveness of interventions. *Journal of Sports Sciences, 22*, 703–725.

Teychenne, M., Ball, K., & Salmon, J. (2008). Physical activity and likelihood of depression in adults: A review. *Preventative Medicine, 46*, 397–411.

Thompson, P. D., & Fahrenbach, M. C. (1994). Risks of exercising: Cardiovascular including sudden cardiac death. In C. Bouchard, R. J. Shephard, & T. Stephens (Eds.), *Physical Activity, Fitness, and Health: International Proceedings and Consensus Statement* (pp. 1019–1028). Champaign, IL: Human Kinetics Publishers.

Thune, I., & Furberg, A. (2001). Physical activity and cancer risk: Does-response and cancer, all sites and site-specific. *Medicine and Science in Sports and Exercise, 33*, S530–S550.

Troiano, R. P., Berrigan, D., Dodd, K. W., Mâsse, L. C., Tilert, T., & Mcdowell, M. (2008). Physical activity in the United States measured by accelerometer. *Medicine & Science in Sports & Exercise, 40*, 181–188.

van Sluijs, E. M., McMinn, A. M., & Griffin, S. J. (2008). Effectiveness of interventions to promote physical activity in children and adolescents: Systematic review of controlled trials. *British Journal of Sports Medicine, 42*, 653–657.

Wannamethee, S. G., & Shaper, A. G. (2001). Physical activity in the prevention of cardiovascular disease: An epidemiological perspective. *Sports Medicine, 3*, 101–114.

Warburton, D. E. R., Nicol, C. W., & Bredin, S. S. D. (2006). Health benefits of physical activity: The evidence. *Canadian Medical Association Journal, 174*, 801–809.

WHO. (2004). *Global Strategy on Diet and Physical Activity*. Geneva: WHO Press.

WHO. (2009). *Global Health Risks: Mortality and Burden of Disease Attributable to Selected Major Risks*. Geneva: WHO Press.

WHO. (2010). *Global Recommendations on Physical Activity for Health*. Geneva: WHO Press.

Williams, N.H., Hendry, M., France, B., Lewis, R., & Wilkinson, C. (2007). Effectiveness of exercise-referral schemes to promote physical activity in adults: Systematic review. *British Journal of General Practice, 57*, 979–986.

4

Distinguishing Between Positive and Negative Exercise Habits

J. Robert Grove, Ben Jackson, Jay-Lee Longbottom, and Nikola Medic

We are what we repeatedly do. Excellence then, is not an act, but a habit.

(Aristotle, 384–322 BC)

Walking is the best possible exercise. Habituate yourself to walk very far.

(Thomas Jefferson, 1743–1826)

Introduction

There is a growing consensus that insufficient physical activity is a global public health concern. In the USA and Canada, recent reports indicate that only about three in 10 people engage in sufficient leisure time physical activity (National Center for Health Statistics, 2008), and the estimates are similar for Europeans and Australians [Australian Institute of Health and Welfare (AIHW), 2008; Sjöström *et al.*, 2006]. This tendency toward sedentary lifestyles is undoubtedly a major contributor to rising levels of overweight and obesity, and it also increases, either directly or indirectly, the risk of numerous chronic diseases (Oldridge, 2008). Approximately 7% of the total burden of disease and disability in Australia is attributable to physical inactivity, with associated financial costs exceeding AUS$1400 million per year (AIHW, 2008).

At the same time, the protective role that exercise plays with respect to physical health status is well-documented in the epidemiological literature. Regular involvement in physical activity has been shown to be an effective mechanism in weight reduction (Miller & Wadden, 2004), and several reviews in the last decade have documented an array of additional health benefits across the lifespan, including reductions in overall mortality risk (e.g., Hallal *et al.*, 2006; Keysor, 2003). More specifically, exercise participation in childhood, adolescence, and adulthood has been shown to play an important role in the primary and/or secondary prevention of health conditions such as cardiovascular disease, diabetes, colon and breast cancer, hypertension, bone and joint disease, and stroke.

Applied Topics in Health Psychology, First Edition. Edited by M. L. Caltabiano and L. Ricciardelli.
© 2013 John Wiley & Sons, Ltd. Published 2013 by John Wiley & Sons, Ltd.

Regular physical activity also has documented benefits for key indicators of social and psychological wellbeing. From a societal perspective, those who participate in physical activity report higher levels of social support, social affiliation, and community involvement (Eyler *et al.*, 1999; Greiner *et al.*, 2004). At a personal level, there is abundant evidence for a wide range of psychological benefits from both acute and chronic physical activity at all stages of life (e.g., Callaghan, 2004; Landers & Arent, 2007). For example, exercise has consistently been shown to enhance mood, improve confidence in the ability to cope with threats, and alleviate stress (e.g., Berger & Motl, 2000; Rodgers & Sullivan, 2001). It has also been shown to reduce the symptoms of anxiety and depression in both clinical and subclinical populations (e.g., Grove & Eklund, 2004; Teychenne *et al.*, 2008). Indeed, the depression-reducing impact of exercise appears to be at least as potent as that typically obtained with group therapy and antidepressant treatments (e.g., Lawlor & Hopker, 2001).

Regular physical activity is also associated with improvements in core self-perceptions such as physical self-concept and global self-esteem (e.g., Spence *et al.*, 2005). In addition, it has been shown to enhance perceived wellbeing and quality of life in various patient populations, including schizophrenics, individuals with bipolar disorder, and cancer survivors (Callaghan, 2004; Courneya & Friedenreich, 1999; Wright *et al.*, 2009). People also tend to appraise their own capabilities more favourably as a result of exercise involvement. Finally, there is substantial evidence for a link between physical activity and improved cognitive functioning in children and adults (e.g., Ellemberg & St Louis-Deschênes, 2010; Gillum & Obisesan, 2010). Moreover, an active lifestyle not only appears to delay the onset of various age-related cognitive impairments such as dementia and Alzheimer's disease (e.g., Rockwood & Middleton, 2007) but also improves cognitive functioning in the presence of these conditions (e.g., Heyn *et al.*, 2004).

In this chapter, we outline a unique, process-oriented framework for evaluating the strength of exercise habits and elaborate on the central components of this framework. Cognitive-behavioral change strategies that might influence these psychological processes are discussed in relation to increasing the strength of exercise habits in the normal population. We then examine the indicators of counterproductive exercise involvement and contrast positive exercise habits with negative exercise habits in the form of exercise dependence.

The Structure of Exercise Habits

Given the plethora of physical and psychological benefits associated with exercise, health practitioners can provide a valuable service to their clients by assisting them to initiate and maintain a regular exercise regime. In order to do so effectively, we believe it is important for healthcare providers to first understand the "structure" of exercise habits. With this background knowledge, they will be in a much better position to facilitate a lasting change in behavior. The characteristics of exercise habits have been an area of research interest in our laboratory for several years, and we offer the following observations based on that research (e.g., Grove *et al.*, unpublished work; Grove & Ortega, 2005; Grove & Zillich, 2003, 2004; Hashim *et al.*, 2008).

As illustrated in Figure 4.1, we believe there are four key processes that underlie the development of exercise habits. These processes are stimulus-response (SR) bonding, automaticity, patterning of action, and negative consequences for nonperformance. This belief is supported by a large body of research. For example, the development of strong SR bonds is a core component of classic learning models and a key determinant of how often any behavior is repeated (Skinner, 1953; Spence, 1956). When these bonds become sufficiently strong, the behavior in question can be directly triggered by

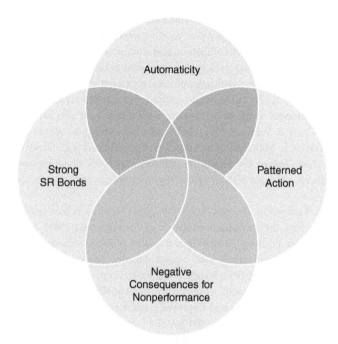

Figure 4.1 Psychological processes associated with exercise habits.

the environmental cues that are associated with the activity (Bargh & Chartrand, 1999; Orbell & Verplanken, 2010). In other words, a key feature of exercise habits is that they can be set in motion when one encounters people, places, or actions that have frequently been associated with exercise in the past (see Wood & Neal, 2007).

Automaticity is also widely acknowledged as a core element of habitual behavior (Aarts & Dijksterhuis, 2000; Ouellette & Wood, 1998; Verplanken & Orbell, 2003). In the early stages of learning, most behaviors require deliberation and conscious monitoring for proper execution. However, as these behaviors are repeated and become well learned, the necessity for deliberation and monitoring decreases (Ajzen, 2002; Ouellette & Wood, 1998; Wood & Neal, 2007). In other words, they become more and more automated, and their execution becomes characterized by lower levels of conscious awareness, less mental effort, and less detailed decision-making (Bargh, 1994; Verplanken *et al.*, 1997).

Response patterning is perhaps less obvious than cueing and automaticity in connection with exercise habits, but we believe there are good reasons for its inclusion as a central element of the construct. Motor learning research clearly shows that repeated practice increases the efficiency and stability of discrete movements (Ericsson *et al.*, 1993; Schmidt & Lee, 2005). There is also considerable support for the notion that a generalized motor program governs the sequencing and relative timing of serial actions, and that this motor program becomes increasingly invariant with more and more repetition (Giuffrida *et al.*, 2002; Shea & Wulf, 2005). These findings are consistent with the view that behavioral habits are characterized by procedural encoding, heuristic processing, and/or scripting (Chen & Chaiken, 1999; Ronis *et al.*, 1989), which produces an integrated, patterned, and predictable action sequence that is highly resistant to change (Ewart, 1993). Thus, with respect to exercise, patterning can be viewed both as an indicator of existing habit strength and as a mechanism for building greater habit strength.

Finally, exercise habit strength is reflected by the extent to which negative psychological consequences are experienced if exercise is not (or cannot be) performed. There is abundant evidence for this assertion in the literature on negative health habits. Regular smokers, for example, report numerous psychological distress symptoms during abstinence (e.g., Hughes, 2007), but neither the severity nor the duration of these symptoms is reliably linked to nicotine intake (Shiffman *et al.*, 2006). Thus, it appears that there is a substantial contribution of expectancies and other cognitive-behavioral factors in the smoking withdrawal syndrome (see Hendricks *et al.*, 2009). This cognitive-behavioral contribution is reinforced by the finding of similar psychological distress symptoms among regular exercisers when their physical activity is restricted for some reason. These exercise-related withdrawal symptoms include guilt, depression, irritability, anxiety, feelings of loss, and somatic complaints such as bloating or fatigue (Acevedo *et al.*, 1992; Szabo, 1995). Importantly, it has been shown that these symptoms disappear when regular exercise is once again possible (Mondin *et al.*, 1996).

Developing Exercise Habits

If these four processes (strengthening of SR bonds, automaticity, patterning of action, and negative consequences for nonperformance) do indeed form the basis of exercise habits, then practitioners should be able to use them in order to build exercise habit strength. We believe they can do so by strategically emphasizing behavior change strategies that are consistent with these processes. Some possibilities along these lines are summarized in Table 4.1 and discussed below.

In discussing exercise behavior change, Marcus *et al.* (1992) provided evidence that: (1) the effectiveness of a given behavior change strategy is likely to depend on the person's current exercise-related stage of change and (2) both experiential processes and behavioral processes are useful for moving people from occasional exercise (preparation stage) to regular exercise (action and maintenance stages). Experiential processes include consciousness raising (increased exposure to information about various forms of exercise and their benefits), dramatic relief (increased exposure to information about the negative consequences of a sedentary lifestyle), environmental reevaluation [reflection on the positive (or negative) impact of increasing (or failing to increase) exercise on those around you], and self-reevaluation [reflection on the positive (or negative) impact of increasing (or failing to increase) exercise on one's self-concept]. Behavioral processes include counterconditioning (framing and engaging in exercise as an activity that allows for time out, relaxation, and recovery), cultivation of helping relationships (associating with and exercising

Table 4.1 Strategies for increasing the strength of exercise habit processes

Strengthening of SR bonds	Increasing automaticity	Patterning of actions	Consequences for nonperformance
Stimulus control	Stimulus control	PODP	Dramatic relief
Counterconditioning	Counterconditioning	Helping relationships	Self-reevaluation
Same activity, same time, same place	Same activity, same time, same place	Same activity, same time, same place	Environmental reevaluation
Exercise partner(s)		Group activities	
PODP	Active transport	Active transport	Reinforcement management

PODP, point-of-decision prompt.

with supportive others), reinforcement management [setting goals for exercise involvement and establishing contingencies for meeting (or failing to meet) targets for exercise involvement], and stimulus control (deliberate enhancement of exercise cues and exercise reminders in the home and work environment). Point-of-decision prompts (PODPs) appear to be a particularly useful stimulus control strategy for increasing the regular use of stairs (Kahn *et al.*, 2002).

A number of additional exercise-specific behavior management strategies can also be mapped against the habit processes as shown in Table 4.1. For example, exercising with a 'buddy' or as part of a group increases the probability of continued involvement (Kahn *et al.*, 2002). Structuring exercise so that it is undertaken on a 'same activity, same time, same place' basis also has been advocated as an effective strategy for increasing exercise frequency and exercise adherence (Dubbert *et al.*, 1987). In terms of our habit framework, it is likely that exercising in this way encourages patterning of action, strengthens exercise-specific SR bonds, and facilitates automaticity. Similarly, behavioral strategies such as deliberately parking further from (rather than closer to) the workplace, consciously using stairs rather than lifts, and regularly adopting 'active transport' for routine, short-distance travel (e.g., to local shops and/or work) are beneficial for increasing energy expenditure and, over time, may become habituated (see McCormack *et al.*, 2003). Again, we would argue that such habituation occurs via the strengthening of habit processes as outlined in Table 4.1.

Too Much of a Good Thing: Training Distress

We certainly believe that healthcare providers should encourage their clients to develop strong exercise habits. At the same time, they should be aware that there is a point at which exercise involvement can produce deleterious physical and mental effects. When individuals fail to appropriately manage the balance between exercise and rest, they may begin to display a profile of negative physiological and psychological symptoms collectively referred to in the literature as training distress, staleness, overreaching, or overtraining syndrome (e.g., Main & Grove, 2009; Meeusen *et al.*, 2006). Although primarily observed in sport settings where exercise workloads are very high, this phenomenon is also apparent in the general population (e.g., Hendrickson & Verde, 1994).

Mood disturbance is a well-documented and consistently observed symptom of training distress. Classic research by Morgan *et al.* (1987), as well as Morgan *et al.* (1988), using the Profile of Mood States showed reliable increases in depression, anger, fatigue, and total mood disturbance as a result of heavy exercise workloads. More recent research has not only substantiated these negative mood effects but also provided evidence of additional psychological and behavioral indicators of training distress (e.g., Meeusen *et al.*, 2006). These indicators include, but are not limited to, increases in perceived stress, insomnia, reduced appetite, increased susceptibility to minor illnesses, lethargy, concentration problems, and irritability (e.g., Main & Grove, 2009; Maso *et al.*, 2004). In addition, disproportionately heavy exercise also causes hormonal fluctuations and reductions in general wellbeing, and, if unresolved, may be associated in the longer term with the onset of clinical depression (Armstrong & Van Heest, 2002; Meeusen *et al.*, 2004).

Far Too Much of a Good Thing: Exercise Dependence

Healthcare providers also need to be aware that exercise involvement can sometimes become all-consuming and evolve into a maladaptive behavior pattern that increases the risk of physical and psychological harm (Gulker *et al.*, 2001). This negative behavior pattern has been labelled "exercise

Table 4.2 Suggested criteria for evaluating exercise dependence

Substantial investment of time/energy
- Perceived need to exercise one or more times each day
- Reduction or elimination of social, occupational, or recreational activities unrelated to exercise
- Compulsive involvement in activities that support or surround exercise behavior

Evidence of tolerance effects
- Perception of decreased benefits from a given frequency, intensity, and/or duration of exercise
- Perceived need to continually increase exercise frequency, intensity, and/or duration

Severe withdrawal symptoms
- Rapid onset of severe actual or perceived withdrawal symptoms when unable to exercise
- Rapid alleviation of withdrawal symptoms when once again able to exercise

Awareness without control
- Subjective awareness of the compulsion to exercise
- Continued involvement despite knowledge of negative physical or psychological consequences

Based on criteria suggested by de Coverley Veale (1987), Hausenblaus and Symons Downs (2002a, 2002b), and Adams *et al.* (2003).

dependence" (Hausenblas & Symons Downs, 2002a, 2002b; Ogden *et al.*, 1997). Although not a formally recognized dependence syndrome, its defining characteristics have been derived from the criteria for existing dependence syndromes in the *Diagnostic and Statistical Manual of Mental Disorders*, 4th edn (DSM-IV; American Psychiatric Association, 1994). As shown in Table 4.2, these characteristics include both biomedical and cognitive-behavioral elements (Veale, 1995). More specifically, exercise dependence is characterized by tolerance effects (i.e., a perceived need to increase the amount undertaken in order to achieve the same results) and a history of unsuccessful attempts to cut down or control exercise (Adams *et al.*, 2003; Hausenblas & Symons Downs, 2002a). Preoccupation with exercise is also evident and is reflected by continuation of exercise despite knowledge of a recurring injury or sickness and/or interference with personal, social, and occupational functioning (Hausenblas & Symons Downs, 2002a). Finally, exercise dependence is characterized by withdrawal symptoms following restraint from exercise. These symptoms include feelings of guilt, decreased self-esteem, depression, anxiety, irritability, sluggishness, lethargy, and fatigue (Adams *et al.*, 2003; Hausenblas & Symons Downs, 2002b). Although some of these symptoms may also be experienced by nondependent habitual exercisers, they are more widespread and severe for dependent exercisers (Szabo, 1995).

Veale (1995) also proposed a diagnostic hierarchy to distinguish between primary and secondary exercise dependence. More specifically, he argued that these two forms of exercise dependence can be differentiated in terms of their motivational objectives. Primary exercise dependence occurs when the individual is intrinsically motivated to exercise and involvement in the activity itself is the desired end-point (see Hausenblas & Symons Downs, 2002a). Secondary exercise dependence occurs as a by-product of another behavioral disorder (e.g., bulimia or anorexia), with compulsive exercise undertaken as a means to an end and performed in an attempt to control or alter body shape, body image, or feelings of self-worth (Hausenblas & Symons Downs, 2002a). In other words, the motivational mechanisms are externally regulated rather than intrinsically regulated (Hall *et al.*, 2009).

From a personality perspective, it has been suggested that neuroticism may be positively associated with the potential for developing exercise dependence (Hausenblas & Giacobbi, 2004). Neuroticism is a known correlate of somatic complaints, health concerns, pessimistic rumination, and poorly developed coping strategies (Costa & McCrae, 1992). In the exercise context, these cognitive tendencies may facilitate rumination and worry about exercise involvement and also increase the likelihood that exercise might be adopted as a strategy for coping with stress (Hausenblas & Giacobbi, 2004). Research examining other trait dimensions has demonstrated a positive association between exercise dependence and obsessive-compulsive tendencies, trait anxiety, and perfectionism (Hall *et al.*, 2009; Spano, 2001). With respect to perfectionism, it appears that a combination of strong concern about personal adequacy and a tendency to set excessively high personal standards is especially important in differentiating exercise dependent individuals from those with strong but more positive exercise habits (Hall *et al.*, 2007; Symons Downs *et al.*, 2004). Indeed, this particular combination of perfectionistic traits is a central feature of maladaptive perfectionism (Bieling *et al.*, 2004), which appears to be associated with a number of counterproductive cognitive, behavioral, and affective outcomes in sport and exercise settings (e.g., Longbottom *et al.*, 2010; Molnar *et al.*, 2006).

Summary and Conclusions

Regular exercise has physical health benefits as well as mental health benefits. Healthcare providers can facilitate the development of positive exercise habits by assisting their clients to utilize cognitive-behavioral strategies that reinforce the psychological processes underpinning habit formation. These processes include patterning of action, strengthening of SR bonds, automaticity, and negative consequences for nonperformance. At the same time, health practitioners should remain vigilant for signs of training distress and exercise dependence. By doing so, they will ensure that the inherent benefits of exercise continue to outweigh the potential costs.

References

Aarts, H., & Dijksterhuis, A. (2000). Habit as knowledge structures: Automaticity in goal-directed behavior. *Journal of Personality and Social Psychology, 78*, 53–63.

Acevedo, E. O., Dzewaltowski, D. A., Gill, D. L., & Noble, J. M. (1992). Cognitive orientations of ultramarathoners. *The Sport Psychologist, 6*, 242–252.

Adams, J. M., Miller, T. W., & Kraus, R. F. (2003). Exercise dependence diagnostic and therapeutic issues for patients in psychotherapy. *Journal of Contemporary Psychotherapy, 33*, 93–107.

AIHW. (2008). *Australia's Health 2008* (Cat. no. AUS 99). Canberra: Australian Institute of Health and Welfare.

Ajzen, I. (2002). Residual effects of past on later behavior: Habituation and reasoned action perspectives. *Personality and Social Psychology Review, 6*, 107–122.

American Psychiatric Association. (1994). *Diagnostic and Statistical Manual of Mental Disorders* (4th edn.). Washington DC: American Psychiatric Association.

Armstrong, L. E., & Van Heest, J. L. (2002). The unknown mechanism of the overtraining syndrome. Clues from depression and psychoneuroimmunology. *Sports Medicine, 32*, 185–209.

Bargh, J. A. (1994). The four horsemen of automaticity: Awareness, intention, efficiency, and control in social cognition. In R. S. Wyer & T. K. Srull (Eds.), *Handbook of Social Cognition*, volume 1 (pp. 1–40). Hillsdale, NJ: Erlbaum.

Bargh, J. A., & Chartrand, T. L. (1999). The unbearable automaticity of being. *American Psychologist, 54*, 462–479.

Berger, B. G., & Motl, R. W. (2000). Exercise and mood: A selective review and synthesis of research employing the Profile of Mood States. *Journal of Applied Sport Psychology, 12*, 69–92.

Bieling, P. J., Israeli, A. L., & Antony, M. M. (2004). Is perfectionism good, bad, or both? Examining models of the perfectionism construct. *Personality and Individual Differences, 36*, 1373–1385.

Callaghan, P. (2004). Exercise: A neglected intervention in mental health care? *Journal of Psychiatric and Mental Health Nursing, 11*, 476–483.

Chen, S., & Chaiken, S. (1999). The heuristic-systematic model in its broader context. In S. Chaiken and Y. Trope (Eds.), *Dual-Process Models in Social Psychology* (pp. 73–96). New York: Guilford Press.

Costa, P. T. Jr., & McCrae, R. R. (1992). *The NEO PI-R: Professional Manual.* Odessa, FL: Psychological Assessment Resources.

Courneya, K. S., & Friedenreich, C. M. (1999). Physical exercise and quality of life following cancer diagnosis: A literature review. *Annals of Behavioral Medicine, 21*, 171–179.

de Coverley Veale, D. M. W. (1987). Exercise and mental health. *Acta Psychiatrica Scandinavica, 76*, 113–120.

Dubbert, P. M., Rappaport, N. B., & Martin, J. E. (1987). Exercise in cardiovascular disease. *Behavior Modification, 11*, 329–347.

Ellemberg, D., & St Louis-Deschênes, M. (2010). The effect of acute physical exercise on cognitive function during development. *Psychology of Sport and Exercise, 11*, 122–126.

Ericsson, K. A., Krampe, R. T., & Tesch-Römer, C. (1993). The role of deliberate practice in the acquisition of expert performance. *Psychological Review, 100*, 363–406.

Ewart, C. K. (1993). Social action theory for a public health psychology. *American Psychologist, 46*, 931–946.

Eyler, A. A., Brownson, R. C., Donatelle, R. J., King, A. C., Brown, D., & Sallis, J. F. (1999). Physical activity social support and middle- and older-aged minority women: Results from a US survey. *Social Science & Medicine, 49*, 781–789.

Gillum, R. F., & Obisesan, T. O. (2010). Physical activity, cognitive function, and mortality in a US national cohort. *Annals of Epidemiology, 20*, 251–257.

Giuffrida, C. G., Shea, J. B., & Fairbrother, J. T. (2002). Differential transfer benefits of increased practice for constant, blocked and serial practice schedules. *Journal of Motor Behavior, 34*, 353–365.

Greiner, K. A., Li, C., Kawachi, I., Hunt, D. C., & Ahluwalia, J. S. (2004). The relationships of social participation and community ratings to health and health behaviors in areas with high and low population density. *Social Science and Medicine, 59*, 2303–2312.

Grove, J. R., & Zillich, I. (2003). Conceptualisation and measurement of habitual exercise. In M. Katsikitis (Ed.), *Proceedings of the 38th Annual Conference of the Australian Psychological Society* (pp. 88–92). Melbourne: Australia Psychological Society.

Grove, J. R., & Eklund, R.C. (2004). Exercise and anxiety. In L. M. LeMura & S. P. Von Duvillard (Eds.), *Clinical Exercise Physiology* (pp. 605–615). Philadelphia, PA: Lippincott Williams & Wilkins.

Grove, J. R., & Zillich, I. (2004). *A Process-Oriented Measure of Habit Strength for Exercise.* Paper presented at the 8th International Congress of Behavioral Medicine, Mainz, Germany.

Grove, J. R., & Ortega, E. (2005). Psychological processes and exercise habits: Criterion-related validity of proposed dimensions. *Proceedings of the 11th World Congress of the International Society of Sport Psychology* (CD-ROM). International Society of Sport Psychology.

Gulker, M. G., Laskis, T. A., & Kuba, S. A. (2001). Do excessive exercises have a higher rate of obsessive-compulsive symptomatology? *Psychology of Health & Medicine, 6*, 387–398.

Hall, H. K., Kerr, A. W., Kozub, S. A., & Finnie, S. B. (2007). Motivational antecedents of obligatory exercise: The influence of achievement goals and multidimensional perfectionism. *Psychology of Sport and Exercise, 8*, 297–316.

Hall, H. K., Hill, A. P., Appleton, P. R., & Kozub, S. A. (2009). The mediating influence of unconditional self-acceptance and labile self-esteem on the relationship between multidimensional perfectionism and exercise dependence. *Psychology of Sport and Exercise, 10*, 35–44.

Hallal, P. C., Victoria, C. G., Azevedo, M. R., & Wells, J. C. K. (2006). Adolescent physical activity and health. *Sports Medicine, 36*, 1019–1030.

Hashim, H. A., Grove, J. R., & Whipp, P. (2008). Relationships between physical education enjoyment processes, physical activity, and exercise habit strength among high school students. *Asian Journal of Exercise and Sports Science, 5*, 23–30.

Hausenblas, H. A., & Giacobbi, P. R. (2004). Relationship between exercise dependence symptoms and personality. *Personality and Individual Differences, 36,* 1265–1273.

Hausenblas, H. A., & Symons Downs, D. (2002a). Exercise dependence: A systematic review. *Psychology of Sport and Exercise, 3,* 89–123.

Hausenblas, H. A., & Symons Downs, D. (2002b). How much is too much? The development and validation of the exercise dependence scale. *Psychology and Health: An International Journal, 17,* 387–404.

Hendricks, P. S., Wood, S. B., & Hall, S. M. (2009). Smokers' expectations for abstinence: Preliminary results from focus groups. *Psychology of Addictive Behaviors, 23,* 380–385.

Hendrickson, C. D., & Verde, T. J. (1994). Inadequate recovery from vigorous exercise. *The Physician and Sports Medicine, 22,* 56–64.

Heyn, P., Abreu, B. C., & Ottenbacher, K. J. (2004) The effects of exercise training on elderly persons with cognitive impairment and dementia: A meta-analysis. *Archives of Physical Medicine and Rehabilitation, 85,* 1694–1704.

Hughes, J. R. (2007). Effects of abstinence from tobacco: Etiology, animal models, epidemiology, and significance: A subjective review. *Nicotine & Tobacco Research, 9,* 329–339.

Kahn, E. B., Ramsey, L. T., Brownson, R. C., Heath, G. W., Howzed, E. H., Powell, K. E. *et al.* (2002). The effectiveness of interventions to increase physical activity: A systematic review. *American Journal of Preventive Medicine, 22,* 73–107.

Keysor, J. J. (2003). Does late-life physical activity or exercise prevent or minimize disablement? A critical review of the scientific evidence. *American Journal of Preventive Medicine, 25,* 129–136.

Landers, D. M., & Arent, S. M. (2007). Physical activity and mental health. In G. Tenenbaum & R. C. Eklund (Eds.), *Handbook of Sport Psychology* (pp. 469–491). Hoboken, NJ: John Wiley & Sons.

Lawlor, D. A., & Hopker, S. W. (2001). The effectiveness of exercise as an intervention in the management of depression: Systematic review and meta-regression analysis of randomised controlled trials. *British Medical Journal, 322,* 763–767.

Longbottom, J.-L., Grove, J. R., & Dimmock, J. A. (2010). An examination of perfectionism traits and physical activity motivation. *Psychology of Sport and Exercise, 11,* 574–581.

Main, L., & Grove, J. R. (2009). A multi-component assessment model for monitoring training distress among athletes. *European Journal of Sport Science, 9,* 195–202.

Marcus, B. H., Rossi, J. S., Selby, V. C., Niaura, R. S., & Abrams, D. B. (1992). The stages of exercise adoption and maintenance in a worksite sample. *Health Psychology, 11,* 386–395.

Maso, F., Lac, G., Filaire, E., Michaux, O., & Robert, A. (2004). Salivary testosterone and cortisol in rugby players: Correlation with psychological overtraining items. *British Journal of Sports Medicine, 38,* 260–263.

McCormack, G., Giles-Corti, B., & Milligan, R. (2003). The test-retest reliability of habitual incidental physical activity. *Australian and New Zealand Journal of Public Health, 27,* 428–433.

Meeusen, R., Piacentini, M. F., Busschaert, B., Buyse, L., De Schutter, G., & Stray-Gundersen, J. (2004). Hormonal responses in athletes: The use of a two-bout exercise protocol to detect subtle differences in (over)training status. *European Journal of Applied Physiology, 91,* 140–146.

Meeusen, R., Duclos, M., Gleeson, M., Rietjens, G., Steinacker, J., & Urhausen, A. (2006). Prevention, diagnosis, and treatment of the overtraining syndrome. *European Journal of Sport Science, 6,* 1–14.

Miller, W. C., & Wadden, T. A. (2004). Exercise as a treatment for obesity. In G. A. Bray & C. Bouchard (Eds.), *Handbook of Obesity: Clinical Applications* (2nd edn.) (pp. 169–183). New York: Marcel Dekker.

Molnar, D. S., Reker, D. L., Culp, N. A., Sadava, S. W., & DeCourville, N. H. (2006). A mediated model of perfectionism, affect, and physical health. *Journal of Research in Personality, 40,* 482–500.

Mondin, G. W., Morgan, W. P., Piering, P. D., Stegner, A. J., Stotesbery, C. L., Trine, M. R., & Wu, M.-Y. (1996). Psychological consequences of exercise deprivation in habitual exercisers. *Medicine and Science in Sports and Exercise, 28,* 1199–1203.

Morgan, W. P., Brown, D., Raglin, J., O'Connor, P. J., & Ellickson, K. A. (1987). Psychological monitoring of overtraining and staleness. *British Journal of Sports Medicine, 21,* 107–114.

Morgan, W. P., Costill, D. L., Flynn, M. G., Raglin, J. S., & O'Connor, P. J. (1988). Mood disturbance following increased training in swimmers. *Medicine and Science in Sport and Exercise, 20,* 408–414.

National Center for Health Statistics (2008). *Chartbook on Trends in the Health of Americans.* Hyattsville, MD: Public Health Service.

Ogden, J., Veale, D., & Summers, Z. (1997). The development and validation of the exercise dependence questionnaire. *Addiction Research, 5,* 343–356.

Oldridge, N. B. (2008). Economic burden of physical inactivity: Healthcare costs associated with cardiovascular disease. *European Journal of Cardiovascular Prevention & Rehabilitation, 15,* 130–139.

Orbell, S., & Verplanken, B. (2010). The automatic component of habit in health behavior: Habit as cue-contingent automaticity. *Health Psychology, 29,* 374–383.

Ouellette, J. A., & Wood, W. (1998). Habit and intention in everyday life: The multiple processes by which past behavior predicts future behavior. *Psychological Bulletin, 124,* 54–74.

Rockwood, K., & Middleton, L. (2007). Physical activity and the maintenance of cognitive function. *Alzheimer's & Dementia, 3,* S38–S44.

Rodgers, W. M., & Sullivan, M. J. L. (2001). Task, coping and scheduling self-efficacy in relation to frequency of physical activity. *Journal of Applied Social Psychology, 31,* 741–753.

Ronis, D. L., Yates, J. F., & Kirscht, J. P. (1989). Attitudes, decisions, and habits as determinants of behavior. In A. R. Pratkanis, S. J. Breckler, & A. G. Greenwald (Eds.), *Attitude Structure and Function* (pp. 213–239). New York: Lawrence Erlbaum.

Schmidt, R. A., & Lee, T. (2005). *Motor Control and Learning: a Behavioral Emphasis* (4th edn.). Champaign, IL: Human Kinetics.

Shea, C. H., & Wulf, G. (2005). Schema theory: A critical appraisal and reevaluation. *Journal of Motor Behavior, 37,* 85–101.

Shiffman, S., Patten, C., Gwaltney, C., Paty, J., Gnys, M., Kassel, J. *et al.* (2006). Natural history of nicotine withdrawal. *Addiction, 101,* 1822–1832.

Sjöström, M., Oja, P., Hagströmer, M., Smith, B. J., & Bauman, A. E. (2006). Health-enhancing physical activity across European Union countries: The Eurobarometer study. *Journal of Public Health, 14,* 291–300.

Skinner, B. F. (1953). *Science and Human Behavior.* New York: Macmillan.

Spano, L. (2001). The relationship between exercise and anxiety, obsessive-compulsiveness, and narcissism. *Personality and Individual Differences, 30,* 87–93.

Spence, J. C., McGannon, K. R., & Poon, P. (2005). The effect of exercise on global self esteem: A quantitative review. *Journal of Sport & Exercise Psychology, 27,* 311–334.

Spence, K. W. (1956). *Behavior Theory and Conditioning.* New Haven, CT: Yale University Press.

Symons Downs, D., Hausenblas, A., & Nigg, C. R. (2004). Factorial validity and psychometric examination of the exercise dependence scale-revised. *Measurement in Physical Education and Exercise Science, 8,* 183–201.

Szabo, A. (1995). The impact of exercise deprivation on well-being of habitual exercisers. *Australian Journal of Science and Medicine in Sport, 27,* 68–75.

Teychenne, M., Ball, K., & Salmon, J. (2008). Physical activity and likelihood of depression in adults: A review. *Preventive Medicine, 46,* 397–411.

Veale, D. (1995). Does primary exercise dependence really exist? In J. Annett, B. Cripps, & H. Steinberg (Eds.), *Exercise Addiction: Motivation for Participation in Sport and Exercise* (pp. 1–5). Leicester: British Psychological Society.

Verplanken, B., & Orbell, S. (2003). Reflections on past behavior: A self-report index of habit strength. *Journal of Applied Social Psychology, 33,* 1313–1330.

Verplanken, B., Aarts, H., & van Knippenberg, A. (1997). Habit, information acquisition, and the process of making travel mode choices. *European Journal of Social Psychology, 27,* 539–560.

Wood, W., & Neal, D. T. (2007). A new look at habits and the habit-goal interface. *Psychological Review, 114,* 843–863.

Wright, K. A., Everson-Hock, E. S., & Taylor, A. H. (2009). The effects of physical activity on physical and mental health among individuals with bipolar disorder: A systematic review. *Mental Health and Physical Activity, 2,* 86–94.

Part 2

Age, Gender, and Cultural Factors in Health

5

Promoting Aging Well

Psychological Contributions

Colette Browning, Chyrisse Heine, and Shane Thomas

The mental and behavioral health of older people is of increasing significance as the population ages. Health and clinical psychologists have a central role in improving quality of life for older people. Health psychologists focus on the assessment, prevention, and management of illness and the behavioral, psychological, and social factors that are associated with mental and physical health. As many aging issues are health-related, health psychologists are well trained to be at the forefront of the care of older people (Australian Psychological Society, 2011a; Matarazzo, 1980; Taylor, 2011). Clinical psychologists can assist older people in the areas of assessment and treatment of depression, anxiety, and suicide, pain management, dementia and substance abuse, and problem behaviors associated with dementia.

The central role of psychologists in the care of older people is highlighted by the promotion of geropsychology through the American Psychological Association and also Australia's Psychology and Ageing interest group (American Psychological Association Office on Aging, 2005; Australian Psychological Society, 2011b). There are also increasing opportunities for psychologists to work in multidisciplinary care teams with older people [Australian Government Department of Health and Ageing (DoHA), 2011; Speer & Schneider, 2003]. Although the work of psychologists in the field of aging leads to substantial cost savings (see, for example, Bird *et al.*, 2007, 2009; Creed *et al.*, 2002; de Jonge *et al.*, 2003), in Australia, psychologists currently have only a minor role in aged-care services and little involvement in working with older people in the community. For the most part, in Australia, psychologists in aged care primarily work in memory clinics with few working in residential and community aged care services or in primary care. Lack of knowledge regarding the efficacy of psychological interventions for older adults may contribute to low referral rates to psychologists from medical practitioners (Koder & Ferguson, 1998). Koder and Helmes (2008) conducted a national survey of Australian psychologists to investigate their exposure to older adults and age-related course content both while they were training and in their everyday practice. Results of this study confirmed low rates of professional involvement with older adult clients. Only 6% of the sample specialized in geropsychology and reported moderate confidence and interest in working with older adults.

Applied Topics in Health Psychology, First Edition. Edited by M. L. Caltabiano and L. Ricciardelli.
© 2013 John Wiley & Sons, Ltd. Published 2013 by John Wiley & Sons, Ltd.

There is thus a need to provide psychology students with enhanced training in services and programs for older people so that the needs of the aging community can be enhanced by good-quality evidence-based professional care (Australian Psychological Society, 2011a). To capitalize on the contribution of psychology to improving the lives of older people, the evidence base for effective interventions, programs, and services needs to be improved and a concerted effort in the training of psychologists in the field of aging needs to occur (Qualls *et al.*, 2002).

In this chapter we will discuss interventions for older people through behavioral and psychological approaches to physical and mental health based on our definition of aging well. First we will examine population aging, aging heterogeneity, the concepts of healthy/successful aging, and the determinants of health and wellbeing in older adults.

Population and Individual Aging

Most countries are experiencing population aging: as the proportion of older people in a population increases the mean and median age of the population rises. Population aging is driven by decreasing fertility, increasing longevity, and migration (Lutz *et al.*, 2008). The causes of increased longevity include genetic influences, early detection and more efficient management of chronic illness due to improved technology and medical, pharmocological, and behavioral interventions, and the promotion of healthy lifestyles.

The older adult age group (those aged 65 years and over) represent the largest-growing segment of the population. On a global level, by 2050 16.5% of the world's population will be aged 65 years and over (Wilson, 2005). In Australia, Gray *et al.* (2008) estimated that 26–28% of the population would be aged over 65 years by 2051. According to the Australian Bureau of Statistics (ABS) (2010), the average life expectancy for non-Indigenous males is 78.7 years and 82.6 years for females while the average life expectancy for Indigenous males is 67.2 years and 72.9 years for females. The increase in the proportion of people who will reach old age is partially due to the addition of the baby boomer generation to the older adult age group. Baby boomers are that segment of the population who were born during the population explosion following World War II (that is, between 1946 and 1964). According to the Australian Government (2007, p. 1), baby boomers will add to the "... older non-working population ... [and] will put a greater strain on Australia's hospitals, aged-care services and pensions," leading to financial strain for individuals and governments. However, there are many opportunities for interventions to improve the health and wellbeing of older age groups and psychologists can make an important contribution.

There has also been a rapid increase in the number of people aged 80 years and older (known as the "old-old" population). By 2051, it is predicted that 1.6 million Australians (6–8% of the total population) will constitute the old-old population (ABS, 2010). Commentators have differentiated between baby boomers, the young-old (65–79 years), and the old-old (80 years and over; see, for example, Suzman *et al.*, 1992). In addition, authors have distinguished between the "Third Age" and "Fourth Age" (e.g., Baltes, 1997; Baltes & Mayer, 1999; Baltes & Smith, 2003), with the Fourth Age describing the old-old population. Centenarians (those who live to 100 years or more) are a further differentiated segment of the old-old population that has received increasing attention in the literature. According to the 2006 Australian census, there were 3154 centenarians living in Australia and this number is expected to increase to 12 000 by 2020 (ABS, 2010). When our current centenarians were born, life expectancy was around 58 years for women and 55 years for men, so their survival to almost 50 years past the turn-of-the-century population life expectancy is exceptional. Yet we know very little about these long-lived survivors in Australia (Richmond, 2008). In a study conducted on 35 centenarians living in Australia, McCormack (2000) found that, overall, centenarians rated their health as fair to good, their social relations as good, and their perception of living to 100 years was generally positive. In this study, the centenarians' health status varied, as did their memory skills. Furthermore, these participants scored lower on most quality-of-life domains compared to the general population. Some centenarian populations have undergone considerable research. For example, the Okinawa Centenarian Study (www.okicent.org/study.html) has investigated aging in a group of centenarians who have much lower rates of cardiovascular disease and cancer than mainland Japanese. These outcomes are associated with genes, diet, spirituality, low body mass index (BMI), and exercise. Similarly the New England Centenarian Study has found that American centenarians are characterized by slow rates of biological aging, delay (or avoidance) in experiencing diseases such as heart disease and cancer, low rates of smoking, and low rates of stress (Evert *et al.*, 2003).

The differentiation of "older people" into different subgroups as discussed above acknowledges that the aging process at the biological, psychological, and social levels is not homogenous. For example, for some, old age may be characterized by aging well: a positive quality of life, active participation in work, family, and society, and financial independence. For others, old age is characterized by illness, frailty, loss of independence, and loss of personal identity (Browning & Heine, 2012; Baltes & Smith, 2003). However the concepts of healthy/successful aging recognize the opportunity for promoting aging well across all older age groups (Browning & Thomas, 2007). These concepts have also been incorporated into policies on aging and we will discuss them in the next section (Andrews, 2002; World Health Organization, 2002).

In addition, by recognizing subgroups within the older adult population, researchers are able to investigate and specify the factors that determine this heterogeneity, and the factors that affect older adults' quality of life. These factors are particularly important for service providers to ensure that services and programs for older adults are well targeted. For example, the old-old population is characterized by features such as an excess of women, higher levels of comorbidity, frailty, and institutionalization (Baltes & Smith, 2003). Their needs will thus differ substantially to the baby boomers and the young-old whose needs are more centered on prevention and management of chronic illness and disability.

In summary, aging covers a number of groups from the baby boomers to centenarians. Psychologists need to recognize the diversity of the experiences of older people and outcomes of the aging process and tailor their interventions accordingly at the individual, group, and community level. However, the majority of published studies of aging focus on 'people aged 65 years and over' with few examining cohort and individual differences across wide age ranges. There are some notable exceptions such as the centenarian studies and more recent studies focusing on the baby boomer cohort. Accordingly, much of what we know about the impact of interventions in older populations suffers from a lack of specificity in terms of who most benefits from these interventions. In addition, while policies on aging have promoted healthy/successful aging approaches to interventions and programs for older people, the specification of what these interventions might look like has been poor mainly due to lack of definitional clarity about what we mean by healthy/successful aging. Below we describe a framework for interventions for older people based on healthy/successful aging concepts and a discussion of our own work in the area.

Concepts of Healthy and Successful Aging

The concept of successful aging was initially identified in the early 1960s (see Havighurst, 1968). During the late 1980s and early 1990s the concept became more popular, with the observation that old age did not merely equate with frailty, illness, and dependence but rather that older people had the capacity for change and adaptation (Baltes & Baltes, 1990). In this way, there was a shift away from the biomedical perspective of successful aging, which focuses on the compression of morbidity and longevity, and the proposition that increasing longevity would inevitably lead to increases in the burden of illness and disability in later life (Fries, 1980, 2002). As noted by Lupien and Wan (2004):

> To strive towards a more optimal view of the ageing process, research on successful ageing needs to focus not only on models of biological and cellular ageing that consider the gradual deterioration of the organism, but also on psychological and sociologically related factors that are related to improvements or maintenance of function. (p. 1423)

Various theories and definitions of successful/healthy aging have been proposed. While these positive approaches to understanding the aging experience are welcome, Holstein and Minkler (2003) have cautioned that the terms potentially stigmatize those older people who age "unsuccessfully" as they do not take into account the varied socioeconomic and cultural contexts and determinants of the aging experience.

Rowe and Kahn (1998) defined successful aging according to three components that are hierarchically arranged, including ". . . low risk of disease and disability, high physical and mental functioning and active engagement with life." Ryff (1989) proposed that successful aging comprises the following dimensions: "self acceptance," "positive relations with others," "autonomy," "environmental mastery," "purpose in life," and "personal growth" (p. 44). In comparison, the National Strategy for an Ageing Australia described healthy aging as an approach that aims to optimize the physical, emotional, and mental wellbeing of people throughout their lives (Andrews, 2002). In one of the few studies of older people's views of what constitutes successful aging Knight and Ricciardelli (2003) proposed the following domains as important for successful aging: health, activity, personal growth, happiness, independence, relationships, appreciation of life, and longevity. Depp and Jeste (2006) proposed the following domains based on a review of the literature: disability/physical functioning, cognitive functioning, life satisfaction/wellbeing, social/productive engagement, presence of illness, longevity, self-rated health, personality, environment/finances, and self-rated successful aging.

The role of adaptive processes in successful/healthy aging has also been examined in the literature. For example, Bryant *et al.* (2001), investigated the domains of physical health and life course and defined successful aging as ". . . the level of health and adaptation to the ageing process acceptable to the individual" (p. 928).

Cognitive aging and its relationship to successful aging has stimulated theoretical development in the field focusing on adaptation. Baltes *et al.* (1984) described cognitive aging as a "process of adaptation" that includes the components of selection (growing older may lead to restrictions in functional capacities), optimization (older people have the capacity to improve their level of functioning), and compensation (older people learn to adapt when capacities are reduced or lost). This SOC model (selection, optimization, and compensation) was ". . . based on the premise that successful, individual development (including aging) is a process" (Baltes & Baltes, 1990, p. 1). Successful aging occurs when the person reaches the goals that they select as important. Baltes and Baltes postulated that those people who age successfully were more likely to make use of the psychological processes of selection, optimization, and compensation, and that those who are rich in sensorimotor, cognitive, personality, and social resources are more likely to use these psychological processes.

A Systematic Review of the Literature:
Successful Aging and Related Terms

There is lack of clarity in the empirical and theoretical literature in terms of defining healthy/ successful aging and how the concepts are operationalized. In addition, to design effective interventions to promote aging well we need to identify the predictors of aging well. To examine this literature in a systematic way, two of the authors, Browning and Thomas (2007), conducted an extensive literature review and consultation on successful aging and related concepts such as healthy, positive, productive, and active aging. They reviewed the varying definitions for successful, healthy, active, positive, and productive aging using the leading published studies and commentaries. To conduct the review the Medline, Ageline, CINAHL, PSYCHINFO, and SOCIOFILE databases were searched over the period 1985 to 2007 using the keywords successful, healthy, active, positive, and productive aging. Key books and policy documents in the area were also searched. In total, 225 publications were extracted that examined the searched concepts.

First, the authors identified a set of domains used in the descriptions and definitions of these terms. Table 5.1 lists the domains and how often the domains were used in the definitions. These data are indicative of substantial disagreement within the respective definitions since the domains that are used in the current definitions are not common across many of the definitions studied in this review. It is noteworthy that many of the domains are central to the work of psychologists, namely the cognitive, behavioral, social, and emotional domains.

A workshop was held with policy and program officials to discuss a working definition of the term successful aging, and the definition and related documents were circulated to a number of

Table 5.1   Frequencies of use of domains across definitions

Successful aging and related concepts domain	*Frequency of use in definitions*
Longevity	4
Physical health	22
Activities of daily living independence	14
Independence/autonomy unspecified	12
Psychological wellbeing	12
Mental health	9
Cognitive health	14
Social relationships: work	4
Social relationships: family	8
Social relationships: friends	8
Paid and unpaid work participation	5
Financial and material security	4
Housing, transport, and the built environment	4
Safety	3
Participation/leisure	12
Quality of life	10
Adaptive/life course perspective	8
Age discrimination/positive attitudes	4

international experts in the field for comment. Following this process the following definition was proposed:

> Ageing well is a process whereby people can achieve or maintain the best possible state of physical, cognitive and mental health and wellbeing, meaningful and positive engagement with people, community and institutions, and a personal sense of security, choice, control and autonomy, with active adaptation to ageing processes from the individual, familial and societal perspectives. (Browning & Thomas, 2007, p. 4)

Next we reviewed longitudinal studies of predictors of successful/healthy aging. The majority of studies focused on predicting the negative aspects of aging, such as functional decline, morbidity, and mortality, while others focused on predicting positive aspects of aging such as happiness and high physical and mental functioning. Based on the searched literature we concluded that the modifiable risk factors for poor outcomes are high blood pressure, high cholesterol levels, and being overweight or underweight. The modifiable protective factors for good outcomes are engaging in social and productive activities, moderate alcohol intake, not smoking, and moderate levels of physical activity. In recent findings from our longitudinal study on aging we found that behavioral factors such as physical activity, healthy nutrition, healthy BMI, and adequacy of social support predicted aging well (Kendig *et al.*, unpublished work).

Many of these modifiable risk and protective factors are linked to the probability of developing diseases such as diabetes and cardiovascular disease which in turn have been shown to be associated with poor outcomes in old age. Depp and Jeste (2006) also note that there are a number of potential predictors of successful aging that have received little attention in the research literature. These include genetic markers, allostatic load, access to health services, nutrition, and psychological variables including spirituality and resilience.

A number of conclusions flow from our review. First there was disjunction between what older people understood as healthy/successful aging and the way that researchers conceptualized the terms. There were few studies where older people were asked to describe what the terms actually meant to them. Second, there was virtually no operationalization of the terms and this makes evaluation of healthy/successful aging programs and interventions problematic. Third, the domains included across the definitions of the various terms varied and did not necessarily follow from theoretical frameworks. Fourth, the longitudinal predictive studies of healthy/successful aging focused on narrow outcomes such as self-rated health or functional health and these outcomes did not reflect the breadth of successful/healthy aging concepts. As discussed below, interventions to promote health and wellbeing in older adults have followed this narrow focus on specific domains of healthy/successful aging.

Interventions to promote aging well

In this section we have used the definition of aging well (as described above) to examine behavioral and psychological interventions to promote aging well. Interventions that flow from this definition are shown in Table 5.2.

It is beyond the scope of this chapter to examine the evidence base for all types of behavioral and psychological intervention across the domains outlined in Table 5.2. Therefore we have selected six examples: physical activity to improve health, physical activity and sleep, self-management of chronic disease, psychological therapies and depression, cognitive training, and seniors as mentors. The first five examples examine specific interventions for older people that focus on the

Table 5.2   Interventions to promote aging well

Aging well domain	Examples of psychological/behavioral intervention domains
Physical health	Health behaviors including physical activity, healthy eating, smoking, alcohol abuse and misuse, incontinence management, falls prevention, self-management of chronic illness, pain management
Cognitive health (including dementia)	Cognitive training, late-life learning, behavioral problems
Mental health	Depression, anxiety, substance abuse and misuse, sleep disorders
Meaningful and positive engagement	Communication skills, sensory rehabilitation, social skills, advocacy skills, interpersonal skills, relationship skills, mentoring programs
Security, choice, control and autonomy	Skills training including life management, assertiveness training, self-efficacy enhancement
Active adaptation	Skills training including memory training, communication skills, relationship skills, self-efficacy enhancement

aging well domains of physical, cognitive, and mental health. The last example focuses on the role of older people in the training of health professionals, and in primary and secondary education as methods of improving the aging well domain of positive and meaningful engagement. Cochrane intervention reviews provide a systematic method for evaluating evidence. Where possible we will use these reviews, systematic reviews, or individual randomized controlled trials to examine the evidence for our six examples.

Physical activity interventions to improve health   There is now strong evidence for the benefits of physical activity for older adults. These benefits include lower rates of mortality, heart disease, diabetes, and related conditions, healthier BMI, enhanced bone health, and higher levels of functional health (American College of Sports Medicine *et al.*, 2009; Taylor *et al.*, 2004; Windle *et al.*, 2010). Physical activity can also improve social interactions. Many organizations now produce specific recommendations for physical activity in older people. For example, the Australian Government recently recommended that older people should do some form of physical activity that incorporates strength, balance, and flexibility, every day for at least 30 min (Sims *et al.*, 2006). Although the determinants of physical activity are many, including the availability of safe and targeted programs for older people, self-efficacy for physical activity, knowledge about the benefits of physical activity, social support for physical activity, and broader policy environments to name a few, psychosocial influences and behavior-change approaches are important components of improving physical activity engagement in older people.

Providing physical activity guidelines and information is normally not sufficient for people to change their behaviors and this is particularly salient in older adults who may not have engaged in physical activity sufficient to gain cardiovascular or strength benefits since they were young. Health psychologists are experts in behavior change and are therefore well placed to work with older people in this area.

An excellent example of a behavioral intervention to increase physical activity in older adults is the US Active for Life program (Wilcox *et al.*, 2008). Active for Life tested the effectiveness of two evidenced-based physical activity programs for older adults (aged 50–75 years and over) in real-life community settings that were based on social cognitive theory (SCT) and the transtheoretical model (TTM). Active Choices (AC) was a 6-month telephone-based behavior change intervention designed to increase physical activity in older adults. It was based on SCT, which outlines a number of key intervention components to assist behavior change (Bandura, 1986). SCT advocates improving self-efficacy to overcome barriers to behavior change and training in self-regulatory skills including goal setting and self-monitoring. Active Living Every Day (ALED) was a 20-week group-based behavior change intervention also designed to increase physical activity in older adults, based on the TTM (Prochaska *et al.*, 1992). The TTM proposes that behavior change is gradual and that interventions should be designed to fit the person's readiness to change. Both programs showed increases in moderate to vigorous physical activity (effect size 0.62 for AC and 0.74 for ALED) and decreases in BMI (effect size −0.05 for AC and −0.06 for ALED). Depressive symptoms and perceived stress decreased in the ALED intervention (effect sizes, −0.17 and −0.29).

Physical activity and sleep   Older adults aged 65 years and over have a high prevalence of sleep disorders with US data estimating the rate to be over 50% in noninstitutionalized older adults (Harbison, 2002). Ohayan (2002) found that the prevalence of sleep disorders ranged from 10 to 65% depending on type and that maintaining sleep is the most common reported problem (Morin & Gramling, 1989). Sleep disorders impact significantly on older adults' quality of life, leading to depression and cognitive impairment (Ford & Kamerow, 1989). These difficulties are often associated with illness and medication use and are therefore not causally linked with aging (Ancoli-Israel & Ayalon, 2006; Foley *et al.*, 1995). Pharmacological treatments are the most common, especially for insomnia. However, Harbison noted that nonpharmacological treatments should be considered, as hypnotic drugs are associated with side effects such as sleep apnea, falls, and increased mortality in older people (Rumble & Morgan, 1992). So what is the evidence for nonpharmacological interventions for sleep disturbance in older people? Below we examine the effectiveness of physical activity.

Montgomery and Dennis (2002) conducted a Cochrane review of physical activity for sleep problems in older people. Physical activity is postulated to raise body temperature and therefore activate sleep mechanisms, and may have an antidepressive effect (Youngstedt, 2000; Van Someren, 2000). Only one study met the inclusion criteria. Montgomery and Dennis (2002) concluded that while the evidence for the effectiveness of physical activity to treat sleep problems in older adults is weak, a small trial by King *et al.* (1997) that included brisk walking and moderate weight training provided encouraging evidence. King *et al.* found that sleep duration, sleep onset latency, and sleep quality improved significantly for all participants (mean age was 62 years) in the trial.

Self-management of chronic disease   Over the last decade patient-centered approaches to the management of chronic disease have focused on partnerships between patients, care givers, and health professionals (Battersby *et al.*, 2010a). As risk behaviors such as a sedentary lifestyle, smoking, alcohol abuse, and overeating underlie the etiology and progress of many chronic illnesses that affect older people, such as arthritis, diabetes, and heart disease, interventions that target changing risk behaviors have been incorporated into programs to manage chronic illness (Lorig & Holman, 2003).

The Stanford Chronic Disease Self Management Program (CDSM), developed by Lorig, is based on SCT and uses a group approach to increase behaviors such as physical activity, pain management, appropriate use of medications, and other self-care behaviors related to chronic illness. It is a structured 6-week program led by a qualified trainer. The Stanford CDSM program has been extensively evaluated and licensed to many countries throughout the world. Jonker *et al.* (2009) conducted a review of effectiveness of the Stanford CDSM program in older people. Nine randomized controlled trials met the inclusion criteria but only three-quarters of these studies included adults aged 49–65 years. Based on the outcomes of the nine randomized controlled trials, Jonker *et al.* concluded that the Stanford CDSM programs resulted in improvements in health behaviors (especially physical activity and self-care), health distress, and self-efficacy. The outcomes of the Stanford CDSM program reinforce the importance of the potential for behavior change in older people through theoretically grounded approaches such as SCT.

In Australia, the Flinders Program™ is a generic program for the assessment and planning for chronic illness management. It uses the principles of the chronic care model (Wagner *et al.*, 1996) and includes case management, self-management support, organizational change, and clinician change. It incorporates cognitive behavior therapy (CBT) and motivational interviewing. Unlike the Stanford CDSM program, it focuses on *both* clinician and patient behavior. As explained by Battersby *et al.* (2010a, p. 199):

> The Program provides a generic set of tools and a structured process that enables health workers and patients to collaboratively assess self-management behaviors, identify problems, set goals, and develop individual care plans covering key self-care, medical, psycho-social and carer issues.

A randomized controlled trial of the Flinders Program™ is currently underway (Battersby *et al.*, 2010b). However, promising results have been found in a pre/post study of the program in 176 patients for whom significant improvements in self-management, pain, and fatigue were shown (Harvey *et al.*, 2008). Like the Stanford CDSM, the Flinders Program provides further evidence for the usefulness of psychological approaches with older people with chronic illnesses.

Managing depression   Depression is a significant health problem for older people. While major depression affects about 2% of older people (Beekman *et al.*, 1999), rates of depression in community-dwelling adults ranges from 10 to 15% (Beyondblue, 2011). There are also a number of barriers to older people seeking and receiving treatment for depression, including stigma, agist attitudes, and lack of training for professionals in late-life depression. In addition, there is debate in the literature concerning the challenges in diagnosing depression in older people that centers on how depression is measured in older adults (Bryant, 2010; O'Connor, 2006). While medication is the usual treatment method, guidelines for the treatment of depression in older groups recommend antidepressant medication supported by psychological interventions (Baldwin *et al.*, 2003). Below we examine the effectiveness of CBT and the depression care management model in the management of depression in older people.

Wilson *et al.* (2008) conducted a review of psychological interventions for older people (aged 55 years and over) with depression and found a lack of high-quality research in the area with few randomized controlled trials. Very few trials met the inclusion criteria and from five included trials with a total of 153 patients the authors concluded that there was some good evidence that CBT was effective in treating depression in older people. The authors noted that further research on psychological treatments for depression needs to address special groups within the older population, including those with pain and sensory loss.

A recent review highlighted the challenges in translating the evidence concerning the treatment of depression in older people into practice (Snowden *et al.*, 2008). The authors used an expert panel of 14 public health and geriatric medicine researcher/practitioner academics to review and rate 97 intervention studies. The depression care management model (DCM) was *strongly recommended* and CBT was *recommended*. The DCM is a team approach based on the chronic care model in primary care settings (see also the Flinders Model discussed above; Wagner *et al.*, 1996). As well as screening for depression and implementing psychotherapy or antidepressant treatment based on evidence-based clinical guidelines, DCM uses a nurse or other trained practitioner to work with the patient in the management of their condition. Based on evidence from randomized controlled trials, DCM has been found to be effective in symptom reduction and improving health-related quality of life in older people with depression (Snowden *et al.*, 2008). Despite the evidence for the effectiveness of both DCM and CBT, Snowden *et al.* (2008) identify a number of challenges in the USA in translating these programs into real-world settings including incorporating routine depression screening in primary care, clients' reluctance to be treated for depression due to stigma, and the funding model for nurse practitioners and DCM programs.

In Australia, while programs through Medicare have targeted older people with mental health issues and chronic illnesses, the costs involved in seeking treatment from psychologists is often prohibitive for older people. The advent of Medicare Locals, a national network of primary healthcare organizations established with the aim of integrating primary healthcare, aged care, and hospitals and meeting the needs of local communities, may provide more opportunities for psychologists to work with older people in the management of depression (DoHA, 2010).

Cognitive training for mild cognitive impairment   With increases in the prevalence of dementia as populations age, the role of cognitive plasticity has received increasing attention from researchers and clinicians. There is evidence that experience can improve performance in areas such as verbal ability and job skills such as decision-making and for the most part older people readily adapt to any minor age-related losses in cognitive functioning such as speed of processing (Baltes & Baltes, 1990; Baltes & Singer, 2001). Mild cognitive impairment is a term used to describe those individuals who do not meet dementia diagnosis criteria but who are showing memory problems beyond normal age-related changes (American Psychiatric Association, 1987). It is in this group that early intervention may slow or prevent the onset of dementia (Hoyer & Verhaegen, 2006).

Martin *et al.* (2011) conducted a review and meta-analysis of cognitive training interventions in healthy and mild cognitively impaired older adults. Cognitive training is defined as "... an intervention providing structured practice on tasks relevant to aspects of cognitive functioning, such as memory, attention, language or executive function" (Martin *et al.*, 2011, p. 80). Based on the pooled results from 24 randomized controlled trials ($n = 2229$ participants) memory training improved immediate and delayed recall in healthy older adults and in those with mild cognitive impairment. However, these effects did not exceed that of alternate interventions such as group discussions, physical training, or drug treatment. Few of the included studies examined speed of processing or executive functioning. Martin *et al.* concluded that there was little evidence for the effectiveness of cognitive training. They recommended standardization of methods to investigate the effects of cognitive training, testing of variations in the types and intensities of cognitive training interventions, and more consistency in the definition of mild cognitive impairment.

Seniors as mentors   A core component of aging well is promoting the contributions that older people make to society rather than focusing on the burden of aging populations. In countries such as China where the wisdom of elders is culturally bound, there are many examples of older people contributing to the education of the young through government-sponsored programs. A number of senior mentor programs have also been developed in US medical schools (Wieland & Eleazer, 2006). For example, in the Seniors Mentor Program at Duke University, second-year medical students meet senior volunteers. The aim of the program is to increase the students' knowledge and skills in geriatric assessment as well as their understanding of the heterogeneity among the older adult population. The University of Missouri-Columbia School of Medicine Senior Mentor Program involved senior volunteers as teachers for first- and second-year students (Hoffman *et al.*, 2006). Qualitative evaluations showed that the students' attitudes to aging and older people improved and that the older volunteers valued their ability to help students understand the heterogeneity of the aging process. One quote from the senior volunteers is indicative: "... [the students] realize that just because you are old doesn't mean you are not healthy" (Hoffman *et al.*, 2006, p. 43).

We have used this approach in our Golden Gurus language program, where older native Chinese, German, and Spanish first-language speakers are paired with high school second-language learners (Monash Intergenerational Languages and Schools Project, http://arts.monash.edu.au/intergenerational/). Our preliminary results have shown that young people benefit in terms of their language skills and improved attitudes to older people and older people benefit in terms of their self-esteem, feelings of positive engagement with younger people, and psychological health.

One mentoring program that has provided strong evidence for its health benefits for older people is the Experience Corps® program (Carlson *et al.*, 2008). This program employs older volunteers from 15 h per week in a reading and library support program in primary schools in Baltimore, MD, USA. The program promotes cognitive, physical, and social activity. A randomized controlled trial of 149 older adults participating in Experience Corps showed improvements in memory and executive functioning at 4–8 months' follow-up. In conclusion, there is some evidence that senior mentor programs provide health benefits for older adults and that they are useful in educating health professionals about aging and older people. We recommend that the training of psychologists involves these approaches.

Conclusion

Population aging presents many challenges and opportunities for society. Psychologists are experts in a number of areas that impact on the health and wellbeing of older people, yet their roles in interventions and programs for older people has been limited. In order to maximize the input of psychology and psychologists to improving the lives of older people, we need to have well-operationalized concepts and measures of healthy/successful aging and evidenced-based interventions that address the range of domains that encapsulate aging well. In addition, the training and continuing education of psychologists needs to increase its focus on aging and older people.

We have outlined a number of interventions and approaches to address a selection of our domains of aging well. However, there is overlap in the intervention types across the aging well domains. For example, a physical activity intervention has the potential to improve physical and mental health and increase social engagement. A program to improve self-management of chronic illness has the potential to improve the sense of personal control and autonomy as well as improve physical health. As demonstrated above, there are evidence-based interventions for *each* aging well domain that we have examined. Surprisingly, however, when rigorous and systematic methods have been used to evaluate these interventions, the evidence is modest. In addition, there has been little development of broader cross-domain interventions for aging well. Interventions or programs that address a number of aging well domains could prove to be an effective and efficient way to promote health and wellbeing in older people. The self-management models used in chronic illness management have the potential to be applied more generally in older groups and we advocate a "self-management of aging" approach. While self-management approaches have focused more on the baby boomers and young-old, further research is needed on the effectiveness of the approach in the old-old.

References

ABS. (2010). *The Health and Welfare of Australia's Aboriginal and Torres Strait Islander peoples. Demographic, social and economic characteristics: Life expectancy.* www.abs.gov.au/AUSSTATS/abs@.nsf/lookup/4704.0Chapter218Oct+2010.

American College of Sports Medicine, Chodzko-Zajko, W. J., Proctor, D. N., Fiatarone Singh, M. A., Minson, C. T., Nigg, C. R. *et al.* (2009). American College of Sports Medicine position stand. Exercise and physical activity for older adults. *Medicine and Science in Sports and Exercise, 41,* 1510–1530.

American Psychiatric Association. (1987). *Diagnostic and Statistical Manual of Mental Disorders* (3rd edn.). Washington DC: American Psychiatric Association.

American Psychological Association Office on Aging. (2005). Psychology and aging: Addressing mental health needs of older adults. www.apa.org/pi/aging/resources/guides/aging.pdf.

Ancoli-Israel, S., & Ayalon, L. (2006). Diagnosis and treatment of sleep disorders in older adults. *American Journal of Geriatric Psychiatry, 14,* 95–103.

Andrews, K. D. (2002). *National Strategy for an Ageing Australia: An Older Australia, Challenges and Opportunities for All.* Canberra: Australian Government Department of Health and Ageing. http://ichal06.longevity-international.com/assets/National%20Strategy%20for%20an%20Ageing%20Australia.pdf.

Australian Government. (2007). Baby Boomers. http://australia.gov.au/about-australia/australian-story/baby-boomers.

Australian Psychological Society. (2011a). *Brief on the Role of Psychologists in Aged Care Services.* www.psychology.org.au/Assets/Files/AgedCareBrief.pdf.

Australian Psychological Society (2011b). *Psychology and Ageing.* www.groups.psychology.org.au/paig/.

Baldwin, R. C., Anderson, D., Black, S., Evans, S., Jones, R., Wilson, K., & Iliffe, S. (2003). Guideline for the management of late-life depression in primary care. *International Journal of Geriatric Psychiatry, 18,* 829–838.

Baltes, P. B. (1997). On the incomplete architecture of human ontogeny: Selection, optimization, and compensation as foundation of developmental theory. *American Psychologist, 52,* 366–380.

Baltes, P. B., & Baltes, M. M. (1990). Psychological perspectives on successful aging: The model of selective optimization with compensation. In P. B. Baltes & M. M. Baltes (Eds.), *Successful Aging: Perspectives from the Behavioral Sciences* (pp. 1–34). New York: Cambridge University Press.

Baltes, P. B., & Mayer, K. U. (1999). *The Berlin Aging Study: Aging from 70 to 100.* New York: Cambridge University Press.

Baltes, P., & Singer, T. (2001). Plasticity and the aging mind. *European Review, 9,* 59–76.

Baltes, P., & Smith, J. (2003). New frontiers in the future of aging: From successful aging of the young old to the dilemma of the fourth age. *Gerontology, 49,* 123–135.

Baltes, P. B., Dittmann-Kohli, F., & Dixon, R. A. (1984). New perspectives on the development of intelligence in adulthood: toward a dual-process conception and a model of selective optimization with compensation. In P. B. Baltes & O. G. Brim (Eds.), *Life-span Development and Behavior,* vol. 6 (pp. 33–76). New York: Academic Press.

Bandura, A. (1986). *Social Foundations of Thought and Action: A Social Cognitive Theory.* Englewood Cliffs, NJ: Prentice-Hall.

Battersby, M., Von Korff, M., Schaefer, J., Davis, C., Ludman, E., Greene, S. M. *et al.* (2010a). Twelve evidence-based principles for implementing self-management support in primary care. *Joint Commission Journal on Quality and Patient Safety, 36,* 561–570.

Battersby, M. W., Harris, M., Reed, R. L., Harvey, P. W., Woodman, R. J., & Frith, P. (2010b). A randomised trial of the Flinders program to improve patient self-management competencies in a range of chronic conditions: Study rationale and protocol. *Australasian Medical Journal, 1,* 198–204.

Beekman, A. T., Copeland, J. R., & Prince, M. J. (1999). Review of community prevalence of depression in later life. *British Journal of Psychiatry, 174,* 307–311.

Beyondblue. (2011). *Depression in Older People.* www.beyondblue.org.au/index.aspx?link_id=101.

Bird, M., Llewellyn-Jones, R., Korten, A., & Smithers, H. (2007). A controlled trial of a predominantly psychosocial approach to BPSD: Treating causality. *International Psychogeriatrics, 19,* 874–891.

Bird, M., Llewellyn-Jones, R., & Korten, A. (2009). An evaluation of the effectiveness of a case-specific approach to challenging behaviour associated with dementia. *Aging and Mental Health, 13,* 73–83.

Browning, C., & Heine, C. (2012). Ageing and health: Biological, social and environmental perspectives. In P. Liamputtong, R. Fanny, & G. Verrinder (Eds.), *Health, Illness and Well-Being: Perspectives and Social Determinants* (pp. 92–106). Oxford: Oxford University Press.

Browning, C., & Thomas, S. (2007). *Definition and Predictors of Successful Ageing and Related Concepts: Final Report.* Melbourne: Victorian Department of Human Services.

Bryant, C. (2010). Anxiety and depression in old age: Challenges in recognition and diagnosis. *International Psychogeriatrics, 22,* 511–513.

Bryant, L. L., Corbett, K. K., & Kutner, J. S. (2001). In their own words: A model of healthy aging. *Social Science & Medicine, 53,* 927–941.

Carlson, M. C., Rebok, G. W., Seeman, T., Glass, T. A., McGill, S., Tielsch, J. *et al.* (2008). Exploring the effects of an "everyday" activity program on executive function and memory in older adults: Experience Corps. *Gerontologist, 48,* 793–801.

Creed, F., Morgan, R., Fiddler, M., Marshall, S., Guthrie, E., & House, A. (2002). Depression and anxiety impair health-related quality of life outcomes and are associated with increased costs in general medical inpatients. *Psychosomatics, 43,* 302–309.

de Jonge, P., Latour, C., & Huyse, F. J. (2003) Implementing psychiatric interventions on a medical ward: Effects on patients' quality of life and length of hospital stay. *Psychosomatic Medicine, 65,* 997–1002.

Depp, C. A., & Jeste, D. V. (2006). The definition and predictors of successful aging: A comprehensive literature review. *American Journal of Geriatric Psychiatry, 14,* 6–20.

DoHA. (2010). *Building a 21st Century Primary Health Care System. Australia's First National Primary Health Care Strategy.* Canberra: Department of Health and Ageing.

DoHA. (2011). *Resident Appraisal and Reviews 2006–2010.* www.health.gov.au/internet/main/publishing .nsf/Content/ageing-resident-appraisal.htm.

Evert, J., Lawler, E., Bogan, H., & Perls, T. (2003). Morbidity profiles of centenarians: Survivors, delayers, and escapers. *Journals of Gerontology A Biological Sciences and Medical Sciences, 58,* 232–237.

Foley, D. J., Monjan, A. A., Brown, S. L., Simonsick, E. M., Wallace, R. B., & Blazer, D. G. (1995). Sleep complaints among elderly persons: An epidemiologic study of three communities. *Sleep, 18,* 425–432.

Ford, D. E., & Kamerow, D. B. (1989). Epidemiologic study of sleep disturbances and psychiatric disorders. *Journal of the American Medical Association, 262,* 1479–1484.

Fries, J. F. (1980). Aging, natural death, and the compression of morbidity. *New England Journal of Medicine, 303,* 130–135.

Fries, J. F. (2002). Successful ageing: An emerging paradigm of gerontology. *Clinics in Geriatric Medicine, 18,* 371–382.

Gray, M., Qu, L., & Weston, R. (2008). *Fertility and Family Policy in Australia.* Australian Institute of Family Studies, research paper no. 41. www.aifs.gov.au/institute/pubs/rp41/rp41.html#table1.

Harbison, J. (2002). Sleep disorders in older people. *Age and Ageing, 31-S2,* 6–9.

Harvey, P. W., Petkov, J. N., Misan, G., Fuller, J., Battersby, M. W., Cayetano, T. N., Holmes, P. (2008). Self-management support and training for patients with chronic and complex conditions improves health-related behaviour and health outcomes. *Australian Health Review, 32,* 330–338.

Havighurst, R. J. (1968). A social psychological perspective on aging. *Gerontologist, 8,* 67–71.

Hoffman, K. G., Gray, P., Hosokawa, M. C., & Zweig, S. C. (2006). Evaluating the effectiveness of a senior mentor program: The University of Missouri-Columbia. *Gerontology & Geriatrics Education, 27,* 37–47.

Holstein, M. B., & Minkler, M. (2003). Self, society and the "new gerontology". *The Gerontologist, 43,* 787–796.

Hoyer, W. J., & Verhaeghen, P. (2006). Memory aging. In J. E. Birren & K. W. Schaie (Eds.), *Handbook of the Psychology of Aging* (6th edn, pp. 209–232). Amsterdam: Academic Press.

Jonker, A. A., Comijs, H. C., Knipscheer, K. C., & Deeg, D. J. (2009). Promotion of self-management in vulnerable older people: A narrative literature review of outcomes of the Chronic Disease Self-Management Program (CDSMP). *European Journal of Ageing, 6,* 303–314.

King, A. C., Oman, R. F., Brassington, G. S., Bliwise, D. L., & Haskell, W. L. (1997). Moderate-intensity exercise and self-rated quality of sleep in older adults. *Journal of the American Medical Association, 277,* 32–37.

Knight, T., & Ricciardelli, L. (2003). Successful ageing: Perceptions of adults aged between 70 and 101 years. *International Journal of Aging and Human Development, 56,* 223–245.

Koder, D. A., & Ferguson, S. J. (1998). The status of geropsychology in Australia: Exploring why Australian psychologists are not working with elderly clients. *Australian Psychologist, 33,* 96–100.

Koder, D., & Helmes, E. (2008). The current status of clinical geropsychology in Australia: A survey of practising psychologists. *Australian Psychologist, 43*, 22–26.

Lorig, K. R., & Holman, H. (2003). Self-management education: History, definition, outcomes, and mechanisms. *Annals of Behavioral Medicine, 26*, 1–7.

Lupien, S. J., & Wan, N. (2004). Successful ageing: From cell to self. *Philosophical Transactions of the Royal Society B: Biological Sciences, 359*, 1413–1426.

Lutz, W., Sanderson,W., & Scherbov, S. (2008). The coming acceleration of global population ageing. *Nature, 451*, 716–719.

Martin, M. A., Algassen, C. L., Cameron, M. A., & Zehnder, F. (2011). Cognition-based interventions for healthy older people with mild cognitive impairment. *Cochrane Library, 1*, 1–48.

Matarazzo, J. D. (1980). Behavioral health and behavioral medicine: Frontiers for a new health psychology, *American Psychologist, 35*, 807–817.

McCormack, J. (2000). Hitting a century: Centenarians in Australia. *Australasian Journal on Ageing, 19*(2), 75–80.

Montgomery, P., & Dennis, J. A. (2002). Physical exercise for sleep problems in adults aged 60+. *Cochrane Database of Systematic Reviews, 4*, CD003404.

Morin, C. M., & Gramling, S. E. (1989). Sleep patterns and aging: Comparison of older adults with and without insomnia complaints. *Psychology and Aging, 4*, 290–294.

O'Connor, D. (2006). Do older Australians truly have low rates of anxiety and depression? A critique of the 1997 National Survey of Mental Health and Wellbeing. *Australian and New Zealand Journal of Psychiatry, 40*, 623–631.

Ohayon, M. M. (2002). Epidemiology of insomnia: What we know and what we still need to learn. *Sleep Medicine Reviews, 6*, 97–111.

Prochaska, J. O., DiClemente, C. C., & Norcross, J. C. (1992). In search of how people change: Applications to addictive behaviors. *American Psychologist, 47*, 1102–1114.

Qualls, S. H., Segal, D. L., Norman, S., Niederehe, G., & Gallagher-Thompson, D. (2002). Psychologists in practice with older adults: Current patterns, sources of training, and need for continuing education. *Professional Psychology: Research and Practice, 33*, 5435–5442.

Richmond, R. (2008). The changing face of the Australian population: Growth in centenarians. *Medical Journal of Australia, 188*, 720–723.

Rowe, J. W., & Kahn, R. L. (1998). *Successful aging.* New York: Pantheon/Random House.

Rumble, R., & Morgan, K. (1992). Hypnotics, sleep, and mortality in elderly people. *Journal of the American Geriatrics Society, 40*, 787–791.

Ryff, C. D. (1989). Happiness is everything, or is it? Explorations on the meaning of psychological well-being. *Journal of Personal and Social Psychology, 57*, 1069–1081.

Sims J., Hill, K., Hunt, S., Haralambous, B., Brown, A., Engel, L. et al. (2006). *National Physical Activity Recommendations for Older Australians: Discussion Document.* Canberra: Department of Health and Ageing.

Snowden, M., Steinman, L., & Frederick, J. (2008). Treating depression in older adults: Challenges to implementing the recommendations of an expert panel. *Preventing Chronic Diseases: Public Health Research, Practice and Policy, 5*, 1–7. www.cdc.gov/pcd/issues/2008/jan/07_0154.htm.

Speer, D. C., & Schneider, M. G. (2003). Mental health needs of older adults and primary care: Opportunities for interdisciplinary geriatric team practice. *Clinical Psychology: Science and Practice, 10*, 109–111.

Suzman, R., Willis, D. P., & Manton, K. G. (1992). *The Oldest Old.* New York: Oxford University Press.

Taylor, A. H., Cable, N. T., Faulkner, G., Hillsdon, M., Narici, M., & Van Der Bij, A. K. (2004). Physical activity and older adults: A review of health benefits and the effectiveness of interventions. *Journal of Sports Sciences, 22*, 703–725.

Taylor, S. E. (2011). *Health Psychology* (8th edn.). New York: McGraw Hill.

Van Someren, E. J. (2000). More than a marker: Interaction between the circadian regulation temperature and sleep, age-related changes, and treatment possibilities. *Chronobiology International, 17*, 313–354.

Wagner, E. H., Austin, B. T., & Von Korff, M. (1996). Organizing care for patients with chronic illness. *Milbank Quarterly, 74*, 511–544.

Wieland, D., & Eleazer, G. P. (2006). Guest editorial. *Gerontology & Geriatrics Education, 27*, 1–2.

Wilcox, S., Dowda, M., Leviton, L. C., Bartlett-Prescott, J., Bazzarre, T., Campbell-Voytal, K., & Wegley, S. (2008). Active for life: Final results from the translation of two physical activity programs. *American Journal of Preventive Medicine, 35*, 340–351.

Wilson, T. (2005). New United Nations world population projections. *People and Place, 13*, 14–22.

Wilson, K. C., Mottram, P. G., & Vassilas, C. A. (2008). Psychotherapeutic treatments for older depressed people. *Cochrane Database of Systematic Reviews, 1*, CD004853.

Windle, G., Hughes, D., Linck, P., Russell, I., & Woods, B. (2010). Is exercise effective in promoting mental well-being in older age? A systematic review. *Aging and Mental Health, 14*, 652–669.

World Health Organization. (2002). *Active Ageing: A Policy Framework*. Geneva: World Health Organization.

Youngstedt, S. D. (2000). The exercise-sleep mystery. *International Journal of Sport Psychology, 30*, 241–255.

6

Gender, Gender-Role Stereotypes, and Health

Robert J. Williams

Background

Persistent differences between males and females continue to be reported across a broad range of issues related to health and wellbeing (Brannon, 2008; Caltabiano *et al.*, 2008; Garfield *et al.*, 2008; Marks *et al.*, 2004). These findings indicate that the gender-related health behaviors would benefit from being studied using the biopsychosocial model of health psychology. Improvement in our understanding of the involvement of the individual's sense of body/mind (intrapersonal) and self in interaction with others (interpersonal) dynamics of gender-related differences will provide more insight into the positive and negative consequences to health and wellbeing. This improvement would be particularly useful in the area of lifestyle behavioral choices as an aid to the further development of preventative education. It would also contribute to the therapeutic science of self-regulation and strategies for supporting the maintenance of behavioral change. For example, men consistently display more drinking problems than women while this gender difference is reversed in terms of incidence of eating disorders and associated problems. Research on these two major areas of health psychology will be used to illustrate the broader principles of the gender-related issues to be covered in this chapter. These particular health-related domains are chosen because of their high rate of incidence and the weight of research evidence that is already available for review. It may well remain the case, as reported by Courtenay (2000), that many of the current and mainstream health perspectives in psychology, sociology, the medical sciences, and epidemiology still do not assign a sufficiently central role to either gender or to cultural variables. However, this is an oversight that simply emphasizes the importance of the contribution that the biopsychosocial model is already making to health psychology.

The focus in this chapter will not be on biological gender differences in health *per se* but on the influence of the stereotyping of gender roles which indicate personal and cultural interpretations of the meaning of biological differences. More specifically, the focus will be on a comparison between gender roles when they are functioning as stereotypes in relation to strategies employed in attempted self-regulation. The evidence of a crucial relationship between stereotyping of gender

Applied Topics in Health Psychology, First Edition. Edited by M. L. Caltabiano and L. Ricciardelli.
© 2013 John Wiley & Sons, Ltd. Published 2013 by John Wiley & Sons, Ltd.

roles and problems with self-control is to be found most readily in the study of potentially modifiable behaviors related to lifestyle practices that are consistently involved in "doing gender" and coping with the challenge to self-concept (Capraro, 2000; Peralta, 2008; Williams *et al.*, unpublished work). For as Courtenay (2000, p. 1385) has also concluded, "health-related beliefs and behaviors, like any other social practices that men and women engage in, are a means for demonstrating femininities and masculinities."

Masculinities and femininities have been conceptualized as existing along a range of dimensions, and measures and debates continue concerning the reevaluation and possible reconstruction of psychological constructs employed (for a review see Ricciardelli & Williams, 2010). There is a particular focus currently being placed on the way that the constructs of stereotypical masculinities tend to support essentialist thinking and a retreat to biological determinism (Addis *et al.*, 2010; Brooks, 2010; O'Neil, 2010). The reasons for reappraisal of this emphasis will become clear during the discussion below.

The point to be stressed at the outset is that despite various methodological differences there is also a strong agreement concerning the intention of working toward a common goal. This agreement takes the form of a shared belief that society's health and wellbeing will be enhanced through the increasing development of the practice of democracy and social equality in inter-personal and sociocultural gendered relationships. Also, the key to the successful development of this aim is mainly reliant upon the evolution of a more balanced, mature, and androgynous sense of intrapersonal gendered being. This development will not only lend itself to a greater fulfilment of individual potential among males and females alike but will also feed back into sociocultural change.

The goal of this chapter is to make a contribution towards fulfilment of the above aims. It is hoped that the discussion will aid in increasing mindfulness of both interpersonal and intrapersonal involvement in the construction and maintenance of problematic gender stereotypes through an increased understanding of the biopsychosocial dynamics involved. The overall orientation will be an investigation of the gender-role dynamics that suggest a ready application to the advance of both preventative educational and counselling strategies. Rose (1996) reminds us that:

> Psychological theories are . . . significant not simply because they have provided an abstract 'science of behavior' but rather because they have represented the self and social interaction in such a way that their properties cannot only be grasped in thought but correlatively transformed into practice. (p. 120)

Gender-Role Prescriptions and Stereotypes

Gender-role prescriptions reflect cultural and personal beliefs formed around configurations of social practices. They provide a necessary, "common-sense" interpersonal framework of expecta-tions used to predict the kind of conduct appropriate to men and women in various psycho-social and interpersonal contexts. The expectations and attributions that gender roles encapsulate are acquired both implicitly and explicitly as individuals learn about the world and their roles within it (Brannon, 2008; Brannon & Feist, 2007; Fiske, 2010; Lillard & Skibbe, 2005). Research stem-ming from Bem's (1981) seminal work has led to clear evidence that the cues related to the social roles attributed to gender memberships and self-identification are among the most highly salient in human interaction. Gender-related schema become internalized during the development of personality/identity and they become assimilated at an early age as the fundamental basis for so-cial comparisons. Once these gender-cognitive schema are established they can play a controlling role in the perception of the appropriateness of subsequent behavior and judgments. Gender-role schema, like all cognitive schemas, can therefore subsequently channel the way that information is processed in terms of the requirements of self-presentation as self-regulation within the social milieu. They also govern the choice of strategies to be used in attempts to influence the behavior of others within that milieu. Learning theory and self-regulation models have provided a solid foundation for the empirical study of these factors (Baumeister & Vohs, 2004; Carver *et al.*, 2000).

Limitations of Stereotypes

Our understanding of the stereotyping of gender roles involves description of the "typical" behaviors and personality type traits that define masculinity and femininity. These descriptions also tend to limit the range of choices that should be available to individuals by emphasizing categorical differences between the genders in terms of the behaviors that are most appropriate to men and women. Stereotypes are exclusive by definition and are likely to promote cognitive rigidity based on biological essentialism. This tendency is particularly problematic in two ways. As well as a conscious influence via social learning they also have an unconscious influence (Chratrand *et al.*, 2005; Ito *et al.*, 2007). In turn this unconscious influence is likely to produce the reactive phenomenon of retreat to stereotypes when there is a perceived threat to individual competence and efficacy (Shapiro & Neuberg, 2007; Smiler & Gelman, 2008; Vick *et al.*, 2008). The net result is that gender-role stereotyping results in a narrowing of the potential repertoire of individual men and/or women in a way that works against the goal of increasing individual adaptability. It also confounds the generally accepted desire to provide a more democratic context for male and female interrelationships.

There is an increasing recognition of the importance of a number of subpopulations within the overall population, for example based on gay and lesbian lifestyles. But gender-role stereotypes reinforce a broad-brush approach that maintains a fundamentalist/essentialist view of masculinity and femininity (Connell & Messerschmidt, 2005; Frosh *et al.*, 2002; Peralta, 2008). In terms of gender-role stereotypes as action schema, Helgeson (1994) defined the kinds of behavior stereotypically attributed to men and women in broader terms. She compared "agency" – efficacy related to an individualistic, outwardly directed focus of motivation commonly attributed to masculinity – with "communion" – a more inward emphasis on interrelationships involving more emotionally aware concerns which are commonly related to femininity. Helgeson also introduced the term "unmitigated" as a description of an unbalanced emphasis that privileges one of these major gender-role dimensions of being at the expense of the other.

Individuals must learn to balance their own attributes of agency and communion as they match their expectations and their behavior to that of others within the changing contexts of personal and social life. Gender roles are ubiquitous in the sense of being a necessary function of social learning but adherence to stereotyping can impose unnecessary restriction on self-esteem and self-image as related to health and wellbeing. Evidence to be outlined below also indicates that a strong self-identification with stereotypical traits also inhibits the learning of more skilful strategies of self-management in pursuit of beneficial change when this is required. Some of these issues will be discussed in the section of this chapter that focuses directly on applications (see below). However, the unmitigated stereotyping of the attributes used to describe masculinity and femininity confuses the interrelationship between the attributes that describe agency and communion by over-estimating their opposition. For example Connell and Messerschmidt (2005) remind us that hegemonic masculinity was initially conceptualized as a gender-role relationship which included stereotypical/essentialist femininity. Femininity was included as a supporting function rather than an oppositional one. The evidence to be covered in this chapter, however, shows that the minimization if not the total repression of femininity has become the *sin qua non* of the hegemonic style of interpersonal interaction. The effect of this unmitigated bias in stereotyping has profound consequences for health-related behaviors in general and upon appetitive-related health issues in particular. It does so because as a gender-role action schema it narrows the potential intra- and interpersonal range of responses that would/should otherwise be available to the individual. The examples of problem drinking and disordered eating that follow will show that adhering to unmitigated stereotypes has problematic repercussions for the strategies self-control and self-expression. The study of adherence to stereotypical gender roles can therefore provide one method for investigating the underlying sociocultural context of health risk behaviors.

The Interaction between Individuals, and the Context of the Gendered Milieu

A large body of the research has examined the role of individual factors in the development and maintenance of health risk behaviors (Brannon & Feist, 2007; Marks *et al.*, 2004; Ogden, 2007; Caltabiano *et al.*, 2008). But individual factors alone cannot fully explain the development and maintenance of health risk behaviors. Health risk behaviors develop and are maintained within a gendered milieu and there is a renewed call for recognition and reconsideration of the powerful role of environmental contexts that support the maintenance of the stereotyping of gender roles (Addis *et al.*, 2010; Blazina & Shen-Miller, 2010). The contextual differences in which stereotyping occurs, as in comparatively private circumstances compared with social environments, suggests that mitigation of stereotyping is indeed possible.

The business of "doing gender" always involves individual–environmental interactions that exists along intrapersonal as well as interpersonal dimensions. The argument being put in this chapter is that the most powerful health-related context is formed by the framework of gender roles *per se*. Gender has been conceptualized as a multidimensional construct and the way that individuals react to and interact with gender roles has already been considered in a number of ways; e.g., adherence to traditional gender-role norms, gender-role conflict, and gender-role stress, etc. (see Ricciardelli & Williams, 2010). The increasing interest in the power of context is to be welcomed because it illustrates the way in which some contexts support more gender-role stereotyping than others. But since the maintenance of gender-role stereotypes also depends upon the choices of individuals negotiating their individual and collective identity within the gendered milieu, the emphasis on self-identification with stereotypes adopted in this chapter will be maintained.

One trait-like measure that has proven useful in offering information about the gendered behavior of individuals within the gender-role context is that of the self-identified extent of adherence to gender-role stereotypes (see Ricciardelli & Williams, 2010; Williams & Ricciardelli, 1999, 2003). All men and all women are not equally gender-schematic and variation in the extent of adherence to stereotypes will emphasize the need to accommodate individual differences in the theory of gender that guides practice. Trait-like measures can be used to place individuals within social dynamics when they are taken to demonstrate the individual's perceptions about the configurations of social practices that are organized in the structure of gender relations. When trait scores are used in this way, rather than demonstrating some permanently embodied personality structure, they can offer some insight into the individual's use of social comparisons. Social comparisons are likely to prefigure the choice of negotiating strategies within the social milieu (Bowker *et al.*, 2003; Connell & Messerschmidt, 2005; Peralta, 2008; Wetherell & Edley, 1999).

The way that men and women describe themselves in terms of adhering to or rejecting the attributed stereotypes of masculinity and femininity can aid in the prediction of their likely strategies for self-presentation as a means of intra- and interpersonal control in social interactions. Few men and women actually live out gender-role stereotypes in an absolute fashion but will adopt stereotypical attitudes and expectancies depending on the circumstances. Some identification markers that offer face validity are required as a point of entry into a discussion of the way that stereotypes are being employed. They can increase mindfulness concerning the individual/context dynamic and its possible modification. Self-descriptions of adherence to stereotypes can indicate who is adopting the style of unmitigated stereotyping that is most likely to give rise to anxieties about identity related to health and wellbeing (Connell & Messerschmidt, 2005; Ricciardelli & Williams, 2010; Wetherell & Edley, 1999).

Stereotypical Gender Traits as Strategies of Control

The consideration of adherence to gender-role stereotypes as a window on strategies of control over self and others has been described above. The rationale for these studies is based on the conceptual similarities between the descriptions of positive and negative gender-role traits attributed to stereotypical masculinity and femininity and the four styles of self-control originally described by Shapiro (1991) using the alternative terms assertion and yielding. In brief, personality type traits attributed to positive masculinity can be equated with an assertive style of control described as acting to change a condition (e.g., assertive, confident, firm). Negative masculinity on the other hand, while also associated with an assertive style of control, is described as attempts to over-control (e.g., aggressive, rude, bossy). Positive femininity is linked to yielding socially while remaining positive about one's own self-control (e.g., responsible, patient, accepting). Negative femininity is associated with a style of yielding of control to others as a result of considering oneself to have too little personal control (e.g., socially dependent, needing approval, timid). Overall the inclusion of the negative as well as the positive dimensions of gender-role stereotypes and the discrimination of higher scores from lower ones can provide a useful framework for further research. The negative attributes of masculinity and femininity can be said to exhibit the more extreme forms of gender roles.

In the following two sections of the chapter these stereotypical attributions will be examined in research on the problems of use of alcohol (a health hazard usually considered to relate mainly to certain dimensions of masculinity) and also disordered eating (a health hazard usually considered to relate mainly to certain dimensions of femininity). The study of gender-role stereotyping related to problem drinking and disordered eating serves to demonstrate the limitations inherent in the hegemonic division between the attributes of masculinity/agency and femininity/communion.

Hegemonic Masculinity and Drinking as a Strategy for "Doing Gender"

The gender gap between men's and women's drinking within the general context of the alcohol milieu can be said to be decreasing in some circumstances (Lemke *et al.*, 2008; Ricciardelli *et al.*, 2001; Williams & Ricciardelli, 1999; Young *et al.*, 2005). However, alcohol use/abuse retains its symbolic as well as its functional status as a predominantly masculine ethos when it comes to "doing gender" which involves "rites of passage" (Capraro, 2000; Peralta, 2007; Williams & Ricciardelli, 1999). Some recent diversification in male drinking has suggested that alternative styles of masculinity need to be better identified (Mullen *et al.*, 2007). But the evidence that the drinking environment, especially among young adults and adolescents, remains a stereotypically gendered environment is strong (Kulis *et al.*, 2008; Peralta, 2007; Williams & Ricciardelli, 2003). Many men are still endorsing the hegemonic style of drinking in terms of stereotypically masculine attributes (de Visser & Smith, 2007; Peralta, 2008) and there is evidence that some women are choosing to adopt a similar approach to alcohol use (Lemke *et al.*, 2008; Ricciardelli *et al.*, 2001; Young *et al.*, 2005).

The hegemonic style of drinking is characterized by both physical and social risk-taking. It is described as an intention to exercise dominance over alternative varieties of masculinity, which might otherwise fail to meet the "ideal" of acting in emotionally toughened ways (Peralta, 2007, 2008). Drinking in a hegemonic fashion has been described as a way of coping with the "emotional hazards" of doing gender within the social milieu (Capraro, 2000; McCreary *et al.*, 1998; Peralta, 2007). Alternative attitudes and behaviors attempting to introduce greater flexibility into one's interactions are judged to be fundamentally nonmasculine (e.g., McQueen & Henwood, 2002). Adherents to this stereotype are therefore required to also exert behavioral dominance over any possible "emotional" interference caused by stereotypically feminine attributes because they might mitigate against the display of increasingly risk-related consumption.

The Repression of Traits Attributed to Stereotypical Femininity

Surveys of drinking among the general population have consistently shown that a higher identification with the attributes of femininity is related to lower levels of drinking (Huselid & Cooper, 1994; Kulis *et al.*, 2008; Nolen-Hoeksema, 2004; Ricciardelli *et al.*, 2001). This of course does not mean that women never drink in the hegemonic fashion. Some women will be as inclined as men to participate in the milieu in a way that promotes the use of alcohol to cope with the emotional and social hazards of doing gender. In fact, the evidence from women drinkers who do drink in this way provides evidence for the argument against the practice of hegemonic drinking by emphasizing the paradoxes and response costs associated with it (Lemke *et al.*, 2008; Young *et al.*, 2005). In terms of social consequences, men who drink at high levels are more likely to be excused for their alcohol-affected behavior when they appeal to the hegemonic stereotype whereas drinking women cannot claim a similar recourse (Williams & Ricciardelli, 1999; Ricciardelli *et al.*, 2001; Young *et al.*, 2005). Thus the hegemonic style of drinking by men and/or women is more likely to maintain gender-role inequality rather than to ameliorate it within the public domain despite the public and personal response costs involved.

The Femininity Hypothesis in Disordered Eating

Disordered eating "is defined as problem eating attitudes and behaviors that occur on a continuum ranging from concerns about body weight and shape, extreme weight control methods which include fasting, and excessive exercise, and binge eating to eating disorders such as anorexia and bulimia nervosa" (Ricciardelli & McCabe, 2004, p. 179). Disordered eating is highly gendered in nature as significantly fewer men develop eating disorders. It is also more difficult to diagnose eating disorders as men are less likely to use extreme weight-loss methods and many of the binge eating patterns that are seen as abnormal or inappropriate in women are socially sanctioned for men for whom terms like "big" can be taken to be an attribute rather than a disadvantage (Ricciardelli & McCabe, 2004).

Nonetheless, a large number of studies have investigated and confirmed the roles of femininity and masculinity in disordered eating (for reviews see Johnson et al., 1996; Lancelot & Kaslow, 1994; Murnen & Smolak, 1997), and several of these have included community and student samples of men. The majority of studies have shown that a high identification with feminine traits is linked to disordered eating in both men and women (Lakkis et al., 1999; Wichstrom, 1995). One of the explanations proposed for the "femininity hypothesis" is that the identification with characteristics typically labeled as "feminine," such as passivity, dependence, and unassertiveness, reflect a need of approval from others and low self-esteem (Paxton & Sculthorpe, 1991). Therefore, both women and men, who identify strongly with feminine traits, and in particular negative feminine traits, may use chronic dieting and other behavioral methods of extreme weight loss as means to alleviate their low self-esteem and to achieve what they perceive to be the ideal body form.

In one study with male university students, which included both heterosexuals and gays, Lakkis et al. (1999) found that gender stereotypes predicted drive for thinness, restrained eating, and binge eating. Moreover, irrespective of sexual orientation, higher scores for negative femininity predicted higher scores on each dimension of disordered eating. These results are consistent with the majority of previous studies which have shown that various aspects of disordered eating are related to higher levels of femininity (Paxton & Sculthorpe, 1991), and they again highlight that negative traits are more important than the positive ones. The femininity hypothesis has also been supported in preadolescent boys (Thomas et al., 2000).

Although the majority of studies have supported the femininity hypothesis, other hypotheses linking gender traits to disordered eating have been proposed (Johnson et al., 1996; Lancelot & Kaslow, 1994; Murnen & Smolak, 1997). One group of studies has demonstrated an overall negative relationship between masculinity and disordered eating (see Murnen & Smolak, 1997 for a review). In other words, a poor identification with masculine traits is linked to disordered eating. This finding is consistent with the femininity hypothesis, as a low identification with masculine traits is also indicative of low self-esteem (Johnson et al., 1996). Another group of studies has shown that higher masculinity is associated with higher levels of disordered eating (Cantrell & Ellis, 1991; Silverstein et al., 1990). However, this relationship may apply more to women as proponents of this view argue that social expectations require women to be both masculine and feminine which then leads to gender-role conflict. To alleviate the stress and tension resulting from conflicting societal demands women may use disordered eating, and in particular binge eating.

Individuals with poorly defined gender attributes are likely to have poor self-definitions and low self-esteem, which makes them more vulnerable to developing disordered eating. This "compensatory style" of eating parallels the compensatory style of drinking described by Williams and Ricciardelli (1999). In order to more fully evaluate this hypothesis, interview studies which examine strategies that men use from their own lived experiences need to be conducted. It is also important to consider that disordered eating, and in particular binge eating, can be viewed as an appetitive behavior. The similarities between disordered eating, in particular, binge eating, and addictions involving alcohol and other drugs have frequently been noted in terms of the development of inefficient strategies of self-regulation (e.g., Baumeister & Heatherton, 1996; Fairburn, 1995; Sayette, 2004; Williams et al., 2009; Williams & Ricciardelli, 2003; Wolfe & Maisto, 2000). Ultimately all of these behaviors share the inevitable requirement for the development of greater self-control because appetitive problems, and the use/abuse of alcohol and disordered eating being prominent among them, can be related to a wide range of issues related to wellbeing and subsequent physical and mental health issues (Ackard et al., 2006; Ensminger et al., 2002; Hüsler & Plancherel, 2007; Wilens et al., 2008).

Appetitive Behavioral Problems and Consequent Difficulties in Self-Management of Emotions

The evidence outlined in this chapter suggests that there is a sense of essentialism occurring when it comes to a self-identification with unmitigated, problematic, gender-role stereotypes. There is clearly an over-identification with the more negative attributes of hegemonic masculinity, which by definition suppresses feminine attributes, in relation to the incidence of problem drinking. Conversely an over-identification with the more negative attributes of femininity and the indication of a low level or lack of positive attributes of masculinity/agency is associated with the incidence of disordered eating. But in both cases it is mainly the adherence to particular stereotypical gender roles rather than biological determinism that is the key to a greater understanding of this process. This must be so because the studies quoted above indicate that some women are increasingly being identified as problem drinkers along with men, and it seems that more men are now also being diagnosed as disordered eaters (Mathews, 2004).

One common strand between the two syndromes is to be found in the consequences of unmitigated stereotyping on the subsequent management of emotions related to appetitive difficulties in self-control (Larsen & Prizmic, 2004; Tracy, Robins & Tangney, 2007). Research into the dynamics of self-regulation (Baumeister *et al.*, 2007) has shown that where a behavior has been previously relied upon as hedonic control over mood and emotion subsequent attempts to exert rational control over its reoccurrence tends to result in a persistent response conflict. Alcohol is a widely used and socially sanctioned mood-change agent that is expected to ease stress and produce emotional wellbeing (Shaol *et al.*, 2008; Sher & Gerkin, 2007). Similar effects associated with "emotional eating" have also been well documented (Schwarze *et al.*, 2003; Spoor *et al.*, 2007).

The requirement of self-regulation over consumption must eventually become paramount. Not only in terms of physical self-preservation but also in the face of the socioemotional consequences of over-indulgence in risky practices (see, for example, Stuewig & Tangney, 2007). Individuals who employ an unmitigated style of control based on gender-role stereotype can subsequently find themselves too poorly equipped, at least initially, to adapt to the necessity of including a more balanced methodology of control by including more of their own neglected aspects of personality described as "feminine" or "masculine" attributes. What is required is the development of a more adaptable and multivocal sense of self (Bosma & Kunnen, 2001; Verhofstadt-Denève, 2001).

Applications and Conclusions

Adopting a psychosocial perspective on self-reported adherence to gender-schematic stereotypes offers a window on the development of a reliance on appetitive behavior as a coping strategy, particularly as related to control of mood and emotion (e.g., Brannon, 2008; Larsen & Prizmic, 2004). It can also shed some light on the individual's interactive strategies based on social comparisons in the negotiation of identity. This is so because stereotypical identification also reflects the way the individual ascribes positive and negative attributions as expectancies related to self-control (Peterson & Park, 2007; Williams & Ricciardelli, 2003). The therapeutic advantage of recognizing the power of stereotypes comes from their immediate, "common-sense" face validity as the basis of ready dialogue leading into the recognition, challenge to, and the potential modification of implicit as well as explicit motivations. Discussion of gender stereotypes can be cast in the form of intrapersonal as well as interpersonal "scripts" that can be of use to practitioners in both health promotion and in clinical health settings. Although stereotypes can be said to be ubiquitous in the general sense they can also prove to be more malleable when the situational demands of particular contexts are taken into account as a level of perceived challenge to the individual's current self-concept. Greater flexibility is suggested in this way. Individuals who have low scores on positive stereotypes will require different therapeutic strategies to those who display high scores on negative stereotypes. The advantage of this stereotyped-script approach is that desired modifications can be rehearsed in order to develop a more "secure sense of self" (Begley, 2000; Brannon, 2008; Hüsler & Plancherel, 2007) as more beneficial strategies for self-regulation are developed (see Mischel & Ayduk, 2004).

References

Ackard, D. M., Neumark-Sztainer, D., Story, M., & Perry, C. (2006). Parent-child connectedness and behavioural and emotional health among adolescents. *American Journal of Preventive Medicine, 30,* 59–66.

Addis, M. E., Mansfield, A. K., & Syzdek, M. R. (2010). Is 'masculinity' a problem? Framing the effects of gendered social learning in men. *Psychology of Men and Masculinity, 11,* 77–90.

Baumeister, R. F., & Heatherton, T. F. (1996). Self-regulation failure: An overview. *Psychological Inquiry, 7,* 1–15.

Baumeister, R. F., & Vohs, K. D. (2004). *Handbook of Self-Regulation: Research, Theory and Applications.* New York: Guilford Press.

Baumeister, R. F., Zell, A. L., & Tice, D. M. (2007). How emotions facilitate and impair self-regulation. In J. J. Gross (Ed.), *Handbook of Emotion Regulation* (pp. 408–426). New York: Guilford Press.

Begley, S. (2000). The trap of stereotype. *Newsweek,* pp. 66–68.

Bem, S. L. (1981). *Bem Sex-Role Inventory: Professional Manual.* Palo Alto, CA: Consulting Psychologists Press.

Blazina, C., & Shen-Miller, D. S. (2010). *An International Psychology of Men: Theoretical Advances, Case Studies, and Clinical Interventions.* New York: Routledge.

Bosma, H. A., & Kunnen, E. S. (2001). *Identity and Emotion: Development Through Self-Organization.* Paris: Cambridge University Press.

Bowker, A., Gadbois, S., & Cornock, B. (2003). Sports participation and self-esteem: Variations as a function of gender and gender orientation. *Sex Roles, 49,* 47–58.

Brannon, L. (2008). *Gender: Psychological Perspectives* (5th edn.). Boston, MA: Allyn and Bacon.

Brannon, L., & Feist, J. (2007). *Health Psychology* (6th edn.). Belmont, CA: Thomson.

Brooks, G. R. (2010). Despite problems, "masculinity" is a vital construct. *Psychology of Men and Masculinity, 11,* 107–108.

Caltabiano, M., Sarafino, E., & Byrne, D. (2008). *Health Psychology: Biopsychosocial Interactions.* Milton, Qld: Wiley & Sons.

Cantrell, P. J., & Ellis, J. B. (1991). Gender role and risk patterns for eating disorders in men and women. *Journal of Clinical Psychology, 47,* 53–57.

Capraro, R. L. (2000). Why college men drink: Alcohol, adventure, and the paradox of masculinity. *Journal of American College Health, 48,* 307–283.

Carver, C. S., Sutton, S. K., & Scheier, M. F. (2000). Action, emotion and personality: Emerging conceptual integration. *Personality and Social Psychology Bulletin, 26,* 741–757.

Chratrand, T. L., Maddux, W. W., & Lakin, J. L. (2005). Beyond the perception-behavior link: The ubiquitous utility and motivational moderators of non-conscious mimicry. In R. R. Hassin, J. S. Uleman, & J. A. Bargh (Eds.), *The New Unconscious* (pp. 334–361). New York: Oxford University Press.

Connell, R. W., & Messerschmidt, J. W. (2005). Hegemonic masculinity: Rethinking the concept. *Gender and Society, 19,* 829–859.

Courtenay, W. (2000). Constructions of masculinity and their influence on men's wellbeing: A theory of gender and health. *Social Science and Medicine, 50,* 1385–1401.

de Visser, R. O., & Smith, J. A. (2007). Alcohol consumption and masculine identity among young men. *Psychology and Health, 22,* 595–614.

Ensminger, M. E., Juon, H. S., & Fothergill, R. E. (2002). Childhood and adolescent antecedents of substance abuse in adulthood. *Addiction, 97*, 833–845.

Fairburn, C. G. (1995). *Overcoming Binge Eating*. New York: Guilford Press.

Fiske, S. T. (2010). *Social Beings: Core Motives in Social Psychology*. New York: Wiley.

Frosh, S., Pheonix, A., & Pattman, R. (2002). *Young Masculinities*. Houndmills: Palgrave.

Garfield, C. F., Isacco, M., & Rogers, T. E. (2008). A review of men's health and masculinity. *American Journal of Lifestyle Medicine, 2*, 474–487.

Helgeson, V. S. (1994). Relation of agency and communion to well-being: Evidence and potential explanations. *Psychological Bulletin, 116*, 412–428.

Huselid, R. F., & Cooper, M. L. (1994). Gender roles as mediators of sex differences in expressions of pathology. *Journal of Abnormal Psychology, 103*, 595–603.

Hüsler, G., & Plancherel, B. (2007). A gender specific model of substance abuse. *Addiction: Research and Theory, 14*, 399–412.

Ito, T. A., Willadsen-Jensen, E., & Correll, J. (2007). Social neuroscience and social perception: New perspectives in categorization, prejudice and stereotyping. In E. Harmon-Jones & P. Winkelman (Eds.), *Social Neuroscience: Integrating Biological and Psychological Explanations of Social Behavior* (pp. 401–424). New York: Guilford Press.

Johnson, M. E., Brems, C., & Fischer, P. (1996). Sex role conflict, social desirability, and eating-disorder attitudes and behaviors. *The Journal of General Psychology, 123*, 75–87.

Kulis, S., Marsiglia, F. F., Lingard, E. C., Nieri, T., & Nagoshi, J. (2008). Gender identity and substance use among students in two high schools in Monterrey, Mexico. *Drug and Alcohol Dependence, 95*, 258–268.

Lakkis, J., Ricciardelli, L. A., & Williams, R. J. (1999). The role of sexual orientation and gender-related traits in disordered eating. *Sex Roles, 41*, 1–16.

Lancelot, C., & Kaslow, N. J. (1994). Sex role orientation and disordered women: A review. *Clinical Psychology Review, 14*, 139–157.

Larsen, R. J., & Prizmic, Z. (2004). Affect regulation. In R. F. Baumeister & K. D. Vohs (Eds.), *Handbook of Self-Regulation: Research, Theory, and Applications* (pp. 40–61). New York: Guilford Press.

Lemke, S., Schutte, K. K., Brennan, P., & Moos, R. H. (2008). Gender differences in social influences and stressors linked to increased drinking. *Journal of Studies on Alcohol and other Drugs, 69*, 695–702.

Lillard, A. S., & Skibbe, L. (2005). Theory of mind: Conscious attribution and spontaneous trait inference. In R. R. Hassin, J. S. Uleman, & J. A. Bargh (Eds.), *The New Unconscious* (pp. 277–308). New York: Oxford University Press.

Mathews, C. R. (2004). Examining problem drinking and eating disorders from a gendered perspective. *Journal of Addiction Disorders, 23*, 67–80.

Marks, D. F., Murray, M., Evans, B., Willig, C., Woodall, C., & Sykes, C. M. (2004). *Health Psychology: Theory, Research and Practice* (2nd edn.). London: Sage.

McCreary, D. R., Newcomb, M. D., & Sadave, S. W. (1998). Dimensions of the male gender role: A confirmatory analysis in men and women. *Sex Roles, 39*, 81–95.

McQueen, C., & Henwood, K. (2002). Young men in 'crisis': Attending to the language of teenage boys in distress. *Social Science and Medicine, 55*, 1493–1509.

Mischel, W., & Ayduk, O. (2004). Willpower in a cognitive-affective processing system: The dynamics of delay of gratification. In R.F. Baumeister & K.D. Vohs (Eds.), *Handbook of Self-Regulation: Research, Theory and Applications* (pp. 99–129). New York: Guilford Press.

Mullen, K., Watson, J., Swift, J., & Black, D. (2007). Young men, masculinity and alcohol. *Drugs: Education, Prevention and Policy, 14*, 151–155.

Murnen, S. K., & Smolak, L. (1997). Femininity, masculinity and disordered eating: A meta-analytic review. *International Journal of Eating Disorders, 22*, 231–242.

Nolen-Hoeksema, S. (2004). Gender differences in risk factors and consequences for alcohol use and problems. *Clinical Psychology Review, 24*, 981–1010.

Ogden, J. (2007). *Health Psychology: A Textbook* (4th edn.). Buckingham: Open University Press.

O'Neil, J. M. (2010). Is criticism of generic masculinity, essentialism, and positive healthy-masculinity a problem for the psychology of men? *Psychology of Men and Masculinity, 11*, 98–106.

Paxton, S. J., & Sculthorpe, A. (1991). Disordered eating and sex role characteristics in young women: Implications for sociocultural theories of disturbed eating. *Sex Roles, 24*, 587–98.

Peralta, R. L. (2007). College alcohol use and the embodiment of hegemonic masculinity among European American men. *Sex Roles, 56*, 741–756.

Peralta, R. L. (2008). 'Alcohol allows you to not be yourself': Towards a structured understanding of alcohol use and gender difference among gay, lesbian, and heterosexual youth. *Journal of Drug Issues, 8*, 373–400.

Peterson, C., & Park, N. (2007). Explanatory style and emotion regulation. In J. J. Gross (Ed.), *Handbook of Emotion Regulation* (pp. 159–179). New York: Guilford Press.

Ricciardelli, L. A., & McCabe, M. P. (2004). A biopsychosocial model of disordered eating and the pursuit of muscularity in adolescent boys. *Psychological Bulletin, 130*, 179–205.

Ricciardelli, L. A., & Williams, R. J. (2010). Role of masculinity and femininity in the development and maintenance of health risk behaviours. In C. Blazina & D. S. Shen-Miller (Eds.), *An International Psychology of Men: Theoretical Advances, Case Studies, and Clinical Interventions* (pp. 57–98). New York: Routledge.

Ricciardelli, L. A., Connor, J. P., Williams, R. J., & Young, R. (2001). Gender stereotypes and drinking cognitions as indicators of moderate and high risk drinking among young women and men. *Drug and Alcohol Dependence, 61*, 129–136.

Rose, N. (1996). *Inventing Ourselves: Psychology, Power and Personhood*. Cambridge: Cambridge University Press.

Sayette, M. A. (2004). Self-regulatory failure and addiction. In R. F. Baumeister & K. D. Vohs (Eds.), *Handbook of Self-Regulation: Research, Theory and Applications* (pp. 447–465). New York: Guilford Press.

Schwarze, N. J., Oliver, J. M., & Handal, P. J. (2003). Binge eating as related to negative self-awareness, depression, and avoidance coping in undergraduates. *Journal of College Student Development, 44*, 644–652.

Shaol, G. D., Gudonis, L. C., Giancola, P. R., & Tarter, R. E. (2008). Negative affectivity and drinking in adolescents: An examination of moderators predicted by affect regulation theory. *Journal of Psychopathology and Behavioral Assessment, 30*, 61–70.

Shapiro, D. H. (1991). *Manual for the Shapiro Control Inventory*. Palo Alto, CA: Behaviordyne.

Shapiro, J. R., & Neuberg, S. L. (2007). From stereotype threat to stereotype threats: Implications of a multi-threat framework for causes, moderators, mediators, consequences, and interventions. *Personality and Social Psychology Review, 11*, 107–130.

Sher, K. J., & Gerkin, E. R. (2007). Alcohol and affect regulation. In J. J. Gross (Ed.), *Handbook of Emotion Regulation* (pp. 560–580). New York: Guilford Press.

Silverstein, B., Carpman, S., Perlick, D., & Perdue, L. (1990). Nontraditional sex role aspirations, gender identity conflict, and disordered eating among college women. *Sex Roles, 23*, 687–695.

Smiler, A. P., & Gelman, S. A. (2008). Determinants of gender: Essentialism in college students. *Sex Roles, 58*, 864–874.

Spoor, S. T. P., Bekker, M. H., Van Strien, T., & van Heck, G. L. (2007). Relations between negative affect, coping, and emotional eating. *Appetite, 48*, 368–376.

Stuewig, J., & Tangney, J. P. (2007). Shame and guilt in antisocial and risky behaviours. In J. L. Tacy, R. W. Robins, & J. P. Tangney (Eds.) *The Self-Conscious Emotions: Theory and Research* (pp. 371–388). New York: Guilford Press.

Thomas, K., Ricciardelli, L. A., & Williams, R. J. (2000). Gender traits and self-concept as indicators of problem eating and body dissatisfaction among children. *Sex Roles, 43*, 441–457.

Tracy, J. L., Robins, R. W., & Tangney, J. P. (2007). *The Self-Conscious Emotions: Theory and Research*. New York: Guilford Press.

Verhofstadt-Denève, L. (2001). Commentary: Affective process in a multi-voiced self in action. In H. A. Bosma & E. S. Kunnen (Eds.), *Identity and Emotion: Development Through Self-Organization* (pp. 141–150). Paris: Cambridge University Press.

Vick, S. B., Seery, M. D., Blascovich, J., & Weisbuch, M. (2008). The effect of gender stereotype activation on challenge and threat motivational states. *Journal of Experimental and Social Psychology, 44*, 624–630.

Wetherell, M., & Edley, N. (1999). Negotiating hegemonic masculinity: Imaginary positions and psycho-discursive practices. *Feminist Psychology, 9*, 335–356.

Wichstrom, L. (1995). Social, psychological and physical correlates of eating problems: A study of the general adolescent population in Norway. *Psychological Medicine, 25*, 567–579.

Wilens, T. E., Biederman, J., Adamson, J. J., Henin, A., Sgambati, S., Gignac, M. *et al.* (2008). Further evidence of an association between adolescent bipolar disorder with smoking and substance use disorders: A controlled study. *Drug and Alcohol Dependence, 95*, 188–198.

Williams, R. J., & Ricciardelli, L. A. (1999). Gender congruence in confirmatory and compensatory drinking. *Journal of Psychology, 133*, 323–331.

Williams, R. J., & Ricciardelli, L. A. (2003). Negative perceptions about self-control and identification with gender-role stereotypes related to binge eating, problem drinking, and to co-morbidity among adolescents. *Journal of Adolescent Health, 32*, 66–72.

Williams, R. J., Richardson, B., & Ricciardelli, L. A. (2009). *The Role of Stereotypes and Misregulation in Binge Eating and Problem Drinking Among Adolescent Girls and Boys.* Unpublished manuscript, Sydney University, Sydney.

Wolfe, W. L., & Maisto, S. A. (2000). The relationship between eating disorders and substance use: Moving beyond co-prevalence research. *Clinical Psychology Review, 20*, 617–631.

Young, A. M., Morales, M., McCabe, S. E., Boyd, C. J., & D'Arcy, H. (2005). Drinking like a guy: Frequent binge drinking among undergraduate women. *Substance Use and Misuse, 40*, 241–267.

7

Culture and Health

An Australian Perspective

Lina A. Ricciardelli, David Mellor, Marita P. McCabe, Alexander J. Mussap, and Christina A. Kolar

With almost 6 million of its population of 23 million being born overseas [Australian Bureau of Statistics (ABS), 2011], and more than half a million Indigenous Australians making up approximately 2.6% of the total population in 2010 (Thomson *et al.*, 2010), Australia is home to many cultures. This highly multicultural population presents great challenges for health service providers and formulators of health policy. Without an adequate knowledge of the issues related to the health status and health-related behaviors of the various subpopulations, health services are unlikely to adequately address the health needs of their members. In addition, we need a better understanding of cultural issues for us to adapt and apply theoretical models of behavior change (see Chapters 1 and 2 in this volume; see also Baumann, 2005) to all cultural groups in Australia. In particular, issues related to migration and acculturation need to be considered. In this chapter we consider these issues, firstly in relation to migrant groups in Australia, and then in relation to Indigenous Australians.

Migrants

Immigrants to Australia come from over 200 countries (ABS, 2011) and represent a quarter of the population. In 2009–2010 the largest groups were people from the UK (1.2 million), New Zealand (544 000), China (380 000 people), India (341 000), and Italy (216 000) (ABS, 2011). Overall, these migrants have good health; they have lower mortality and hospitalization rates than the Australian-born population, as well as lower rates of disability and risk factors for health problems, such as obesity and high blood pressure (Anikeeva *et al.*, 2010). This is known as the "healthy migrant effect," and is primarily attributable to the fact that individuals with poor health are unlikely to migrate or even be accepted for migration (Anikeeva *et al.*, 2010). For some migrants, this health advantage is maintained, and this is often attributed to the adherence to some of their cultural traditions, particularly diet. However, for many other migrants, this health advantage dissipates with increasing length of residence in Australia, as individuals' lifestyles change, often adopting the host country's unhealthy behaviors. Other factors that can also contribute to declines in health

Applied Topics in Health Psychology, First Edition. Edited by M. L. Caltabiano and L. Ricciardelli.
© 2013 John Wiley & Sons, Ltd. Published 2013 by John Wiley & Sons, Ltd.

include a lack of knowledge about the healthcare system of the host country, difficulties in communication with health practitioners, and cultural beliefs that present barriers to health-seeking or healthy behaviors (Chiswick *et al.*, 2008). A decline in health has also been linked to negative consequences of immigration such as unemployment and low economic integration (Khoo, 2010).

The most recent data relating to death rates for persons born overseas is from 2005–2007 [Australian Institute for Health and Welfare (AIHW), 2010]. These data are consistent with earlier studies showing that, overall, overseas-born populations experience lower rates of mortality than Australian-born individuals (Strong *et al.*, 1998). The only exceptions were the overall death rates for persons born in New Zealand and Poland, which were similar to those for people born in Australia, and the death rates for individuals born in the UK and Ireland, which were slightly higher than those for Australian-born people (AIHW, 2010).

Migrants with the lowest death rates were born in Asian countries. These rates were 41% lower for persons born in Vietnam, 40% lower for the Philippines, 35% lower for China, and 33% lower for Malaysia (AIHW, 2010). In accordance with the lowest death rates, migrants from South Asia are less likely than Australian-born people to smoke, drink alcohol at risky or high levels, and be overweight or obese (AIHW, 2010). Moreover, and in line with the lower death rates for Asian migrants, Asian mortality from cardiovascular disease is significantly less than that for the Australian-born population, but rates tend to rise with increasing length of residence in Australia (Daly *et al.*, 2002). This is consistent with the fact that the prevalence of chronic illnesses such as diabetes and osteoporosis are increasing among Asian-Australians (Wahlqvist, 2002). These increases are in part attributable to some of the changes in diet that often follow migration to Australia (Daly *et al.*, 2002; Wahlqvist, 2002). The role of diet as one of the main lifestyle factors in relation to a migrants' health will be examined in the next section.

Migrants from Southern Europe are an interesting group. Overall, in a recent review, Greek and Italian migrants, who constitute the largest Southern European groups in Australia, were found to have the greatest health advantage primarily because of low mortality rates from many cancers and cardiovascular diseases (Anikeeva *et al.*, 2010). This health advantage has been primarily attributed to their close and supportive environment, which fosters the maintenance of their traditional diet (Anikeeva *et al.*, 2010). However, their prevalence of Type 2 diabetes (a risk factor for cardiovascular disease) is more than three times higher than that of Australian-born individuals (Hodge *et al.*, 2004). A major risk factor for Type 2 diabetes among Southern European migrants is obesity, as indicated by their higher body mass index (BMI). Other measures of obesity, which include waist/hip ratio, waist circumference, hip circumference, fat mass, and fat mass as a percentage of body mass, have also been found to be higher among Greek and Italian migrants than among Australian-born people (Hodge *et al.*, 2004).

Another group who are at higher risk of developing Type 2 diabetes in comparison to Australian-born are Indian migrants, and this has also been primarily attributed to their higher rates of obesity (Anikeeva *et al.*, 2010; Ibiebele *et al.*, 2000). High levels of obesity are becoming a major concern in other cultural groups as well, including migrants from Middle Eastern countries such as Turkey and Iran (Gholizadeh *et al.*, 2009), and migrants from Africa (Saleh *et al.*, 2002). For example, in one study, Gholizadeh *et al.* (2009) found that 84% of women in a sample of Middle Eastern women living in Australia were either overweight or obese.

Lifestyle factors

Diet The main lifestyle factor that has been examined in relation to migrants' health is diet. Overall, with increased length of residence in Australia, many migrants often eliminate positive aspects of their traditional diets, and replace these with less desirable elements of typical "Western-style dietary patterns." This often includes reduced consumption of fruits and vegetables, and an increased consumption of foods with high content of sodium, fats, saturated fats, sugars, and energy (Pereira *et al.*, 2010). It also includes the wide array of already prepared and packaged foods available in supermarkets; the range of sweetened drinks, which include soft and energy drinks, flavoured milk, and sweetened teas; and the wide availability and affordability of fast foods (Renzaho *et al.*, 2010).

With reference to the Asian diet in Australia, decreases in the intake of foods with a low glycemic index that contain legumes, green leafy vegetables, fish, and tea, and an increase in the intake of saturated and *trans*-fatty acids and sodium have been documented (Wahlqvist, 2002). This may be due to the Westernization of Asian foods in Australia. This includes noodles that are ready made and more fatty, stir fries with more fat, vegetable dishes with less tofu, more meat in vegetable dishes, less beans and lentils, and the use of less fish (Wahlqvist, 2002).

Changes in dietary behaviors and associated health risks have been directly observed in Asian migrants. In one study Richman *et al.* (2000) found that although older Koreans had resided in Australia for relatively short periods of time, dietary intakes higher in fat and lower in carbohydrate compositions were evident when compared to their Korean counterparts. There was also evidence of increased cardiovascular disease risk factors such as increased adiposity in women and men, and increased prevalence of higher cholesterol levels in men. However, there were also increases in protective factors. Australian Koreans were more physically active and less likely to be smokers than those still living in Korea. Thus these protective factors may help to counteract some of the other health risk factors.

In another more recent study, changes in diet were also implicated in observed weight gain and increased risk for health problems among Taiwanese women living in Australia (Lee *et al.*, 2007). The main focus was the comparison of waist circumference and hip circumference among Taiwanese women living in Australia with those living in Taiwan. Importantly, weight circumference measurement has been shown to be the best single measurement of abdominal fat at a population level and to be an independent risk factor for cardiovascular disease and diabetes (Lee *et al.*, 2007). Women living in Australia had significantly higher waist circumference and hip circumference than women living in Taiwan. In addition, women who had been living in Australia for more than 5 years had significantly higher weight, weight circumference, hip circumference, BMI, and higher percentage of total body fat compared with women living in Australia less than 5 years. The differences in waist and hip circumference were primarily explained by differences in diet rather than physical activity. The intake of total energy and percentage of saturated fat were found to be significantly higher in Australian Taiwanese women than the women living in Taiwan. It was also found that only about 50% of women participated in any regular exercise whether they were living in Australia or Taiwan. The average amount of exercise each day for women in Australia was only 14 min, and 16 min for those in Taiwan, which is well below the recommended Australian government guidelines of at least 30 min of moderate-intensity physical activity each day (Department of Health and Ageing, 2005).

Also of concern are the changes in diet that have been observed among more recently arrived African migrant groups. In one study of Somali women, Burns (2004) found that some new foods included in their diet were cordial and soft drink, potato crisps, white baked bread, breakfast cereal, processed food such as cake and biscuits, instant pasta and pizza, and margarine on bread. However, on the whole, Somali women were able to maintain many aspects of their traditional diet as meals were largely prepared at home, and their uptake of new fruits and vegetables was far higher than of processed foods.

Similarly, one study showed that within the first year of settlement, the diet of African refugees is likely to retain an emphasis on what might generally be described as "African-style" foods and eating patterns (Pereira *et al.*, 2010). This included lower intake of meat, takeaway foods, and fat, and higher consumption of vegetables, whole grains, legumes, and fruit. In addition, much of the food was largely prepared at home. Interestingly, exposure to foods more typical of those reported among the general Australian population (including juices, fruits, soft drinks, breads, rice, cakes, and salads) occurred outside of their home at orientation events such as classes, workshops, and training programs. Thus it is important that foods provided at orientation events include a range of healthy options to assist migrants in learning about the new foods to include in their diets.

In another study, West African women reported that they had made significant dietary changes after their arrival in Australia (Drummond *et al.*, 2011). The women reported a decrease in consumption of cassava, palm oil, and fish but an increase in the consumption of meat, chicken, apples, potatoes, and lettuce/salad. Other studies have also highlighted the increases in the consumption of high-energy takeaway foods, soft drinks, cordials, frozen foods, and other fast foods. In combination with reduced physical activity, this marked change of diet would be a major contributing factor to weight gain among migrants and refugees (Drummond *et al.*, 2011).

One type of diet that is frequently associated with positive health outcomes is the traditional Mediterranean diet. It has been estimated that 40% of excess mortality among older Australians of Anglo-Celtic origin in comparison to Greek migrants living in Australia can be explained in terms of their dietary habits and specifically the extent to which they adhere to the traditional Mediterranean diet (Kouris-Blazos *et al.*, 1999). The traditional Mediterranean diet includes a higher monounsaturated/saturated fat ratio, moderate alcohol consumption, high consumption of legumes, high consumption of cereals (including bread and potatoes), high consumption of fruits, high consumption of vegetables, low consumption of meat and meat products, and a low consumption of milk and dairy products. Interestingly, the advantages of the Greek migrant diet have been found to even surpass those of Greeks in their native country (Wahlqvist *et al.*, 2005). For example, in one study Greeks in Greece were found to have higher mortality risk whereas Greeks in Australia had the lowest risk. The factors which predicted this lower risk were both social patterns and diet. Social networks were greater and social activity was higher for Greeks in Australia, and their diet was more in line with a traditional Mediterranean diet than their counterparts in Greece. Specifically, Greek migrants living in Australia consumed more vegetables, legumes, meat, and fish than Greeks in Greece (Wahlqvist *et al.*, 2005). Moreover, diet was found to be more important in predicting mortality risk than exercise and social activity (Wahlqvist *et al.*, 2005).

On the contrary, some evidence suggests that Greek diets have changed upon migration since the 1960s (Kouris-Blazos, 2002). This is most likely due to a lack of familiar foods in Australia, the memory of premigration hunger, and meat and animal products being not only cheaper and readily available, but also being prescribed a higher "food status" due to their high energy density (Kouris-Blazos, 2002). However, Greek Australians in the 1990s continued to consume large amounts of protective foods such as leafy green vegetables, tomatoes, garlic, and fish, and as a result have been found to have over double the concentration of antioxidants in their bloodstream in comparison to Australians of Anglo-Celtic origin (Kouris-Blazos, 2002; Kouris-Blazos *et al.*, 1996).

Diet interventions   With regards to healthy eating interventions, a study conducted with Pacific Islander and African migrants showed that the current approach to healthy eating interventions is not ideal (Williams & Harris, 2010). When migrants first arrive in Australia, they are bombarded with information, which is often forgotten since many migrants and refugees are likely to be experiencing culture shock and are unlikely to possess good English language skills. Newly arrived migrants are also likely to be preoccupied with adapting to the new environment and enrolling their children in schools and themselves in English classes (Williams & Harris, 2010). Furthermore, the nature of interventions is often unsuitable since they do not take cultural issues into consideration. For example, written information is unlikely to be effective if migrants have not yet learned English, so a more hands-on approach such as cooking demonstrations is more likely to be effective, especially during early settlement. The format of interventions has also been found to be important, with bilingual delivery being preferred by migrants. Based on Williams and Harris' (2010) study, an ideal healthy eating intervention would involve food safety and budgeting information within the first 6 months of migration, and gradual information on dietary guidelines and healthy lunchboxes after 6 months. After 16 months, education needs to include information on nutrition and how it relates to disease risks as well as information regarding the benefits and risks of physical activity/inactivity. Wilson *et al.* (2010) also found that nutritional messages and nutritional panels are too difficult to comprehend for migrants when they are not fluent in English. Furthermore, other studies have shown that many migrants often have low literacy skills in both their native language and English, thus reliance on printed materials is problematic (Walker *et al.*, 2005).

Physical activity   In addition, many migrants report lower levels of physical activity in comparison to Australian-born persons (e.g., AIHW, 2010; Hodge *et al.*, 2004). This is particularly notable among migrant women who report about a 20% lower participation rate in sport and physical activity compared to Australian-born women (Caperchione *et al.*, 2011). The main groups that report lower levels of exercise are from Southern and Eastern Europe, North Africa, the Middle East, and Southeast Asia (AIHW, 2010). Frequently it is changes in lifestyle that have led to marked decreases in physical activity. For example, migrants often report being more active in their country of origin than in Australia due to the more physical nature of everyday life (Caperchione *et al.*, 2011; Renzaho *et al.*, 2010). In many of the less industrialized countries there would have been less reliance on cars and more emphasis on walking, and also less access to labor-saving devices such as vacuum cleaners and washing machines.

The main reasons that migrant women give for their physical inactivity are their high family commitments and lack of social support from family and friends (Caperchione *et al.*, 2011). This is especially the case among Arabic-speaking women and Sudanese women, who have migrated more recently, and often report feeling socially isolated. Arabic-speaking women have larger than average family sizes and they report that there are strong cultural expectations that women would do the bulk of the domestic work around their family life, thus giving them very little free time to take part in physical activity. Furthermore, Arabic women tend to avoid mixed-gender activities for religious reasons (Dassanayake *et al.*, 2011). Similarly, Sudanese women report childcare and other family home duties as significant barriers to undertaking more physical activity (Caperchione *et al.*, 2011). Other reasons for physical inactivity include feeling unsafe, since many women live in areas with higher than average crime rates, and being unaware of community initiatives in their areas. Many migrant women also report other barriers to engaging in physical activity, which include high levels of mental health issues such as post-traumatic stress from their war experiences, depression, and other stressors associated with feeling socially isolated (Caperchione *et al.*, 2011).

Social exclusion has been identified as a major factor associated with physical inactivity among Indian migrant women (Sawrikar & Muir, 2010). With regards to sport, a study found that female migrants felt that they did not belong, most likely due to a lack of representation of ethnic minority women playing sport in the media. Despite Australia's multicultural diversity, migrants view sport to be a cliquish, "White" institution (Sawrikar & Muir, 2010).

Physical activity interventions   Although there has been extensive research on the role of physical activity and how it promotes physical health, none of the current theoretical models take into account cultural issues (see Chapter 3 in this volume). Interventions to increase physical activity among migrants need to take into consideration cultural issues. Kousar and colleagues (2008) conducted a study on sedentary, overweight, and obese Pakistani women. They implemented a 12 week culturally appropriate diet and lifestyle intervention. This intervention featured bilingual educators and facilitators, educational material which was translated into women's native language, one-on-one or small-group health education for women's family and peers, as well as in-home sessions to ease the burdens of transport, time constraints, and family commitments. The results of this intervention indicated that the average number of steps taken daily by participants increased from 4000 to 8617, BMI values dropped from 29.2 to 27.8 kg/m^2, blood pressure was reduced to a healthy level, and blood cholesterol declined from 6.8 to 5.5 mmol/L. Although there was no comparison group, the results suggest that well-designed interventions which take into account cultural issues are likely to improve migrants' health behaviors. However, more studies and evaluations are clearly needed.

An important cultural program in Australia has been established by the Ethnic Communities Council of Queensland (2011). This Chronic Disease program, which is part of the Queensland Strategy for Chronic Disease 2005–2015, aims to address the prevalence of chronic disease among culturally and linguistically diverse (CALD) populations by:

- delivering culturally tailored programs to create opportunities for CALD populations to make informed healthy lifestyle choices to reduce their risk of developing chronic disease,
- expanding partnerships with healthcare providers, government departments, and nongovernment organizations to promote greater awareness for multicultural health,
- working with healthcare providers to effectively target and deliver culturally appropriate health services to CALD populations,
- conducting research to improve information and resources on multicultural populations and chronic disease in Queensland.

However, no evaluation of the program is yet available.

Health behavior and barriers

It is well documented that migrants from non-English-speaking backgrounds are less likely to make use of health services when in need (AIHW, 2010; Daly *et al.*, 2002). This is often because they lack knowledge of the services they can access, but they also often have difficulties gaining access to health and welfare services. For example, Chinese migrants have double the risk of dying from cerebrovascular disease, and this has been attributed in part to poor communication and delays in seeking medical attention (Anikeeva *et al.* 2010). Interpreters are often available, but migrants are not always satisfied with these services, and often report feeling misunderstood (Butow *et al.*, 2011).

Although many migrants identify language barriers and discrimination as being issues in accessing healthcare, others do not report these occurrences (Garrett *et al.*, 2011). This phenomenon is known as the "happy migrant effect" (Garrett *et al.*, 2011). It has been suggested that these migrants do not complain as they feel powerless and, in any case, they view the Australian healthcare system as more favorable than the one in their old country. However, research from the USA shows that ethnic discrimination is associated with negative health outcomes (i.e., high blood pressure) and behaviors (i.e., higher levels of smoking) (Contrada *et al.*, 2000).

In addition to language difficulties, cultural beliefs also need to be considered and are often a barrier to seeking help (Baumann, 2005; Gholizadeh *et al.*, 2009). For example, Chinese older people tend to take a passive role in expressing their needs and rely more on their extended family for assistance with their rehabilitation (Daly *et al.*, 2002). These attitudes and behaviors are viewed to be in line with traditional Chinese philosophies of Confucianism, Taoism, and Buddhism which emphasize the centrality of the family in the management of life problems, and view stresses as being determined by fate. Further, any associated suffering is valued because it develops character and repays the debts of previous lives (Daly *et al.*, 2002).

Oral health services, too, are often under-utilized by migrants (Marino *et al.*, 2002, 2007). For example, the findings of one study of older Italian and Greek migrants indicated low rates of dental visits, and this was reported to be due to the high cost, which was for most pensioners unaffordable (Marino *et al.*, 2002). Excessively long waiting lists acted as deterrents to free oral health services and language was seen as another barrier, especially when dentists were conveying complex information, such as prevention techniques. Distance was another barrier for migrants since suburban oral health services were reported to be sparsely dispersed. Moreover, participants were of the view that tooth loss and dentures were just a part of growing old (Marino *et al.*, 2002).

Breast and cervical cancer screening are also significantly lower among migrant women compared with Australian-born women (Anikeeva *et al.*, 2010). This is especially the case among migrants from Southern Europe, Southern Asia, the Middle East, and Southeast Asia, with some of the lowest levels among Muslim and Thai women. For example, one study showed that only 39% of Thai women had undergone a Pap smear within the last 5 years (Jirojwong *et al.*, 2001). Reasons for low Pap smear rates among Thai women include viewing the referral system as a barrier to healthcare since this does not occur in Thailand, and the perception that general practitioners are unkind and at times racist (Jirojwong & Manderson, 2002).

Sexual health among Chilean and Filipino women is another domain that has been studied. Many of the Chilean women in one study were of the view that doctors and Western medicine are enough to both prevent and heal sexually transmitted diseases, and there is no need to prevent sexually transmitted diseases with the use of condoms (Dawson *et al.*, 2000). In addition, the women were not willing to use condoms as they reported that men did not like to use them. Filipino women have also been found to experience barriers to contraception and prevention of sexually transmitted diseases, since they do not wish to disappoint their families and wish to maintain their honor; therefore, the subject of sex is rarely discussed, thereby limiting access to information and services (Manderson *et al.*, 2002).

Breast cancer is one of the most common causes of cancer morbidity among Chinese-Australian women (Kwok *et al.*, 2006), and this may be partly attributable to the participation of Chinese women in Australia in breast cancer screening being 50% lower than that of Australian-born women. Several cultural factors are associated with this lower level of screening. For example, many of the women in Kwok *et al.*'s (2006) study were of the view that White women were more likely to develop breast cancer as they were open to sexual activity and had bigger breasts. Another barrier to screening was modesty and embarrassment. The Chinese women in Kwok *et al.*'s study were uneasy talking about their breasts and believed it was inappropriate to expose their breasts to anyone except their husband. They were also uncomfortable about self-examining their breasts, and believed that it was inappropriate to do so. In addition, several of the women were of the view that breast cancer was shameful and that this was the result of immoral behavior. Other beliefs held by the women included a larger focus on destiny and the view that negative thoughts, such as those about cancer, should not be discussed.

Religious belief is one of the main reasons given by many Muslim women for not participating in physical activity (Caperchione *et al.*, 2011). For example, they interpret the *Qur'an* as prohibiting physical activity as this is seen to be in conflict with family responsibilities. These women are highly committed to caring for children and other family members and believe that taking time out for themselves to engage in physical activities would signify that they were neglecting their role as mother and family caregiver. Thus there is a need to develop physical activity programs in environments that are mother/child friendly, where mothers can participate in activities with their children, and which would also provide mothers with the opportunity to benefit from physical activity (Caperchione *et al.*, 2011).

Specific attitudes and beliefs about food and body size also need to be taken into account when considering changes in some migrants' eating patterns. For example, among African migrants, high-fibre foods such as vegetables are considered to be a "poor man's diet" and this may explain why West African women report eating vegetables less often than Australian women (Drummond *et al.*, 2011). Healthy eating among migrants is often equated with giving up traditional food and conforming to the eating habits of the dominant culture (Drummond *et al.*, 2011). In addition, many Africans believe that a larger body size is a sign of higher status and wealth, while thinness is associated with war, poverty, malnutrition, and chronic diseases (Renzaho *et al.*, 2010). Similarly, Greek Australians view larger body sizes to be indicative of wealth, and thin bodies to be indicative of poverty, and such views may contribute to more weight gain (Kouris-Blazos, 2002). The extent to which these views are also maintained among other migrant groups, and the extent to which this is changing, has yet to be examined.

Other health risk behaviors that are increasing among some migrant groups include substance use. For example, one study showed that smoking and drinking rates in migrant Thai women were similar to those of Australian-born women (Jirojwong & Manderson, 2002), and significantly higher than Thai women living in Thailand. However, one of the most under-used health services by migrant women is drug and alcohol services (Lee *et al.*, 2009). This is most likely a result of the stigma attached to substance abuse but may also be due to other barriers experienced by migrant women including time restraints, family commitments, and lack of transport (Lee *et al.*, 2009).

Unemployment among migrant groups also needs to be considered, as this has been found to be associated with poor health, particularly among those who have migrated for humanitarian reasons, including refugees (Khoo, 2010). Specifically, one study showed that, for this group of migrants, those with poor physical health were significantly less likely to be in the workforce than their healthy counterparts, and this relationship was stronger for men than women (Khoo, 2010). However, many migrants in this study had poorer health to begin with, and the extent to which unemployment further exacerbated poor physical and mental health was not examined. Given that unemployment is associated with greater mortality, worse physical and mental health and more disability (AIHW, 2010), it is important that more research examines the effects of unemployment among migrant groups in Australia.

Indigenous Australians

Overall, the physical health of our Indigenous people is the worst in Australia and very poor in comparison to other first nations (Hunter, 2003, 2007). One of the main indicators of their poorer health in comparison to other Australians is life expectancy. Life expectancy for the average Indigenous male who was born in the period 2005–2007 is 67.2 years (Thomson *et al.*, 2010). This is about 11.5 years less than for a non-Indigenous male. The life expectancy for the average

Indigenous female born in the same period is 72.9 years, which is about 10 years less than for a non-Indigenous female (Thomson *et al.*, 2010).

Other indicators of health status which also demonstrate the significant gap between Indigenous and non-Indigenous Australians include burden of disease, disability prevalence, and hospitalization rates (AIHW, 2010). A summary measure that takes into account both illness and death is disability-adjusted life years (DALYs), which is the sum of years of life lost due to premature death and the healthy years of life lost due to disability (AIHW, 2010). The overall DALYs for Indigenous Australians is 2.5 times higher than that of the total Australian population (AIHW, 2010). The prevalence of disability among Indigenous Australians is about 4%, which is almost twice as high as that found among non-Indigenous Australians (AIHW, 2010). Similarly, hospitalization rates of Indigenous Australians are 2.5 times higher than for non-Indigenous Australians (AIHW, 2010).

The leading cause of death for Indigenous Australians is cardiovascular disease and this is three times higher than that found among non-Indigenous Australians (Brown, 2009; Thomson *et al.*, 2010). Two of the other main chronic illnesses affecting Indigenous Australians are diabetes and renal diseases (Brown, 2009; Thomson *et al.*, 2010). Together, cardiovascular disease, diabetes, and renal disease account for almost 50% of the difference in life expectancy between Indigenous and non-Indigenous Australians (Brown, 2009). Another significant health problem among Indigenous Australians is respiratory disease, which has been reported in about 27% of Indigenous people (Thomson *et al.*, 2010).

The data informing on cancer incidence and mortality comparisons between Indigenous and non-Indigenous Australians are considered less reliable than other data (Newman *et al.*, 2008). However, small-scale studies suggest that the incidence rates of overall cancers is slightly lower for Indigenous people than non-Indigenous people (Newman *et al.*, 2008; Thomson *et al.*, 2010). Specifically, incidence rates are lower for colorectal, breast, and prostate cancers, and lymphomas, but are higher for lung and other smoking-related cancers, and cervical cancers (Thomson *et al.*, 2010). In addition, although overall incidence rates of cancer are lower, diagnoses of advanced disease are higher, and Indigenous Australians are more likely to die from cancer than non-Indigenous people (Newman *et al.*, 2008; Thomson *et al.*, 2010). The main reasons for this discrepancy is that, among Indigenous Australians, screening uptake is low, diagnosis is late, referral for treatment and care services is delayed, uptake of treatment and care services is low, and compliance and follow-up tends to be poor (Newman *et al.*, 2008).

One additional factor to consider when examining the health patterns of Indigenous Australians is one's living location as defined by the ABS (2001). Indigenous Australians living in remote areas show higher rates of all-cause, cardiovascular, diabetes, and renal mortality rates than Indigenous Australians in outer regional and very remote areas (Andreasyan & Hoy, 2010). This may in part be due to Indigenous people with chronic illnesses living in very remote areas needing to relocate to less remote areas for better access to healthcare services (Andreasyan & Hoy, 2010). However, very remote areas may also be better due to more favorable social environments, stronger family support, more physical activity, and healthier diets (Andreasyan & Hoy, 2010). Studies which specifically examine the different physical and social environments, and how they impact on physical and emotional health, are needed.

One of the main factors contributing to the poor health among Indigenous Australians is socioeconomic disadvantage (AIHW, 2009). Indigenous Australians, on average, report lower incomes, higher rates of unemployment, lower education attainment, and more overcrowded households than other Australians (AIHW, 2009). Associated with this socioeconomic disadvantage are higher levels of health risk behaviors, and these are known to be significant contributors to several health problems among all populations (Caltabiano *et al.*, 2008). Among Indigenous Australians these include poor nutrition, physical inactivity, high BMI, smoking, and alcohol consumption (AIHW, 2010; Vos *et al.*, 2009).

The traditional diet of Indigenous Australians was rich in fibre, high in protein, and low in saturated fat but this is a stark contrast to the modern diet, which is high in refined carbohydrates and saturated fats (AIHW, 2010). Only 41% of Indigenous Australians living in non-remote areas report eating the recommended daily intake of fruit in comparison to over half of non-Indigenous Australians, and only 10% report the recommended daily intake of vegetables in comparison to 14% of non-Indigenous Australians (AIHW, 2010). The consumption of fruit and vegetables among Indigenous Australians living in remote areas is even lower. In remote areas, 20% of Indigenous Australians report no usual daily intake of fruit and 15% no intake of vegetables. In non-remote areas 12% of Indigenous Australians report no daily intake of fruit and 2% no intake of vegetables. The lower intake of fruit and vegetables in remote communities is largely attributable to the limited access to such foods given the high costs of transportation, the lack of appropriate storage facilities, and the lack of suitable local produce (AIHW, 2010).

Surveys have shown that three-quarters of the Indigenous population aged 15 and older who live in non-remote areas report low levels of physical activity, and this is even more notable among women than men (AIHW, 2009). In addition, among Indigenous Australians, 29% have been found to be overweight and 31% are obese (AIHW, 2009). Moreover, Indigenous women were around 1.5 times as likely to be overweight or obese in comparison to non-Indigenous women, but no differences were found for men (AIHW, 2009).

It has also been consistently shown across studies that smoking is higher among Indigenous Australians than other Australians (AIHW, 2010; Thomson *et al.*, 2010). Approximately, 45% of Indigenous Australians over the age of 15 are current smokers as compared to 19% of the non-Indigenous population (Thomson *et al.*, 2010). Overall, Indigenous Australians are less likely to drink alcohol than non-Indigenous Australians (AIHW, 2010; Thomson *et al.*, 2010). However, among those that drink, a higher number of Indigenous Australians than other Australians are more likely to consume alcohol at risky or high-risk levels for harm in the short term (Thomson *et al.*, 2010).

Our recent study, using a participatory action research framework, has specifically examined the role of risk and/or protective factors that influence physical activity and healthy eating among Indigenous men aged between 20 and 40 from the inner suburbs in the city of Melbourne, and a regional town, Mildura, in Victoria (Ricciardelli *et al.*, 2011). In both locations, the men talked about four main factors that they viewed as affecting men's health behavior (Ricciardelli *et al.*, 2011). These were a low motivation to engage in physical activity and healthy eating, reluctance for many men to obtain health checks, sedentary lifestyles, and negative role models.

The majority of the men were informed about eating well, keeping physically active, and the negative impact of other unhealthy behaviors such as smoking and high levels of alcohol consumption (Ricciardelli *et al.*, 2011). Similarly, in another recent study, older Indigenous men and women (aged 45 years and above) were fully aware of the main health conditions affecting the Indigenous Australian population; that is, diabetes, cardiovascular disease, emphysema, asthma, obesity, cancer, kidney disease, arthritis, higher blood pressure, and high cholesterol (Waugh & Mackenzie, 2011). Moreover, in our study it was also noted that change had to come from "yourself" or "your own willpower" (Ricciardelli *et al.*, 2011). As explained by one man, "they already know what's healthy" but it's "up to the individual to change what they eat and drink. . . . You can't force someone to do something really." Thus more work is needed to help shift men's "awareness" to taking "action." However, this needs to be done in a way that is congruent with Indigenous men's focus on family and community relationships. As discussed by Nelson *et al.* (2010), some Indigenous adults view "individual health and fitness activities as a 'disconnecting and shameful experience' because it focused on them as an individual rather than on social relationships" (p. 502). Current and well-accepted health behavior change models (see Chapters 1 and 2 in this volume) need to consider and address cultural issues (see also Baumann, 2005).

Another major barrier to improving health is the reluctance of men to obtain health checks (Ricciardelli *et al.*, 2011). Clearly, this is not an issue that is exclusive to Indigenous men, as men, overall, are less likely to have annual health checks with their doctor or seek help for physical and/or emotional problems because they want to be seen as independent, self-sufficient, and strong because these characteristics are thought to be associated with a "masculine" gender role, and this image is believed to be compromised if men seek health advice (Addis & Mahalik, 2003). This may be an even greater barrier for Indigenous Australian men, who have been described as fearful, confused, ashamed, angry, and lost by Richard Akbar, a Mental Health Support Worker from Derbari Yerrigan Health Service in Western Australia. Akbar (1999), who spoke at the first National Indigenous Male Health Convention Conference in Alice Springs, Australia, explains that these are "not qualities we could describe as ideally male or masculine." Moreover, "Aboriginal men no longer see themselves as the warrior, providers for the families or role models in their own community." Rather, Indigenous men see themselves as "welfare dependents with no voice and if suffering from mental illness no real future." Similarly, Adams has argued that "Aboriginal men have lost the roles that generated prestige and self-esteem (or relational self-esteem); they have lost the ability to achieve and excel in an area beyond the family or household" (Adams, 2006, p. 70).

Several of the men from our study in both Melbourne and Mildura also talked about how their lifestyle had changed over the years from being highly active to one that now had become more "lazy" (Ricciardelli *et al.*, 2011). In part this was due to giving up sporting activities as one became older and having more family commitments. However, this was also due to a major shift from living off the land and being out in the bush to "city living." Other men talked about sitting around, "not doing enough stuff," and a boring life. This was also viewed as a major contributor to problem drinking and feeling down. A suggested underlying factor to this problem was the need for more community activities and events for men to attend which would provide more opportunities for getting together. Several of the men in Mildura also talked about wanting to get more connected with their traditional culture, and doing more traditional activities such as hunting trips, camping, and fishing. In addition, they mentioned wanting more mentoring and guidance from elders to learn about traditional ways of living. Other scholars have further highlighted the importance of "country" for Indigenous Australians, and view their connection to the land as a key aspect of improving Indigenous wellbeing (Ganesharajah, 2009). This involves caring for their physical country, maintaining cultural and community bonds, and also a better diet and more exercise (Ganesharajah, 2009).

The other main health-disrupting r factor identified by men in our study was "negative role models" (Ricciardelli *et al.*, 2011). Several of the men talked about the negative health behaviors being modelled by parents and the influence of peer pressure. For example, as one man explained about smoking and drinking: "it's been in their family and they know nothing else but that." Although the men in our study talked about negative role models, they also mentioned positive role models. Family members and friends were discussed as important influences and role models who encouraged healthy eating habits and physical activity. This result was also found in another study where grandchildren were viewed as a motivating factor in remaining healthy to fulfil the grandparent's role, and this was seen as a great source of happiness and satisfaction (Waugh & Mackenzie, 2011).

It also needs to be noted that Indigenous Australians do not understand their physical health in the same way as European Australians (Nelson *et al.*, 2010; Newman *et al.*, 2008). In fact many traditional Indigenous concepts of health are entirely incongruent to Western views of health, and it is these Western views which underpin current models of health psychology and allied disciplines that are used to develop health programs for Indigenous people (Caltabiano *et al.*, 2008; Chapter 1 in this volume). As argued by Anderson and coworkers (2007), Indigenous people do not make the Platonic and Cartesian divide between mental and physical being, but "health includes the physical, social, emotional, cultural and spiritual wellbeing . . . and this is not only of the individual but of the whole community" (Anderson, 1996, p. 68). Similarly, McCoy (2004, p. 220) has pointed out that "a desert person is healthy or *palya* when their body (*yarnangu*) is in a right relationship with their inner spirit (*kurrun*) and with others (*walytja*)" (also see Baumann, 2005). Therefore, we need to incorporate these views in any future health promotion work with Indigenous Australians (Anderson *et al.*, 2007). In addition, there has been "a call for a more meaningful and substantive inclusion or, and responsiveness to, Indigenous voice and worldviews in analyses of Indigenous wellbeing" (Prout, 2011, p. 2).

Conclusions

Although Australia is home to many cultures, we still have only a limited understanding of how culture may promote and/or impede physical health. Much of the research has focused on the effects of diet on physical health among both migrants and Indigenous Australians. We have not yet empirically researched important sociocultural factors such as acculturation, intergenerational and interpersonal relationships, limited education and work opportunities, and discrimination and alienation, which are likely to impact on the physical health of migrant and Indigenous Australians (Baumann, 2005; Contrada *et al.*, 2000). In addition, although we know that some modifiable health behaviors (i.e., poor diet and physical inactivity) are higher among some migrant groups and Indigenous Australians, an important challenge facing health psychologists is how to best assist these cultural groups in better managing and reducing these health risk behaviors.

References

ABS. (2001). *ABS View on Remoteness.* Canberra: Australian Bureau of Statistics.

ABS. (2011). *Migration, Australia, 2009–10* (catalogue no. 3412.0). www.abs.gov.au/ausstats/abs@.nsf/Latest products/3412.0Media%20Release12009–10?opendocument&tabname=Summary&prodno=3412.0&issue=2009-10&num=&view=.

Adams, M. (2006). Raising the profile of Aboriginal and Torres Strait Islander men's health: An Indigenous man's perspective. *Australian Aboriginal Studies, 2,* 68–74.

Addis, M. E., & Mahalik, J. R. (2003). Men, masculinity, and the contexts of help seeking. *American Psychologist, 58,* 5–14.

AIHW. (2009). *Aboriginal and Torres Strait Islander Health Performance Framework 2008 Report: Detailed Analyses* (catalogue no. IHW 22). Canberra: Australian Institute for Health and Welfare.

AIHW. (2010). *Australia's Health 2010* (catalogue no. AUS 122). Canberra: Australian Institute for Health and Welfare.

Akbar, R. (1999). *Masculinity and Mental Health: An Aboriginal Mental Health Worker's Perspective.* Paper presented at the First National Indigenous Male Health Convention, Alice Springs, Australia. www.ethicalnutrition.com.au/menshealth/akbar.htm.

Anderson, I. (1996). Aboriginal wellbeing. In C. Grbich (Ed.), *Health in Australia: Sociological Concepts and Issues* (pp. 57–78). Sydney: Prentice Hall.

Anderson, I., Baum, F., & Bentley, M. (Eds.). (2007). *Beyond Bandaids: Exploring the Underlying Social Determinants of Aboriginal Health.* Casuarina: Cooperative Research Centre for Aboriginal Health.

Andreasyan, K., & Hoy, W. E. (2010). Recent patterns in chronic disease mortality in remote living Indigenous Australians. *BMC Public Health, 10,* 483.

Anikeeva, O., Peng, B., Hiller, J. E., Ryan, P., Roder, D., & Han, G. (2010). The health status of migrants in Australia: A review. *Asia-Pacific Journal of Public Health, 22,* 159–193.

Baumann, L. C. (2005). Culture and illness representation. In L. D. Cameron & H. Leventhal (Eds.), *The Self-Regulation of Health and Illness Behavior* (pp. 242–253). New York: Routledge.

Brown, A. (2009). Bridging the survival gap between Indigenous and non-Indigenous Australians: Priorities for the road ahead. *Heart, Lung and Circulation, 18,* 96–100.

Burns, C. (2004). Effect of migration on food habits of Somali women living as refugees in Australia. *Ecology of Food and Nutrition, 43,* 213–229.

Butow, P. N., Sze, M., Dugal-Beri, P., Mikhail, M., Eisenbruch, E., Jefford, M. *et al.* (2011). From inside the bubble: Migrants' perceptions of communication with the cancer team. *Support Care Cancer, 19,* 281–290.

Caltabiano, M. L., Sarafino, E. P., & Byrne, D. (2008). *Health Psychology: Biopsychosocial Interactions.* Milton, Qld: John Wiley & Sons.

Caperchione, C. M., Kolt, G. S., Tennet, R., & Mummery, W. K. (2011). Physical activity behaviours of culturally and linguistically diverse (CALD) women living in Australia: A qualitative study of socio-cultural influences. *BMC Public Health, 11,* 26.

Chiswick, B. R., Lee, Y. L., Miller, P. W. (2008). Immigrant selection systems and immigrant health. *Contemporary Economic Policy, 26,* 555–578.

Contrada, R. J., Ashmore, R. D., Gary, M. L., Coups, E., Egeth, J. D., Sewell, A. *et al.* (2000). Ethnicity-related sources of stress and their effects on well-being. *Current Directions in Psychological Sciences, 19,* 136–139.

Daly, J., Davidson, P., Chang, E., Hancock, K., Rees, D., & Thompson, D. R. (2002). Cultural aspects of adjustment to coronary heart disease in Chinese-Australians: A review of the literature. *Journal of Advanced Nursing, 39,* 391–399.

Dassanayake, J., Dharmage, S. C., Gurrin, L., Sundararajan, V., & Payne, W. R. (2011). Are Australian immigrants at a risk of being physically inactive? *International Journal of Behavioral Nutrition and Physical Activity, 8,* 53–58.

Dawson, M. T., Gifford, S., & Amezquita, R. (2000). ¿DoÂnde hay doctor?: Folk and cosmopolitan medicine for sexual health among Chilean women living in Australia. *Culture, Health and Sexuality, 2,* 51–68.

Department of Health and Ageing. (2005). *National Physical Activity Guidelines for Adults.* Canberra: Department of Health and Ageing.

Drummond, P., Mizan, A., Burgoyne, A., & Wright, B. (2011). Knowledge of cardiovascular risk factors in West African refugee women living in Western Australia. *Journal of Immigrant and Minority Health/Center For Minority Public Health, 13,* 140–148.

Ethnic Communities Council of Queensland. (2011). *Chronic Disease Program.* www.eccq-cd.com.au/.

Ganesharajah, C. (2009). *Indigenous Health and Wellbeing: The Importance of Country.* Canberra: Australian Institute of Aboriginal and Torres Strait Islander Studies.

Garrett, P. W., Dickson, H. G., Young, L., & Klinken Whelan, A. (2011). "The happy migrant effect": Perceptions of negative experiences of healthcare by patients with little or no English: A qualitative study across seven language Groups. *Quality and Safety, 17,* 101–103.

Gholizadeh, L., Salamonson, Y. M., Worrall-Carter, L., DiGiacomo, M., & Davidson, P. M. (2009). Awareness and causal attributions of risk factors for heart disease among immigrant women living in Australia. *Journal of Women's Health, 18,* 1385–1393.

Hodge, A. M., O'Dea, K., English, D. R., & Giles, G. G. (2004). Increased diabetes incidence in Greek and Italian migrants to Australia. *Diabetes Care, 27,* 2330–2334.

Hunter, E. (2003). Staying tuned to developments in Indigenous health: Reflection on a decade of change. *Australasian Psychiatry, 11,* 418–423.

Hunter, E. (2007). Disadvantage and discontent: A review of issues relevant to the mental health of rural and remote Indigenous Australians. *Australian Journal of Rural Health, 15,* 88–93.

Ibiebele, T. I., Wattanapenpaiboon, N., Hsu-Hage, B. H. H., & Wahlqvist, M. L. (2000). Prevalence of non-insulin dependent diabetes mellitus in Indian migrants in Melbourne, Australia, using fasting plasma glucose. *International Journal of Diabetes and Metabolism, 8,* 56–68.

Jirojwong, S., & Manderson, L. (2002). Physical health and preventive health behaviours among Thai women in Brisbane, Australia. *Health Care for Women International, 23,* 197–206.

Jirojwong, S., Maclennan, R., & Manderson, L. (2001). Health beliefs and pap smears among Thai women in Brisbane, Australia. *Asia-Pacific Journal of Public Health, 13,* 20–23.

Khoo, S. (2010). Health and humanitarian migrants' economic participation. *Journal of Immigrant and Minority Health, 12,* 327–339.

Kouris-Blazos, A. (2002). Morbidity mortality paradox of 1st generation Greek Australians. *Asia Pacific Journal of Clinical Nutrition, 11,* 569–575.

Kouris-Blazos A., Wahlqvist, M. L., Trichopoulou A., Polychronopoulos E., & Trichopoulos D. (1996). Health and nutritional status of elderly Greek migrants to Melbourne, Australia. *Age Ageing, 25,* 177–189.

Kouris-Blazos, A., Gnardellis, C., Wahlqvist, M. L., Trichopoulos, D., Lukito, W., & Trichopoulou. A. (1999). Are there advantages of the Mediterranean diet transferable to other populations? A cohort study in Melbourne, Australia. *British Journal of Nutrition, 82,* 57–61.

Kousar, R., Burns, C., & Lewandowski, P. (2008). A culturally appropriate diet and lifestyle intervention can successfully treat the components of metabolic syndrome in female Pakistani immigrants residing in Melbourne, Australia. *Metabolism Clinical and Experimental, 57,* 1502–1508.

Kwok, C., Sullivan, G., & Cant, R. (2006). The role of culture in breast health practice among Chinese-Australian women. *Patient Education and Counselling, 64,* 268–276.

Lee, S. K., Thompson, S. C., & Amorin-Woods, D. (2009). One service, many voices: Enhancing consumer participation in a primary health service for multicultural women. *Quality in Primary Care, 17,* 63–69.

Lee, W. P., Lingard, J., & Bermingham, M. (2007). Insulin, lipid profiles and measures of fatness in Taiwanese women in relation to duration of residence in Australia. *Asia Pacific Journal of Clinical Nutrition, 16,* 254–261.

Manderson, L., Kelaher, M., Woelz-Stirling, N., Kaplan, J., & Greene, K. (2002). Sex, contraception and contradiction among young Filipinas in Australia. *Culture, Health & Sexuality, 4,* 381–391.

Marino, R., Minichiello, V., Wright, C., & Schofield, M. (2002). Oral health beliefs and practices among Greek and Italian older Australians: A focus group approach. *Australasian Journal on Ageing, 21,* 193–198.

Marino, R., Calache, H., Wright, C., Morgan, M., Schofield, M., & Minichiello, V. (2007). Profile of the oral health among ambulant older Greek and Italian migrants living in Melbourne. *Australian Dental Journal, 52,* 198–204.

McCoy, B. F. (2004). *Kanyirninpa: Health, Masculinity and Wellbeing of Desert Aboriginal Men.* Unpublished doctoral dissertation, University of Melbourne, Australia.

Nelson, A., Abbott, R., & Macdonald, D. (2010). Indigenous Australians and physical activity: Using a social-ecological model to review the literature. *Health Education Research, 25,* 498–509.

Newman, C., Butow, P., Knight, R., McMillan, K., Treloar, D., Kippax, S., & Eades, S. (2008). Cancer and Aboriginal people in Australia: A review of the literature. *Critical Public Health, 18,* 65–75.

Pereira, C. A. N., Larder, N., & Somerset, S. (2010). Food acquisition habits in a group of African refugees recently settled in Australia. *Health & Place, 16,* 934–941.

Prout, S. (2011). Australia: Indigenous wellbeing frameworks in Australia and the quest for quantification. *Social Indicators Research,* doi:10.1007/s11205-011-9905-7.

Renzaho, A. M. N., Green, J., Mellor, D., & Swinburn, B. (2010). Parenting, family functioning and lifestyle in a new culture: The case of African migrants in Melbourne, Victoria, Australia. *Child and Family Social Work, 16,* 228–240.

Ricciardelli, L. A., Mellor, D., McCabe, M. P., & Mussap, A. J. (2011). *Promoting Fit Bodies, Healthy Eating and Physical Activity Among Indigenous Australian Men: Preliminary Findings.* Unpublished report, Deakin University, Melbourne.

Richman, R. M., Bermingham, M., Ko, J., Mahajan, D., Steinbeck, K., & Caterson, I. D. (2000). Cardiovascular risk factors in elderly Koreans in Australia and Korea. *Asia-Pacific Journal of Clinical Nutrition, 9,* 46–52.

Saleh, A., Amanatidis, S., & Samman, S. (2002). Cross-sectional study of diet and risk factors for metabolic diseases in Ghanian population in Sydney, Australia. *Asia-Pacific Journal of Clinical Nutrition, 11,* 210–216.

Sawrikar, P., & Muir, K. (2010). The myth of a 'fair-go': Barriers to sport and recreational participation among Indian and other ethnic minority women in Australia. *Sports Management Review, 13,* 355–367.

Strong, K., Trickett, P., & Bhatia, K. (1998). The health of overseas-born Australians, 1994–1996. *Australian Health Review, 21,* 124–133.

Thomson, N., MacRae A., Burns, J., Catto, M., Debuyst, O., Krom, I. *et al.* (2010). *Summary of Australian Indigenous Health, 2010.* www.healthinfonet.ecu.edu.au/health-facts/summary.

Vos, T., Barker, B., Begg, S., Stanley, L., & Lopez, A. D. (2009). Burden of disease and injury in Aboriginal and Torres Strait Islander Peoples: The Indigenous health gap. *International Journal of Epidemiology, 38,* 470–477.

Wahlqvist, M. L. (2002). Asian migration to Australia: Food and health consequences. *Asia Pacific Journal of Clinical Nutrition, 11,* 562–568.

Wahlqvist, M. L., Darmadi-Blackberry, I., Kouris-Blazos, A., Jolley, D., Steen, N., Lukito, W., & Horie, Y. (2005). Does diet matter for survival in long-lived cultures? *Asia Pacific Journal of Clinical Nutrition, 14,* 2–6.

Walker, C., Weeks, A., McAvoy, B., & Demetriou, E. (2005). Exploring the role of self-management programmes in caring for people from culturally and linguistically diverse backgrounds in Melbourne, Australia. *Health Expectations, 8,* 315–323.

Waugh, E., & Mackenize, L. (2011). Ageing well from an urban Indigenous Australian perspective. *Australian Occupational Therapy Journal, 58,* 25–33.

Williams, E., & Harris, N. (2010). Understanding the nutrition information needs of migrant communities: The needs of African and Pacific Islander communities of Logan, Queensland. *Public Health Nutrition, 14,* 989–944.

Wilson, A., Renzaho, A. M. N., McCabe, M., & Swinburn, B. (2010). Towards understanding the new food environment for refugees from the Horn of Africa in Australia. *Health and Place, 16,* 969–976.

Part 3
Health and Wellbeing

8

The Relationship Between Subjective Wellbeing and Health

Robert A. Cummins

Subjective wellbeing (SWB) has been a topic of scientific study for over 35 years. It was launched into scientific prominence by the publications of Andrews and Withey (1976) and Campbell *et al.* (1976). Both texts demonstrated that SWB data could be reliably measured and that levels of SWB were remarkably stable over time. It is these characteristics that have made SWB such an attractive new area for quantitative investigation within psychology in general, and health psychology in particular. However, its popularity as a topic of research has also led to difficulties for those who attempt to systematize this area of knowledge. The two major obstacles are inconsistent terminology and measurement.

The problems with terminology are horrendous, as exemplified by the term happiness. It may be used as a blanket term to include all positive feelings about the self (Veenhoven, 2010), as a synonym for SWB (e.g., Chang & Nayga, 2010), as referring to average levels of positive and negative affect (Seidlitz & Diener, 1993), and as a single affect within the classification system described by the circumplex model of affect (Russell, 2003). Happiness is also used to imply different temporal durations, as a long-duration positive mood trait (Seidlitz & Diener, 1993), or as a short-duration positive emotion. The latter is consistent with the term happy in common English usage, which refers to a transient, positive state of mind that has been caused by a specific experience, such as a pleasant social interaction (Diener *et al.*, 2004).

In 2006, Diener made a determined attempt to create a standardized taxonomy and nomenclature for this area. Unfortunately, the negotiated endorsement by multiple senior researchers seems to have diluted the recommendations, most of which lack specificity. Perhaps for this reason, few authors pay heed and terminological anarchy remains the order of the day. Nevertheless, for the purpose of this chapter and in accordance with Diener's recommendations, SWB will be used to refer to a combined affective and cognitive evaluation of one's own life. The term mood happiness will refer to the positive affective trait located on the circumplex.

In the presence of terminological confusion it is hardly surprising to find a corresponding diversity of opinion as to what should be measured. This problem is compounded by the fact that a surprisingly high proportion of researchers consider it necessary to invent their own scale.

The result is a huge legacy of instruments. The Australian Centre on Quality of Life (2011) lists many hundreds of scales that purport to measure SWB in one form or another. This has greatly limited progress in understanding SWB since these scales are of very mixed psychometric quality and many measure quite different constructs. The unfortunate result is a confused and massive literature that, despite over three decades of research, has low conceptual cohesion.

Notwithstanding these difficulties, SWB is gaining prominence as an interesting new facet of the human condition, most particularly in relation to health. Traditionally, the dimension of health has been conceived only in objective terms but more recently it is understood as a dual construct. Health also comprises a subjective dimension of "perceived health" which is finding its way into national surveys of health in Australia [Australian Bureau of Statistics (ABS), 2009]. Perceived health is typically measured through questions of satisfaction, such as "How satisfied are you with your health?" When measured in this form, health satisfaction is a life domain that is included in numerous scales which purport to measure SWB (e.g., Psychological General Wellbeing Index: Dupuy, 1984; Quality of Life Inventory: Frisch, 1995; Personal Wellbeing Index: International Wellbeing Group, 2006).

A curious feature of the objective and subjective dimensions of health is their relative independence from one another. The reason, we propose, is the management system called SWB homeostasis (Cummins, 2003, 2010; Cummins *et al.*, 2002).

The following sections will explain homeostasis theory using results from surveys conducted as the Australian Unity Wellbeing Index. These national Australian surveys have been conducted several times each year since 2001. At the end of 2010, a total 24 surveys had been conducted, each one comprising 2000 respondents, newly recruited for each survey, representing the geographical distribution of the population. Each survey includes the Personal Wellbeing Index (International Wellbeing Group, 2006) to measure SWB, as well as standard demographic questions and items unique to each survey. People respond to a 0–10 scale, from completely dissatisfied to completely satisfied, and data are standardized for reporting to a 0–100 format. The reports and data from each of these surveys are available from the website of the Australian Centre on Quality of Life (http://www.deakin.edu.au/research/acqol/index.php).

SWB Homeostasis

The theory of subjective wellbeing homeostasis proposes that, in a manner analogous to the homeostatic maintenance of body temperature, SWB is actively controlled and maintained by automatic neurological processes (see Cummins & Nistico, 2002, for an extended description). The purpose of SWB homeostasis is to maintain a normally positive sense of wellbeing that is generalized and rather abstract. It can be measured by the classic question "How satisfied are you with your life as a whole?" Given the extraordinary generality of this question, the response that people give does not represent a cognitive evaluation of their life. Rather it reflects the deep, and stable, positive mood state that is the core of SWB. It is this general and abstract sense of positive wellbeing which the homeostatic system seeks to defend. As one consequence, the level of satisfaction people record to this question has some interesting characteristics.

SWB is normally stable and positive

The stability of SWB at the level of population sample mean scores is remarkable. Figure 8.1 shows the levels of SWB represented by the 26 survey mean scores from 2001 to 2010 (Cummins

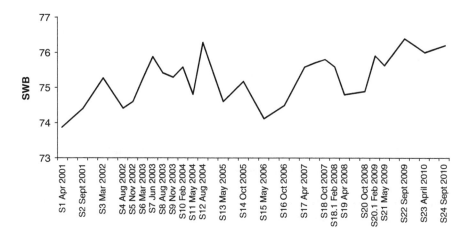

Figure 8.1 SWB over a 10-year period in Australia.

et al., 2010). The horizontal axis of the figure indicates the date of each survey. The total variation between these means is less than three percentage points.

As can also be seen from Figure 8.1, the average person feels that their general satisfaction with life is held at about three-quarters of its maximum extent (Cummins, 1995, 1998), rating 75 on the 0–100 scale. The supporting frequency distribution of SWB is shown in Figure 8.2, with SWB measured by the Personal Wellbeing Index (International Wellbeing Group, 2006). This shows aggregated data from our surveys 10 to 24 (Cummins *et al.*, 2010).

From the distribution shown in Figure 8.2, it is evidently normal for people to feel positive about themselves. Only 4.4% of respondents in these general population surveys fall below 50 points, and these people are at high risk of depression (see below).

The distribution of SWB is under genetic control

To explain this positive stability in SWB, it is proposed that each person has a set point for their SWB that constitutes a genetically determined, individual difference. We also propose, on the

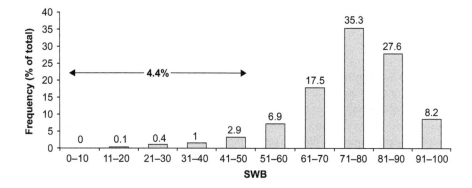

Figure 8.2 Frequency distribution of the Personal Wellbeing Index.

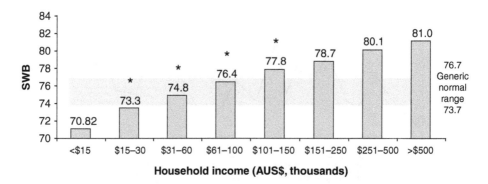

Figure 8.3 Income versus SWB. The stars above columns indicate a significant difference from the group immediately to the left.

basis of empirical deduction (Cummins, 2010), that the range of set points within large normative samples is from 60 to 90 points, with a mean of 75. We also calculate that each set-point range has a width of about six percentage points on either side of its set point, and that homeostasis seeks to maintain SWB within this range for each person.

The normal distribution of set points within large samples, together with the set-point ranges, explains why no population group chosen on the basis of demographic criteria has a reliable SWB higher than about 81–82 points (Cummins *et al.*, 2007b). That is, if all members of a demographically advantaged sample, such as people who are very wealthy, are operating at the top of their respective set-point ranges, then the sample SWB should be about $75 + 6 = 81$ points.

This is confirmed in Figure 8.3 which shows the relationship between income and SWB. These results come from Cummins *et al.* (2010) and are cumulative, derived from around 30 000 people involved in our general population surveys over the past 7 years. In our surveys, household income is the demographic variable which, of itself, evidences the highest group mean SWB.

The median household income in Australia lies within the range of AUS$61 000–100 000 per annum (see Flood & Baker, 2010). The largest proportion of respondents ($n = 6888$) lies within this range while the smallest proportion ($n = 80$) has the highest income (>$500 000). The generic normal range is calculated by using the 26 survey mean scores shown in Figure 8.1 as data. The range represents two standard deviations on either side of the mean. Clearly SWB is rising with income and the upper value of 81.0 points accords well with theory.

SWB is homeostatically protected

While SWB is normally held positive with remarkable tenacity, it is not immutable. A sufficiently adverse level of challenge can defeat the homeostatic system and, when this occurs, the level of SWB falls below its homeostatic range. This is demonstrated in relation to body mass index (BMI), calculated as the body weight in kilograms divided by the square of the height in meters. Data are gathered through the question "What is your approximate height and weight?" Figure 8.4 has been extracted from Report 16.0 of the Australian Unity Wellbeing Index (Cummins *et al.*, 2006) and represents data cumulated over several surveys.

The literature is emphatic in documenting a negative correlation between obesity and wellbeing (for a meta-analysis see de Wit *et al.*, 2010). However, from Figure 8.4 it is evident that SWB is

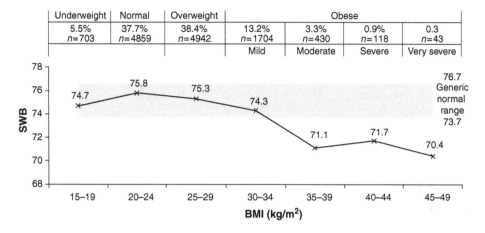

Figure 8.4 BMI vs. SWB.

relatively insensitive to BMI. Even mild obesity does not take SWB below the normal range. It is not until BMI reaches the level of moderate obesity (35–39 kg/m^2) that the level of chronic negative challenge to the maintenance of wellbeing is sufficient to increase the frequency of homeostatic failure, and SWB significantly falls ($P < 0.001$). It is interesting to observe that this information is lost if results are simply analysed by linear correlation.

So, how does homeostasis *work* to defend SWB against the unusually good and the unusually bad experiences of life? The answer we propose is that there are three levels of defense and we call these defensive systems "buffers."

Homeostatic buffers

The first line of defense is behavior. People are generally adept at avoiding strong challenges through established life routines that make daily experiences predictable and manageable. However, strong and unexpected events will inevitably occur from time to time. They will shift SWB out of its normal range, as attention shifts to the emotion generated by the event. Such deviations from the set-point range will usually last for a brief period of time, until adaptation occurs. Adaptation to unusual positive challenges is very predictable and well understood (Helson, 1964). Adaptation to negative challenges is less certain but is assisted by the buffering capacity of money and relationship intimacy.

Money and relationships Of these two homeostatic buffers, the most powerful is a relationship with another human being that involves mutual sharing of intimacies and support (Cummins *et al.*, 2007a). Almost universally, the research literature attests to the power of good relationships to moderate the influence of potential stressors on SWB (for reviews see Henderson, 1977; Sarason *et al.*, 1990)

Money is also a powerful external buffer, but there are misconceptions as to what money can and cannot do in relation to SWB. It cannot, for example, shift the set point to create a perpetually happier person. Set points for SWB are genetically determined (Lykken & Tellegen, 1996; Røysamb *et al.*, 2002; Stubbe *et al.*, 2005) so in this sense money cannot buy happiness. No matter how rich someone is, their average level of SWB cannot be sustained higher than a level that lies towards the

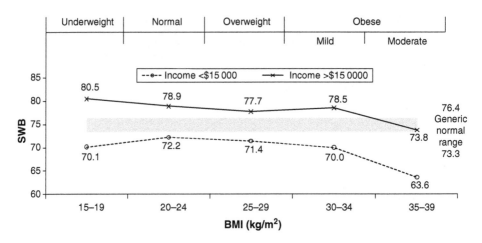

Figure 8.5　BMI vs. household income.

top of their set-point range. People adapt readily to luxurious living standards, so genetics trumps wealth after a certain level of income has been achieved.

The true power of wealth is to protect wellbeing through its potential as a highly flexible resource (Cummins, 2000) that allows people to defend themselves against the negative potential inherent within their environment. Wealthy people pay others to perform tasks they do not wish to do themselves. Poor people, who lack such resources, must fend for themselves to a much greater extent. Poor people, therefore, have a level of SWB that is far more at the mercy of their environment. One consequence is that their mean SWB is low with high within-group variance. This principle of wealth as a flexible resource is demonstrated in Figure 8.5, which shows how the relationship between BMI and SWB is moderated by income.

These results come from cumulated survey data reported by Cummins *et al.* (2006). The degree of SWB difference across the BMI range, within the <$15 000 and >$150 000 income groups, is 8.6 and 6.7 points respectively. The smaller difference within the higher-income group is consistent with greater buffering capacity counteracting the negative effects of obesity.

In conclusion, the external buffers assist with homeostatic management of SWB, but if such defenses fail then the experience of SWB moves outside the set-point range. When this occurs, the internal buffers are activated.

Internal buffers　The internal buffers comprise protective cognitive devices designed to minimize the impact of personal failure on positive feelings about the self. Such devices have been variously described as downward social comparisons (Wills, 1981), secondary control (Rothbaum *et al.*, 1982), benefit reminding (Affleck & Tennen, 1996), and positive reappraisal (Folkman & Moskowitz, 2002).

A detailed discussion of these internal buffers in relation to SWB is provided by Cummins and Nistico (2002) and Cummins *et al.* (2002). Internal buffers protect SWB by altering the way we see ourselves in relation to homeostatic challenge, such that the negative potential in the challenge is deflected away from the core view of self. The ways of thinking that can achieve this are highly varied. For example, one can find meaning in the event ("God is testing me"), fail to take responsibility for the failure ("it was not my fault"), or regard the failure (such as dropping a fragile object) as unimportant ("I did not need that old vase anyway").

In summary, the combined external and internal buffers ensure that our wellbeing is robustly defended. There is, therefore, considerable stability in the SWB of populations and, as has been stated, the means for Western societies like Australia are consistently at about 75 points on a 0–100 scale. But what is the composition of SWB at the level of affect and cognition?

What is homeostasis defending?

Most contemporary theorists regard the composition of SWB, obtained through a verbal or written response, to involve both affective and cognitive components. This was first recognized by Campbell *et al.* (1976) who suggested that this amalgam should be measured through questions of "satisfaction." This form of question has since become standard for SWB measurement. However, relatively little research has been directed to examining the relative contribution of affect and cognition. Certainly the two components are separable (Lucas *et al.*, 1996) but whether, as claimed by Diener *et al.* (2004), SWB represents a dominantly cognitive evaluation, is moot. Indeed, to the contrary, more recent research (Davern *et al.*, 2007) weighs the balance in favor of affect as the central element in the form of a deep and stable positive mood state. Following Russell (2003) we initially called this construct "core affect" (Russell, 2003) but now refer to it as homeostatically protected mood (HP mood; Cummins, 2010). We propose that it has the following characteristics.

1. Following Russell (2003), we consider HP mood to be a genetically based, neurophysiologically generated state, that is experienced as stable positive mood. Being a trait, the presence of HP mood is not tied to any acute causative agent in the manner of an emotional response. Instead, it represents how each individual senses themselves in an abstract and personal way. Again following Russell (2003), HP mood may be described as analogous to felt body temperature in that it is always there, it can be assessed when attention is drawn to it, extremes are most obvious, and it exists without words to describe it. In conformity with the circumplex model of affect, HP mood comprises a blend of hedonic (pleasant) and arousal values (activation).
2. While we initially hypothesized that the origin of this trait positive mood was from personality, as has been suggested by numerous prior researchers (e.g., Oishi & Diener, 2001), this now appears incorrect. As initially demonstrated by Davern *et al.* (2007) and confirmed by Blore *et al.* (2011) and Tomyn and Cummins (2011), structural modelling has revealed that the positive affect in HP mood drives both personality and SWB. In other words, personality correlates with SWB only because both variables are being influenced by HP mood.
3. SWB is highly saturated with HP mood and is a proxy measure of the latter construct. This is most evident when SWB is measured by "satisfaction with life as a whole." The abstract and personal nature of this item means that people respond using mood as information (Schwarz & Clore, 1983, 1996) and use an affect heuristic to tap HP mood.
4. HP mood appears to comprise three main affects. These are dominated by a sense of contentment, flavored with a touch of happiness and arousal. We propose that the genetically generated level of HP mood provides each person with a unique level of felt positivity, which constitutes an individual difference between people. This level represents their set point and is the level that SWB homeostasis seeks to defend.

In summary, the underlying neurophysiological state being homeostatically defended is proposed to be HP mood. However, SWB is a good proxy measure of this construct since it is heavily saturated with positive affect. The relationship between these constructs helps to explain the link between SWB and depression.

SWB, Health, and Depression

As has been described, strong positive or negative experience will shift SWB out of its set-point range to higher or lower values, usually for a brief period of time. However, if negative experience is sufficiently strong and sustained, it will cause SWB to remain below its set-point range.

A critical requirement for homeostatic defeat is that the threat must be consciously experienced. Thus, in order for any health condition to impact on SWB, people must be consciously aware of their condition or its sequelae. If they are not, then even a serious medical condition will have no impact on SWB. This is demonstrated in Figure 8.6. The results come from Australian Unity Report 17 (Cummins *et al.*, 2007b) and show the combined data from several surveys.

It is evident that medical conditions which involve heart or blood pressure problems have little impact on SWB. Very commonly, the people concerned have little or no ongoing, conscious awareness of their condition, other than when reminded by their physician. So the conditions in Figure 8.6 impact SWB proportionally to their perceived homeostatic threat, rather than their medical severity. In confirmation of this, conditions that likely involve stress or pain (cancer, arthritis, diabetes) are quite effective in reducing SWB below the normal range.

The condition with the strongest link to SWB is depression. While the essence of SWB is positive affect from HP mood, the essential diagnostic feature of depression is the loss of positive mood (see American Psychiatric Association, 2000). Thus, we propose that loss of positive mood is the essence of both constructs, which makes SWB a good marker for an elevated risk of depression (Cummins, 2010).

Implications for Practice

There are several ideas for practicing psychologists that may be derived from this chapter, both for the promotion of population health generally and for psychological practice. In terms of health promotion, encouraging healthy lifestyles will diminish the probability of compromised health. This, in turn, will make normally healthy people more resilient to homeostatic defeat and, in relatively unhealthy groups, can even raise SWB (see Mo & Winnie, 2010).

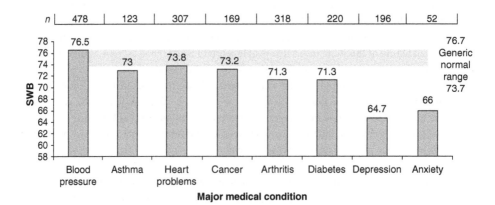

Figure 8.6 Major medical condition versus Personal Wellbeing Index.

In terms of psychological practice, perhaps the most important aspect of SWB is its nonlinear relationship with physical ill health. This means, among other things, that people with significant medical illness may have normal levels of SWB. The significance of this is considerable. It means that preconceptions must be abandoned when faced with, for example, an elderly disabled and medically compromised person. They may well have quite normal levels of SWB and any proxy assumption, by the psychologist, that their SWB is low may quite probably be wrong. The only way to know someone's level of SWB, and therefore their risk of depression, is through direct measurement.

Finally, if SWB is to be used as a measure of intervention efficacy, then reliable baseline measurements are essential. If the person has normal SWB prior to the intervention, then homeostasis will probably defeat any further rise. There is no literature of which I am aware showing that people with normal-range SWB can increase their level, on a chronic basis, by more than three or four percentage points. Despite this, even a small persistent rise in SWB may be useful. It may indicate the person has successfully developed resources to become more resilient. While this idea is appealing and consistent with homeostatic theory, it remains to be empirically demonstrated.

If, on the other hand, SWB is low at baseline, then it will be a very good marker of the extent to which an intervention has succeeded in counteracting the challenges that led to homeostatic defeat. Under such conditions, very large increases in SWB may follow successful intervention. Indeed, the observation of such marked changes has led some researchers to question set-point theory (e.g., Fujita & Diener, 2005; Headey, 2008; Lucas, 2007). Using data from the German Socio-Economic Panel Study, from 1984 to 2000, Fujita and Diener showed that, over this 16 year period, about 10% of the sample showed a change in satisfaction of about 30 points. They conclude that SWB "can and does change for some people" and take this as evidence of set-point change. However, homeostasis theory and HP mood offers an alternative explanation.

The period in question included the tumultuous German Reunification in 1990, which substantially raised the living circumstances of many East Germans. For many of these people, their living circumstances had been sufficiently harsh to defeat normal homeostasis. Their level of SWB was being controlled by powerful negative emotions that overwhelmed homeostasis, and so dominated their awareness, causing them to report low SWB. Within this conception, each person's HP mood and set-point remains unaltered and the abnormal level of SWB reflects attention to the dominating emotional state.

This explanation applies equally to the area of health psychology. If someone is suffering homeostatic defeat due, for example, to overwhelming pain or anxiety, then the success of an intervention which directs resources to the restoration of homeostasis will be evidenced by a substantial increase in SWB. For these reasons, screening clients with an instrument such as the Personal Wellbeing Index (International Wellbeing Group, 2006) is recommended as an effective way of both detecting initial depression and as a reference for future progress.

References

ABS. (2009). *4364.0 National Health Survey: Summary of Results, 2007–08.* www.ausstats.abs.gov.au/Ausstats/subscriber.nsf/0/CC0FB5A08570984ECA25762E0017CF2B/$File/4363055001_2007-08.pdf.

Affleck, G., & Tennen, H. (1996). Construing benefits from adversity: Adaptational significance and dispositional underpinnings. *Journal of Personality and Social Psychology, 64,* 899–922.

American Psychiatric Association. (2000). *Diagnostic and Statistical Manual of Mental Disorders* (4th edn.). Washington DC: American Psychiatric Association.

Andrews, F. M., & Withey, S. B. (1976). *Social Indicators of Well-Being: American's Perceptions of Life Quality*. New York: Plenum Press.

Australian Centre on Quality of Life. (2011). *Instruments*. www.deakin.edu.au/research/acqol/instruments/instrument.php.

Blore, J., Stokes, M. A., Mellor, D., Firth, L., & Cummins, R. A. (2011). Comparing multiple discrepancies theory to affective models of subjective well-being. *Social Indicators Research, 100,* 1–16.

Campbell, A., Converse, P. E., & Rodgers, W. L. (1976). *The Quality of American life: Perceptions, Evaluations, and Satisfactions*. New York: Russell Sage Foundation.

Chang, H. H., & Nayga, R. M. (2010). Childhood obesity and unhappiness: The influence of soft drinks and fast food consumption. *Journal of Happiness Studies, 11,* 261–276.

Cummins, R. A. (1995). On the trail of the gold standard for life satisfaction. *Social Indicators Research, 35,* 179–200.

Cummins, R. A. (1998). The second approximation to an international standard of life satisfaction. *Social Indicators Research, 43,* 307–334.

Cummins, R. A. (2000). Personal income and subjective well-being: A review. *Journal of Happiness Studies, 1,* 133–158.

Cummins, R. A. (2003). Normative life satisfaction: Measurement issues and a homeostatic model. *Social Indicators Research, 64,* 225–256.

Cummins, R. A. (2010). Subjective well-being, homeostatically protected mood and depression: A synthesis. *Journal of Happiness Studies, 11,* 1–17.

Cummins, R. A., & Nistico, H. (2002). Maintaining life satisfaction: The role of positive cognitive bias. *Journal of Happiness Studies, 3,* 37–69.

Cummins, R. A., Gullone, E., & Lau, A. L. D. (2002). A model of subjective well being homeostasis: The role of personality. In E. Gullone & R. A. Cummins (Eds.), *The Universality of Subjective Well-Being Indicators: Social Indicators Research Series* (pp. 7–46). Dordrecht: Kluwer.

Cummins, R. A., Woerner, J., Tomyn, A., Gibson, A., & Knapp, T. (2006). *Australian Unity Well-Being Index: Report 16.0. The Well-Being of Australians – Mortgage Payments and Home Ownership*. Melbourne, Australian Centre on Quality of Life, School of Psychology, Deakin University. www.deakin.edu.au/research/acqol/index_well-being/index.htm.

Cummins, R. A., Walter, J., & Woerner, J. (2007a). *Australian Unity Well-Being Index: Report 16.1. The Well-Being of Australians – Groups with the Highest and Lowest Well-Being in Australia*. Melbourne, Australian Centre on Quality of Life, School of Psychology, Deakin University. www.deakin.edu.au/research/acqol/index_well-being/index.htm.

Cummins, R. A., Woerner, J., Tomyn, A., Gibson, A., & Knapp, T. (2007b). *Australian Unity Well-Being Index: Report 17.0. The Well-Being of Australians – Work, Wealth and Happiness*. Melbourne, Australian Centre on Quality of Life, School of Psychology, Deakin University. www.deakin.edu.au/research/acqol/index_well-being/index.htm.

Cummins, R. A., Woerner, J., Weinberg, M., Perera, C., Gibson, A., Collard, J., & Horfiniak, K. (2010). *Australian Unity Well-Being Index: – Report 24.0. The Well-being of Australians – Trust, Life Better/Worse and Climate Change*. Melbourne, Australian Centre on Quality of Life, School of Psychology, Deakin University. www.deakin.edu.au/research/acqol/index_well-being/index.htm.

Davern, M., Cummins, R. A., & Stokes, M. (2007). Subjective well-being as an affective/cognitive construct. *Journal of Happiness Studies, 8,* 429–449.

de Wit, L., Luppino, F., van Straten, A., Penninx, B., Zitman, F., & Cuijpers, P. (2010). Depression and obesity: A meta-analysis of community-based studies. *Psychiatry Research, 178,* 230–235.

Diener, E. (2006). Guidelines for national indicators of subjective well-being and ill-being. *Applied Research in Quality of Life, 1,* 151–157.

Diener, E. D., Napa-Scollon, C. K., & Lucas, R. E. (2004). The evolving concept of subjective well-being: The multifaceted nature of happiness. In P. T. Coista & I. C. Siegler (Eds.), *Recent Advances in Psychology and Aging* (pp. 187–220). Amsterdam: Elsevier Science BV.

Dupuy, H. J. (1984). The Psychological General Well-Being (PGWB) Index. In N. K. Wenger, M. E. Mattson, & C. D. Furberg (Eds.), *Assessment of Quality of Life in Clinical Trials of Cardiovascular Therapies* (pp. 170–183). New York: Elinson J. Le Jacq Publishing.

Flood, J., & Baker, E. (2010). *Housing Implications of Economic, Social, and Spatial Change*. AHURI final report no. 150. Melbourne: Australian Housing and Urban Research Institute. www.apo.org.au/research/housing-implications-economic-social-and-spatial-change.

Folkman, S., & Moskowitz, J. T. (2002). Positive affect and the other side of coping. *American Psychologist, 55,* 647–654.

Frisch, M. B. (1995). *Quality Of Life Inventory*. San Antonio, TX: Pearson Assessments.

Fujita, F., & Diener, E. (2005). Life satisfaction set point: Stability and change. *Journal of Personality and Social Psychology, 88,* 158–164.

Headey, B. (2008). The set-point theory of well-being: Negative results and consequent revisions. *Social Indicators Research, 85,* 389–404.

Helson, H. (1964). *Adaptation-Level Theory*. New York: Harper & Row.

Henderson, S. (1977). The social network, support and neurosis. The function of attachment in adult life. *British Journal of Psychiatry, 131,* 185–191.

International Wellbeing Group. (2006). *Personal Wellbeing Index Manual*. Melbourne, Deakin University. www.deakin.edu.au/research/acqol/instruments/well-being_index.htm.

Lucas, R. E. (2007). Adaptation and the set-point model of subjective well-being: Does happiness change after major life events? *Current Directions in Psychological Science, 16,* 75–79.

Lucas, R. E., Diener, E., & Suh, E. (1996). Discriminant validity of well-being measures. *Journal of Personality and Social Psychology, 71,* 616–628.

Lykken, D., & Tellegen, A. (1996). Happiness is a stochastic phenomenon. *Psychological Science, 7,* 186–189.

Mo, P. K. H., & Winnie, W. S. M. (2010). The influence of health promoting practices on the quality of life of community adults in Hong Kong. *Social Indicators Research, 95,* 503–518.

Oishi, S., & Diener, E. (2001). Re-examining the general positivity model of subjective well-being: The discrepancy between specific and global domain satisfaction. *Journal of Personality and Social Psychology, 69,* 641–666.

Rothbaum, F., Weisz, J. R., & Snyder, S. S. (1982). Changing the world and changing the self: A two-process model of perceived control. *Journal of Personality and Social Psychology, 42,* 5–37.

Røysamb, E., Harris, J. R., Magnus, P., Vitterso, J., & Tambs, K. (2002). Subjective well-being. Sex-specific effects of genetic and environmental factors. *Personality and Individual Differences, 32,* 211–223.

Russell, J. A. (2003). Core affect and the psychological construction of emotion. *Psychological Review, 110,* 145–172.

Sarason, I. G., Sarason, B. R., & Pierce, G. R. (1990). Social support: The search for theory. *Journal of Social and Clinical Psychology, 9,* 137–147.

Schwarz, N., & Clore, G. L. (1983). Mood, misattribution, and judgements of well-being: Informative and directive functions of affective states. *Journal of Personality and Social Psychology, 45,* 513–523.

Schwarz, N., & Clore, G. L. (1996). Feelings and phenomenal experience. In E. T. Higgins & A. W. Kruglandski (Eds.), *Social Psychology: Handbook of Basic Principles* (pp. 433–465). New York: Guilford Press.

Seidlitz, L., & Diener, E. (1993). Memory for positive versus negative life events: Theories for the differences between happy and unhappy persons. *Journal of Personality and Social Psychology, 64,* 654–664.

Stubbe, J. H., Posthuma, D., Boomsma, D. I., & de Geus, E. J. C. (2005). Heritability of life satisfaction in adults: A twin-family study. *Psychological Medicine, 35,* 1581–1588.

Tomyn, A. H., & Cummins, R. A. (2011). Subjective wellbeing and homeostatically protected mood: theory validation with adolescents. *Journal of Happiness Studies, 12*(5), 897–914.

Veenhoven, R. (2010). Greater happiness for a greater number – Is that possible and desirable? *Journal of Happiness Studies, 11,* 605–629.

Wills, T. A. (1981). Downward comparison principles in social psychology. *Psychological Bulletin, 90,* 245–271.

9

Developing Conceptual Models of Psychosocial Wellbeing

Pursuing Better Health Outcomes

Lyn G. Courtney, Nerina J. Caltabiano, and Marie L. Caltabiano

Subjective wellbeing (SWB), often referred to as quality of life (QOL) or satisfaction with life, is a predictor of better mental health, improved overall health, superior prognosis in times of illness, reduced mortality, and increased longevity (Diener & Chan, 2011; Seligman, 2008). For more than four decades, the theoretical structure of SWB has been subjected to extensive empirical investigation in order to determine the dimensions that comprise SWB (see review Diener *et al.*, 2009). However, the study of SWB is considered to be in its formative stages with little consensus on the theoretical structure, composition, conceptual characteristics, measurement, and consequences of SWB.

This chapter has four objectives. First, this chapter will introduce SWB within a positive psychology framework (Seligman 1998, 2003) and the emerging field of positive health (Seligman, 2008). Next, to provide the context from which the field of SWB has emerged, a brief review of QOL and wellbeing is presented. Third, we will compare and contrast four well-established models and measures of SWB in order to elucidate some of the challenges that need to be resolved by SWB researchers. Finally, this chapter will present an argument for viewing SBW from an integrative, holistic perspective that takes into account the differing life contexts, histories, experiences, beliefs, values, perceptions, and expectations of subpopulations (e.g., gender, age, personality, culture). A holistic perspective of SWB would incorporate factors that have recently been shown to contribute to SWB, such as spirituality/religiosity (e.g., McCullough *et al.*, 2000; Strawbridge *et al.*, 2001), generativity (e.g., An & Cooney, 2006; Cheng, 2009), and autonomy (e.g., Deci & Ryan, 2008). Precise, targeted conceptual models of SWB may facilitate the development of interventions that promote and enhance physical and psychosocial health.

Positive Psychology and Positive Health

In 1946 the World Health Organization (WHO) introduced a revised definition of health as "a state of complete physical, mental and social wellbeing and not merely the absence of disease or

Applied Topics in Health Psychology, First Edition. Edited by M. L. Caltabiano and L. Ricciardelli.
© 2013 John Wiley & Sons, Ltd. Published 2013 by John Wiley & Sons, Ltd.

infirmity" (WHO, 1946, p. 100). However, the traditional "disease model" of human functioning, which focused primarily on pathology, weaknesses, and treating illness, persisted. By including psychological and social aspects of individual health, concerns regarding wellbeing and satisfaction with life began to emerge.

Martin Seligman (2002, 2003) proposed a paradigm shift to a positive model of psychology, which focused on positive subjective experiences, strengths, and promoting health and wellbeing. Seligman and Csikszentmihalyi (2000) predicted that positive psychology would "allow psychologists to understand and build those factors that allow individuals, communities, and societies to flourish" (p. 13). Positive psychology, as a theoretical framework, does not imply the dichotomization of human experience into positive or negative; rather it views experience as a continuum that spans the whole spectrum of human experiences from health to illness and from distress to wellbeing (Keyes, 2002; WHO, 2005). For example, positive and negative psychological states can occur contiguously or even simultaneously, and even when faced with highly stressful circumstances, positive psychological states can occur (Folkman & Moskowitz, 2000).

Gable and Haidt (2005) defined positive psychology as "the study of the conditions and processes that contribute to the flourishing or optimal functioning of people, groups, and institutions" (p. 104). Seligman (2003) forwarded three pillars of positive psychology: positive subjective experiences (e.g., optimism, hope, happiness); positive individual characteristics (e.g., personal strengths that promote mental health); and positive social institutions and communities (e.g., those that contribute to individual happiness and health). According to Seligman and Csikszentmihalyi (2000), "the aim of Positive Psychology is to begin to catalyse a change in the focus of psychology from a preoccupation only with repairing the worst things in life to also building positive qualities" (p. 5).

A key contribution made by proponents of positive psychology has been the classification system forwarded by Peterson and Seligman's (2004) character strengths and virtues (CSV) model designed to provide a theoretical framework and common language to assist in developing interventions to enable human thriving. The CSV model provided six universal virtues endorsed by almost every culture and generation: wisdom and knowledge, courage, humanity, justice, temperance, and transcendence. The six virtues are comprised of 24 character strengths that can be reliably measured and used to sustain and even increase wellbeing (see Dahlsgaard *et al.*, 2005). Shared strength profiles can then be utilized to facilitate the development of specific interventions to enhance wellbeing and improve health outcomes.

Positive health

Seligman (2008) extended positive psychology to include the discipline of positive health. Seligman operationalized positive health as a combination of biological, subjective, and functional measures that promote emotional and physical wellbeing. Positive health interventions have been shown to enhance wellbeing and alleviate the effects of negative states, such as depression (see meta-analysis by Sin & Lyubomirsky, 2009), and provide a buffer against physical and mental illness, and future stress (Seligman, 2008).

Positive health outcomes are well documented in the epidemiological literature, which recognizes that promoting positive psychological health benefits physical health by improving overall health (see review Chida & Steptoe, 2008), lowering mortality, and increasing longevity (Diener & Chan, 2011). For example, positive emotions are associated with reduced incidences of stroke and improved poststroke survival rates (Ostir *et al.*, 2001), provide protection from coronary heart disease (Sanjuán *et al.*, 2010), and may influence inflammatory and coagulation factors that are involved in cardiovascular disease (Chida & Steptoe, 2008). Furthermore, positive emotions have been shown to decrease depression (Fava *et al.*, 2005), provide higher immune functioning (Segerstrom & Sephton, 2010), be protective against the rapid progression of HIV (Taylor *et al.*, 2000), are negatively correlated with obesity (de Wit *et al.*, 2010), and lower mortality rates among older people (Cohen & Pressman, 2006). Additionally, Chida and Steptoe's (2008) meta-analysis examining positive wellbeing and mortality in both healthy and diseased populations indicated that positive psychological wellbeing was related to lower mortality and increased longevity in both populations. Consequently, the last 50 years of wellbeing research have been focused on understanding, defining, operationalizing, and delineating the measurement of wellbeing in order to improve QOL.

Quality of Life and Wellbeing

Quality of Life emerged as a discipline in the 1970s and in 1975 McCall suggested that the best way to approach QOL was to measure the extent to which the individual's "happiness requirement" was met. However, there is little consensus of what constitutes happiness (see review by Schalock, 2000) and debate continues over the contributions of objective happiness (captured through measurement of brain waves) and subjective happiness (asking people how happy they feel) (Frey & Stutzer, 2002). Therefore, as the determinants of happiness are unresolved, it has been more productive at times to retreat and to measure QOL, which has received more rigorous empirical investigation (Eid & Larsen, 2008).

The construct of QOL is prominent in the health literature; however, there are over 100 definitions (Cummins 1997; Rapley 2003), which consist of a wide range of interpretations generating considerable conceptual confusion (Rapley 2003). Early efforts to define QOL took an objective (or economic indicator) approach to assessing the state of a nation's health; however, objective measures account for only a small proportion of an individual's subjectively reported QOL (Diener & Suh, 1997). For example, physical health can be ascribed to longevity statistics or the number of people with major illnesses. An aggregate of family wellbeing may be measured in divorce rate or incidents of domestic violence.

Previous research has established that measures of objective wellbeing, often referred to as social indicators, are easily measured (e.g., gross national product, infant mortality rate) and facilitate making comparisons between groups and across nations (Diener & Suh, 1997) Objective indicators also reflect aspects beyond economic indices, such as social issues (e.g., climate change, deforestation), which provide opportunities to initiate global solutions to societal problems (Diener & Suh, 1997). However, objective wellbeing measures fail to account for individual preferences, interests, goals, attitudes, and life history/experiences (Haq, 2009) and are only weakly correlated with life satisfaction (Cummins, 2000a, 2000b; Diener, 2000).

Australian and international research has confirmed that the power of more money to increase happiness is only significant at low incomes, and that once basic needs are met happiness does not increase as income rises (Cummins, 2006). Rojas (2006) found no correlation between income and subjective wellbeing (SWB). Recent studies have indicated that "relative income" in poor and middle-income countries, even in the context of extreme poverty, may be a better predictor of QOL than absolute income (Fafchamps & Shilpi, 2008; Guillen-Royo, 2011). Therefore, objective wellbeing indicators have been shown to be misleading indicators of life satisfaction as they provide an incomplete picture of one's QOL (Cummins, 1996, 2000a; Diener, 2003).

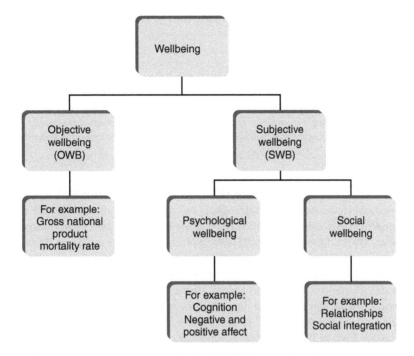

Figure 9.1 Conceptual diagram of the basic structure of wellbeing, consisting of both objective and subjective wellbeing.

The WHO Quality of Life Group (1995) defined QOL as "individuals' perception of their position in life in the context of the culture and value systems in which they live and in relation to their goals, expectations, standards, and concerns" (p. 1404). While the ideals of the WHO Quality of Life Group are admirable goals, a more precise definition is required to operationalize QOL for research purposes. Despite considerable debate about how to define QOL, the operational definition of wellbeing forwarded by Cummins (1996) has been widely accepted (Rapley, 2003) and adopted by the Australian Centre on Quality of Life (ACQOL), "Quality of life is both objective and subjective. Each of these two axes comprises several domains which, together, define the total construct. Objective domains are measured through culturally relevant indices of objective wellbeing. Subjective domains are measured through questions of satisfaction" (ACQOL, 2011, n.p.). SWB directly reflects an individual's self-assessment about individual preferences, satisfaction with life as a whole, sense of community, and happiness (Cummins, 1996; Diener, 1984). To assist in distinguishing QOL, objective wellbeing, and SWB, and based on a general synthesis of the literature, Figure 9.1 provides the structure of wellbeing as conceptualized by the authors of this chapter.

Subjective Wellbeing

The theoretical structure of SWB has been subjected to extensive empirical investigation for more than four decades (see reviews by Diener, 1984; Diener *et al.*, 1999); however, the study of SWB is still considered to be in its formative stages with considerable debate about theoretical structure, composition, conceptual characteristics, and how best to measure SWB. For the purpose of this discourse, a broad definition of SWB forwarded by Diener (2006) captures the essence of SWB:

> Subjective wellbeing refers to all of the various types of evaluations, both positive and negative, that people make of their lives. It includes reflective cognitive evaluations, such as life satisfaction and work satisfaction, interest and engagement, and affective reactions to life events, such as joy and sadness. Thus, subjective wellbeing is an umbrella term for the different valuations people make regarding their lives, the events happening to them, their bodies and minds, and the circumstances in which they live. (pp. 399–400)

Seminal research conducted by Bradburn (1969) provided evidence that SWB was at least a two-dimensional construct where positive affect (PA) and negative affect (NA) were shown to be independent of each other and influenced by different variables. Diener and colleagues (e.g., Diener *et al.*, 1985; Kuppens *et al.*, 2008) have conducted exhaustive studies on the two-factor (PA and NA) model of SWB and proposed that SWB had three distinct components: PA, NA, and life satisfaction (LS). Lucas *et al.* (1996) reported that SWB was comprised of multiple, separable components that were not strictly independent. High PA does not necessarily result in low NA, and LS was separable into specific life domains, such as domain satisfaction (or DS) (Oishi & Diener, 2001). Cognitive appraisals of LS and positive functioning have led to both global and domain-specific levels of SWB gaining prominence (e.g., Argyle, 2001; Diener *et al.*, 1999).

Further complicating the exploration into the composition and structure of SWB are bottom-up (e.g., social demographic status, such as education) and top-down (e.g., derived from personality traits) theories (see review by Diener, 1984). Early proponents of the bottom-up theory of SWB (e.g., Andrews & Withey, 1976) argued that the accumulation of satisfaction in many domains leads to satisfaction with life overall. Conversely, top-down theorists of SWB (e.g., Brief *et al.*, 1993) proposed that satisfaction with life as a whole can be attributed to satisfaction with life in specific domains. Bottom-up perspectives have been criticized for explaining only a small amount of the variance in wellbeing (Diener *et al.*, 1999), and top-down approaches have been criticized for explaining too much variance due to the overlap of predictor and criterion variables (Schmitte & Ryff, 1997). Other researchers (e.g., Mallard *et al.*, 1997) argued for a bidirectional model of SWB where bottom-up and top-down theories of SWB occur simultaneously and bidirectionally. Finally, more recent research conducted by González *et al.* (2010) provided an argument, based on the bottom-up approach, for the value of adopting a nonlinear approach to the measurement of life satisfaction and SWB.

Despite disagreement about the structure of SWB, it is generally accepted that there is no sole determinant of SWB and thus most SWB models are multidimensional. These include Ryff's (1989a, 1989b, 1995) six dimensions of psychological wellbeing (PWB) and Keyes' (1998; Keyes & Shapiro, 2004) five dimensions of social wellbeing. Due to possible confusion between acronyms, SWB will be used in this chapter to denote subjective wellbeing and Keyes' (1998) model will be referred to as the social wellbeing model. The International Wellbeing Group's (IWbG; 2006) model of personal wellbeing consisted of eight dimensions of SWB and a separate global measure of SWB. Recently, spirituality has been added as a new dimension of the personal wellbeing index–adult (PWI-A) version (Casas *et al.*, 2009; IWbG, 2006). Also recently, Diener *et al.* (2009) forwarded a conceptual hierarchical model of SWB, which consisted of four dimensions and 24 subdimensions. To assist in understanding some of the major models of SWB, Table 9.1 presents four models of SWB that are frequently used both nationally and internationally. They were selected based on their theoretical framework, their cross-national validation, and the extensive

Table 9.1 Prominent models of SWB, measures, dimensions, and psychometric strengths

Author(s)	Model	Measure	Dimensions	Psychometric properties
Cummins/ACQOL and the International Wellbeing Group (2003–2011) Australian Unity Wellbeing Index Project has measured the SWB of the Australian population twice a year since 2003.	Theory and model of subjective wellbeing homeostasis Represents a first-level deconstruction of satisfaction with life as a whole and adopts a domain-level approach to measure satisfaction with eight life areas. SWB is not free to vary as a function of changing external circumstances. It is actively managed to lie within a narrow, positive set point (mean is 75) by a system of homeostasis; however, in times of prolonged challenges it can fail (Cummins, 2010).	Personal wellbeing index–adult (PWI-A) Eight forced response questions rated on an 11-point Likert scale 0–10 that transform onto a 0–100 scale. And a one-item global satisfaction with life as a whole question reliably predicts 50% of the variance of satisfaction with life as a whole (Cummins et al., 2002).	Eight dimensions: 1. Standard of living 2. Health 3. Achievements 4. Relationships 5. Safety 6. Community 7. Future security 8. Spirituality	Construct validity, Cronbach's alpha = 0.71–0.85. Convergent validity = correlation of 0.78 with the satisfaction with life scale (Diener et al., 1985). Interdomain correlations 0.30–0.55 and item-total correlations are at least 0.50. Test–retest reliability across 1–2 week interval with an intra-class correlation coefficient of 0.84 (Lau et al., 2005). Emphasis on cross-cultural validity, which is useful considering multicultural societies and has been translated into 20 languages.
Diener et al. (1985) Most widely used scale in SWB research (Eid & Larsen, 2008)	Global satisfaction with life Diener's (2000) SWB model comprises three dimensions: (1) SWB covers the entire range of wellbeing from extremely unhappy to extremely happy; (2) it is solely the individual's internal experience, or perspective, that constitutes SWB; (3) SWB focuses on long-term states rather than momentary moods.	Satisfaction with life scale (SWLS)	Two dimensions: 1. Positive affect 2. Negative affect	Construct validity, Cronbach's alpha = 0.87. Convergent reliability with numerous SWB measures (Diener et al., 1985). Test–retest coefficient of 0.82 with a 2 month interval (Diener et al., 1985; Pavot & Diener, 2009). Similar findings by Yardley and Rice (1991). Temporal stability of 0.54 for 4 years and discriminant validity from emotional wellbeing measures (Pavot & Diener, 2009). Translated into 28 languages.

(continued)

Table 9.1 Prominent models of SWB, measures, dimensions, and psychometric strengths (*Continued*)

Author(s)	Model	Measure	Dimensions	Psychometric properties
Keyes (1998)	Social wellbeing	Social wellbeing scale Fifteen forced-response questions rated on an 6-point Likert scale (strongly agree to strongly disagree)	Five dimensions: 1. Social integration 2. Social acceptance 3. Social contribution 4. Social actualisation 5. Social coherence	Internal consistency, Cronbach's alpha = 0.57, identical to the average reliability of 0.57 with the general social survey over 6 years. Goodness of fit for the five-factor model ranged from 0.86 (small study) to 0.95 for large study (Keyes, 1998). Translated into at least three languages: French, Romanian, and Italian. The author acknowledged possible dimension overlap and suggests that social wellbeing may be unequally distributed in the population (Keyes, 1998; Keyes & Shapiro, 2004).
Ryff (1989a, 1989b)	Psychological wellbeing (PWB) The PWB scale has been used extensively to evaluate life change. For example, the change of self-concept through life's transitions (Kling *et al.*, 1997), variations of self in adult and elderly life (Ryff, 1995), success in growing older (Ryff, 1989a), and autonomy and wellbeing during life transitions (Showers & Ryff, 1996).	PWB scale Eighty-four forced-response questions rated on an 6-point Likert scale (strongly agree to strongly disagree)	Six dimensions: 1. Autonomy 2. Environmental mastery 3. Personal growth 4. Positive relations with others 5. Purpose in life 6. Self-acceptance	Internal consistency, Cronbach's alpha = 0.83–0.91) for each dimension and correlation with 20-item parent scale = 0.97–0.98 (Ryff & Keyes, 1995). Subscale intercorrelations were 0.30–0.76. Test–retest reliability 0.81–0.88 at 6 weeks (Ryff, 1989b). Translated into at least 18 different languages (Ryff & Singer, 1996). Construct validity failed to show six distinct dimensions (Springer *et al.*, 2006).

118

investigations focusing on their reliability and validity. Therefore, they provide some insight into the strengths and weaknesses of SWB models.

An early biological or set-point theory of SWB, the hedonic treadmill (Brickman & Campbell, 1971), proposed that positive and negative events temporarily disrupt the individual's average level of SWB; however, hedonic adaptation eventually returns to the individual's generally stable baseline level of SWB. However, extensive investigation of adaptation theory (see Diener, 2006; Fujita & Diener, 2005; Headey, 2008) has revealed that a person's set point is not neutral, and that coping temperament plays a role in the person's set point. Additionally, a person may have several set points, set points can be modified under certain conditions, and there are individual differences in rates of adaptation (Fujita & Diener 2005). Cummins' (1998, 2003, 2010) findings from the extensive data collected by the ACQOL since 2001 have provided substantial support that homeostasis is a key component of SWB, which is described as "a dispositional brain system that acts to keep each individual's wellbeing within a narrow positive range" (Cummins, 2010, p. 5). However, when the individual is stressed over time, the homeostasis system can fail, which can result in depression). Cummins also reported that SWB is "highly stable . . . normally restricted to the positive half of the dissatisfied – satisfied continuum" (Cummins, 2010, p. 3).

Diener and colleagues' perspectives on the effects of PA and NA have been validated repeatedly, and there is abundant evidence that PA and NA are important components of SWB (Diener, 2008; Eid & Larson, 2008). However, Diener and colleagues (2009) have recently proposed a more sophisticated model of SWB, which supports the multidimensional hypothesis of SWB and provided evidence for a hierarchical structure of SWB.

Keyes (1998) and Ryff (1989a, 1989b) proposed multidimensional, integrative models and measures of wellbeing. Ryff's six-dimensional PWB model was a forerunner of Keyes' five dimensional social wellbeing model. However, Keyes expressed uncertainty as to whether his social wellbeing dimensions overlap with some of Ryff's psychological wellbeing dimensions and he speculated that social wellbeing may be culture-bound and unequally distributed in the population (Keyes, 1998; Keyes & Shapiro, 2004). The structural validity of Ryff's model has been contested (see Burne & Machin, 2004; Springer *et al.*, 2006), however, Ryff (1995) conceded that two dimensions (self-acceptance and environmental mastery) were "highly correlated . . . and data – not theory – suggested a possible five-factor model" (p. 725). She also suggested augmenting data with information from other sources (e.g., observational methods) to increase the veracity of findings (Ryff & Keyes, 1995).

We propose that SWB is comprised of both psychological (e.g., cognition, affect) and social (e.g., relationships, social integration) dimensions, as well as other known but under-studied or undetermined factors, such as spirituality (Helliwell, 2003; Meyers, 2008; Myers & Diener, 1995) and generativity (e.g., Courtney, 2006; Courtney *et al.*, 2007a, 2007b; Strawbridge *et al.*, 2001). Figure 9.2 represents the authors' conceptualization of SWB.

Subpopulations

There are numerous SWB measurement issues that are pertinent to determining the structure of SWB and developing a testable framework, which is beyond the scope of this chapter. This chapter proposes that subpopulation differences need to be considered when developing SWB models so that precise interventions can be developed that address the specific needs of each subpopulation. Research has shown that many factors, such as gender (e.g., Alesina *et al.*, 2004), age (e.g., Easterlin, 2006), culture (e.g., Tov & Diener, 2009), personality (De Neve & Cooper, 1998), religion (e.g., Helliwell, 2003), ethnicity (e.g., Luttmer, 2005); political persuasion

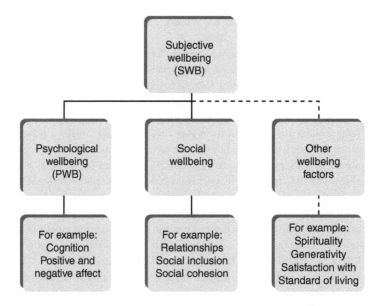

Figure 9.2 Proposed structure of SWB, which consists of psychological wellbeing, social wellbeing, and other wellbeing factors that are emerging in the literature (depicted with a dashed line).

(e.g., Graham & Pettinato, 2001), and so forth, are associated with differing levels of SWB. In order to elucidate subpopulation differences, the following section will briefly review gender, age, culture, personality, and spirituality as examples of personal characteristics that are not homogeneous.

Gender

When assessing health and wellbeing, Eckermann (2000) reported that QOL is not gender-neutral. Eckermann stressed how important it is for wellbeing measures to be "gender specific" (p. 37) in order to capture the subtle effects of gender and to fully understand the diversity between men and women's health experiences. For example, men in the USA suffer more severe chronic health conditions and a shorter lifespan of nearly seven years compared to women (Courtenay, 2011). Australian health statistics indicate that in 2008 men's death rates were 50% higher than women's (Australian Bureau of Statistics, 2010), yet men were less likely to engage in health behaviors linked with increased health and longevity (Courtenay, 2000, 2011). Compared to women, insufficient attention has been undertaken to address men's health and wellbeing, particularly to men in later life (Arber *et al.*, 2003); therefore, the sociostructural factors that contribute to men's health beliefs and behaviors are unidentified or under-studied (Courtenay, 2000, 2011).

Gender has been reported to have a greater influence on wellbeing than chronological age and gender differences have been attributed to the dramatic changes in gender roles over the last 50 years (Arber *et al.*, 2003). For instance, 21st century Western women are marrying later or not at all, delaying parenthood and having fewer children, and are likely to be engaged in full-time employment as well as being the primary family caregiver (Arber *et al.*, 2003). However, women typically have lower earnings, tremendous variability in their work history, and contribute less to superannuation than men (Arber *et al.*, 2003; Lalive & Stutzer, 2010). Despite women's disadvantaged living situation, women are not less satisfied with life than men (Arber *et al.*, 2003; Lalive & Stutzer, 2010). Men, on the other hand, are frequently not in the role of 'breadwinner', which can result in a loss of male identity, contribute to lower self-esteem and decreased SWB in men (Arber *et al.*, 2003; Courtenay, 2000, 2011).

While gender identity is commonly described as dichotomous, either male or female (McLean, 2008), sexual identity is better conceptualized as a bipolar continuum (Pedersen & Kristiansen, 2008). Individuals who fail to conform to heterosexual norms include lesbian women, gay men, bisexual women and men, and transgender people (LGBT people). Transgender is used as an umbrella term for people who identify as transsexual, cross-dressers, intersex, gender-queer, drag queens, and drag kings, which is consistent with terminology currently used by Queensland Association for Healthy Communities (2008). Nonconformity to heterosexual norms by LGBT individuals has resulted in discrimination toward this minority group, resulting in serious negative health and wellbeing consequences (Goodman & Moradi, 2008). LGBT individuals represent a significantly under-researched population with fewer than 1% of published studies; therefore, the factors that contribute to SWB for this minority group is relatively unknown (Kelley *et al.*, 2008).

Age

The effects of generational differences have been subjected to insufficient research (Reeves & Oh, 2007). Distinguishing between individuals who share historical and social experiences, and shared developmental stages, may lead to a better understanding of the effects of age on SWB (Kupperschmidt, 2000). Many studies suggest a U-shaped curve with higher levels of SWB at younger and older ages and the lowest levels of SWB in middle age (between 32 and 50 years of age) (Easterlin, 2006). Investigations of generational differences have been hampered by a lack of standardization in categorization (generational labels) and in chronology (span of years) that comprise specific generations (see review by Reeves & Oh, 2007). Additionally, researchers have acknowledged that individuals born close to the edges of given generations may share characteristics of more than one generation (Lancaster & Stillman, 2002). Reeves and Oh (2007), confirmed by Wong *et al.* (2008), cautioned that there are a variety of methodological limitations (e.g., cross-sectional, self-report research design, narrow demographic profiles) that reduce the reliability, validity, and generalizability of generational differences. However, other researchers (e.g., Lyons *et al.*, 2007) have found that generation is a useful variable in examining differences in social values. The impact of generational differences on psychological traits has led to a better understanding of the consequences of generational differences (e.g., such as in the workplace) (Twenge & Campbell, 2008). While stereotyping an entire group of individuals to a specific generation may fail to consider individual differences, it is logical to assume that individuals who share similar economic, historic, social, and technological environments would share distinct values and beliefs, such as attitudes towards career goals, education, and political orientation (see Debard, 2004). Despite disagreement on generational labels, and birth years that comprise each label, the chapter authors have distilled from the research commonly held generational labels and dates, which are presented in Table 9.2.

There is value in considering generational differences when conceptualizing SWB models for subpopulations. For example, baby boomers (individuals born from 1946 to 1964) have historically been investigated as one homogeneous cohort. However, research conducted by Courtney (2006) and Courtney *et al.* (2007a, 2007b) has provided evidence that there are at least two distinct cohorts of Australian baby-boomer career women – early baby boomers born from 1946 to 1954 and late

Table 9.2 Commonly used generational labels and birth dates

Label	Silent generation	Baby boomer generation	Generation X	Generation Y	Generation Z
Birth date	1925–1945	1946–1964	1965–1980	1981–2000	2001–present

baby boomers born from 1955 to 1964 – with evidence that there may be three or four distinct baby-boomer cohorts. Therefore, when developing SWB conceptual models, generational subgroups may provide insight into the development of interventions that are salient to specific cohorts.

Culture

More than 10 years ago Diener and colleagues (Diener *et al.*, 1999; Diener & Suh, 1997, 2000) cautioned that one of the central weaknesses of SWB models is that they may not adequately reflect a particular geographical location or culture and that SWB measures may have different meanings in different cultures. For example, a consistent finding in the SWB literature is that individuals from Eastern cultures tend to report lower levels of SWB compared with Western cultures (Lau *et al.*, 2005). Even within a country, such as the USA, levels of ethnic diversity mirror cross-national findings: Asian-Americans reported lower SWB than European-Americans (e.g., Okazaki, 2000; Schkade & Kahneman, 1998); therefore, it is difficult to disentangle cultural differences.

Further complicating issues of cross-cultural comparisons were revealed in a recent study conducted by Scollon *et al.* (2009) investigating European-American, Asian-American, Japanese, Indian, and Hispanic students. Their findings revealed that the three Asian groups (Asian, Japanese, and Indian) had lower levels of pleasant emotions compared with European-Americans and Hispanic groups, a finding consistent with cultural norms. Additionally, European-Americans' global past-week satisfaction with life was more positive than their average satisfaction for each day of the week (Scollon *et al.*, 2009). Asian-American participants did not demonstrate a significant difference between global and daily satisfaction (Oishi, 2002). Similar findings have been reported by Kim-Prieto (2005) researching European-Americans and Asians. Therefore, Tov and Diener (2009) cautioned that "by equating entire nations with single cultures, we risk overlooking important differences within nations, as well as similarities that extend beyond national borders" (p. 33). For example, when making cross-cultural comparisons about SWB, the effects of gender and age (e.g., the effects of shared experiences and common histories) need to be considered (Lucas & Gohm, 2000).

Personality

A considerable amount of research has been conducted exploring the relationship between personality and SWB. For example, early empirical research by Costa and McCrae (1980) posited that much of the variance of SWB could be accounted for by personality. Specifically, PA was shown to be correlated with extroversion and NA correlated with neuroticism. De Neve and Cooper (1998) summarized the correlations of 137 personality traits with SWB. These findings were subsequently replicated repeatedly (see review by De Neve & Cooper, 1998). More recently, personality has been shown to be one of the strongest predictors of SWB (see meta-analyses by Ozer & Benet-Martínez, 2006; Steel *et al.*, 2008). For example, individuals who are extroverts are thought to create more positive life events and have more socially fulfilling relationships, and therefore they are considered happier compared with individuals with a neurotic personality type (Hills *et al.*, 2000). Ozer and Benet-Martínez (2006) found that personality is also correlated with SWB behaviors, such as occupational choice and community involvement. Additionally, the similarity between PA and extroversion, and NA and neuroticism, suggests that if these are not the same constructs then there is considerable overlap (Lucas & Fujita, 2000).

There are abundant studies that report a strong correlation between optimism, pessimism, and SWB (see review Carver & Scheier, 2002) and optimism is a significant predictor of positive health outcomes (see review by Rasmussen *et al.*, 2009). Scheier and Carver (1985) proposed that optimists and pessimists have different expectations of their ability to achieve goals. Optimists believe that their actions will achieve their goals, so therefore they tend to persist in those actions longer than pessimists. Also, optimists manage critical life situations better than pessimists and deal with stress using a problem-focused coping strategy, which is more successful than the emotion-focused coping strategy of pessimists (Scheier & Carver, 1985; Scheier *et al.*, 1994). Chang's (2002) review provided a model where optimism/pessimism influenced life satisfaction indirectly but was mediated by PA and NA. However, there is no consensus regarding whether optimism/pessimism affects SWB directly or indirectly, or is instead a mediator between positive and negative outcome expectancies. Additionally, when considering dispositional optimism/pessimism and their effects on SWB, there are many other factors, such as considerations of age and cultural differences on dispositional optimism, that need to be considered (e.g., You *et al.*, 2009). However, what is known about optimism is that it is a learned skill and that once it has been learned it increases positive health outcomes (Seligman, 1993).

Spirituality and religiosity

Previous research has established a link between spirituality and/or religiosity with SWB (e.g., Cohen, 2002; Wills, 2009) and yet these factors are generally absent from SWB models. The relationship between spirituality, religion, and health has received increased interest. For example, more than 1000 studies have reported positive correlations of spirituality and/or religiosity with health and healing (Meyers, 2008) and with longevity (McCullough & Laurenceau, 2005). The most recent edition of the *Diagnostic and Statistical Manual of Mental Disorders* (American Psychiatric Association, 1994) acknowledges religions and spiritual issues as normal and important factors to be considered in diagnosis. Spirituality/religiosity has been shown to be a predictor of health and longevity that even rivals nonsmoking and the effects of exercise (Oman *et al.*, 2002). Over 20 studies have associated attendance at religious services with lower mortality from all causes, even when the contributions of age, gender, healthy behaviors, and social support were controlled for (see meta-analysis by McCullough *et al.*, 2000). Abundant research has established that spirituality and religious participation is associated with a myriad of health-related benefits, such as lower incidence of disabilities among older people (Idler & Kasl, 1997), reduced alcohol and substance abuse (Zemore & Kaskutas, 2004), reduced risk of depression, especially for individuals experiencing stressful circumstances (Smith *et al.*, 2003), and better health practices in adolescents (Wallace & Forman, 1998). Unfortunately, most of the studies are correlational, and it is conceded that individuals who engage in religious and/or spiritual practices regularly generally lead healthier lifestyles and have superior social support, which may contribute to these positive correlations (Strawbridge *et al.*, 2001). Nevertheless, these findings provide a compelling argument for spirituality and religion to be included in models of SWB.

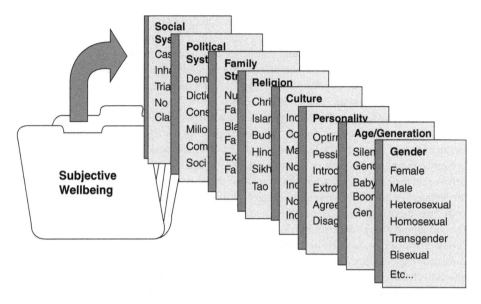

Figure 9.3 This figure provides some of the many types of subgroups that may need to be considered when developing conceptual models of SWB.

Other individual differences

In order to develop conceptual SWB models it is necessary to consider how well a measurement model fits a population. The previous section has clarified that populations are not homogenous groups of people sharing the same life experiences. With globalization and multicultural societies it is essential to consider population heterogeneity, or distinct subpopulations, in order to develop conceptual SWB models that are sensitive to differing attitudes and expectations. Figure 9.3 provides an illustration of just some of the many subpopulations that may warrant consideration.

Future Directions

Advances in psychometrics (e.g., reliability, validity, improved construction of self-report measures) have contributed to the development of more sophisticated models and measures of SWB. However, the state of SWB measurement issues was summarized by Diener and Seligman (2004) as "a haphazard mix of different measures of varying quality, usually taken from non-representative samples of respondents" (p. 4). Here we present four measurement issues: definitional issues, research design issues, measurement issues, and more sophisticated data-analysis techniques. Detailed accounts of measurement issues are available from Diener *et al.* (2009) and Pavot (2008).

Definitional issues

The debate regarding the definition of SWB is understandable as the components of SWB are still emerging. However, Diener proposed a set of guidelines and recommendations for the development of national indicators of SWB (Diener, 2006; Diener & Seligman, 2004) which could have been used to provide standardized terminology, which might have been useful in working towards more comprehensive assessments of wellbeing (Diener & Seligman, 2004). Unfortunately, the guidelines proposed by Diener (2006) have not been widely accepted and terminological confusion is exacerbating the progress toward a conceptual definition of SWB. On the other hand, while consensus on a definition of SWB is desirable to operationalize SWB, definitions provided by current theorists (e.g., Cummins, Diener) are fairly explicit and have been open to revision when new SWB dimensions have become apparent from advances in research.

Research design issues

Pavot (2008) suggested that despite advances in SWB research and assessment, there are a number of research design issues, "such as over-reliance on single method, cross-sectional designs and the use of narrow measures that provide only a partial assessment of SWB, have combined to limit the generality of the findings from individual studies" (p. 125). Diener (2008) advocated more experimental and longitudinal studies of SWB and proposed using multimethod approaches to capture external validation of self-report measures. Multimethod approaches could combine self-report questionnaires with peer reports, observational methods, handwritten autobiographies, or physiological methods (Diener, 2008; Ryff & Keyes, 1995). Furthermore, cross-sectional and cross-national studies need to use the same measure and standard sampling strategies. Alternative strategies, such as experience sampling methodology (ESM) (Diener, 2000) and the day reconstruction method (DRM) (Kahneman *et al.*, 2004), may also contribute to capturing aspects of SWB.

Measurement issues

The reliability and validity of SWB rating scales were initially challenged in the literature; however, current scales have been empirically tested and generally demonstrate strong psychometric properties (Donohue *et al.*, 2003). Recognition of reliability and validity weaknesses have resulted in reviews of SWB scales to address shortcomings (e.g., Ryff & Keyes, 1995; Springer *et al.*, 2006). For example, Diener and Seligman (2004) reported that a high percentage of SWB studies use only one or two of the three SWB components that they identified (e.g., many studies include PA and NA, but not LS). In short, they provide incomplete assessments of SWB.

As the configuration of SWB is evolving, it is crucial that SWB measures are sensitive to emerging factors. For example, the PWI-A is a reliable, valid, and sensitive instrument (IWbG, 2006); however, Cummins (2002) reminds us that this measure is a work in progress. Recently, Diener and colleagues (2010) introduced two new wellbeing measures – the flourishing scale (FS) and the scale of positive and negative experiences (SPANE) – which are intended to compliment other SWB measures. Therefore, SWB measures require review to accommodate new knowledge and more sophisticated data-analysis techniques, which may capture the complexity of SWB.

Sophisticated data-analysis techniques

Advances in structural equation modelling using AMOS (Arbuckle, 2009) and MPlus (Muthén & Muthén, 2009) have contributed to a better understanding of multidimensional, hierarchical constructs, such as SWB. Gruenewald *et al.* (2008) proposed that recursive partitioning can be employed as an analytical technique, which is especially useful in delineating subgroup differences and detecting meaningful patterns in complex datasets. Tay *et al.* (2011) suggested that multilevel mixed-measurement item response theory (MMM-IRT) analysis should be considered in SWB research to assist in cross-cultural and cross-national self-report analysis. MMM-IRT analysis is a methodological approach that "uses information from observed hierarchical groups and item responses to infer individual-level measurement classes and hierarchical classes simultaneously" (Tay *et al.*, 2011, p. 201). More sophisticated data-analysis techniques will make it possible to investigate the relationships between the determinates of SWB more decisively, which will contribute to the understanding of SWB.

Conclusion

It has been more than 60 years since the WHO (1946) redefined health as "a state of complete physical, mental and social wellbeing". Moreover, 25 years have elapsed since the WHO referred to health as "a resource for everyday life...health is a positive concept emphasizing social and personal resources, as well as physical capacities" (WHO, 1986, n.p.). Achieving the health goals as set forth by WHO depend on our understanding of SWB and the health consequences of both negative and positive SWB.

Over the last few decades, considerable progress has been made in the development of theoretical models of SWB, with new dimensions, models, and measures of SWB being refined by prominent researchers (e.g., Cummins, Deci, Diener, Ryan, Ryff, Keyes, Seligman). Despite the considerable contributions that have been made to the study of SWB, there remains a lack of consensus on the definition, composition, and structure of SWB. Rather than a shortcoming, this debate has enhanced the exploration of the many facets of SWB, which have contributed tremendously to the understanding of this field of research. However, current models and measures of SWB probably provide an incomplete picture of an individual's subjective level of life satisfaction.

The field of positive psychology has gained traction in the last 10 years and Seligman and colleagues' (2005) review found specific interventions that make people happier, which has implications for the future of positive interventions and perhaps for clinical interventions. However, positive psychology has been critiqued by Christopher *et al.* (2008) as "one-sided individualism of American society with its stress on personal autonomy and individually-defined fulfilment" (p. 557). Progress in research using a positive health perspective has focused researchers on the potential that advances in the understanding of SWB has on health. This chapter has forwarded abundant evidence-based research that confirms that SWB is a strong predictor of physical and mental health, reduced mortality, and increased longevity. Therefore, it is crucial to continue to investigate the structure and composition of SWB, and to disentangle the varied interpretations of SWB, so that it can be accurately measured and monitored. Monitoring changes in SWB will provide an insight into the factors that increase or decrease one's SWB so that interventions can be evaluated for effectiveness.

One strategy to developing effective SWB interventions would be to develop SWB conceptual models that recognize subpopulation differences. This would allow for interventions to be developed that target factors that are most salient to specific subpopulations and therefore increase the effectiveness of the intervention. Development of SWB conceptual models should also contribute to the overall understanding of the composition and structure of SWB, thus ensuring that people are not only happier but also healthier.

> [H]ealth is a state of wellbeing in which the individual realizes his or her own abilities, can cope with the normal stresses of life, can work productively and fruitfully, and is able to make a contribution to his or her community. (WHO, 2001, n.p.)

References

ACQOL. (2011). *Introduction: Definition of Quality of Life.* www.deakin.edu.au/research/acqol/introduction/.

Alesina, A. R., Di Tella, R., & McCullough, R. J. (2004). Inequality and happiness: Are Europeans and Americans different? *Journal of Public Economics, 88,* 2009–2042.

American Psychiatric Association. (1994). *Diagnostic and Statistical Manual of Mental Disorders IV* (4th edn.). Washington DC: American Psychiatric Association.

An, J. S., & Cooney, T. (2006). Psychological well-being in mid to late life: The role of generativity development and parent-child relationships across the lifespan. *International Journal of Behavioral Development, 30,* 20–31.

Andrews, F. M., & Withey, S. B. (1976). *Social Indicators of Well-Being: American's Conception of Life Quality.* New York: Plenum.

Arber, S., Davidson, K., & Ginn, J. (2003). Changing approaches to gender and later life. In S. Arber & K. Davidson (Eds.), *In Gender and Ageing: Changing Roles and Relationships* (pp. 1–13). Philadelphia, PA: McGraw-Hill.

Arbuckle, J. L. (2009). *Amos 18 User's Guide.* Crawfordville, FL: AMOS Development.

Argyle, M. (2001). *The Psychology of Happiness.* New York: Taylor & Francis.

Australian Bureau of Statistics. (2010). *Men's Health.* www.ausstats.abs.gov.au/ausstats/.

Bradburn, M. M. (1969). *The Structure of Psychological Well-Being.* Chicago, IL: Aldine.

Brickman, P., & Campbell, D. T. (1971). Hedonic relativism and planning the good society. In M. H. Apley (Ed.), *Adaptation-Level Theory: A Symposium* (pp. 287–302). New York: Academic Press.

Brief, A. P., Butcher, A. H., George, J. M., & Link, K. E. (1993). Integrating bottom-up and top-down theories of subjective well-being: The case of health. *Journal of Personality and Social Psychology, 64*(4), 646–653.

Burne R. A., & Machin, A. (2008). Investigating the structural validity of Ryff's Psychological Well-being Scale across two samples. *Social Indicators Research, 93*(2), 359–375.

Carver, C. S., & Scheier, M. F. (2002). Optimism. In C. R. Snyder & S. J. Lopez (Eds.), *Handbook of Positive Psychology* (pp. 31–52). Oxford: Oxford University Press.

Casas, F., González, M., Figuer, C., & Malo, S. (2009). Satisfaction with spirituality and with religion, and personal well-being among Spanish adolescents and young university students. *Applied Research in Quality of Life, 4*(1), 23–45.

Chang, E. (2002). Optimism-pessimism and stress appraisal: Testing a cognitive interactive model of psychological adjustment in adults. *Cognitive Therapy and Research, 26,* 675–690.

Cheng, S. (2009). Generativity in later life: Perceived respect from younger generations as a determinant of goal disengagement and psychological well-being. *Journals of Gerontology, Series B: Psychological Science and Social Science, 64B*(1), 45–54.

Chida, Y., & Steptoe, A. (2008). Positive psychological well-being and mortality: A quantitative review of prospective observational studies. *Psychosomatic Medicine, 70,* 741–756.

Christopher, J. C., Richardson, F. E., & Slife, B. D. (2008). Thinking about positive psychology. *Theory & Psychology, 18,* 555–561.

Cohen, A. B. (2002). The importance of spirituality in well-being for Jews and Christians. *Journal of Happiness Studies, 3,* 287–310.

Cohen, S., & Pressman, S.D. (2006). Positive affect and health. *Current Directions in Psychological Science, 15,* 122–125.

Costa, P. T., & McCrae, R. R. (1980). Still stable after all these years: Personality as a key to some issues in adulthood and old age. In P. B. Baltes & O. G. Brim (Eds.), *Lifespan Development and Behaviour* (3rd edn.) (pp. 65–102). New York, NY: Academic Press.

Courtenay, W. (2000). Constructions of masculinity and their influence on men's well-being: A theory of gender and health. *Social Science & Medicine, 50,* 1385–1401.

Courtenay, W. (2011). *Dying to be Men: Psychosocial, Environmental, and Biobehavioral Directions in Promoting the Health of Men and Boys.* New York: Routledge.

Courtney, L. (2006). *Voices of Australian baby boom career women: Preliminary findings from focus groups.* Paper presented at the Australasian Centre on Aging 5th National Conference for Emerging Researchers in Ageing (pp. 86–93), 21 November, Sydney.

Courtney, L., Caltabiano, N., & Caltabiano, M. (2007a). *Focus group findings: Successful ageing of Australian Baby Boom Career Women.* Paper presented at the 42nd Annual Conference of the Australian Psychology Society (pp. 254–260), 25–29 September, Brisbane.

Courtney, L., Caltabiano, N., & Caltabiano, M. (2007b). *Psychosocial well-being predictors of successful ageing of Australian baby boom career women: Main focus group findings.* Paper presented at the 39th Annual National Conference of the Association of Gerontology (pp. 41–51), November 23–24, 2006, Sydney.

Cummins, R. A. (1996). The domains of life satisfaction: An attempt to order chaos. *Social Indicators Research, 38,* 303–328.

Cummins, R. A. (1997). Assessing quality of life. In R. I. Brown (Ed.), *Quality of Life for People with Disabilities: Models, Research and Practice* (2nd edn.) (pp. 116–150). Cheltenham: Stanley Thornes.

Cummins, R. A. (1998). The second approximation to an international standard of life satisfaction. *Social Indicators Research, 43,* 307–334.

Cummins, R. A. (2000a). Objective and subjective quality of life: An interactive model. *Social Indicators Research, 52,* 55–72.

Cummins, R. A. (2000b). Personal income and subjective well-being: A review. *Journal of Happiness Studies, 1,* 133–158.

Cummins, R. A. (2002). *Vale ComQol: Caveats to Using the Comprehensive Quality of Life Scale: Welcome the Personal Wellbeing Index.* Melbourne: Deakin University. http://acqol.deakin.edu.au/instruments/ Caveats_ComQol_scales.doc.

Cummins, R. A. (2003). Normative life satisfaction: Measurement issues and a homeostatic model. *Social Indicators Research, 64,* 225–256.

Cummins, R. A. (2006). *Australian Unity Well-being Index: Report 16.0 The Well-being of Australians – Mortgage Payments and Home Ownership.* Melbourne: Australian Centre on Quality of Life, School of Psychology, Deakin University.

Cummins R. A. (2010). Subjective wellbeing, homeostatically protected mood and depression: A synthesis. *Journal of Happiness Studies, 11,* 1–17.

Cummins, R. A., Eckersley, R., Pallant, J., Van Vugt, J., & Misajon, R. (2002). *The Australian Unity Wellbeing Index Survey 4: Australian Centre on Quality of Life.* Melbourne: Deakin University.

Dahlsgaard, K., Peterson, C., & Seligman, M.E.P. (2005). Shared virtue: The convergence of valued human strengths across culture and history. *Review of General Psychology, 9,* 203–213.

Debard, R. D. (2004). Millennials coming to college. In R. D. Debard & M. D. Coomes (Eds.), *Serving the Millennial Generation: New Directions for Student Services* (pp. 33–45). San Francisco, CA: Jossey-Bass.

Deci, E. L., & Ryan, R. M. (2008). Facilitating optimal motivation and psychological well-being across life's domains. *Canadian Psychology, 49,* 14–23.

De Neve, K. M., & Cooper, H. (1998). The happy personality: A meta-analysis of 137 personality traits and subjective well-being. *Psychological Bulletin, 124,* 197–229.

de Wit, L., Luppino, F., van Straten, A., Penninix, B., Zitman, F., & Cuijpers, P. (2010). Depression and obesity: A meta-analysis of community-based studies. *Psychiatry Research, 178,* 230–235.

Diener, E. (1984). Subjective well-being. *Psychological Bulletin, 95,* 542–575.

Diener, E. (2000). Subjective well-being: The science of happiness, and a proposal for a national index. *American Psychologist, 55,* 34–43.

Diener, E. (2003). What is positive about positive psychology: The curmudgeon and Pollyanna. *Psychological Inquiry, 14,* 115–120.

Diener, E. (2006). Guidelines for national indicators of subjective well-being and ill-being. *Applied Research in Quality of Life, 1,* 151–157.

Diener, E. (2008). Myths and directions for future research. In M. Eid & Larsen, R. J. (Eds.), *The Science of Subjective Well-Being* (pp. 493–514). New York: Guilford Press.

Diener, E., & Suh, E. (1997). Measuring quality of life: Economic, social, and subjective indicators. *Social Indicators Research, 40,* 189–216.

Diener, E., & Suh, E. M. (Eds.) (2000). *Culture and Subjective Well-being.* Cambridge, MA: MIT Press.

Diener, E., & Seligman, M. E. P. (2004). Beyond money: Toward and economy of well-being. *Psychological Science in the Public Interest, 5,* 1–31.

Diener, E., & Chan, M. (2011). Happy people live longer: Subjective well-being contributes to health and longevity. *Applied Psychology: Health and Well-being, 2,* 1–43.

Diener, E., Emmons, R. A., Larsen, R. J., & Griffin, S. (1985). The Satisfaction with Life scale. *Journal of Personality Assessment, 49,* 71–75.

Diener, E., Suh, E. M., Lucas, R. E., & Smith, H. E. (1999). Subjective well-being: Three decades of progress. *Psychological Bulletin, 125,* 276–302.

Diener, E., Lucas, R., & Scollon, C. N. (2009). Beyond the hedonic treadmill: Revising the adaptation theory of well-being. In E. Diener (Ed.), *The Science of Well-Being: The Collected Works of Ed Diener* (pp. 103–118). Social Indicators Research Series 37. London: Springer.

Diener, E., Wirtz, D., Tov, W., Kim-Prieto, C., Choi, D.-W., Oishi, S., & Biswas-Diener, R. (2010). New well-being measures: Short scales to assess flourishing and positive and negative feelings. *Social Indicators Research, 97,* 143–156.

Donohue, B., Teichner, G., Azrin, N., Weintraub, N., Crum, T. A., Murphy, L., & Sliver, N. C. (2003). Initial reliability and validity of the Life Satisfaction scale for problem youth in a sample of drug abusing and conduct disordered youth. *Journal of Child and Family Studies, 12,* 453–464.

Easterlin, R. (2006). Life cycle happiness and its sources. Intersections of psychology, economics and demography. *Journal of Economic Psychology, 27,* 463–482.

Eckermann L. (2000). Gendering indicators of health and well being: Is quality of life gender neutral? *Social Indicators Research, 52,* 29–54.

Eid, M., & Larsen, R. J. (Eds.) (2008). *The Science of Subjective Well-Being.* New York: Guilford Press.

Fafchamps, M., & Shilpi, F. (2008). Subjective welfare, isolation, and relative consumption. *Journal of Development Economics, 86,* 43–60.

Fava, G. A., Ruine, C., Rafanelli, C., Finos, L., Salmaso, L., Mangelli, L., & Sirigatti, S. (2005). Well-being therapy of generalized anxiety disorder. *Psychotherapy and Psychosomatics, 74,* 26–30.

Folkman, S., & Moskowitz, J. T. (2000). Positive affect and the other side of coping. *American Psychologist, 55,* 647–654.

Frey, B., & Stutzer, A. (2002). *Happiness and Economics: How the Economy and Institutions Affect Well-Being.* Princeton, NJ: Princeton University Press.

Fujita, F., & Diener, E. (2005). Life satisfaction set-point: Stability and change. *Journal of Personality and Social Psychology, 88,* 158–164.

Gable, S. L., & Haidt, J. (2005). What (and why) is positive psychology? *Review of General Psychology, 9,* 103–110.

González, M., Coenders, G., Saez, M., & Casas, F. (2010). Non-linearity, complexity and limited measurement in the relationship between satisfaction with specific life domains and satisfaction with life as a whole. *Journal of Happiness Studies, 11,* 335–352.

Goodman, M., & Moradi, B. (2008). Attitudes and behaviors toward lesbian and gay persons: Critical correlates and mediated relations. *Journal of Counseling Psychology, 55,* 371–384.

Graham, C., & Pettinato, S. (2001). Happiness, markets and democracy: Latin America in comparative perspective. *Journal of Happiness Studies, 2,* 237–268.

Gruenewald, T. L., Ryff, C. D., Mroczek, D. K., & Singer, B. H. (2008). Diverse pathways to positive and negative affect in adulthood and later life: An integrative approach using recursive partitioning. *Developmental Psychology, 44,* 330–343.

Guillen-Royo, M. (2011). Reference group consumption and the subjective wellbeing of the poor in Peru. *Journal of Economic Psychology, 32,* 259–272.

Haq, R. (2009). Measuring human wellbeing in Pakistan: Objective versus subjective indicators. *European Journal of Social Sciences, 9,* 516–529.

Headey, B. (2008). The set-point theory of well-being: Negative results and consequent revisions. *Social Indicators Research, 85,* 389–404.

Helliwell, J. F. (2003), "How's life?" Combining individual and national variables to explain subjective well-being. *Economic Modelling, 20,* 331–360.

Hills, P., Argyle, M., & Reeves, R. (2000). Individual differences in leisure satisfactions: An investigation of four theories of leisure motivation. *Personality and Individual Differences, 28,* 763–779.

Idler, E. L., & Kasl, S. V. (1997). Religion among disabled and nondisabled persons: Attendance at religious services as a predictor of the course of disability. *Journals of Gerontology. Series B, Psychological Sciences and Social Sciences, 52,* S306–S316.

International Wellbeing Group (IWbG) (2006). *Personal Wellbeing Index Manual.* Melbourne: Deakin University. www.deakin.edu.au/research/acqol/instruments/well-being_index.htm.

Kahneman, D., Krueger, A., Schkade, D., Schwarz, N., & Stone, A. (2004). A survey method for characterizing daily life experience: The day reconstruction method (DRM). *Science, 306,* 1776–1780.

Kelley, L., Chou, C. L., Dibble, S. L., & Robertson, P. A. (2008). A critical intervention in lesbian, gay, bisexual, and transgender health: Knowledge and attitude outcomes among second-year medical students. *Teaching and Learning in Medicine, 20,* 248–253.

Keyes, C. L. M. (1998). Social wellbeing. *Social Psychology Quarterly, 61,* 121–140.

Keyes, C. L. M. (2002). The mental health continuum: From languishing to flourishing in life. *Journal of Health and Social Behavior, 43,* 207–222.

Keyes, C. M., & Shapiro, A. D. (2004). Social wellbeing in the United States: A descriptive epidemiology. In O. Brim, C. Ryff, & R. C. Kessler (Eds.), *How Healthy are We? A National Study of Wellbeing at Midlife* (pp. 350–372). Chicago, IL: University of Chicago Press.

Kim-Prieto, C. Y. (2005). *Culture's Influence on Experienced and Remembered Emotions.* Unpublished doctoral dissertation, University of Illinois, Urbana-Champaign, IL.

Kling, K. C., Ryff, C. D., & Essex, M. J. (1997). Adaptive changes in the self-concept during a life transition. *Personality and Social Psychology Bulletin, 23,* 989–998.

Kuppens, P., Realo, A., & Diender, E. (2008). The roles of positive and negative emotions in life satisfaction judgement. *Journal of Personality and Social Psychology, 95,* 66–75.

Kupperschmidt, B. R. (2000). Multigeneration employees: Strategies for effective management. *The Health Care Manager, 19,* 65–76.

Lalive, R., & Stutzer, A. (2010). Approval of equal rights and gender differences in well-being. *Journal of Population Economics, 23,* 933–962.

Lancaster, L. C., & Stillman, D. (2002). *When Generations Collide. Who They Are? Why They Clash? How to Solve the Generational Puzzle at Work.* New York: Collins Business.

Lau, A. L. D., Cummins, R. A., & McPherson, W. (2005). An investigation into the cross-cultural equivalence of the Personal Wellbeing Index. *Social Indicators Research, 72,* 403–430.

Lucas, R. E., & Fujita, F. (2000). Factors influencing the relation between extraversion and pleasant affect. *Journal of Personality and Social Psychology, 79,* 1039–1056.

Lucas, R., & Gohm, C. L. (2000). Age and sex differences in subjective well-being across cultures. In E. Diener & E. M. Suh (Eds.), *Culture and subjective well-being* (pp. 291–317). Cambridge, MA: The MIT Press.

Lucas, R., Diener, E., & Suh, E. (1996). Discriminate validity of wellbeing measures. *Journal of Personality and Social Psychology, 71,* 616–628.

Luttmer, E. F. (2005). Neighbors as negatives: Relative earnings and well-being. *The Quarterly Journal of Economics, 120,* 963–1002.

Lyons, S. T., Duxbury, L., & Higgins, C. (2007). An empirical assessment of generational differences in basic human values. *Psychological Reports, 101,* 339–352.

Mallard, A. G. C., Lance, C. E., & Michalos, A. C. (1997). Culture as a moderator of overall life satisfaction – life facet satisfaction relationships. *Social Indicators Research, 40,* 259–284.

McCall, S. (1975). Quality of life. *Social Indicators Research, 2,* 229–248.

McCullough, M. E., & Laurenceau, J. P. (2005). Religiousness and the trajectory of self-rated health across adulthood. *Personality and Social Psychology Bulletin, 31,* 560–573.

McCullough, M. E., Hoyt, W. T., Larson, D. B., Koenig, H. G., & Thoresen, C. (2000). Religious involvement and mortality: A meta-analytic review. *Health Psychology, 19,* 211–222.

McLean, K. (2008). Inside, outside, nowhere: Bisexual men and women in the gay and lesbian community. *Journal of Bisexuality, 8,* 63–80.

Meyers, D. (2008). Religion and human flourishing. In M. Eid & R. J. Larsen (Eds.), *The Science of Subjective Well-Being* (pp. 323–346). New York: Guilford Press.

Muthén, L. K., & Muthén, B. O. (2009). *M-Plus® Statistical Analysis with Latent Variables: User's Guide* (5th edn.). Los Angeles, CA: Muthén & Muthén.

Myers, D. G., & Diener, E. (1995). Who is happy? *Psychological Science, 6,* 10–19.

Oishi, S. (2002). Experiencing and remembering of well-being: A cross-cultural analysis. *Personality and Social Psychology Bulletin, 28,* 1398–1406.

Oishi, S., & Diener, E. (2001). Re-examining the general positivity model of subjective well-being: The discrepancy between specific and global domain satisfaction. *Journal of Personality, 69,* 641–666.

Okazaki, S. (2000). Asian American and White American differences on affective distress symptoms: Do symptom reports differ across reporting methods? *Journal of Cross-Cultural Psychology, 31,* 603–625.

Oman, D., Kurata, J. H., Strawbridge, W. J., & Cohen, R. D. (2002). Religious attendance and cause of death over 31 years. *International Journal of Psychiatry in Medicine, 32,* 69–89.

Ostir, G. V., Markides, K. S., Peek, M. K., & Goodwin, J. S. (2001). The association between emotional well-being and the incidence of stroke in older adults. *Psychosomatic Medicine, 63,* 210–215.

Ozer, D. J., & Benet-Martínez, V. (2006). Personality and the prediction of consequential outcomes. *Annual Review of Psychology, 57,* 401–412.

Pavot, W. (2008). The structure of well-being. In M. Eid & R. J. Larsen (Eds.), *The Science of Subjective Well-Being* (pp. 124–140). New York: Guilford Press.

Pavot, W., & Diener, E. (2009). Review of the Satisfaction with Life scale. In E. Diener (Ed.), *Assessing Well-Being: The Collected Works of Ed Diener* (pp. 101–117). Social Indicators Research Series 39. London: Springer.

Pedersen, W., & Kristiansen, H. (2008). Homosexual experience, desire and identity among young adults. *Journal of Homosexuality, 54,* 68–102.

Peterson, C., & Seligman, M. E. P. (2004). *Character Strengths and Virtues: A Classification and Handbook.* New York: American Psychological Association.

Queensland Association for Healthy Communities (2008). *Supporting Transgender and Sistergirl Clients.* Eagle Farm, Qld: QAHC Inc.

Rapley, M. (2003). *Quality of Life Research: A Critical Introduction.* Thousand Oaks, CA: Sage.

Rasmussen, H., Scheier, M., & Greenhouse, J. (2009). Optimisim and physical health: A meta-analytic review. *Annals of Behavioural Medicine, 37,* 239–256.

Reeves, T. C., & Oh, E. J. (2007). Generation differences and educational technology research. In J. M. Spector, M. D. Merrill, J. J. G. van Merriënboer, & M. Driscoll (Eds.), *Handbook of Research on Educational Communications and Technology* (pp. 295–303). Mahwah, NJ: Lawrence Erlbaum Associates.

Rojas, M. (2006). Well-being and the complexity of poverty: A subjective well-being approach. In M. McGillivray & M. Clarke (Eds.), *Understanding Human Well-Being* (pp. 182–206). Tokyo: United Nations University Press.

Ryff, C. D. (1989a). Beyond Ponce de Leon and life satisfaction: New directions in the quest for successful aging. *International Journal of Behavioral Development, 12,* 35–55.

Ryff, C. D. (1989b). Happiness is everything, or is it? Explorations on the meaning of psychological well-being. *Journal of Personality and Social Psychology, 57,* 1069–1081.

Ryff, C. D. (1995). Psychological well-being in adult life. *Current Directions in Psychological Science, 4,* 99–104.

Ryff, C. D., & Keyes, C. M. (1995). The structure of psychological well-being revisited. *Journal of Personality and Social Psychology, 69,* 719–727.

Ryff, C. D., & Singer, B. (1996). Psychological well-being: Meaning, measurement and implications for psychotherapy research. *Psychotherapy and Psychosomatics, 65,* 14–23.

Sanjuán, P., Ruiz, A., & Pérez, A. (2010). Life satisfaction and positive adjustment as predictors of emotional distress in men with coronary heart disease. *Journal of Happiness Studies.* 1035–1047.

Schalock, R. L. (2000). Three decades of quality of life. *Focus on Autism and Other Developmental Disabilities, 15,* 116–127.

Scheier M. F., & Carver C. S. (1985). Optimism, coping, and health: Assessment and implications of generalized outcome expectancies. *Health Psychology, 4,* 219–247.

Scheier, M. F., Carver, C. S., & Bridges, M. W. (1994). Distinguishing optimism from neuroticism (and trait anxiety, self-mastery, and self-esteem): A reevaluation of the Life Orientation Test. *Journal of Personality and Social Psychology, 67*, 1063–1078.

Schkade, D., & Kahneman, D. (1998). Does living in California make people happy? A focusing illusion in judgments of life satisfaction. *Psychological Science, 9*, 340–346.

Schmitte, P. S., & Ryff, C. D. (1997). Personality and well-being: Reexamining methods and meanings. *Journal of Personality and Social Psychology, 73*, 549–559.

Scollon, C. N., Diener, E., Oishi, S., & Biswas-Diener, R. (2009). Emotions across cultures and methods. In E. Diener (Ed.), *Culture and Well-Being: The Collected Works of Ed Diener* (pp. 203–228). Social Indicators Research Series 38. London: Springer.

Segerstrom, S. C., & Sephton, S. E. (2010). Optimistic expectancies and cell-mediated immunity: The role of positive affect. *Psychological Science, 21*, 448–455.

Seligman, M. E. P. (1993). *What you can Change . . . and What you Can't: The Complete Guide to Successful Self-Improvement.* New York: Fawcett Books.

Seligman, M. E. P. (1998). Positive social science. *American Psychology Association Monitor, 29*(4), 2–5.

Seligman, M. E. P. (2002). *Authentic Happiness: Using the New Positive Psychology to Realize Your Potential for Lasting Fulfilment.* New York: Free Press.

Seligman, M. E. P. (2003). The past and future of positive psychology [Foreword]. In C. L. M. Keyes & J. Haidt (Eds.), *Flourishing: Positive Psychology and the Life Well Lived* (pp. xi–xx). Washington DC: American Psychological Association.

Seligman, M. E. P. (2008). Positive health. *Applied Psychology: An International Review, 57*, 3–18.

Seligman, M., & Csikszentmihalyi, M. (2000). Positive psychology: An introduction. *American Psychologist, 55*, 5–14.

Seligman, M. E. P., Steen, T. A., Park, N., & Peterson, C. (2005). Positive psychology progress: Empirical validation of interventions. *American Psychologist, 60*, 410–421.

Showers, C. J., Ryff, C (1996). Self-differentiation and well-being in a life transition. *Personality and Social Psychology Bulletin, 22*, 448–460.

Sin, N. L., & Lyubomirsky, S. (2009). Enhancing well-being and alleviating depressive symptoms with positive psychology interventions: A practice-friendly meta-analysis. *Journal of Clinical Psychology: In Session, 65*, 467–487.

Smith, T.B., McCullough, M. E., & Poll, J. (2003). Religiousness and depression: Evidence for a main effect and the moderating influence of stressful life events. *Psychological Bulletin, 129*, 614–636.

Springer, K. W., Hauser, R. M., & Freese, J. (2006). Bad news indeed for Ryff's six-factor model of well-being. *Social Science Research, 35*, 1120–1131.

Steel, P., Schmidt, J., & Shultz, J. (2008). Refining the relationship between personality and subjective well-being. *Psychological Bulletin, 134*, 138–161.

Strawbridge, W. J., Shema, S. J., Cohen, R. D., & Kaplan, G. A. (2001). Religious attendance increases survival by improving and maintaining good health behaviors, mental health, and social relationships. *Annuals of Behavioral Medicine, 23*, 68–74.

Tay, L., Diener, E., Drasgow, F., & Vermunt, J. K. (2011). Multilevel mixed-measurement IRT analysis: An explanation and application to self-reported emotions across the world. *Organizational Research Methods, 14*, 177–207.

Taylor, S.E., Kemeny, M. E., Reed, G. M., Bower, J. E., & Gruenewald, T. L. (2000). Psychological resources, positive illusions, and health. *American Psychologist, 55*, 99–109.

Tov, W., & Diener, E. (2009). Culture and well-being. In E. Diener (Ed.), *The Science of Well-Being: The Collected Works of Ed Diener* (pp. 9–42). Social Indicators Research Series 38. London: Springer.

Twenge, J. M., & Campbell, S. M. (2008). Generational differences in psychological traits and their impact on the workplace. *Journal of Managerial Psychology, 23*, 862–877.

Veenhoven, R. (2006). The study of life satisfaction. In W.E. Saris, R. Veenhoven, A. C. Scherpenzeel, & B. Bunting (Eds.), *A Comparative Study of Satisfaction with Life in Europe* (pp. 11–48). Budapest: Eötvö University Press.

Wallace, J. M. Jr, & Forman, T. A. (1998). Religion's role in promoting health and reducing risk among American youth. *Health Education and Behavior, 25,* 721–741.

Wills, E. (2009). Spirituality and subjective well-being: Evidences for a new domain in the Personal Well-being Index. *Journal of Happiness Studies, 10,* 49–69.

WHO. (1946). *Preamble to the Constitution of the World Health Organization as adopted by the International Health Conference,* New York, 19–22 June. Official Records of the WHO, no. 2, p. 100; and entered into force on 7 April 1948. www.who.int/about/definition/en/.

WHO. (1986). *Ottawa Charter for Health Promotion.* First International Conference on Health Prevention, 21 November, Geneva. WHO/HPR/HEP/95.1. www.who.int/hpr/NPH/docs/ottawa_charter_hp.pdf.

WHO. (2001). *Mental Health: Strengthening Mental Health Promotion.* Fact sheet no. 220. www.who.int/mediacentre/factsheets/fs220/.

WHO. (2005). *Promoting mental health: Concepts, emerging evidence, practice: A report of the World Health Organization, Department of Mental Health and Substance Abuse in collaboration with the Victorian Health Promotion Foundation and the University of Melbourne.* www.who.int/mental_health/evidence/en/promoting_mhh.pdf.

WHO Quality of Life Group. (1995). The World Health Organization Quality of Life Assessment: Position paper from the World Health Organization. *Social Science & Medicine, 41,* 1403–1409.

Wong, M., Gardiner, E., Lang, W., & Coulon, L. (2008). Generational differences in personality and motivation. *Journal of Managerial Psychology, 23,* 878–890.

Yardley, J. K., & Rice, R. W. (1991). The relationship between mood and subjective well-being. *Social Indicators Research, 24,* 101–111.

You, J. Fung, H. H. L., & Isaacowitz, D. M. (2009). Age differences in dispositional optimism: A cross-cultural study. *European Journal of Ageing, 6,* 247–252.

Zemore, S. E., & Kaskutas, L. A. (2004). Helping, spirituality, and Alcoholics Anonymous in recovery. *Journal of Studies on Alcohol and Drugs, 65,* 383–391.

10

Companion Animals and Physical Health

The Role of Health Psychology

Anna Chur-Hansen and Helen R. Winefield

Dedication

The first author would like to dedicate this chapter to her West Highland White Terriers, Hamish McBeth, Angus Davis (deceased), and Clarence Jones, and also to her childhood and young adult canine companions, Miss Fanny Adams and Suzie Wong (both deceased), who from very early in her life fostered her interest in the human–companion animal bond and its relationship to psychological and physical health.

It is widely accepted that companion animals promote good physical and mental health. Animals, both domesticated and "wild," have shared their environment and their lives with humans since prehistoric times (Serpell, 2000). In modern Australian society, the most likely companion animals that people choose are cats and dogs. More than 63% of Australian households include a companion animal, with 40% of these being a dog and 26% a cat (Australian Companion Animal Council, 2008). The people who decide to include a companion animal in their lives are presumably motivated to do so because of some perceived positive outcome for themselves. For example, researchers have found that people want an animal for companionship (Wood *et al.*, 2007) or as a reason to exercise (Cutt *et al.*, 2007). Yet not all animals become valued members of their human family, with animal shelters in Australia overflowing with unwanted cats (Marston & Bennett, 2009). Similarly, not all dogs are included in any physical exercise despite their owner's good intentions (Cutt *et al.*, 2008a).

Wells (2009) has written an excellent review of the literature on the effects of companion animals on human health. Serpell (2009) wrote of this review that it:

> evoked vague feelings of frustration . . . not because of the quality of the review but because, after nearly 30 years of research, the evidence still remains quite equivocal. Although beneficial effects of pet ownership continue to be widely assumed, and often alluded to in the popular press, there is an extreme dearth of well-designed studies that demonstrate such effects convincingly. (p. 637)

Applied Topics in Health Psychology, First Edition. Edited by M. L. Caltabiano and L. Ricciardelli.

A recent paper by Chur-Hansen *et al.* (2010) outlines the numerous conceptual and methodological weaknesses in past and current research that make the connection between companion animals and human health almost impossible to state definitively. In summary, these include a reliance on anecdotal reports, cross-sectional research designs, and a failure to control for other variables that might better explain any positive or negative findings, such as human social supports, health habits, and the attachment to the animal. Attachment in early research tended to suppose that participants reporting "love" for the animal is equivalent to the concept of attachment. More recently researchers have become more sophisticated in their definition, drawing upon the theoretical foundations proposed by Bowlby (Winefield *et al.*, 2008). Nevertheless, how attachment may or may not mediate health benefits is still poorly understood.

With the caveat that at this time claims about the benefits of companion animals for human health at both individual and population levels may be dubious and lacking an evidence base, this chapter outlines some of the areas in which the health psychologist might utilize knowledge regarding companion animals in health promotion, in clinical practice, in interprofessional education, and in research. The chapter does not aim to review the health benefits of companion animals, as that has been done elsewhere (see for example Barker & Wolen, 2008; Cutt *et al.*, 2007; Wells, 2007, 2009). Nor does this chapter pretend to offer a comprehensive discussion of all of the areas in which health psychology is relevant to human–companion animal interactions and physical and psychological health. However, some pertinent domains are outlined in which health psychology can make significant contributions.

Companion Animals and Health Promotion

Health promotion aims to promote positive health behaviors and reduce harmful health behaviors including physical inactivity, in order to reduce community obesity and illnesses such as heart disease. Health psychologists design programs and public health campaigns to assist people to improve their health and to promote wellness. The epidemiological arm of health promotion includes estimating the distribution of disease, health behavior, and modifiable determinants (Australian Psychological Society College of Health Psychologists, 2010). There are several ways in which health promotion might incorporate companion animals.

Public health campaigns that incorporate companion animals

Cutt *et al.* (2008a) studied why some people with dogs do not walk them: in their research that was 23% of dog owners. The authors conclude that there would be a significant impact on community physical activity levels if those who currently own a dog but do not exercise it could be persuaded to do so. They identify barriers to walking, such as not considering the dog as a motivator or a social support for walking. There is an opportunity here for the health psychologist to design public health campaigns that capitalize on dog ownership. Understanding more about what might motivate people with dogs to exercise them (and thus themselves) would be an important part of any campaign (Cutt *et al.*, 2008b). As well as benefitting the human's health, walking improves the health of the dog (Bland *et al.*, 2009), so this message might be one way to motivate people to reconsider their hesitation to pick up the leash. Public health campaigns focusing on companion animals are consistent with trends in health promotion to engage urban people with nature and the environment, as upstream preventative interventions for populations (Maller *et al.*, 2005; St Leger, 2003).

Advocating for the importance of companion animals in people's lives

A number of people living in the community who share their lives with a companion animal struggle to manage because of disability, chronic illness, or frailty (Fitzpatrick, 2008). The animal may be their sole source of socioemotional support and companionship. There are anecdotal reports of ill and elderly people refusing to go to hospital or to accept any medical interventions that might separate them from their animal. There are also reports of grief-stricken owners who must surrender their animal as they move into a residential care facility (McNicholas *et al.*, 2005). The animal may need to be euthanized, causing anguish and grief for their owner. The health psychologist can play an important role in raising the awareness of the negative health implications of both threatened and actual separation from a cherished companion animal. Working with other health professionals and government, health psychologists can work towards finding and evaluating solutions for situations such as these.

Cost-benefit analyses of companion animals and human health

In 1994, Headey (1999) conducted the first national survey in Australia ($n = 1011$) to estimate the magnitude of benefits of companion animals for human health. Survey data showed that dog and cat owners made fewer annual visits to medical practitioners and were less likely to be on medication for heart problems and sleeping difficulties. He reiterated the links between human health and companion animals in longitudinal German and Australian surveys (Headey & Grabka, 2007), concluding that for both countries people who continuously own a pet are the healthiest group and people who cease to have a pet or never had one are less healthy, and that the relationship is most likely causal, not correlational. However, mechanisms for causality cannot be identified at this stage, and thus these are areas for further investigation. Headey (1999) postulated that an important public policy implication of the data is that companion animals probably reduce national health expenditure, and he made a preliminary estimate of savings of AUS$988 million for Australia for financial year 1994–1995. There is a great deal of scope for health psychologists to contribute to the debate and to the literature by studying the costs of living with a companion animal (be those costs financial, physical, or psychological) and comparing those with the corresponding benefits.

Epidemiological studies of companion animals and human health

Large-scale epidemiological studies conducted by health psychologists would be valuable in understanding more about the relationships or otherwise between companion animals and health. There has been a tendency in companion animal research to focus on particular groups, such as the elderly, at the expense of collecting data on populations as a whole. It has been argued that companion animals facilitate social capital, a sense of community (Wood *et al.*, 2005, 2007). This is an area where epidemiological research methods would be instructive. In their epidemiological research conducted in New South Wales, Bauman *et al.* (2001) identified the human health benefits of dog walking, and argued that there is a need to encourage those with dogs to walk them more. This, then, brings us back to the need for health promotion campaigns, designed using the principles of health psychology.

Companion Animals and Clinical Health Psychology Practice

In clinical health psychology the practitioner's role includes supporting people with chronic illness, and providing psychological treatments for problems associated with physical illness, such as chronic pain, addiction, poor sleep, eating problems, anxiety, depression, and emotional reactions such as anger and grief (Australian Psychological Society College of Health Psychologists, 2010). There are a number of ways in which companion animals may be important in clinical settings for individuals suffering with physical illness or disability.

Animal-assisted therapy

Fine (2006) has produced a comprehensive handbook of animal-assisted therapies for children and adults, to which the reader is referred. The Delta Society of Australia (2010) defines animal-assisted therapy (AAT) as:

> designed to improve the physical, social, emotional and/or cognitive functioning of the patient, as well as provide educational and motivational effectiveness for participants. AAT can be provided on an individual or group basis. During AAT, therapists document records and evaluate the participant's progress.

Research on psychologists' knowledge of and attitudes toward AAT is virtually nonexistent. Black *et al.* (2011a) conducted a qualitative study exploring Australian psychologists' knowledge of and attitudes toward AAT, and found positive attitudes in those who volunteered to participate, with some utilizing such therapies in their clinical practice. However, professional training in AAT is lacking in Australian postgraduate psychology programs and, alarmingly, some psychologists appear to be incorporating animals into their therapy without the consent of the client and without any attempt at formal evaluations of efficacy. Furthermore, psychologists in the study did not seem to draw upon research evidence in any way. Wilson (2006) has reviewed the evidence for the efficacy of animal-assisted interventions. She concludes that as with all research into the human–companion animal bond flaws in research methodologies make definitive statements impossible. Despite the inadequate evidence base there is anecdotal and cross-sectional evidence that AAT can be a useful intervention for some people (Morrison, 2007; Podberscek, 2006). There is also evidence that AAT might be potentially harmful for some, with risk of bites, allergies, or zoonoses (any infectious diseases that can be passed from nonhuman animals to humans) (Khan & Farrag, 2000; Morrison, 2007). An aversion to animals or a phobia of them is also a potential issue, which is one reason why it is essential to seek informed consent before instigating AAT with any client. The suitability and welfare of the animal must also be considered in any AAT intervention.

Service animals

The role of service animals from the perspective of health psychology has not been well researched. Service animals, such as guide dogs for the visually impaired or those with mobility or hearing problems, bring the person a number of positive and negative experiences in domains including social and psychological functioning, activities of daily living, physical health, health-related activities and safety, and changed social supports (from the dog as a companion and also from others, including strangers, who may engage with or be repelled by the dog) (Rintala *et al.*, 2008; Wiggett-Barnard & Steel, 2008). There is a role for the health psychologist to assist individuals at the time of acquiring a service dog, helping them adjust to living with it, and helping them when the service dog must be relinquished.

Companion animals as social supports

It is important, when consulting with a client for the first time, to draw a genealogy which includes the person's significant others, as part of history-taking. This is standard clinical practice. Usually the psychologist asks about family and friends. Whether the individual shares his or her life with a companion animal or not is another social support question that should be asked. It should be noted here that this does not necessarily mean that the person lives with an animal. Chur-Hansen *et al.* (2008) found in a qualitative study that elderly people sometimes engage with animals that belonged to neighbors or relatives, or with wildlife, in ways that gave them pleasure and a sense of meaning. For those people who do live with an animal, it has been well documented that, for many, the animal is regarded as a member of the family (Downey & Ellis, 2008; Walsh, 2009). The role of the companion animal as a "fur-child" has resulted in a burgeoning industry in pet food, veterinary services and products, and other services such as grooming, toys, housing, and clothing. In 2007, Australian expenditure on pet care (including dogs, cats, and other animals) was $4736 million (Australian Companion Animal Council, 2008). The economic benefits of promoting companion animals as family members are obvious.

Grief and bereavement

Asking about companion animals is also important because if the person does rely upon an animal for social support there may be significant grief reactions if the bond between them is broken (Chur-Hansen, 2010). The health psychologist should respect and validate such grief, and use established counselling methods, as would be done with any other situation where the person was suffering a loss. The loss might be through natural death, but with companion animal loss (unlike most human losses), the loss could be through death via euthanasia, theft, relinquishment (from moving house, moving to residential care, complaints from neighbours, lack of finances and so on), or because the animal has literally been lost (after a thunderstorm, or because someone left the gate open). Each of these scenarios may bring with them different emotional reactions for different people. The psychologist should be mindful that it is what the animal means to the person, and what the situation of loss means for them, that is important. Dismissive approaches, or ones where the person feels that the psychologist is looking for the "real" reason for their grief (such as that they lack human social supports, or are really in fact grieving over another human relationship loss) are unhelpful and disrespectful.

Companion Animals and Interprofessional Education

One of the roles of the health psychologist is to collaborate with and educate other healthcare professionals (Australian Psychological Society College of Health Psychologists, 2010). The role of the psychologist in educating students of medicine and medical practitioners is a well-established one. With regards to companion animals there is scope for the health psychologist to collaborate with and educate students and practitioners of veterinary medicine.

Education, collaboration, and support for veterinary medicine students and practitioners

Health psychologists, as educators, have a great deal to offer students and practitioners of veterinary medicine. The situation of a companion animal and its owner during a veterinary consultation could be seen as analogous to a parent and preverbal child visiting the pediatrician or general practitioner. The human in a veterinary consultation is the one with whom the practitioner must gather data, seek consent, build a relationship of trust, and demonstrate respect and empathy (Shaw *et al.*, 2004). These communication skills are core to health psychology. Also, with training in evaluation methods, any interventions provided by a health psychologist educator to improve either trainee or qualified veterinary practitioner communication skills can be assessed, drawing upon the scientist–practitioner paradigm.

In addition to teaching skills to utilize with human clients and animal patients, the health psychologist can provide training in dealing with veterinary workers' work-related distress, anxiety, and depression, which have been identified as significant issues in the profession in a recent Australian study (Fritschi *et al.*, 2009). These self-care personal and professional skills are important, as veterinarians have been identified as a group with higher than expected rates of suicide. Platt *et al.* (2010) indicate that suicide rates in UK veterinarians may be at least three times the general population rate. In an Australian study estimates of veterinarian suicide were again three to four times higher than in the general population (Jones-Fairnie *et al.*, 2008). Burn-out, compassion fatigue, and self-medication with alcohol and other substances are all areas in which the health psychologist can provide preventative strategies as well as management.

Education, collaboration, and support for animal health workers

The communication skills and self-care skills that health psychologists can offer to veterinary trainees and practitioners are also valuable to others working in the animal care industry. Compared with veterinarians, veterinary nurses have less occupational control, and the prestige and financial remuneration is less. Thus it is plausible that they will experience high rates of burn-out, job dissatisfaction, and psychological stress (Black *et al.*, 2011b). This is likely true for others working in the field, such as animal welfare officers and dog management officers, and people working in abattoirs, zoos, and animal research laboratories. Chur-Hansen *et al.* (2011) found that those working in the animal cremation industry experience a great deal of psychological stress, as they cope with little or no training with the demands of grieving animal owners seeking practical and emotional support. Health psychologists could run group training programs and assist with individual interventions, for animal support workers finding it difficult to cope with their occupation and lacking the self-care skills to deal with both others' emotions and their own.

Companion Animals and Health Psychology Research

The health psychologist holds valuable research skills and knowledge that can benefit the current status of human–companion animal research. Identified in many of the areas discussed in this chapter are research questions that remain unanswered or answered in an unsatisfactory, tentative fashion. The overall question that is yet to be addressed in a methodologically rigorous way is "are companion animals beneficial to human health?" A multitude of related questions, about which animals may benefit which humans, in what ways and in what circumstances, still await systematic exploration. With a scientist–practitioner orientation and strong training in psychosocial research methods, health psychologists are well placed to contribute to our knowledge. Specific suggestions for research design have been proposed in Chur-Hansen *et al.* (2010) so will not be repeated here. Wilson (2006) also makes suggestions for the way forward in human–companion animal research into health and wellbeing.

While we await the results of future studies, this chapter has indicated areas in which health psychology and its practitioners can draw upon existing knowledge and work with those people, who regardless of any research are certain that their companion animal is "good for their health."

References

Australian Companion Animal Council. (2008). *Australians and Their Pets. The Facts.* St Leonards, NSW: Australian Companion Animal Council Inc.

Australian Psychological Society College of Health Psychologists (2010). *Health Psychology.* www.psychology .org.au/community/specialist/health/.

Barker, S. B., & Wolen, A. R. (2008). Purdue conference on the human-animal bond. The benefits of human–companion animal interaction: A review. *Journal of Veterinary Medical Education, 35,* 487–495.

Bauman, A. E., Russell, S. J., Furber, S. E., & Dobson, A. J. (2001). The epidemiology of dog walking: An unmet need for human and canine health. *Medical Journal of Australia, 175,* 632–634.

Black, A., Chur-Hansen, A., & Winefield, H. R. (2011a). Psychologists' knowledge of and attitudes toward animal assisted therapy (AAT). *Clinical Psychologist, 15,* 69–77.

Black, A., Winefield, H. R., & Chur-Hansen, A. (2011b). Occupational stress in veterinary nurses: roles of the work environment and own companion animal. *Anthrozoos, 24,* 191–202.

Bland, I. M., Guthrie-Jones, A., Taylor, R. D., & Hill, J. (2009). Dog obesity: Owner attitudes and behaviour. *Preventative Veterinary Medicine, 92,* 333–340.

Chur-Hansen, A. (2010). Grief and bereavement issues and the loss of a companion animal: People living with a companion animal, owners of livestock, and animal support workers. *Clinical Psychologist, 14,* 14–21.

Chur-Hansen, A., Winefield, H. R., & Beckwith, M. (2008). Reasons given by elderly men and women for not owning a pet, and the implications for clinical practice and research. *Journal of Health Psychology, 13,* 988–995.

Chur-Hansen, A., Stern, C., & Winefield, H. (2010). Gaps in the evidence about companion animals and human health: Some suggestions for progress. *International Journal of Evidence-Based Healthcare, 8,* 140–146.

Chur-Hansen, A., Black, A., Gierasch, A., Pletneva, A., & Winefield, H. R. (2011) Cremation services on the death of a companion animal: Views of service providers and service users. *Society and Animals, 19,* 248–260.

Cutt, H., Giles-Corti, B., Knuiman, M., & Burke, V. (2007). Dog ownership, health and physical activity: A critical review of the literature. *Health & Place, 13,* 261–272.

Cutt, H., Giles-Corti, B., & Knuiman, M. (2008a). Encouraging physical activity through dog walking: Why don't some owners walk with their dog? *Preventive Medicine, 46,* 120–126.

Cutt, H., Giles-Corti, B., Knuiman, M., Timperio, A., & Bull, F. (2008). Understanding dog owners' increased levels of physical activity: Results from RESIDE. *American Journal of Public Health, 98,* 66–69.

Delta Society of Australia (2010). *Helping Dogs Help People.* http://www.deltasocietyaustralia.com.au/ taxonomy/term/4?page=1.

Downey, H., & Ellis, S. (2008). Tails of animal attraction: Incorporating the feline into the family. *Journal of Business Research, 61*, 434–441.

Fine, A. H. (Ed.) (2006). *Animal-Assisted Therapy. Theoretical Foundations and Guidelines for Practice* (2nd edn.). London: Elsevier.

Fitzpatrick, L. (2008). *Identifying the Need for Companion Animal Support for the Home and Community Care Target Population*. Melbourne: National Ageing Research Institute.

Fritschi, L., Morrison, D., Shirangi, A., & Day, L. (2009). Psychological well-being of Australian veterinarians. *Australian Veterinary Journal, 87*, 76–81.

Headey, B. (1999). Health benefits and health cost savings due to pets: Preliminary estimates from an Australian national survey. *Social Indicators Research, 47*, 233–243.

Headey, B., & Grabka, M. M. (2007). Pets and human health in Germany and Australia: National longitudinal results. *Social Indicators Research, 80*, 297–311.

Jones-Fairnie, H., Ferroni, P., Silburn, S., & Lawrence, D. (2008). Suicide in Australian veterinarians. *Australian Veterinary Journal, 86*, 114–116.

Khan, M., & Farrag, N. (2000). Animal-assisted activity and infection control implications in a healthcare setting. *Journal of Hospital Infection, 46*, 4–11.

Maller, C., Townsend, M., Pryor, A., Brown, P., & St Leger, L. (2005). "Healthy nature healthy people": 'Contact with nature' as an upstream health promotion intervention for populations. *Health Promotion International, 21*, 45–53.

Marston, L. C., & Bennett, P. C (2009). Admissions of cats to animal welfare shelters in Melbourne, Australia. *Journal of Applied Animal Welfare Science, 12*, 189–213.

McNicholas, J., Gilbey, A., Rennie, A., Ahmedzai, S., Dono, J., & Ormerod, E. (2005). Pet ownership and human health: A brief review of evidence and issues. *British Medical Journal, 331*, 1252–1254.

Morrison, M. L. (2007). Health benefits of animal-assisted interventions. *Complementary Health Practice Review, 12*, 51–62.

Platt, B., Hawton, K., Simkin, S., & Mellanby, R. J. (2010). Systematic review of the prevalence of suicide in veterinary surgeons. *Occupational Medicine, 60*, 436–446.

Podberscek, A. L. (2006). Positive and negative aspects of our relationship with companion animals. *Veterinary Research Communications, 30*, 21–27.

Rintala, D. H., Matamoros, R., & Seitz, L. L. (2008). Effects of assistance dogs on persons with mobility or hearing impairments: A pilot study. *Journal of Rehabilitation Research & Development, 45*, 489–504.

Serpell, J. A. (2000). Animal companions and human well-being: An historical exploration of the value of human-animal relationships. In A. H. Fine (Ed.), *Handbook on Animal Assisted Therapy: Theoretical Foundations and Guidelines for Practice* (pp. 3–19). New York: Academic Press.

Serpell, J. A. (2009). Having our dogs and eating them too: Why animals are a social issue? *Journal of Social Issues, 65*, 633–644.

Shaw, J. R., Adams, C. L., & Bonnett, B. N. (2004). What can veterinarians learn from studies of physician-patient communication about veterinarian-client-patient communication? *Journal of the American Veterinary Medical Association, 224*, 676–684.

St Leger, L. (2003). Health and nature: New challenges for health promotion. *Health Promotion International, 18*, 173–175.

Walsh, F. (2009). Human-animal bonds II: The role of pets in family systems and family therapy. *Family Process, 48*, 481–499.

Wells, D. L. (2007). Domestic dogs and human health: An overview. *British Journal of Health Psychology, 12*, 145–156.

Wells, D. L. (2009). The effects of animals on human health and well-being. *Journal of Social Issues, 65*, 523–543.

Wiggett-Barnard, C., & Steel, H. (2008). The experience of owning a guide dog. *Disability and Rehabilitation, 30*, 1014–1026.

Wilson, C. (2006). Human-animal interactions and health: Best evidence and where we go from here. In A. H. Fine (Ed.), *Animal-Assisted Therapy. Theoretical Foundations and Guidelines for Practice* (2nd edn.) (pp. 499–512). London: Elsevier.

Winefield, H. R., Black, A., & Chur-Hansen, A. (2008). Health effects of ownership of and attachment to companion animals in an older population. *International Journal of Behavioral Medicine, 15*, 303–310.

Wood, L. J., Giles-Corti, B., & Bulsara, M. K. (2005). The pet connection: Pets as a conduit for social capital? *Social Science and Medicine, 61*, 1159–1173.

Wood, L. J., Giles-Corti, B., Bulsara, M. K., & Bosch, D. A. (2007). More than a furry companion: The ripple effect of companion animals on neighborhood interactions and sense of community. *Society and Animals, 15*, 43–56.

11

Oral Health and Wellbeing

Evelyn L. C. Howe

Despite advances in oral health and epidemiology and political initiatives such as the fluoridation of water, current human and treatment resources in dentistry remain challenged by an epidemic of two essentially preventable diseases, dental caries (decay) and periodontal disease (gum disease, now linked to cardiovascular disease and preterm labor). Increased prevalence of oral cancer is linked to tobacco use, bulimia and child sexual abuse are often first diagnosed by dentists, and other mental and systemic illnesses have oral implications. Lifestyle factors important in control of oral diseases include diet and nutrition, oral and sexual hygiene, and regular preventive dental visits. The dietary factors exacerbating oral disease are similar to those implicated in obesity and diabetes. Oral hygiene strategies (such as brushing and flossing) are complex motor habits which need to be trained to achieve effective removal of dental plaque. Regular preventive dental visits are necessary for topical fluoride applications which can arrest and reverse tooth demineralization, thus preventing caries. Motivational interviewing is effective in facilitating the required behavioral changes for control of oral disease. However, communities do not know that dental caries can be stopped, reversed, and prevented. They know even less about periodontal disease or oral sexually transmissible infections. Without this knowledge they will neither implement appropriate self-care nor attend for preventive treatment and will remain anxious about the invasive dental treatment necessitated by their uncontrolled oral disease. Sustainable praxis in oral health is not possible without thinking outside professional boundaries. Although the number of health psychologists currently working in dentistry is small, their impact in clinical treatment (e.g., orofacial pain management), primary prevention (e.g., tobacco cessation), community education (e.g., oral health promotion), and health policy development is of growing significance for population oral health and wellbeing.

To work effectively at the interface of psychology and dentistry, health psychologists need an understanding of oral diseases, their etiology, presenting symptoms, treatment and prevention, and knowledge of psychological treatment programs for oral behavioral disorders, community oral health promotion strategies, and oral health coaching. Dentists also need an understanding of what health psychology has to offer. However, until recent years, few psychologists have been attracted to this important area of health. Research at the interface is still in its early stages. This chapter provides an introduction to current progress in the field in relation to the two broad arms of health psychology: clinical health psychology and health promotion.

Oral Health and Disease

A comprehensive definition of oral health, extending the World Health Organization (WHO) definition of health (1980), which has been the most widely utilized definition in the dental literature, was provided by Mouradian (2001, p. 822):

> Oral health encompasses all the immunologic, sensory, neuromuscular, and structural functions of the mouth and craniofacial complex. It influences and is related to nutrition and growth, pulmonary health, speech production, communication, self-image, and social functioning. Oral health includes the interrelationship with all aspects of the child's developmental processes, genetic potential, and environmental circumstances.

There are two main and essentially preventable diseases, that is, dental caries (tooth decay) and periodontal disease (gum disease); both of which involve transmissible infectious processes (Harris & Garcia-Godoy, 1999). Dental caries is estimated to be five times more common than asthma and is one of the most frequently cited causes of missed school days in children (Hendricson & Cohen, 2001). Early childhood caries, often resulting when babies are put to sleep with a bottle of milk or other sweetened drink (Casamassimo *et al.*, 2009), is correlated with compromised oral function, inadequate nutrition, and adversely affected height and weight (Hendricson & Cohen, 2001). The etiological factor in both oral diseases is bacterial plaque, a biological film adhering to teeth and gums, which, in the presence of dietary sugars, produces acids that demineralize tooth enamel to create dental caries and lead to periodontal breakdown through chronic tissue inflammation (Fejerskov & Kidd, 2008). Both diseases can be prevented by drinking fluoridated water, application of topical fluorides such as toothpaste, reduction of dietary sugars and acidic drinks, and regular dislodgement of the bacterial plaque by brushing and flossing (Fejerskov & Kidd, 2008).

Certain systemic diseases, such as diabetes mellitus and HIV, increase susceptibility to periodontal disease; conversely periodontal disease is a risk factor for systemic conditions such as cardiovascular disease, preterm labor, and infant mortality (Offenbacher *et al.*, 1998). Approximately 23% of Australian adults suffer from moderate to severe periodontal disease (Slade *et al.*, 2007). Prevalence is positively correlated with age but young adults who smoke are nearly three times more likely than non-smokers to experience periodontitis by their mid 20s (Hashim *et al.*, 2001). The disease usually requires surgical intervention, which can be both expensive and disfiguring (Hendricson & Cohen, 2001).

Many modifiable lifestyle factors are implicated in oral diseases and injuries. Those increasing susceptibility to dental caries and periodontal disease include dietary sugar, carbonated drinks, oral piercing, and smoking while commonly prescribed medications, such as antidepressants or asthma medications, which decrease saliva production, may also increase risk (de Moor *et al.*, 2005; Elter *et al.*, 2002; Maguire *et al.*, 1996). Oral and nasopharyngeal cancers, the sixth most common type of cancer with survival rates of approximately 52%, are linked to poor nutrition and consumption of tobacco, alcohol, and areca nut (paan) and show varied epidemiological rates in different countries (Winn, 2001). Unprotected oral sex, often believed to be "safe sex," has become a significant risk factor for sexually transmitted diseases in recent years, especially in younger age groups (Remez, 2000). Oral sexual abuse may result in oral injuries, often diagnosed by dentists (Maguire *et al.*, 2007) and two-thirds of physical abuse experienced by children involves orofacial trauma which is also treated by dentists (Needleman, 1986).

A review of oral needs in the Australian and US populations found that oral health has significant impact on quality of life (Sanders *et al.*, 2009) while dental caries, periodontal disease, and edentulism (absence or loss of teeth) are the most prevalent conditions requiring intervention (Australian Health Ministers Advisory Council Steering Committee for National Oral Health, 2001) and orofacial pain (Macfarlane *et al.*, 2001), trauma to the face or mouth (Welbury & Murphy, 1998), and craniofacial birth defects, also linked to maternal tobacco use (Wyszynski *et al.*, 1997), contribute to the current unmet need for dental treatment (Slade *et al.*, 2007). Projective analysis of the supply and demand for dental treatment indicates an increase in demand for diagnostic, preventive, and restorative services while resources supplying those services remain static, a finding with implications for oral health policy and tertiary education (Spencer *et al.*, 2003; Teusner *et al.*, 2008).

The historic separation of medicine and dentistry, which was originally a branch of surgery, has resulted in inadequate knowledge of oral health and disease among both medical and allied health practitioners (Lewis *et al.*, 2000), while the development of allied health specialties, notably dietetics and speech pathology, have tended to focus attention on specific functions of the mouth, thus limiting the needed holistic focus (Wilder *et al.*, 2008). Effective national oral health planning initiatives have been hampered by lack of collaboration between these professional silos of expertise (Huston & Wood, 2009). The dental profession acting alone to improve access to oral health services is unlikely to have the power to sway governments to provide the necessary funding for effective oral health services (Hopkins, 2007; Spencer, 2004).

A positive move forward has been stimulated by the development of the International Classification of Functioning, Disability and Health or ICF (WHO, 2001) to incorporate specific reference to oral structures and functions and to include the mouth and face in activity and participation. The ICF classification has provided a needed framework for psychological, behavioral, social, and cultural factors, implicated in oral diseases, and has stimulated development of a range of methods for evaluating oral health. Slade and Sanders (2003) argue that, while many scales measure only negative outcomes of oral diseases, the dental impact profile (Strauss & Hunt, 1993) and the oral health related quality of life questionnaire (McGrath & Bedi, 2001) assess both positive and negative aspects of oral status. The oral health impact profile (Slade & Spencer 1994) and its 14-item abbreviated version (Slade, 1997) have been used to assess oral health in a number of Australian studies and have also enabled comparisons of the oral health status of people of different nationalities (Steele *et al.*, 2004). An important finding emerging from recent research in this field was that pain plays a significant role in escalating the level of debilitation attributable to oral conditions and may mediate transitions in the ICF categories of activity and participation (Slade & Sanders, 2003).

Clinical Oral Health Psychology

Treatment of orofacial disorders and diseases is important for biological, social, and psychological reasons. Because suckling, eating, breathing, smiling, speech, music, and love-making are all functions of the mouth critical for good social interaction, oral disease and disfigurement may have destructive effects on human wellbeing beyond the medical and functional aspects of the condition (Eli, 1992). Biologically, the significance of the mouth can be understood in terms of the size of its representation in the somatic, sensory, and motor cerebral cortices and its limbic links to genital and aggressive behavior (Miyamoto *et al.*, 2006). The mouth also mediates gustatory and olfactory sensation and halitosis (bad breath) may adversely impact social interaction (Hughes & McNab, 2008).

Giddon and Anderson (2006) conceptualize oral significance sequentially in terms of survival, socialization, and self-actualization. As the route for nutrition, the mouth provides the infant's first nurturing emotional contact with the world and also the first prototype of pain or threat in the experiences of hunger and choking. Evolutionary psychology links facial symmetry to mating preferences and judgments of oral esthetics. The mouth and eyes are prominent features in judgments of physical attractiveness, fitness, age, fecundity, gender, and emotion and these judgments appear to be innate as they are consistent cross-culturally (Rhodes, 2006). Perceived oral dysmorphia, rather than functional concerns, remains the prime reason for seeking orthodontic treatment to change these structures (Giddon & Anderson, 2006).

Conditions seen by dentists, with psychological, social, and behavioral components, include acute and chronic orofacial pain, parafunctional habits (bruxism, clenching, jaw posturing, thumb-sucking, and fingernail biting), abnormal gagging, and craniofacial anomalies (e.g., cleft lip and palate). Psychological conditions with specific oral presentations include dental anxiety, specific phobias of dental treatment, and stress. Certain medical or psychological conditions (e.g., eating disorders, depression, or autism) and trauma (e.g., oral, sexual, or physical abuse) may require special management within the surgery environment and referral to multidisciplinary teams for further intervention. Psychological treatment protocols for these conditions are briefly described below.

Pain

The most common reason for acute oral pain is dental caries, where demineralization of tooth tissue results in exposure of sensitive dentine or the pulp chamber. This may also be a route for bacterial infection of the pulp resulting in a tooth abscess, which creates severe acute pain due to inflammation within dense tissue (Sharav *et al.*, 1984). Periodontal disease rarely generates pain until quite advanced (Wilson *et al.*, 2000). Pain may result from bruxism or clenching, which may be triggered when the teeth do not bite together evenly (malocclusion), sometimes because of a previous extraction or restoration (van der Meulen *et al.*, 2006). Acute pain may be associated with other oral conditions (e.g., aphthous ulcers, herpes, burning mouth syndrome, or trigeminal neuralgia) or trauma (e.g., accidental biting of soft tissues or rubbing of orthodontic appliances) (Krukemeyer *et al.*, 2009). Some patients experience acute pain with administration of oral injections because anxious anticipation and misperception of pressure lead an otherwise innocuous sensation to be perceived as pain (Howe, 1998). However, perception of oral pain is subject to modifying emotional and environmental variables, as is the case in other parts of the body (McNeil *et al.*, 2006).

Acute pain usually subsides following dental restoration or extraction of the affected tooth. However, where there is acute tissue inflammation (e.g., with an abscess) local anesthesia may be ineffective in managing pain and the dentist may have to open the pulp chamber to drain the abscess without being able to anesthetize the tooth (Nusstein *et al.*, 2010). Health psychologists counselling people after this type of emergency must understand that this experience does not imply incompetence in dental treatment.

Psychological management of acute pain in dental surgeries involves empathic communication (Maggiras & Locker, 2002), enhancing patient control (Thrash *et al.*, 1982), effective relaxation, and distraction. Brief arousal control relaxation procedures, which can be administered quickly in the surgery are recommended, e.g., breathing and jaw relaxation or the miniTRIP, a brief tension-reducing imagery procedure using all five senses to recreate a pleasant place chosen by the patient (Williams, 1996). Distraction procedures such as visualization or redirection of attention to a competing difficult activity (e.g., holding one leg up in the air) may assist in surgical management of acute pain (Frere *et al.*, 2001).

Chronic orofacial pain affects more than 20% of adults (Hendricson & Cohen, 2001) and can result from infection or conditions such as trigeminal neuralgia (Graff-Radford, 2009). It is frequently experienced as a symptom of temporomandibular dysfunction (van der Meulen *et al.*, 2006). This condition is associated with occlusal problems or parafunctional habits such as bruxism (grinding) or jaw posturing and is sometimes described by patients as "dental migraine" because the chronic tension of temporalis or neck muscles produces headache (Glaros & Lausten, 2003). Tension or spasm of the oral musculature due to biting forces on poorly occluding (misaligned) teeth or habitual posturing of the jaw to avoid sensitive teeth may in turn compromise diagnostic accuracy (Liu *et al.*, 1999). For this reason, relaxation of the oral musculature must be achieved to enable correct diagnosis of the occlusal problem.

Muscle spasm and habitual tension have been treated using biofeedback-monitored relaxation, with surface electrodes placed on masseter or temporalis muscles (Crider & Glaros, 1999). In some studies this treatment has been effectively combined with cognitive-behavioral skills training (Gardea *et al.*, 2001). However, biofeedback may be ineffective where the underlying lateral ptery-goid muscles are involved, since these may be monitored only by insertion of needle electrodes. Oral splints, which impede habituated patterns of muscle tension, may be effective in reducing pain but patients may show poor treatment adherence in wearing them as required (Wassall *et al.*, 2006).

A treatment protocol for a parafunctional habit such as bruxing comprises administration of a pain /bruxing diary to identify times and activities where bruxing occurs (usually stressful activities such as driving or those requiring intense concentration such as computer work). Following biofeedback-monitored muscle relaxation training the patient is exposed to situations likely to trigger the habit but consciously relaxes the masseter muscles as a response-prevention strategy (Shulman, 2001). Nocturnal bruxism has been treated using alarmed electronic pressure monitors attached to masseter muscles that awaken the sleeper when bruxism commences, a program similar to that for treatment of enuresis (Cassisi *et al.*, 1987). Motivational interviewing or health coaching may be required to identify and treat nonadherence to occlusal splint therapy and to ensure that the patient completes the recommended dental treatment plan.

Abnormal Gagging

The gag reflex acts to protect the airway from accidental obstruction and is usually triggered by stimulation of the soft palate, pharynx, and posterior third of the dorsal surface of the tongue. These areas are enervated by the glossopharyngeal nerve. However, in abnormal gagging, the urge to gag is stimulated by other areas of the mouth and even by anticipation of touch. The etiology of the condition appears to be multifactorial (Dickinson & Fiske, 2005a) but there is a history of medical or dental aversive experience in many severe gaggers, frequently oral abuse (Howe, 1985). However, any condition that hampers nasal breathing (e.g., asthma) is likely to trigger gagging when the patient is unable to breathe through the mouth (i.e., when supine, with instruments or water in the mouth). Smoking is also a risk factor for development of abnormal gagging. A nasal decongestant may be all that is required to manage cases where impedance of breathing is the key factor (Dickinson & Fiske, 2005b).

Gagging is effectively treated through graded exposure to exercises that extend tolerance to stimulation of tissues anterior to the soft palate and the anterior two-thirds of the tongue. These exercises include tooth-brushing, commencing with the incisors and gradually extending range of brushing to molar teeth, at no time triggering the gag reflex. Sucking safe objects (e.g., a large spoon handle) gradually deeper into the oral cavity, tolerating fluid in an open mouth, tongue-brushing, and chewing of large wads of chewing gum to simulate impression materials can effectively reduce sensitivity of specific areas of the mouth to gagging triggered by similar sensations (Dickinson & Fiske, 2005b; Howe, 1985).

Thumb-Sucking and Fingernail Biting

Thumb-sucking is implicated in class II malocclusion (protruding upper incisors), a condition affecting normal tooth and jaw development requiring orthodontic surgery for correction. Children with this malocclusion may develop other dental problems including temporomandibular disorders, abnormal tooth wear, and psychological problems associated with teasing or bullying because of the defect (Miltenberger & Rapp, 2006). Fingernail biting, a risk factor for temporomandibular disorder, is implicated in abnormal wear of the incisor teeth and leads to increased exposure to pathogens carried by the hands to the mouth (Baydas *et al.*, 2007). There is also a social stigma attached to fingernail biting and to a lesser extent to thumb-sucking that can adversely affect the self-image of sufferers. Habit reversal of both conditions involves keeping a diary to identify frequency, timing, and triggers for the behavior followed by a response-prevention program. Reward incentives for older children can further assist in the development of habit control (Miltenberger & Rapp, 2006; Twohig *et al.*, 2003).

Craniofacial Anomalies

WHO data reveal that craniofacial anomalies affect approximately 1:500–700 live births, with cleft lip and palate being the most common and the ratio varying widely across geographic locations (Mossey, 2004; WHO, 2007). Some conditions, e.g., Moebius syndrome, which prevents the ability to smile, affect soft tissue; most anomalies are disfiguring. Many craniofacial anomalies are comorbid with psychological disorders and learning difficulties (de Sousa, 2008). Maternal cigarette smoking has been identified as a significant risk factor for these disorders (Mossey, 2004; Wyszynski *et al.* 1997).

Extensive surgical and rehabilitative interventions are required to treat most of these defects as can be seen with treatment for the most common condition, cleft lip and palate, which is undertaken throughout childhood and adolescence. Initially the cleft is closed and special feeding bottles are provided to enable the baby to create the vacuum required for sucking. Parents are trained to manage choking, as any threat to the airway may endanger the child's life. Multiple surgical corrections follow as the child's face grows from birth to adolescence. Psychological counselling of parents may be needed to address their reactions to having an affected child, their fears for the child's wellbeing and safety, particularly beliefs that the child is wounded or in pain, and their need for information or reassurance about future reproductive plans (Eiserman, 2001; Trulsson & Klingberg, 2003). Critical to adjustment is exposure to pictures of similar children before and after corrective treatment and introduction to self-help and support groups such as Cleftpals (www.cleftpals.org.au). Intervention with school peer groups to reduce social stigmatization may be beneficial (Edwards *et al.*, 2011) but, although boys appear more willing to interact with peers with a craniofacial difference, children's reactions appear to be influenced by judgments of overall attractiveness rather than craniofacial distinctions alone (Reed *et al.*, 1999).

Dental Anxiety

Anxiety is the most common psychological problem presenting in dentistry, affecting approximately 70% of patients to some degree and leading to avoidance of needed treatment in approximately 10%, especially older patients (Armfield, 2010). Anxiety exacerbates pain, complicates patient management, decreases retention of information provided during treatment, and decreases likelihood of return for regular dental check-ups. Dental anxiety is associated with a history of past painful experience, usually surgical, but more rarely abuse or trauma; it may also be acquired vicariously through contact with other anxious people (Mendola *et al.*, 1991).

Specific phobias in dentistry include blood-injury-injection phobia, drilling, extractions, surgical sounds, smells, and prophylaxis (Armfield, 2010; Howe, 1985) but other specific phobias may be triggered by dental situations, e.g., patients with claustrophobia find it difficult to accept a rubber dam (a means of protecting the mouth from debris during treatment) or children with clown phobia may react adversely to dental gowns and masks.

Because people use avoidance of preventive dental treatment as a coping strategy for anxiety or phobia, they often present with severe acute pain from oral abscess or tooth fracture requiring emergency dental treatment. In severe cases of phobia, this will be administered in conjunction with general anaesthetic, intravenous sedation, or relative analgesia, allowing resolution of pain but leaving the phobia untreated. Thus there arises a vicious circle of ongoing anxiety or phobia reinforced both by dental pain symptoms and painful crisis treatment (Eli, 1992). Patients experiencing severe dental pain, usually as intense as heart attack or renal colic, often develop posttraumatic stress symptoms in relation to dental treatment (Liedl *et al.*, 2010). Furthermore, description of such experiences by parents may be the vector for vicarious acquisition of anxiety and phobia in children (Eli, 1992).

Treatment for dental anxiety involves relaxation training, particularly arousal control procedures such as breathing control relaxation or the miniTRIP (Williams, 1996) and effective use of distraction strategies such as music or protective glasses with embedded television screens (Botto, 2006). Portable vibrating massage machines also effectively distract patients from oral procedures when placed against the skin of the face during dental treatment (Baba *et al.*, 2010). When combined with motivational interviewing to assist adoption of effective dietary and hygiene measures for disease prevention, the need for surgical dental treatment is avoided and anxiety about regular prophylactic visits is significantly reduced (Botto, 2006).

Specific Dental Phobias

Effective treatment for phobias includes guided imagery desensitization, graduated *in vivo* and simulated-exposure treatments, and hypnosis (Peltier, 2006). Treatment for phobic anxiety involves identification of anxiety triggers and challenge of unhelpful or irrational beliefs. For example, a patient who fears that dental injections enter the brain may actually perceive the dental syringe with plunger extended as a "huge needle," all of which disappears from the visual field during injection; with no understanding of human anatomy, the actual length of the needle tip or the way in which the plunger operates to force fluid from the carpule, an irrational belief may develop from perceptual "evidence." Such misperceptions can be alleviated through explanation and handling of the instrument. One frequently held belief is that injections are severely painful. The actual sensations experienced are pinprick and pressure. Where patients are desensitized to these sensations, the injection process becomes tolerable and the phobia can be extinguished (Howe, 1985). This is achieved by using a toothpick or paper clip lying flat against the palm of the hand to simulate the sensation of a prick (without breaking the skin) and then applying pressure against the shaft. This simulated exposure to the injection sensations can be graded from calloused to more sensitive parts of the body, including the gums, and repeated until anxiety about these sensations is extinguished (Howe, 1998). The dental injection, which is administered to topically anesthetized tissues, is then experienced as less painful than the simulation exercise.

Treatment for drill phobia involves desensitization to the sensation of vibration transmitted through bone. This can be simulated by an electric toothbrush, first used conventionally to brush teeth and then used with the plastic back of the brush placed in contact with the teeth (avoiding any teeth with crowns or veneer restorations). Desensitization to the smell of dental surgeries, which is oil of cloves, an antiseptic used in restorations, can be achieved by providing a small amount of this fluid for the patient to take home and smell increasingly frequently until inurement occurs (Howe, 1985).

Vasovagal syncope is a common complication of blood and injection phobia, occurring in about 70% of cases. For this reason, patients with a history of fainting during medical or dental procedures or with a family history of injection phobia benefit from training in tensing (instead of relaxing) major muscle groups to prevent the sudden drop in blood pressure resulting in syncope (Marchiondo, 2010).

Stress

Although dental treatment is recognized as stressful by the majority of people requiring it, less is known about the effect of stress on oral wellbeing. An important oral indicator of health and disease is saliva. It plays a significant role in protection of oral structures from microbial attack, mechanical irritation, and chemical erosion (Eli, 1992). Disease, medication, and emotional states such as depression can affect quality and quantity of saliva (Navazesh, 2006). Xerostomia (dry mouth) is a side effect of many medications and treatments including antidepressants, drugs with anticholinergic or sympathomimetic actions, radiation, and chemotherapy. It is a symptom of chronic systemic diseases such as Sjogren's syndrome, HIV, uncontrolled diabetes, Alzheimer's disease, bulimia nervosa, and depression and is a vector for transmission of diseases such as herpes and hepatitis C (Bergdahl & Bergdahl, 2000). Xerostomia is a causative factor in dental caries, periodontal disease, and opportunistic infections of oral soft tissues (e.g., oral moniliasis). In menopausal women, altered salivary composition may result from sympathetic activation due to psychological stress (Ben Aryeh *et al.*, 1996). Where stress is identified as a contributing factor to dental problems, as is the case with xerostomia, parafunctional habits, and chronic pain, referral for psychological treatment of stress has been shown to be effective in lowering levels of cortisol and amylase in the saliva and improving oral comfort and wellbeing (Brennan *et al.*, 2002).

Oral Health Promotion and Health Coaching

Oral diseases comprise a serious health problem with significant cost to the community in terms of the healthcare budget, school and work absence, and quality of life (Croucher *et al.*, 2006). Because expressive ability can be compromised by oral disease, edentulism, ill-fitting dentures, orthodontic appliances, injury, and congenital defects, the appearance of the oral area may be for many people more important than its function both in recognizing disease and in motivating hygiene practice and preventive dental visits. However, oral disease is often asymptomatic in its early stages and easily recognizable only when advanced. The task for the dental profession remains to educate the population about dental disease, change the behaviors and beliefs of individual patients from secondary to primary prevention, and move health policy from a downstream to an upstream focus (Schou & Locker, 1997).

One of the challenges facing dentists in health promotion is lack of skill not only in communication and education but also in planning, strategy development, community liaison, and political lobbying (Hopkins, 2007; Watt & Fuller, 1999). Historically, dentistry has been focused on mastery of oral restorative and surgical techniques, which are secondary and tertiary interventions, whereas primary prevention requires communication and health promotion skills. These skills are currently being introduced into dental curricula at the same time as dental schools are increasing medical science training in order to facilitate the growing role of dentists as oral physicians (Hendricson & Cohen, 2001). Thus dental curricula are now extremely dense and many schools teaching communication and health promotion do so passively, as knowledge, rather than actively, as skill. As a consequence, many oral health promotion campaigns are poorly designed and lack evidence of audience analysis or market testing of effectiveness in achieving attitudinal or behavioral change (Howe & Schnabel, 2012).

A prime barrier for population oral health has been the failure to link oral health with health promotion campaigns targeting other major health issues such as diabetes, cardiovascular disease, tobacco use, and obesity, which have etiological lifestyle factors in common and may be comorbid. The common risk factor approach offers a cost-effective basis for oral health campaigns such as health promoting schools (Kwan *et al.*, 2005). Recent development of scales for assessment of oral health literacy has informed development of campaigns that are more effectively designed to meet the needs of specific population groups (Horowitz, 2008). A key problem appears to be that the oral health literacy of medical and allied health professionals is no better than that of the general population. Thus an important primary task for dentists is education of these professional groups so that better collaboration can be achieved (Douglass *et al.*, 2009).

Sheiham (1995) identified six policy areas as essential in improving oral health: reduction of sugar consumption, smoking cessation, accident reduction (e.g., through use of mouthguards), improvement of oral hygiene, water fluoridation, and access to primary preventive dental care. Social equity is an issue for oral health, as it is for general health (Lalloo *et al.*, 1999). Low socioeconomic status is linked to high disease rates, poorer nutrition, greater tobacco use, and less access to treatment services.

Mass media campaigns are costly and may not prove effective in changing community oral health. A British campaign to encourage dental visits raised community awareness of the need for regular dental attendance but did not lead to an increased number of dental visits (Anderson & Morgan, 1992). On the other hand, focusing health promotion efforts on dental treatment visits provides the opportunity for health education and encouragement of behavior change. To dislodge the plaque biofilm and remineralize acid-leached tooth tissue requires effective tooth-brushing and topical fluoride application; however, most people have never been taught a brushing technique that ensures all plaque is removed and that teeth are exposed to fluoride dentifrices for the needed period of time. To train tooth-brushing, which is a complex motor habit, requires regular health coaching to ensure that the technique is effective and does not create iatrogenic erosion of tooth enamel (Chander & Rees, 2010). There is an urgent need for research in the application of coaching techniques in training tooth-brushing. Recent application of motivational interviewing to oral health behavior change has shown promising results in early evaluations (Ramseier & Suvan, 2010). Although patient attitudes and anxiety may initially pose a barrier, most dental treatment plans involve a series of visits, which offer multiple opportunities for motivational interviewing and health coaching. Because dental surgeries usually carry high overhead costs, procedures must be efficient and cost effective, preferably also ensuring patient retention. For this reason brief motivational interviewing and health coaching techniques are likely to be best accepted in practice (Dunn & Deroo, 2001).

Professional Liaison

Historically, dentistry has been such a professional silo that dentists may have difficulty in convincing patients to accept referral for psychological intervention. Although dentists are often the first practitioners to identify conditions such as bulimia nervosa or childhood sexual abuse, they have not been linked to multidisciplinary treatment teams for these disorders, a problem that all members of these teams must now actively address (Halstrom, 2007). Many types of mental illness are readily diagnosed in dental surgeries, where the stress of undergoing dental treatment exacerbates recognizable symptoms (Eli, 1992), yet there are few clinical placements for health psychologists in dental hospitals. Some psychiatric disorders such as specific phobia or body dysmorphic disorder have specifically dental presentations, which remain relatively unfamiliar in clinical or health psychology programs. There is a need for greater collaboration between the professions of dentistry and psychology.

Health psychologists may also need to address the health needs of dentists. Although, contrary to popular myth, dentists do not have a higher suicide rate than other professional groups (Alexander, 2001; Sancho & Ruiz, 2010; Skegg *et al.*, 2010), they do have other occupational health issues (Leggat *et al.*, 2007). They are exposed on a daily basis to serious blood- and saliva-borne infections, chemicals, and sounds that produce selective deafness over time (Cristina *et al.*, 2009). Their work requires intense concentration, good eyesight, and manual dexterity, all human attributes that deteriorate with age. Although with improved ergonomic surgery design, postural problems are less, the necessity of maintaining sustained operating postures for prolonged periods of time remains an issue. As with other private practitioners, before they graduate they carry a large debt at a time in life when they are forming partnerships and starting families and thus must work very hard to establish a practice, sometimes at a cost to family and leisure life; in addition, their working life is limited by their physical and emotional fitness to practice. Key factors for maintenance of health are work/life balance, good financial management, and retirement planning. Psychologists working in liaison with the dental profession to foster professional health and wellbeing may provide life coaching and mentoring for which there is a clear need within the dental profession (Holt & Ladwa, 2010). In health promotion and clinical healthcare the future is attractive for interprofessional collaboration and likely to be mutually beneficial.

Summary and Conclusion

The contribution of psychology to dentistry is evident in clinical oral health psychology, oral health promotion, and interprofessional liaison. In clinical oral health psychology, strategies are required for management of psychological and social conditions that present in dental surgeries and which can seriously affect oral health, complicate the dental treatment and sometimes require nondental interventions, e.g., bulimia nervosa or child sexual abuse. Further, the etiology of many oral disorders (e.g., dental phobias, stress-related temporomandibular dysfunction, or abnormal gagging) includes cognitive and behavioral factors that must be treated using psychological interventions to achieve the best oral health outcomes. Although psychological treatment procedures have been developed for these conditions, there is an urgent need for further research, especially randomized controlled trials of these treatments.

In oral health promotion, psychologists have made an important contribution to oral health and wellbeing, both in chairside delivery and public communication forms. Application of motivational interviewing to oral health behavior change has significantly reduced oral disease in target populations. However, more research is required to maximize the potential of this intervention for oral health applications. Dentistry also requires research to develop better understanding of communication skills appropriate for oral health promotion using mass media. A complicating factor is the historical separation of medicine and dentistry, which implies that oral conditions and treatments are somehow different or separate from those of other parts of the body. A result of this artificial separation of treatment responsibilities is a failure to include oral health in major health initiatives, which have lifestyle factors in common, such as obesity and diabetes. Development of effective collaboration between health teams to reduce these counterproductive stereotypes is another important area of research.

References

Alexander, R. E. (2001). Stress-related suicide by dentists and other health care workers. Fact or folklore? *Journal of the American Dental Association, 132,* 786–794.

Anderson, R. J., & Morgan, J. D. (1992). Marketing dentistry: A pilot study in Dudley. *Community Dental Health, 9* (suppl. 1), 69–126.

Armfield, J. M. (2010). The extent and nature of dental fear and phobia in Australia. *Australian Dental Journal, 55,* 368–377.

Australian Health Ministers Advisory Council Steering Committee for National Oral Health. (2001). *Oral Health of Australians: National Planning for Oral Health Improvement.* www.arcpoh.adelaide.edu.au/publications/report/miscellaneous/pdf_files/oral_health_of_Australians_cover.pdf.

Baba, L. R., McGrath, J. M., & Liu, J. (2010). The efficacy of mechanical vibration analgesia for relief of heel stick pain in neonates: a novel approach. Journal of Perinatal & Neonatal Nursing, 24, 274–283.

Baydas, B., Uslu, H., Yavuz, I., Ceylan, I., & Dagsuyu, I. M. (2007). Effect of a chronic nail-biting habit on the oral carriage of Enterobacteriaceae. *Oral Microbiology & Immunology, 22,* 1–4.

Ben Aryeh, H., Gottlieb, I., Ish-Shalom, S., David, A., & Laufer, D. (1996). Oral complaints related to menopause. *Maturitas, 24,* 185–189.

Bergdahl, M., & Bergdahl, J. (2000). Low unstimulated salivary flow and subjective oral dryness: Association with medication, anxiety, depression and stress. *Journal of Dental Research, 79,* 1652–1658.

Botto, R. W. (2006). Chairside techniques for reducing dental fear. In D. I. Mostofsky, A. G. Forgione, & D. B. Giddon (Eds.), *Behavioral Dentistry* (pp. 115–125). Oxford: Blackwell Munksgaard.

Brennan, M. T., Shariff, G., Lockhart, P. B., & Fox, P. C. (2002). Treatment of xerostomia: A review of therapeutic trials. *Dental Clinics of North America, 46,* 847–856.

Casamassimo, P. S., Thikkurissy, S., Edelstein, B. L., & Maiorini, E. (2009). Beyond the dmft: The human and economic cost of early childhood caries. *Journal of the American Dental Association, 140,* 650–657.

Cassisi, J. E., McGlynn, F. D., & Belles, D. R. (1987). EMG-activated feedback alarms for the treatment of nocturnal bruxism: Current status and future directions. *Biofeedback & Self Regulation, 12,* 13–30.

Chander, S., & Rees, J. (2010). Strategies for the prevention of erosive tooth surface loss. *Dental Update, 37,* 12–16.

Crider, A. B., & Glaros, A. G. (1999). A meta-analysis of EMG biofeedback treatment of temporomandibular disorders. *Journal of Orofacial Pain, 13,* 29–37.

Cristina, M. L., Spagnolo, A. M., Sartini, M., Dallera, M., Ottria, G., Perdelli, F., & Orlando, P. (2009). Investigation of organizational and hygiene features in dentistry: A pilot study. *Journal of Preventive Medicine & Hygiene, 50*, 175–180.

Croucher, R., Marcenes, W., & Pau, A. (2006). Community health promotion. In D. I. Mostofsky, A. G. Forgione, & D. B. Giddon (Eds.), *Behavioral Dentistry* (pp. 265–276). Oxford: Blackwell Munksgaard.

de Moor, R. J., De Witte, A. M., Delmé, K. I., De Bruyne, M. A., Hommez, G. M., Goyvaerts, D. (2005). Dental and oral complications of lip and tongue piercings. *British Dental Journal, 199*, 506–509.

de Sousa, A. (2008). Psychological issues in oral and maxillofacial reconstructive surgery. *British Journal of Oral & Maxillofacial Surgery, 46*, 661–664.

Dickinson, C. M., & Fiske, J. (2005a). A review of gagging problems in dentistry: I. Aetiology and classification. *Dental Update, 32*, 26–28.

Dickinson, C. M., & Fiske, J. (2005b). A review of gagging problems in dentistry: 2. Clinical assessment and management. *Dental Update, 32*(2), 74–80.

Douglass, A. B., Douglass, J. M., & Krol, D. M. (2009). Educating pediatricians and family physicians in children's oral health. *Academic Pediatrics, 9*, 452–456.

Dunn, C., & Deroo, L. (2001). The use of brief interventions adapted from motivational interviewing across behavioral domains: A systematic review. *Addiction, 96*, 1725–1742.

Edwards, T. C., Topolski, T. D., Kapp-Simon, K. A., Aspinall, C. A., & Patrick, D. L. (2011). What difference can a minute make? Social skills and first impressions of youth with craniofacial differences. *Cleft Palate Craniofacial Journal, 48*, 91–97.

Eiserman, W. (2001). Unique outcomes and positive contributions associated with facial difference: expanding research and practice. *Cleft Palate Craniofacial Journal, 38*, 236–244.

Eli, I. (1992). *Oral Psychophysiology: Stress, Pain and Behavior in Dental Care.* Boca Raton, FL: CRC Press.

Elter, J. R., White, B. A., Gaynes, B. N., & Bader, J. D. (2002). Relationship of clinical depression to periodontal treatment outcome. *Journal of Periodontology, 73*, 441–449.

Fejerskov, O., & Kidd, E. (2008). *Dental Caries: The Disease and its Clinical Management.* Oxford: Blackwell Munksgaard.

Frere, C. L., Crout, R., Yorty, J., & McNeil, D. W. (2001). Effects of audiovisual distraction during dental prophylaxis. *Journal of the American Dental Association, 132*, 1031–1038.

Gardea, M. A., Gatchel, R. J., & Mishra, K. D. (2001). Long-term efficacy of behavioural treatment of temporomandibular disorders. *Journal of Behavioural Medicine, 24*, 341–389.

Giddon, D. B., & Anderson, N. K. (2006). The oral and craniofacial area and interpersonal attraction. In D. I. Mostofsky, A. G. Forgione, & D. B. Giddon (Eds.), *Behavioral Dentistry* (pp. 3–18). Oxford: Blackwell Munksgaard.

Glaros, A. G., & Lausten, L. (2003). Temporomandibular disorders. In M. S. Schwartz and F. Andrasik (Eds.), *Biofeedback: A Practitioner's Guide* (3rd edn.) (pp. 349–368). New York: Guilford Press.

Graff-Radford, S. B. (2009). Facial pain. *Neurologist, 15*, 171–177.

Halstrom, W. (2007). Let's put the mouth back in the body. *Canadian Medical Association Journal, 176*, 145–147.

Harris, N. O., & Garcia-Godoy, F. (1999). *Primary Preventive Dentistry.* Stamford, CT: Appleton & Lange.

Hashim, R., Thomson, W. M., & Pack, A. R. C. (2001). Smoking in adolescence: A predictor of early loss of periodontal attachment. *Community Dentistry and Oral Epidemiology, 29*, 130–135.

Hendricson, W. D., & Cohen, P. A. (2001). Oral health care in the 21st century: Implications for dental and medical education. *Academic Medicine, 76*, 1181–1206.

Holt, V. P., & Ladwa, R. (2010). Developing a mentoring culture in dentistry. Making a difference in a changing world. *Primary Dental Care, 17*, 93–98.

Hopkins, S. (2007). Wait no more: The use of private dental services by welfare recipients in Australia. *Journal of Economic and Social Policy, 12*, 1–18.

Horowitz, A. (2008). Oral health literacy: The new imperative to better oral health. *Dental Clinics of North America, 52*, 333–344.

Howe, E. L. C. (1985). *Behaviour Therapy in the Treatment of Oral Behavioural Disorders.* Doctoral thesis, University of Sydney.

Howe, E. L. C. (1998). A treatment protocol for injection anxiety. *Newsletter of the APS College of Health Psychologists, 2,* 3–4.

Howe, E. L. C., & Schnabel, M. A. (2012). The changing face of problem-based learning: Social networking and interprofessional collaboration. In S. Bridges, C. McGrath, & T. Whitehill (Eds.), *Problem-Based Learning in Clinical Education: The Next Generation* (pp. 121–137). Innovation and Change in Professional Education 8. London: Springer.

Hughes, F. J., & McNab, R. (2008). Oral malodour: A review. *Archives of Oral Biology, 53*(suppl. 1), S1–S7.

Huston, J., & Wood, A. J. (2009). Sharing early preventive oral health with medical colleagues: A dental pain prevention strategy. *Journal of the California Dental Association, 37,* 723–734.

Krukemeyer, A. M., Arruda, A. O., & Inglehart, M. R. (2009). Pain and orthodontic treatment. *Angle Orthodontist, 79,* 1175–1181.

Kwan, S. Y. L., Petersen, P. E., Pine, C. M., & Borutta, A. (2005). Health-promoting schools: An opportunity for oral health promotion. *Bulletin of the World Health Organization, 83,* 677–685.

Lalloo, R., Myburgh, N. G., & Hobdell, M. H. (1999). Dental caries, socio-economic development and national oral health policies. *International Dental Journal, 49,* 196–202.

Leggat, P. A., Kedjarune, U., & Smith, D. R. (2007). Occupational health problems in modern dentistry: A review. *Industrial Health, 45,* 611–621.

Lewis, C. W., Grossman, D. C., Domoto, P. K., & Deyo, R. A. (2000). The role of the pediatrician in the oral health of children: A national survey. *Pediatrics, 106.* www.pediatrics.org/cgi/content/full/106/6/e84.

Liedl, A., O'Donnell, M., Creamer, M., Silove, D., McFarlane, A., Knaevelsrud, C., & Bryant, R. A. (2010). Support for the mutual maintenance of pain and post-traumatic stress disorder symptoms. *Psychological Medicine, 40,* 1215–1223.

Liu, Z. J., Yamagata, K., Kasahara, Y., & Ito, G. (1999). Electromyographic examination of jaw muscles in relation to symptoms and occlusion in patients with temporomandibular joint disorders. *Journal of Oral Rehabilitation, 26,* 33–47.

Macfarlane, T. V., Glenny, A. M., & Worthington, H. V. (2001). Systematic review of population-based epidemiological studies of oro-facial pain. *Journal of Dentistry, 29,* 451–467.

Maggiras, J., & Locker, D. (2002). Psychological factors and perceptions of pain associated with dental treatment. *Community Dentistry and Oral Epidemiology, 30,* 151–159.

Maguire, A., Rugg-Gunn, A. J., & Butler, T. J. (1996). Dental health of children taking antimicrobial and non-antimicrobial liquid oral medications long-term. *Caries Research, 30,* 16–21.

Maguire, S., Hunter, B., Hunter, L., Sibert, J. R., Mann, M., Kemp, A. M., & Welsh Child Protection Systematic Review Group. (2007). Diagnosing abuse: A systematic review of torn frenum and other intra-oral injuries. *Archives of Disease in Childhood, 92,* 1113–1117.

Marchiondo, K. J. (2010). Recognizing and treating vasovagal syncope. *American Journal of Nursing, 110,* 50–53.

McGrath, C., & Bedi, R. (2001). An evaluation of a new measure of oral health related quality of life: OHQoL-UK(W). *Community Dental Health, 18,* 138–143.

McNeil, D. W., Sorrell, J. T., & Vowles, K. E. (2006). Emotional and environmental determinants of dental pain. In D. I. Mostofsky, A. G. Forgione & D. B. Giddon (Eds.), *Behavioral Dentistry* (pp. 79–97). Oxford: Blackwell Munksgaard.

Mendola, P., O'Shea, R. M., Corah, N. L., Moretti, R., & Ayer, W. A. (1991). General practitioners' opinions on the treatment of anxious patients. *General Dentistry, 39,* 6, 444–447.

Miltenberger, R. G., & Rapp, J. T. (2006). Behavior management in dentistry: Thumb sucking. In D. I. Mostofsky, A. G. Forgione, & D. B. Giddon (Eds.), *Behavioral Dentistry* (pp. 163–174). Oxford: Blackwell Munksgaard.

Miyamoto, J. J., Honda, M., Saito, D. N., Okada, T., Ono, T., Ohyama, K., & Sadato, N. (2006). The representation of the human oral area in the somatosensory cortex: A functional MRI study. *Cerebral Cortex, 16,* 669–675.

Mossey, P. (Chief ed.) (2004). *Addressing the Global Challenges of Craniofacial Anomalies.* Report of a WHO meeting on International Research on Craniofacial Anomalies, December 2–4. Geneva: World Health Organization.

Mouradian, W. E. (2001). The face of a child: children's oral health and dental education. *Journal of Dental Education, 65*(9), 821–831.

Navazesh, M. (2006). Saliva in health and disease. In D. I. Mostofsky, A. Forgione, & D. B. Giddon (Eds.), *Behavioral Dentistry* (pp. 37–50). Oxford: Blackwell Munksgaard.

Needleman, H. L. (1986). Orofacial trauma in child abuse: Types, prevalence, management and the dental profession's involvement. *Pediatric Dentistry, 8*, 71–80.

Nusstein, J. M., Reader, A., & Drum, M. (2010). Local anesthesia strategies for the patient with a "hot" tooth. *Dental Clinics of North America, 54*, 237–247.

Offenbacher, S., Jared, H. L., & O'Reilly, P. G. (1998). Potential pathogenic mechanisms of periodontitis associated pregnancy complication. *Annals of Periodontology, 3*, 233–250.

Peltier, B. (2006). Hypnosis in dentistry. In D. I. Mostofsky, A. G. Forgione, & D. B. Giddon (Eds.), *Behavioral Dentistry* (pp. 65–78). Oxford: Blackwell Munksgaard.

Ramseier, C. A., & Suvan, J. E. (2010). *Health Behaviour Change in Dental Practice.* Ames, IO: Wiley Blackwell.

Reed, J., Robathan, M., Hockenhull, A., Rostill, H., Perrett, D., & Lees, A. (1999). Children's attitudes toward interacting with peers with different craniofacial anomalies. *Cleft Palate Craniofacial Journal, 36*, 441–447.

Remez, L. (2000). Oral sex among adolescents: is it sex or is it abstinence? *Family Planning Perspective, 32*, 298–304.

Rhodes, G. (2006). The evolutionary psychology of facial beauty. *Annual Review of Psychology, 57*, 199–226.

Sancho, F. M., & Ruiz, C. N. (2010). Risk of suicide amongst dentists: myth or reality? *International Dental Journal, 60*, 411–418.

Sanders, A. E., Slade, G. D., Lim, S., & Reisine, S. T. (2009). Impact of oral disease on quality of life in the US and Australian populations. *Community Dentistry & Epidemiology, 37*, 171–181.

Schou, L., & Locker, D. (1997). Principles of oral health promotion. In C. Pine (Ed.), *Community Oral Health* (pp. 177–187). Oxford: Wright.

Sharav, Y., Leviner, E., Tzukert, A., & McGrath, P. A. (1984). The spatial distribution, intensity and unpleasantness of acute dental pain. *Pain, 20*, 363–370.

Sheiham, A. (1995). Development of oral health strategies. In E. Kay (Ed.), *Turning Strategy into Action* (pp. 9–46). Manchester: Eden Bianchi Press.

Shulman, J. (2001). Teaching patients how to stop bruxing habits. *Journal of the American Dental Association, 132*, 1275–1277.

Skegg, K., Firth, H., Gray, A., & Cox, B. (2010). Suicide by occupation: does access to means increase the risk? *Australian and New Zealand Journal of Psychiatry, 44*, 429–434.

Slade, G. D. (1997). Derivation and validation of a short-form oral health impact profile. *Community Dentistry & Oral Epidemiology, 25*, 284–290.

Slade, G. D., & Spencer, A. J. (1994). Development and evaluation of the Oral Health Impact Profile. *Community Dental Health, 11*, 3–11.

Slade, G. D., & Sanders, A. E. (2003). *10.9 The ICF and Oral Health. Australian Institute of Health and Welfare ICF Australian User Guide, Version 1.0.* Disability Series. AIHW cat. no. DIS 33. Canberra: Australian Institute of Health and Welfare.

Slade, G. D., Spencer, A. J., & Roberts-Thomson, K. F. (Eds.) (2007). *Australia's Dental Generations: The National Survey of Adult Oral Health 2004–2006.* Dental Statistics and Research Series No. 34. AIHW cat. no. DEN 165. Canberra: Australian Institute of Health and Welfare.

Spencer, A. J. (2004). *Narrowing the Inequality Gap in Oral Health and Dental Care in Australia.* Commissioned Paper Series 2004. Australian Health Policy Institute, University of Sydney. www.menzieshealth policy.edu.au/other_tops/pdfs_hpa/spencernarrowing.pdf.

Spencer, A. J., Teusner, D. N., Carter, A. D., & Brennan, D. S. (2003). *The Dental Labour Force in Australia: The Position and Policy Directions.* Population Oral Health Series no. 2. AIHW cat. no. POH 2. Canberra: Australian Institute of Health and Welfare.

Steele, J. G., Sanders, A. E., Slade, G. D., Allen, P. F., Lahti, S., Nuttall, N., & Spencer, A. J. (2004). How do age and tooth loss affect oral health impacts and quality of life? A study comparing two national samples. *Community Dentistry & Oral Epidemiology, 32*, 107–114.

Strauss, R. P., & Hunt, R. J. (1993). Understanding the value of teeth to older adults: Influences on the quality of life. *Journal of the American Dental Association, 124,* 105–110.

Teusner, D. N., Chrisopoulos, S., & Spencer, A. J. (2008). *Projected Demand and Supply for Dental Visits in Australia: Analysis of the Impact of Changes in Key Inputs.* Dental Statistics and Research Series no. 38. AIHW cat. no. DEN 171. Canberra: Australian Institute of Health and Welfare.

Thrash, W., Marr, J., & Box, T. (1982). Effects of continuous patient information in the dental environment. *Journal of Dental Research, 61,* 1063–1065.

Trulsson, U., & Klingberg, G. (2003). Living with a child with a severe orofacial handicap: Experiences from the perspectives of parents. *European Journal of Oral Sciences, 111,* 19–25.

Twohig, M. P., Woods, D. W., Marcks, B. A., & Teng, E. J. (2003). Evaluating the efficacy of habit reversal: Comparison with a placebo control. *Journal of Clinical Psychiatry, 64,* 40–48.

van der Meulen, M. J., Lobbezoo, F., Aartman, I. H. A., & Naeije, M. (2006). Self-reported oral parafunctions and pain intensity in temporomandibular disorder patients. *Journal of Orofacial Pain, 20,* 31–35.

Wassell, R. W., Adams, N., & Kelly, P. J. (2006). The treatment of temporomandibular disorders with stabilizing splints in general dental practice: One-year follow-up. *Journal of the American Dental Association, 137,* 1089–1098.

Watt, R. G., & Fuller, S. S. (1999). Dental public health: Oral health promotion – opportunity knocks! *British Dental Journal, 186,* 3–6.

Welbury, R. R., & Murphy, J. M. (1998). The dental practitioner's role in protecting children from abuse. 2. The orofacial signs of abuse. *British Dental Journal, 184,* 7–10.

WHO. (2001). *International Classification of Functioning, Disability and Health (ICF).* Geneva: World Health Organization.

WHO (2007). *International Database of Craniofacial Anomalies (IDCFA).* Geneva: World Health Organization.

Wilder, R. S., O'Donnell, J. A., Barry, M., Galli, D. M., Foroud, F. H., Holyfield, L. J., & Robbins, M. R. (2008). Is dentistry at risk? A case for interprofessional education. *Journal of Dental Education, 72,* 1231–1237.

Williams, D. (1996). Acute pain management. In R. J. Gatchel & D. C. Turk (Eds.), *Psychological Approaches to Pain Management* (pp. 55–77). London: Guilford Press.

Wilson, K. E., Dorman, M. L., Moore, P. A., & Girdler, N. M. (2009). Pain control and anxiety management for periodontal therapies. *Periodontology 2000, 46,* 42–55.

Winn, D. (2001). Tobacco use and oral disease. *Journal of Dental Education, 65,* 306–312.

Wyszynski, D. S., Duffy, D. L., & Beaty, T. H. (1997). Maternal cigarette smoking and oral clefts: A meta-analysis. *Cleft Palate Craniofacial Journal, 34,* 206–210.

12

Health Psychology in Relation to Employment

Helen R. Winefield

The Changing Workplace

As the world of work occupies such a large portion of time over the lifespan of the majority of adults, health psychologists need to understand both how work impacts on health and wellbeing, and how workplaces can promote and sustain health. The focus of this chapter is paid employment, with acknowledgement that people undertake considerable amounts of unpaid purposeful work, for example in caring for family members, running households, and engaging in volunteering. However, these valuable contributions to society and to individual wellbeing are beyond the scope of this chapter. Similarly, "emotion work," as in the control of one's own emotional expression in the service of company goals or of relationship maintenance, although a fascinating subject (see Goldberg & Grandey, 2007; Strazdins, 2000), will not be explored here.

Employment comes in many forms: part-time and full-time, permanent or casual, contracted, or precarious. Work has been changing dramatically in recent decades, with increases in casual and short-term contract work, which is often less stable and reliable than a permanent position. Workers may or may not appreciate the uncertainties and flexibility of this change: financial insecurities may cause great anxiety, and casual workers may experience less control over the timing and duration of their work, making it harder to plan child care and other competing time demands. Many women have been adversely affected by this casualization of the modern workforce. Other changes are the disappearance of many unskilled jobs, taken over by machines and technology, and thus fewer employment opportunities for the less educated or those with disabilities.

In addition to improved financial status, satisfying work provides many other benefits of a more psychological nature including contact with others outside the home, regular time demands and learning opportunities which keep mind and body active and allow personal growth, and a sense of purpose and fulfilment from engagement in something useful (Jahoda, 1982). While this is the ideal, many jobs provide inadequate levels of these psychological benefits and some are so unsatisfying as to be aversive. Others are unsafe, physically or emotionally (for example through bullying or

Applied Topics in Health Psychology, First Edition. Edited by M. L. Caltabiano and L. Ricciardelli.
© 2013 John Wiley & Sons, Ltd. Published 2013 by John Wiley & Sons, Ltd.

harassment), or threaten the worker's health in other ways such as intruding excessively on time and energy for other aspects of the worker's life. Jobs of poor psychosocial quality such as those with high demands, low decision latitude or control, lack of social support, effort/reward imbalance, and insecurity can be worse for health and wellbeing than being unemployed (Butterworth *et al.*, 2011).

Just as employment potentially benefits health and wellbeing, the unemployed typically experience poorer health and wellbeing. There is a large research literature about the psychology of unemployment and questions of causality such as whether unemployment damages health or poor health reduces employability; again, these issues are beyond the scope of this chapter (see Dooley *et al.*, 1996; Goldney, 1996). It is worth noting, however, that the poorest health is reported overall by those who are neither employed nor unemployed, but by those who are out of the workforce due to disability that makes them unable to work. Results from the South Australian Monitoring and Surveillance System, July 2003 to June 2007, show approximately double the numbers of "unable to work" compared with unemployed among those aged 35–64 years. People in this category reported psychological distress at much the highest rate, whereas others out of the workforce by choice or due to retirement or studenthood report comparable wellbeing to the employed (Gill *et al.*, 2009).

Working-age Australians who are unemployed or out of the workforce make up 42.7% of the population (Australian Bureau of Statistics, 2009), and most of these receive some form of government pension or benefit. This fact concerns demographers and policy makers because the pensions need to be paid from taxes collected from the workers, of whom there is a diminishing number due to falling birth rates. Thus we are seeing extensions or abolition of compulsory retirement ages and encouragement (officially at least) for workers to continue in employment into their 70s. All these social changes have interesting consequences for the way work is organized and for the resources needed by older and younger members of the workforce.

Another major change in the workforce is the increasing proportion of women employees (46.1% of the employed, in the 2006 census: Australian Bureau of Statistics, 2009). The current generation of Australian women is the best-educated ever (Australian Bureau of Statistics, 2009), and their workforce participation rates are much higher than in previous generations. There are many resulting changes to how families operate and what goods and services are provided by family members and in turn, demanded by them. Potentially, the wellbeing of women workers has rippling effects on their partners, children, and the older (grandparent) generation, as well as their employers. The American Psychological Association's *Journal of Occupational Health Psychology* has been published since 1995, and an Occupational Health Psychology Interest Group of the Australian Psychological Society was established in 2010. The medical specialty of occupational medicine has concentrated on issues such as physical hazards of work, and rehabilitation of injured or disabled workers, but the Australasian Faculty of Occupational and Environmental Medicine has recently formulated a consensus statement about the health benefits of work which signals their developing interest in broadening this involvement. Health psychologists too have in the past often been involved in injury rehabilitation and chronic pain management, whether in hospital or community settings. The relatively new subspecialty of occupational health psychology has emerged to address work-related issues, as in this chapter. This area draws from both health psychology and organizational psychology as well as being influenced by their contributory disciplines including occupational medicine, occupational health and safety, health economics, sociology of health, epidemiology, rehabilitation, and human resource management. This chapter will briefly outline three main component areas: the sources and health effects of work stress, workplace wellness programs, and work–life balance (WLB). Interested readers are encouraged to pursue some of these ideas by searching the evidence base themselves, making use of the terms and conceptual frameworks introduced here, and of the understanding of research design strengths and weaknesses which are inherent in psychology training.

Sources and Health Effects of Work Stress

Work stress has been studied by psychologists for some time, although the term is often used rather loosely to refer to both the sources of dissatisfaction with work, and the psychological outcomes. More than sheer quantity of work, the sources of work stress are usually found to include workers' perception of a lack of control or autonomy in their workplace, in a context of high demands and lack of social support from coworkers and also supervisors and managers (Clarke & Cooper, 2004; Karasek, 1979; Muchinsky, 2009; O'Driscoll & Brough, 2005). The psychological outcomes include distress, anxiety and depression, burnout (the main expression of which is emotional exhaustion), and low commitment to the employer. Behaviorally, outcomes tend to be increased absences, reduced productivity, and, in extreme cases, retaliatory actions such as theft or sabotage.

The health effects of work stress (or, more correctly, of work strain) have been found to include pain, cardiovascular disease, and poor health habits. Many studies are cross-sectional, allowing the possibility that dissatisfaction with employment conditions is a result, instead of or as well as a cause, of reports of poor mental and physical health. However, we now have some longitudinal studies which make a stronger case for the causal influence of adverse work conditions. For example, Brunner *et al.* (2007) found in the prospective Whitehall II Study ($n > 10\,000$) a dose–response relationship between work stress and risk of general obesity (body mass index 30 kg/m^2) and central obesity (waist circumference >102 cm in men, >88 cm in women) that was largely independent of covariates including age, socioeconomic position, and adverse health behaviors. Similarly Lallukka *et al.* (2005) found in another large sample ($n > 8700$) that work fatigue and working overtime were associated with weight gain in both sexes. Women who were dissatisfied with combining paid work and family life were more likely to have gained weight, while men with low job demands were less likely to have gained weight. Such findings support calls for a systemic perspective on workplace wellness and health promotion programs, as discussed below.

Making a worker's compensation claim is one action available to workers who believe their health has been damaged in the work environment. Dollard *et al.* (1999) found that workers often use compensation claims as a last resort, after using up their sick leave entitlement, believing that claimants are regarded unfavourably by managers in terms of their future career prospects. The traditional occupational health and safety framework developed for sprains and strains and industrial accidents is not necessarily appropriate for work stress-related claims – which in Australia must be categorized as "psychological injury" – and these claims tend to take a long time to resolve and thus to result in high costs for both the employer and the claimant (Comcare, 2008; Haines *et al.*, 2004). Winefield *et al.* (2010) used a case-control design to compare workers who subsequently made a workers' compensation claim for psychological injury with matched controls. The clearest differences were that, up to 2 years before the claim, claimants had reported lower perceptions of procedural fairness, job autonomy, and trust in their immediate manager/supervisor (interactional justice). It is important for managers and supervisors to understand the connection between perceived injustice at work, in performance appraisal, appointment, promotion, and redundancy procedures, and the lodging of claims for compensation and bullying complaints. The important topic of organizational justice has received intensive research attention in the last three decades (Colquitt *et al.*, 2010).

Workplace Health Promotion

As seen above, employment conditions can powerfully affect worker health and wellbeing in a negative way, but to take a positive orientation, what may be the possibilities for workplace health promotion? This idea has stimulated a great deal of activity and advocacy in recent years, resulting in programs aimed to modify a variety of health-related behaviors including physical activity (Dugdill *et al.*, 2008), stress management, smoking, and nutrition, as well as safe lifting, ergonomics, and back pain prevention. Usually the goals are not only to improve worker health and wellbeing, but to reduce costs to employers from sickness absences, staff turnover, and compensation claims. But wider benefits may follow as well, as summarized by Whitehead (2006), who was alert to the need for organizations to consider their human resource management, and their training, marketing, and communication policies – in short, the whole culture and capacity-building commitment of the employing agency – in efforts to improve worker wellbeing and productivity. Management styles that advocate "negotiation, empowerment, participation and team unity" (p. 63) were recommended and obviously these go well beyond providing a gymnasium or dietary advice for the workers. Noblet (2003) also identified relatively early that the findings of the job stress literature, as above, such as seeking to enhance worker autonomy and social supports, offer immediate suggestions about how to protect and enhance worker health.

Meta-analyses show that workplace wellness or health promotion programs tend to reduce absenteeism and increase job satisfaction (Parks & Steelman, 2008; Richardson & Rothstein, 2008). However, it has proven difficult to translate these results into the reliable evidence of benefit and cost-effectiveness which managers look for in making decisions about program implementation. One problem is that employees, especially those with the poorest health initially, do not necessarily participate in the offered programs. Even getting workers to attend a health risk assessment is difficult, especially for smokers, older and male workers, workers with low socioeconomic status, and/or those who are not already preparing to change their health-related behaviors (Dobbins *et al.*, 1998; Simpson *et al.*, 2000).

In a randomized controlled trial of a fitness program at a casino, Atlantis *et al.* (2006) found that only 6.4% of the workforce were interested in participating, 42% of those then dropped out of the study, and compliance with treatments was far from perfect. Those who completed the study – mainly healthy but sedentary shift workers – showed reduced waist circumference and better aerobic fitness, although not improved body mass index; the results illustrate how barriers to adoption of and adherence to exercise at the worksite need further study. A more successful intervention at a fly-in-fly-out mine reported by Devine *et al.* (2008) used action research methodology. Their paper usefully details the long process of consultations and trust-building between workers, managers, unions, and researchers, which allowed the identification of health and safety issues and then the planning, implementation, and evaluation of interventions. Nöhammer *et al.* (2010) investigated the determinants of worker participation using interviews, and found that workers prefer information about the program which is personally targeted and which respects their autonomy. Then they are more likely to participate if they expect a benefit and if the costs in money, time, and inconvenience are low.

A crucial factor is the active support of participation by top management, a feature which requires that the management sees economic advantages for the business as well as for worker health. As a case example of how to achieve that, Lee *et al.* (2010) have described how they set up their health promotion program in a busy and resource-stretched hospital, as a business. They utilized a 3-year grant to get started but always sought financial independence after that, and succeeded such that they began to earn a healthy profit, felt they were responsible for employee loyalty to the organization, and had produced a social, organizational, and physical environment promoting staff and student health. However, they do not report hard data on sickness absence and turnover.

The latter were the kinds of benefits which Zwetsloot *et al.* (2010) had hoped to be able to trace in four Dutch health management organizations. Instead they found limited and fragmented outcome data which still tended to overlook the real but intangible benefits of a health promotion program, such as the company being seen to care about employees and therefore being more attractive to potential employees. A less ambitious and comprehensive study by Yen *et al.* (2010) followed employees over 1999–2007 and found a return on investment to the company amounting to US$180 per participant per year. In the same year a systematic literature review by Goldgruber and Ahrens (2010) cataloged results of interventions in stress, physical activity and nutrition, organizational development, smoking, and ergonomics and back pain. While they found inconsistent evidence for singular interventions and outcomes, there was stronger evidence for the effectiveness of multimodal or systemic programs including behavioral and relational (organizational) elements. Like all other researchers, they call for further research to elucidate which interventions work best for which workers and workplaces.

It is better than nothing, but not enough, to screen workers at their workplaces and then refer those with high risk of illness to their doctor. Aoun and Samar (2002) found that 76% of those so advised, who were men from 27 rural industries, did visit their general practitioner. However, the doctors reported that they had neither the time nor the resources to follow-up lifestyle advice such as "lose weight" or "exercise more," and would appreciate being able to refer those at risk but without established disease as yet to other health professionals for education and preventive care. In some cases this other professional will be a nurse, dietitian, or exercise specialist; in others it may be a health psychologist.

The special skills that psychologists can bring to tasks such as workplace-based health promotion include not only an understanding of how to motivate sustainable health-related behavior change (smoking, diet, exercise, etc.) but also an understanding of how the interpersonal environment at work (perceptions of support and fairness) impacts on worker wellbeing. The implications for involvement of psychologists in management training are clear, although this does not seem to be an area where psychological contributions are given much recognition. The other way that occupational health psychologists could add value to workplace health promotion would be in evaluation of the effectiveness of change efforts conducted, probably by multidisciplinary teams.

Work-Life Balance

What is the permeability of the boundaries between work and other aspects of life, such as home, family, and leisure, for working adults? Role incompatibility arises when there is just not enough time or energy for people to feel satisfied that they are giving enough or gaining enough satisfaction in either domain. Ford *et al.* (2007) found that a considerable amount of variability in family satisfaction is explained by work domain-specific variables, whereas a considerable amount of variability in job satisfaction is explained by family domain-specific variables, with job and family stress having the strongest effects on work–family conflict and cross-domain satisfaction. Their meta-analysis showed that organizations cannot optimize employee satisfaction without considering nonwork influences, so if organizations can positively impact family outcomes, that may in turn enhance employee satisfaction and commitment in the long run, such investments are worth their cost.

WLB "from an employee perspective, is the maintenance of a balance between responsibilities at work and at home" (De Cieri *et al.*, 2005, p. 2). When a good balance cannot be achieved, workers may experience various forms of work–home conflict or spillover and consequent emotional exhaustion, mood disorders, or substance-dependence disorders such as heavy drinking (Frone, 2000, 2003; Hall *et al.*, 2010; Parasuraman & Greenhaus, 2002).

Unpaid work or leisure activities may compete with employment, for adults' time and attention, but working parents have particularly been the focus of WLB research. Nearly all (92%) of Australian fathers with dependent children in the home are employed, as are two-thirds of couple mothers, and 30% of lone mothers, with rates increasing substantially when the youngest child starts school (De Vaus, 2004). Poor WLB is associated with strains in role relationships and conflicts between time and energy demands of employment and family (Baxter & Alexander, 2008; Pocock, 2003). For women, overload and a poor fit between work hours and demands outside of work have major influences on their work–life conflict (Skinner & Pocock, 2008).

Grandparents often have an important role in providing child care (Goodfellow & Laverty, 2003), and thus older people in the workforce may, like their adult children, need to balance family and work responsibilities (Winefield & Air, 2010). In the USA a higher percentage of employed grandparents provide child care than those who are retired/not employed (Guzman, 2004), and in Australia employed and nonemployed grandmothers are equally likely to be providing child care (Millward, 1998).

Working long hours can become part of a workplace culture, which interprets spending more time there as being more loyal and dedicated to the organization, but it does not necessarily follow that working fewer or part-time hours increases wellbeing. Part-time is often associated with casual or insecure jobs, low pay, and unpredictable demands for availability (Burchielli *et al.*, 2008; Skinner & Pocock, 2008). The role of long work hours in contributing to poor WLB is moderated by job status. Some demanding jobs where long hours are normal, are of high status and autonomy, and very rewarding to the worker (Weston *et al.*, 2004), are also associated with levels of pay which facilitate purchase of supplementary services. For women in Europe, Warren (2010) found that it is vital to take account of unpaid household and care-giving work, as well as of the number of hours and rates of pay of employment, in trying to understand WLB.

Work–home conflict may itself contribute to excessive workload because of the exhaustion and reduced efficiency it causes (Dikkers *et al.*, 2007). In fact, Bakker and Geurts (2004) reported a "loss spiral" where high job demands, fatigue, and work–home interference reinforce each other in their effects. The consequences or concomitants of work–home conflict include sleep problems, poorer health, and more sickness absences for workers (Clay *et al.*, 2009; Jansen *et al.*, 2006; Krantz & Lundberg, 2006). Not surprisingly these in turn predict lower worker retention and productivity (Beauregard & Henry, 2009; Peeters *et al.*, 2005; Skinner & Pocock, 2008; Steinmetz *et al.*, 2008). Hoobler *et al.* (2010) showed in a meta-analysis of 96 studies that both work-to-family conflict and family-to-work conflict were negatively associated with work performance, as rated by both self and manager. As a follow-up they recommend more study of gender influences, as managers tend to perceive women as more affected than men by family to work conflict, and accordingly to see them as less promotable. As noted by Cheung and Halpern (2010, p. 183): "The presence of children signals stability and responsibility for men, who are assumed to be better workers because of their roles as breadwinners. The identical situation for women has the opposite effect."

The management literature has advocated various strategies to reduce work–home conflict and thus improve worker wellbeing and productivity. WLB policies such as allowing flexible hours or working from home have shown some success in improving worker job performance and retention (Glass & Finley, 2002; Jacob *et al.*, 2008; Konrad & Mangel, 2000). However, the consequences can sometimes be unexpected. For example, Breaugh and Frye (2008) found that while flexible hours helped full-time employed parents, being able to take work home made things worse, perhaps due to blurring of the work–home boundary. Beauregard and Henry's (2009) review highlighted the fact that family friendly work–life policies do not necessarily result in reduced conflict between work and family. Employees may fail to utilize these concessions because they fear appearing uncommitted to the organization. Nonetheless, work–life policies are associated with improved organizational performance and advantages in recruitment and retention (Glass & Finley, 2002; Konrad & Mangel, 2000).

On the positive side, work–life enhancement can occur when workers report they bring benefits from their work, such as skills and capabilities, back to their nonwork lives. In fact, Gordon *et al.* (2007) found this associated with job and career satisfaction and organizational commitment, in a sample of 489 women aged 50+ who were working in healthcare and financial services. Regarding the opposite direction of home to work enhancement, Cheung and Halpern (2010) and others have concluded that the confidence and skills such as time management and interpersonal relations which women develop in running a household help them to become efficient workers and transformational leaders. It is highly relevant for psychologist practitioners, who are predominantly women, to consider issues of WLB and enhancement as they apply to their own self-care and personal/professional development.

Conclusions

This chapter has briefly reviewed some prominent topics within occupational health psychology: the health effects of work stress, the usefulness of the workplace as a location to promote health, and the wider question of how employers can contribute to worker health by aiding their WLB. It is hoped that readers may be stimulated to add to the knowledge base in this fascinating and crucial field of study at the interface between employment and health, each area with its heritage of theories and conceptual schemes. There has been a relative lack of psychological input to topics such as health promotion at work, or management training to increase worker perceptions of justice and understanding. This is one direction that health psychology can very usefully expand to encompass, to the benefit of all those in the workforce and their dependents, and to the benefit of our understanding of how to apply psychological knowledge to improve human health.

References

Australian Bureau of Statistics. (2009). *2006 Census of Population and Housing.* Canberra: Australian Bureau of Statistics.

Aoun, S., & Samar, L. (2002). Men's health promotion by general practitioners in a workplace setting. *Australian Journal of Rural Health, 10*, 268–272.

Atlantis, E., Chow, C., Kirby, A., & Fiatarone Singh, M. A. (2006). Worksite intervention effects on physical health: A randomized controlled trial. *Health Promotion International, 21*, 191–199.

Bakker, A. B., & Geurts, S. A. E. (2004). Toward a dual-process model of work-home interference. *Work and Occupations, 31*, 345–366.

Baxter, J., & Alexander, M. (2008). Mothers' work-to-family strain in single and couple parent families. *Australian Journal of Social Issues, 43*, 195–214.

Beauregard, T. A., & Henry, L. C. (2009). Making the link between work-life balance practices and organizational performance. *HRM Review, 19*, 9–22.

Breaugh, J. A., & Fry, N. K. (2008). Work-family conflict: The importance of family-friendly employment practices and family-supportive supervisors. *Journal of Business Psychology, 22*, 345–353.

Brunner, E. J., Chandola, T., & Marmot, M. G. (2007). Prospective effect of job strain on general and central obesity in the Whitehall II Study. *American Journal of Epidemiology, 165*, 828–837.

Burchielli, R., Bartram, T., & Thanacoody, R. (2008) Work-family balance or greedy organizations? *Relations Industrielles/Industrial Relations, 63*, 108–133.

Butterworth, P., Leach, L. S., Strazdins, L., Olesen, S. C., Rodgers, B., & Broom, D. H. (2011). The psychosocial quality of work determines whether employment has benefits for mental health: Results from a longitudinal national household panel survey. *Occupational and Environmental Medicine, 68*, 806–812.

Cheung, F. M., & Halpern, D. F. (2010). Women at the top. *American Psychologist, 65*, 182–193.

Clarke, S., & Cooper, C. L. (2004). *Managing the Risk of Workplace Stress: Health and Safety Hazards.* London: Routledge.

Clay, E., Kittel, F., Godin, I., Bacquer, D. D., & Backer, G. D. (2009). Measures of work-family conflict predict sickness absence from work. *Journal of Occupational and Environmental Medicine, 51*, 879–86.

Colquitt, J. A., Wesson, M. J., & Lepine, J. A. (2010). *Organizational Behavior: Improving Performance and Commitment in the Workplace.* New York: McGraw-Hill.

Comcare. (2008). *Working Well: An Organisational Approach to Preventing Psychological Injury.* Pub 47. Canberra: Commonwealth of Australia.

De Cieri, H., Holmes, B., Abbot, J., & Petit, T. (2005) Achievements and challenges for work/life balance strategies in Australian organisations. *International Journal of Human Resource Management, 6*, 90–103.

De Vaus, D. (2004). *Diversity and Change in Australian Families: Statistical Profiles.* Melbourne: Aust Institute Family Studies.

Devine, S. G., Muller, R., & Carter, A. (2008). Using the framework for health promotion action to address staff perceptions of occupational health and safety at a fly-in/fly-out mine in north-west Queensland. *Health Promotion Journal of Australia, 19*, 196–202.

Dikkers, J. S. E., Guerts, S. A. E., Kompier, M. A. J., Taris, T. W., Houtman, I.L. D., & van den Heuvel, F. (2007). Does workload cause work-home interference or is it the other way around? *Stress and Health, 23*, 303–314.

Dobbins, T. A., Simpson, J. M., Oldenburg, B., Owen, N., & Harris, D. (1998). Who comes to a workplace health risk assessment? *International Journal of Behavioral Medicine, 5*, 323–334.

Dollard, M. F., Winefield, H. R., & Winefield, A. H. (1999). Predicting work stress compensation claims and return to work in welfare workers. *Journal of Occupational Health Psychology, 4*, 279–287.

Dooley, D., Fielding, J., & Levi, L. (1996) Health and unemployment. *Annual Review of Public Health, 17*, 449–465.

Dugdill, L., Brettle, A., Hulme, C., McCluskey, S., & Long, A.F. (2008). Workplace physical activity interventions: a systematic review. *International Journal of Workplace Health Management, 1*, 20–40.

Ford, M. T., Heinen, B. A., & Langkamer, K. L. (2007). Work and family satisfaction and conflict: A meta-analysis of cross-domain relations. *Journal of Applied Psychology, 92*, 57–80.

Frone, M. (2000). Work–family conflict and employee psychiatric disorders: The National Comorbidity Survey. *Journal of Applied Psychology, 85*, 888–95.

Frone, M. R. (2003). Work–family balance. In J. C. Quick & L. E. Tetrick (Eds.), *Handbook of Occupational Health Psychology* (pp. 143–162). Washington DC: American Psychological Association.

Gill, T., Koster, C., Taylor, A., Chittleborough, C., & Winefield, H. (2009). *Employment Status and Psychological Distress in South Australia: Summary of Results.* Discipline of Psychiatry, University of Adelaide. www.health.sa.gov.au/pros/default.aspx?PageContentID=384&tabid=120.

Glass, J., & Finley, A. (2002). Coverage and effectiveness of family-responsive workplace policies. *Human Resources Management Review, 12*, 313–337.

Goldberg, L. S., & Grandey, A. A. (2007). Display rules versus display autonomy: Emotion regulation, emotional exhaustion, and task performance in a call center simulation. *Journal of Occupational Health Psychology, 12*, 301–318.

Goldgruber, J., & Ahrens, D. (2010) Effectiveness of workplace health promotion and primary prevention interventions: A review. *Journal of Public Health, 18*, 75–88.

Goldney, R. (1996). Unemployment and health. *Australian and New Zealand Journal of Psychiatry, 30*, 309–311.

Goodfellow, J., & Laverty, J. (2003). Grandparents supporting working families. *Family Matters, 66*, 14–19.

Gordon, J. R., Whelan-Berry, K. S., & Hamilton, E. A. (2007). The relationship among work-family conflict and enhancement, organizational work-family culture, and work outcomes for older working women. *Journal of Occupational Health Psychology, 12*, 350–364.

Guzman, L. (2004). *Grandma and Grandpa Taking Care of the Kids*. Child Trends Research Brief *17*. Washington DC: Child Trends.

Haines, J., Williams, C. L., & Carson, J. (2004). Workers' compensation for psychological injury: Personal and environmental correlates. *Work, 22*, 183–194.

Hall, G. B., Dollard, M. F., Tuckey, M. R., Winefield, A. H., & Thompson, B. (2010). A longitudinal study of spillover of job demands and emotional exhaustion to work-family conflict. *Journal of Occupational and Organisational Psychology, 83*, 237–250.

Hoobler, J. M., Hu, J., & Wilson, M. (2010). Do workers who experience conflict between work and family domains hit a "glass ceiling?": A meta-analytic examination. *Journal of Vocational Behavior, 77*, 481–494.

Jacob, J. I., Bond, J. T., Galinsky, E., & Hill, E. J. (2008). Six critical ingredients in creating an effective workplace. *The Psychologist-Manager Journal, 11*, 141–161.

Jahoda, M. (1982). *Employment and Unemployment: A Social-Psychological Analysis*. Cambridge: Cambridge University Press.

Jansen, N. W. H., Kant, I. J., van Amelsvoort, L. G. P. M., Kristensen, T. S., Swaen, G. M. H., & Nijhuis, F. J. N. (2006). Work-family conflict as a risk factor for sickness absence. *Occupational and Environmental Medicine, 63*, 488–494.

Karasek, R. A. (1979). Job demands, job decision latitude, and mental strain: Implications for job redesign. *Administrative Science Quarterly, 24*, 285–308.

Konrad, A. M., & Mangel, B. (2000). The impact of work-life programs on firm productivity. *Strategic Management Journal, 21*, 1225–1237.

Krantz, G., & Lundberg, U. (2006). Workload, work stress, and sickness absence in Swedish male and female white-collar employees. *Scandinavian Journal of Public Health, 34*, 238–246.

Lallukka, T., Laaksonen, M., Martikainen, P., Sarlio-Lähteenkorva, S., & Lahelma, E. (2005). Psychosocial working conditions and weight gain among employees. *International Journal of Obesity, 29*, 909–915.

Lee, S., Blake, H., & Lloyd, S. (2010). The price is right: Making workplace wellness financially sustainable. *International Journal of Workplace Health Management, 3*, 58–69.

Millward, C. (1998). *Family Relationships and Intergenerational Exchange in Later life*. AIFS Working Paper No. 15. Melbourne: Australian Institute of Family Studies.

Muchinsky, P. M. (2009). *Psychology Applied to Work: An Introduction to Industrial and Organizational Psychology* (9th edn.). Summerfield, NC: Hypergraphic Press.

Noblet, A. (2003). Building health promoting work settings: Identifying the relationship between work characteristics and occupational stress in Australia. *Health Promotion International, 18*, 351–359.

Nöhammer, E., Schusterschitz, C., & Stummer, H. (2010). Determinants of employee participation in workplace health promotion. *International Journal of Workplace Health Management, 3*, 97–110.

O'Driscoll, M., & Brough, P. (2005). Job stress and burnout. In M. O'Driscoll, P. Taylor, & T. Kalliath (Eds.), *Organisational Psychology in Australia and New Zealand* (pp. 188–211). Melbourne: Oxford University Press.

Parasuraman, S., & Greenhaus, J. H. (2002). Toward reducing some critical gaps in work-family research. *Human Resource Management Review, 12*, 299–312.

Parks, K. M., & Steelman, L. A. (2008). Organizational wellness programs: A meta-analysis. *Journal of Occupational Health Psychology, 13*, 58–68.

Peeters, M. C. W., Montgomery, A. J., Bakker, A. B., & Schaufeli, W. B. (2005). Balancing work and home: How job and home demands are related to burnout. *International Journal of Stress Management, 12*, 43–61.

Pocock, B. (2003). *The Work/Life Collision*. Adelaide: Federation Press.

Richardson, K. M., & Rothstein, H. R. (2008). Effects of occupational stress management programs: A meta-analysis. *Journal of Occupational Health Psychology, 13*, 69–93.

Simpson, J. M., Oldenburg, B., Owen, N., Harris, D., Dobbins, T., Salmon, A. *et al.* (2000). The Australian national workplace health project: Design and baseline findings. *Preventive Medicine, 31*, 249–260.

Skinner, N., & Pocock, B. (2008). Work-life conflict: Is work time or work overload more important? *Asia Pacific Journal of Human Resources, 46*, 303–315.

Steinmetz, H., Frese, M., & Schmidt, P. (2008). A longitudinal panel study on antecedents and outcomes of work-home interference. *Journal of Vocational Behavior, 73*, 231–241.

Strazdins, L. M. (2000). Integrating emotions: Multiple role measurement of emotional work. *Australian Journal of Psychology, 52*, 41–50.

Warren, T. (2010). Work time. Leisure time. On women's temporal and economic well-being in Europe. *Community, Work & Family, 13*, 365–392.

Weston, R., Gray, M., Qu, L., & Stanton, D. (2004). *Long Work Hours and the Wellbeing of Fathers and their Families*. Research Paper No. 35. Melbourne: Australian Institute of Family Studies.

Whitehead, D. (2006). Workplace health promotion: The role and responsibility of health care managers. *Journal of Nursing Management, 14*, 59–68.

Winefield, H., & Air, T. (2010). Grandparenting: Diversity in grandparent experiences and needs for health care and support. *International Journal of Evidence-Based Healthcare, 8*, 277–283.

Winefield, H. R., Saebel, J., & Winefield, A. H. (2010). Employee perceptions of fairness as predictors of workers' compensation claims for psychological injury: An Australian case-control study. *Stress and Health, 26*, 3–12.

Yen, L., Schultz, A. B., Schaefer, C., Bloomberg, S., & Edington, D. W. (2010). Long-term return on investment of an employee health enhancement program at a Midwest utility company from 1999 to 2007. *International Journal of Workplace Health Management, 3*, 79–96.

Zwetsloot, G. I., van Scheppingen, A. R., Dijkman, A. J., Heinrich, J., & den Besten, H. (2010). The organizational benfits of investing in workplace health. *International Journal of Workplace Health Management, 3*, 143–159.

Part 4

Health Conditions
and Health Issues

13

"My Genes are my Destiny"

Psychosocial Aspects of Genetic Risk Assessment for Illness Susceptibility

Kerry Sherman and Nadine Kasparian

Genetic testing for disease susceptibility is becoming increasingly available for a range of diseases (e.g., hereditary cancer, Huntington's disease, heart disease, Alzheimer's disease). The decision to undergo genetic testing is not straightforward as in many cases the outcomes of testing may be uncertain and do not always lead to clearly indicated risk reduction or preventive measures. Adopting a broad psychological perspective, this chapter will delineate the key challenges facing individuals undergoing genetic risk assessment for disease susceptibility, and the range of psychological, social, and behavioral responses to the genetic testing process. Focus will be on key phases of the genetic testing process including decision-making for initial uptake of testing, responses to the testing process and to receipt of test results, and decision-making, family communication, and adjustment following test result disclosure. Finally, this chapter will explore avenues for psychological intervention within the genetic testing context.

What is Genetic Risk and Genetic Testing?

Scientific and technological advances, along with the decoding of the human genome sequence in 2003, paved the way for links to be made between disease susceptibility and genetic mutations (Patenaude, 2005). There are currently more than 1000 known links between specific genetic mutations and disease risk across a spectrum of conditions ranging from cancer, heart disease, and diabetes through to Alzheimer's disease. Genetic testing for disease susceptibility is currently available for those conditions linked to specific gene mutations, with the number of available links increasing at a rapid rate. As a consequence, the availability and use of genetic testing is expanding (National Cancer Institute, 2011). One example of this is pre-implantation genetic diagnosis, a process that provides couples who have a personal or strong family history of a specific disease with the opportunity to screen embryos for particular genetic mutation(s) prior to implantation through *in vitro* fertilization techniques. This allows only embryos unaffected with the genetic mutation to be implanted (Patenaude, 2005).

Applied Topics in Health Psychology, First Edition. Edited by M. L. Caltabiano and L. Ricciardelli.
© 2013 John Wiley & Sons, Ltd. Published 2013 by John Wiley & Sons, Ltd.

Some diseases (e.g., cystic fibrosis, muscular dystrophy, Huntington's disease) are caused by a genetic mutation in one specific gene (monogenic disorder). Other diseases are linked with a range of genetic mutations which alone can confer some increased risk, but in combination may greatly increase the likelihood of future disease (multifactorial inheritance disorder) (National Human Genome Research Institute, 2011). Conditions such as hereditary nonpolyposis colorectal cancer (HNPCC) and hereditary breast and ovarian cancer (HBOC) are diseases that have been linked with multiple gene mutations. With HBOC, for example, mutations on genes *BRCA1* and *BRCA2* are associated with increased disease risk. For individuals carrying mutations on both these genes their lifetime risk for breast cancer is 60%, along with a 40% lifetime risk of ovarian cancer (Lindor *et al.*, 2008), compared with the estimated lifetime risk for women not carrying these mutations of 12% for breast cancer, and less than 2% for ovarian cancer.

What Information Can Genetic Testing Provide?

One of the prime reasons for undertaking genetic testing is to obtain more definite estimates of disease risk (Patenaude, 2005). However, the outcomes of the genetic testing process are often fraught with uncertainty and ambiguity. There are a number of possible testing outcomes. A *mutation-positive* outcome indicates that the specific gene mutation being tested is present, and the individual concerned is a mutation carrier. A *mutation-negative* result indicates that no mutation is present, and that the tested individual is not a carrier of the known mutation. However, for an individual to receive a mutation-negative outcome, a member of the family who has already been affected with the specific condition needs to have undergone testing for the mutation; without this information, a tested individual will not receive a definite negative outcome. This presents a considerable barrier to testing if the affected family member(s) is no longer alive or available to participate in the testing process. Also, a mutation-negative result does not mean that the individual is not at risk of developing the condition; rather, it indicates that the person's risk is likely to be similar to that of the general population. Some individuals will receive a result indicating that there are mutations present, but that the significance of these mutations is currently unknown: an *inconclusive* test result. It is likely that as knowledge about the role of specific genetic mutations increases many of the currently unknown mutation variants will be linked to disease, but with the present level of scientific understanding there is a considerable number of individuals for whom the testing outcome will end with uncertainty, and will perhaps provide no further insight into their risk of disease compared with what was known prior to testing.

The *penetrance*, or extent to which a genetic mutation confers increased disease risk, differs between conditions, and is another source of ambiguity or uncertainty. For some disorders, such as Huntington's disease and early-onset alzheimer's disease, the penetrance approaches 100%, meaning that an individual carrying the specific gene will likely develop the disease at some point in their life. For many conditions, however, the penetrance is much less than 100%, sometimes as low as 5% (Waalen & Beutler, 2009). In such instances, the genetic mutation is only one of a number of possible causal factors, with exogenous factors, including gene–environment interactions, implicated to a considerable extent. Moreover, with multiple genes, the interpretation of genetic testing outcomes is considerably more difficult than for single-gene conditions and this may lead to greater ambiguity regarding disease risk.

Given that the desire for greater certainty about one's disease susceptibility is a prime motivator for genetic testing (Esplen *et al.*, 2007), the level of uncertainty implicated here is likely to be a source of frustration and disappointment. Indeed, in some cases, individuals may not even be offered testing based on the findings of the genetic counselling process, creating yet another source of frustration (Patenaude, 2005).

Who Provides Genetic Testing?

Until recently, genetic risk-assessment services were typically offered only through hospital-affiliated clinics. Technological advances in DNA extraction and analysis have vastly improved the accessibility of genetic testing services, and have also lowered the cost for obtaining these services. As a result, there has been a rapid expansion in the number of testing providers, and genetics services are now also available through direct-to-consumer marketing (Botkin *et al.*, 2010), via nonhospital-affiliated enterprises and Internet-based providers (Cameron *et al.*, 2009). A key difference between the organizations offering genetic risk-assessment services lies not with the genetic testing *per se*, but with the level of information, support, and counselling provided throughout the risk-assessment process. Genetic risk-assessment services at hospital-based clinics typically provide information and counselling prior to blood collection through genetic coun-sellors and clinical geneticists, entailing an overview of the individual's family history of disease, explanation of the links between genetic mutations and disease, and estimation of the likelihood that the individual has acquired a specific gene mutation based on their pedigree (Butow *et al.*, 2003). Available screening and preventive options for the specific disease of concern are also typ-ically discussed. It is critical that the individual understands fully the possible implications of genetic testing (e.g., from a medical, emotional, social, occupational, and insurance perspective), particularly since for some conditions there is currently a "therapeutic gap" whereby genetic test-ing for disease susceptibility is available, but there is no known cure or treatment for the disease (Patenaude, 2005). Following the initial visit, the individual then decides whether to provide blood for testing, following which additional counselling is provided by the genetic counsellors and clinical geneticists prior to, and at the time of, test result disclosure. At any stage throughout the genetic testing process, individuals and family members may be referred to a psychologist to address any psychological concerns or emotional distress they may be experiencing (Thewes *et al.*, 2003).

In contrast to the high level of information and support provided by specialist genetics clinics, direct-to-consumer providers of testing services focus on the provision of test results and provide minimal counselling about the process and possible implications, and generally do not provide psychological support services (Bloss *et al.*, 2011). Lack of counselling and information about genetic testing can leave the tested individual vulnerable to a range of difficulties including mis-interpretation of testing results, inappropriate decisions regarding the uptake or abandonment of surveillance or preventive options, and psychological and social difficulties arising from the receipt of results (Hock *et al.*, 2011). The potential for such difficulties highlights the importance of support provision in this setting.

Eligibility for genetic testing is typically governed by the individual having a strong family history of the disease in question, although this is not always the case. Online genetics services will provide genetic testing without information on family history of disease, and this may make interpretation of genetic test results very difficult, if not impossible. Nevertheless, once testing outcomes are known, the individual is faced with decisions about appropriate actions to take regarding surveillance and risk reduction, and also decisions about strategies for communicating test outcomes to family members. By its very nature, genetic risk assessment entails familial risk, thus the testing process has implications not only for the tested individual, but also for other family members (Patenaude, 2005).

Frameworks for Understanding Responses
to Genetic Risk Assessment

Genetic risk assessment carries with it the assumption that receipt of genetic risk information will guide and motivate future health behaviors and health-related decisions (Bloss *et al.*, 2011). That is, genetic risk information may serve as a motivator of future health-promoting behaviors such as diet and exercise choices, as well as decisions relating to disease screening and prophylactic options. Self-regulation models [e.g., Cognitive-Social Health Information Processing (C-SHIP); Leventhal *et al.*, 1998; Miller *et al.*, 1996] provide a conceptual basis from which to understand psychosocial responses in this context. Central to this theorizing is the notion that responses to a health threat will not necessarily follow a rational model of thinking or behavior, and that responses are mediated by a range of psychological, social, and environmental factors (Leventhal *et al.*, 2003).

Thinking about individual dynamics, self-regulation theory identifies five core dimensions of illness representations which may influence responses to genetic risk assessment: identity of the threat (i.e., perceived signs and symptoms of, as well as past experiences with, a disease); causal attributions (i.e., beliefs about the cause of an illness such as genetics or stress); time-line (i.e., beliefs about illness onset and duration); controllability in terms of disease prevention and cure; and consequences (relating to both physical and psychosocial aspects) (Leventhal *et al.*, 2003; Shiloh, 2006). Within the context of familial melanoma, for example, an individual may hold specific beliefs about the signs, symptoms, and risk factors associated with melanoma; the extent to which genetic factors play a role in the development of the disease; the anticipated trajectory of the disease (e.g., child versus adult onset; chronic versus acute nature of the disease); available preventive, risk reduction or treatment options for melanoma; and the anticipated impact of melanoma or melanoma risk on their physical, psychological, and social functioning. Variations in these representations, as well as in perceived risk (i.e., the way in which an individual construes personal disease risk or susceptibility), demographic variables, personality factors, and early life experiences and attachment relationships, will evoke different responses to the same health threat (Shiloh, 2006). Coping skills or self-regulatory competencies are also important and may involve strategies for dealing with specific barriers to, and maintenance of, physical and psychological adjustment to risk information, such as acceptance of risk status and distress tolerance (Miller *et al.*, 1996). These skills will impact on the individual's ability to understand genetic risk information, make appropriate decisions for them, and adjust their behavior as recommended by the specific testing outcome (de Ridder & Kuijer, 2006).

Moreover, the family systems model of illness developed by Rolland and Williams (2005) supplements these self-regulatory approaches by focusing on how the threat of disease may impact on the family as a whole, depending on the type of condition, the likely psychosocial demands of the illness over time, and the degree of certainty following the genetic testing process. The focus of this latter developmental framework is on understanding the implications of genetic testing for disease risk within the context of family relationships, cultural beliefs, and the wider healthcare and societal systems. In doing so, this model offers a structure for organizing our thinking about the complex interplay between: (a) genetic and other factors placing individuals at risk of disease; (b) significant family and relationship factors; and (c) the professionals involved in providing care (Rolland & Williams, 2005). There is also a strong emphasis on recognizing the ways in which individual and family responses to health threat or illness may change over time, and across the life span. Applied to the genetic testing process, the family systems genetic illness model posits that individuals and families move through a number of phases or developmental challenges associated with genetic testing. These include initial awareness of familial disease risk, "crises" such as contemplation of genetic risk assessment and receipt of genetic test results, and adaptation (Rolland & Williams, 2005). The ways in which individuals and families move through these phases may vary considerably, reflecting the complexities inherent in individual and family dynamics, as well as differences in medical, cultural, and environmental factors.

Factors Underlying Interest in Genetic Testing

Early research assessing hypothetical interest in uptake of genetic testing across a range of diseases reported generally high levels of interest (e.g., Bernhardt *et al.*, 2009; Bottorff *et al.*, 2002; Doukas *et al.*, 2004; Kasparian *et al.*, 2009). High levels of motivation to undertake testing, as well as beliefs in the genetic cause of disease and positive consequences of testing (e.g., Barnoy *et al.*, 2009; Doukas & Li, 2004), are associated with interest in testing. Moreover, evidence from at-risk individuals considering testing for Huntington's disease supports the notion that these decisions do not necessarily follow a rational approach (Etchegary, 2006). In the case of prenatal testing, or the genetic testing of children, additional factors consistent with the family systems approach (Rolland & Williams, 2005) also appear to influence the decisions of parents (or prospective parents). For example, in considering prenatal testing for fragile X syndrome, factors such as the woman's reproductive stage of life and her experience with illness and disability, along with her perceptions of the consequences of knowing her carrier status, influenced decision-making (Archibald *et al.*, 2009; Sparbel & Williams, 2009). Similarly, when parents who are carriers of a genetic disorder make decisions about testing for their child, they consider not only the likely medical consequences, but also their personal experiences of learning about their genetic status, and the possible psychological and emotional consequences for the child and other family members (Clarke *et al.*, 2010).

Hypothetical interest, however, has not necessarily translated into actual uptake of genetic testing (e.g., Bernhardt *et al.*, 2009; Kasparian *et al.*, 2009). This difference between attitudes towards genetic testing and actual behavior may, in part, be attributed to the influence of genetic counselling, which has been found to considerably change the attitudes of prospective testers, often leading to deferment of testing (Li *et al.*, 2007). Given that genetic counselling provides information on the possible benefits, limitations, and negative consequences of genetic testing, it is likely that many people initially interested in testing do not have a realistic perception of the process. Following genetic counselling, women withdrawing from testing for breast cancer susceptibility cited fear of the psychological effects of testing as a major reason for not continuing with the process (Godard *et al.*, 2007). Evidence indicates that, for most individuals, decisions about genetic testing rest primarily with that individual, but other sources of influence may include the individual's spouse, other family members (e.g., Jaques *et al.*, 2004; Klitzman *et al.*, 2007), and also their health professionals (Salkovskis *et al.*, 2010).

Psychosocial Challenges of Genetic Testing

Once individuals opt for genetic testing, they are faced with a number of additional decision-making challenges, including: receipt of test results, disclosure of test results to other family members or significant others, and actions to take in light of the outcomes of genetic testing. There is also the need to understand and manage strong emotional and psychological reactions to the testing process. The majority of tested individuals agree to receive their test results; however, not all tested individuals choose to share this information with other family members (DeMarco & McKinnon, 2006). Disclosure of results typically occurs most with first-degree relatives, and then less often with second- and third-degree relatives (Gaff *et al.*, 2007). Family communication is often facilitated by perceived physical and emotional closeness of the tested individual to family members (Wiseman *et al.*, 2010), and the perceived receptivity of the family member is ascertained prior to disclosure (Gaff *et al.*, 2007). The process of communicating genetic test results to family members appears to fulfil a number of functions including the sharing of responsibility for informing family members, seeking emotional support and information from the family and, in some cases, preventing future illness by informing others of their potential risk (Wiseman *et al.*, 2010). Testees are often uncomfortable conveying a mutation-positive result and, for this reason, may elect not to share this information with their family (Wiseman *et al.*, 2010), or may want to try to protect their family (particularly young children) from undue distress (DeMarco & McKinnon, 2006). While there is no legal obligation for a testee to disclose his or her genetics information to others, the decision to withhold this information may be deleterious over time to the health of other blood-related kin who may also be mutation carriers.

Following results disclosure, decisions will need to be made about whether it is necessary or appropriate to undertake preventive actions to minimize disease risk, particularly where the lifetime risk of disease can be greater than 80%. Uptake of recommended risk-reducing options varies considerably by disease, and by type of recommendation. In some instances the recommended risk-reducing options entail relatively simple lifestyle changes (such as adopting sun-safe practices for individuals at high risk of developing melanoma), as well as undergoing frequent screening when this option is available (e.g., skin surveillance for melanoma, colonoscopy for familial colorectal cancer) (Loescher *et al.*, 2009; Metcalfe *et al.*, 2008). Frequently the preventive options offered are highly invasive (e.g., removal of the stomach to prevent hereditary gastric colorectal cancer, bilateral prophylactic mastectomy to prevent breast cancer), and may be associated with severe side effects (e.g., infertility resulting from drug interventions or prophylactic removal of the ovaries). Moreover, for some diseases (e.g., ovarian cancer) the effectiveness of screening is unproven and prophylactic surgery is regarded as the most effective risk-reduction approach (Metcalfe *et al.*, 2008). As described in the brief case study below, there is no one clear path and the decisions about one's medical future rest with the tested individual.

Case Study: Justine

Justine, a 25 year-old woman with a strong family history of HNPCC, (hereditary colon cancer), has just undergone genetic testing and found out that she is a mutation carrier, and has a more than 80% chance of developing the disease at some point in her life. From the day that the genetic counsellor disclosed the testing results, Justine's mind has been in a whirlwind. She feels angry, sad, scared, and confused, all at once. She has no idea how she is going to tell her boyfriend of 2 years, and she is fearful of the implications of this result for future children. The geneticist has suggested that Justine consider the possibility of having surgery to completely remove her colon: the only safe way to eliminate her risk. At 25 and with her life ahead of her, is this really what she wants? What does all this mean for her future?

The challenges of communication and decision-making throughout the testing process can take their toll on both the tested individual and other family members. It is not unusual for individuals undergoing testing to experience heightened psychological distress (anxiety and depression), particularly at the time of test result disclosure, and for months thereafter if the test result is positive (Hamilton *et al.*, 2009; Landsbergen *et al.*, 2009). Distress is not only experienced by the tested individual; there is evidence that spouses frequently experience similar levels of psychological distress as the testee themselves (Mireskandari *et al.*, 2007). Spousal distress may be associated with difficulties in understanding the testing process, as well as uncertainty about how best to support the testee (Sherman *et al.*, 2010). Siblings who are not found to be mutation carriers may also experience a degree of distress in the form of "survivor guilt" (e.g., Graceffa *et al.*, 2009). Also, "transmission guilt" is a common experience of parents who are found to have a child affected by a genetic mutation, and may be accompanied by feelings of self-blame as well as changes in their reproductive plans compared to carriers without affected children (Lewis *et al.*, 2010).

Fortunately, several studies indicate that distress associated with the genetic testing process is relatively short-lived in most, but not all, cases. Individuals receiving negative results typically revert to pretest levels of adjustment within weeks of results disclosure, whereas for those with positive results heightened distress may persist for up to 18 months (Hendriks *et al.*, 2008; Landsbergen *et al.*, 2010). Perhaps reflecting the high degree of uncertainty associated with receipt of inconclusive results, individuals receiving this outcome have also been found to experience heightened distress for months after test receipt (van Dijk *et al.*, 2008). Other more subtle psychological difficulties which may not be detected using general or standard measures of psychological distress, but are still of great importance, include feelings of shame or guilt relating to genetic risk, fear of cancer development, use of emotion-regulation strategies such as denial or immersion in work activities, difficulties in discussing genetic test results with family, and ongoing uncertainty and worry about the future (Cameron & Muller, 2009). These difficulties may be experienced not only by those who receive a positive genetic test result, but also by those who receive negative or inconclusive results, and, as such, it is important that health professionals try to understand the idiosyncratic meanings and beliefs patients form in relation to their results, irrespective of medical outcome.

Another important consideration is whether individuals who undergo genetic testing change their behaviors in response to the results. Depending on the condition, it is implicit that the receipt of risk-related information will prompt actions to minimize disease risk, whether through increased disease surveillance, healthier lifestyle, or surgical or drug-based preventive actions. While some studies report improvement in preventive or risk-reducing behaviors (Hughes Halbert *et al.*, 2004; Kasparian *et al.*, 2009), many tested individuals elect not to undergo recommended preventive actions (e.g., risk-reducing breast and ovary removal) or to increase their disease-screening regimen (Bloss *et al.*, 2011; Marteau *et al.*, 2010; Metcalfe *et al.*, 2008). Age appears to be a factor related to uptake of risk reducing options with older individuals less likely to opt for prophylactic surgery (Beattie *et al.*, 2009). Similarly, the extent to which the individual believes that environmental and behavioral factors, such as diet, exercise, and medication, may modify genetic disease risk is likely to influence willingness to accept recommended risk-reducing options (Cameron & Muller, 2009). There is preliminary evidence from genetic testing in the areas of Alzheimer's disease and lung cancer that genetic risk information may serve as a motivator to initiate and maintain health protective behaviors (Chao *et al.*, 2008; Sanderson *et al.*, 2008). Reluctance to change health behaviors may also be a reflection of individuals simply needing to figure out the right time to act in terms of their circumstances, having sufficient time to think about options, and being able to deal emotionally with the decisions and associated consequences (Howard *et al.*, 2010).

Psychological Interventions in the Genetic Risk-Assessment Context

In view of the medical and psychological complexities involved in genetic risk assessment, there is increasing recognition of the need for psychosocial interventions to supplement and support individuals as they navigate their way through the testing process, particularly for those who may be more vulnerable to experiencing difficulty (e.g., individuals with limited social support or re-ported difficulties adjusting emotionally to the testing outcome). To date, a range of intervention approaches have been developed and trialled, although there is limited evidence for the efficacy of these approaches beyond the familial cancer context. There is also ambiguity as to the 'active ingredients' which contribute to improved outcomes for participants. Broadly, and in addition to standard genetic counselling (Meiser *et al.*, 2008), the two main approaches to the provision of supportive care for individuals participating in genetic risk assessment are: (1) information and decisional support, typically utilizing static (Juan *et al.*, 2008) or interactive (Green *et al.*, 2004; Kaufman *et al.*, 2003) decision aids; and (2) enhanced counselling, which may include psycho-education, skills-based training (e.g., distress tolerance, problem solving, relaxation tech-niques), assistance with communication of genetic test results, and opportunities for support, self-expression, and exploration of emotional, social, and cognitive responses (e.g., Roussi *et al.*, 2010). In the genetic counselling setting, psychosocial care may feature one or both of these ap-proaches and may be tailored to the specific needs of the individual and his or her family. Within these approaches individuals may be offered variations on psychotherapeutic modalities such as psychodynamic, cognitive-behavioral, or supportive-expressive therapies (e.g., Esplen *et al.*, 2004; McInerney-Leo *et al.*, 2004), and support may be delivered through a variety of formats, including face-to-face interaction, written materials, web-based or multimedia resources, group therapy, or telephone-based support (e.g., McKinnon *et al.*, 2007). Indeed, several interventions have supple-mented face-to-face counselling with the use of resources which can be taken home for participants to review and share with others (Wakefield *et al.*, 2008a).

The provision of decisional support is increasingly regarded as a key part of the genetic testing process. A number of decision aids that provide information about available testing options, likely outcomes of testing, and the pros and cons of testing have been developed for a number of genetic testing environments (e.g., hereditary colorectal cancer, Hall *et al.*, 2011; male breast cancer, Juan *et al.*, 2008; Li–Fraumeni syndrome, Peterson *et al.*, 2006; breast cancer, Wakefield *et al.*, 2008a; prostate cancer, Wakefield *et al.*, 2011). Evidence to date indicates that these decision aids have the potential to reduce decisional conflict through increasing knowledge and perceived benefits of testing, clarifying values, and increasing preparedness to have the test (Hall *et al.*, 2011; Peterson *et al.*, 2006; Wakefield *et al.*, 2008a, 2008b).

Overall, interventions in the genetics setting have been found to improve cognitive outcomes for participants, such as knowledge and risk perception, without generating anxiety or depression (van Roosmalen *et al.*, 2004; Wakefield *et al.*, 2008a). Few interventions, however, have been shown to be efficacious in reducing psychological distress (Esplen *et al.*, 2004; Roussi *et al.*, 2010), improving satisfaction with decision-making, or increasing health-oriented behaviors (Miller *et al.*, 2005). Despite this, it is often the supportive or emotional elements of counselling interventions that participants perceive as providing the greatest benefit, rather than the informational or educational components (Edwards *et al.*, 2008). This highlights the importance of striking a balance between imparting health- and risk-related information, and addressing individuals' need for support around experiences of loss, unresolved grief, decisional conflict, health-related worry, changing self-concept, and relationship difficulties.

An example of an enhanced counselling (EC) intervention was recently developed and trialled by Roussi *et al.* (2010). Drawing on the principles of a self-regulatory approach, this intervention was designed to improve knowledge about genetic testing, and reduce risk-related distress, in women with a strong family history of breast and/or ovarian cancer. The face-to-face intervention was delivered by a health educator over a 45 min period, immediately following each woman's initial standard genetic counselling session. The EC session featured opportunities for the women to role-play various possible genetic testing outcomes (positive, negative, and inconclusive), as well as to engage in preparatory planning and thinking about ways of coping, both emotionally and practically. Results from the randomised clinical trial showed that, in the short-term, women who received EC exhibited greater knowledge compared to women in the control group. Further, EC was found to have emotional benefits around the time of test result disclosure, particularly for women who tested mutation-positive. Another approach utilizing a cognitive-behavioral problem solving training intervention focused on developing effective coping strategies and skills to manage stressors and problems, and to make effective decisions among *BRCA1/2* mutation carrier families (McInerney-Leo *et al.*, 2004). The problem solving training was found to reduce depressive symptoms at 6–9 months following results disclosure for all individuals tested for the *BRCA1/2* mutation, indicating that this approach has the potential to enhance psychological wellbeing. Similarly, a psychosocial telephone-based intervention delivered after the disclosure of positive *BRCA1/2* test results, and as an adjunct to standard genetic counselling, was found to reduce distress and anxiety among women with a genetic mutation at 6 months, but not 12 months following results disclosure (Graves *et al.*, 2010). These studies are part of a growing body of evidence that psychosocial interventions may provide benefits to genetic testing participants, in terms of reduced distress and greater wellbeing, at least in the short term following results disclosure.

An ongoing challenging aspect of genetic disease risk is to maintain, in the long-term, recommended health-protective and risk-reducing actions (Cameron & Muller, 2009). Adhering to these recommendations requires not only initiation, but also ongoing persistence (Bellg, 2003; Mechanic & Cleary, 1980). Emotional distress associated with a health threat may impede an individual's ability to undertake the long-term health-related behavior, but self-regulation of affect, the process by which individuals manage their emotions in order to maintain a sense of normal functioning, may allow an individual to continue carrying out the required risk-management actions with minimal hindrance (de Ridder & Kuijer, 2006). Therefore, the ability to manage or self-regulate risk-related distress, should it arise, is likely to be an important coping mechanism associated with adherence to risk-management strategies. Few studies have addressed this issue. One simple approach entailed a 1 day workshop to support families with hereditary *BRCA* mutations (McKinnon *et al.*, 2007). The purpose of this workshop was to provide education about medical management and privacy issues, as well as to address psychological and family issues. Six months following the workshop, the majority of participants had undertaken positive steps towards reducing their cancer risk including increasing their cancer screening, initiating chemoprevention, or planning for prophylactic surgery. In addition, one half of attendees had initiated positive lifestyle changes (i.e., increased exercise, decreased fat intake, decreased alcohol, increased vitamin intake) at the 6 month assessment. These findings are promising, and the combined approach of education along with addressing psychological concerns, suggests that the increased adherence to the risk-reduction recommendations may have stemmed, at least in part, from improved self-regulation in these at-risk individuals.

Given that the testing process has the potential to impact negatively on all family members, particularly those close to the tested family member (e.g., Graceffa *et al.*, 2009), one final aspect that needs to be considered is whether interventions can address family-related concerns. Very little work has been carried out in this area, but one study provides some insight into an approach that may provide benefits in this context. Speice *et al.* (2002) describe a family-oriented psycho-education intervention approach that encompasses a broad range of topics related to genetic testing participation. In a group setting, tested individuals and their accompanying family members attend six 90 min sessions with therapists who facilitate discussion of family reactions to the testing process, timing and disclosure of results, and treatment options, as well as emotional responses, coping strategies, body image, sexuality, and relationship concerns. As yet there are no data available regarding the benefits to be derived from this inclusive approach.

Despite these positive findings, however, intervention studies in the field are fraught with a number of challenges, including relatively small sample sizes, low uptake rates, high drop-out rates, cultural and educational biases, and limited capacity to influence emotional and behavioral responses to genetic testing outcomes. Further, there have been few rigorous trials of psychosocial interventions beyond the familial cancer setting. Thus it is clear that there is a need for more work in this area.

Conclusions

Genetic testing for disease susceptibility is fraught with psychological and social challenges for the individuals concerned and their family members. Interventions designed not only to enhance understanding of hereditary disease risk and the genetic testing process, but also to facilitate processing of this information, are critical to ensure informed decision-making and adjustment to the genetic risk-assessment process. In addition, there is a need for counselling approaches that supplement and complement the role of the genetic counsellor by assisting the tested individual and close family members to manage distress arising from genetic testing and the challenges of decision-making that arise through the course of testing and thereafter. While the field of genetic testing for disease susceptibility is expanding at a rapid rate, the future of genetic research is the harbinger of even more psychological challenges with the proposed development of genetics-based delivery of treatment for diseases. In particular, research currently underway is exploring ways in which to apply pharmacogenomics, a new era of personalized medicine whereby individuals may receive personalized medicine via the use of gene chips. The use of genetic information to provide tailored health treatment is likely to be fraught with at least as many ethical and psychological challenges that arise from genetic testing for disease susceptibility. It is critical that health psychologists learn to embrace and understand these new technologies, and to adapt existing psychosocial interventions to these new medical technology contexts to ensure the psychological wellbeing of all individuals concerned.

References

Archibald, A. D., Jaques, A. M., Wake, S., Collins, V. R., Cohen, J., & Metcalfe, S. A. (2009). "It's something I need to consider": Decisions about carrier screening for fragile X syndrome in a population of non-pregnant women. *American Journal of Medical Genetics, 149A,* 2731–2738.

Barnoy, S., Zelikaman, L., & Bar-Tal, Y. (2009). To take or not to take genetic carrier tests: Personal characteristics associated with taking recommended and nonrecommended tests. *Genetic Testing and Molecular Biomarkers, 13,* 453–458.

Beattie, M. S., Crawford, B., Lin, F., Vittinghoff, E., & Ziegler, J. (2009). Uptake, time course, and predictors of risk-reducing surgeries in BRCA carriers. *Genetic Testing and Molecular Biomarkers, 13,* 51–56.

Bellg, A. J. (2003). Maintenance of health behavior change in preventive cardiology. Internalization and self-regulation of new behaviors. *Behavior Modification, 27,* 103–131.

Bernhardt, C., Schwan, A. M., Kraus, P., Epplen, J. T., & Kunstmann, E. (2009). Decreasing uptake of predictive testing for Huntington's disease in a German centre: 12 years' experience (1993–2004). *European Journal of Human Genetics*, *17*, 295–300.

Bloss, C. S., Schork, N. J., & Topol, E. J. (2011). Effect of direct-to-consumer genomewide profiling to assess disease risk. *New England Journal of Medicine*, *364*, 524–534.

Botkin, J. R., Teutsch, S. M., Kaye, C. I., Hayes, M., Haddow, J. E., Bradley, L. A. *et al.* (2010). Outcomes of interest in evidence-based evaluations of genetic tests. *Genetic Medicine*, *12*, 228–235.

Bottorff, J. L., Ratner, P. A., Balneaves, L. G., Richardson, C. G., McCullum, M., Hack, T. *et al.* (2002). Women's interest in genetic testing for breast cancer risk: The influence of sociodemographics and knowledge. *Cancer Epidemiology, Biomarkers and Prevention*, *11*, 89–95.

Butow, P. N., Lobb, E. A., Meiser, B., Barratt, A., & Tucker, K. M. (2003). Psychological outcomes and risk perception after genetic testing and counselling in breast cancer: A systematic review. *Medical Journal of Australia*, *178*, 77–81.

Cameron, L. D., & Muller, C. E. (2009). Psychosocial aspects of genetic testing. *Current Opinion in Psychiatry*, *22*, 218–223.

Cameron, L. D., Sherman, K. A., Marteau, T. M., & Brown, P. M. (2009). Impact of genetic risk information and type of disease on perceived risk, anticipated affect, and expected consequences of genetic tests. *Health Psychology*, *28*, 307–316.

Chao, S., Roberts, J. S., Marteau, T. M., Silliman, R., Cupples, L. A., & Green, R. C. (2008). Health behavior changes after genetic risk assessment for Alzheimer disease: The REVEAL Study. *Alzheimer Disease and Associated Disorders*, *22*, 94–97.

Clarke, A., Sarangi, S., & Verrier-Jones, K. (2010). Voicing the lifeworld: Parental accounts of responsibility in genetic consultations for polycystic kidney disease. *Social Science and Medicine*, *72*, 1743–1751.

DeMarco, T. A., & McKinnon, W. C. (2006). Life after BRCA1/2 testing: Family communication and support issues. *Breast Disease*, *27*, 127–136.

de Ridder, D., & Kuijer, R. G. (2006). Managing immediate needs in the pursuit of health goals: The role of coping in self-regulation. In D. de Ridder & J. de Wit (Eds.), *Self-Regulation in Health Behaviour* (pp. 147–168). Chichester: Wiley.

Doukas, D. J., & Li, Y. (2004). Men's values-based factors on prostate cancer risk genetic testing: A telephone survey. *BMC Medical Genetics*, *5*, 28–35.

Doukas, D. J., Localio, A. R., & Li, Y. (2004). Attitudes and beliefs concerning prostate cancer genetic screening. *Clinical Genetics*, *66*, 445–451.

Edwards, A., Gray, J., Clarke, A., Dundon, J., Elwyn, G., Gaff, C. *et al.* (2008). Interventions to improve risk communication in clinical genetics: Systematic review. *Patient Education & Counseling*, *71*, 4–25.

Esplen, M. J., Hunter, J., Leszcz, M., Warner, E., Narod, S., Metcalfe, K. *et al.* (2004). A multicenter study of supportive-expressive group therapy for women with BRCA1/BRCA2 mutations. *Cancer*, *101*, 2327–2340.

Esplen, M. J., Madlensky, L., Aronson, M., Rothenmund, H., Gallinger, S., Butler, K. *et al.* (2007). Colorectal cancer survivors undergoing genetic testing for hereditary non-polyposis colorectal cancer: Motivational factors and psychosocial functioning. *Clinical Genetics*, *72*, 394–401.

Etchegary, H. (2006). Genetic testing for Huntington's disease: How is the decision taken? *Genetic Testing*, *10*, 60–67.

Gaff, C. L., Clarke, A. J., Atkinson, P., Sivell, S., Elwyn, G., Iredale, R. *et al.* (2007). Process and outcome in communication of genetic information within families: A systematic review. *European Journal of Human Genetics*, *15*, 999–1011.

Godard, B., Pratte, A., Dumont, M., Simard-Lebrun, A., & Simard, J. (2007). Factors associated with an individual's decision to withdraw from genetic testing for breast and ovarian cancer susceptibility: Implications for counseling. *Genetic Testing*, *11*, 45–54.

Graceffa, A., Russo, M., Vita, G. L., Toscano, A., Dattola, R., Messina, C. *et al.* (2009). Psychosocial impact of presymptomatic genetic testing for transthyretin amyloidotic polyneuropathy. *Neuromuscular Disorders*, *19*, 44–48.

Graves, K. D., Wenzel, L., Schwartz, M. D., Luta, G., Wileyto, P., Narod, S. *et al.* (2010). Randomized controlled trial of a psychosocial telephone counseling intervention in BRCA1 and BRCA2 mutation carriers. *Cancer Epidemiology,* Biomarkers and Prevention, *19*, 648–654.

Green, M. J., Peterson, S. K., Baker, M. W., Harper, G. R., Friedman, L. C., Rubinstein, W. S., & Mauger, D. T. (2004). Effect of a computer-based decision aid on knowledge, perceptions, and intentions about genetic testing for breast cancer susceptibility: A randomized controlled trial. *JAMA, 292,* 442–452.

Hall, M. J., Manne, S. L., Winkel, G., Chung, D. S., Weinberg, D. S., & Meropol, N. J. (2011). Effects of a decision support intervention on decisional conflict associated with microsatellite instability testing. *Cancer Epidemiology, Biomarkers and Prevention, 20,* 249–254.

Hamilton, J. G., Lobel, M., & Moyer, A. (2009). Emotional distress following genetic testing for hereditary breast and ovarian cancer: A meta-analytic review. *Health Psychology, 28,* 510–518.

Hendriks, K. S. W. H., Hendriks, M. M. W. B., Birnie, E., Grosfeld, F. J. M., Wilde, A. A. M., van den Bout, J. *et al.* (2008). Familial disease with a risk of sudden death: A longitudinal study of the psychological consequences of predictive testing for long QT syndrome. *Heart Rhythm, 5,* 719–724.

Hock, K. T., Christensen, K. D., Yashar, B. M., Roberts, J. S., Gollust, S. E., & Uhlmann, W. R. (2011). Direct-to-consumer genetic testing: An assessment of genetic counselors' knowledge and beliefs. *Genetic Medicine, 13,* 325–332.

Howard, A. F., Bottorff, J. L., Balneaves, L. G., & Kim-Sing, C. (2010). Women's constructions of the 'right time' to consider decisions about risk-reducing mastectomy and risk-reducing oophorectomy. *BMC Womens Health, 10,* 24.

Hughes Halbert, C., Lynch, H., Lynch, J., Main, D., Kucharski, S., Rustgi, A., & Lerman, C. (2004). Colon cancer screening practices following genetic testing for hereditary nonpolyposis colon cancer (HNPCC) mutations. *Archives of Internal Medicine, 164,* 1881–1887.

Jaques, A. M., Bell, R. J., Watson, L., & Halliday, J. L. (2004). People who influence women's decisions and preferred sources of information about prenatal testing for birth defects. *Australian and New Zealand Journal of Obstetrics and Gynaecology, 44,* 233–238.

Juan, A. S., Wakefield, C. E., Kasparian, N. A., Kirk, J., Tyler, J., & Tucker, K. (2008). Development and pilot testing of a decision aid for men considering genetic testing for breast and/or ovarian cancer-related mutations (BRCA1/2). *Genetic Testing, 12,* 523–532.

Kasparian, N. A., Meiser, B., Butow, P. N., Simpson, J. M., & Mann, G. J. (2009). Genetic testing for melanoma risk: A prospective cohort study of uptake and outcomes among Australian families. *Genetic Medicine, 11,* 265–278.

Kaufman, E. M., Peshkin, B. N., Lawrence, W. F., Shelby, R., Isaacs, C., Brown, K. *et al.* (2003). Development of an interactive decision aid for female BRCA1/BRCA2 carriers. *Journal of Genetic Counseling, 12,* 109–129.

Klitzman, R., Thorne, D., Williamson, J., & Marder, K. (2007). The roles of family members, health care workers, and others in decision-making processes about genetic testing among individuals at risk for Huntington disease. *Genetic Medicine, 9,* 358–371.

Landsbergen, K. M., Prins, J. B., Brunner, H. G., Kraaimaat, F. W., & Hoogerbrugge, N. (2009). Genetic testing for Lynch syndrome in the first year of colorectal cancer: A review of the psychological impact. *Familial Cancer, 8,* 325–337.

Landsbergen, K. M., Prins, J. B., Brunner, H. G., & Hoogerbrugge, N. (2010). Shortened time interval between colorectal cancer diagnosis and risk testing for hereditary colorectal cancer is not related to higher psychological distress. *Familial Cancer, 10,* 51–57.

Leventhal, H., Leventhal, E. A., & Contrada, R. J. (1998). Self-regulation, health, and behavior: A perceptual-cognitive approach. *Psychology & Health, 13,* 717–733.

Leventhal, H., Brissette, I., & Leventhal, E. A. (2003). The common-sense model of self-regulation of health and illness. In L. D. Cameron & H. Leventhal (Eds.), *The Self-Regulation of Health and Illness Behaviour* (pp. 42–65). London: Routledge.

Lewis, C., Skirton, H., & Jones, R. (2010). Living without a diagnosis: The parental experience. *Genetic Testing and Molecular Biomarkers, 14,* 807–815.

Li, Y., Steinberg, A. G., Bain, L., Yaeger, D., Bieler, A., Ewing, R. *et al.* (2007). Assessing parental attitudes toward genetic testing for childhood hearing loss: Before and after genetic consultation. *American Journal of Medical Genetics, 143A,* 1546–1553.

Lindor, N. M., McMaster, M. L., Lindor, C. J., & Greene, M. H. (2008). Concise handbook of familial cancer susceptibility syndromes – second edition. *Journal of the National Cancer Institute Monographs, 2008*(38), 3–93.

Loescher, L. J., Crist, J. D., & Siaki, L. A. (2009). Perceived intrafamily melanoma risk communication. *Cancer Nursing, 32*, 203–210.

Marteau, T. M., French, D. P., Griffin, S. J., Prevost, A. T., Sutton, S., Watkinson, C. *et al.* (2010). Effects of communicating DNA-based disease risk estimates on risk-reducing behaviours. *Cochrane Database of Systematic Reviews 2010*, 10, CD007275.

McInerney-Leo, A., Biesecker, B., Hadley, D., Kase, R., Giambarresi, T., Johnson, E. *et al.* (2004). BRCA1/2 testing in hereditary breast and ovarian cancer families: Effectiveness of problem-solving training as a counseling intervention. *American Journal of Medical Genetics, 130A*, 221–227.

McKinnon, W. C., Naud, S., Ashikaga, T., Colletti, R., & Wood, M. (2007). Results of an intervention for individuals and families with BRCA mutations: A model for providing medical updates and psychosocial support following genetic testing. *Journal of Genetic Counseling, 16*, 433–456.

Mechanic, D., & Cleary, P. D. (1980). Factors associated with the maintenance of positive health behavior. *Preventive Medicine, 9*, 805–814.

Meiser, B., Irle, J., Lobb, E., & Barlow-Stewart, K. (2008). Assessment of the content and process of genetic counseling: A critical review of empirical studies. *Journal of Genetic Counseling, 17*, 434–451.

Metcalfe, K. A., Birenbaum-Carmeli, D., Lubinski, J., Gronwald, J., Lynch, H., Moller, P. *et al.* (2008). International variation in rates of uptake of preventive options in BRCA1 and BRCA2 mutation carriers. *International Journal of Cancer, 122*, 2017–2022.

Miller, S. M., Shoda, Y., & Hurley, K. (1996). Applying cognitive-social theory to health-protective behavior: Breast self-examination in cancer screening. *Psychology Bulletin, 119*, 70–94.

Miller, S. M., Roussi, P., Buzaglo, J. S., Sherman, K., Godwin, A. K., Balshem, A., & Atchison, M. E. (2005). Enhanced counselling for women undergoing BRCA1/2 testing: Impact on subsequent decision making about risk reduction behaviours. *Health Education & Behavior, 32*, 654–667.

Mireskandari, S., Sherman, K. A., Meiser, B., Taylor, A. J., Gleeson, M., Andrews, L., & Tucker, K. M. (2007). Psychological adjustment among partners of women at high risk of developing breast/ovarian cancer. *Genetics in Medicine, 9*, 311–320.

National Cancer Institute. (2011). *Genetics of Breast and Ovarian Cancer: Major Genes.* www.cancer.gov/cancertopics/pdq/genetics/breast-and-ovarian/HealthProfessional/page2.

National Human Genome Research Institute. (2011). *Genetic Testing.* www.genome.gov/10002335.

Patenaude, A. F. (2005). *Genetic Testing for Cancer: Psychological Approaches for Helping Patients and Families.* Washington DC: American Psychological Association.

Peterson, S. K., Pentz, R. D., Blanco, A. M., Ward, P. A., Watts, B. G., Marani, S. K. *et al.* (2006). Evaluation of a decision aid for families considering p53 genetic counseling and testing. *Genetics in Medicine, 8*, 226–233.

Rolland, J., & Williams, J. (2005). Toward a biopsychosocial model for 21st century genetics. *Family Process, 44*, 3–24.

Roussi, P., Sherman, K. A., Miller, S. M., Buzaglo, J. S., Daly, M. B., Taylor, A. *et al.* (2010). Enhanced counselling for women undergoing BRCA1/2 testing: Impact on knowledge and psychological distress-results from a randomised clinical trial. *Psychology & Health, 25*, 401–415.

Salkovskis, P. M., Rimes, K. A., Bolton, J., & Wroe, A. L. (2010). An experimental investigation of factors involved in the decision to undertake genetic testing for schizophrenia. *Journal of Mental Health, 19*, 202–210.

Sanderson, S. C., Humphries, S. E., Hubbart, C., Hughes, E., Jarvis, M. J., & Wardle, J. (2008). Psychological and behavioural impact of genetic testing smokers for lung cancer risk: A phase II exploratory trial. *Journal of Health Psychology, 13*, 481–494.

Sherman, K. A., Kasparian, N. A., & Mireskandari, S. (2010). Psychological adjustment among male partners in response to women's breast/ovarian cancer risk: A theoretical review of the literature. *Psycho-Oncology, 19*, 1–11.

Shiloh, S. (2006). Illness representations, self-regulation, and genetic counseling: A theoretical review. *Journal of Genetic Counseling, 15*, 325–337.

Sparbel, K. J., & Williams, J. K. (2009). Pregnancy as foreground in cystic fibrosis carrier testing decisions in primary care. *Genetic Testing and Molecular Biomarkers, 13,* 133–142.

Speice, J., McDaniel, S. H., Rowley, P. T., & Loader, S. (2002). Family issues in a psychoeducation group for women with a BRCA mutation. *Clinical Genetics, 62,* 121–127.

Thewes, B., Meiser, B., Tucker, K., & Schnieden, V. (2003). Screening for psychological distress in women at increased risk for breast cancer: A review of the literature. *Psychology, Health & Medicine, 8,* 289–304.

van Dijk, S., Otten, W., Tollenaar, R. A., van Asperen, C. J., & Tibben, A. (2008). Putting it all behind: Long-term psychological impact of an inconclusive DNA test result for breast cancer. *Genetic Medicine, 10,* 745–750.

van Roosmalen, M., Stalmeier, P., Verhoef, L., Hoekstra-Weebers, J., Oosterwijk, J., Hoogerbrugge, N. *et al.* (2004). Randomised trial of a decision aid and its timing for women being tested for a BRCA1/2 mutation. *British Journal of Cancer, 90,* 333–342.

Waalen, J., & Beutler, E. (2009). Genetic screening for low-penetrance variants in protein-coding genes. *Annual Review of Genomics and Human Genetics, 10,* 431–450.

Wakefield, C. E., Meiser, B., Homewood, J., Taylor, A. J., Gleeson, M., Williams, R. *et al.* Australian GENetic testing Decision Aid Collaborative Group. (2008a). A randomized trial of a breast/ovarian cancer genetic testing decision aid used as a communication aid during genetic counseling. *Psycho-Oncology, 17,* 844–854.

Wakefield, C. E., Meiser, B., Homewood, J., Ward, R., O'Donnell, S., & Kirk, J. (2008b). Randomized trial of a decision aid for individuals considering genetic testing for hereditary nonpolyposis colorectal cancer risk. *Cancer, 113,* 956–965.

Wakefield, C. E., Watts, K. J., Meiser, B., Sansom-Daly, U., Barratt, A., Mann, G. J. *et al.* (2011). Development and pilot testing of an online screening decision aid for men with a family history of prostate cancer. *Patient Education and Counseling, 83,* 64–72.

Wiseman, M., Dancyger, C., & Michie, S. (2010). Communicating genetic risk information within families: A review. *Familial Cancer, 9,* 691–703.

14

Psychological Implications of Infertility and Assisted Reproductive Technologies

Sarah Nowoweiski

Primary infertility is typically defined as the failure to conceive following 12 months or more of regular sexual intercourse without contraception (Benyamini *et al.*, 2004). Secondary infertility is when a couple is unable to conceive again after having one child or more (Hammarberg, 2010). Estimates of the prevalence of infertility vary but are estimated to affect around 15% of couples (Benyamini *et al.*, 2004). Further, data from the Australian Institute of Health and Welfare (2010) reveal an increase in the trend of the number of births from assisted reproductive technology (ART) each year. For example, in 2008 there were 61 929 ART cycles undertaken in Australia and New Zealand clinics with 22.6% (13 983) resulting in a clinical pregnancy and 17.2% (10 633) resulting in a live delivery (the birth of at least one live born baby). In total there were 11 528 live born babies following ART in 2008 (84.4% singletons, 15% twins, 0.6% higher-order multiples). The number of treatment cycles undertaken in 2008 represents a 9% increase in the number of cycles undertaken since 2007 and a 47.8% increase in the number of cycles undertaken since 2004. There was also a steady increase in the number of clinical pregnancies and live deliveries resulting from ART between 2004 and 2008. This increase represents a growth of 1270 clinical pregnancies per year and 939 live deliveries per year between 2004 and 2008 (Australian Institute of Health and Welfare, 2010). Ambiguity exists regarding the cause of this increasing trend, with some researchers suggesting that increases in infertility may be related to the effects of environmental pollutants and/or occupational exposure on human reproduction (Feveile *et al.*, 2011), whereas others postulate that the prevalence of infertility is unchanged, despite an increase in both the number of women seeking medical care for infertility and the proportion reporting pregnancies (Oakley *et al.*, 2007). Regardless of the origins of infertility, it is clear that there has been a medicalization of infertility. Medicalization is a process whereby a previously natural, social, or behavioral entity is transformed into a medical one, therefore requiring medical treatment. Since the advent of reproductive technologies in the 1970s and 1980s, infertility has increasingly been constructed as a disease and something to be treated rather than a social construction or natural part of life (Bates & Bates, 1996).

Applied Topics in Health Psychology, First Edition. Edited by M. L. Caltabiano and L. Ricciardelli.
© 2013 John Wiley & Sons, Ltd. Published 2013 by John Wiley & Sons, Ltd.

Broadly speaking, infertility can be divided into four categories: female factor, male factor, combined factors, and unexplained factors. Interestingly, the prevalence of male and female factors are equivalent (around 30% each), in contrast to previously held societal beliefs about infertility being a female problem (Miles *et al.*, 2009). Common medical reasons for infertility include abnormal sperm analyses, blocked or damaged fallopian tubes, polycystic ovaries and polycystic ovarian syndrome (PCOS), endometriosis, or advanced maternal and/or paternal age. Less commonly, known and unknown chromosomal abnormalities may impact on a couple's ability to conceive a healthy fetus or to carry a pregnancy to term.

Two of the most common types of ART are intrauterine insemination (IUI) and *in vitro* fertilization (IVF). In IUI, the female partner is inseminated with a prepared sperm sample at the time of ovulation. To time the procedure correctly, she most likely has blood tests and ultrasound scans. This form of ART is less invasive and is best suited to younger couples with less severe or unexplained types of infertility. However, it is cautioned that couples do not spend too many months on "low-tech" treatments such as IUI because as age increases the chances of conceiving decrease and IVF may be the most effective treatment at this stage (Hammarberg, 2010). There are numerous types of IVF cycle and each cycle is tailored to the specific needs of the couple, but generally speaking the female partner is required to take a series of medications to stimulate follicular development in the ovaries. Following this an oocyte pick up is performed under anesthetic. A sperm specimen is collected from the male partner and fertilization is attempted using standard insemination or intracytoplasmic sperm injection (commonly used to overcome male infertility). Two to five days later the female partner has an embryo-transfer procedure and is then required to wait approximately 2 weeks until a blood test can be used to determine whether a pregnancy has been achieved. Patients are required to be informed of all possible medical risks associated with the procedure, side effects of the medications including mood swings, headaches, and nausea (Hammarberg, 2010), and the probabilities of success, which have been found to be associated with specific individual factors such as age and reason for infertility. Patients embarking on any form of ART are also informed that even if a pregnancy is achieved they are exposed to the normal risks of pregnancy, including miscarriage. Miscarriage is one of the most common complications of pregnancy with between 12 and 24% of clinically recognized pregnancies aborting spontaneously (Carter *et al.*, 2007). During the early years of ART, multiple embryo transfer was accepted as a routinely used method in IVF to achieve acceptable pregnancy rates, as cryopreservation of surplus embryos was not yet possible. This practice resulted in a remarkable increase in multiple deliveries (Schieve *et al.*, 1999). Despite the introduction of elective single-embryo transfer at the end of the 1990s as a method of reducing multiple delivery rates after ART multiple pregnancies are still common and carry more risks for both the mother and the unborn children, including miscarriage and premature birth (Helmerhorst *et al.*, 2004; Vilska *et al.*, 2009).

In Australia, the majority of presentations to ART clinics are by couples experiencing medical infertility, with a smaller proportion of individuals and couples presenting for "social" infertility reasons. Social infertility is defined as single women or same sex couples who wish to conceive but cannot due to their social circumstances, and need to conceive with the use of donor sperm. While these individuals and couples may require similar treatment to medically infertile couples, their experiences are unique and also raise specific issues including, but not limited to, parenting a nonbiological child and the impact of donor conception and disclosure. Whereas these considerations are important they are extremely varied and are therefore not the main focus of this chapter. Readers interested in these topics are directed to the resources of the Victorian Assisted Reproductive Treatment Authority (www.varta.org.au).

Psychological Impact of Infertility and Infertility Treatment

The psychological impact of infertility can vary enormously between individuals and couples and may be associated with factors such as the amount of time the couple have been trying to conceive, the reason for their infertility, and the meaning of becoming a parent (Glover *et al.*, 2009; Smith *et al.*, 2009). Initially, the couple may experience a sense of failure and loss (Applegarth, 1999) due to their inability to conceive naturally. Further, after being referred to an infertility specialist they will be required to undertake a number of medical tests, which can also exacerbate this sense of failure and loss. After this process, a diagnosis of infertility may be obtained, which commonly results in further feelings of guilt, shame, failure, and grief (Faramarzi *et al.*, 2008), which can be experienced as a threat to one's femininity or masculinity. However, a couple may also be given an "unexplained" diagnosis whereby the couple's test results are within normal limits where no medical explanation for their inability to conceive could be found. This situation often leads to feelings of frustration and confusion about the circumstances surrounding the inability to conceive naturally, leading to doubt about one's partner or one's self, as individuals tend to want explanations about the causes for their inability to conceive. As such, couples who choose to undertake ART such as IVF or IUI may experience a wide range of emotional responses, which can vary depending on the number of cycles (length of treatment) it may take to conceive and the constant reminder that a pregnancy is not guaranteed despite the enormous investment and effort required.

Infertility can also be experienced as an unanticipated life crisis for which individuals and couples sometimes lack sufficient coping skills (Applegarth, 1999). This is due to the threat of infertility impacting on the major developmental milestone of parenthood and because infertility may impede the acquisition of generativity (a concern with establishing and guiding the next generation), which Erikson (1963) postulated as a central developmental task of adulthood. It is suggested that, for most people, to have a child is to continue the human life cycle, which is seen as a renewal of life; as a form of immortality (Applegarth, 1999). For many women, the ability to conceive and give birth to a child can be paramount to their lifelong notions of femininity, and ultimately associated with the meaning of life. Further, bearing children and parenting are often the foundations around which a couple build a relationship (Applegarth, 1999). When efforts to achieve parenthood fail, life is put "on hold," and many individuals are left with deep feelings of guilt, self-blame, and inadequacy (Applegarth, 1999). Further, as infertility requires couples to undergo medical treatment that can be ongoing with no guarantee of success, its emotional impact is comparable to that of serious chronic diseases such as cancer (Domar *et al.*, 1993). Previous researchers have found that when compared to women with heart disease, cancer, chronic pain, or HIV-positive status, infertile women reported equivalent levels of anxiety and depression to all but patients with chronic pain (Domar *et al.*, 1999). Not surprisingly, infertility and infertility treatment have been shown to be a trigger for both depression and anxiety for some women (Peterson & Eifert, 2011). Researchers have found a higher level of depression and anxiety symptoms in individuals undergoing infertility treatment, as compared to the general population (van Balen & Trimbos-Kemper, 1993), although such findings are to be interpreted with caution due to the difficulty in using fertile matched controls. The social cognitive theory of depression proposes that women for whom motherhood is a highly valued role may be particularly vulnerable to depression if events or difficulties threaten this role (Champion & Power, 1995).

The impact of anxiety and depression can be broadly categorized into two areas: the impact on the individual's emotional wellbeing and their ability to cope with treatment, and the impact on treatment outcomes. Research in these areas is continually developing with results showing that anxiety and depression scores change following failed cycles for women, but not men (Verhaak *et al.*, 2005), higher depression scores being correlated with low egg numbers and poor sperm motility (Gurhan *et al.*, 2009), and higher levels of anxiety at the time of procedure being associated with decreases in pregnancy, implantation, and fertilization rates in women (Klonoff-Cohen, 2008). Researchers have also found that for females higher depression and anxiety scores prior to beginning IVF treatment were associated with a greater likelihood for treatment termination after only one cycle (Domar, 2004), which impacts not only IVF outcomes but also further opportunities to conceive. These examples of recent research findings highlight that regardless of the impact on IVF outcomes it would be beneficial for health professionals to have a better understanding of the factors that may contribute to greater psychological stress before and after starting IVF in order to better guide and support individuals and couples seeking infertility treatment.

The cognitive appraisals that patients apply when experiencing infertility and infertility treatment have also received attention. Researchers have found that the meaning attributed to one's infertility experience is likely to have a great effect on how one copes with treatment (Kraaij *et al.*, 2008). Couples typically perceive infertility as potentially both harmful (e.g., role loss) and challenging (e.g., marriage-strengthening). Researchers have found that couples reported the experience to have either brought them together and strengthened their relationship, or if there were already strains or unresolved relationship issues, infertility and infertility treatment highlighted these vulnerabilities and couples experienced a greater sense of relationship dissatisfaction which at times has lead to separations (Peterson *et al.*, 2003). Assisting couples to find positive meaning in infertility has been found to predict better adjustment, as compared to blaming oneself for a fertility problem, which is related to poorer adjustment (Morrow *et al.*, 1995). Greater perceived control is also related to better adjustment, for example, if the infertility diagnosis is related to a modifiable lifestyle issue such as smoking or obesity. Providing behavior-modification techniques has been found to increase perceived control and improve satisfaction with treatment (Lord & Robertson, 2005). Regarding specific coping strategies, it has consistently been demonstrated that approach-oriented strategies such as problem-focused coping or emotion-focused coping are more effective than avoidant-oriented strategies such as avoiding painful emotions (Morrow *et al.*, 1995). When considering the psychological impact of infertility, it is also crucial to remember that men and women cope quite differently due to a number of factors such as gender differences and differences in medical treatment requirements. Further, in many circumstances one partner's ability to cope may negatively affect the other partner's ability to cope, highlighting the need to be mindful of focusing therapy on individual and couple factors.

Gender Differences in the Experience of Infertility and Infertility Treatment

Although male factor infertility contributes to half of all infertility problems in couples, historically women have disproportionately borne the medical, social, and cultural burden of the couple's failure to conceive (Fisher, Baker & Hammarberg, 2010). Anecdotally, women still remain the main focus of social pressure and primarily experience questions, assumptions, and expectations regarding their fertility status. One of the most common presenting problems at infertility treatment counselling services relates to difficulties coping with questions about when they are going to have children from family, friends, acquaintances, and work colleagues, as well as the impact of their childless status on their progress in career and their position within the family unit. Women commonly report a desire to withdraw from child-focused events and celebrations, or other family gatherings in general. When close friends and relatives announce pregnancies, women report an inner conflict of wishing to express happiness for them, but intense sadness and loss for themselves. This is particularly difficult when the "other" (family or friend) is younger and may have achieved a pregnancy relatively quickly and easily. While all of these factors may also impact men, studies comparing men and women have found that women react more strongly overall (Holter *et al.*, 2007).

It has been reported that as fertility problems arise women worry more, are more self-blaming, and take a more active responsibility for problem solving (Newton & Houle, 1993). Furthermore, when struggling with infertility women may also suffer from low self-esteem, loss of self-confidence, and feelings of incompetence, isolation, loneliness, guilt, fear, anger, shame, and frustration (Eunpu, 1995). The type of infertility diagnosis may also impact on gender differences in coping. For example, Beutel *et al.* (1999) surveyed 281 men who had undergone ART and found that men with male factor infertility were more distressed than men in couples with other causes of infertility. Similarly, Newton *et al.* (1999) found higher global stress and more social and sexual concern in both men and women in couples with a male infertility diagnosis than in couples with female infertility. However, a more recent, prospective study by Peronance *et al.* (2007) of 256 men assessed prior to and after 12 months of unsuccessful ART found that distress increased over time for all men irrespective of diagnosis. It is possible that mens' experiences of infertility are connected to threats to their masculinity and feelings of role failure (Edelmann *et al.*, 1994) but that these responses must also be considered in the context of socially constructed gender roles and cultural factors regarding fertility.

Researchers have also found that women are more likely than men to report distress specific to infertility (Newton *et al.*, 1999). There are a number of explanations for this difference. Firstly, women most often bear infertility's physical burdens, typically engaging in more monitoring and medical procedures than men. Secondly, parenthood is emphasized as a more central role to women, and thus infertility represents a more profound loss. Women rate becoming a parent as more important than men do in infertile couples (Abbey *et al.*, 1991), and partners who differ in the importance placed on having a child are likely to have poorer marital adjustment (Berg & Wilson, 1995). Thirdly, women have also reported feeling more strain from managing fertility issues in the couple's social circle (Tennen *et al.*, 1991). Consequently, a higher level of support may be needed for women experiencing infertility and infertility treatments compared with men. Nevertheless, support should be targeted at normalizing, validating, and exploring these common emotional responses to relieve some of the stress associated with infertility and infertility treatment. However, it is disingenuous to assume that male "baby hunger" does not exist, given that there are surveys showing routinely that men value the significance of babies. For example, a recent US survey showed that 78% of men believed that being a father is the most important role in a man's life (Rasmussen Report, 2009). Others have reported that to become a parent is often considered to be one of the main goals in life for men as well as for women (Hjelmstedt *et al.*, 2007). Subsequently, the needs of a male experiencing infertility and infertility treatment should not be viewed as secondary to his partner's.

Impact of Infertility and Infertility Treatment on a Couple's Sexual Relationship, and Cultural and Social Considerations

Infertility can also affect men's and women's sexual functioning in different ways. When a couple is unsuccessful in trying to conceive naturally it is not uncommon for one or both of the individuals to become concerned with being a failure, which subsequently impacts on their sexual desire and levels of arousal. Further, sexual intercourse often becomes a routine requirement; men feel as though they are being reduced to sperm donors, and women can become obsessed about the timing of intercourse with both partners reporting a loss of enjoyment from sex. The meaning of sex may also change, particularly when couples start ART whereby sexual intercourse is not necessary for reproduction. Sexual intercourse may have started out being a pleasurable activity, but during infertility treatment many couples report that it becomes an activity designed to achieve a pregnancy (Nene *et al.*, 2005), and when undergoing infertility treatment sexual intercourse becomes unnecessary. Couples therefore often report a cessation or significant reduction in their sexual activity after beginning infertility treatment. Couples report that reasons for this are due to feeling as though they need a break from sex because sex has become associated with failure, which leads to feelings of worthlessness, loss of enjoyment, which in turn is influenced by other emotional and medical implications of treatment (e.g., if a woman is feeling moody and bloated while taking the medication, she is less likely to feel desirable). While these are quite common changes, less commonly sexual dysfunction problems may also occur such as erectile dysfunction for males and sexual desire disorders for women. Although such problems are not common in an infertile population, compared to a fertile population infertile men have been found to have a higher prevalence of erectile dysfunction. However, conflicting results have been reported regarding whether infertile women have more sexual dysfunction than the general population (Khademi *et al.*, 2008). Accurate estimates of prevalence to assist in understanding the true burden of sexual dysfunction in infertile people are impeded by interactions between many domains of sexual functioning and risk factors such as psychological distress (Khademi *et al.*, 2008).

When a couple experience both infertility and sexual dysfunction, the couple prefer the infertility label, which has relatively more acceptance in society, than "sexual dysfunction" (Nene *et al.*, 2005). Another important consideration is the intrusiveness of infertility treatment on men and women's bodies, such as consistent monitoring via vaginal ultrasound or having a testicular assessment or biopsy. These physically intrusive procedures, the sense of being monitored, and the need for sex on demand (e.g., postcoital tests, semen analysis) in infertility treatment can affect sexual self-image, desire, and performance, and often results in constant worry and marital conflicts, strained sexual relationship, and diminished sexual desire (Donnelly, 1993; Nene *et al.*, 2005).

As with disruptions in sexual functioning, the situation of childlessness is also culturally defined, and meanings and experiences of infertility have been studied and described in a variety of cultural settings. In some Western countries such as Europe, for example, being childless is acceptable (van Balen & Bos, 2004). However, among most non-Western countries childlessness is viewed as reproductive failure (Runganga *et al.*, 2001). In Indian society, for example, childless women are seen by society as incomplete as Indian women are only able to gain security in their marriage after achieving motherhood (Widge, 2002). Women must have children, otherwise they do not count. Stereotyped views of infertility and class also exist in many cultures and have led to common notions about socioeconomic divides (McCormack, 2005). Infertility is commonly seen to be a middle- and upper-class Western woman's problem due to delayed childbearing, whereas working-class women's infertility is more likely to be perceived to be caused by sexually transmitted infections or environmental and occupational hazards (Green *et al.*, 2001). Despite having similar rates of infertility, women of low socio economic status receive less treatment (Bell, 2009). Additionally, within the field of infertility there is a much larger focus on the treatment rather than the prevention of infertility, which some argue reflects an implicit policy focus on women of higher socioeconomic status (Bell, 2009), whose fertility problems are more likely because of their late marriages and delayed childbearing rather than factors that could be resolved through preventive public health interventions (Green *et al.*, 2001).

Whether the individual or couple disclose their infertility to family, friends, or others is also likely to influence the amount of social support they receive. When disclosure does occur, most often family and friends attempt to provide support and are well intentioned in their comments and behaviors. However, this can also elicit anxiety in others and unhelpful and unsolicited advice can impact on these relationships. Common responses from family and friends include advising the individual or couple to relax, to reduce the stress in their life, or making jokes or comments about the benefits of a childfree life. Such comments can lead to feelings of anger and hurt, leading to isolation, which may contribute to the commonly held belief by infertile couples that no one can understand what they are experiencing. In addition, "support" can take on many different meanings, which may lead to misunderstandings or miscommunication about what is a supportive stance. For example, some people may think giving the couple space and not discussing infertility is being supportive, whereas others may think that asking for regular updates about the progress of infertility treatment shows interest and is supportive.

Clearly, all of these factors contribute to an individual's and couple's experience of infertility and how they cope with treatment. The impact of infertility and its treatment affects not only the couple's emotional and physical wellbeing, but can disrupt their family life, work and career decisions, and other opportunities such as travel, sexual and relationship functioning, and their social networks and it is important for the treating psychologist to keep these factors in mind when providing interventions. What was initially a very private problem between two people, becomes a very public experience when the couple engage with an ART clinic with medical specialists and family and friends knowing intimate details about their lives.

Efficacy of Psychological Interventions

Despite advances in the knowledge of the impact of infertility on individuals and couples, relatively few studies exist which examine the effectiveness of psychosocial interventions used to treat infertility-related distress. Peterson and Eifert (2011) recently reported that there is a significant gap between the number of treatment outcomes studies (6%) and the number of studies that provide general treatment information (94%). A relatively recent meta-analysis conducted by de Liz and Strauss (2005) using 22 outcomes studies concluded that therapy is effective in reducing infertility stress, depression, and anxiety symptoms with individuals and couples. However, there is a clear need for further research examining the effectiveness of treatment interventions in reducing infertility-related distress.

In the absence of a thorough evidence base on efficacy, anecdotal and case-based reports remain useful in describing responses to specific therapeutic interventions. For example, given that infertility and its associated treatment is often completely unexpected and overwhelming for many people, validation, normalization, and empathy can provide enormous relief (Ustunsoz, 2011). Individuals often feel greatly unprepared for the challenges involved in treatment, and the personal impact can change the couple's relationship. Therefore, assisting the couple to feel less isolated and less "abnormal" will reduce a lot of stress and concern. Normalizing a couple's changes in their sexual relationship, validating the different ways men and women respond and providing empathy for their current circumstance can assist greatly in relieving anxiety.

For individuals and couples whose main concern is their grief reaction over infertility, grief counselling may be useful to help them acknowledge the loss of the fantasized pregnancy, which commonly involves feelings of shock and an assault on self-worth. Infertility treatment creates a unique setting for grief in that it can involve not only acute losses, but can bring to the surface more chronic loss experiences. Acute losses include pregnancy loss and failed treatment cycles; however, these acute losses are embedded within a structure of overall chronic losses an individual may have experienced throughout their lives. As such, individuals may not only grieve for their current loss (e.g., inability to conceive naturally or recent failed pregnancy test), but may also need to discuss other losses that they have previously experienced, along with anticipatory grief due to the lack of guarantee that their treatment will be successful. Assisting individuals and couples to acknowledge their grief and to find healthy ways of coping is an important task for the treating psychologist. Additionally, experiencing the loss of an embryo or fetus during treatment can be similar to the loss of a young child for some couples but may not be seen as important by the couple's social support network, so providing validation for any disenfranchised grief and acknowledging that these losses are indeed significant (including the loss of dreams and hopes) is imperative in assisting the couple through this process.

A number of different theoretical models have been used to guide therapeutic work with individuals and couples faced with infertility. Some of these models include stress and coping (Zucker, 1999), the close relationship model of infertility (Higgins, 1990), self-discrepancy theory (Kikendall, 1994), object relations (Greenbaum, 2005), self-regulation (Benyamini *et al.*, 2004), the relational model of development (Gibson & Myers, 2000), a family systems approach (McDaniel *et al.*, 1992), and attachment (Amir *et al.*, 1999). A stress and coping framework (Lazarus & Folkman, 1984) is commonly used in guiding interventions for psychologists in these settings, as infertility is commonly perceived as a major stressor. Couples experiencing infertility commonly face stressors that are emotional, social, and financial in nature, and each stress reaction is unique to each person and is based on individual characteristics. Therapists can assist the individual or couple in evaluating the effectiveness of their coping strategies employed to manage these stressors (e.g., avoidance versus approach strategies), which may lead to better adjustment to infertility. Research has shown that both emotion-focused and problem-focused interventions are effective in men and women coping with infertility, with emotion-focused interventions providing better outcomes in the short term, and problem-focused interventions providing better outcomes in the long term (McQueeney *et al.*, 1996).

Object relations theory focuses on the mental representations of objects and the relationship of the self to one's world of inner objects. This approach highlights the fundamental importance of reproductive ability in defining an individual's sense of self and the powerful influence of reproductive ability on identity formation (Sewell & Burns, 2006). The family life cycle perspective defines a series of stages with expectable time lines that most people imagine as their predictable life course (Carter & McGoldrick, 1980), with the decision to have children as an implicit part of most marital relationships. However the infertile couple who are unable to achieve the next stage find themselves indefinitely stuck in the "couple" stage. Furthermore, the stress of infertility can unbalance family relationships and increase the possibility for triangulation, which reduces anxiety in one relationship by focusing on a third party, commonly the fantasy child or infertility process itself (Mikesell & Stohner, 1995). However a rigid triangle may translate into an unhealthy focus on the child when the couple do achieve a pregnancy, therefore a family systems therapeutic approach may provide appropriate interventions to improve family outcomes. Finally, the importance of attachment implications for treatment of infertile patients is illustrated by research findings that suggest that the predictor of a healthy attachment relationship between mother and infant may be evident well before a baby's birth. Through the world of the mother's (and father's) fantasy life, the development of a secure attachment with an infant starts to take shape (Frank *et al.*, 1998). Bowlby (1969) noted that when attachment behavior is activated by separation and no reunion takes place, as happens for infertile patients in treatment failures, people exhibit a prolonged distress of grief (Nelson, 1998). Using an attachment framework, a therapist may assist the individual or couple in examining how they are functioning within interpersonal relationships and assist in the prevention of insecure or anxious attachments.

Group therapy approaches have also been evaluated in infertile populations and have been shown to exert positive outcomes. For example, the application of cognitive behavior therapy (CBT) to infertile women in a group format has been shown to contribute to significant psychological improvement. In three separate, randomized controlled studies (Domar *et al.*, 1990, 1992, 1999), infertile women who attended a 10-session CBT program experienced significant improvement pre- to postprogram on all assessments of depressive symptoms, anxiety, and anger. Similarly, Tarabusi *et al.* (2004) investigated the effects of a 12-session CBT group treatment program on 10 infertile couples who were waiting to begin IVF treatment, and compared their outcomes to an observational group who were also waiting to begin IVF but received no intervention. The researchers showed that their CBT group treatment program attenuated the distress of waiting for IVF, as the CBT group participants showed a significant decrease in anxiety as compared to the observational (no-treatment) group. Group formats have also been reported by patients as useful in decreasing isolation and providing a sense of connection with individuals and couples facing similar circumstances. Melbourne IVF, a large Victorian clinic, therefore offer groups specifically targeting separate needs such as the "Single Mums' Group," "Donor Egg Group," and "Donor Embryo Program Group," and the "Moving On Group" for people who have been unsuccessful in achieving a pregnancy. Each group is designed and targeted to address the sensitive issues and challenges faced by group members and provides a safe place for support and information.

The provision of groups, however, does not attenuate the need for support from one's own social network. Therefore evaluating and addressing the level of social support is an important component of treatment. Often individuals and couples can benefit from assistance in establishing boundaries in relationships and increasing assertiveness regarding how they wish to be treated (e.g., managing unsolicited advice). Psycho-education regarding communicating effectively and practicing assertiveness can assist patients to feel more in control of how they are managing their situation. Factors such as quality of life, interpersonal communication and coping strategies can be improved through therapy, and thus help the individual and couple to maintain their morale for treatment. Finally, it is essential for the therapist to acknowledge that infertility cannot be treated in isolation, because it affects both the spouses (Nene *et al.*, 2005). Therefore even though one individual in a couple may access psychological support, it is the therapist's role to consider this presentation in the context of the couple relationship.

Use of Third-Party Reproduction Methods such as Donor Gametes and Surrogacy

If a couple are unsuccessful in achieving a pregnancy with their own gametes, the option of using a sperm, egg, or embryo donor, or a surrogate, may be an option. Many ART clinics in Australia have sperm, egg, and embryo donor programs available for infertile couples. There are many circumstances in which using a sperm, egg, or embryo donor may be beneficial, but it is essential that the couple be thoroughly familiar with the emotional, legal, and psychosocial issues that this treatment option presents. Couples must consider how they would feel about conceiving a child that is not genetically related to one or both of them, how this may impact family relationships, and who, when, and how they would disclose the donor origins to the child and others. Additionally, they must consider the type of relationship the donor may have in their and the child's life, the legal rights and responsibilities of donors and recipients, and many other issues for the potential child, recipient, and donor. Legislation in Australia prohibits payment for sperm, egg, and embryo donation; therefore donors enter into these arrangements for altruistic reasons. The use of any donor material can raise significant issues for an individual and couple, and it is essential that all parties involved feel fully informed and entirely comfortable with the possible outcomes and issues before proceeding. Research regarding the outcomes of donor conception has largely shown that donor-conceived families do not differ with respect to the quality of parenting or psychological adjustment of the child (Golombok *et al.*, 2003). In fact, in their study comparing 21 egg-donation families, 45 donor-insemination families, 55 adoptive families, and 41 families created by IVF, Golombok *et al.* (2003) found greater psychological wellbeing among mothers and fathers in families where there was no genetic link between the mother and the child. Whereas space constraints in this chapter prohibit a full exploration of the issues involved, extensive resources are fully accessible elsewhere (see www.varta.org.au).

Finally, if a woman is unable to carry a child herself, surrogacy may be an option. Surrogacy is a method of reproduction whereby a woman agrees to become pregnant and deliver a child for a commissioning party. The practice of surrogacy occurs worldwide. However, legislation in most of Australia stipulates that surrogacy must be altruistic (i.e., the surrogate is not financially rewarded), and the surrogate must not use her own eggs in the fertilization procedure (i.e., is not the genetic parent of the child she relinquishes). This is called gestational surrogacy, which differs from traditional surrogacy where the surrogate's egg is used in fertilization as occurs in some other countries, but is prohibited in Australia. Surrogacy is a reasonably new practice in Australia and requires all parties of the arrangement to consent to extensive counselling, psychological, and medical assessments, as well as seeking independent legal advice, in order to ensure that informed consent is provided and a full consideration of the possible outcomes of surrogacy is considered by all parties. Most of the previous research in this area has been conducted overseas and has shown that despite the unconventional nature of this treatment option few problematic outcomes have occurred with the majority of arrangements, resulting in successful relinquishment of the baby with little negative impact on the surrogate, commissioning couple, and baby (Teman, 2008).

Conclusion

Although infertility has historically been exposed to stigmatization, in recent years the process of medicalization of infertility has resulted in a shift in emphasis from coping with childlessness through social means (e.g., participating in the raising of another person's child) to a dependence on medical intervention. While social conditions have limited the availability of children for adoption, infertility treatment options have increased the likelihood of achieving successful pregnancies for many infertile couples (Vilska *et al.*, 2009). Consequently, couples not only have to deal with cultural and social pressures surrounding their childlessness, but also with the pressure to use the medical treatments available to them, often at great emotional, physical, and financial cost. Medical intervention can also delay a couple coming to terms with their infertility and finding other meaningful ways to experience life. This can have significant impact on individuals' and couples' self esteem and quality of life, particularly those who continue with treatment for long periods of time and try a wide range of interventions.

Infertility and infertility treatment experiences can vary greatly for each individual or couple, and their experiences are greatly affected by social, individual and couple factors. Common sense can be used to guide an understanding of the types of pressures and expectations that individuals and couples feel when thrust into this situation and psychologists are well positioned to assist patients in acknowledging the grief and loss, anger and disappointment, and conflicting thoughts and emotions about the threat of infertility on a major life goal. Individual and group psychological interventions have been shown to be effective yet further research is needed, and range from providing validation, normalization and empathy, to more in-depth CBT or psychodynamic and systems therapy approaches. It is clear that the impact of reproductive issues is wide-ranging and may affect crucial aspects of one's self-identity, core values and beliefs, and closest relationships. Thus, it is imperative that psychological interventions are appropriate to the individual or couple, well timed, and delivered efficiently to relieve some of the enormous pressure of infertility and infertility treatment.

References

Abbey, A., Andrews, F. M., & Halman, L. J. (1991). Gender's role in response to infertility. *Psychology of Women Quarterly, 15,* 295–316.

Amir, M., Horesh, N., & Lin-Stein, T. (1999). Infertility and adjustment in women: The effects of attachment style and social support. *Journal of Clinical Psychology in Medical Settings, 6,* 463–463.

Applegarth, L. D. (1999). Individual counselling and psychotherapy. In L. H. Burns & S. N. Covington (Eds.), *Infertility Counselling: A Comprehensive Handbook for Clinicians.* New York: The Parthenon Publishing Company.

Australian Institute of Health and Welfare. (2010). *Assisted Reproductive Technology in Australia and New Zealand 2008.* Assisted Reproduction Technology Series no. 14. Cat. no. PER 49. Canberra: Australian Institute of Health and Welfare.

Bates, G. W., & Bates, S. R. (1996). Infertility services in a managed care environment. *Current Opinion in Obstetrics and Gynecology, 8,* 300–304.

Bell, A. V. (2009). "It's way out of my league": Low-income women's experiences of medicalized infertility. *Gender & Society, 23,* 688–709.

Benyamini, Y., Gozlan, M., & Kokia, E. (2004). On the self-regulation of a health threat: Cognitions, coping, and emotions among women undergoing treatment for infertility. *Cognitive Therapy and Research, 28,* 577–592.

Berg, B. J., & Wilson, J. F. (1995). Patterns of psychological distress in infertile couples. *Journal of Psychosomatic Obstetrics and Gynecology, 16,* 65–78.

Beutel, M., Kupfer, J., Kirchmeyer, P., Kehde, S., Kohn, F. M. *et al.* (1999) Treatment-related stresses and depression in couples undergoing assisted reproductive treatment by IVF or ICSI. *Andrologia, 31,* 27–35.

Bowlby, J. (1969). *Attachment and Loss: Vol. 1. Attachment.* New York: Basic Books.

Carter, E., & McGoldrick, M. (1980). *The Family Life Cycle.* New York: Gardner.

Carter, D., Misri, S., & Tomfohr, L. (2007). Psychological aspects of early pregnancy loss. *Clinical Obstetrics and Gynecology, 50,* 154–165.

Champion, L. A., & Power, M. J. (1995). Social and cognitive approaches to depression: Towards a new synthesis. *British Journal of Clinical Psychology, 34,* 485–503.

de Liz, T. M., & Strauss, B. (2005). Differential efficacy of group and individual couple psychotherapy with infertile patients. *Human Reproduction, 20,* 1324–1332.

Domar, A. (2004). Impact of psychological factors on dropout rates in insured infertility patients. *Fertility and Sterility, 81,* 271–273.

Domar, A., Siebel, M., & Benson, H. (1990). The mind/body program for infertility: A new behavioural treatment approach for women with infertility. *Fertility and Sterility, 53,* 246–249.

Domar, A., Zuttermeister, P., Seibel, M., & Benson, H. (1992). Psychological improvement in infertile women after behavioural treatment: A replication. *Fertility and Sterility, 58,* 144–147.

Domar, A., Zuttermeister, P., & Friedman, R. (1993). The psychological impact of infertility: A comparison to patients with other medical conditions. *Journal of Psychosomatic Obstetrics and Gynecology, 14,* 45–52.

Domar, A., Zuttermeister, P., & Friedman, R. (1999). The relationship between distress and conception in infertile women. *Journal of the American Women's Association, 54,* 196–198.

Donnelly, D. (1993). Sexually inactive marriages. *Journal of Sexual Research, 30,* 171–9.

Edelmann, R., Humphrey, M., & Owens, D. J. (1994). The meaning of parenthood and couple reactions to male infertility. *British Journal of Medical Psychology, 67*, 291–299.

Erikson, E. H. (1963). *Childhood and society* (revised edn.). New York: W. W. Norton.

Eunpu, D. (1995). The impact of infertility and treatment guidelines for couples therapy. *The American Journal of Family Therapy, 23*, 115–128.

Faramarzi, A., Alipor, A., Esmaelzadeh, S., Kheirkhah, F., Poladi, K., & Pash, H. (2008). Treatment of depression and anxiety in infertile women: Cognitive behavioral therapy versus fluoxetine. *Journal of Affective Disorders, 108*, 159–164.

Feveile, H., Schmidt, L., Hannerz, H., & Hougaard, K. (2011). Industrial differences in female fertility treatment rates – a new approach to assess differences related to occupation? *Scandanavian Journal of Public Health, 39*, 164–171.

Fisher, J., Baker, G., & Hammarberg, K. (2010). Long-term health, well-being, life satisfaction, and attitudes towards parenthood in men diagnosed as infertile: challenges to gender stereotypes and implications for practice. *Fertility and Sterility, 94*, 574–580.

Frank, M., Tuber, S., Slade, A., & Garrod, E. (1998). Mother's fantasy representations and infant security of attachment: A Rorschach study of first pregnancy. *Psychoanalytic Psychology, 11*, 476–486.

Gibson, D. M., & Myers, J. E. (2000). Gender and infertility: A relational approach to counseling women. *Journal of Counseling and Development, 78*, 400–410.

Glover, L., McLellan, A., & Weaver, S. M. (2009). What does having a fertility problem mean to couples? *Journal of Reproductive and Infant Psychology, 27*, 401–418.

Golombok, S., Murray, C., Brinsden, P., & Abdallah, H. (2003). Social versus biological parenting: Family functioning and the socioemotional development of children born by egg or sperm donation. In M. E. Hertzig & E. A. Farber (Eds.), *Annual Progress in Child Psychiatry and Child Development: 2000–2001* (pp. 155–175). New York: Brunner-Routledge.

Green, J. A., Robins, J. C., Scheiber, M., Awadalla, S., & Thomas, M. A. (2001). Racial and economic demographics of couples seeking infertility treatment. *American Journal of Obstetrics and Gynecology, 184*, 1080–1082.

Greenbaum, M. (2005). Integrated reproductive healthcare: An object relational model for treatment and collaboration. *Dissertation Abstracts International, 66*(5-B), 2820–2887.

Gurhan, N., Aygul, A., Derya, A., & Sezer, K. (2009). Association with depression and anxiety with occyte and sperm numbers and pregnancy outcomes during in vitro fertilisation treatment. *Psychological Reports, 3*, 796–806.

Hammarberg, K. (2010). *IVF & Beyond for Dummies.* Australia: Wiley Publishing.

Helmerhorst, F. M., Perquin, D. A., Donker, D., & Keirse, M. J. (2004). Perinatal outcome of singletons and twins after assisted conception: a systematic review of controlled studies. *British Medication Journal, 328*, 261–265.

Higgins, B. S. (1990). Couple infertility: From the perspective of the close-relationship model. *Family Relations, 39*, 81–86.

Hjelmstedt, A., Widstrom, A., & Collins, A. (2007). Prenatal attachment in Swedish IVF fathers and controls. *Journal of Reproductive and Infant Psychology, 25*, 296–307.

Holter, H., Anderheim, L., Bergh, C., & Moller, A. (2007). The psychological influence of gender infertility diagnoses among men about to start IVF or ICSI treatment using their own sperm. *Human Reproduction, 22*, 2559–2565.

Khademi, A., Alleyassin, A., Amini, M., & Ghaemi, M. (2008). Evaluation of sexual dysfunction prevalence in infertile couples. *Journal of Sexual Medicine, 5*, 1402–1410.

Kikendall, K. A. (1994). Self-discrepancy as an important factor in addressing women's emotional reactions to infertility. *Professional Psychology, Research and Practice, 25*, 214–220.

Klonoff-Cohen, H. (2008). The role of procedural vs. chronic stress and other psychological factors in IVF success rates. In A. Turley, G. Hofmann, & N. Hauppauge (Eds.). *Life Style and Health Research Progress* (pp. 67–85). New York: Nova Biomedical Books.

Kraaij, V., Garnefski, N., & Vlietstra, A. (2008). Cognitive coping and depressive symptoms in definitive infertility: A prospective study. *Journal of Psychosomatic Obstetrics & Gynecology, 29*, 9–16.

Lazarus, R., & Folkman, S. (1984). *Stress, Appraisal and Coping*. New York: Springer.

Lord, S., & Robertson, L. (2005). The role of patient appraisal and coping in predicting distress in IVF. *Journal of Reproductive and Infant Psychology, 23,* 319–332.

McCormack, K. (2005). Stratified reproduction and poor women's resistance. *Gender and Society, 19,* 660–79.

McDaniel, S. H., Hepworth, J., & Doherty, W. (1992). Medical family therapy with couples facing infertility. *The American Journal of Family Therapy, 20,* 101–122.

McQueeney, D. A., Stanton, A. L., & Sigmon, S. (1996). Efficacy of emotion-focused and problem-focused group therapies for women with fertility problems. *Journal of Behavioral Medicine, 20,* 313–331.

Mikesell, S. G., & Stohner, M. (1995). Infertility and pregnancy loss: The role of the family consultant. In R. Mikesall, D. Lusterman & S. McDaniel (Eds.), *Integrating Family Therapy: Handbook of Family Psychology and Systems Theory* (pp. 421–436). Washington DC: American Psychological Association.

Miles, L. M., Keitel, M., Jackson, M., Harris, A., & Licciardi, F. (2009). Predictors of distress in women being treated for infertility. *Journal of Reproductive and Infant Psychology, 27,* 238–257.

Morrow, K. A., Thoreson, R. W., & Penney, L. L. (1995). Predictors of psychological distress among infertility clinic patients. *Journal of Consulting and Clinical Psychology, 63,* 163–167.

Nelson, J. (1998). The meaning of crying based on attachment theory. *Clinical Social Work Journal, 2,* 9–22.

Nene, U. A., Coyaji, K., & Apte, H. (2005). Infertility: A label of choice in the case of sexually dysfunctional couples. *Patient Education and Counseling, 59,* 234–238.

Newton, C. R., & Houle, M. (1993). Gender differences in psychological response to infertility treatment. *Canadian Journal of Human Sexuality, 2,* 129–139.

Newton, C. R., Sherrard, W., & Glavac, I. (1999). The Fertility Problem Inventory: Measuring perceived infertility-related stress. *Fertility and Sterility, 72,* 54–62.

Oakley, L., Doyle, P., & Maconochie, N. (2007). Lifetime prevalence of infertility and infertility treatment in the UK: Results from a population-based survey of reproduction. *Human Reproduction, 23,* 447–450.

Peronance, L. A., Boivin, J., & Schmidt, L. (2007). Patterns of suffering and social interactions in infertile men: 12 months after unsuccessful treatment. *Journal of Psychosomatic Obstetrics and Gynecology, 28,* 105–114.

Peterson, B. D., & Eifert, G. H. (2011). Using acceptance and commitment therapy to treat infertility stress. *Cognitive and Behavioral Practice, 18,* 577–587.

Peterson, B. D., Newton, C. R., & Rosen, K. H. (2003). Examining congruence between partners perceived infertility-related stress and its relationship to marital adjustment and depression in infertile couples. *Family Process, 42,* 59–70.

Rasmussen Report. (2009). *Most Agree that Being a Father is a Man's Most Important Role*. www .rasmussenreports.com/public_content/lifestyle/holidays/june_2009/most_agree_that_being_a_father_is_a _man_s_most_important_role.

Runganga, A. O., Sundby, J., & Aggleton, P. (2001). Culture, identity and reproductive failure in Zimbabwe. *Sexualities, 4,* 315–332.

Schieve, L. A., Peterson, H. B., Meikle, S. F., Jeng, G., Danel, I., Burnett, N. M., & Wilcox, L. S. (1999). Live-birth rates and multiple-birth risk using in vitro fertilization. *Journal of the American Medical Association, 282,* 1832–1838.

Sewell, G., & Burns, L. H. (2006). Involuntary childlessness. In S. N. Covington & L. H. Burns (Eds.), *Infertility Counselling: A Comprehensive Handbook for Clinicians* (pp. 167–194). Cambridge: Cambridge University Press.

Smith, J. F., Walsh, T. J., Shindel, A. W., Turek, P. J., Wing, H., Pasch, L., & Katz, P. P. (2009). Sexual, marital and social impact of a man's perceived infertility diagnosis. *Journal of Sexual Medicine, 6,* 2505–2515.

Tarabusi, M., Volpe, A., & Facchinetti, F. (2004). Psychological group support attenuates distress of waiting in couples scheduled for assisted reproduction. *Journal of Psychosomatic Obstetrics and Gynecology, 25,* 273–279.

Teman, E. (2008). The social construction of surrogacy research: An anthropological critique of the psychosocial scholarship on surrogate motherhood. *Social Science and Medicine, 67,* 1104–1112.

Tennen, H., Affleck, G., & Mendola, A. (1991). Causal explanations for infertility: Their relation to control appraisals and psychological adjustments. In A. L. Stanton & C. Dunkel-Schetter (Eds.), *Infertility: Perspectives from Stress and Coping Research* (pp. 109–132). New York: Plenum Press.

Ustunsoz, A. (2011). To be an infertile woman. *Patient Education and Counseling, 82,* 182–183.

van Balen, F., & Trimbos-Kemper, T. C. M. (1993). Long-term infertile couples: A study of their well-being. *Journal of Psychosomatic Obstetrics and Gynecology, 14,* 53–60.

van Balen, F., & Bos, H. M. (2004). Infertility, culture, and psychology in worldwide perspective. *Journal of Infant and Reproductive Psychology, 22,* 245–7.

Verhaak, C., Smeenk, J., van Minnen, A., Kremer, J., & Kraaimaat, F. (2005). A longitudinal, prospective study on emotional adjustment before, during and after consecutive fertility treatment cycles. *Human Reproduction, 20,* 2253–2260.

Vilska, S., Unkila-Kallio, L., Punamki, R. L., Poikkeus, P., Repokari, L., Sinkkonen, J. *et al.* (2009). Mental health of mothers and fathers of twins conceived via assisted reproduction treatment: A 1-year prospective study. *Human Reproduction, 24,* 367–377.

Widge, A. (2002). Sociocultural attitudes towards infertility and assisted reproduction in India. In E. Vayena, P. J. Rowe, & P. D. Griffin (Eds.), *Current Practices and Controversies in Assisted Reproduction.* Geneva: World Health Organization.

Zucker, A. N. (1999). The psychological impact of reproductive difficulties on women's lives. *Sex Roles, 40,* 767–786.

15

The Psychological Management of Sexually Transmitted Infections and Human Immunodeficiency Virus

Danielle C. Newton

Sexual health, as defined by the World Health Organization (WHO), is "a state of physical, mental and social wellbeing in relation to sexuality" (WHO, 2010c). Viewing sexual health from this biopsychosocial perspective recognizes the contribution of biological, psychological and social factors to sexual wellbeing. The World Psychiatric Association definition of sexual health goes on to explain that sexual health is "a dynamic and harmonious state involving erotic and reproductive experiences and fulfilment, within a broader physical, emotional, interpersonal, social and spiritual sense of wellbeing, in a culturally informed, freely and responsibly chosen, and ethical framework; not merely the absence of disorders" (Mezzich & Hernandez-Serrano, 2006).

Sexually transmitted infections (STIs) are a major health concern in Western society. At the individual level, a person's sexual health can be seriously impacted by STIs, with a diagnosis resulting in adverse consequences affecting physical, reproductive, psychological, and social wellbeing. The way in which the effects of an STI diagnosis are managed has significant implications not only for the individual but also for the effective management and prevention of transmission at the community level.

This chapter provides a comprehensive analysis of the psychological and behavioral impact of STIs on sexual health. Psychological distress is most commonly associated with viral STIs, since these often result in chronic infections. For this reason, this review summarizes the impact of a diagnosis with herpes simplex virus (HSV), genital human papillomavirus (HPV), and human immunodeficiency virus (HIV). While all three viruses produce persistent infections, the severity of resulting conditions varies greatly. This provides a useful framework around which to base a discussion of the observed psychosocial impacts and interventions that are common and distinct between different STIs.

The Psychological Impact of a Genital Herpes or Genital HPV Diagnosis

Two of the most common viral STIs are genital herpes and genital HPV, some serovars of which can cause genital warts. Both genital herpes and genital warts are medically incurable, may be

Applied Topics in Health Psychology, First Edition. Edited by M. L. Caltabiano and L. Ricciardelli.
© 2013 John Wiley & Sons, Ltd. Published 2013 by John Wiley & Sons, Ltd.

physically evidenced on the body, may cause the infected individual pain, and may be transmitted to sexual partners even in the absence of any notable symptoms.

Being diagnosed and living with an STI can have a significant psychosocial impact on an individual (Carney *et al.*, 1994; Green, 2004; Holt *et al.*, 2010; Lee & Craft, 2002; Mark *et al.*, 2009; Nack, 2008; Newton & McCabe, 2005). While acquiring any health condition can potentially be a source of distress, the societal stigma of "sexual immorality" and "uncleanliness" associated with having an STI make a diagnosis of this kind all the more troubling (British Psychological Society, 2002). A STI diagnosis can have drastic effects on quality of life (Mark *et al.*, 2009), affecting intimate relationships (Newton & McCabe, 2008b), and individuals' sexual identity and feelings of desirability (Melville *et al.*, 2003; Nack, 2000, 2008; Newton & McCabe, 2008a, 2008b; Zacharioudakis, 2001).

Genital herpes is caused by the HSV. Globally, approximately 16% of 15–49 year olds are living with HSV type 2 (HSV-2) (Looker *et al.*, 2008). The infection may be asymptomatic, or may periodically cause the development of painful fluid-filled blisters or ulcerations of the genital skin (Centers for Disease Control and Prevention, 2010). Living with herpes is complicated by the fact that even when asymptomatic the infected individual may still shed viral particles and be capable of transmitting the virus to others. Irrespective of the frequency of symptoms, genital herpes may cause psychological distress in people who are aware that they are infected (Centers for Disease Control and Prevention, 2010) and transmission of the genital herpes virus is a primary concern of those infected (Carney *et al.*, 1994). This is despite the transmission of HSV-2 to uninfected partners being relatively low. In research by Corey and colleagues (2004) the HSV-2 transmission rate to partners over an 8 month period was 3.6%, decreasing to 1.9% among individuals taking daily antiviral medication (Corey *et al.*, 2004). The often unpredictable nature of the virus may render it more likely to impact on intimate relationships than other STIs that manifest differently.

More than 40 types of HPV can infect the genital area and may manifest as either visible warts or as a cervical infection that can lead to cervical cancer (Centers for Disease Control and Prevention, 2009). Warts are typically visible as a small bump or cluster of bumps in the genital area, that may be cauliflower-shaped in appearance (Centers for Disease Control and Prevention, 2009). Genital warts are among the most commonly diagnosed STIs in Australia, the USA, and the UK. Among Australians aged 16–59 years, the estimated prevalence of genital warts is 4%, while among Americans aged 18–59 years genital wart prevalence is approximately 5.6% (Dinh *et al.*, 2008; Grulich *et al.*, 2003). Genital warts are the most common viral STI in the UK; between 2000 and 2009, first-episode genital wart diagnoses at genitourinary medicine clinics increased by 30% (Microbiology and Epidemiology of STIs and HIV Department, 2010).

Research into the psychosocial impact of genital herpes and/or genital HPV indicates that a diagnosis may have an adverse effect on sexual identity and feelings of desirability, and may result in a lowered quality of life (Barnack-Tavlaris *et al.*, 2011; Newton & McCabe, 2008a, 2008b; Patrick *et al.*, 2004). Anxiety and depression are also frequently reported among individuals living with herpes and/or HPV (Mark *et al.*, 2009; Newton & McCabe, 2008b).

Disclosure of STI to Sexual Partners

Disclosure of an STI to sexual partners can be one of the most distressing aspects of an STI diagnosis. Historically, individuals with STIs were seen to have acquired the infection through lax behaviors and poor lifestyle preferences; infections were perceived to be self-inflicted (Brandt, 1987; Hall, 2001). The stigma associated with having an STI is a significant emotional burden for individuals living with STIs and may be a barrier to seeking adequate healthcare and treatment (British

Psychological Society, 2002). Furthermore, the stigma attached to diagnosis can have a significant impact on whether an individual chooses to disclose their condition to others (Lee & Craft, 2002).

When disclosing their STI to a partner, infected individuals must confront not only the social perception of their condition but also their fear of rejection. The disclosure of STI status is a process that may be fraught with anxiety and fear, and negative partner reactions to disclosure may cause individuals to retreat from future disclosure of their STI. Disclosure is viewed as a difficult process, and while notions of morality and responsibility may compel one individual with an STI to disclose their condition to their partner, fears of rejection and moral judgment may prompt another to keep their condition hidden. A personal dilemma therefore ensues for the individual diagnosed with an STI. Issues of personal morality, responsibility, and ethics intertwine to create feelings of intrapersonal conflict surrounding the issue of whether or not to disclose their STI to their partner (Lehr & Lee, 1990). The consequences of their decision can also be considerable, impacting on the degree of trust, intimacy, and communication in the relationship.

Research on STI disclosure has focused primarily on the manner in which individuals disclose their STI (Lee & Craft, 2002; Swanson & Chenitz, 1993), and the reasons for disclosure versus nondisclosure (Green *et al.*, 2003; Keller *et al.*, 2000; Lee & Craft, 2002; Temple-Smith *et al.*, 2010). Other people's reactions to the disclosure of STI status can have a significant impact on the infected individual's feelings of self. Negative disclosure experiences, where the individual is rejected based on their disclosure, have been shown to have detrimental effects on individuals with herpes and HPV. In situations where disclosure of their STI to a sexual partner resulted in rejection or judgment, individuals often felt badly about themselves and retreated from future disclosure to sexual partners or from entering into future sexual relationships (Newton & McCabe, 2008b).

Often individuals will choose not to disclose their STI to their sexual partner; however, those who do not disclose have been shown to be more sexually anxious, have lower sexual esteem, be more sexually depressed, and be less sexually satisfied than individuals who had disclosed their STI status to their current partner (Newton & McCabe, 2008a). These findings may be accounted for by a number of explanations. It is possible that individuals who do not disclose their STI status to their partner have experienced difficulties in adjusting to their diagnosis. They may experience feelings such as discomfort or depression about their sexual lives as a result of having an STI, and this may lead them to fear rejection if they reveal their STI status to their partner. An alternative possibility is that not having revealed their STI status to their partner, an individual may feel even more anxious and depressed about the sexual aspects of their lives, and doubt their capacity to experience their sexual life in a satisfying manner. The burden of secrecy may cause feelings of guilt or anxiety to develop, leading to inhibition and to negative feelings about the sexual aspects of themselves. Moreover, there are many factors that potentially could play a mediating role in the effects of disclosure of one's STI status to their partner and impact on sexual self-concept. For example, in situations where a newly infected partner holds their partner responsible for the acquirement of their STI, they may be more likely to disclose their STI status to their partner. It is possible that the impact of having an STI on the sexual self-concept of an individual in this situation may be less, as the individual is perhaps less likely to blame themselves for the acquisition of their STI (Newton & McCabe, 2008a).

Psychological Interventions to Assist in Coping with an STI Diagnosis and Modifying Risk Behavior

A number of interventions aimed at mitigating the adverse effects of diagnosis have been reported, and indicate that the psychological care of individuals diagnosed with an STI should begin at the time of diagnosis. Medical practitioners involved in the diagnosis and management of individuals with an STI can make a significant difference to how well these individuals adjust to their diagnosis (Warren & Ebel, 2005). Research has shown that patients attending general practice for STI-related care are dissatisfied with their care when they feel their medical practitioner has given them little information about their symptoms or diagnosis (Sutcliffe *et al.*, 2011). In addition, at the time of diagnosis with herpes, a person's primary concerns are about the psychosocial aspects of the condition particularly transmission and its likely impact on their sex life (Melville *et al.*, 2003; Patrick *et al.*, 2004). It is therefore essential that medical practitioners give the newly diagnosed individual time to process their diagnosis, and provide them with reassurance and emotional support to mitigate any distress. Newly diagnosed patients should be provided with the opportunity to ask questions about their condition and be provided with information not only about the physical aspects but also the potential psychosocial impact.

Referral to a psychologist for additional information and support may be necessary if a patient is exhibiting high levels of distress that are not lessening over time. Psychological therapies have been shown to be effective in addressing many of the issues associated with sexual health problems, such as depression, anxiety, adjustment issues, poor/lowered self-esteem, and relationship difficulties, and as such are well placed to address these issues when associated with an STI diagnosis (British Psychological Society, 2002). Since anxiety and depression are particularly common among individuals living with herpes or HPV (Mark *et al.*, 2009; Newton & McCabe, 2008b), psychological intervention can assist individuals in addressing these issues. Research has also found that, compared to individuals experiencing a lower number of herpes recurrences, individuals experiencing a greater number of herpes recurrences are less likely to use problem-focused coping strategies of planning and active coping and the coping skill of positive reinterpretation and growth (Cassidy *et al.*, 1997). Therefore, psychologists may have a role to play in assisting clients to adapt their coping styles in order to make greater use of problem and emotion focused strategies. Psycho-education can be used to decrease the stigma associated with having an STI and to reassure the individual that all sexually active people are at risk of contracting an STI. In situations where an individual's particular sexual behavior has put them at risk, psychological intervention may also play a role in modifying sexual health risk behaviors (Roth & Fonagy, 1996).

In the interests of public health, fears surrounding disclosure to sexual partners should be addressed by those involved in the care of individuals infected with STIs. Psychologists can assist individuals in developing techniques to aid in disclosing their STI status to partners. They can also work with the individual to develop useful coping strategies to assist them in adapting to the potential negative outcome of such disclosure. Inevitably, for some individuals, being diagnosed with an STI may result in relationship difficulties. Psychological intervention can also play a role in assisting an individual and their partner to cope with the issues introduced into the relationship as a result of the diagnosis. In serodiscordant relationships (relationships where only one partner has an STI), this may involve developing practical strategies to manage the risk of transmission or assisting the couple to manage issues of conflict or distrust that may have arisen in the relationship as a result of the diagnosis.

Psychological Aspects of Living with HIV/AIDS

HIV is a blood-borne virus producing long-term chronic symptoms in infected individuals. A person living with HIV may experience symptoms such as extreme fatigue, flu-like symptoms, rapid weight loss, diarrhoea, and muscular aches. HIV weakens the body's immune system, leaving it vulnerable to various infections and cancers. Without treatment individuals with HIV will eventually become ill and may develop acquired immune deficiency syndrome (AIDS) within a period of 5–10 years (WHO, 2010a). The advent of highly active antiretroviral therapy (HAART) in the mid-1990s had a dramatic effect in changing HIV infection from a death sentence to a chronic illness requiring lifetime management. However, living with HIV infection today is certainly not without challenges, not the least of which is the uncertainty and unpredictable nature surrounding disease progression. In addition to coping with the deteriorations in one's health state, HIV-positive individuals are confronted with complex medication regimens and their associated side effects, and changing personal relationships with partners, family members, and friends.

By the end of 2009 it was estimated that 33.3 million people across the world were living with HIV, with 2.6 million of these people newly infected in 2009 (WHO, 2009). In Australia an estimated 18 000 adults and children were living with HIV in 2007 (WHO, 2008a), and diagnoses have been steadily increasing since 1999 (WHO, 2008b). Due to their engagement in risky behaviors, some populations are more at risk of HIV infection than others. These include sex workers and their clients, injecting drug users, men who have sex with men, and prisoners (WHO, 2010b).

It is widely recognized that persons living with HIV may experience a variety of psychological challenges throughout the duration of their illness. As with all chronic conditions, these issues may be remitting and relapsing over the term of their illness and do not necessarily follow any linear pattern. As a result, psychological support is now viewed as an essential component of holistic HIV healthcare (British Psychological Society, 2002).

Adjustment to and coping with an HIV diagnosis

Due to the serious nature of a diagnosis with HIV, psychological support should begin prior to diagnosis, at the time of HIV testing. Individuals should always receive adequate pretest counselling prior to receiving the results of a HIV test. Pretest counselling should include education in relation to HIV and an assessment of the risk behaviors engaged in by the individual (Cohen & Ankus, 2009). In the event that the patient expresses concern about their behavior, practitioners should attempt to empower and support patients in modifying their risk behaviors (Cohen & Ankus, 2009). At this time, the practitioner should attempt to establish a relationship of trust with the individual and focus on developing rapport. Time should be spent hypothetically developing potential coping strategies that the individual might use in the event that they are HIV-positive (Cohen & Ankus, 2009).

At the time of being given a positive HIV diagnosis, the diagnosed individual may experience a range of emotions such as shock, fear, anxiety, sadness, confusion, anger, and guilt. All of these reactions are a normal and expected response to being diagnosed with any type of chronic illness (Remien & Rabkin, 2002). For most individuals the distress associated with their HIV diagnosis will resolve over time and they will adjust to and learn to cope with their new health status. However, for others, distress experienced as a result of their diagnosis may be prolonged and may necessitate psychological intervention (Chippindale & French, 2001). Preexisting psychiatric conditions, comorbid disorders, or the presence of suicidal ideation may further hinder a patient's adjustment to a diagnosis of HIV (Chippindale & French, 2001).

Being diagnosed with HIV can be considered a life crisis, and utilizing a model of crisis intervention can be useful for guiding and supporting the patient through this time. Such an approach suggests that, in contrast to situations where an individual is given a herpes or HPV diagnosis, an individual diagnosed with HIV should be provided with minimal education on

HIV at the time of diagnosis, because patients are likely to be emotionally overwhelmed and it is considered best practice to focus on mobilizing their coping resources. The patient should then be provided with more information about their condition over time. The practitioner should aim to identify the patient's primary concerns, and reassure them that their reactions to the diagnosis are completely normal. They should provide the patient with empathic, nonjudgmental support and work with the patient to identify and draw on external and internal coping strategies to assist them in managing their immediate reactions to their diagnosis. The practitioner should ensure that the individual has a support network or, at the very least, can nominate one person to whom they feel they will be able to turn to for support. The person should also be provided with appropriate referrals for psychological support if required (Cohen & Ankus, 2009).

In assisting a newly diagnosed individual in adjusting to their HIV diagnosis, it is essential that practitioners are vigilant towards the social, cultural, or religious factors that may influence how HIV and HIV testing is perceived by the patient or within their community. For example, in some cultural communities open discussion of sexual practices and sexuality is not the norm and for these individuals their levels of knowledge in relation to sexual behavior may be low (Cohen & Ankus, 2009). A focus on providing the patient with nonjudgmental, factual information about HIV transmission should be provided by the practitioner.

Depression and anxiety among individuals with HIV/AIDs

Depression is one of the most common psychiatric diagnoses among people with HIV/AIDS (Pence, 2009; Penzak *et al.*, 2002). The prevalence of major depression among people living with HIV is estimated to be 22–45% (Bing *et al.*, 2001; Komiti *et al.*, 2003; Orlando *et al.*, 2002; Penzak *et al.*, 2002) and varies depending on the population. In addition to the psychosocial implications, research has indicated that depression among individuals with HIV/AIDS also has significant implications for medical care. For example, individuals with HIV/AIDs suffering from depression are likely to experience greater delays in being prescribed antiretroviral therapy (ART) (Fairfield *et al.*, 1999) and are more likely to exhibit poorer ART adherence (Gordillo *et al.*, 1999). Women living with HIV/AIDS are particularly vulnerable to depression and among these women depression has been associated with negative outcomes such as higher levels of HIV plasma viral loads and higher mortality (Cook *et al.*, 2004; Evans *et al.*, 2002; Ickovics *et al.*, 2001), higher perceived stress (Remien *et al.*, 2006), poorer quality of life, and poorer social support (Tostes *et al.*, 2004).

Symptoms of depression may present in a variety of ways among individuals living with HIV/AIDS. Typical behavioral indicators include reduced adherence to treatment regimen, difficulty in making choices in relation to medical care, reduced ability to engage in tasks of daily living, and increasing social isolation. Individuals suffering from depression may also exhibit poorer adjustment to their diagnosis, demonstrate a preoccupation with seemingly minor problems, and experience interpersonal difficulties (New York State Department of Health, 2010b). Individuals living with HIV/AIDS who experience depression may also complain of unexplained somatic symptoms such as pain or fatigue (New York State Department of Health, 2010b). It is important to note that people living with HIV infection also have a high risk of suicide or attempted suicide (WHO, 2008c). A past history of depression, feelings of hopelessness, and comorbid substance-use disorders are psychological predictors of suicidal ideation among HIV-positive individuals (WHO, 2008c).

Antidepressant use has been found to be effective in treating depression among individuals with HIV/AIDS; however, this form of treatment is not acceptable to all patients (Himelhoch

& Medoff, 2005). Both individual and group cognitive behavior therapy (CBT) have also been found to be effective in reducing depressive symptomatology among HIV-positive individuals (Himelhoch *et al.*, 2007; Safren *et al.*, 2009).

It is likely that people living with any form of chronic illness will experience some periods of distress or anxiety. The illness trajectory is such that anxiety symptoms such as worry, fear, stress, and tension may be commonly experienced. Aspects of medical care such as uncertain prognosis, treatment side effects, or treatment failure may cause fear and distress. In addition, individuals may worry about disclosing their condition to others and may be fearful of potential rejection based on their disclosure. As to be expected, periods of anxiety are likely to occur at various times throughout the course of the illness. It is therefore not surprising that anxiety disorders are pervasive among the HIV-positive population. Among HIV-infected patients receiving medical care, 20.3% have been found to have an anxiety disorder, with 12.3% meeting the criteria for panic disorder, 10.4% for posttraumatic stress disorder, and 2.8% for generalized anxiety disorder (Vitiello *et al.*, 2003). It is not uncommon for patients suffering from major depression to also have an anxiety disorder. Anxiety disorders are associated with higher rates of nonadherence to antiretroviral therapies (Tucker *et al.*, 2003; Turner *et al.*, 2003), more rapid disease progression (Leserman *et al.*, 2002), and higher levels of pain (Tsao *et al.*, 2004).

An anxiety disorder may be present if the symptoms are causing a marked interference with the individual's daily functioning (e.g., the patient is unable to work, leave home, attend to medical care), if they are interfering with their personal relationships, or if the symptoms are causing the individual clear distress (New York State Department of Health, 2010a). CBTs may be useful in treating anxiety among this population. This may involve psycho-education about anxiety, identifying the psychological factors contributing to anxiety, modifying unhelpful thinking styles, assisting in the development of coping mechanisms, and teaching simple relaxation exercises. For more severe cases a combination of CBT and medication may be required (New York State Department of Health, 2010a).

Medication adherence

Adherence is the degree to which an individual is able and willing to follow medical and health advice. Adherence to pharmacological therapy for any individual living with a chronic illness can be problematic. Since the introduction of HAART in the mid-1990s the quality of life of people living with HIV/AIDS has improved tremendously. Compared to previous therapies, HAART is associated with less frequent side effects and increased life expectancy. However, this form of treatment is efficacious only if adherence is consistently maintained (Altice *et al.*, 2001; Mannheimer *et al.*, 2005). Adherence is a critical determinant of progression to AIDS and long-term survival (Bangsberg *et al.*, 2001; Wood *et al.*, 2003) and an adherence level of less than 95% may lead to the development of viral resistance (Paterson *et al.*, 2000; WHO, 2008c).

The literature shows that medication adherence and mental health are intricately linked. For example, adherence to HAART in higher-income countries is significantly poorer among individuals suffering from depression, cognitive impairment, or alcohol- and substance-use disorders (WHO, 2008c). Women are less likely to start HAART regimens and demonstrate lower adherence to HAART than men (Mocroft *et al.*, 2000; Turner *et al.*, 2003). Among individuals with HIV/AIDS, predictors of adherence include social stability and support, beliefs and knowledge about medications, a high degree of self-efficacy/confidence in their ability to adhere successfully to the regimen, a regimen that fits well into the structure of their daily life, and a strong and trusting patient–provider relationship (New York State Department of Health, 2006). Psychosocial factors that may affect adherence include lack of social support, homelessness, family instability, domestic violence, and fear of stigma (New York State Department of Health, 2006).

The complexity of many of the medication regimens, which often include a high pill burden, varied dosing schedules, and dietary restrictions, is a significant barrier for many individuals with HIV/AIDS (Ferguson *et al.*, 2002). HAART necessitates frequent medical attention for the monitoring of viral load and management of treatment side effects, and it is not uncommon for HAART to produce a number of unpleasant and distressing side effects, including nausea, vomiting, diarrhoea, nervousness, hallucination, depression, and psychosis (WHO, 2008c). Individuals with HIV/AIDs experiencing more severe side effects are likely to have poorer adherence than those with more mild side effects (Catz *et al.*, 2000). Compared to men, women are significantly more likely to experience side effects from HAART, necessitating engagement in complex side-effect-related treatment decision-making (Kremer *et al.*, 2009). Maintaining adherence to a treatment regimen in the face of so many barriers is a significant challenge for many individuals living with HIV/AIDS.

Psychological intervention, in the form of psycho-education and cognitive-behavioral strategies, may be useful in addressing some of the mental health factors that have been shown to impact on adherence, such as depression, or substance and alcohol use. It is worthwhile for healthcare workers to explore some of the barriers that the patient may be experiencing, their concerns about the treatment, and their fears about their ability to adhere to HAART. Checking the patient's knowledge and understanding of HAART and addressing any gaps in their knowledge is mandatory as patients who believe that HAART will be effective are likely to demonstrate better adherence (Gellaitry *et al.*, 2005). Cognitive-behavioral methods are useful if the individual has difficulties with recall or memory or if they feel overwhelmed by the medication regimen. Useful strategies might include personalizing the drug schedules by integrating treatment into the patient's lifestyle or linking medications to daily activities, utilizing memory prompts such as written instructions or illustrations, pill timers, diaries, or phone calls from family members or friends (New York State Department of Health, 2006). Another increasingly used patient-centered method of health behavior change is motivational interviewing. Motivational interviewing, when combined with the building of cognitive skills, has also been found to be effective in increasing treatment adherence among individuals living with HIV/AIDS (Parsons *et al.*, 2007).

Procreation/parenting decisions

Since the advent of HAART, individuals with HIV are now living longer and increasing numbers are electing to become parents (Schuster *et al.*, 2000). Technologies are now available that significantly reduce the likelihood of infant infection, but they are not without risks (Fakoya *et al.*, 2008). Individuals with HIV/AIDS who wish to conceive should receive comprehensive preconception counselling with their partner to ensure that they are aware of their reproduction options, are fully cognisant of the risks involved, and are emotionally prepared for the impact this decision will have on their lives (Fakoya *et al.*, 2008). It is common for HIV-infected individuals to experience fertility problems, and the process of reproductive interventions can be emotionally taxing (Fakoya *et al.*, 2008).

Individuals with HIV/AIDS attempting to conceive must be prepared for unwanted outcomes such as the inability to successfully conceive and the small possibility of transmission of the virus to the child. The couple must also be prepared for the emotional impact of the decision to have a child on their relationship and consider how they would cope if the health status of one or both partners were to change or deteriorate in the future (Fakoya *et al.*, 2008). This is important as the perceived stress of the parenting role has been shown to negatively impact on healthcare behaviors such as medication adherence and attendance of medical appointments among HIV-positive individuals (Goldstein *et al.*, 2005; Mellins *et al.*, 2003). Furthermore, maternal distress among HIV-infected women is negatively associated with a broad range of parenting skills including engaging children in family routines, parent–child communication, and parenting discipline (Murphy *et al.*, 2010). Evidence of psychological distress such as anxiety and depression are not uncommon among HIV-infected parents (Goldstein *et al.*, 2005).

Psychological interventions can assist individuals with HIV/AIDS in the development of parenting skills and coping strategies to assist them in managing the demands of parenting when experiencing ill health. Interventions may also have a role to play in supporting parents living with HIV/AIDS to prioritize their healthcare over other competing demands, assist them in planning for the future care of their child in the event of ill health, and help them to develop strategies for the disclosure of their HIV infection to their child when they are ready to do so.

Summary

Like all aspects of health, optimal sexual health should encompass a state of biological, psychological, and social wellbeing. Being diagnosed with an STI or HIV has the potential to impact on individuals in myriad ways and may significantly impact on or alter their physical health, feelings about themselves, sexual behavior, and interpersonal relationships. It is clear that psychological interventions have an important role to play in assisting individuals to manage the impact of a diagnosis of a chronic sexual health condition such as genital herpes, genital HPV, or HIV/AIDS. Such interventions may be utilized at various stages of the illness course. For example, psychological intervention may be useful in helping individuals to cope with their initial diagnosis and to manage psychiatric dysfunction such as depression and anxiety that may arise as a result of their diagnosis. Psychological strategies may also play a role in assisting individuals to reduce their engagement in risk behaviors such as unprotected sexual intercourse, or drug and alcohol use. The process of disclosing their health condition to others can be made less anxiety-provoking and more likely to occur through the provision of psychological support and the teaching of strategies to enable the disclosure process. In the case of HIV, adherence to complex treatment regimens may be promoted through the use of psychological strategies and support. Parenting considerations among individuals with HIV, including decisions about future parenting and parental skills building, can also be facilitated by psychological intervention. It is essential that the provision of healthcare to individuals living with these conditions is holistic in its approach. Health practitioners should ensure that when providing healthcare to these individuals the physical, psychological, and social impacts of these conditions are given full consideration.

References

Altice, F. L., Mostashari, F., & Friedland, G. H. (2001). Trust and the acceptance of and adherence to antiretroviral therapy. *Journal of Acquired Immune Deficiency Syndromes, 28*, 47–58.

Bangsberg, D. R., Perry, S., Charlebois, E. D., Clark, R. A., Roberston, M., Zolopa, A. R., & Moss, A. (2001). Nonadherence to highly active antiretroviral therapy predicts progression to AIDS. *AIDS, 15*, 1181–1183.

Barnack-Tavlaris, J. L., Reddy, D. M., & Ports, K. (2011). Psychological adjustment among women living with genital herpes. *Journal of Health Psychology, 16*, 12–21.

Bing, E. G., Burnam, M. A., Longshore, D., Fleishman, J. A., Sherbourne, C. D., London, A. S. *et al.* (2001). Psychiatric disorders and drug use among human immunodeficiency virus-infected adults in the United States. *Archives of General Psychiatry, 58,* 721–728.

Brandt, A. M. (1987). *No Magic Bullet: A Social History of Venereal Disease in the United States since 1880.* New York: Oxford University Press.

British Psychological Society. (2002). *Clinical Psychology Services in HIV and Sexual Health: A Guide for Commissioners of Clinical Psychology Services.* www.bps.org.uk/downloadfile.cfm?file_uuid=B38FC081-1143-DFD0-7E20-6987AF78345E&ext=pdf.

Carney, O., Ross, E., Bunker, C., Ikkos, G., & Mindel, A. (1994). A prospective study of the psychological impact on patients with a first episode of genital herpes. *Genitourinary Medicine, 70,* 40–45.

Cassidy, L., Meadows, J., Catalán, J., & Barton, S. (1997). Are reported stress and coping style associated with frequent recurrence of genital herpes? *Genitourinary Medicine, 73,* 263–266.

Catz, S. L., Kelly, J. A., Bogart, L. M., Benotsch, E. G., & McAuliffe, T. L. (2000). Patterns, correlates, and barriers to medication adherence among persons prescribed new treatments for HIV disease. *Health Psychology, 19,* 124–133.

Centers for Disease Control and Prevention. (2009). *Genital HPV Infection.* www.cdc.gov/std/HPV/STDFact-HPV.htm.

Centers for Disease Control and Prevention. (2010). *Genital Herpes.* www.cdc.gov/std/herpes/stdfact-herpes.htm.

Chippindale, S., & French, L. (2001). ABC of AIDS: HIV counselling and the psychosocial management of patients with HIV or AIDS. *British Medical Journal, 322,* 1533–1535.

Cohen, J., & Ankus, J. M. (2009). Counselling and testing for HIV. In A. Menon & A. Kamarulzaman (Eds.), *Is it HIV? A Handbook for Health Care Providers* (pp. 93–99). Darlinghurst: Australasian Society for HIV Medicine.

Cook, J. A., Grey, D., Burke, J., Cohen, M. H., Gurtman, A. C., Richardson, J. L. *et al.* (2004). Depressive symptoms and AIDS-related mortality among a multisite cohort of HIV-positive women. *American Journal of Public Health, 94,* 1133–1140.

Corey, L., Wald, A., Patel, R., Sacks, S. L., Tyring, S. K., Warren, T. *et al.* (2004). Once-daily valacyclovir to reduce the risk of transmission of genital herpes. *New England Journal of Medicine, 350,* 11–20.

Dinh, T. H., Sternberg, M., Dunne, E. F., & Markowitz, L. E. (2008). Genital warts among 18- to 59-year-olds in the United States: National health and nutrition examination survey, 1999–2004. *Sexually Transmitted Diseases, 35,* 357–360.

Evans, D. L., Ten Have, T. R., Douglas, S. D., Gettes, D. R., Morrison, M., Chiappini, M. S. *et al.* (2002). Association of depression with viral load, CD8 T lymphocytes and natural killer cells in women with HIV infection. *American Journal of Psychiatry, 159,* 1752–1759.

Fairfield, K. M., Libman, H., Davis, R. B., & Eisenberg, D. M. (1999). Delays in protease inhibitor use in clinical practice. *Journal of General Internal Medicine, 14,* 395–401.

Fakoya, A., Lamba, H., Mackie, N., Nandwani, R., Brown, A., Bernard, E. J. *et al.* (2008). British HIV Association, BASHH and FSRH guidelines for the management of the sexual and reproductive health of people living with HIV infection 2008. *HIV Medicine, 9,* 681–720.

Ferguson, T. F., Stewart, K. E., Funkhouser, E., Tolson, J., Westfall, A. O., & Saag, M. S. (2002). Patient-perceived barriers to antiretroviral adherence: Associations with race. *AIDS Care, 14,* 607–617.

Gellaitry, G., Cooper, V., Davis, C., Fisher, M., Date, H. L., & Horne, R. (2005). Patients' perceptions of information about HAART: Impact on treatment decisions. *AIDS Care, 17,* 367–376.

Goldstein, R. B., Johnson, M. O., Rotheram-Borus, M. J., Kirshenbaum, S. B., Pinto, R. M., Kittel, L. *et al.* National Institute Mental Health Healthy Living Project Team, (2005). Psychological distress, substance use, and adjustment among parents living with HIV. *Journal of the American Board of Family Practice, 18,* 362–373.

Gordillo, V., del Amo, J., Soriano, V., & Gonzalez-Lahoz, J. (1999). Sociodemographic and psychological variables influencing adherence to antiretroviral therapy. *AIDS, 13,* 1763–1769.

Green, J. (2004). Psychosocial issues in genital herpes management. *Herpes, 11,* 60–62.

Green, J., Ferrier, S., Kocsis, A., Shadrick, J., Ukoumunne, O. C., Murphy, S., & Hetherton, J. (2003). Determinants of disclosure of genital herpes to partners. *Sexually Transmitted Infections, 79,* 42–44.

Grulich, A. E., de Visser, R. O., Smith, A. M., Rissel, C. E., & Richters, J. (2003). Sex in Australia: Sexually transmissible infection and blood-borne virus history in a representative sample of adults. *Australian and New Zealand Journal of Public Health, 27,* 234–241.

Hall, L. A. (2001). Venereal disease and society in Britain, from the Contagious Diseases Act to the National Health Service. In R. Davidson & L. A. Hall (Eds.), *Sex, Sin, and Suffering: Venereal Disease and European Society since 1870* (pp. 120–136). London: Routledge.

Himelhoch, S., & Medoff, D. R. (2005). Efficacy of antidepressant medication among HIV-positive individuals with depression: A systematic review and meta-analysis. *AIDS Patient Care & STDS, 19,* 813–822.

Himelhoch, S., Medoff, D. R., & Oyeniyi, G. (2007). Efficacy of group psychotherapy to reduce depressive symptoms among HIV-infected individuals: A systematic review and meta-analysis. *AIDS Patient Care & STDS, 21,* 732–739.

Holt, M., Bernard, D., & Race, K. (2010). Gay men's perceptions of sexually transmissible infections and their experiences of diagnosis: 'Part of the way of life' to feeling 'dirty and ashamed'. *Sexual Health, 7,* 411–416.

Ickovics, J. R., Hamburger, M. E., Vlahov, D., Schoenbaum, E. E., Schuman, P., Boland, R. J., & Moore, J. (2001). Mortality, CD4 cell count decline, and depressive symptoms among HIV-seropositive women: longitudinal analysis from the HIV Epidemiology Research Study. *Journal of the American Medical Association, 285,* 1466–1474.

Keller, M. L., von Sadovszky, V., Pankratz, B., Hermsen, J., Sowell, R. L., & Demi, A. S. (2000). Self-disclosure of HPV infection to sexual partners. *Western Journal of Nursing Research, 22,* 285–302.

Komiti, A., Judd, F., Grech, P., Mijch, A., Hoy, J., Williams, B. *et al.* (2003). Depression in people living with HIV/AIDS attending primary care and outpatient clinics. *Australian and New Zealand Journal of Psychiatry, 37,* 70–77.

Kremer, H., Sonnenberg-Schwan, U., Arendt, G., Brockmeyer, N. H., Potthoff, A., Ulmer, A. *et al.* German Competence Network HIV/AIDS. (2009). HIV or HIV-therapy? Causal attributions of symptoms and their impact on treatment decisions among women and men with HIV. *European Journal of Medical Research, 14,* 139–146.

Lee, J. D., & Craft, E. A. (2002). Protecting one's self from a stigmatized disease . . . once one has it. *Deviant Behavior, 23,* 267–299.

Lehr, S. T., & Lee, M. E. (1990). The psychosocial and sexual trauma of a genital HPV infection. *Nurse Practitioner Forum, 1,* 25–30.

Leserman, J., Petitto, J. M., Gu, H., Gaynes, B., Barroso, J., Golden, R. *et al.* (2002). Progression to AIDS, a clinical AIDS condition and mortality: Psychosocial and physiological predictors. *Psychological Medicine, 32,* 1059–1073.

Looker, K. J., Garnett, G. P., & Schmid, G. P. (2008). An estimate of the global prevalence and incidence of herpes simplex virus type 2 infection. *Bulletin of the World Health Organization, 86,* 805–812.

Mannheimer, S. B., Matts, J., Telzak, E., Chesney, M., Child, C., Wu, A. W., & Friedland, G. (2005). Quality of life in HIV-infected individuals receiving antiretroviral therapy is related to adherence. *AIDS Care, 17,* 10–22.

Mark, H., Gilbert, L., & Nanda, J. (2009). Psychosocial well-being and quality of life among women newly diagnosed with genital herpes. *Journal of Obstetric, Gynecologic & Neonatal Nursing, 38,* 320–326.

Mellins, C. A., Kang, E., Leu, C. S., Havens, J. F., & Chesney, M. A. (2003). Longitudinal study of mental health and psychosocial predictors of medical treatment adherence in mothers living with HIV disease. *AIDS Patient Care & STDs, 17,* 407–416.

Melville, J., Sniffen, S., Crosby, R., Salazar, L., Whittington, W., Dithmer-Schreck, D. *et al.* (2003). Psychosocial impact of serological diagnosis of herpes simplex virus type 2: A qualitative assessment. *Sexually Transmitted Infections, 79,* 280–285.

Mezzich, J. E., & Hernandez-Serrano, R. (2006). Conceptual bases of sexual health. In J. E. Mezzich & Hernandez-Serrano (Eds.), *Psychiatry and sexual health: An integrative approach* (pp. 14–85). New York: Jason Aronson.

Microbiology and Epidemiology of STIs and HIV Department. (2010). *Number of Selected STI Diagnoses made at Genitourinary Medicine Clinics in the UK and England: 2000–2009.* www.hpa.org.uk/web/HPAwebFile/HPAweb_C/1215589013442.

Mocroft, A., Gill, M. J., Davidson, W., & Philips, A. N. (2000). Are there gender differences in starting protease inhibitors, HAART, and disease progression despite equal access to care? *Journal of Acquired Immune Deficiency Syndromes, 24,* 475–482.

Murphy, D. A., Marelich, W. D., Armistead, L., Herbeck, D. M., & Payne, D. L. (2010). Anxiety/stress among mothers living with HIV: Effects on parenting skills and child outcomes. *AIDS Care: Psychological and Socio-medical Aspects of AIDS/HIV, 22,* 1449–1458.

Nack, A. (2000). Damaged goods: Women managing the stigma of STDs. *Deviant Behavior, 21,* 95–121.

Nack, A. (2008). *Damaged Goods: Women Living with Incurable Sexually Transmitted Diseases.* Philadelphia: Temple University Press.

New York State Department of Health. (2006). *Adherence to Antiretroviral Therapy among HIV-Infected Patients with Mental Health Disorders.* www.hivguidelines.org/clinical-guidelines/hiv-and-mental-health/adherence-to-antiretroviral-therapy-among-hiv-infected-patients-with-mental-health-disorders/.

New York State Department of Health. (2010a). *Anxiety Disorders in Patients with HIV/AIDS HIV Clinical Resource.* www.hivguidelines.org/clinical-guidelines/hiv-and-mental-health/anxiety-disorders-in-patients-with-hivaids/.

New York State Department of Health. (2010b). *Depression and Mania in Patients with HIV/AIDS: Clinical Guidelines.* www.hivguidelines.org/clinical-guidelines/hiv-and-mental-health/depression-and-mania-in-patients-with-hivaids/.

Newton, D. C., & McCabe, M. P. (2005). A theoretical discussion of the impact of stigma on psychological adjustment to having a sexually transmissible infection. *Sexual Health, 2,* 63–69.

Newton, D. C., & McCabe, M. P. (2008a). Effects of sexually transmitted infection status, relationship status, and disclosure status on sexual self-concept. *Journal of Sex Research, 45,* 187–192.

Newton, D. C., & McCabe, M. P. (2008b). Sexually transmitted infections: Impact on individuals and their relationships. *Journal of Health Psychology, 13,* 864–869.

Orlando, M., Burnam, M. A., Beckman, R., Morton, S. C., London, A. S., Bing, E. G., & Fleishman, J. A. (2002). Re-estimating the prevalence of psychiatric disorders in a nationally representative sample of persons receiving care for HIV: Results from the HIV Cost and Services Utilization Study. *International Journal of Methods in Psychiatric Research, 11,* 75–82.

Parsons, J. T., Golub, S. A., Rosof, E., & Holder, C. (2007). Motivational interviewing and cognitive-behavioral intervention to improve HIV medication adherence among hazardous drinkers: a randomized controlled trial. *Journal of Acquired Immune Deficiency Syndromes, 46,* 443–450.

Paterson, D. L., Swindells, S., Mohr, J., Brester, M., Vergis, E. N., Squier, C. *et al.* (2000). Adherence to protease inhibitor therapy and outcomes in patients with HIV infection. *Annals of Internal Medicine, 133,* 21–30.

Patrick, D. M., Rosenthal, S. L., Stanberry, L. R., Hurst, C., & Ebel, C. (2004). Patient satisfaction with care for genital herpes: Insights from a global survey. *Sexually Transmitted Infections, 80,* 192–197.

Pence, B. W. (2009). The impact of mental health and traumatic life experiences on antiretroviral treatment outcomes for people living with HIV/AIDS. *Journal of Antimicrobial Chemotherapy, 63,* 636–640.

Penzak, S. R., Reddy, Y. S., & Grimsley, S. R. (2002). Depression in patients with HIV infection. *American Journal of Health-System Pharmacy, 57,* 376–386.

Remien, R. H., & Rabkin, J. G. (2002). Managing chronic disease: individual counseling with medically ill patients. In M. A. Chesney & M. H. Antoni (Eds.), *Innovative Approaches to Health Psychology: Prevention and Treatment Lessons from AIDS* (pp. 117–119). Washington DC: American Psychological Association.

Remien, R. H., Exner, T., Kertzner, R. M., Ehrhardt, A. A., Rotheram-Borus, M. J., Johnson, M. O. *et al.* NIMH Healthy Living Project Trial Group. (2006). Depressive symptomatology among HIV-positive women in the era of HAART: A stress and coping model. *American Journal of Community Psychology, 38,* 275–285.

Roth, A., & Fonagy, P. (1996). *What Works for Whom: A Critical Review of Psychotherapy Outcome Research.* London: Guilford Press.

Safren, S. A., O'Cleirigh, C., Tan, J. Y., Raminani, S. R., Reilly, L. C., Otto, M. W., & Mayer, K. H. (2009). A randomized controlled trial of cognitive behavioral therapy for adherence and depression (CBT-AD) in HIV-infected individuals. *Health Psychology, 28,* 1–10.

Schuster, M. A., Kanouse, D. E., Morton, S. C., Bozzette, S. A., Miu, A., Scott, G. B., & Shapiro, M. F. (2000). HIV-infected parents and their children in the United States. *American Journal of Public Health, 90,* 1074–1081.

Sutcliffe, L. J., Sadler, K. E., Low, N., & Cassell, J. A. (2011). Comparing expectations and experiences of care for sexually transmitted infections in general practice: A qualitative study. *Sexually Transmitted Infections, 87,* 131–135.

Swanson, J. M., & Chenitz, W. C. (1993). Regaining a valued self: The process of adaptation to living with genital herpes. *Qualitative Health Research, 3,* 270–297.

Temple-Smith, M., Hopkins, C., Fairley, C., Tomnay, J., Pavlin, N., Parker, R. *et al.* (2010). The right thing to do: Patients' views and experiences of telling partners about chlamydia. *Family Practice, 27,* 418–423.

Tostes, M. A., Chalub, M., & Botega, N. J. (2004). The quality of life of HIV-infected women is associated with psychiatric morbidity. *AIDS Care, 16,* 177–186.

Tsao, J. C., Dobalian, A., & Naliboff, B. D. (2004). Panic disorder and pain in a national sample of persons living with HIV. *Pain, 109,* 172–180.

Tucker, J. S., Burnam, M. A., Sherbourne, C. D., Kung, F. Y., & Gifford, A. L. (2003). Substance use and mental health correlates of nonadherence to antiretroviral medications in a sample of patients with human immunodeficiency virus infection. *American Journal of Medicine, 114,* 573–580.

Turner, B. J., Laine, C., Cosler, L., & Hauck, W. (2003). Relationship of gender, depression, and health care delivery with antiretroviral adherence in HIV-infected drug users. *Journal of General Internal Medicine, 18,* 248–257.

Vitiello, B., Burnam, M. A., Bing, E. G., Beckman, R., & Shapiro, M. F. (2003). Use of psychotropic medications among HIV-infected patients in the United States. *American Journal of Psychiatry, 160,* 547–554.

Warren, T., & Ebel, C. (2005). Counseling the patient who has genital herpes or genital human papillomavirus infection. *Infectious Disease Clinics of North America, 19,* 459–476.

WHO. (2008a). *Epidemiological Fact Sheet on HIV and AIDS: Core Data on Epidemiology and Response: Australia.* http://apps.who.int/globalatlas/predefinedReports/EFS2008/full/EFS2008_AU.pdf.

WHO. (2008b). *HIV and AIDS Estimates and Data, 2007 and 2001: 2008 Report on the Global AIDS Epidemic.* http://data.unaids.org/pub/GlobalReport/2008/jc1510_2008_global_report_pp211_234_en.pdf.

WHO. (2008c). *HIV/AIDS and Mental Health.* http://apps.who.int/gb/ebwha/pdf_files/EB124/B124_6-en.pdf.

WHO. (2009). *Global Summary of the AIDS Epidemic 2009.* www.who.int/hiv/data/2009_global_summary .png.

WHO. (2010a). *Health Topics: HIV/AIDS.* www.who.int/topics/hiv_aids/en/.

WHO. (2010b). *HIV/AIDs: Most at-Risk Populations.* www.who.int/hiv/topics/populations/en/index.html.

WHO. (2010c). *Sexual Health.* www.who.int/topics/sexual_health/en/.

Wood, E., Hogg, R. S., Yip, B., Harrigan, P. R., O'Shaughnessy, M. V., & Montaner, J. S. (2003). Is there a baseline CD4 cell count that precludes a survival response to modern antiretroviral therapy? *AIDS, 17,* 711–720.

Zacharioudakis, M. A. (2001). Doing psychotherapy with patients with genital herpes: Issues and interventions. *Scandinavian Journal of Behaviour Therapy, 30,* 108–133.

16

Identification and Treatment of Depression in the Perinatal Period

Jeannette Milgrom and Alan W. Gemmill

Antenatal depression (AND) and postnatal depression (PND) are prevalent and often experienced as devastating by those affected, at a time when personal, familial, and societal expectations are of joy and fulfilment. Depression before and after childbirth constitutes a major public health problem due to the adverse consequences not only for women but their infants and their families (Milgrom *et al.*, 2004; Murray & Cooper, 1996).

Antenatal depression is linked to poor maternal self-care and inadequate nutrition (Zuckerman *et al.*, 1989) as well as premature labor and adverse obstetric outcomes (Chung *et al.*, 2001; Dayan *et al.*, 2006; Kurki *et al.*, 2000), all of which can potentially affect infant health and wellbeing (Zuckerman *et al.*, 1989). Furthermore, AND can have direct negative consequences for the fetus. A clear association between maternal emotional distress in pregnancy and suboptimal infant development has been established in both animal and human studies (Talge *et al.*, 2007; Van den Bergh *et al.*, 2005). In humans, there is a direct association between maternal depression and anxiety in pregnancy and effects on the fetus *in utero*, resulting in sizeable and lasting problems in child cognitive, behavioral, and emotional development (Talge *et al.*, 2007).

Postnatally, maternal depression also has detrimental effects on infant development as confirmed in several longitudinal studies (e.g., Cooper & Murray, 1997; Milgrom *et al.*, 1999, 2004; Murray & Cooper, 1997). Many postnatally depressed mothers experience difficulties in interacting with their infants in a positive way (e.g., Diego *et al.*, 2006) and make less eye contact, with less well-timed responsiveness in mother–infant interactions. Clinically depressed mothers have been characterized as emotionally flat, displaying less warmth, and being insensitive, disengaged, and uninvolved (Field, 1992; Murray & Cooper, 1997; Murray *et al.*, 2003; Reck *et al.*, 2004; Righetti-Veltema *et al.*, 2002).

An emotionally attuned and responsive mother has been identified by developmental theorists as critical to a "good-enough" mother–infant interaction, necessary for optimal development (Brazelton *et al.*, 1974; Stern, 1985; Tronick & Weinberg, 1997; Winnicott, 1974). Emotional unavailability following depression can result in escalating, self-perpetuating cycles of dysfunctional

Applied Topics in Health Psychology, First Edition. Edited by M. L. Caltabiano and L. Ricciardelli.

behavior by both mother and child, which in turn impacts on child development (Milgrom *et al.*, 2004, 2006).

A number of research studies, including meta-analyses of published data, have found significant effects of PND (effect size ranging from $d = 0.36$ to 0.45) on both emotional development and cognitive outcomes for infants (e.g., Beck, 1998; Hay *et al.*, 2001; Lyons-Ruth *et al.*, 1986). These problems may persist into early childhood (Sharp *et al.*, 1995), and include behavioral difficulties at least up to the age of 5 (Murray *et al.*, 1999). Longer-term follow-up data are still emerging (Murray *et al.*, 2010).

Women's partners are not immune to the impact of mood disorders in the perinatal period. Maternal depression is a risk factor for depression in a male partner, and for men the rates of psychological distress in general (not just depression) do appear to rise during their partner's pregnancy (around 18%; Boyce *et al.*, 2007).

In summary, untreated depression leaves women, their infants, and their families vulnerable to a range of negative and lasting consequences, making effective identification vitally important.

Definitions

AND and PND can be defined as a major or minor depressive episode with an onset either during pregnancy and in the first year postpartum respectively. These are the definitions most commonly applied by researchers and clinicians. Depression in this perinatal period is characterized by the same symptoms as depression at other life stages and includes the affective, behavioral, physiological, and cognitive changes listed below.

Recognition of Symptoms

According to the *Diagnostic and Statistical Manual of Mental Disorders* (4th edn, text revision; DSM-IV-TR; American Psychiatric Association, 2000) criteria, for a diagnosis of major depression at least five of the symptoms listed below must be present (at least one of which must be symptom a or symptom b), occurring on most days in the previous 2 weeks:

a   depressed mood,
b   diminished interest in activities,
c   significant weight or appetite change,
d   sleeping problems, e.g., insomnia or hypersomnia,
e   fatigue,
f   feelings of worthlessness/guilt,
g   inability to think clearly or concentrate,
h   recurrent thoughts of death and/or suicide,
i   psychomotor agitation and/or retardation,

For a DSM-IV-TR diagnosis of minor depression at least two symptoms (but fewer than five) are needed, again one of which must be symptom a or symptom b. The International Classification of Diseases (ICD-10) classification (World Health Organization, 1993) provides a comparable list of diagnostic criteria.

While the symptoms of depression and diagnostic criteria for a major or minor depressive episode in the perinatal period are the same as at any other time, identification can be more problematic since some changes that accompany childbearing overlap with symptoms of depression (e.g., changes in eating patterns, fatigue). Symptoms of PND can also take on a particular significance due to the presence of an infant, so that inability to sleep for instance may be further exacerbated by infant demands.

The DSM-IV-TR lists a "specifier" for postpartum depression as depression with an onset within 4 weeks of childbirth. Unfortunately this definition is problematic given that, during this early postpartum period, around 85% of women suffer the transitory "postnatal blues" or "baby blues" (Pearlstein, 2008). Furthermore, the "peak" prevalence of PND is probably around 3 months postpartum or later (Gavin *et al.*, 2005). Thus, the DSM-IV-TR specifier is at odds with our understanding of PND based on existing research and with the meaning as widely applied by working clinicians. There is no equivalent DSM specifier for AND, but it is usually thought of as a diagnosis of depression with an onset during pregnancy. The ICD-10 (World Health Organization, 1993) currently has a specifier which is also of limited utility in classifying perinatal mood disorders.

Prevalence

A wide range of prevalence rates are reported for depression in the perinatal period, usually estimated on the basis of the proportion of women scoring above a certain threshold on a self-report instrument. However, determining the number of cases that fulfil diagnostic criteria through a diagnostic interview is clearly the best route to determining prevalence. On this basis, the point prevalence of PND (that is, the number of cases at any single time point as a proportion of the perinatal population) has been cited to be around 13% (O'Hara & Swain, 1996), with point estimates for major and minor depression ranging from approximately 5 to 20% depending on which time point is considered (Gavin *et al.*, 2005). Probably the most robust estimate, based on diagnostic criteria, is that at 3 months postpartum the point prevalence of major and minor depression combined is 12.9%. Similarly, in any of the three trimesters of pregnancy around 9% of women are suffering major or minor depression (Gavin *et al.*, 2005). Thus, the period prevalence of AND/PND (that is, the total proportion of women experiencing depression across an extended interval of time) is almost certainly higher than 12.9%. However, as there are still few studies that have measured period prevalence using a diagnostic standard (even the confidence limits of the best meta-estimates are relatively wide) it is not possible to state with certainty whether depression is more common in perinatal women than in the general adult female population (Gavin *et al.*, 2005).

The Need for Active Identification

Women from every walk of life can have difficulty in seeking or accepting help for emotional distress in the perinatal period (Dennis & Chung-Lee, 2006). Reasons include perceived stigma, lack of knowledge about depression, beliefs that they should be coping, feelings of failure, being seen as a bad mother, fear of contact with mental health services, and fear of disclosing emotional difficulties. As a consequence, most women with PND do not actively seek treatment (MacLellan *et al.*, 1996). Frequently, perinatal women are unaware that effective help for depression is available. Coupled with symptoms of depression, such as lack of energy, this can result in women feeling overwhelmed, demotivated, and unable to make decisions about accessing help (Bilszta *et al.*, 2010). Thus there is considerable interest in the potential of using screening tools to aid identification. The context of screening, however, needs to be based on positive relationships with health professionals as screening is only the first step in a process of identification. A positive relationship with health professionals is known to facilitate treatment uptake (Dennis & Chung-Lee, 2006). Among the attributes perinatal women perceive as "ideal" in health professionals are empathy, kindness, knowledge, availability, active assistance, and continuity of care (Bilstza *et al.*, 2010).

Is Screening Worthwhile?

If any health condition is serious, prevalent and treatable, screening can be an effective option in principle (Shakespeare, 2002). A further prerequisite is a tolerable, affordable screening procedure, the accuracy of which is well established.

The Edinburgh Postnatal Depression Scale (EPDS) meets key criteria for an effective screening tool for perinatal depression.

- The EPDS is a rapid, inexpensive screening tool for perinatal women that is widely available, with well-established accuracy and psychometric properties. It is a simple 10-item self-report scale that is straightforward to complete (Cox *et al.*, 1987).
- Screening with the EPDS is acceptable to a majority of perinatal women, both depressed and nondepressed (Gemmill *et al.*, 2006; Leigh & Milgrom, 2007) and the vast majority of women view screening as desirable (Gemmill *et al.*, 2006).
- In practical terms, about six out of 10 women who score positive (meaning a score of 13 points or higher) on the EPDS will meet diagnostic criteria for major depression.

Reasons to undertake screening in the case of PND and AND include:

- perinatal depression is serious and has lasting consequences,
- perinatal depression is common,
- depression can be successfully treated,
- most depressed women will not be detected by other contacts with the health system and will not actively seek help.

Internationally, governmental health agencies have developed different sets of criteria for recommending the implementation of widespread perinatal depression programs (e.g., British Columbia Reproductive Care Program, 2003; National Institute for Health and Clinical Excellence, 2007; Scottish Intercollegiate Guidelines Network, 2002). In Australia, the federally funded National Perinatal Depression Initiative aims to screen and assess every perinatal woman at least once in pregnancy and at least once in the postpartum (Beyondblue, 2011). However, while the spread of routine screening worldwide reflects the fact that a number of key prerequisite criteria for successful screening are met, implementation of universal screening is still short of meeting policy guidelines in some countries (e.g., the UK National Health Service; Shakespeare, 2002). This is due primarily to insufficient formal research evidence on the reduction of morbidity achieved by screening and cost-effectiveness.

How should screening be deployed?

There is clearly a potential for a numerical increase in identification generated by screening. The higher the positive predictive value (PPV) of a screening tool, the more "real" cases of depression will be included in the screen-positive group. The PPV can be understood as simply the percentage of individuals with a positive result who are truly depressed. Diagnostic-stage procedures can then be better targeted, resulting in an increased identification of cases. One recent analysis demonstrates that the EPDS always has numerical utility in circumscribing a high-prevalence subpopulation (Milgrom *et al.*, 2011a) and an average PPV of 62%. In practical terms this means that for every 100 women with a positive screening result, 62 will meet diagnostic criteria for major depression. From a wider health-system point of view, a policy of diagnostic testing following all positive screening results would seem wise in economic terms, as suggested by one recent analysis (Paulden *et al.*, 2009).

How acceptable is screening?

Most, but not all, perinatal women report that screening for emotional health difficulties is acceptable. An Australian study of 403 pregnant women found 100% acceptability (Leigh & Milgrom, 2007). No women reported feeling upset, labeled, stigmatized, or distressed by screening. Similarly, in a sample of 479 postnatal women (half depressed and half nondepressed; Gemmill *et al.*, 2006) the great majority of both depressed and nondepressed women were comfortable being screened. Although acceptability appears high, it cannot be assumed to be the case for all women and may depend on the way screening is carried out (e.g., Shakespeare *et al.*, 2003).

Emotional Health Assessment

In Australia, the federally funded National Perinatal Depression Initiative encourages universal screening for AND and PND in the context of full psychosocial assessment for all perinatal women, alongside a recommendation for training for all health professionals involved (Department of Health and Ageing, 2009).

Nevertheless it is vital to be aware that screening is not a diagnostic test, only a first step. Screening tools do not diagnose, they can only facilitate an increase in cases diagnosed. No one should be considered "diagnosed" with a depressive condition and have an active treatment commenced on the basis of a screening result. Therefore, following a positive screening result, a full diagnostic assessment based on standard clinical criteria should be offered by a trained professional.

Screening and diagnosis

It is both inaccurate and potentially harmful for women to be told they are depressed on the basis of a positive screening result. If entered into a medical record, such a distorted interpretation may even prove prejudicial to future healthcare. A diagnostic interview must follow a positive screening result, and only at that point can a diagnosis be made. In talking to women, terms such as "at risk" are misleading and should not be used (Krantz *et al.*, 2008; Matthey, 2009). For example, at risk could be interpreted as meaning that a woman is likely to develop depression at some future time: no existing instrument (including the EPDS) can establish this.

Likewise, a negative screen indicates a lower-than-average chance of a depression diagnosis, but should never be communicated as "you are not depressed." Rather, a woman can be informed that her high score on the EPDS indicates that further assessment is recommended to better understand whether she has PND. The criteria for diagnosing a major or minor depressive episode were described above.

Even if no diagnosis of depression is ultimately reached, following up a positive screen may be worthwhile. For example, in a study of 4168 women (Milgrom *et al.*, 2005a) among "false-positive" women (those scoring positive on the screening instrument, but found to be free of depression at diagnostic interview), other common mental disorders were highly prevalent. Eighty-five per cent of women scoring over the EPDS threshold had a DSM-IV-TR diagnosis of a common mental disorder of some kind (bipolar, dysthymic, or anxiety disorder, etc.).

Psychosocial assessment

In addition to screening for depression, the current best-practice recommendation is that all perinatal women should be assessed to identify psychosocial factors associated with increased vulnerability to mental health issues. In doing this it is important to consider a range of risk factors that are associated with depression in perinatal women (Beck, 1996, 2001; O'Hara & Swain, 1996; Robertson *et al.*, 2004; Rubertsson *et al.*, 2005). The major established risk factors for PND which are consistently found to have large effects in meta-analyses are:

- a past history of depression and/or anxiety,
- AND and/or anxiety,
- lack of support from partner or marital problems,
- a family history of depression or other mental health difficulties,
- a lack of practical, financial, social, and/or emotional support, and
- life stresses and adverse life events (for example, moving house, stopping or restarting work, major illness, bereavement). Concurrent stresses in women's lives may include isolation, financial difficulties, relationship breakdown, or an unexpectedly difficult birth or pregnancy.

Other factors that have a documented association with PND and/or anxiety are:

- severe "baby blues" (the drop in mood that around 85% of women feel a short time after childbirth),
- complications in labor/delivery,
- problems with the baby's health,
- breastfeeding difficulties,
- difficulties in close/family relationships,
- single parenthood,
- an unsettled baby,
- unrealistic expectations about motherhood,
- low self-esteem,
- being a victim of past abuse,
- personality factors (e.g., being a "perfectionist"),
- previous reproductive loss, and
- young maternal age.

Screening tools often pave the way for further discussions by making it routine to ask questions about feelings (Austin *et al.*, 2008; Milgrom *et al.*, 2008; Webster *et al.*, 2003). A full psychosocial assessment then allows a holistic, integrated approach to understanding each woman's circumstances by exploring any other stressors, be they physical, emotional, or social/partner-related. A full assessment requires sufficient time to develop both a rapport and an atmosphere in which the mother feels accepted, understood, and valued so that she can explore and disclose any concerns in a context and place where privacy is ensured.

Anxiety

Anxiety is frequently comorbid with depression and is also prevalent in nondepressed perinatal women. Anxiety is a debilitating mental health condition which, just like depression, requires assertive management. Anxiety disorders involve excessive worry, on most days, that is difficult to control. The prevalence of generalized anxiety disorder has been estimated at 8.5% in pregnancy and up to 8.2% in the postpartum (Ross & McLean, 2006). Estimates vary depending on which anxiety disorders are included. Diagnostic criteria for generalized anxiety disorder (the most common anxiety disorder) include anxiety/worry that is hard to control will be present on most days, accompanied by at least three of the following additional symptoms: restlessness or feeling keyed up or on edge, becoming fatigued easily, difficulty concentrating, irritability, muscle tension, and disturbed sleep (American Psychiatric Association, 2000).

Other anxiety disorders that may affect perinatal women include panic disorder, obsessive compulsive disorder, and posttraumatic stress disorder. Even when a woman does not meet diagnostic criteria for an anxiety disorder she may still suffer severe levels of anxiety affecting normal functioning. Three of the questions (items 3, 4, and 5) in the EPDS tap into symptoms of anxiety, but there is no currently recommended tool to screen for anxiety in perinatal women. However, if scores on these items are high, discussion around the issue of anxiety may be helpful.

Treatment: What Works?

For women diagnosed with a major or minor depressive disorder, often with comorbid anxiety, structured psychological therapies have a good evidence base for efficacy.

Group-based cognitive behavior therapy

In previous studies, we evaluated a structured 12 week group cognitive behavior therapy (CBT) program designed specifically for women suffering PND. The manualized program, called Getting Ahead of Postnatal Depression (Milgrom *et al.*, 1999) was successful at lowering depressed mood (Milgrom & Meager, 1996; Milgrom *et al.*, 2005b) and was superior both to a group counselling intervention and to routine care. This program was developed by adapting Lewinsohn's Coping With Depression course (Lewinsohn *et al.*, 1984, 1992) and modifying this effective cognitive-behavioral program to meet the unique needs of new mothers, with the addition of partner sessions. The order of sessions is also rearranged so that behavioral interventions precede cognitive ones. For example, relaxation is deferred in favor of earlier introduction of pleasant activities and time management, as for most mothers organizing themselves and their babies to attend sessions is challenging and can be overwhelming for some. Further, content was adapted to be less demanding in terms of time and information processing (e.g., by providing techniques of "relaxation-on-the-run" etc.). New components were added including a module on getting support and on family of origin issues. The program was evaluated in a randomized controlled trial (RCT) comparing women assigned to a number of treatments including the group CBT treatment (*n* = 46) and routine primary care (*n*=33). Significant amelioration of depressive symptoms in the CBT treatment group was achieved compared to the control (Milgrom *et al.*, 2005b). This group-based program has also proven readily adaptable for different groups of perinatal women. For example, as part of the Australian National Postnatal Depression Program, which screened over 40 000 pregnant women (Beyondblue, 2005), an antenatal-to-postnatal adaptation was developed which aimed to prevent early parenting difficulties and coping difficulties. Milgrom and colleagues then conducted a full RCT of this new Toward Parenthood program which again proved effective (Milgrom *et al.*, 2011b). The essential program content has also been adapted for the indicated treatment of AND (Beating The Blues Before Birth).

Using treatment of maternal depression as a starting point, this line of research has also begun to successfully address the impairment of mother–infant interactions through the addition of a targeted mother–baby module, Happiness, Understanding, Giving, and Sharing (HUGS; Milgrom *et al.*, 1999, 2006).

Psychological treatment of PND (not limited to CBT) also has support from other existing research (Dennis & Hodnett, 2007). From the available evidence worldwide, CBT-based treatments and interpersonal psychotherapy appear to achieve the best outcomes among the psychological therapies that have been evaluated, although fewer studies have evaluated the interpersonal psychotherapy approach in depressed perinatal women (e.g., Mulcahy *et al.*, 2009; O'Hara *et al.*, 2000).

In the UK Cooper *et al.* (2003) also reported short-term improvement with three psychological treatments (CBT, non-directive counselling, and psychodynamic therapy). In this cohort of moderately depressed perinatal women, psychodynamic therapy appeared to yield the best reduction in depressive symptomatology at 4.5 months postpartum.

Combination therapy

There is good evidence that, for depression in general, antidepressants and psychological treatments are both effective (Cuijpers *et al.*, 2008b). Although there is some support for combination therapy for depression in general (Cuijpers *et al.*, 2008a; de Matt *et al.*, 2007) this appears to depend on severity and chronicity and on the type of antidepressant used. Where the psychological component of combination therapy is CBT, the addition of an antidepressant appears to make the smallest difference to outcome. Currently there is little published evidence to support combination therapy in the particular case of PND. Existing work reports no benefit of combining antidepressants with psychological therapy (Appleby *et al.*, 1997; Misri *et al.*, 2004). Appelby *et al.* reported the results of a controlled study of fluoxetine and cognitive behavior counselling in the treatment of PND. Either fluoxetine or one or six sessions of cognitive behavior-focused counselling were found to be effective treatments. Misri *et al.* reported paroxetene alone and in combination with CBT as similarly effective. Neither study found any additive benefit of combination therapy in reducing depressive symptoms on average (Appleby *et al.*, 1997; Misri *et al.*, 2004). Furthermore, many women are reluctant to take medication due to potential effects on the fetus or on breastfeeding infants.

Nevertheless, on a case-by-case basis, medication may well be an appropriate treatment option to include in a management plan, and more details are provided in the section below.

Antidepressants

In practice, when recommending that antidepressant medication is likely to be helpful for an individual woman, clinicians must balance factors such as pregnancy, lactation, overall physical health, contraindication with any concurrent medication, the severity of depression (and the urgency of alleviating symptoms), the ability and willingness to engage in "talk therapy," and any prior response or nonresponse to a particular treatment (pharmacological or nonpharmacological) in previous depressive episodes.

If antidepressants are considered for treating depression in the perinatal period a collaborative decision is important between doctor and patient, including a consideration of the known effects of medication on the fetus. Medications used to treat depression will enter the fetal circulatory system and will be passed to breast milk in low concentrations. In both pregnancy and the postpartum, balancing the potential risks to the fetus/infant posed by exposure to medication against the risks that mental illness pose for the mother, the fetus, and the future development of the infant, is at the centre of the decision. Where a pregnant woman is already medicated, the risks of cessation (and possible relapse) must be weighed carefully. The selective serotonin reuptake inhibitors (SSRIs) are the class of antidepressants about which the most information is available. Current evidence of risk posed to infants is limited. However, there are now several studies reporting no increased risk of overall birth defects or malformations above the general population risk (which is 2–3%) with early pregnancy exposure to the SSRIs (e.g., Bellantuono *et al.*, 2007). Nevertheless there are reports of "neonatal withdrawal syndromes" in babies exposed to SSRI and tricyclic antidepressants in late pregnancy.

The information on possible long-term neurodevelopmental effects of SSRIs and benzodiazepines on breastfeeding is also limited. The SSRIs are currently not contraindicated for women who are breastfeeding on the basis of current evidence (Beyondblue, 2011). When any medication is prescribed it should be prescribed at the lowest effective dose and for the shortest duration. The medication with the shortest half-life (among the effective alternatives) should be prescribed and the first trimester of pregnancy should be avoided if possible. Medication should be regularly reviewed and dispensed as single repeats. Similarly, for the treatment of severe anxiety, if benzodiazepines are necessary then current evidence suggests that intermittent use is preferable and long-acting forms are best avoided.

Treatment Preferences

In terms of improving adherence to a treatment plan, patient preference is known to be important in pharmacological and nonpharmacological treatment of both depression and mental health difficulties in general (Kwan *et al.*, 2010; Swift & Callahan, 2009). Several studies have found that antidepressants are unpopular among pregnant and breastfeeding women (e.g., Boath *et al.*, 2004) and that, in general, "talking" options are women's treatments of preference (Dennis & Chung-Lee, 2006). In weighing the pros and cons of taking medication, perinatal women have reported that finding enough information to allow an informed choice is difficult (Bilstza *et al.*, 2010; Dennis & Chung-Lee, 2006). Fear of "addiction" and a perceived stigma of "being medicated" are also common. Having the "permission" to talk openly and in detail about difficult emotions, and being taken seriously by a nonjudgmental listener, have emerged as centrally important (Dennis & Chung-Lee, 2006). Finally, it needs to be recognized that a fraction of perinatal women do actively prefer medication as their first choice for treatment (Turner *et al.*, 2008). For some women, natural and complimentary therapies (e.g., herbal supplements, yoga, naturopathy) are attractive (Beyondblue, 2005) but there is a limited evidence base for their effectiveness.

Social Support

It is not surprising that most depressed women desire emotional support from their partners and families and that practical, hands-on assistance with day-to-day tasks is seen as equally important (Bilstza *et al.*, 2010; Dennis & Chung-Lee, 2006). Social support can involve several aspects (Honikman, 2008) including practical support, emotional support, information provision (someone to answer questions, offer advice, etc.), and peer support (e.g., sharing of common experiences).

Positive interpersonal interactions, social participation, social services, social support, and community networks are recognized by the World Health Organization (2004) as protective factors for good mental health. Lack of support (and in particular lack of support from a partner) is frequently found to be associated with an elevated risk of PND (e.g., Milgrom *et al.*, 2008).

Management plans therefore need to be supplemented with a focus on mobilizing social support. Depressed women often find it difficult to communicate to those around them their need for support and in many cases reduce their social contact as their depression deepens. Accepting help when it is offered can also be problematic as for some women it reinforces feelings of not coping.

Involving partners in sessions to inform them of the diagnosis and collaborative problem solving about what might be helpful can start to mobilize available family and community support. Both practical support with everyday tasks and obligations, and emotional support (e.g., sympathy, encouragement, affection) are therefore an essential part of effective care.

Further, women's partners may themselves require increased emotional and practical supports at this time. However, this can be problematic as men's engagement in a couple's counselling (Englar-Carlson & Shepard, 2005) and in mental health service uptake in the perinatal period (Matthey *et al.*, 2009) is generally poor.

Parent–Infant Intervention

There is increasing recognition of the importance of early interventions to improve infant outcomes following PND, as treating maternal depression does not appear to be sufficient (Forman *et al.*, 2007; Milgrom *et al.*, 2006). However, the evidence base is still limited for the efficacy of interventions that specifically target the mother–infant interaction in the context of maternal PND. Although some published intervention studies are encouraging, many are limited methodologically and are based on small samples (Clark *et al.*, 2003; Murray *et al.*, 2003; Gelfand *et al.*, 1996; Lyons-Ruth *et al.*, 1986; Onozawa *et al.*, 2001). Further, many are intensive or long-term interventions and so not easily delivered in primary care.

We developed the HUGS program (Milgrom *et al.*, 2006) as a brief intervention to bolster and protect the mother–infant relationship and it has proved effective in uncontrolled trials. Since untreated maternal depression expressed as emotional unavailability interferes with building successful interactions, HUGS is designed to strengthen relationships and is delivered immediately following maternal treatment of depression through our group CBT program. It draws on the program by Muir (1992) and the work of Selma Fraiberg (Fraiberg, 1980).

There remains a need, however, for brief interventions addressing mother–infant difficulties following PND to be evaluated in controlled studies (HUGS is currently the subject of an RCT).

Prevention

There have been numerous reviews of antenatal interventions designed to reduce the incidence of new cases of PND. A number of reviews (Austin & Lumley, 2003; Lumley, 2005) have shown that most attempts at prevention have failed to have a significant impact. Similarly, meta-analyses of studies designed to prevent the onset of PND have found no major effect of psychological interventions (Dennis & Creedy 2004). However, those individual studies that hold the most promise tended to be those targeted at high-risk women, i.e., women pre-identified with a number of psychosocial risk factors and/or displaying subsyndromal depressive symptoms. Recently, Mihalopoulos *et al.* (2011) conducted a cost-effectiveness modeling exercise using data from studies aimed at preventing depression in general (not just in perinatal women). They found that preventative psychosocial interventions, again targeted at subsyndromal individuals identified by screening, did reduce morbidity and proved a cost-effective option for health systems in some circumstances. In our own recent work with the Towards Parenthood intervention (which begins in pregnancy; Milgrom *et al.*, 2011b) a small reduction in rates of PND emerged. Clearly, the possibility of prevention of AND and PND holds promise, but the area requires considerable further research.

Concluding Remarks

Making screening an effective population health measure

In nonperinatal populations, treatments for existing depression, such as CBT or antidepressant medication, and preventative interventions in high-risk individuals can give value for money (Mihalopoulos *et al.*, 2011); that is, they restore an individual's quality of life at a price the health system is willing to pay. Although the value of one-time screening for depression has been quantified successfully (e.g., Mihalopoulos *et al.* 2011; Valenstein *et al.*, 2001), for PND specifically the results from economic modeling depend on how women with a positive screen are subsequently managed. In the only published cost-effectiveness model of one-time perinatal screening with the EPDS (Paulden *et al.*, 2009), screening with the EPDS achieved cost-effectiveness only when all positive results were followed by a formal diagnostic interview. This key finding, that the initial management of women with positive screening results determines the economic cost of screening, complements the clinical view that active treatment should never commence solely on the basis of a positive screen before a formal diagnostic procedure.

As there is some evidence from meta-estimates that prevalence of PND is highest at around 3 months postpartum (Gavin *et al.*, 2005) this may be an opportune time to screen in order to maximize the efficiency of screening. If screening is to be effective on a population level, options for effective, accessible treatment must be in place and all positive screening results must be followed, systematically, by an offer to undergo a second, diagnostic stage procedure (Gilbody *et al.*, 2009).

The evidence discussed in this chapter suggests that most of the key elements for effective PND screening are in place. Further, while evidence that the burden of morbidity is ultimately lessened by screening remains scarce, it is beginning to emerge. In the only published RCT of this kind (Leung *et al.*, 2010) a significant reduction in morbidity was found due to the implementation of PND screening. Again, the key to effectiveness proved to be the systematic follow-up of all positive screening results with further clinical assessment for depression and access to effective management.

Key points for effective identification, treatment, and recovery

- Acting on all positive screening results by offering a diagnostic procedure maximizes the usefulness of screening.
- Screening and assessment need to be conducted in the context of broader psychosocial factors and with consideration given to possible comorbid conditions (e.g., anxiety).
- Psychological interventions based on CBT and interpersonal psychotherapy are likely to be the most helpful.
- Medication can be an effective treatment but must be weighed carefully along with women's preferences and the potential risks involved.
- Social supports need to be mobilized, as far as possible.
- Women's partners should be included in supporting their management plan and may themselves require support, counselling, or treatment.
- Preventative strategies are not yet demonstrated to be effective in the case of perinatal depressive disorders.
- Mother–infant therapies are indicated but more research is needed to confirm the most effective and practicable approaches.

References

American Psychiatric Association. (2000). *Diagnostic and Statistical Manual of Mental Disorders* (4th edn., Text revision). Washington DC: American Psychiatric Association.

Appleby, L., Warner, R., Whitton, A., & Faragher, B. (1997). A controlled study of fluoxetine and cognitive-behavioural counselling in the treatment of postnatal depression. *British Medical Journal, 314,* 932–936.

Austin, M. P., & Lumley, J. (2003). Antenatal screening for postnatal depression: A systematic review. *Acta Psychiatrica Scandinavica, 107,* 10–17.

Austin, M.-P., Priest, S. R., & Sullivan, E. A. (2008). Antenatal psychosocial assessment for reducing perinatal mental health morbidity. *Cochrane Database of Systematic Reviews, 4,* CD005124.

Beck, C. T. (1996). A meta-analysis of predictors of postpartum depression. *Nursing Research, 45,* 297–303.

Beck, C. T. (1998). The effects of postpartum depression on child development: A meta-analysis. *Archives of Psychiatric Nursing, 12,* 12–20.

Beck, C. T. (2001). Predictors of postpartum depression, an update. *Nursing Research, 50,* 275–285.

Bellantuono, C., Milgliarese, G., & Gentile, S. (2007). Serotonin reuptake inhibitors in pregnancy and the risk of major malformations: A systematic review. *Human Psychopharmacology, 22,* 121–128.

Beyondblue. (2005). *Final Report of the National Postnatal Depression Program, 2001–2005. 1, 2.* Melbourne: Beyondblue.

Beyondblue. (2011). *Clinical Practice Guidelines for Depression and Related Disorders – Anxiety, Bipolar Disorder and Puerperal Psychosis – in the Perinatal Period. A Guideline for Primary Care Health Professionals.* Melbourne: Beyondblue.

Bilszta, J., Ericksen, J., Buist, A., & Milgrom, J. (2010). Women's experiences of postnatal depression: Beliefs and attitudes as barriers to care. *Australian Journal of Advanced Nursing, 27,* 44–54.

Boath, E., Bradley, E., & Henshaw, C. (2004). Women's views of antidepressants in the treatment of postnatal depression. *Journal of Psychosomatic Obstetrics and Gynecology, 25,* 221–233.

Boyce, P., Condon, J., Barton, J., & Corkindale, C. (2007). First-time fathers study: Psycholoical distress in expectant fathers during pregnancy. *Australian and New Zealand Journal of Psychiatry, 41,* 718–725.

Brazelton, T. B., Koslowski, B., & Main, M. (1974). Origins of reciprocity: The early mother-infant interaction. In M. Lewis & L. Rosenbloom (Eds.), *Effects of the Infant on its Caregiver* (pp. 49–79). New York: John Wiley & Son.

British Columbia Reproductive Care Program. (2003). *Reproductive Mental Health Guideline 3: Identification and Assessment of Reproductive Mental Illness During the Preconception and Perinatal Periods*. Vancouver: British Columbia Reproductive Care Program.

Chung, T. K. H., Lau, T. K., Yip, A. S. K., Chiu, H. F. K., & Lee, D. T. S. (2001). Antepartum depressive symptomatology is associated with adverse obstetric and neonatal outcomes. *Psychosomatic Medicine, 63*, 830–834.

Clark, R., Tluczek, A., & Wenzel, A. (2003). Psychotherapy for postpartum depression: A preliminary report. *American Journal of Orthopsychiatry, 73*, 441–454.

Cooper, P., & Murray, L. (1997). The role of infant and maternal factors in postpartum depression, mother-infant interactions, and infant outcome. In L. Murray & P. J. Cooper (Eds.), *Postpartum Depression and Child Development* (pp. 111–135). New York: Guilford Press.

Cooper, P. J., Murray, L., Wilson, A., & Romaniuk, H. (2003). Controlled trial of the short- and long-term effect of psychological treatment of post-partum depression 1: Impact on maternal mood. *British Journal of Psychiatry, 182*, 412–419.

Cox, J., Holden, J., & Sagovsky, R. (1987). Detection of postnatal depression: Development of a 10 item postnatal depression scale. *British Journal of Psychiatry, 150*, 782–786.

Cuijpers, P., Brannmark, J. G., & van Straten, A. (2008a). Psychological treatment of postpartum depression: A meta-analysis. *Journal of Clinical Psychology, 64*, 103–118.

Cuijpers, P., van Straten, A., van Oppen, P., & Andersson, G. (2008b). Are psychological and pharmacologic interventions equally effective in the treatment of adult depressive disorders? A meta-analysis of comparative studies. *Journal of Clinical Psychiatry, 69*, 1675–1685.

Dayan, J., Creveuill, C., Marks, M. N., Conroy, S., Herlicoviez, M., Dreyfus, M., & Tordjman, S. (2006). Prenatal depression, prenatal anxiety, and spontaneous preterm birth: A prospective cohort study among women with early and regular care. *Psychosomatic Medicine, 68*, 938–946.

de Matt, S., Dekker, J., Schoevers, R., & de Jonghe, F. (2007). Relative efficacy of psychotherapy and combined therpay in the treatment of depression: A meta-analysis. *European Psychiatry, 22*, 1–8.

Dennis, C. L., & Creedy, D. (2004). Psychosocial and psychological interventions for preventing postpartum depression. *Cochrane Database of Systematic Reviews* (4), CD001134.

Dennis, C. L., & Chung-Lee, L. (2006). Postpartum depression help-seeking barriers and maternal treatment preferences: a qualitative systematic review. *Birth, 33*, 323–331.

Dennis, C. L., & Hodnett, E. (2007). Psychosocial and psychological interventions for treating postpartum depression. *Cochrane Database of Systematic Reviews, 4*, CD006116.

Diego, M. A., Field, T., Jones, N., & Hernandez-Reif, M. (2006). Withdrawn and intrusive maternal interaction style and infant frontal EEG asymmetry shifts in infants. *Infant Behavior & Development, 29*, 220–229.

Department of Health and Ageing. (2009). *National Perinatal Depression Framework*. www.health.gov.au/internet/mentalhealth/publishing.nsf/Content/perinatal-depression-2.

Englar-Carlson, M., & Shepard, D. (2005). Engaging men in couples counseling: Strategies for overcoming ambivalence and inexpressiveness. *The Family Journal, 13*, 383–391.

Field, T. (1992). Infants of depressed mothers. *Development and Psychopathology, 4*, 49–66.

Forman, D. R., O'Hara, M. W., Stuart, S., Gorman, L. L., Larsen, K. E., & Coy, K. C. (2007). Effective treatment for postpartum depression is not sufficient to improve the developing mother-child relationship. *Development & Psychopathology, 19*, 585–602.

Fraiberg, S. (1980). *Clinical Studies in Infant Mental Health*. New York: Basic Books.

Gavin, N. I., Gaynes, B. N., Lohr, K. N., Meltzer-Brody, S., Gartlehner, G., & Swinson, T. (2005). Perinatal depression: A systematic review of prevalence and incidence. *Obstetrics & Gynecology, 106*, 1071–1083.

Gelfand, D. M., Teti, D. M., Seiner, S. A., & Jameson, P. B. (1996). Helping mothers fight depression: Evaluation of a home-based intervention program for depressed mothers and their infants. *Journal of Clinical Child Psychology, 25*, 406–422.

Gemmill, A. W., Leigh, B., Ericksen, J., & Milgrom, J. (2006). A survey of the clinical acceptability of screening for postnatal depression in depressed and non-depressed women. *BMC Public Health, 6*, 211.

Gilbody, S., House, A., & Sheldon, T. (2009). Screening and case finding instruments for depression. *Cochrane Database of Systematic Reviews, 4*, CD002792.

Hay, D. F., Pawlby, S., Sharp, D., Asten, P., Mills, A., & Kumar, R. (2001). Intellectual problems shown by 11-year-old children whose mothers had postnatal depression. *Journal of Child Psychology and Psychiatry*, *42*, 871–889.

Honikman, J. (2008). The role of social support in the prevention, intervention and treatment of perinatal mood disorders. In S. Dowd Stone & A. Menken (Eds.), *Perinatal and Postpartum Mood Disorders* (pp. 339–355). New York: Springer.

Krantz, I., Eriksson, B., Lundquist-Persson, C., Ahlberg, B. M., & Nilstun, T. (2008). Screening for postpartum depression with the Edinburgh Postnatal Depression Scale (EPDS): An ethical analysis. *Scandinavian Journal of Public Health*, *36*, 211–216.

Kurki, T., Hiilesmaa, V., Raitasalo, R., Mattila, H., & Ylikorkala, O. (2000) Depression and anxiety in early pregnancy and risk for preeclampsia. *Obstetrics and Gynaecology*, *95*, 487–493.

Kwan, B., Dimidjian, S., & Rizvi, S. (2010). Treatment preference, engagement, and clinical improvement in pharmacotherapy versus psychotherapy for depression. *Behaviour Research and Therapy*, *48*, 799–804.

Leigh, B., & Milgrom, J. (2007). Acceptability of antenatal screening for depression in routine antenatal care. *Australian Journal of Advanced Nursing*, *24*, 14–18.

Leung, S., Leung, C., Lam, T., Hung, T., Chan, R., Yeung, T. *et al.* (2011). Outcome of a postnatal depression screening programme using the Edinburgh Postnatal Depression Scale: A randomized controlled trial. *Journal of Public Health*, *33*, 292–301.

Lewinsohn, P. M., Antonuccio, D. O., Steinmetz, J. L., & Teri, L. (1984). *The Coping with Depression Course: A Psycho-Educational Intervention for Unipolar Depression*. Eugene: Castalsa Publishing Company.

Lewinsohn, P. M., Munoz, R. F., Youngren, M. A., & Zeiss, A. M. (1992). *Control your Depression*. New York: Simon & Schuster.

Lumley, J. (2005). Attempts to prevent postnatal depression. *BMJ*, *331*(7507), 5–6.

Lyons-Ruth, K., Zoll, D., Connell, D., & Grunebaum, H. U. (1986). The depressed mother and her one-year-old infant: Environment, interaction, attachment and infant development. In E. Z. Tronick & T. Field (Eds.), *Maternal Depression and Infant Disturbance: New Directions for Child Development*, vol. 34 (pp. 61–82). San Francisco, CA: Jossey Bass.

MacLellan, A., Wilson, D., & Taylor, A. (1996). The self-reported prevalence of postnatal depression. *Australian and New Zealand Journal of Obstetrics and Gynaecology*, *36*, 313–313.

Matthey, S. (2009). Are we overpathologising motherhood? *Journal of Affective Disorders*, *120*, 263–266.

Matthey, S., Reay, R., & Fletcher, R. (2009). Service strategies for engaging fathers in the perinatal period: What have we learned so far? *The International Journal of Mental Health Promotion*, *11*, 29–41.

Mihalopoulos, C., Vos, T., Pirkis, J., Smit, F., & Carter, R. (2011). Do indicated preventive interventions for depression represent good value for money? *Australian and New Zealand Journal of Psychiatry*, *45*, 36–44.

Milgrom, J., & Meager, I. (1996). Group treatment for post-partum depression: A pilot study. *Australian and New Zealand Journal of Psychiatry*, *30*, 750–758.

Milgrom, J., Martin, P. R., & Negri, L. M. (1999). *Treating Postnatal Depression. A Psychological Approach for Health Care Practitioners*. Chichester: Wiley.

Milgrom, J., Westley, D., & Gemmill, A.W. (2004). The mediating role of maternal responsiveness in some longer-term effects of postnatal depression on infant development. *Infant Behavior & Development*, *27*, 443–454.

Milgrom, J., Ericksen, J., Negri, L., & Gemmill, A. (2005a). Screening for postnatal depression in routine primary care: Properties of the Edinburgh Postnatal Depression Scale in an Australian sample. *Australian and New Zealand Journal of Psychiatry*, *39*, 843–849.

Milgrom, J., Negri, L. M., Gemmill, A. W., McNeil, M., & Martin, P. R. (2005b). A randomized controlled trial of psychological interventions for postnatal depression. *British Journal of Clinical Psychology*, *44*, 529–542.

Milgrom, J., Ericksen, J., McCarthy, R., & Gemmill, A. (2006). Stressful impact of depression on early mother-infant relations. *Stress and Health*, *22*, 229–238.

Milgrom, J., Gemmill, A. W., Bilszta, J. L., Hayes, B., Barnett, B., Brooks, J. *et al.* (2008). Antenatal risk factors for postnatal depression: A large prospective study. *Journal of Affective Disorders*, *108*, 147–157.

Milgrom, J., Mendelsohn, J., & Gemmill, A. W. (2011a). Does postnatal depression screening work? Throwing out the bathwater, keeping the baby. *Journal of Affective Disorders*, *132*, 301–310.

Milgrom, J., Schembri, C., Ericksen, J., Ross, J., & Gemmill, A. W. (2011b). Towards parenthood: An antenatal intervention to reduce depression, anxiety and parenting difficulties. *Journal of Affective Disorders, 130,* 385–394.

Misri, S., Reebye, P., Corral, M., & Milis, L. (2004). The use of paroxetine and cognitive-behavioral therapy in postpartum depression and anxiety: A randomized controlled trial. *Journal of Clinical Psychiatry, 65,* 1236–1241.

Muir, E. (1992) Watching, waiting and wondering: Applying psychoanalytic principals to mother-infant intervention, *Infant Mental Health Journal, 13,* 319–328.

Mulcahy, R., Reay, R. E., Wilkinson, R. B., & Owen, C. (2009). A randomised control trial for the effectiveness of group interpersonal psychotherapy for postnatal depression. *Archives of Women's Mental Health, 13,* 125–139.

Murray, L., & Cooper, P. J. (1996). The impact of postpartum depression on child development. *International Review of Psychiatry, 8,* 55–63.

Murray, L., & Cooper, P. (Eds.). (1997). *Postpartum Depression and Child Development.* New York: Guilford Press.

Murray, L., Sinclair, D., Cooper, P., Ducournau, P., Turner, P., & Stein, A. (1999). The socioemotional development of 5-year-old children of postnatally depressed mothers. *Journal of Child Psychology and Psychiatry, 40,* 1259–1271.

Murray, L., Cooper, P. J., Wilson, A., & Romaniuk, H. (2003). Controlled trial of the short-and long-term effect of psychological treatment of post-partum depression 2: Impact on the mother-child relationship and child outcome. *British Journal of Psychiatry, 182,* 420–427.

Murray, L., Arteche, A., Fearon, P., Halligan, S., Croudace, T., & Cooper, P. (2010) The effects of maternal postnatal depression and child sex on academic performance at age 16 years: a developmental approach. *Journal of child psychology and psychiatry, and allied disciplines, 51,* 1150–1159.

National Institute for Health and Clinical Excellence. (2007). *Antenatal and Postnatal Mental Health: Clinical Management and Service Guidance.* www.nice.org.uk/CG45.

O'Hara, M., & Swain, A. (1996). Rates and risk of postpartum depression: A meta-analysis. *International Review of Psychiatry, 8,* 37–54.

O'Hara, M. W., Stuart, S., Gorman, L., & Wenzel, A. (2000). Efficacy of interpersonal psychotherapy for postpartum depression. *Archives of General Psychiatry, 57,* 1039–1045.

Onozawa, K., Glover, V., Adams, D., Modi, N., & Kumar, R. C. (2001). Infant massage improves mother-infant interaction for mothers with postnatal depression. *Journal of Affective Disorders, 63,* 201–207.

Paulden, M., Palmer, S., Hewitt, C., & Gilbody, S. (2009). Screening for postnatal depression in primary care: Cost effectiveness analysis. *British Medical Journal, 339,* b5203.

Pearlstein, T. (2008). Perinatal depression: Treatment options and dilemmas. *Journal of Psychiatry & Neuroscience, 33,* 302–318.

Reck, C., Hunt, A., Fuchs, T., Weiss, R., Noon, A., Moehler, E. *et al.* (2004). Interactive regulation of affect in postpartum depressed mothers and their infants: an overview. *Psychopathology, 37,* 272–280.

Righetti-Veltema, M., Conne-Perreard, E., Bousquet, A., & Manzano, J. (2002). Postpartum depression and mother-infant relationship at 3 months old. *Journal of Affective Disorders, 70,* 291–306.

Robertson, E., Grace, S., Wallington, T., & Stewart, D. E. (2004). Antenatal risk factors for postpartum depression: A synthesis of recent literature. *General Hospital Psychiatry, 26,* 289–295.

Ross, L., & McLean, L. (2006). Anxiety disorders during pregnancy and the postpartum period: A systematic review. *Journal of Clinical Psychiatry, 67,* 1285–1298.

Rubertsson, C., Wickberg, B., Gustavsson, P., & Radestad, I. (2005). Depressive symptoms in early pregnancy, two months and one year postpartum-prevalence and psychosocial risk factors in a national Swedish sample. *Archives of Women's Mental Health, 8,* 97–104.

Shakespeare, J. (2002). *Evaluation of Screening for Postnatal Depression against the NSC Handbook Criteria.* Working party document. www.nelh.nhs.uk/screening/adult_pps/postnatal_depresion.html.

Shakespeare, J., Blake, F., & Garcia, J. (2003). A qualitative study of the acceptability of routine screening of postnatal depression using the Edinburgh Postnatal Depression Scale. *British Journal of General Practice, 53,* 614–619.

Sharp, D., Hay, D., Pawlby, S., Schmucher, G., Allen, H., & Kumar, R. (1995). The impact of postnatal depression on boys intellectual development. *Journal of Child Psychology and Psychiatry, 36*, 1315–1337.

Scottish Intercollegiate Guidelines Network. (2002). *Postnatal Depression and Puerperal Psychosis: A National Clinical Guidance.* Edinburgh: Royal College of Physicians.

Stern, D. N. (1985). *The Interpersonal World of the Infant: A View from Psychoanalysis and Developmental Psychology.* New York: Basic Books.

Swift, J., & Callahan, J. (2009). The impact of client treatment preferences on outcome: A meta-analysis. *Journal of Clinical Psychology, 56*, 368–381.

Talge, N., Neal, C., & Glover, V. (2007). Antenatal maternal stress and long-term effects on child neurodevelopment: how and why? *Journal of Child Psychology and Psychiatry, 48*, 245–261.

Tronick, E. Z., & Weinberg, M. K. (1997). Depressed mothers and infants: Failure to form dyadic states of consciousness. In L. Murray & P. Cooper (Eds.), *Postpartum depression and child development* (pp. 54–84). New York: Guilford Press.

Turner, K. M., Sharp, D., Folkes, L., & Chew-Graham, C. (2008). Women's views and experiences of antidepressants as a treatment for postnatal depression: A qualitative study. *Family Practice, 25*, 450–455.

Valenstein, M., Sandeep, V., Zeber, J. E., Boehm, K., & Buttar, A. (2001). The cost-utility of screening for depression in primary care. *Annals of International Medicine, 134*, 345–360.

Van den Bergh, B. R. H., Mulder, E. J. H., Mennes, M., & Glover, V. (2005). Antenatal maternal anxiety and stress and the neurobehavioural development of the fetus and child: Links and possible mechanisms. A review. *Neuroscience and Biobehavioral Reviews, 29*, 237–258.

Webster, J., Pritchard, M. A., Creedy, D., & East, C. (2003). A simplified predictive index for the detection of women at risk for postnatal depression. *Birth, 30*, 101–108.

World Health Organization. (1993). *The ICD-10 Classification of Mental and Behavioural Disorders: Diagnostic Criteria for Research.* Geneva: World Health Organization.

World Health Organization. (2004). *Prevention of Mental Disorders: Effective Interventions and Policy Options.* Summary report. Geneva: World Health Organization.

Winnicott, D. W. (1974). *Playing and Reality.* London: Pelican.

Zuckerman, B., Amaro, H., Bauchner, H., & Cabral, H. (1989). Depressive symptoms during pregnancy: Relationship to poor health behaviours. *American Journal of Obstetrics and Gynaecology, 160*, 1107–1111.

17

From Insomnia to Healthy Sleep

Cognitive-Behavioral Applications

Delwyn Bartlett and Moira Junge

In this chapter we examine the development of insomnia, diagnostic considerations, and the treatments available. Humans spend approximately one-third of their lives attempting or achieving sleep, yet this is an area of psychology which is often overlooked or dismissed as a symptom of mood or some other medical condition. Insomnia is the most common of all sleep disorders, and one of the most prevalent health complaints in the general population (Buysse *et al.*, 2006). There is an enormous prevalence range in the literature due to the word "insomnia" being used to refer to both insomnia symptoms and insomnia disorder (Siebern & Manber, 2011). Psychosocial, behavioral, and biological factors are implicated in the development and maintenance of insomnia as a disorder.

Health psychologists utilize psychological principles to enhance wellbeing and health, with the primary goal of reducing the impact of illness. Psychological skills and knowledge are also required in the field of sleep disorders to treat the whole patient. One of the aims of this chapter is to give the reader a sound understanding of the difference between insomnia as a symptom and insomnia, the sleep disorder. To help alleviate this ambiguity sleep researchers have reserved the term "insomnia symptoms" to differentiate it from insomnia as a sleep disorder (Edinger *et al.*, 2004).

Sleep is an essential element of optimal mental and physical health, and difficulties with sleep result in suboptimal health. Insomnia frequently results in lost working days (Leger & Bayon, 2010; Simon & VonKorff, 1997), exacerbates other medical and pain-related symptoms (Katz & McHorney, 1998), and has a strong bidirectional relationship with both depression and anxiety (Breslau *et al.*, 1996; Riemann & Voderholzer, 2003). Insomnia may present as the primary issue or in parallel with coexisting medical or psychiatric conditions.

Insomnia involves difficulty with initiating or maintaining sleep or waking too early (all greater than 30 min) where there has been sufficient opportunity to sleep and symptoms have been occurring at least three nights per week (American Academy of Sleep Medicine, 2005). According to the *International Classification of Sleep Disorders* (ICSD; American Academy of Sleep Medicine, 2005), 6 months is the point at which insomnia becomes chronic. If the insomnia is present for less than 1 month, then is it classified as acute (American Academy Of Sleep Medicine, 2005).

Applied Topics in Health Psychology, First Edition. Edited by M. L. Caltabiano and L. Ricciardelli.
© 2013 John Wiley & Sons, Ltd. Published 2013 by John Wiley & Sons, Ltd.

Table 17.1 Diagnosis and Differentiation of the Insomnias, Based on ICSD-II

Classification	Sleep disorder/type of insomnia	Essential features: complaint of insomnia plus . . .
Insomnias	Psychophysiological insomnia	Learned sleep-preventing associations, conditioned arousal, "racing mind" phenomenon
	Paradoxical insomnia	Complaint of poor sleep disproportionate to sleep pattern and sleep duration
	Idiopathic insomnia	Insomnia typically begins in childhood or from birth; unknown cause generally
	Insomnia due to a mental disorder	Course of sleep disturbance concurrent with mental disorder
	Inadequate sleep hygiene	Daily living activities inconsistent with maintaining good-quality sleep
	Insomnia due to a medical disorder	Course of sleep disturbance concurrent with mental disorder
	Insomnia due to drug or substance	Sleep disruption caused by prescription medication, recreational drug, caffeine, alcohol or foodstuff
	Adjustment insomnia	Presence of identifiable stressor; insomnia resolves or is expected to resolve when stressor removed

Using another classification, the *Diagnostic and Statistical Manual of Mental Disorders* (4th edn, text revision; DSM-IV-TR; American Psychiatric Association, 2000), insomnia is defined as chronic if it exceeds a month. Both classifications include daytime symptoms, where social and/or occupational functioning is impaired along with dissatisfaction with sleep. Individuals may feel sleep-deprived but they spend sufficient time in bed whereas in true sleep deprivation the individual only *allows* for a few hours, or no hours, in bed per night. Overall, sleep quality is chronically nonrestorative despite adequate sleep opportunity, and is distressing for the individual.

Table 17.1 outlines the different types of insomnia classified using the second edition of the ICSD (ICSD-II). However, mental health practitioners typically use the DSM-IV-TR, which includes fewer subtypes of insomnias: primary insomnia, insomnia related to a substance or another medication, a psychiatric or medical condition. The classification systems differ mainly in terms of the time frames.

Interestingly, the DSM-V advisory committee on sleep nosology has proposed a single diagnosis of "insomnia disorder" including what was previously called primary insomnia as well as insomnia related to a medical or psychiatric condition. The DSM-V advisory committee has also proposed qualifying statements to specify the presence of medical and/or psychiatric comorbidities (Siebern & Manber, 2011).

Symptoms and Features

The individual with insomnia often presents as being "wired and tired," reporting high levels of fatigue on questionnaires but is rarely sleepy on the Epworth Sleepiness Scale (ESS) (Johns, 1991). This scale is used to measure excessive daytime sleepiness in individuals with other sleep disorders and in shift workers. Individuals with insomnia experience physiological hyperarousal and cognitive hypervigilance which is thought to mask any usual sleepiness. Individuals with insomnia are generally not sleepy day or night. If high levels of sleepiness are found then it is important to look at the possibility of other sleep disorders such as obstructive sleep apnea, restless legs syndrome, narcolepsy/cataplexy, an undiagnosed medical disorder, head injury, and/or severe depression. Consultation with the general practitioner (GP) is advised at this point.

Insomnia also causes daytime impairments, including fatigue, inattention, and mood changes with depression, anxiety, worry, and irritability (Buckner *et al.*, 2008; Jansson-Frojmark & Lindblom, 2008). Apprehension about the next day can also reduce sleep quality (Kecklund & Akersted, 2004). Less frequently, cognitive and performance abilities may be affected (Backhaus *et al.*, 2006; Reidel & Lichstein, 2000). Sleep or lack of perceived sleep becomes a major negative preoccupation for the individual with insomnia (Morin & Espie, 2003). Concerns include sleep onset, the possibility of waking and not returning to sleep, the unpredictability of sleep, and ability to be effective in their various roles with reduced sleep. Perfectionism which is commonly associated with insomnia is likely to exacerbate these symptoms (Azevado *et al.*, 2010)

Women report insomnia more often than men, with a ratio of 4:1, are diagnosed with insomnia more often, and report more sleep dissatisfaction (Ohayon, 2002). It is unclear why women are more vulnerable to insomnia. Some research suggests the timing of melatonin and lowering of core body temperature, which is necessary for sleep onset, is different in women. Recent research found the melatonin curve (showing the diurnal levels of melatonin in the body) in women was advanced compared with men (Cain *et al.*, 2010), which has implications in terms of timing and quantity of sleep achieved by women compared with men. Melatonin is generally not found in the bloodstream during the daytime, becoming apparent around 10 pm and peaking between 2 and 3 am. However, being in a younger age group and/or having a history of mental illness explains most of the variability, rendering gender differences nonsignificant (Hale *et al.*, 2009). There is still an underrecognition of the role of sleep. In a recent review of health in women throughout life, sleep was mentioned, but not as an integral component of good health (Zender & Olshansky, 2009).

Comorbidity and Insomnia

Being 45 years or older, overweight/obese, having pain, hypertension, cardiovascular disease, upper airway disease, anxiety, bipolar disorder, major depression, or consuming moderate to large amounts of alcohol or coffee on a daily basis is associated with difficulty returning to sleep (Ohayon, 2010). Insomnia was previously perceived as merely a symptom of depression, not requiring any treatment in its own right. Research has now shown that untreated insomnia leads to depression (Riemann & Voderholzer, 2003). When individuals have previously experienced depression, sleep disturbance in the form of insomnia is often a prodromal symptom of a recurring bout of depression and is therefore an important marker requiring treatment (Breslau *et al.*, 1996). The bidirectional negative nature of mood and sleep is well described in a recent community study of 3000 Swedish residents who were followed-up at 1 year (Jansson-Frojmark & Lindblom 2008). This prospective study found that high anxiety and depression at baseline resulted in insomnia 1 year later and untreated insomnia at baseline resulted in depression and anxiety at the 1 year follow-up. It is important to note that even when individuals have been successfully treated for a major depressive episode the most common residual symptoms is sleep disturbance which can in turn predispose them to further depression (Nierenberg *et al.*, 2010).

Shift Work and Insomnia

Few shift workers become nocturnal even when they are on permanent night shifts. Anecdotal data suggest that a schedule of 70 working nights in a row is necessary for the average human to become nocturnal. Generally, social and family responsibilities prevent the shift to a nocturnal schedule. Night-shift workers lose 5–7 h of sleep per night and battle to maintain sleep during the daytime due to the circadian rhythm desynchrony of managing a rising core body temperature, light, and noise factors (Akerstedt *et al.*, 2002; Kecklund & Akersted, 2004). Most shift workers report difficulties with sleep onset and "too little sleep" but many see this sleep disturbance as being part of the job. However, the addition of insomnia was associated with higher stress levels whereas better-sleeping shift workers appear to self-select shift work (Akerstedt *et al.*, 2008).

Pain Conditions and Insomnia

Pain conditions increase depression and depressive symptoms intensify the experience of pain, as does sleep deprivation (Leprin & Briley, 2004). Yet insomnia is a neglected area in chronic pain with pharmacological interventions perceived as the only treatment intervention (Lacks & Morin, 1992). Sleep disturbance is very common in pain conditions with a prevalence of 23.1% in arthritis sufferers (similar to figures in other chronic conditions) compared with 16.4% with no arthritis (Louie *et al.*, 2011). When individuals have pain alongside anxiety and or depression the increased risk of developing insomnia is even greater. Treating individuals with pain and insomnia is difficult. Currie and colleagues (2000) undertook a randomized controlled trial of cognitive behavior therapy, aimed at treating insomnia (CBT-i), for individuals with insomnia secondary to pain. A 7 week group intervention showed initial improvements in sleep/wake measures of sleep-onset latency, wake time, and sleep efficiency which were maintained at 3 months. Interestingly, most of these patients had been recruited from other pain clinic programs, showing that in complex cases such as pain and insomnia additional treatments are often required for long-term success (Currie *et al.*, 2002).

Insomnia and Increasing Age

Sleep quality is reduced with increasing age and insomnia symptoms increase with age, with an estimated prevalence of 25% (Ohayon, 2002). Age-related sleep-stage changes include reduced slow-wave sleep or deep sleep, increased transitional sleep or Stage 1 sleep, and an increase in the number of wakes. Stage 2 sleep (light sleep) is relatively maintained although more fragmented, as is rapid-eye-movement sleep (REM sleep). Comorbid medical and psychiatric conditions plus increased usage of hypnotic drugs are factors in the increased prevalence of insomnia. When older adults are healthy (actively using brain and body) the prevalence rate for insomnia is similar to the general population (Vitiello *et al.*, 2002). Unrealistic expectations about sleep and age impact on perception.

Electroencephalography and Insomnia

It is unclear whether the physiological changes associated with insomnia precede onset or are a consequence. High-frequency electroencephalographic (EEG) activity is exaggerated in individuals with insomnia, suggesting a central nervous system arousal (elevated cortisol and adrenocorti-cotrophins) (Vgontzas *et al.*, 2001). Adrenocorticotrophins elevated in individuals with insomnia raises the question of whether increased stress/arousal hormones reflect an adaptation to poor sleep or is a yet-discovered genotype.

Development and Maintenance of Insomnia

Approximately one-thirds of adults will report occasional insomnia symptoms, but when daytime impairment and sleep dissatisfaction are added the prevalence is approximately 6% (Ohayon & Shapiro, 2002). In Australia, information on insomnia prevalence is somewhat scant. In one cross-sectional study 33% of individuals randomly selected from the electoral roll reported insomnia symptoms but only 11.1% sought medical treatment (Bartlett *et al.*, 2007, 2008). These findings are very similar to international prevalence data (Morin *et al.*, 2005) and those from comorbid conditions (Siversten *et al.*, 2009).

Proposed Models of Etiology of Insomnia

Several models have been developed to explain the development and maintenance of insomnia. However, none of the models completely explain the etiology of insomnia as it is complex and usually multifactorial.

Spielman model

The Spielman model of insomnia proposes that there are three main factors (predisposing, precipitating, and perpetuating: the three Ps) involved in the establishment and maintenance of insomnia (Spielman *et al.*, 1987). The most common types of predisposing factors include demographic factors (e.g., aging, female gender, living alone), familial/hereditary conditions (a personal or family history of insomnia), psychological factors (e.g., anxiety, depression, personality traits), and physiological and lifestyle factors (e.g., increased arousability, caffeine and alcohol intake, and smoking). There is little or no longitudinal research at present to identify whether these factors are a trigger or an effect. Precipitating factors include stressful life events (e.g., relationships, divorce, grief, financial worries, work-related stressors), as well as psychological and health-related factors (e.g., pain, cardiovascular disease, mental health problems). These precipitating factors push the individual over the threshold, resulting in acute insomnia. Perpetuating factors include maladaptive sleep habits, such as spending excessive amounts of time in bed to make up for perceived sleep loss. However, the main perpetuating factor is "distress and concern about poor sleep," leading to "performance anxiety" and dysfunctional/unhelpful beliefs about the ability to sleep, which becomes a self-fulfilling prophecy (Bonnet & Arand, 1998).

With effective and early treatment of insomnia, patients may revert to their premorbid, noninsomniac state, but without early intervention the insomnia condition is likely to become chronic (Spielman *et al.*, 1987). The identifiable insomnia trigger is generally resolved within weeks or months (75%) yet the insomnia can remain untreated for years (Bastien *et al.*, 2004). The individual generally fails to recognize that the combination of poor sleep, sleep anxiety, and an inability to "down-regulate" arousal levels at bedtime is what feeds the insomnia on a nightly basis. Explaining this model to individuals is very useful and helps them to have a better understanding of their insomnia and how it is perpetuated.

Harvey model

The hyperarousal state frequently seen in insomnia can also be caused by cognitive arousal and distress. Harvey (2002) proposed a cognitive model of the maintenance of chronic insomnia where excessive and negative cognitive activity leads to increased physiological hyperarousal and selective attention. The five factors proposed by Harvey in this model of maintenance of chronic insomnia are worry, unhelpful beliefs about sleep, use of safety behaviors, monitoring of sleep-related threats, and inaccurate perceptions of sleep and consequences of sleep loss. *Worry* can either precipitate or perpetuate the insomnia. However, worry about the daytime consequences of not obtaining enough sleep can become the defining point, resulting in absenteeism and performance anxiety. This worry cycle triggers an autonomic physiological arousal and further exacerbates emotional distress and wakefulness (Bonnet & Arand, 1997). *Unhelpful beliefs* about sleep include statements such as "I need 8 hours of sleep every night to feel refreshed" or "I am concerned that if I go for 2–3 nights without sleep I shall have a nervous breakdown." These statements exemplify the unrealistic beliefs which are partly maintained by worry. The use of *safety behavior* is a paradox in that the individual engages in behavior that is more likely to make their sleep worse (e.g., napping, sleeping late, and consuming large amounts of caffeine/alcohol) which is the feared outcome they are often attempting to prevent. *Monitoring of sleep-related threats* further perpetuates the worry and this attentional bias contributes to negative cognitive intrusions about sleep. At bedtime, on waking and during the day individuals engage in monitoring body sensations (muscle tension and a racing mind) and using environmental cues (clock watching), which support the premise that sleep will not occur, that it was insufficient in length, and has negative effects on daytime mood and performance. An *inaccurate perception of sleep* is common and individuals overestimate their sleep loss. The difference on objectively measured sleep between good sleepers and those with insomnia was 35 min, which does not account for the severity of sleep complaints (Chambers & Keller, 1993). Consequences of sleep loss have been covered within the five components listed. Treatment entails targeting false attributions about causes of insomnia, the false expectations about sleep (always waking refreshed), and the ensuing faulty beliefs, challenging the perceptions of the consequences of poor sleep, and introducing tools (e.g., thought blocking) to aid cognitive restructuring.

Treatment of Insomnia: Nonpharmacological

CBT-i targets maladaptive behaviors and thoughts described by the two models above. CBT-i is considered the gold standard, being the most effective treatment for insomnia (Morin *et al.* 2006), as measured objectively and compared with hypnotic medication (Morin *et al.*, 1999; Siversten *et al.*, 2006), and is effective in older age groups (Lichstein *et al.*, 2000), community groups (Espie *et al.*, 2007), and when used with depressed individuals (Manber *et al.*, 2008). There is strong empirical evidence for the effectiveness of CBT-i with demonstrable large effect size changes in primary outcomes (sleep latency, increased total sleep time and sleep efficiency, fewer wakes), maintained at long-term follow-up (12–24 months) (Irwin *et al.*, 2006; Morin *et al.*, 1994; Murtagh & Greenwood, 1995; Smith *et al.*, 2002).

Table 17.2 outlines the components of CBT-i. The essential headings include stimulus control, sleep restriction (also known as sleep consolidation or bed restriction), cognitive therapy, relaxation techniques, and sleep hygiene education. Typically CBT-i is delivered in four to ten sessions, either individually or in a group setting. When delivered in a group setting ideal group numbers would be four to eight participants. Both groups and individual settings have been shown to be equally effective (Verbeek *et al.*, 2006) but with group settings treating more individuals is possible. Anecdotally groups have the additional advantage of helping individuals to feel less isolated in relation to their chronic disorder.

Table 17.2 Description of CBT-i Components

Intervention	General description	Specific techniques
Stimulus control	Bed=sleep. Set of instructions aimed at conditioning the patient to expect that bed is for sleeping and not other stimulating activiites. The only exception is sexual activity. Aim is to promote a positive association between bedroom environment and sleepiness.	Go to bed only when sleepy/ comfortable and intending to fall asleep. If unable to sleep within what feels like 15–20 min (without watching the clock), leave the bed and bedroom and go to another room and do nonstimulating activity. Return to bed only when comfortable enough to sleep again. Do not read, watch TV, talk on phone, pay bills, tweet, visit Facebook, worry, or plan activities in bed.
Sleep-/bed- restriction therapy	A technique that increases sleep "drive" and reduces time in bed lying awake. It limits the time in bed to match the patient's average reported *actual* sleep time. Slowly allows more time in bed as sleep improves.	Set strict bedtime and rising schedule limited to average expected hours of sleep reported in the average night. Increase time in bed by 15–30 min when the time spent asleep is at least 85% of the allowed time in bed. Keep a fixed wake-up time, regardless of actual sleep duration.
Relaxation techniques	Various breathing techniques, use of visual imagery, use of meditation.	Progressive muscle relaxation (practice at least daily) and encourage shorter relaxation periods (2 min) a number of times per day; use of breathing and self-hypnosis techniques.
Cognitive therapy	Identification of, and targeting of, beliefs that may be interfering with adherence to Stimulus control and Sleep restriction. Use of mindfulness to alter approach to sleep	Unhelpful beliefs can include: over-estimation of hours of sleep required each night to maintain health; over-estimation of the power of sleeping tablets; under-estimation of actual sleep obtained; fear of stimulus control or sleep restriction for fear of missing the time when sleep will come.
Sleep hygiene education	Sleep "hygiene" emphasizes: environmental factors, physiological factors, behaviors, habits which promote sound sleep. (Hauri, 1982).	Avoid long naps in daytime, short naps (less than 30 min) are OK. Regular exercise, maintain regular sleep/wake schedule 7 days per week (particularly wake times), avoid stimulants (caffeine and nicotine). Limit alcohol intake, especially before bed. Avoid visual access to clock when in bed. Keep bedroom dark, quiet, clean, and comfortable.

Stimulus control

Stimulus control is a reconditioning treatment forcing discrimination between daytime and sleeping environments (Bootzin, 1972). For the poor sleeper, the bedroom triggers associations with being awake and aroused. Treatment involves removing all stimuli that are potentially sleep-incompatible (reading and watching television) and excluding sleep from living areas. The individual is instructed to get up if not asleep within 15–20 min or when wakeful during the night or experiencing increasing distress.

Sleep-restriction therapy/bed-restriction therapy

Sleep restriction, also known as bed restriction (or sleep consolidation) relates to the ratio of time asleep with time spent in bed, and involves recording average nightly sleep duration (Spielman *et al.*, 1987). The name change is to reduce the emphasis on restricting sleep and to increase sleep time and quality by slowly reducing time in bed to match recorded sleep duration. This effective intervention induces natural sleepiness (reduced time in bed), and gives the individual a sense of assurance that bed is now a safe place to sleep.

Relaxation techniques

Relaxation methods include progressive relaxation, imagery training, biofeedback, meditation, hypnosis, and autogenic training, with little evidence to indicate superiority of any one approach. Patients are encouraged to practice relaxation techniques throughout the day and early evening. Even a few minutes two to four times a day is useful. A last-minute relaxation attempt a short time before sleep will not work miracles. Muscular tension and cognitive arousal (a "chattering mind") are incompatible with sleep. At the cognitive level, these techniques may act by distraction. Relaxation reduces physical and mental arousal but is less effective as a stand-alone treatment and is better used in combination with other treatment interventions.

Cognitive therapy

An important component of cognitive therapy is to help the client recognize how unhelpful and negative thinking about sleep increases physiological and psychological arousal levels. Setting aside 15–20 min in the early part of the evening to write down any worries, make plans for the following day, and to address any concerns that may be raised during the night allows the day to be put to rest. Challenging thoughts that appear at night with "I have already addressed this and now I can let go of it!" is helpful. "Time out" time is some form of soothing activity before bed and is useful in reducing arousal levels. Thought-stopping attempts or "blocking" techniques, such as repeating the word "the" every 3 seconds, occupy the short-term memory store (used in processing information), potentially allowing sleep to happen. Cognitive restructuring challenges unhelpful beliefs such as "if I don't get enough sleep tonight tomorrow is going to be a disaster," which maintain both wakefulness and helplessness. Another cognitive and behavioral technique is paradoxical intention. Clients are encouraged to put the effort into remaining awake rather than "trying" to fall asleep (decatastrophizing technique), strengthening the sleep drive, and reducing performance effort (Morin *et al.*, 2006).

Sleep hygiene education

There is limited evidence to suggest that, on its own, sleep hygiene is efficacious (Morin *et al.*, 2006). However, it is an essential component of CBT-i. and is a term used to "clean up" or improve an individual's sleep environment to promote better sleep quality and duration. It can be useful to provide a patient with a handout with these instructions/suggestions (see Table 17.2).

Mindfulness and insomnia

In recent years, the technique of mindfulness has become increasingly popular and is likely to be efficacious in helping to promote sleep by reducing cognitive and physiological arousal. Mindfulness treatment interventions have demonstrated statistically and clinically significant improvements in several nighttime symptoms of insomnia as well as reductions in presleep arousal, sleep effort, and dysfunctional sleep-related cognitions (Ong *et al.*, 2008). In many cases it is combined with CBT-i (Lundh, 2005; Ong & Scholtes, 2010; Ong *et al.*, 2008). As an adjunct to CBT-i, mindfulness can be used for psycho-education to help the client develop a more functional schematic model of sleep and dealing with sleeplessness, including the detrimental role of hyperarousal. Typically, the "chattering mind" is focused on past or future events, whereas mindfulness emphasizes being nonjudgmental in the present, which potentially can reduce mind activation.

Acceptance and commitment therapy and insomnia

Acceptance and commitment therapy (or ACT) has also grown in popularity yet no randomized controlled trials of its efficacy exist at present. The principles of acceptance and commitment therapy, however, could be useful in teaching people with insomnia to be more accepting of wakefulness or having a chattering mind. Lundh (2005) argues that acceptance and commitment therapy is an appropriate framework in which to conceptualize a client's insomnia and to help teach them about hyperarousal.

Drug therapy

Drug therapy is still the most common intervention for insomnia in Australia (Charles *et al.*, 2009). Historically benzodiazepine compounds superseded barbiturates and the most commonly used ones include nitrazepam and temazepam. Effective in the short term, these drugs are associated with long-term tolerance and withdrawal is often accompanied by relapse to hypnotic use (Sullivan & Guilleminault, 2009). Current hypnotic therapy includes so-called BzRAs (z drugs, such as Zolpidem and Imovane), which are thought to offer fewer adverse effects but the long-term effectiveness of which is less clear. More recently, melatonin receptor agonists (such as Ramelteon) (Rajaratnam *et al.*, 2008) have become available. Circadin (prolonged-release melatonin) has been suggested for an older age group with sleep maintenance difficulties. Increasingly (off-label) sedative antidepressants are used along with an anecdotal increase in the use of antipsychotic medications such as Seroquel. Melatonin, the pineal hormone, triggers sleep onset by lowering core body temperature and is a useful chronobiotic (changing timing of sleep) in delayed sleep-phase disorder. However, a careful assessment of the sleep/wake cycle and an objective estimation of minimum core body temperature occurrence is essential before melatonin is given. Without this information melatonin will not be effective and is likely to exacerbate the delay in sleep-onset times (Lewy, 2010). The use of natural products such as valerian has increased remarkably in the last 10 years. In a systematic review of valerian there are currently methodological problems in terms of standardized preparations and correct dosages for health and safety (Bent *et al.*, 2006).

Drug Therapy Over CBT-i?

Despite the evidence for the efficacy of CBT-i, in Australia at present most patients who consult their GP for insomnia will be prescribed benzodiazepines. In the Australian Bettering the Evaluation and Care of Health (BeAcH) program between April 2006 and March 2008, insomnia was the most common sleep disorder (occurring in eight out of 10 cases) managed by GPs with medication being prescribed for 95.2 per 100 insomnia problems (Charles *et al.*, 2009). Lower than average rates of advice/counselling were found and referral rates per 100 insomnia problems were considerably lower than the BeAcH average (0.8 versus 8.3). All health practitioners need to be aware of the efficacy of nonpharmacological approaches for managing insomnia, and the need for referral to specialists in the sleep field.

Educating Patients about Sleep and Biological Clock and Light/Dark Cycle

Educating the patient about sleep is an important aspect of treating insomnia: these are understanding what sleep is, how sleep changes with age, and what behaviors enable healthy sleep (reviewing all lifestyle factors including reducing caffeine and alcohol, etc.). Good objective information about sleep and sleep loss are helpful starting points for self-management.

Bright light is a potent marker for human circadian rhythm resetting of sleep times (evening light) in advanced sleep-phase syndrome and (morning light) delayed sleep-phase syndrome (Bjorvatn & Palleson, 2009). Sleep-initiation insomnia is improved with morning light and reduced evening light.

Exercise can positively influence sleep quality, particularly in the late afternoon or early evening (Stepanski & Wyatt, 2003). Morning exercise with light exposure suppresses melatonin and circadian rhythm is further enhanced by adhering to a constant waking time. Sunglasses or a hat with a brim should not be worn when out early. Sleeping in a safe environment includes minimizing disruption from external factors (e.g., heating, noise, violence) and internal factors relating to previous experiences.

Investigations: What to Look For and What to Ask as a Practitioner

Treatment of insomnia should include assessment for known extrinsic causes of certain sleep disorders and alcohol, stimulants, or proprietary drugs which interfere with sleep. Individuals need to be encouraged to seek advice early rather than to self-administer treatment. Avoiding the use of hypnotic agents would substantially reduce the number of iatrogenic cases of chronic insomnia. If patients who are seeking treatment for insomnia have already been commenced on hypnotic medication they can commence CBT-i and remain on medication and gradually withdraw from it. It has been reported in a study with three different groups – individuals receiving CBT-i, those taking medication, and those receiving a combination of CBT-i plus medication – that those in the third group had better sleep improvements in the long term, provided they had ceased medication after the sixth session of CBT-i (Morin *et al.*, 2009).

A thorough history incorporating questions regarding mood, lifestyle, restlessness, limb movements, and breathing is important. Monitoring with a sleep diary is a useful form of assessment in addition to questionnaires on beliefs and moods (Morin *et al.*, 2006). Wrist actigraphy estimates sleep/wakefulness based on body movement for 10 consecutive 24 h periods and can identify paradoxical insomnia, along with circadian anomalies. An overnight sleep study, known as a polysomnography is undertaken only when another sleep disorder or paradoxical insomnia is suspected.

Summary

Insomnia is complex and the disorder is usually chronic by the time the individual consults a health practitioner. A full assessment of the patient's physical and psychological wellbeing is necessary. Cognitive, behavioral, and social factors are usually involved in the onset and maintenance of insomnia. Ignored or untreated insomnia has a significant detrimental effect on quality of life and daytime function as well as increasing the likelihood of anxiety and depression. Treatment needs to focus on sleep parameters, mood, and perception of daytime function with the primary goal of increasing the individual's wellbeing.

References

Akerstedt, T., Fredlund, P., Gillberg, M., & Jansson, B. (2002). Work load and work hours in relation to disturbed sleep and fatigue in a large representative sample. *Journal of Psychosomatic Research, 53*, 585–588.

Akerstedt, T., Ingre, M., Broman, J. E., & Keckland, G. (2008). Disturbed sleep in shift workers, day workers and insomniacs. *Chronobiology International, 25*, 333–348.

American Academy of Sleep Medicine. (2005). *ICSD – International Classification of Sleep Disorders: Diagnostic and Coding Manual* (2nd edn.). Westchester, IL: American Academy of Sleep Medicine.

American Psychiatric Association. (2000). *Diagnostic and Statistical Manual of Mental Disorders* (4th edn, Text revision). Washington DC: American Psychiatric Association.

Azevado, M. H., Carvalho Bos, S., Joa O Soares, M., Marques, M., Telma Pereira, A., Maia, B. *et al.* (2010). Longitudinal study on perfectionism and sleep disturbance. *The World Journal of Biological Psychiatry, 11*, 476–485.

Backhaus, J., Junghanns, K., Born, J., Hohaus, K., Faasch, F., & Hohagen, F. (2006). Impaired declarative memory consolidation during sleep in patients with primary insomnia: Influence of sleep architecture and nocturnal cortisol release. *Biological Psychiatry, 60*, 1324–1330.

Bartlett, D. J., Marshall, N. S., Williams, A., & Grunstein, R. R. (2007). Sleep health New South Wales: Chronic sleep restriction and daytime sleepiness. *Internal Medicine Journal, 38*, 24–31.

Bartlett, D. J., Marshall, N. S., Williams, A., & Grunstein, R. R. (2008). Predictors of primary medical care consultations for sleep disorders. *Sleep Medicine, 9*, 857–864.

Bastien, C. H., Morin, C. M., Quellet, M.-C., Blais, F. C., & Bouchard, S. (2004). Cognitive-Behavioral Therapy for insomnia: Comparison of individual therapy, group therapy and telephone consultations. *Journal of Consulting and Clinical Psychology, 72*, 653–659.

Bent, S., Padula, A., Moore, D., Patterson, M., & Mehling, W. (2006). Valerian for sleep: A systematic review and meta-analysis. *American Journal of Medicine, 119*, 1005–1012.

Bjorvatn, B., & Palleson, S. (2009). A practical approach to circadian rhythm sleep disorders. *Sleep Medicine Reviews, 13*, 47–60.

Bonnet, M. H., & Arand, D. L. (1997). Hyperarousal and insomnia. *Sleep Medicine Reviews, 1*, 97–108.

Bonnet, M. H., & Arand, D. L. (1998). The consequences of a week of insomnia II: Patients with insomnia. *Sleep, 21*, 359–368.

Bootzin, R. R. (1972). Stimulus control treatment for insomnia. *Proceedings of the 80th Annual Convention of the American Psychological Association, 7*, 395–396.

Breslau, N., Roth, T., Rosenthal, L., & Andreski, P. (1996). Sleep disturbance and psychiatric disorders: A longitudinal epidemiological study of young adults. *Biological Psychiatry, 39*, 411–418.

Buckner, J. D., Bernert, R. A., Cromer, K. R., Joiner, T. E., & Schmidt, N. B, (2008). Social anxiety and insomnia: The mediating role of depressive symptoms. *Depression and Anxiety, 25*, 124–130.

Buysse, D. J., Ancoli-Israel, S., Edinger, J. D., Lichstein, K. L., & Morin, C. M. (2006). Recommendations for a standard research assessment of insomnia. *Sleep, 29*, 1155–1173.

Cain, S. W., Dennison, C. F., Zeitzer, J. M., Guzik, A. M., Khalsa, S. B. S., Santhi, N. *et al.* (2010). Sex differences in phase angle of entrainment and melatonin amplitude in humans. *Journal of Biological Rhythms, 25*, 288–296.

Chambers, M. J., & Keller, B. (1993). Alert inosmniacs: Are they areally sleep deprived? *Clinical Psychology Review, 13*, 649–666.

Charles, J., Harrison, C., & Britt, H. (2009). Insomnia. *Australian Family Physician, 38*, 283–283.

Currie, S. R., Wilson, K. G., Pontefract, A. J., & deLaplante, L. (2000). Cognitive-behavioral treatment of insomnia secondary to chronic pain. *Journal of Consulting and Clinical Psychology, 68*, 407–416.

Currie, S. R., Wilson, K. G., & Curran, D. (2002). Clinical significance and predictors of treatment response to cognitive behavioral treatment for insomnia secondary to chronic pain. *Journal of Behavorial Medicine, 25*, 135–153.

Edinger, J. D., Means, M. K., Stechuchak, K. M., & Olsen, M. K. (2004). A pilot study of inexpensive sleep-assessment devices. *Behavioral Sleep Medicine, 2*, 41–49.

Espie, C. A., MacMahon, K. M. A., Kelly, H.-L., Broomfield, N. M., Douglas, N. J., Engleman, H. M. *et al.* (2007). Randomised clinical effectiveness trial of nurse-administered small-group cognitive behavior therapy for persistent insomnia in general practice. *Sleep, 30*, 574–584.

Hale, L., Do, D. P., Basurto-Davila, R., Heron, M., Finch, B. K., Dubowitz, T. *et al.* (2009). Does mental health history explain gender disparities in insomnia symptoms among young adults. *Sleep Medicine, 10*, 1118–1123.

Harvey, A. G. (2002). A cognitive model of insomnia. *Behaviour Research and Therapy, 40*, 869–893.

Hauri, P. J. (1982). *The Sleep Disorders*. Michigan: Upjohn.

Irwin, M. R., Cole, J. C., & Nicassio, P. M. (2006). Comparative meta-analysis of behavioral interventions for insomnia and their efficacy in middle aged adults and in older adults aged 55+ years of age. *Health Psychology, 25*, 3–14.

Jansson-Frojmark, M., & Lindblom, K. (2008). A bidirectional relationship between anxiety and depression, and insomnia? A prospective study in the general population. *Journal of Psychosomatic Research, 64*, 443–449.

Johns, M. W. (1991). A new method for measuring daytime sleepiness: The Epworth sleepiness scale. *Sleep, 14*, 540–545.

Katz, D. A., & McHorney, C. A. (1998). Clinical correlates of insomnia in patients with chronic illness. *Archives of Internal Medicine, 158*, 1099–1107.

Kecklund, G., & Akersted, T. (2004). Apprehension of the subsequent working day is associated with a low amount of slow wave sleep. *Biological Psychiatry, 66*, 169–176.

Lacks, P., & Morin, C. (1992). Recent advances in the assessment and treatment of insomnia. *Journal of Consulting and Clinical Psychology, 60*, 586–594.

Leger, D., & Bayon, V. (2010). Societal costs of insomnia. *Sleep Medicine Reviews, 14*, 379–389.

Leprin, J., & Briley, M. (2004). The epidemiology of pain in depression. *Human Psychopharmacology, 19*, S3–S7.

Lewy, A. (2010). Clinical implications of the melatonin phase response curve. The *Journal of Clininical Endocrinology and Metabolism, 95*, 3158–3160.

Lichstein, K. L., Wilson, N. M., & Johnson, C. T. (2000). Psychological treatment of secondary insomnia. *Psychology and Aging, 15*, 232–240.

Louie, G. H., Tektonidou, M. G., Caban-Martinez, A. J., & Ward, M. (2011). Sleep disturbances in adults with arthritis: Prevalence, mediators and subgroups at greatest risk. Data from the 2007 National Health Interview Survey. *Arthritis Care & Research, 63*, 247–260.

Lundh, L. (2005). The role of acceptance and mindfulness in the treatment of insomnia. *Journal of Cognitive Psychotherapy, 19*, 29–31.

Manber, R., Edinger, J. D., Gress, J. L., San Pedro-Salcedo, M. G., Kuo, T. F., & Kalista, T. (2008). Cognitive behavioral therapy for insomia enhances depression outcomes in patients with comorbid major depressive disorder and insomnia. *Sleep, 31*, 489–495.

Morin, C. M., & Espie, C. A. (2003). *Insomnia: A Clinical Guide to Assessment and Treatment.* New York: Kluwer Academic.

Morin, C. M., Culbert, J. P., & Schwartz, S. M. (1994). Nonpharmocological interventions for insomnia: A meta-analysis of treatment and efficacy. *The American Journal of Psychiatry, 151*, 1172–1180.

Morin, C. M., Hauri, P., Espie, C. A., Spielman, A. J., Buysse, D. J., & Bootzin, R. R. (1999). Nonpharmacologic treatment of chronic insomnia. *Sleep, 22*, 1134–1156.

Morin, C. M., Beaulieu-Bonneau, S., Le Blanc, M., & Savard, J. (2005). Self help treatment for insomnia: A randomized controlled trial. *Sleep, 28*, 1319–1327.

Morin, C. M., Bootzin, R. R., Buysse, D. J., Edinger, J. D., Espie, C. A., & Lichstein, K. L. (2006). Psychological and behavioral treatment of insomnia: Update of the recent evidence (1998–2004). *Sleep, 29*, 1398–1414.

Morin, C., Vallières, A., Guay, B., Ivers, H., Savard, J., Merette, C. *et al.* (2009). Cognitive behavioral therapy, singly and combined with medication, for persistent insomnia: A randomized controlled trial. *JAMA, 301*, 2005–2015.

Murtagh, D. R., & Greenwood, K. M. (1995). Identifying effective psychologcial treatments for insomnia: A meta-analysis of treatment efficacy. *Journal of Consulting and Clinical Psychology, 63*, 79–89.

Nierenberg, A. A., Husain, M. M., Trivedi, M. H., Fava, M., Warden, D., Wisniewski, S. R. *et al.* (2010). Residual symptoms after remission of major depressive disorder with citalopram and risk of relapse: A STARD report. *Psychological Medicine, 40*, 41–50.

Ohayon, M. M. (2002). Epidemiology of insomnia: What we know and what we still need to learn. *Sleep Medicine Reviews, 6*, 97–111.

Ohayon, M. M. (2010). Nocturnal awakenings and difficulty resuming sleep: Their burden in the European general population. *Journal of Psychsomatic Research, 69*, 565–571.

Ohayon, M. M., & Shapiro, C. M. (2002). Tenses of insomnia epidemiology. *Journal of Psychosomatic Research, 53*, 525–527.

Ong, J., & Scholtes, D. (2010). A mindfulness-based approach to the treatment of insomnia. *Journal of Clinical Psychology, 66*, 1175–1184.

Ong, J. C., Shapiro, C. M., & Manber, R. (2008). Combining mindfulness meditation with cognitive behavior therapy for insomnia: A treatment development study. *Behavior Therapy, 39*, 171–182.

Rajaratnam, S. M. W., Polymeropoulos, M. H., Fisher, D. M., Roth, T., Scott, C., Birznieks, G., & Klerman, E. B. (2008). Melatonin agonist tasimelteon (VEC-162) for transient insomnia after sleep-time shift: Two randomised controlled multicentre trials. *The Lancet, 6736*, 61812–61817.

Reidel, B. W., & Lichstein, K. L. (2000). Insomnia and daytime functioning. *Sleep Medicine Reviews, 4*, 277–298.

Riemann, D., & Voderholzer, U. (2003). Primary insomnia: A risk factor to develop depression? *Journal of Affective Disorders, 76*, 255–259.

Siebern, A. T., & Manber, R. (2011). Insomnia and its effective non pharmacologic treatment. *Medical Clinics of North America, 94,* 581–591.

Simon, G., & VonKorff, M. (1997). Prevalence, burden and treatment of insomnia in primary care. *American Journal of Psychiatry, 154,* 1417–1423.

Siversten, B., Omvik, S., Pallesen, S., Bjorvatn, B., Havik, O. E., Kvale, G. *et al.* (2006). Cognitive behavioral therapy vs Zopicone for treatment of chronic primary insomnia in older adults. *JAMA, 295,* 2851–2858.

Siversten, B., Krokstad, S., Overland, S., & Mykletun, A. (2009). The epidemiology of insomnia: Associations with physical and mental health. The HUNT-2 study. *Journal of Psychosomatic Research, 67,* 109–116.

Smith, M. T., Perlis, M. L., Park, A., Smith, M. S., Pennington, J. M., Giles, D. E., & Buysse, D. J. (2002). Comparative meta-analysis of pharmacotherapy and behavior therapy for persistent insomnia. *American Journal of Psychiatry, 159,* 5–11.

Spielman, A. J., Saskin, P., & Thorpy, M. J. (1987). Treatment of chronic insomnia by restriction of time in bed. *Sleep, 10,* 45–56.

Stepanski, E. J., & Wyatt, J. K. (2003). Use of sleep hygiene in the treatment of insomnia. *Sleep Medicine Reviews, 7,* 215–225.

Sullivan, S., & Guilleminault, C. (2009). Emerging drugs for insomnia: New frontiers for old and novel targets. *Expert Opinion on Emerging Drugs, 14,* 411–422.

Verbeek, I. H., Konings, G. M., Aldenkamp, A. P., Declerek, A. C., & Klip, E. C. (2006). Cognitive behavioral treatment in clinically referred chronic insomniacs: Group vs individual treatment. *Behavior Sleep Medicine, 4,* 135–151.

Vgontzas, A. N., Bixler, E. O., Lin, H.-M., Prolo, P., Mastorakos, G., Vela-Bueno, A. *et al.* (2001). Chronic insomnia is associated with nyctohemeral activation of the hypothalamic-pituitary-adrenal axis: Clinical implications. *Journal of Clinical Endocrinology and Metabolism, 86,* 3787–3794.

Vitiello, M. V., Moe, K. E., & Prinz, P. N. (2002). Sleep complaints cosegregate with illness in older adults: Clinical research informed by and informing epidemiological studies of sleep. *Journal of Psychosomatic Research, 53,* 555–559.

Zender, R., & Olshansky, E. (2009). Promoting wellness in women across the life span. *Nursing Clinics of North America, 44,* 281–291.

18

Living with a Craniofacial Condition

Rachel M. Roberts and Jane L. Mathias

Craniofacial conditions result from a wide range of congenital deformities that affect the growth of the head and facial bones. Approximately one in 500 Australians are affected by a craniofacial condition, the most common being a cleft lip and/or palate, which affects around one in 750 newborn children (Tolarova & Cervenka, 1998). This rate is comparable to that seen in other westernized countries (Mastroiacova & International Perinatal Database of Typical Oral Clefts Working Group, 2011). Other conditions that affect craniofacial development are relatively rare, but together are estimated to occur at the rate of one in every 1600 newborn babies (World Health Organization, 2003).

Children with craniofacial conditions often experience one or more of a range of associated physical and cognitive complications, including problems with dental development and feeding, chronic ear infections and hearing problems, respiratory difficulties, and speech, language, and learning problems. While surgical treatments are often able to reduce both the functional and appearance-related effects of these conditions, many adults experience ongoing functional problems and permanent differences in appearance (Chuo *et al.*, 2008).

This chapter is designed to assist psychologists working with people with craniofacial conditions by critically reviewing the existing research on the psychosocial and cognitive functioning of children and adults with craniofacial conditions, with an emphasis on recent Australian research. It begins by providing some background information about craniofacial conditions that psychologists who are working in this area need to be familiar with, and concludes with evidence-based recommendations for the treatment and prevention of the psychological problems that are identified.

Applied Topics in Health Psychology, First Edition. Edited by M. L. Caltabiano and L. Ricciardelli.

Case Study: Tom

Tom, now in his 20s, was born with hemifacial microsomia, a condition in which one side of the face is smaller than the other. In Tom's case, the left half of his face was smaller, resulting in a malformed left ear and left-sided deafness. He required speech therapy and experienced some learning problems at school. Tom had eight operations to manage his condition throughout his childhood and adolescence, with his final surgery taking place at the age of 19.

He has also had multiple other clinical appointments and orthodontic treatments throughout his life. Now his appearance is normal, except for his reconstructed left ear, which is still visibly different. He reflects on his experience by saying, "as I get older it doesn't bother me as much" and "it has made me realise more that everyone is different. What matters is what's on the inside. Also there are people out there worser [*sic*] off and I should be thankful for who I am and my family. I don't judge people on how they look. I treat people how I want to be treated."

Craniofacial Conditions

There are a wide variety of congenital conditions that can affect the head and face, causing disfigurements that can be partially or totally resolved using surgical procedures. The etiology of these conditions is not well understood but is likely to be multifactorial, with both genetic and intrauterine environmental factors, such as maternal cigarette smoking, alcohol use, and nutrition during pregnancy, contributing to their development (Cobourne, 2004; Cunningham *et al.*, 2007). The most common condition is that of a cleft lip and/or palate (Tolarova & Cervenka, 1998). A cleft lip involves cleft(s) of the upper lip due to failure of the two sides of the upper lip and nose to fuse during development, while a cleft palate involves a fissure in the midline of the roof of the mouth where the two sides of the palate fail to join normally (Mosby, 2009). Children may have clefts of the lip, the palate, or both. The second most common congenital craniofacial anomaly is hemifacial microsomia, which involves an underdeveloped jaw, a lateral cleft-like extension of the corner of the mouth, and ear anomalies, and is asymmetric (Jones, 2006). Numerous other craniofacial conditions exist, the most common of which are summarized in Table 18.1.

As is evident from these descriptions, craniofacial conditions affect the appearance of the head and face in many different ways. In addition, these conditions may also be associated with abnormal development of the brain, resulting in cognitive impairments, as well as impacting on the development of sensory functions as a result of abnormal eye and ear development. Abnormal development of the face can also result in problems with speech, eating, and breathing.

People with craniofacial conditions share the experience of having a congenital, low-incidence condition that is likely to affect both appearance and function (e.g., hearing impairment), and of having received significant medical and surgical treatments throughout an extended part of their lives. For example, a review of adults who had completed treatment for their cleft lip and palate found that the number of surgeries that were required ranged from three to 12 (Schnitt *et al.*, 2004). They also usually undergo long-term treatments with multidisciplinary teams in tertiary hospitals. Numerous medical investigations, clinical appointments, assessments, orthodontic treatments, and operations are usually required to manage all of these conditions, with final

Table 18.1 Summary description of some of the most common craniofacial syndromes

Syndrome	Description
Crouzon syndrome	A congenital genetic abnormality involving the appearance of prominent eyes due to shallow orbits, frontal bossing (rounded prominent forehead), undergrowth of the upper jaw, and premature fusion of the sutures (Jones, 2006).
Coronal synostosis	The premature fusion of the coronal suture (the lines of junction between the bones of the skull), resulting in an abnormally tall, wide head (David *et al.*, 1987).
Binder syndrome	A condition involving a flat midface with poorly developed cheek bones and a flattened nose (David *et al.*, 1987).
Treacher Collins syndrome	A congenital genetic anomaly involving bilateral facial clefts. The appearance is of notching of the lower eyelids with slanted eyelids, a small lower jaw, and flattening of the cheek bones (Magalini & Magalini, 1997).
Apert syndrome	A genetic condition involving a short anteroposterior diameter with a high, full forehead and flat back of the head, premature fusion of the cranial sutures, flat face, shallow orbits, wide space between the eyes, narrow palate, and complex syndactyly (fusion) of the hands and feet (Jones, 2006).
Saethre–Chotzen syndrome	A condition involving disturbances of cranial development including premature fusion of the coronal, lambdoid, and/or metopic sutures, a high, flat forehead, low frontal hairline, small ears, shallow orbits, wide spaces between eyes, and partial fusion of the soft tissue of the fingers and toes (Jones, 2006).
Waardenberg syndrome	A condition involving the inner angles of the eyes being widely spaced, thick eyebrows, broad root of the nose, and hearing impairment (David *et al.*, 1987).
Goldenhar syndrome	A congenital anomaly involving underdevelopment of the jaw, a lateral cleft-like extension of the corner of the mouth, and a small ear; which tends to be asymmetric (Jones, 2006).
Oro-facial-digital syndrome	A syndrome that causes changes in the oral structures, including the teeth and jaw; the facial structures, including the head, eyes, and nose; and the fingers and toes (Mosby, 2009).

surgery often only undertaken when facial development is complete in late adolescence or early adulthood (see Schnitt *et al.*, 2004 for a protocol for the management of cleft lip and palate). However, some adults continue to require healthcare throughout their lives as a result of the craniofacial condition (Chuo *et al.*, 2008). These experiences combine to make living with a craniofacial condition a long-term challenge.

What are the challenges of living with a craniofacial condition?

Given both the focus on physical appearance in Western cultures and the importance of the face in communication, it might be expected that children and adults who are living with a condition that affects facial appearance would experience particular challenges. Existing research has identified a number of such challenges, including teasing, staring, low self-esteem, and learning difficulties (Rumsey & Harcourt, 2005).

With this in mind, a recent Australian qualitative study examined the experiences of children and adolescents with congenital craniofacial conditions from both the child's and parent's perspectives (Roberts & Shute, 2010). Interview data from both parties revealed that children with craniofacial conditions frequently experience negative responses from others to their appearance, such as *teasing* and *staring*. These were commonly reported stressors, although far from universal, with interviews revealing many examples of being teased, such as name-calling and being laughed at or made fun of. For example, the mother of a 16 year-old girl with a cystic hygroma (large cystic mass) on the face and neck reported that when her daughter was younger "there was a lot of teasing and a lot of 'big chin' and stuff like that," and an 8 year-old boy with Apert syndrome recalled how "with other kids, they call me like weird names, like fish head 'cos of my eyes" (Roberts & Shute, 2010, p. 7). Interestingly, this contrasts with the findings of an earlier Australian study, which compared self-reports of teasing among children with craniofacial conditions to that of a healthy control group and found that children with craniofacial conditions were not being teased any more (or less) frequently than their peers (Carroll & Shute, 2005). While Roberts and Shute (2010) reported that parents gave examples of their child being teased, many parents also commented that teasing is likely to be experienced by children for a variety of reasons, highlighting the need to support all children in the development of effective responses to teasing and the potential risk of misattributing teasing to the craniofacial condition, rather than to a more general societal problem.

Similar issues have been described in a US qualitative study with adolescents with Treacher Collins syndrome (Beaune *et al.*, 2004), a syndrome that leads to the abnormal development of the eyes, cheeks, ears and lower jaw (Magalini & Magalini, 1997). These adolescents reported being treated as different or special by others and experiencing problems with making friends.

The available research also suggests that these issues continue to cause problems for adults. Lanigan and Cotterill (1989), for example, examined the questionnaire responses of adults with port wine stains and noted that many respondents (75%) reported that people stare at them or that they had been hurt by others' comments about their condition (73%).

The examination of the impact of craniofacial conditions on the development of *self-concept* has revealed mixed findings. While difficulties with how children felt about their own appearance were described as a problem by both parents and children in the Roberts and Shute (2010) study, quantitative work has found minimal or no differences between groups with craniofacial conditions and their peers (Endringa & Kapp-Simon, 1999). Moreover, recent Australian work has found better self-esteem among adults with craniofacial conditions (Roberts & Mathias, 2011b), which contrasts with an earlier study that reported lower self-esteem in adults with craniofacial conditions (Sarwer *et al.*, 1999).

The persistent and distressing nature of these concerns is illustrated by responses to a recent Australian study examining the impact of living with a craniofacial condition (Roberts & Mathias, 2011a) in which a 19 year-old woman with oro-facial-digital syndrome wrote, "I feel very alone, very shy and I am not self-confident at all. I am very hard on myself. I never feel beautiful and I am always ready for someone to comment on my appearance" (p. 5).

The *cognitive impairments* that are related to the craniofacial condition (e.g., learning diffi- culties) have also been described as significant stressors by children and adults (Roberts & Shute, 2010). In fact, it is estimated that nearly half of all craniofacial conditions are associated with cognitive deficits, making this a significant issue for many (Gorlin *et al.*, 1990).

Finally, the *treatment* itself (e.g., painful surgical procedures) has been identified as a source of stress (Roberts & Shute, 2010). The regular clinic visits, which serve as a reminder of the condition, and anxiety about surgery and its outcomes, have been described by Rumsey and Harcourt (2005) as contributing to this stress.

People with craniofacial conditions therefore clearly contend with a number of potential challenges in their lives. However, the experience is not always a negative one.

Positive aspects of living with a craniofacial condition

When examining the growing field of positive psychology, Aspinwall and Staudinger (2003) discussed the human strength that is evident when people draw on the positive aspects of their lives to better manage the negative aspects. As such, it might be expected that adults and children with craniofacial conditions would also be able to describe some positive aspects of their life that they attribute to their condition.

Indeed, the stressors identified by the children and adolescents in the Roberts and Shute (2010) study were balanced against several positive aspects of living with a craniofacial condition, including the development of positive personal qualities, such as kindness and determination. Parents and children both reported personal experiences that resulted in them having an increased understanding of the problems that are experienced by people with other disabilities or differences. This translated to children with craniofacial conditions deliberately choosing not to tease other children, trying not to be prejudiced toward others, having a well-developed understanding of others' feelings, and being more compassionate, tolerant, or empathic than they might otherwise have been. This is illustrated by the example of a 15 year-old boy who spoke of his friends judging girls by appearance alone. He described himself as being more sensitive than his friends, stating:

> I don't judge people 'cos I'm no one to judge. I really don't criticize many people. One of my mates especially, he's really, he's pretty top stuff and he judges, she's pretty ugly or whatever, and I'm like, well man, you don't know her. I like to get to know people and I don't know if I'd be like that if I hadn't had this and stuff. If I hadn't been through so much, to know what it's like. (Roberts and Shute, 2010, p. 11)

Similar positive themes were described in the aforementioned qualitative study of adolescents with Treacher Collins syndrome, including enjoying being unique, being optimistic about life, receiving more help from others (e.g., learning support), and being motivated to excel in other areas, such as sport or school (Beaune *et al.*, 2004). These positive outcomes are also evident in overseas studies of adults with a range of craniofacial conditions (e.g., Cochrane & Slade, 1999; Eiserman, 2001; Meyerson, 2001). For example, Eiserman's (2001) interviews with adults revealed positive outcomes in a number of areas, including greater sensitivity toward others, the ability to move on in the face of challenges, the ability to help others, an acceptance of life's challenges, more gratitude for the little things in life, and a greater self-determination and sense of purpose in life. Comparable findings have been reported in Australian research in which adults with craniofacial conditions were asked about the impact of their condition on their lives (Roberts & Mathias, 2011b). For example, the 19 year-old woman, quoted above, when describing the positive impact of living with her oro-facial-digital syndrome, also wrote, "In my opinion it has made me a more tolerant person and a more sensitive person. I really like my personality and I don't believe it would be how it is if I didn't have a craniofacial condition" (Roberts & Mathias, 2011a, p. 6).

Given both the challenges and the positive aspects of living with a craniofacial condition, it is important to consider the impact that this has for a person's psychological wellbeing by reviewing research with children and adolescents, and with adults.

Psychological wellbeing in childhood and adolescence

Research indicates that during childhood and adolescence the presence of a craniofacial condition increases the likelihood of a young person experiencing psychological problems (Endringa & Kapp-Simon, 1999), most commonly in the areas of shyness, social withdrawal, social competence, and behavior (Rumsey & Harcourt, 2005). In a unique study by Kapp-Simon and McGuire (1997), the social interactions of adolescents with a craniofacial condition were observed in a natural environment. Adolescents with craniofacial conditions were more often found at the periphery of the group and tended to be observers rather than participants in conversations when compared with their peers, providing additional evidence for the increased risk of problems with social interactions.

Australian research supports these findings, reporting a relatively high incidence of adjustment difficulties, particularly in the area of social problems, as assessed by both parents and children (Child Behaviour Checklist and Youth Self Report; Achenbach & Rescorla, 2001; Roberts & Shute, 2012). Similarly, a qualitative study by Roberts and Shute (2010), which examined the impact of a craniofacial condition, found that both children and their parents frequently described problems with social acceptance. Specifically, they encountered problems with being accepted by others, making and keeping friends, and not being invited to spend time with their peers or to attend social occasions. For example, the mother of a 10 year-old girl explained that "She's hardly got any friends. When she goes to school they won't play with her. They just ignore her. If there's games they won't include her. No one picks her in the class for anything. It's like they just don't want to have anything to do with her" (Roberts and Shute, 2010, p. 6).

Psychological wellbeing in adulthood

The psychosocial outcomes of *adults* with congenital craniofacial conditions, on the other hand, are less well understood as there has been less research in this area. Among the problems reported by adults with cleft lip and/or palate are emotional problems, including elevated levels of social anxiety and social avoidance (Berk *et al.*, 2001). Adults with cleft lip and palate have also reported higher levels of depression and anxiety than their healthy peers, with these problems being associated with appearance-related concerns (Ramstad *et al.*, 1995). Similarly, certain aspects of quality of life, such as perceived meaningfulness of life and family life, are also reportedly worse in adults with cleft lip and palate (Marcusson *et al.*, 2001), with a recent study reporting that mental-health-related quality of life was lower in a group of adults with cleft lip and palate compared with their peers (Mani *et al.*, 2010).

Moreover, a study with adults who had been treated as children for either of two craniofacial conditions (hemifacial microsomia or orbital hypertelorism, in which the eyes are very widely spaced) reported lower levels of self-esteem, less satisfaction with their facial appearance, and poorer quality of life compared with adults seen in the same hospital with minor conditions, such as moles or other facial lesions requiring removal (Sarwer *et al.*, 1999). These findings suggest that, like children, adults with craniofacial conditions are at an increased risk of developing problems.

Recent Australian work with adults who were born with a range of craniofacial conditions has additionally found that they were living in areas of higher socioeconomic status, and were more likely to have completed secondary schooling and to have higher levels of postsecondary school education than their healthy peers (Roberts & Mathias, 2011a). Possibly related to their higher level of education, they were also less likely to report their occupation as being "home duties" than the general population. Moreover, compared with the general population, adults with craniofacial conditions were less likely to be married and more likely to be receiving a disability or other type of pension, and females were less likely to have children. Appearance-related concerns were reported more frequently and mental-health-related quality of life was lower, as were perceived levels of social support from their friends.

Importantly, there were many areas of functioning where there were no differences between adults with craniofacial conditions and the general population, including occupational status, levels of unemployment, and several measures of psychosocial functioning; namely anxiety, depression, social anxiety, satisfaction with life, and perceived levels of social support from family and a significant other (Roberts & Mathias, 2011a). These findings may reflect the resilience of this population due to the psychosocial support provided to participants by their treating craniofacial unit and other professional agencies, and their families and communities, as well as the individual's own ability to draw upon the positive aspects of living with a craniofacial condition. Overall, this Australian study provides additional evidence from a large sample to suggest that adults with a variety of craniofacial conditions experience numerous positive outcomes that may help offset some of the aforementioned negative consequences. However, further work in this area is still needed, particularly research that is less reliant on the use of normative data and, instead, compares the outcomes of persons with craniofacial conditions to those of matched control groups.

Moreover, psychological wellbeing is not the only aspect of people's lives that needs to be considered. The impact of craniofacial conditions on cognitive development is another important consideration for psychologists in their work with this group, both in terms of assessing and monitoring cognitive development, and in ensuring psychological interventions are tailored to the client's level of cognitive development.

Cognitive functioning

There has been limited research, to date, examining the cognitive functioning of either children or adults with craniofacial conditions, with the exception of cleft lip and palate, largely due to the low incidence of each of these conditions. A recent meta-analysis examined the cognitive functioning of infants, children, and adults with cleft lip, cleft palate, or cleft lip and palate in order to establish both the nature and severity of cognitive impairments that are associated with nonsyndromal clefts (cleft conditions that are not part of a syndrome involving a range of other malformations) when compared to their healthy peers (Roberts *et al.*, 2010). A comprehensive search of the literature identified 27 studies that compared the cognitive functioning of participants with cleft lip and/or palate to that of a community control group. Cohen's *d* effect sizes were calculated to estimate the magnitude of the cognitive impairments, independently of sample size, where a *d* value of 0.2, 0.5, and 0.8 reflected small, medium, and large impairments, respectively. The presence of a cleft was associated with poorer cognitive performance, particularly in the areas of processing speed ($d_w = -0.75$), attention/executive functioning ($d_w = -0.71$), language ($d_w = -0.59$), and memory (immediate recall; $d_w = -0.52^*$) (* indicates a statistically significant effect). More modest deficits were also apparent in academic ability ($d_w = -0.47$), sensorimotor ($d_w = -0.47^*$) and motor ($d_w = -0.42^*$) functions, general cognition ($d_w = -0.37$), memory (delayed recall; $d_w = -0.31$), and visuospatial ability ($d_w = -0.10$). These findings indicate that cleft lip and/or palate is associated with sizeable cognitive impairments across a wide range of cognitive functions.

More research is required to establish the impact of other craniofacial conditions on cognitive functioning; however, existing research suggests that many of these other conditions are also associated with cognitive impairments, although the patterns of impairment have not yet been established. For example, Apert syndrome is associated with high rates of intellectual disability

(Cohen & Kreiborg, 1990). Moreover, single-suture craniosynostosis, which is caused by premature fusing of the cranial sutures (junction between the bones of the skull), is associated with high rates of learning and language disorders (Speltz *et al.*, 2004).

Although the research literature provides general guidance about the likelihood of people with particular craniofacial conditions experiencing cognitive impairments, there is considerable variability in cognitive outcomes, even within the same condition. As such, clinicians need to consider their client's level of cognitive functioning and the potential for this to contribute to the psychosocial outcomes of these clients.

Predictors of psychosocial functioning

Recently there has been an increased interest in identifying the factors that help to predict the psychosocial outcomes of people with craniofacial conditions, with research suggesting that a person's satisfaction with their appearance (Billaud Feragen *et al.*, 2009) and levels of social anxiety and perceived social support (Shute *et al.*, 2007) are important contributing factors. While interesting and useful, much of this research has failed to adopt a theoretical model to guide the research or build our understanding of the variables that contribute to the psychosocial outcome of people born with craniofacial conditions.

A variety of models of the determinants of health-related outcomes for people with chronic illness and disability have been proposed over the years. These models are designed to improve our ability to predict the psychosocial outcomes of persons with various disabilities and provide a theoretical basis for the development of interventions to improve their outcomes. One such model is that of Moos and Holahan (2007) who have proposed that personal resources (e.g., self-esteem and demographic characteristics), condition-related factors (e.g., severity of the condition), social and physical context (including social support), cognitive appraisal, adaptive responses (such as managing treatment), and coping skills collectively contribute to a person's health and wellbeing. Alternatively, Rumsey and Harcourt (2005) have proposed a model that specifically focuses on understanding the outcomes of people with disfigurements. While some of the variables that these authors identify overlap with those of Moos and Holahan (e.g., demographic, peer, family, and societal influences), their model has a greater focus on the intervening role of cognitive processes, including self-perceptions, social comparisons, and appearance-related beliefs on outcomes. Neither model explicitly considers a person's level of cognitive functioning.

Certain aspects of both of these models have been examined in adults with cleft lip and/or palate (e.g., Cochrane & Slade, 1999). However, the variables that are predictive of psychosocial outcomes in the broader group of adults with craniofacial conditions remain poorly understood; a likely contributor to the paucity of evidence-based interventions for this population (Rumsey & Harcourt, 2005).

A recent Australian study of the psychosocial outcomes of adults with noncleft craniofacial conditions (Roberts & Mathias, 2012) used the aforementioned two models as a basis for selecting potential predictor variables, which included self-esteem, appearance-related concerns, social support, fear of negative evaluation, satisfaction with facial appearance, and demographic variables. Psychosocial outcome was assessed using measures of anxiety, depression, and quality of life. This study found that mental-health-related quality of life was better in people with higher levels of perceived social support, higher levels of self-esteem, and fewer appearance-related concerns. Anxiety levels were lower in people who had higher levels of perceived social support, better self-esteem, and fewer fears of being evaluated negatively. Depression was lower in people who had higher levels of perceived social support and self-esteem. Interestingly, satisfaction with facial appearance, age, gender, education, and social disadvantage were *not* related to psychosocial outcome (anxiety, depression, quality of life). These findings identify some potential targets for both interventions that may improve the psychosocial wellbeing of adults with craniofacial conditions and earlier interventions with adolescents to prevent or minimize the potential negative effects of having a craniofacial condition. Specifically, interventions that focus on increasing perceived social support and self-esteem, and reducing fear of negative evaluation and concerns with appearance, are all indicated on the basis of this research.

Interventions

The potential exists for psychologists to provide a range of early interventions that are designed to prevent or reduce the likelihood of children, adolescents, and adults with craniofacial conditions developing psychological problems, as well as providing individual or group interventions to treat any psychological problems these individuals may have developed. There is a clear need for psychologists to be core members of healthcare teams that work with people with craniofacial conditions and this is now recognized in the treatment protocols that have been developed for use in both North America and Europe. In particular, the Standards for Approval of Cleft Palate and Craniofacial Teams that have been developed by the the American Cleft Palate-Craniofacial Association and Cleft Palate Foundation (2010) identify psychological services as an essential component of care. This includes initial and periodic assessments of the psychological needs of patients and their families, assessments of cognitive development and learning disabilities in children and adolescents, and the use of psychological interventions to address the needs of both patients and families. Similarly, European practice guidelines state that emotional support and professional advice should be provided to parents, patients, and all other relevant persons (Shaw *et al.*, 2001). Moreover, the Craniofacial Society of Great Britain and Ireland (2005) provides specific recommendations for the timing of psychological assessments for people with cleft lip and palate; these being at 0–6 weeks, 18 months, and at 5, 10, 15, and 18 years of age, although the reasons for choosing these particular ages are not given. Unfortunately, despite the existence of these standards, it has been estimated that only 20% of cleft teams worldwide carry out any form of psychological assessment (Turner *et al.*, 1998), highlighting a very large unmet need.

In addition, there is currently only a small evidence-base upon which psychologists can draw when working with this population (for a review of interventions see Bessell & Moss, 2007). The aforementioned study by Roberts and Mathias (2012) is useful from this perspective, as it serves to identify some potential targets for interventions. As noted above, interventions that focus on increasing people's perceived social support and self-esteem, and reducing their fear of negative evaluation and concerns with appearance, are indicated. While social support is one possible area for intervention, Smith *et al.* (1994) have previously suggested that a good understanding of an individual's social support needs and his/her existing social support structure is necessary, prior to implementing an intervention, as some forms of social support can be seen as negative (e.g., viewed as an invasion of privacy or overdependence). Therefore, a focus on social skills training may be a more useful alternative.

To date, the social skills training and cognitive-behavioral interventions described below have shown some promise in this clinical context (Bessell & Moss, 2007). In addition, the field of positive psychology highlights the possibility of supporting people with craniofacial conditions in order to "thrive," rather than focusing solely on those with psychological problems. In a review of adjustment to chronic illness, de Ridder *et al.* (2008) suggested that interventions that support participants to focus on potential positive outcomes of their condition result in improved outcomes.

Further, they suggest that cognitive-behavioral therapy, which includes encouragement to identify advantages and strategies to promote realistic but optimistic thinking about the chronic condition, has the potential to result in better levels of adjustment.

Social skills training

Recent research has shown that when youths with a craniofacial condition adopted a set of positive social skills, such as making good eye contact, initiating social interactions, and explaining their craniofacial condition to others, rather than negative social skills, such as confrontation and distancing themselves, other people's perceptions of them were more positive (Edwards *et al.*, 2011). Thus, it appears that the development and promotion of positive social skills in people with craniofacial conditions may be effective in reducing the negative perceptions of others.

There have also been promising initial reports of interventions that are designed to improve the social skills of adolescents with conditions affecting facial appearance. For example, a study by Kapp-Simon *et al.* (2005) reported that adolescents with a range of facially disfiguring conditions demonstrated increased levels of social interaction with their peers after 12 group sessions of social skills training. This program taught a variety of skills, such as attending skills (nonverbal communication, including eye contact and posture to show interest in others), self-awareness, social initiation and conversation, responding to uncomfortable questions and stares, anxiety management, and conflict resolution. Similarly, positive findings have been reported for social skills training delivered in a small-group residential setting for adolescents with facial differences caused by burns (Blakeney *et al.*, 2005). This intervention was based on a social skills training program that has also been shown to effectively reduce social anxiety in adults with craniofacial conditions (Robinson *et al.*, 1996).

Cognitive-behavioral interventions

Cognitive-behavioral interventions have also been used with people who have a range of disfiguring conditions and, although the existing research suggests these interventions are promising, the efficacy of these interventions when used with people who have craniofacial conditions has not yet been comprehensively evaluated (Bessell & Moss, 2007; Kish & Lansdown, 2000). Based on research with adults who are dissatisfied with their appearance, Liossi (2003) recommends that cognitive-behavioral interventions should include components that address the following issues: appearance schemas (cognitive generalizations about the importance, meaning, and effects of appearance in a person's life; Cash & Labarge, 1996), negative thoughts about body image, cognitive errors in evaluating appearance, unhelpful behavioral strategies, and psychological distress about appearance.

Several studies have reported interventions based on these components with adults with conditions affecting appearance. Papadopoulos *et al.* (1999) evaluated the effects of eight 1-hour cognitive behavior therapy sessions provided to adults with a condition affecting the appearance of their skin, called vitiligo (a progressive skin condition in which pigment is lost, resulting in white patches over the skin surface). These sessions included cognitive-behavioral techniques, as well as training in practical skills that were designed to help manage negative social attention, such as staring, and questions and comments from strangers. When followed-up 5 months after treatment, the intervention group continued to show improved self-esteem, quality of life, and body image, compared to both their pre-intervention levels and those of a control group.

Other support for the use of a cognitive-behavioral approach for people with disfigurements comes from a study by Kleve *et al.* (2002), which used cognitive-behavioral interventions in a hospital-based psychology service for clients with disfigurements to the face and head. Clinical interventions were individually tailored and included social skills training, assertiveness training, anxiety management, and cognitive restructuring. An evaluation of treatment efficacy at 6 months showed improvements in a range of areas, including social anxiety, depression, and satisfaction with life.

In a related area, Newell and Clarke (2000) evaluated the effectiveness of providing self-help information to adults with a facial disfigurement and found a modest decrease in the symptoms of anxiety and depression after receiving a self-help booklet that included a cognitive-behavioral explanation for anxiety and the relationship between anxiety and avoidance, as well as strategies for reducing anxiety. While a variety of sources of self-help information for both children and adults with facial disfigurement is available, their usefulness has not yet been formally evaluated (e.g., Clarke, 2001; information provided by the UK charity Changing Faces, which supports people with facial disfigurement, including craniofacial conditions; www.changingfaces.org.uk/Links-&-Resources).

Thus, there are promising models for interventions to improve the psychological outcomes of children and adults with craniofacial conditions; however, these interventions have not been adequately evaluated in this client group. Additional research is therefore required to establish a stronger evidence-base for clinical services with people with craniofacial conditions.

Conclusion

Despite the low incidence of individual craniofacial conditions, approximately one in 500 Australians have a diagnosed congenital craniofacial condition and are at an increased risk of developing psychosocial problems, which may impact negatively on social relationships. However, it is important to balance the problems associated with living with a craniofacial condition against the significant positive aspects that are also reported. For the problems that do arise, there are a range of psychological interventions that show promise for use with this clinical group. In particular, treatments that focus on social skills training and cognitive-behavioral interventions are indicated, with the former focusing on improving problem solving, coping, and social skills, and the latter addressing negative beliefs about appearance and poor self-image. Any such intervention must also take into consideration the cognitive impairments that may be associated with a particular craniofacial condition.

References

Achenbach, T. M., & Rescorla, L. (2001). *Manual for the ASEBA School-Age Forms and Profiles*. Burlington: Research Center for Children, Youth, and Families.

American Cleft Palate-Craniofacial Association and Cleft Palate Foundation. (2010). *Standards for Approval of Cleft Palate and Craniofacial Teams*. www.acpa-cpf.org/standards.

Aspinwall, L. G., & Staudinger, U. M. (2003). A psychology of human strengths: Some central issues of an emerging field. In L. G. Aspinwall & U. M. Staudinger (Eds.), *A Psychology of Human Strengths: Fundamental Questions and Future Directions for a Positive Psychology*. Washington DC: American Psychological Association.

Beaune, L., Forrest, C. R., & Keith, T. (2004). Adolescents' perspectives on living and growing up with Treacher Collins Syndrome: A qualitative study. *Cleft Palate-Craniofacial Journal, 41*, 343–350.

Berk, N. W., Cooper, M. E., Liu, Y., & Marazita, M. L. (2001). Social anxiety in Chinese adults with oral-facial clefts. *Cleft Palate-Craniofacial Journal, 38,* 126–133.

Bessell, A., & Moss, T. P. (2007). Evaluating the effectiveness of psychosocial interventions for individuals with visible differences: A systematic review of the empirical literature. *Body Image, 4,* 227–238.

Billaud Feragen, K., Borge, A. I. H., & Rumsey, N. (2009). Social experiences in 10-year-old children born with a cleft: Exploring psychosocial resilience. *Cleft Palate-Craniofacial Journal, 45,* 65–74.

Blakeney, P., Thomas, C., Holzer, C., Rose, M., Berniger, T., & Meyer, W. J. (2005). Efficacy of a short-term, intensive social skills training program for burned adolescents. *Journal of Burn Care and Rehabilitation, 26,* 546–555.

Carroll, P., & Shute, R. (2005). School peer victimization of young people with craniofacial conditions: A comparative study. *Psychology Health and Medicine, 10,* 291–304.

Cash, T. F., & Labarge, A. S. (1996). Development of the Appearance Schemas Inventory: A new cognitive body-image assessment. *Cognitive Therapy and Research, 20,* 37–50.

Chuo, B., Searle, Y., Jeremy, A., Richard, B. M., Sharp, I., & Slator, R. (2008). The continuing multidisciplinary needs of adult patients with cleft lip and/or palate. *Cleft Palate Craniofacial Journal, 45,* 633–638.

Clarke, A. (2001). Managing the psychological aspects of altered appearance: The development of an information resource for people with disfiguring conditions. *Patient Education and Counseling, 43,* 305–309.

Cobourne, M. T. (2004). The complex genetics of cleft lip and palate. *European Journal of Orthodontics, 26,* 7–16.

Cochrane, V. M., & Slade, P. (1999). Appraisal and coping in adults with cleft lip: Associations with well-being and social anxiety. *British Journal of Medical Psychology, 72,* 485–503.

Cohen, M. M., & Kreiborg, S. (1990). The central nervous system in the Apert Syndrome. *American Journal of Medical Genetics, 35,* 36–45.

Craniofacial Society of Great Britain and Ireland. (2005). *Recommendations for Minimum Records for Cleft Audit.* www.craniofacialsociety.org.uk/info/audit.html.

Cunningham, M. L., Seto, M.L., Ratisoontorn, C., Heike, C. L., & Hing, A. V. (2007). Syndromic craniosynostosis: From history to hydrogen bonds. *Orthodontics & Craniofacial Research, 10,* 67–81.

David, D. J., Henriksson, T. G., & Cooter, R. D. (1987). *Craniofacial Deformities: An Introductory Guide.* North Adelaide: Australian Cranio-maxillo-facial Foundation.

de Ridder, D., Geenen, R., Kuijer, R., & van Middendorp, H. (2008). Psychological adjustment to chronic disease. *Lancet, 372,* 246–245.

Edwards, T. C., Topolski, T. D., Kapp-Simon, K. A., Aspinall, C. L., & Patrick, D. L. (2011). What difference can a minute make? – Social skills and first impressions of youth with craniofacial differences. *Cleft Palate-Craniofacial Journal, 48,* 91–97.

Eiserman, W. (2001). Unique outcomes and positive contributions associated with facial difference: Expanding research and practice. *Cleft Palate-Craniofacial Journal, 38,* 236–244,

Endringa, M. C., & Kapp-Simon, K. A. (1999). Psychological issues in craniofacial care: State of the art. *Cleft Palate-Craniofacial Journal, 36,* 3–11.

Gorlin, R. J., Cohen, M. M., & Levin, L. S. (1990). *Syndromes of the Head and Neck* (3rd edn.). New York: Oxford University Press.

Jones, K. L. (2006). *Smith's Recognizable Patterns of Human Malformation* (6th edn.). Philadelphia: W.B. Saunders Company.

Kapp-Simon, K. A., & McGuire, D. E. (1997). Observed social interaction patterns in adolescents with and without craniofacial conditions. *Cleft Palate-Craniofacial Journal, 34,* 380–384.

Kapp-Simon, K. A., McGuire, D. E., Long, B. C., & Simon, D. J. (2005). Addressing quality of life issues in adolescents: Social skills interventions. *Cleft Palate-Craniofacial Journal, 42,* 45–50.

Kish, V., & Lansdown, R. (2000). Meeting the psychosocial impact of facial disfigurement: Developing a clinical service for children and families. *Clinical Child Psychology and Psychiatry, 5,* 497–512.

Kleve, L., Rumsey, N., Wyn-Williams, M., & White, P. (2002). The effectiveness of cognitive-behavioural interventions provided at Outlook: A disfigurement support unit. *Journal of Evaluation in Clinical Practice, 8,* 387–395.

Lanigan, S. W., & Cotterill, J. A. (1989). Psychological disabilities amongst patients with port wine stains. *British Journal of Dermatology, 121,* 209–215.

Liossi, C. (2003). *Appearance Related Concerns across the General and Clinical Populations.* Unpublished thesis, City University, London.

Magalini, S. I., & Magalini, S. C. (1997). *Dictionary of Medical Syndromes* (4th edn.). Philadelphia: Lippicott-Raven Publishers.

Mani, M., Carlsson, M., & Marcusson, A. (2010). Quality of life varies with gender and age among adults treated for unilateral cleft lip and palate. *Cleft Palate-Craniofacial Journal. 47,* 491–498. doi:10.1597/08-281.

Marcusson, A., Akerlind, I., & Paulin, G. (2001). Quality of life in adults with repaired complete cleft lip and palate. *Cleft Palate-Craniofacial Journal, 38,* 379–385.

Mastroiacova, P., & International Perinatal Database of Typical Oral Clefts Working Group. (2011). Prevalence at birth of cleft lip with or without cleft palate. Data from the International Perinatal Database of Typical Oral Clefts (IPDTOC). *Cleft Palate-Craniofacial Journal, 48,* 66–81.

Meyerson, M. D. (2001). Resilience and success in adults with Moebius syndrome. *Cleft Palate Craniofacial Journal, 38,* 231–230.

Moos, R. H., & Holahan, C. J. (2007). Adaptive tasks and methods of coping with illness and disability. In E. Martz & H. Livneh (Eds.) *Coping with Chronic Illness and Disability: Theoretical, Empirical, and Clinical Aspects* (pp. 107–126). New York: Springer.

Mosby. (2009). *Mosby's Medical Dictionary* (8th edn.). St. Louis, MO: Mosby.

Newell, R., & Clarke, M. (2000). Evaluation of a self-help leaflet in treatment of social difficulties following facial disfigurement. *International Journal of Nursing Studies, 37,* 381–388.

Papadopoulos, L., Bor, R., & Legg, C. (1999). Coping with the disfiguring effects of vitiligo: A preliminary investigation into the effect of cognitive-behavioural therapy. *British Journal of Medical Psychology, 72,* 385–396.

Ramstad, T., Ottem, E., & Shaw, W. C. (1995). Psychosocial adjustment in Norwegian adults who had undergone standardised treatment of complete cleft lip and palate II: Self-reported problems and concerns with appearance. *Scandinavian Journal of Plastic and Reconstructive Surgery and Hand Surgery, 29,* 329–336.

Roberts, R. M., & Shute, R. (2010). Children's experience of living with a craniofacial condition: Perspectives of children and parents. *Clinical Child Psychology and Psychiatry, 16,* 317–334.

Roberts, R. M., & Shute, R. (2012). A prospective study of coping and adjustment in adolescents with craniofacial conditions. *Children's Health Care, 41*(2), in press.

Roberts, R. M., & Mathias, J. L. (2011a). Discrimination and other experiences of living with a craniofacial condition in adulthood. Unpublished manuscript.

Roberts, R. M., & Mathias, J. L. (2011b). Psychosocial functioning in adults with congenital craniofacial conditions. *Cleft Palate-Craniofacial Journal,* doi:10.1597/10-143.

Roberts, R. M., & Mathias, J. L. (2012). Predictors of mental health in adults with congenital craniofacial conditions attending the Australian Craniofacial Unit. *Cleft Palate-Craniofacial Journal,* doi: http://dx.doi.org/10.1597/11-105.

Roberts, R. M., Mathias, J., & Wheaton, P. (2010). *Cognitive outcomes in cleft: A meta-analysis.* Abstracts of the 16th Annual Conference of the APS College of Clinical Neuropsychologist, 66.

Robinson, E., Rumsey, N., & Partridge, J. (1996). An evaluation of the impact of social interaction skills training for facially disfigured people. *British Journal of Plastic Surgery, 49,* 281–289.

Rumsey, N., & Harcourt, D. (2005). *The Psychology of Appearance.* Maidenhead: Oxford University Press.

Sarwer, D. B., Bartlett, S. P., Whitaker, L. A., Paige, K. T., Pertschuk, M. J., & Wadden, T. A. (1999). Adult psychological functioning of individuals born with craniofacial anomalies. *Plastic and Reconstructive Surgery, 103,* 412–418.

Schnitt, D. E., Agir, H., & David, D. J. (2004). From birth to maturity: A group of patients who have completed their protocol management. Part 1. Unilateral cleft lip and palate. *Plastic and Reconstructive Surgery, 113,* 805–817.

Shaw, W. C., Semb, G., Nelson, P., Brattstrom, V., Molsted, K., Prahl-Anderses, B., & Gundlach, K. K. H. (2001). The Eurocleft Project 1996–2000: Overview. *Journal of Cranio-Maxillofacial Surgery, 29,* 1–10.

Shute, R., McCarthy, K. R., & Roberts, R. (2007). Predictors of social competence in young adolescents with craniofacial anomalies. *International Journal of Health and Clinical Psychology, 7*, 575–613.

Smith, C. E., Fernengel, K., Holcroft, C., & Gerald, K. (1994). Meta-analysis of the associations between social support and health outcomes. *Annals of Behavioral Medicine, 16*, 352–362.

Speltz, M. L., Kapp-Simon, K. A., Cunningham, M., Marsh, J., & Dawson, G. (2004). Single-suture craniosynostosis: A review of neurobehavioural research and theory. *Journal of Pediatric Psychology, 29*, 651–668.

Tolarova, M. M., & Cervenka, J. (1998). Classification and birth prevalence of orofacial clefts. *American Journal of Medical Genetics, 75*, 126–137.

Turner, S. R., Rumsey, N., & Sandy, J. R. (1998). Psychological aspects of cleft lip and palate. *European Journal of Orthodontics, 20*, 407–415.

World Health Organization. (2003). *Global Registry and Database on Craniofacial Anomalies: Report of a WHO Registry Meeting on Craniofacial Anomalies.* Geneva: World Health Organization.

Part 5

Body Image, Eating Problems, and Obesity

19

Body Image and Health

Matthew Fuller-Tyszkiewicz, Lina A. Ricciardelli, Marita P. McCabe, and Brigitte Laville

Body image is a multidimensional construct defined as an individual's perception of, and attitudes towards, his or her body and appearance (Cash *et al.*, 2002). Body image encompasses a range of cognitive, affective, and perceptual phenomena (Thompson *et al.*, 1999). Disturbances to body image are of clinical interest as they are thought to play a central role in the development and/or maintenance of a range of adverse psychosocial conditions, including depression, eating disorders, and low self-esteem.

Body image is a significant issue affecting women and men across the lifespan and in different cultural groups. In a recent survey of 29 000 Australians aged 11–24 years, 70% of respondents reported dissatisfaction with their body weight and shape, and body image was consistently rated as the most important issue for this cohort, ahead of family conflict and coping with stress (Mission Australia, 2010). Similarly, in a recent study from the USA, 63% of women and 48% of men were dissatisfied with their appearance. While body image concerns appear to be highest in Western cultures, such as Australia, the USA, the UK, and New Zealand, research suggests that body image concerns are also increasing in non-Western cultures, such as China, Malaysia, Fiji, and Turkey (Swami *et al.*, 2010).

In this chapter we examine how different dimensions of body image (body dissatisfaction, weight and muscle concerns, appearance concerns, importance and investment, and perceptual distortion) relate to eating disorders and subclinical levels of disordered eating, muscle dysmorphia, cosmetic surgery, unhealthy weight-loss behaviors, obesity, depression, low self-esteem, and relationships. A particular focus is on how idealized physiques differ for men and women, and how these translate into different health risks for the two gender groups. In addition, we address the health implications and the treatment options for the different types of body image concerns.

Body Image and Body Change Behaviors

Body image disturbances (most notably, body dissatisfaction, and weight, shape, and muscle concerns) have been consistently linked with a range of body change-related attitudes and behaviors.

Applied Topics in Health Psychology, First Edition. Edited by M. L. Caltabiano and L. Ricciardelli.
© 2013 John Wiley & Sons, Ltd. Published 2013 by John Wiley & Sons, Ltd.

These include drive for thinness or muscularity, steroid use, supplements for diuretic purposes, severe restriction of food intake, obligatory exercise, and cosmetic surgery (Cafri *et al.*, 2005). The body change-related consequences of negative body image are perhaps best understood by considering the underlying roles played by (1) the appearance ideal to which one aspires and (2) the importance an individual places on physical appearance. In this section we evaluate the literature related to gender- and age-related differences in psychological investment in appearance and in the body shape an individual aspires to, and the type and severity of body change behaviors. We also consider the health consequences of these body change behaviors.

Gender differences in body change strategies

Sociocultural messages about what constitutes an attractive physique are pervasive, and feature heavily in the marketing campaigns of a variety of industries, including pharmaceutical, cosmetic, physical fitness, fashion, and medical. In current Western cultures, the idealized male physique features a lean, muscular V-shaped frame with a well-defined upper torso (Leit *et al.*, 2001), whereas the idealized female physique is thin and lean (Syspeck *et al.*, 2006). As a consequence, the methods that men and women adopt to reach their appearance-related goals diverge markedly. Among female populations, weight and appearance management typically involves some form of weight loss, which may include high-level exercise, dieting (through reduction of caloric intake or through restriction of food types, such as carbohydrates), purging, or the use of diuretics and weight-loss pills (Celio *et al.*, 2006; McCabe & Ricciardelli, 2009).

Exercise is a commonly used method of weight control in both clinical and nonclinical populations (Mond *et al.*, 2006). While individuals may engage in exercise for a variety of reasons, girls and women are more likely to report exercising to improve appearance or muscle tone, and as a means to control one's weight (Furnham *et al.*, 2002; Kilpatrick *et al.*, 2005). Furthermore, individuals with a clinical or subclinical eating disorder are more likely to engage in an unhealthy form of exercise known as excessive exercise. This more extreme form of exercise is characterized by frequent episodes of exercise which significantly interfere with daily activities (e.g., work, relationships, etc.). The individual is likely to continue exercising despite injury or other medical conditions, and they may experience feelings of guilt for missing an exercise session (Mond *et al.*, 2006).

Dieting is another commonly used body change strategy for weight loss. It is estimated that the majority of women from Western cultures have dieted at some point in their lives (Allaz *et al.*, 1998). However, these levels have also increased to high levels among non-Western cultures (Mellor *et al.*, 2008, 2010c; Xu *et al.*, 2010). Adolescence and early adulthood have been considered peak periods for dieting, as these periods typically coincide with developmental changes in one's body (adolescence) and transition from high school to college or full-time work (early adulthood) (Vohs *et al.*, 2001). Consistent with this view, it has been shown that 29–60% of adolescent and young adult females from Western cultures reported dieting in the past year (Celio *et al.*, 2006; McVey *et al.*, 2004), and 38–60% admitted to dieting on a regular basis (Patton *et al.*, 1997, 1999). Among adolescent samples, the prevalence rates (35–57%) are almost as high for more serious weight-loss behaviors, such as fasting, crash dieting, vomiting, and laxative use (Ricciardelli & McCabe, 2004).

Although the incidence rates of these more extreme weight-loss behaviors are generally lower among preadolescent than adolescent and adult populations, there is evidence to suggest that preadolescent children also engage in dieting. Estimates for dieting to lose weight vary from 20 to 56% for preadolescent girls and 31–39% for preadolescent boys (Ricciardelli & McCabe, 2001). Furthermore, information from responses to the Children's Eating Attitudes Test (ChEAT) scores has shown that 9–14% of preadolescent girls and 5–8% of boys score above the threshold (>20), indicative of disordered eating (Ricciardelli & McCabe, 2001).

While dieting behaviors are also observed in male populations, the incidence of dieting behavior tends to be lower than for age-matched female cohorts, and the goal of dieting is more often for muscle gain than to decrease weight (Cafri *et al.*, 2005, 2006). Estimates of dieting among male populations range from 13 to 26% for adolescent samples (Ricciardelli & McCabe, 2004), and from 14 to 20% for preadolescent samples for weight-gain-related dieting (Field *et al.*, 2003). In addition to dieting, many males also use supplementary methods in pursuit of the muscular ideal, such as use of chemical supplements, such as creatine, anabolic steroids, prohormones, or ephedrine (Cafri *et al.*, 2005). Although the estimated incidence of chemical supplement use in the general community ranges from 3 to 12% (Cafri *et al.*, 2005), prevalence rates vary as a function of the perceived severity of the method (e.g., anabolic steroid use is less commonly used than over-the-counter chemical supplements; Cafri *et al.*, 2005), perceived side effects (Evans, 1997), level of dissatisfaction with one's physique, including body dysmorphia (Wroblewska, 1997), and membership of groups which directly or indirectly emphasize physical appearance (e.g., gym attendees, athletes, body builders, etc.) (Kanayama *et al.*, 2001).

Tanning is another behavior that many individuals, particularly females, use as a body change strategy to increase attractiveness and because of the perception that tanning makes one appear slimmer (Cafri *et al.*, 2006, 2009). In a recent Australian study, 44% of females and 57% of males aged between 18 and 30 years engaged in tanning behavior, and consistent with previous research the main variable found to predict tanning was the motive to improve appearance (Smith & Ricciardelli, 2011). For young people, the immediate benefits of a tan are often felt to outweigh the distant (and indefinite) risks of skin cancer (Calder & Aiken, 2008; Kulik *et al.*, 2008).

Finally, there has been a recent increase in Western countries, such as Australia, the USA, and UK, in the use of cosmetic surgery (e.g., breast augmentation, liposuction, and facelift) and minimally invasive surgical procedures (e.g., chemical peels, microdermabrasion, etc.). The American Society of Plastic Surgeons (2010) reports that cosmetic surgeries are most prevalent in the USA, with over 1.5 million cosmetic surgeries and a further 11.5 million minimally invasive procedures documented in 2010. Australia ranked 22nd in total number of cosmetic procedures, but when this figure is adjusted for population the occurrence of these procedures is almost as common as in the USA. The majority of these procedures are conducted on women (roughly 90%). Although many of these procedures were for legitimate physical defects (i.e., those that impair functionality), individuals with an eating disorder or body dysmorphic disorder represent a significant minority of this patient population. Buhlmann *et al.* (2010) found that the prevalence rate of cosmetic surgery was roughly five times higher among body dysmorphic populations than the general population. However, what differentiates the use of cosmetic surgery among clinical populations and the general community is that the former group are more likely to seek treatment for minimal or nonexistent perceived defects. The risk of medical complications during surgery is greater for individuals with an eating disorder (particularly, anorexia nervosa) due to their underweight body status (Sarwer *et al.*, 2007). Furthermore, whereas individuals who seek treatment for physical defects without an eating disorder or body dysmorphic disorder tend to report improvements in self-esteem and wellbeing following treatment, individuals with an eating disorder or body dysmorphic disorder tend to report no improvements and many actually experience worsening of their appearance-related concerns (Willard *et al.*, 1996).

Age-related decline in body change behaviors

While the majority of studies have focused on adolescent and young adult populations, the available data from surveys of middle-aged and older women (usually defined as 40 years and above) suggest that body dissatisfaction may exert less influence on body change behaviors (or at the very least, they may engage in less extreme body change behaviors). Although Allaz *et al.* (1998) found that 31% of women in their sample who were aged over 65 reported dieting in the last 5 years, this figure was still lower than the average for the sample as a whole (42%), which included younger adults. Bennett and Stevens (1996) found that 20% of women aged 50–84 in their sample were currently dieting. However, when stricter criteria are applied to "dieting" status, the proportions drop significantly. Juhaeri *et al.* (2001) estimated that between 3.5 and 6.5% of women and 2.3% of men in their sample of 10 554 individuals aged between 45 and 64 had dieted for weight-loss purposes for more than 1 year. One explanation for the lower prevalence of dieting among older populations is that body image becomes less important for an individual's overall sense of self-worth as we age and, therefore, body dissatisfaction is less likely to motivate older individuals to engage in body change behaviors (Fredrickson & Roberts, 1997; Tiggemann, 2004). Consistent with this view is the finding that motives for exercising, healthy eating, and dieting in later life differ from younger adults and adolescents (Bennett & Stevens, 1996; Steptoe *et al.*, 1995). Whereas younger cohorts are concerned primarily with appearance-related aspects of their bodies, older adults also cite health concerns as a key motivator for engaging in weight-loss strategies (Clarke, 2002).

Health consequences of use of body change strategies

Dieting has been linked to a range of psychological and physical health issues. Patton *et al.* (1999) showed that adolescent girls who dieted moderately (as determined by midrange scores on the Adolescent Dieting Scale, ADS; Patton *et al.*, 1997) were five times more likely than nondieting adolescents to develop an eating disorder, whereas adolescents who dieted severely (scores above the midrange for the ADS) were 18 times more likely to develop an eating disorder. Moreover, individuals who diet before the age of 15 are more prone to depression, low iron levels, lethargy, and (in females) menstrual irregularities (Lee, 2001). Koenig and Wasserman (1995) argue that the link between dieting and depression may be driven by psychological investment in appearance and body dissatisfaction. They found that college women who were dissatisfied with their appearance were more likely to diet, and that subsequent dieting failure was, in turn, predictive of depressive symptoms.

Adolescent and young adult males who are dissatisfied with their physique and/or who attend gyms or play sports are considerably more likely to abuse chemical supplements in an attempt to increase muscularity. As a consequence, they are at risk for a range of adverse health implications of use. The main physical and psychological health risks associated with the use of anabolic steroids include athereosclerosis, mood changes, aggression, and dependence on the substance (Cafri *et al.*, 2005). The acute effects associated with ephedrine/caffeine combinations include increased systolic blood pressure, increased heart rate, other symptoms of excitatory central nervous system stimulation, increased plasma glucose, headaches, irritability, motor restlessness, nausea, sleeplessness, tachycardia, urinary disorders, vomiting, and dependence on the substance (Cafri *et al.*, 2005).

Body Image and Obesity

The relationship between body image and obesity is well established, especially among adult women from European backgrounds (e.g., Sarwer *et al.*, 2005; Schwartz & Brownell, 2004). Moreover, among preadolescents, adolescents, and adults (which include both females and males) a higher body mass index (BMI) is associated with greater body dissatisfaction, and weight and shape concerns about wanting to be thinner (Ricciardelli & McCabe, 2004, 2007; Schwartz & Brownell, 2004; Stice, 2002). However, the size of the relationship is often modest, suggesting that weight-related body dissatisfaction may be contingent upon other factors.

The relationship between body dissatisfaction and BMI is not always found among overweight and obese women in treatment for weight-related issues (Sarwer *et al.*, 2005; Schwartz & Brownell, 2004). This is because we are dealing with a narrow range of body image concerns and the levels of body dissatisfaction experienced by obese women are very high (Schwartz & Brownell, 2004). Other features that characterize obese individuals with the higher levels of body dissatisfaction include a childhood onset of obesity, weight-related teasing during childhood, binge eating disorder, and a history of weight cycling (Sarwer *et al.*, 2005; Schwartz & Brownell, 2004).

On the other hand, gender and cultural background are also important factors to consider. Overweight males are often protected from experiencing body dissatisfaction because they often perceive themselves as "big" and "strong" rather than "fat" (Schwartz & Brownell, 2004). Similarly, some cultures are more accepting of a greater diversity of body sizes, and traditionally place a greater value on larger body sizes. This includes African-American culture for females, and the Pacific Islands for both females and males (Ricciardelli *et al.*, 2007; Schwartz & Brownell, 2004). Although many of these non-Western cultures are rapidly changing and adopting Western values, these cultures often still place more importance on family, the community, and religion, and much less importance on appearance or body shape (Kirk *et al.*, 2008; McCabe *et al.*, 2009). In fact, the messages they get from family and the broader community is that a large body is valued.

Explaining the relationship between body image and obesity

A certain level of body dissatisfaction among individuals who are overweight and obese is to be expected, given the widespread sociocultural pressures for women to be thin (Schwartz & Brownell, 2004), and there are increasingly similar sociocultural pressures for males (Ricciardelli & McCabe, 2004). This body dissatisfaction has at times been considered adaptive (Schwartz & Brownell, 2004), as it is expected that it may motivate individuals to lose weight; however, this is not always the case. Often the body dissatisfaction is closely linked with societal discrimination and stigma, which may lead to social isolation, relationship difficulties, and poor physical and mental health (Annis *et al.*, 2004; Schwartz & Brownell, 2004).

The relationship between body dissatisfaction and the motivation to lose weight has been found to follow an inverted-U-shaped curve (Heinberg *et al.*, 2001). If an overweight person has no body dissatisfaction then he/she may feel less motivated to make health behavior changes than someone with a moderate level of body dissatisfaction. Consistent with this view, it has been found that obese women with lower levels of body dissatisfaction may display increased self-efficacy and this has been linked to rapid weight loss and lower drop-out rates when in treatment (Schwartz & Brownell, 2004). On the other hand, someone with extreme body image distress may be caught in a destructive cycle of negative self-talk that is debilitating and inhibits change (Schwartz & Brownell, 2004). Thus, people who feel badly about their bodies may be more prone to depression, anxiety, and poor self-esteem, and may be less able to motivate themselves to make healthy behavioral changes (Schwartz & Brownell, 2004).

Another view in the literature is that a higher BMI leads to increased social pressure to be thin and thus increased body dissatisfaction. It is this body dissatisfaction that may increase negative affect and motivate weight-loss strategies (Stice, 2002). However, many attempts to lose weight often fail and these failures counterproductively perpetuate cycles of negative affect (Foreyt *et al.*,

1995) and binge eating (Sherwood *et al.*, 1999; Venditti *et al.*, 1996), which then lead individuals to gain further weight (McGuire *et al.*, 1999). In addition, individuals with a subjective view of themselves as "weight cyclers" are more likely to be dissatisfied with their bodies and to have lower self-esteem and life satisfaction (Schwartz & Brownell, 2004). These issues need to be addressed before any weight-management program is commenced.

It is important to consider that individuals with a negative body image are also less likely to engage in positive health behaviors and more likely to engage in negative health behaviors. Relationships have been found between smoking rates and body dissatisfaction in samples of women with both clinical and nonclinical eating disorders (Peñas-Lledó *et al.*, 2002; Wiseman *et al.*, 1998), and negative body image has been found to be predictive of more difficulty quitting smoking (King *et al.*, 2005). One reason for the higher rates of smoking among individuals with disordered eating symptoms is that smoking serves as a weight-management strategy by reducing appetite. Fear of subsequent weight gain is one factor associated with difficulty in quitting smoking (King *et al.*, 2005).

Higher use of alcohol among women has also been associated with body dissatisfaction (Peñas-Lledó *et al.*, 2002). Although Peñas-Lledó *et al.* (2002) found that body dissatisfaction was correlated with lower levels of exercise for men, this relationship was not found for females. Finally, body dissatisfaction has been found to be predictive of poor eating habits such as binge eating (Barker & Galambos, 2007; Stice, 2002). It is these types of negative health behavior that may contribute to gaining weight, and the maintenance of the weight gain. Moreover, this weight gain may lead to further increases in body dissatisfaction. More research is needed to more fully understand gender differences.

Improving body image

Several studies have examined the changes in body image for overweight and obese women who take part in weight-loss programs (e.g., Palmeira *et al.*, 2010; Sarwer *et al.*, 2005). In one recent study (Palmeira *et al.*, 2010) that examined the impact of a weight-loss program on body satisfaction and related factors, it was found that the greatest improvement for women was in body satisfaction, depressive symptoms, and mood. There were significant weight changes at 4 and 16 months relative to baseline measures. The program focused on educating women about exercise and nutrition and used cognitive behavior therapy (CBT). The physical activity part of the program involved educating about the energy consumption of various forms of exercise. The nutritional component of the program incorporated information on caloric, fat, and fibre content of various foods and importance of portion size and meal frequency in managing weight. Cognitive-behavioral strategies involved self-monitoring, enhancing body image, and dealing with lapses and relapses.

Some interventions are also designed to help individuals improve their body image without losing weight. One study by Ramirez and Rosen (2001) randomly assigned 65 obese men and woman to a combined body image therapy program with a 16 week behavioral weight control intervention or a behavioral weight control alone, to assess which intervention would be more effective in improving body image. The weight-control-only program consisted of weekly 1 hour sessions with a dietician promoting nutritional eating and exercise. The combined program in-cluded 12 weeks of 2 hour sessions with a psychologist or graduate student for cognitive-behavioral body image therapy. This therapy used cognitive restructuring to reduce negative views of body appearance and techniques for gradual exposure to distressing interpersonal situations where self-conscious bodily feelings generally arose. Methods to handle social discrimination were also discussed. Both groups lost approximately 10% of their initial weight and reported significant improvements in body image, self-esteem, and eating concerns. Also at 1 year follow-up, the two groups did not differ on weight maintenance or body image. This suggests that weight reduction alone is as effective in improving body image as a combined weight loss/body image treatment.

Given that weight loss can often be difficult to achieve in the short term, difficult to maintain in the long term, and requires major lifestyle changes, the improvement of body image for many researchers and clinicians is seen as important as the actual weight loss. Some overweight and obese individuals may be motivated to lose weight to improve their health, but the majority of people desire to lose weight to improve their physical appearance (Sarwer *et al.*, 2005). Even among those with serious comorbid health problems, such as diabetes and osteoarthritis, improving physical appearance and not health is often the primary motivator for weight loss (Sarwer *et al.*, 2005). Clearly, the motivation for the weight loss and the expectation of body image improvement needs to be taken into account by clinicians.

Bauchowitz *et al.* (2005) recommend that clinicians challenge patients' belief that surgery is a panacea for their weight-related problems. While surgery can immediately reduce body weight, it does not address the unhealthy eating behaviors which initially prompted weight gain. As a consequence, many patients regain their presurgery weight, and some even put on additional weight (Margro *et al.*, 2008).

It is also important to assess the expectations of morbidly obese patients who undergo bariatric surgery. Many of these individuals experience improvement in body image, but others also demonstrate dissatisfaction with their bodies following the massive weight loss (Sarwer *et al.*, 2005). Some may experience phantom fat while others may experience dissatisfaction with nonweight concerns such as the development of loose or sagging skin at different areas of the body (Sarwer *et al.*, 2005). In addition, given that body dissatisfaction among overweight and obese individuals is often related to lower self-esteem and increased symptoms of depression (Sarwer *et al.*, 2005), they also need assistance to deal with these broader and related psychological factors before they can begin to more fully and effectively address their body image concerns and weight management.

Body Image and Mental Health

The relationship between negative body image and a range of adverse psychosocial outcomes, including depression, anxiety, low self-esteem, poor quality of life, and suicidal ideation, has been amply demonstrated in cross-sectional studies (e.g., Crow *et al.*, 2008; Tiggemann, 2005; Yuan, 2010). Despite the relative paucity of experimental and longitudinal studies in this area, the findings suggest that adolescents may be particularly vulnerable to the mental health consequences of negative body image.

Experimental and longitudinal findings

It has been shown that exposure to stimuli which target one's body image (e.g., exposure to images of models, appearance-related feedback, or weight-related teasing) tends to increase negative mood states, such as depression, anger, and anxiety, and reduce self-esteem for both men and women (Agliata & Tantleff-Dunn, 2004; Hargreaves & Tiggemann, 2002). Moreover, these effects seem particularly pronounced for individuals with elevated disordered eating symptoms, including negative body image, internalization of unrealistic appearance standards, and dietary restraint (Halliwell & Dittmar, 2004; Yamamiya *et al.*, 2005).

Findings from longitudinal studies of adolescents suggest that body image may also have more sustained and long-term effects on mental health. While the interval between time points varied across studies (ranging from 1 to 5 years), it was consistently found that body dissatisfaction at time 1 prospectively predicted lower self-esteem and psychological wellbeing, and heightened rates of depressive symptoms, suicidal ideation, and suicide attempts for both boys and girls (Grabe *et al.*, 2007; Holsen *et al.*, 2001; Rodriguez-Cano *et al.*, 2006; Stice *et al.*, 2000; Tiggemann, 2005). However, initial levels of depression and subjective wellbeing failed to predict time 2 levels of body image disturbances (Mellor *et al.*, 2010a; Stice & Whitenton, 2002; Tiggemann, 2005), suggesting that it is not a bidirectional, causal relationship.

Interestingly, there may be age- and gender-related differences in the influence of body image on mental health. Whereas body dissatisfaction influenced self-esteem and suicidal ideation in early adolescence for girls, these longitudinal relationships were only significant for mid- to late-adolescent boys (Grabe *et al.*, 2007). In the only study to longitudinally evaluate the link between body image and self-esteem in a population more representative of the adult lifespan (age ranges 20–84 years), Mellor *et al.* (2010b) found that time 1 body dissatisfaction was predictive of self-esteem 2 years later for women, but not for men. However, time 1 body dissatisfaction was not predictive of time 2 subjective wellbeing for men or women. Thus, it is possible that body image may exert greatest influence on mental health in adolescence.

Age-related influences on the relationship between body image and mental health

It has been argued that the physical, social, and emotional changes that typically occur in adolescence make this cohort increasingly vulnerable to the development of negative body image and mental health issues (e.g., Ge *et al.*, 2001; Yuan, 2007). Physical changes due to puberty (e.g., breast development, weight gain, and menarche for girls, and muscle development, deepened voice, and increased body hair for boys) coincide with increasing self-awareness about, and desire to improve, one's physical appearance (Harter, 1999). It is not surprising then to find that the relationship between negative body image and poor mental health (notably, depressive mood, diminished psychological wellbeing, and low self-esteem) is particularly strong for adolescent boys and girls who exhibit the physical signs of puberty earlier or later than their same-sex peers (Ge *et al.*, 2001; Yuan, 2007, 2010). Furthermore, weight- and appearance-related teasing from peers often reinforces the self-consciousness that adolescents feel about their appearance, and this teasing has been shown to mediate the relationship between negative body image due to pubertal status and diminished mental health (Eisenberg *et al.*, 2006).

Aside from these physical changes, adolescence is also an important period for the development of one's self-concept. More so than at other periods in one's life, self-worth appears to be heavily influenced by the satisfaction that one has towards one's appearance, particularly for adolescent girls (Harter, 1999). Consistent with this view, negative body image is associated with negative, global assessments of self-worth in adolescent samples (Paxton *et al.*, 2006; Tiggemann, 2005). The relationship between body image and self-esteem has also been observed in young adult populations (Tiggemann & Lynch, 2001; Wade & Cooper, 1999).

However, the extent to which negative body image and self-esteem are associated in mid- to late adulthood may depend on other factors, such as psychological investment in appearance. Fredrickson and Roberts (1997) argued that the impact that the physical aging process has on body dissatisfaction and mental health will depend on the extent to which an individual is able to relinquish or modify the unrealistic appearance standards that have been internalized throughout youth and early adulthood. For individuals who fail to modify their appearance-related beliefs, we may anticipate a worsening of body dissatisfaction and its negative consequences. Conversely, for individuals who de-emphasize the importance of physical appearance in later life, body image concerns may exert less impact on their wellbeing and feelings of self-worth. Interestingly, in several studies which failed to find a decline in the link between body image and self-esteem across the adult lifespan for men or women (e.g., Tiggemann & Stevens, 1999; Wilcox, 1997), body image importance was also found to be stable across age groups.

Body Image and Relationships

The way an individual feels about their appearance is thought to influence – and perhaps be influenced by – interactions with others. For instance, Hinrichsen *et al.* (2003) asserted that individuals with negative body image may be hesitant to expose themselves to public scrutiny and, as a consequence, their fear of negative evaluation may diminish the number and quality of social interactions in their daily lives. Wiederman (2000) suggested that negative body image may also have adverse effects on an individual's willingness to engage in acts of intimacy with a partner. In this section, we examine (1) body image and sexual functioning, and (2) body image and interpersonal relationships.

Body image and sexual functioning

While strength or quality of intimate interpersonal relationships can be measured in a variety of ways, many researchers have focused on sexual functioning. As Wiederman (2002) noted, sexual functioning is an important aspect of interpersonal relationships to target in individuals with negative body image because the sexual act is so heavily reliant on bodily functions and appearance. Although the majority of available data in this area comes from cross-sectional studies of college or university students, the evidence supports a link between body image and different aspects of sexual functioning.

First, it has been consistently demonstrated that body dissatisfaction is associated with lower frequency of, and less varied, sexual experiences (McDonagh *et al.*, 2007; Meana & Nunnink, 2006; Wiederman, 2000). Among adolescent boys and girls, positive body image has been associated with the earlier onset of sexual experiences and sexual assertiveness, whereas negative body image (including body dissatisfaction, overvaluation of the importance of physical attractiveness, and frequent body self-surveillance) is linked with lower self-efficacy to act upon one's sexual desires (Hirschman *et al.*, 2006; Impett *et al.*, 2006). While the link between body image and sexual functioning has rarely been explored in male and/or middle-aged populations, available data suggest that body image is associated with sexual functioning in ways that are comparable to results found in female populations (Davison & McCabe, 2005).

Body image may also influence quality of sexual experiences. Dissatisfaction with one's appearance in general and with genitals in particular, investment in appearance, and low self-rated physical attractiveness have been linked with lower sexual satisfaction, reduced pleasure from sexual intercourse, lower arousability, reduced libido, anxiety about sexual intimacy, and greater cognitive distraction during sex (Davison & McCabe, 2005; Meana & Nunnink, 2006; Puyols *et al.*, 2010; Schick *et al.*, 2010). The content of these cognitive distractions for men typically involves performance concerns, whereas women report being distracted by body image self-consciousness (Meanna & Nunnink, 2006).

Despite the paucity of literature on the topic, available evidence suggests that individuals with negative body image may be more likely to engage in risky sexual behaviors. Littleton *et al.* (2005) found that among a sample of 1547 women seeking services at a family planning clinic, individuals with negative body image were more likely to report infrequent use of condoms, having sex with multiple partners, and having sex while under the influence of alcohol or drugs. In light of other findings which suggest that individuals with negative body image are less confident and assertive in sexual relationships, and report anxiety about negotiating terms in intimate relationships (Schooler *et al.*, 2005), it is possible that the risky sexual behaviors of individuals with body image disturbances are a byproduct of diminished sexual assertiveness. Such an explanation is also consistent with the observation that individuals with negative body image are more inclined to feel regret for previous sexual encounters (Hirschman *et al.*, 2006).

Body image and interpersonal relationships

The relationship between body image and other aspects of interpersonal relationships have also been demonstrated. In particular, individuals with elevated levels of body dissatisfaction tend to exhibit an attachment style characterized by anxiety and feelings of insecurity (Barone & Guiducci, 2009). Body dissatisfaction has been linked with separation anxiety, reduced confidence in relationships, and greater discomfort with romantic intimacy, a need for approval from one's partner, and preoccupation with the status or stability of one's relationship (Barone & Guiducci, 2009; Pinger & Crittenden, 2007; Sharpe *et al.*, 1998). For example, reports from married couples show that when one partner is cognizant of the other's negative body image, they report that this anxiety interferes with the dynamic of the relationship, and identify the anxiety as a key source of dissatisfaction in their relationship (Boyes *et al.*, 2007; Meltzer & McNulty, 2010).

It has also been shown that aspects of the relationship may also influence body image. Pole *et al.* (2004) found an association between level of body dissatisfaction and frequency/severity of appearance comments received from one's spouse. Sanchez *et al.* (2008) found that body dissatisfaction increased in single men and women as a function of (1) the role of relationships in their evaluations of self-worth (relationship contingency) and (2) their self-reported feelings of urgency to find a mate. Interestingly, Boyes *et al.* (2007) found that the influence of partner on body dissatisfaction differed by gender; whereas women were more dissatisfied with their appearance and more likely to diet if their partner was unhappy, men reported greater motivation to change their appearance when their partners were contented and well-adjusted.

Much less attention has been given to either the quality or quantity of platonic relationships and friendships among individuals with body image disturbances. While there is no evidence to suggest that the number of people within one's social network is linked to body image disturbances or that individuals with negative body image engage in more social avoidant behaviors, men and women with body dissatisfaction do report greater self-consciousness about their appearance and greater fear about being negatively evaluated in social settings (Cash *et al.*, 2004). They also feel less confident about acceptance from friends or their ability to provide support to their friends (Gerner & Wilson, 2005). Such findings are consistent with the anxious attachment style exhibited by individuals with negative body image in their romantic relationships.

There is also evidence to suggest that individuals within a friendship clique share similar attitudes and behaviors related to appearance and dieting (Hutchinson & Rapee, 2007; Paxton *et al.*, 1999). While it is possible that individuals with body dissatisfaction benefit from association with like-minded individuals through empathy, re-assurance, and comforting (Gapinski *et al.*,

2003), body dissatisfaction is also linked to perceived teasing and appearance-related comments from other members of the friendship circle (Hutchinson & Rapee, 2007; Phares *et al.*, 2004), suggesting that friendship cliques may exert positive and negative influences on body image.

Body image attitudes and behaviors also tend to aggregate in families. Adolescents report modelling their appearance values and behaviors on those observed in the home setting (Keery *et al.*, 2004). Children and adolescents with elevated body image concerns are more likely to report that their family members comment on their appearance, criticize them, and even tease them when they fail to meet an appearance standard (Paxton *et al.*, 1999; Stice, 1998).

Body Image and Treatment Options

Although a variety of options are available for the treatment of body image disturbances, by far the most commonly used approach is CBT. CBT is a multicomponent approach to treatment of psychological disorders which seeks to identify and challenge dysfunctional thoughts, feelings, and behaviors (Cash & Strachan, 2002). Within the context of body image disturbances, CBT typically involves a range of complementary techniques which target the cognitive-evaluative (e.g., psycho-education, exposure and desensitization, and monitoring and cognitive restructuring of one's appearance-related cognitions), behavioral (strategies to minimize avoidant behaviors and appearance-checking tendencies, building skills in problem solving and assertiveness), and perceptual aspects of body image disturbance (training in accurate body size estimation) (Cash & Strachan, 2002).

Evidence from efficacy studies suggests that CBT is an effective approach to treatment of body image disturbances in nonclinical and clinical populations (Cash & Hrabosky, 2004; Cash & Strachan, 2002; Jarry & Berardi, 2004), although the effects tend to be more pronounced in clinical populations (Jarry & Ip, 2005). Not surprisingly, the effect sizes for change in body image due to CBT are larger when body image disturbances are the primary focus of intervention than in instances when treatment of negative body image is incidental to or embedded within treatment of eating disorders (Jarry & Ip, 2005; Rosen, 1996). Moreover, negative body image is a key indicator of resistance to treatment for disordered eating symptoms, and in instances where body image is left untreated there is an increased likelihood of relapse into disordered eating behaviors (Allen & Hollander, 2002).

Jarry and Ip (2005) conducted a meta-analysis of studies which evaluated the effectiveness of stand-alone CBT for body image. They found that although CBT was effective for all three components of body image disturbance (attitudinal, behavioral, and perceptual), the largest effects were observed for the behavioral component of body image, whereas CBT had least impact on the attitudinal component (i.e., psychological investment in appearance). They also found that treatment approaches were more efficacious if they targeted all three components of body image than if they targeted attitudinal and behavioral components combined.

It is important to emphasize that although CBT has been beneficial for many individuals with negative body image, there are instances when it may be less effective. For instance, in severe cases of body dysmorphic disorder, CBT plus psychopharmacological interventions have been shown to be more effective than CBT alone (Allen & Hollander, 2002). Allen and Hollander argue that failure to treat the comorbid symptoms, such as obsessive-compulsive aspects of body dysmorphic disorder, means that an individual may experience relief of negative body image but still experience clinically significant levels of psychological dysfunction.

Some individuals may be unwilling or unable to seek treatment for body image because of costs involved in treatment, feelings of shame and embarrassment in seeking help, aversion to one-on-one or group contact, or lack of available counselling services within a reasonable distance of home and/or place of work. Increasingly, researchers are looking to inexpensive, self-guided alternatives to in-person treatment. Online programs in psycho-education or CBT have demonstrated moderate positive effects relative to nontreatment control groups (Geraghty *et al.*, 2010; Strachan & Cash, 2002; Winzelberg *et al.*, 2002). However, it has also been shown that minimal contact with clinicians for CBT interventions yields clinically significant improvements over the effects of self-guided CBT, and that minimal and consistent contact-based CBTs yield comparable results (Cash & Hrabosky, 2003). It is argued that contact with a therapist is advantageous to the treatment process as it increases compliance with treatment protocols and decreases the likelihood of dropping out (Strachan & Cash, 2002). Thus, Winzelberg *et al.* (2002) suggest that self-guided therapies may be used as an initial screening strategy in a multifaceted treatment regimen. In many instances, self-guided treatment may sufficiently reduce body image concerns to the point that further treatment in unnecessary. However, in cases where symptoms persist, the client may then be referred to clinician-guided therapy.

Recently, there has been a proliferation of alternatives to CBT for body image disturbances, such as use of mindfulness-based techniques to reduce the influence of negative body image cognitions (Blevins, 2008), gratitude diaries to train individuals to focus more so on the positive aspects of their lives (Geraghty *et al.*, 2010), and ecological and activist approaches (e.g., Levine & Smolak, 2002) which seek to facilitate positive change in body image by targeting social and environmental influences on negative body image. While it is presently unclear whether these approaches will yield comparable effects to CBT, or whether they may instead be complementary to CBT, Jarry and Ip (2005) argue that there is a need to explore these alternatives as they may be suitable alternatives for individuals who are unresponsive to traditional, CBT approaches.

Further research is also needed to evaluate potential gender effects in the efficacy of CBT and other approaches to treatment of body image disturbances. Much of the treatment literature cited in this section has had female-only samples, and the few studies that also included males had insufficient cases to make meaningful gender-based comparisons. While this gender imbalance may, in part, be attributable to gender differences in the prevalence of clinically significant body image disturbances, it is also possible that men are less likely to seek treatment for body image issues. Clearly, an examination of the factors which predict treatment seeking behavior would complement current knowledge about efficacy of treatment options for body image disturbances.

Conclusion

In this chapter we have seen that body image is broadly related to a range of health behaviors and cognitions, including use of body change strategies, functioning in interpersonal relationships, mental health, and obesity. It is also evident that the strength of these relationships is dependent on the ideal physique to which one aspires. Men in Western cultures seek a lean and muscular physique and therefore use a variety of body change behaviors which allow them to increase muscularity (e.g., chemical supplements, steroid use, and weight-lifting). In contrast, women tend to use dietary restraint and/or exercise to achieve a thin physique. Regardless of gender, the impact of negative body image on mental health is greater for individuals who psychologically invest in appearance.

Of the range of treatment options and modes currently available to alleviate the symptoms and sequelae of negative body image, one-on-one CBT with a psychologist has been shown to be most efficacious. Web-based applications of CBT appear promising, although they have a higher drop-out rate than in-person therapy and therefore should be supplemented with at least a minimal amount of contact with a therapist. Therapists should be mindful of the presence and potential impact of negative body image on the success of treatment, even if their primary focus is on another condition (e.g., eating disorder, comorbid mood disorder, etc.). If left untreated, negative body image can lead to relapse of these treated symptoms.

Further research is needed to more fully investigate the impact of body image on health across the adult lifespan. To date, the majority of research in this area has examined the link between body image and health in samples of adolescents and young adults, as this age range coincides with a peak in negative body image (Grogan, 2008). While recent studies demonstrate that negative body image and body change behaviors also occur in preadolescent samples, much less is known about the extent to which body image affects health in middle to later adulthood. Longitudinal studies show that negative body image in adolescence is predictive of mental health issues, obesity, and onset of eating disorders in early adulthood. However, it is unclear whether the body image issues that develop in these formative years continue to affect individuals in later life, or whether later-onset body image issues (e.g., in one's 30s or 40s) are also predictive of adverse health outcomes.

Research is also needed to explore the origin and stability of cultural differences in body image and related health outcomes. Although earlier studies suggested that body image disturbances and eating disorders were a primarily Western phenomenon, globalization and, in particular, the increasing reach of Western media coincides with increased body image concerns in previously unaffected regions of the world. Even so, some individuals remain resistant to these changing cultural values. Identifying protective factors that prevent an individual from internalizing unrealistic appearance standards and engaging in unhealthy body-image-related behaviors remains a research priority.

References

Agliata, D., & Tantleff-Dunn, S. (2004). The impact of media exposure on males' body image. *Journal of Social and Clinical Psychology, 23,* 7–22.

Allaz, A., Bernstein, M., Rouget, P., Archinard, M., & Morabia, A. (1998). Body weight preoccupation in middle-age and ageing women: A general population survey. *International Journal of Eating Disorders, 23,* 287–294.

Allen, A., & Hollander, E. (2002). Psychopharmacological treatments for body image disturbances. In T. F. Cash & T. Pruzinski (Eds.), *Body Image: A Handbook of Theory, Research, and Clinical Practice* (pp. 450–458). New York: Guilford Press.

American Society of Plastic Surgeons (2010). *Report of the 2010 Plastic Surgery Statistics.* www.plasticsurgery.com/News-and-Resources/Statistics.html.

Annis, N. M., Cash, T. F., & Hrabosky, J. I. (2004). Body image and psychological differences among stable average-weight, currently overweight and formerly overweight women: The role of stigmatizing experiences. *Body Image, 1,* 155–167.

Barker, E. T., & Galambos, N. L. (2007). Body dissatisfaction, living away from parents, and poor social adjustment predict binge eating symptoms in young women making the transition to university. *Journal of Youth and Adolescence, 36,* 904–911.

Barone, L., & Guiducci, V. (2009). Mental representations of attachment in eating disorders: A pilot study using the Adult Attachment Interview. *Attachment & Human Development, 11,* 405–417.

Bauchowitz, A. U., Gonder-Frederick, L. A., Olbrisch, M., Azarbad, L., Ryee, M., Woodson, M. *et al.* (2005). Psychosocial evaluation of bariatric surgery candidates: A survey of present practices. *Psychosomatic Medicine, 67,* 825–832.

Bennett, K., & Stevens, R. (1996). Weight anxiety in older women. *European Eating Disorders Review, 4,* 32–39.

Blevins, N. C. (2008). Mindfulness meditation as an intervention for body image and weight management in college women: A pilot study. Unpublished manuscript.

Boyes, A. D., Fletcher, G. J. O., & Latner, J. D. (2007). Male and female body image and dieting in the context of intimate relationships. *Journal of Family Psychology, 21,* 764–768.

Buhlmann, U., Glaesmer, H., Mewes, R., Fama, J. M., Wilhelm, S., Brahler, E., & Rief, W. (2010). Updates on the prevalence of body dysmorphic disorder: A population-based survey. *Psychiatry Research, 178,* 171–175.

Cafri, G., Thompson, J. K., Ricciardelli, L., McCabe, M., Smolak, L., & Yesalis, C. (2005). Pursuit of the muscular ideal: Physical and psychological consequences and putative risk factors. *Clinical Psychology Review, 25,* 215–239.

Cafri, G., Thompson, J. K., Roehrig, M., van den Berg, P., Jacobsen, P. B., & Stark, S. (2006). An investigation of appearance motives for tanning: the development and evaluation of the Physical Appearance Reasons for Tanning Scale (PARTS) and its relation to sunbathing and indoor tanning intentions. *Body Image, 3,* 199–209.

Cafri, G., Thompson, J. K., Jacobsen, P. B., & Hillhouse, J. (2009). Investigating the role of appearance-based factors in predicting sunbathing and tanning salon use. *Journal of Behavioural Medicine, 32,* 532–544.

Calder, N., & Aitken, R. (2008). An exploratory study of the influences that compromise the sun protection of young adults. *International Journal of Consumer Studies, 32,* 579–587.

Cash, T. F., & Strachan, M. D. (2002). Cognitive behavioural approaches to changing body image. In T. F. Cash & T. Pruzinsky (Eds.), *Body Image: A Handbook of Theory, Research, and Clinical Practice* (pp. 478–486). New York: Guilford Press.

Cash, T. F., & Hrabosky, J. I. (2003). The effects of psychoeducation and self-monitoring in a cognitive behavioral program for body image improvement. *Eating Disorders, 11,* 255–270.

Cash, T. F., & Hrabosky, J. I. (2004). Treatment of body image disturbances. In J. K. Thompson (Ed.), *Handbook of Eating Disorders and Obesity* (pp. 515–541). New York: Wiley.

Cash, T. F., Fleming, E. C., Alindogan, J., Steadman, L., & Whitehead, A. (2002). Beyond body image as a trait: The development and validation of the Body Image States Scale. *Eating Disorders: Journal of Treatment & Prevention, 10,* 103–113.

Cash, T. F., Theriault, J., & Annis, N. M. (2004). Body image in an interpersonal context: Adult attachment, fear of intimacy, and social anxiety. *Journal of Social and Clinical Psychology, 23,* 89–103.

Celio, C. I., Luce, K. H., Bryson, S. W., Winzelberg, A. J., Cunning, D., Rockwell, R. *et al.* (2006). Use of diet pills and other dieting aids in a college population with high weight and shape concerns. *International Journal of Eating Disorders, 39,* 492–497.

Clarke, L. H. (2002). Older women's perceptions of ideal bodyweights: The tensions between health and appearance motivations for weight loss. *Ageing and Society, 22,* 751–773.

Crow, S., Eisenberg, M. E., Story, M., & Neumark-Sztainer, D. (2008). Are body dissatisfaction, eating disturbances, and body mass index predictors of suicidal behaviour in adolescents? A longitudinal study. *Journal of Consulting and Clinical Psychology, 76,* 887–892.

Davison, T., & McCabe, M. (2005). Relationships between men's and women's body image and their psychological, social, and sexual functioning. *Sex Roles, 52,* 463–475.

Eisenberg, M. E., Neumark-Sztainer, D., Haines, J., & Wall, M. (2006). Weight-teasing and emotional wellbeing in adolescents: Longitudinal findings from Project EAT. *Journal of Adolescent Health, 38,* 675–683.

Evans, N. A. (1997). Gym and tonic: A profile of 100 male steroid users. *British Journal of Sports Medicine, 31,* 54–58.

Field, A. E., Austin, S. B., Taylor, C. B., Malspeis, S., Rosner, B., Rockett, H. R. *et al.* (2003). Relation between dieting and weight change among preadolescents and adolescents. *Pediatrics, 112,* 900–906.

Foreyt, J. P., Brunner, R. L., Goodrick, G. K., Cutter, G., Brownell, K., & St Jeor, S. T. (1995). Psychological correlates of weight fluctuation. *International Journal of Eating Disorders, 17,* 263–275.

Fredrickson, B. L., & Roberts, T. (1997). Objectification theory: Toward understanding women's lived experiences and mental health risks. *Psychology of Women Quarterly, 21,* 173–206.

Furnham, A., Badmin, N., & Sneade, I. (2002). Body image dissatisfaction: Gender differences in eating attitudes, self-esteem, and reasons for exercise. *The Journal of Psychology, 136,* 581–596.

Gapinski, K. D., Brownell, K. D., & LaFrance, M. (2003). Body objectification and "fat talk": Effects on emotion, motivation, and cognitive performance. *Sex Roles, 48,* 377–388.

Ge, X., Elder Jr., G. H., Regnerus, M., & Cox, C. (2001). Pubertal transitions, perceptions of being overweight, and adolescents' psychological maladjustment: Gender and ethnic differences. *Social Psychology Quarterly*, *64*, 363–375.

Geraghty, A. W. A., Wood, A. M., & Hyland, M. E. (2010). Attrition from self-directed interventions: Investigating the relationship between psychological predictors, intervention content and dropout from a body dissatisfaction intervention. *Social Science & Medicine*, *71*, 30–37.

Gerner, B., & Wilson, P. H. (2005). The relationship between friendship factors and adolescent girls' body image concerns, body dissatisfaction, and restrained eating. *International Journal of Eating Disorders*, *37*, 313–320.

Grabe, S., Hyde, J. S., & Lindberg, S. M. (2007). Body objectification and depression in adolescents: The role of gender, shame, and rumination. *Psychology of Women Quarterly*, *31*, 164–175.

Grogan, S. (2008). *Body image: Understanding Body Dissatisfaction in Men, Women, and Children*. New York: Routledge.

Halliwell, E., & Dittmar, H. (2004). Does size matter? The impact of model's body size on women's body-focused anxiety and advertising effectiveness. *Journal of Social and Clinical Psychology*, *23*, 104–122.

Hargreaves, D., & Tiggemann, M. (2002). The effect of television commercials on mood and body dissatisfaction: The role of appearance-schema activation. *Journal of Social and Clinical Psychology*, *21*, 287–308.

Harter, S. (1999). *The Construction of the Self. A Development Perspective*. New York: The Guilford Press.

Heinberg, L. J., Thompson, J. K., & Matzon, J. L. (2001). Body image dissatisfaction as a motivator for healthy lifestyle change: Is some distress beneficial? R. H. Striegel-Moore & L. Smolak (Eds.), *Eating Disorders: Innovative Directions in Research and Practice* (pp. 215–232). Washington DC: American Psychological Association.

Hinrichsen, H., Wright, F., Waller, G., & Meyer, C. (2003). Social anxiety and coping strategies in the eating disorders. *Eating Behaviours*, *4*, 117–126.

Hirschman, C., Impett, E. A., & Schooler, D. (2006). Disembodied voices: What late-adolescent girls can teach us about objectification and sexuality. *Sexual Research & Social Policy: A Journal of the NSRC*, *3*, 8–20.

Holsen, I., Kraft, P., & Roysamb, E. (2001). The relationship between body image and depressed mood in adolescence: A 5-year longitudinal panel study. *Journal of Health Psychology*, *6*, 613–627.

Hutchinson, D. M., & Rapee, R. M. (2007). Do friends share similar body image and eating problems? The role of social network and peer influences in early adolescence. *Behavior Research and Therapy*, *45*, 1557–1577.

Impett, E. A., Schooler, D., & Tolman, D. L. (2006). To be seen and not heard: Femininity ideology and adolescent girls' sexual health. *Archives of Sexual Behaviour*, *35*, 131–144.

Jarry, J. L., & Berardi, K. (2004). Characteristics and effectiveness of stand-alone body image treatments: A review of the empirical literature. *Body Image*, *1*, 319–333.

Jarry, J. L., & Ip, K. (2005). The effectiveness of stand-alone cognitive-behavioural therapy for body image: A meta-analysis. *Body Image*, *2*, 317–331.

Juhaeri, J., Stevens, L. E., Chambless, L. E., Tyroler, H. A., Harp, J., Jones, D., & Arnett, D. (2001). Weight change among self-reported dieters and non-dieters in white and African American men and women. *European Journal of Epidemiology*, *17*, 917–923.

Kanayama, G., Gruber, A. J., Pope, Jr., H. G., Borowiecki, J. J., & Hudson, J. I. (2001). Over-the-counter drug use in gymnasiums: An underrecognised substance abuse problem? *Psychotherapy and Psychosomatics*, *70*, 137–140.

Keery, H., van den Berg, P., & Thompson, K. (2004). An evaluation of the tripartite influence model of body dissatisfaction and eating disturbance with adolescent girls. *Body Image*, *1*, 237–251.

Kilpatrick, M., Hebert, E., & Bartholomew, J. B. (2005). College students' motivation for physical activity: Differentiating men's and women's motives for sport participation and exercise. *Journal of American College Health*, *54*, 87–94.

King, T. K., Matachin, M., White, K. S., & Marcus, B. H. (2005). A prospective examination of body image and smoking cessation in women. *Body Image*, *2*, 19–28.

Kirk, S., Cockbain, A. J., & Beazley, J. (2008). Obesity in Tonga: A cross-sectional comparative study of perceptions of body size and beliefs about obesity in lay people and nurses. *Obesity Research & Clinical Practice*, *2*, 35–41.

Koenig, L. J., & Wasserman, E. L. (1995). Body image and dieting failure in college men and women: Examining links between depression and eating problems. *Sex Roles, 32,* 225–249.

Kulik, J. A., Butler, H., Gerrard, M., Gibbons, F. X., & Mahler, H. (2008). Social norms information enhances the efficacy of an appearance-based sun protection intervention. *Social Science & Medicine, 67,* 321–329.

Lee, C. (2001). *Women's Health Australia: What Do We Do? What Do We Need to Know? Progress on the Australian Longitudinal Study of Women's Health 1995–2000.* Brisbane: Australian Academic Press.

Leit, R. A., Pope, Jr., H. G., & Gray, J. J. (2001). Cultural expectations of muscularity in men: The evolution of Playgirl centrefolds. *International Journal of Eating Disorders, 29,* 90–93.

Levine, M. P., & Smolak, L. (2002). Body image development in adolescence. In T. F. Cash & T. Pruzinsky (Eds.), *Body Image: A Handbook of Theory, Research, and Clinical Practice* (pp. 74–82). New York: Guilford Press.

Littleton, H., Breitkopf, C. R., & Berenson, A. (2005). Body image and risky sexual behaviours: An investigation in a tri-ethnic sample. *Body Image, 2,* 193–198.

Margro, D. O., Geloneze, B., Delfini, R., Pareja, B. C., Callejas, F., & Pareja, J. C. (2008). Long-term weight regain after gastric bypass: A 5-year prospective study. *Obesity Surgery, 18,* 648–651.

McCabe, M., & Ricciardelli, L. (2009). Extreme weight change behaviours: Are overweight and normal weight adolescents different, and does this vary over time? *European Eating Disorders Review, 17,* 301–314.

McCabe, M., Ricciardelli, L., Waqa, G., Gounder, R., & Fotu, K. (2009). Body image and body change strategies among adolescent males and females from Fiji, Tonga, and Australia. *Body Image, 6,* 299–303.

McDonagh, L. K., Morrison, T. G., & McGuire, B. E. (2007). The naked truth: Development of a scale designed to measure male body image self-consciousness during physical intimacy. *The Journal of Men's Studies, 16,* 253–265.

McGuire, M. T., Wing, R. R., Klem, M. L., Lang, W., & Hill, J. O. (1999). What predicts weight regain in a group of successful weight losers? *Journal of Consulting and Clinical Psychology, 67,* 177–185.

McVey, G., Tweed, S., & Blackmore, E. (2004). Dieting among preadolescent and young adolescent females. *Canadian Medical Association Journal, 170,* 1559–1561.

Meanna, M., & Nunnink, S. E. (2006). Gender differences in the content of cognitive distraction during sex. *Journal of Sex Research, 43,* 59–67.

Mellor, D., McCabe, M., Ricciardelli, L., & Merino, M. E. (2008). Body dissatisfaction and body change behaviors in Chile: The role of sociocultural factors. *Body Image, 5,* 205–215.

Mellor, D., Fuller-Tyszkiewicz, M., McCabe, M., & Ricciardelli, L. (2010a). The moderating influences of age and gender in the relationship between self-esteem and body dissatisfaction. Unpublished manuscript, Deakin University, Melbourne.

Mellor, D., Fuller-Tyszkiewicz, M., McCabe, M., & Ricciardelli, L. (2010b). Body image and self-esteem across age and gender: A short-term longitudinal study. *Sex Roles, 63,* 672–681.

Mellor, D., Ricciardelli, L., McCabe, M., Yeow, J., Hidayah bt Mamat, N., & Hapidzal, F. (2010c). Psychosocial correlates of body image and body change behaviors among Malaysian adolescent boys and girls. *Sex Roles, 63,* 386–398.

Meltzer, A. L., & McNulty, J. K. (2010). Body image and marital satisfaction: Evidence for the mediating role of sexual frequency and sexual satisfaction. *Journal of Family Psychology, 24,* 156–164.

Mission Australia (2010). *National Survey of Young Australians 2010: Key and Emerging Issues.* www.missionaustralia.com.au/downloads/national-survey-of-young-australians/2010/.

Mond, J. M., Hay, P. J., Rodgers, B., & Owen, C. (2006). An update on the definition of "excessive exercise" in eating disorders research. *International Journal of Eating Disorders, 39,* 147–153.

Palmeira, A. L., Branco, T. L., Martins, S. C., Minderico, C. S., Silva, M. N., Vieira, P. N. *et al.* (2010). Changes in body image and psychological wellbeing during behavioural obesity treatment: Associations with weight loss and maintenance. *Body Image, 7,* 187–193.

Patton, G. C., Carlin, J. B., Shao, Q., Hibbert, M. E., Rosier, M., Selzer, R., & Bowes, G. (1997). Adolescent dieting: Healthy weight control or borderline eating disorder? *Journal of Child Psychology and Psychiatry, 38,* 299–306.

Patton, G. C., Selzer, R., Coffey, C., Carlin, J. B., & Wolfe, R. (1999). Onset of adolescent eating disorders: Population based cohort study over 3 years. *British Medical Journal, 318,* 765–768.

Paxton, S. J., Schutz, H. K., Wertheim, E. H., & Muir, S. L. (1999). Friendship clique and peer influences on body image concerns, dietary restraint, extreme weight-loss behaviours, and binge eating in adolescent girls. *Journal of Abnormal Psychology, 108,* 255–266.

Paxton, S. J., Neumark-Sztainer, D., Hannan, P. J., & Eisenberg, M. E. (2006). Five year change in body satisfaction among adolescents. *Journal of Psychosomatic Research, 61,* 521–527.

Peñas-Lledó, E., Sancho, L., & Waller, G. (2002). Eating attitudes and the use of alcohol, tobacco, and exercise among male and female adolescents. *Eating Behaviors, 3,* 101–111.

Phares, V., Steinberg, A. R., & Thompson, J. K. (2004). Gender differences in peer and parental influences: Body image disturbance, self-worth, and psychological functioning in preadolescent children. *Journal of Youth & Adolescence, 33,* 421–429.

Pinger, F., & Crittenden, P. M. (2007). Eating disorders and attachment: The effects of hidden family processes on eating disorders. *European Eating Disorders Review, 15,* 119–130.

Pole, M., Crowther, J. H., & Schell, J. (2004). Body dissatisfaction in married women: The role of spousal influence and marital communication patterns. *Body Image, 1,* 267–278.

Puyols, J., Meston, C. M., & Brooke, N. S. (2010). The association between sexual satisfaction and body image in women. *Journal of Sexual Medicine, 7,* 905–916.

Ramirez, E. M., & Rosen, J. C. (2001). A comparison of weight control and body image therapy for obese men and women. *Journal of Consulting and Clinical Psychology, 69,* 440–446.

Ricciardelli, L. A., & McCabe, M. P. (2001). Children's body image concerns and eating disturbance: A review of the literature. *Clinical Psychology Review, 21,* 325–344.

Ricciardelli, L. A., & McCabe, M. P. (2004). A biopsychosocial model of disordered eating and the pursuit of muscularity in adolescent boys. *Psychological Bulletin, 130,* 179–205.

Ricciardelli, L. A., & McCabe, M. (2007). Pursuit of muscularity among adolescents. In J. K. Thompson & G. Cafri (Eds.), *The Muscular Ideal: Psychological, Social, and Medical Perspectives* (pp. 199–216). Washington: American Psychological Association.

Ricciardelli, L. A., McCabe, M. P., Williams, R. J., & Thompson, J. K. (2007). The role of ethnicity and culture in body image and disordered eating among males. *Clinical Psychology Review, 27,* 582–606.

Rodriguez-Cano, T., Beato-Fernandez, l., & Llario, A. B. (2006). Body dissatisfaction as a predictor of self-reported suicide attempts in adolescents: A Spanish community prospective study. *Journal of Adolescent Health, 38,* 684–688.

Rosen, J. C. (1996). Body image assessment and treatment in controlled studies of eating disorders. *International Journal of Eating Disorders, 20,* 331–343.

Sanchez, D. T., Good, J. J., Kwang, T., & Saltzman, E. (2008). When finding a mate feels urgent: Why relationship contingency predicts men's and women's body shame. *Social Psychology, 39,* 90–102.

Sarwer, D. B., Thompson, J. K., & Cash, T. F. (2005). Body image and obesity in adulthood. *Psychiatric Clinics of North America, 28,* 69–87.

Sarwer, D. B., Crerand, C. E., & Gibbons, L. M. (2007). Cosmetic procedures to enhance body shape and muscularity. In J. K. Thompson & G. Cafri (Eds.), *The Muscular Ideal: Psychological, Social, and Medical Perspectives* (pp. 183–198). Washington, DC: American Psychological Association.

Schick, V. R., Calabrese, S. K., Rima, B. N., & Zucker, A. N. (2010). Genital appearance dissatisfaction: Implications for women's genital image self-consciousness, sexual esteem, sexual satisfaction, and sexual risk. *Psychology of Women Quarterly, 34,* 394–404.

Schooler, D., Ward, L. M., Merriwether, A., & Caruthers, A. (2005). Cycles of shame: Menstrual shame, body shame, and sexual decision-making. *Journal of Sex Research, 42,* 324–334.

Schwartz, M. B., & Brownell, K. D. (2004). Obesity and body image. *Body Image, 4,* 43–56.

Sharpe, T. M., Killen, J. D., Bryson, S. W., Shisslak, C. M., Estes, L. S., Gray, N. *et al.* (1998). Attachment style and weight concerns in preadolescent and adolescent girls. *International Journal of Eating Disorders, 23,* 39–44.

Sherwood, N. E., Jeffery, R. W., & Wing, R. R. (1999). Binge status as a predictor of weight loss treatment outcome. *International Journal of Obesity and Related Metabolic Disorders, 23,* 485–493.

Smith, C., & Ricciardelli, L. A. (2011). Sun protection motives: The importance of a tanned appearance to young Australian adults. Unpublished manuscript, Deakin University, Melbourne.

Steptoe, A. W., Pollard, T. M., & Wardle, J. (1995). Development of a measure of the motives underlying the selection of food: The Food Choice Questionnaire. *Appetite, 25,* 267–284.

Stice, E. (1998). Modeling of eating pathology and social reinforcement of the thin-ideal predict onset of bulimic symptoms. *Behaviour Research & Therapy, 36,* 931–944.

Stice, E. (2002). Risk and maintenance factors for eating pathology: A meta-analytic review. *Psychological Bulletin, 128,* 825–848.

Stice, E., & Whitenton, K. (2002). Risk factors for body dissatisfaction in adolescent girls: A longitudinal investigation. *Developmental Psychology, 38,* 669–678.

Stice, E., Hayward, C., Cameron, R. P., Killen, J. D., & Taylor, C. B. (2000). Body image and eating disturbances predict onset of depression among female adolescents: A longitudinal study. *Journal of Abnormal Psychology, 109,* 438–444.

Strachan, M. D., & Cash, T. F. (2002). Self-help for a negative body image: A comparison of components of a cognitive-behavioural program. *Behavior Therapy, 33,* 235–251.

Swami, V., Frederick, D. A., Aavik, T., Alcalay, L., Allik, J., Anderson, D. *et al.* (2010). The attractive female body weight and female body dissatisfaction in 26 countries across 10 world regions: Results of the international body project I. *Personality and Social Psychology Bulletin, 36,* 309–325.

Syspeck, M. F., Gray, J. J., Etu, S. F., Ahrens, A. H., Mosimann, J. E., & Wiseman, C. V. (2006). Cultural representations of thinness in women, redux: Playboy magazines' depiction of beauty from 1979 to 1999. *Body Image, 3,* 229–235.

Thompson, J. K., Heinberg, L., Altabe, M., & Tantleff-Dunn, S. (Eds.). (1999). *Exacting Beauty: Theory, Assessment, and Treatment of Body Image Disturbance.* Washington DC: American Psychological Association.

Tiggemann, M. (2004). Body image across the adult life span: Stability and change. *Body Image, 1,* 29–41.

Tiggemann, M. (2005). Body dissatisfaction and adolescent self-esteem: Prospective findings. *Body Image, 2,* 129–135.

Tiggemann, M., & Stevens, C. (1999). Weight concern across the life-span: Relationship to self-esteem and feminist identity. *International Journal of Eating Disorders, 26,* 103–106.

Tiggemann, M., & Lynch, J. E. (2001). The impact of adolescent girls' life concerns and leisure activities on body dissatisfaction, disordered eating, and self-esteem. *Journal of Genetic Psychology, 162,* 133–142.

Venditti, E. M., Wing, R. R., Jakicic, J. M., Butler, B. A., & Marcus, M. D. (1996). Weight cycling, psychological health, and binge eating in obese females. *Journal of Consulting and Clinical Psychology, 64,* 400–405.

Vohs, K. D., Heatherton, T. F., & Herrin, M. (2001). Disordered eating and the transition to college: A prospective study. *International Journal of Eating Disorders, 29,* 280–288.

Wade, T. J., & Cooper, M. (1999). Sex differences in the links between attractiveness, self-esteem, and the body. *Personality and Individual Differences, 27,* 1047–1056.

Wiederman, M. W. (2000). Women's body image self-consciousness during physical intimacy with a partner. *Journal of Sex Research, 37,* 60–68.

Wiederman, M. W. (2002). Body image and sexual functioning. In T. F. Cash & T. Pruzinsky (Eds.), *Body Image: A Handbook of Theory, Research, and Clinical Practice* (pp. 287–294). New York: Guilford Press.

Wilcox, S. (1997). Age and gender in relation to body attitudes: Is there a double standard of aging? *Psychology of Women Quarterly, 21,* 549–565.

Willard, S. G., McDermott, B. E., & Woodhouse, L. (1996). Lipoplasty in the bulimic patient. *Plastic and Reconstructive Surgery, 98,* 276–278.

Winzelberg, A. J., Abascal, L. B., & Taylor, C. B. (2002). Psychoeducational approaches to the prevention and change of negative body image. In T. F. Cash & T. Pruzinsky (Eds.), *Body Image: A Handbook of Theory, Research, and Clinical Practice* (pp. 487–496). New York: Guilford Press.

Wiseman, C. V., Turco, R. M., Sunday, S. R., & Halmi, K. A. (1998). Smoking and body image concerns in adolescent girls. *International Journal of Eating Disorders, 24,* 429–433.

Wroblewska, A. (1997). Androgenic-anabolic steroids and body dysmorphia in young men. *Journal of Psychosomatic Research, 42,* 225–234.

Xu, X., Mellor, D., Kiehne, M., Ricciardelli, L., McCabe, M., & Xu, Y. (2010). Body dissatisfaction, engagement in body change behaviours and sociocultural influences on body image among Chinese adolescents. *Body Image, 7,* 156–164.

Yamamiya, Y., Cash, T. F., Melnyk, S., Posavac, H. D., & Posavac, S. S. (2005). Women's exposure to thin-and-beautiful media images: Body image effects of media-ideal internalisation and impact-reduction interventions. *Body Image, 2*, 74–80.

Yuan, A. S. V. (2007). Gender differences in the relationship of puberty with adolescents' depressive symptoms: Do body perceptions matter? *Sex Roles, 57*, 69–80.

Yuan, A. S. V. (2010). Body perceptions, weight control behavior, and changes in adolescents' psychological wellbeing over time: A longitudinal examination of gender. *Journal of Youth & Adolescence, 39*, 927–939.

20

Maladaptive Eating Practices as Precursors to Eating Disorders

A Method of Assessment

Justine L. Ebenreuter and Richard E. Hicks

Maladaptive eating practices develop into eating disorders as defined by the *Diagnostic and Statistical Manual of Mental Disorders* (4th edn, text revision; DSM-IV-TR; American Psychiatric Association, 2000) in 40% of reported cases. Eating disorders as defined by the DSM-IV-TR are limited to fully established eating disorders. Therefore current tests do not capture maladaptive eating practices, or eating disorders in the formative stages. This chapter examines maladaptive eating practices and identifies subdiagnostic indicators relating to cognitive, emotional, and behavioral processes, assessed through the development of a new questionnaire. An eating disorder framework is used to better understand the outcomes of maladaptive eating practices.

Maladaptive eating practices are represented by a group of disorders in which there are significant disturbances in eating (Fox & Leung, 2008; Pott *et al.*, 2009). According to the DSM-IV-TR, these practices include three distinct eating disorder diagnoses: anorexia nervosa, bulimia nervosa, and eating disorder not otherwise specified (EDNOS; American Psychiatric Association, 2000; Enten & Golan, 2008). Each differs in presentation, symptoms, and severity (McLaughlin *et al.*, 2006; Slane *et al.*, 2010). Severe food restriction, bingeing, and purging behaviors may be present within a clinical diagnosis. Anorexia nervosa is characterized by a fear of gaining weight, weight loss that is considered to be unhealthy, and modified eating practices (Katzman, 2005). Bulimia nervosa is characterized by unusually secretive high-kilojoule food intake and bingeing sessions (Budd, 2007). These sessions are accompanied by compensating practices such as heavy exercise, vomiting, or strict dieting periods, and many incur emotional responses such as shame and loss of control (Perkins *et al.*, 2006). The primary distinction between anorexia nervosa and bulimia nervosa diagnostic criteria is reflected in the anorexic's refusal to maintain normal body weight and amenorrhea in postmenarcheal females (Crossfield, 2005). EDNOS encompasses a wider spectrum of disordered eating practices and is frequently used for individuals who fulfill some but not all of the diagnostic criteria of anorexia nervosa or bulimia nervosa (Marcus & Wildes, 2009). One example of EDNOS is binge eating disorder (BED), which is marked by uncontrollable binge eating in the absence of compensatory behaviors. It is important to note that obesity is not recognized as an eating disorder by the DSM-IV-TR, because it has not been associated with a psychological or

Applied Topics in Health Psychology, First Edition. Edited by M. L. Caltabiano and L. Ricciardelli.
© 2013 John Wiley & Sons, Ltd. Published 2013 by John Wiley & Sons, Ltd.

behavioral syndrome. However, the study reported in this chapter obesity was included in the definition of maladaptive eating practices for individuals who reported using maladaptive weight-control techniques that impact negatively on their physical and psychological health.

While a lot is known about eating disorders, certain areas such as subdiagnostic indicators have not been given much attention. This is because eating behavior is often assessed via a number of psychometrically sound instruments, which look for a specific DSM-IV-TR diagnostic outcome. For example, the Eating Disorder Diagnostic Scale (EDDS) diagnoses anorexia, bulimia, and BED (Stice *et al.*, 2000), the Questionnaire for Eating Disorder Diagnoses (Q-EDD) differentiates between eating disorder, symptomatic, and asymptomatic individuals and between those with anorexia, bulimia, and EDNOS diagnoses (Mintz *et al.*, 1997) and the Eating Disorder Inventory-3 (EDI-3; Garner *et al.*, 1983) assesses the presence of an eating disorder specifying both restricting and binge-eating/purging type of anorexia, bulimia, and EDNOS including BED, also aligned specifically to the DSM-IV-TR criteria.

The literature on eating disorders currently includes relevant psychological, sociocultural, and relational domains that also need to be assessed. Within the psychological domain, the designation of maladaptive eating practices includes cognitive, affective/emotional, and physical/behavioral dimensions. The cognitive dimension is typified by dysfunctional thoughts about food and one's poor sense of identity relative to others. The affective/emotional dimension includes feelings of shame, guilt, depression, and hopelessness as well as perfectionism, tied to body image. The physical/behavioral dimension is characterized by rituals. These rituals may include daily weigh-ins, heavy exercise, observance of strict food rules, obsessive calorie counting, and episodic, unrestrained, eating behaviors (Blodgett *et al.*, 2007). Similarly cultural and environmental factors add pressure for thinness, increase body dissatisfaction, dieting, and negative affect (e.g., anxiety, depression, and low self-esteem), which reinforce a range of maladaptive eating practices. Alternatively, high levels of social support from family and friends tends to counteract the effects of stress on maladaptive eating behaviors, as feeling accepted and appreciated by others is believed to help people feel more positively about themselves and their bodies (Stice *et al.*, 2000).

Maladaptive eating practices also impact on physical health. The literature on eating disorders highlights a number of health risks associated with maladaptive eating practices that range from benign to life-threatening (Garner, 1997). Behavioral consequences most frequently cited include starvation, inadequate nutrient intake, bingeing and purging, and laxatives and diuretics abuse. These behaviors can result in a number of significant health consequences such as cardiovascular complications (e.g., loss of heart muscle mass and cardiac failure), lowered bone mineral density (e.g., osteoporosis), gastrointestinal (e.g., constipation, ulcers, esophagus tears, and gastrointestinal bleeding), and disrupted hormone functioning (e.g., reduced fertility; Garner, 1997; Lock *et al.*, 2001). Individuals with long-standing or entrenched maladaptive eating behaviors place themselves at a higher risk for developing a significant health problem. However, individuals who engage in periodic malnutrition (e.g., fasting, meal skipping, and dieting) are common among those who partially meet the criteria for a clinical eating disorder and remain at risk (Perkins *et al.*, 2006). Biochemical abnormalities associated with individuals who engaged in less frequent maladaptive practices such as inadequate nutrient intake and purging tend to report reduced energy levels and overall physical and psychological functioning. These findings highlight the importance of attending to all individuals who display disordered eating practices including those who may not meet the threshold for a clinical eating disorder diagnosis.

The DSM-IV-TR definitions are useful, but they do not give attention to the subdiagnostic aspects of maladaptive eating practices. Until recently the substantial number of individuals with a significant eating pathology who did not meet full clinical diagnostic criteria were unrepresented in both the clinical arena and research and literature. Currently there are no satisfactory indicators of who will acquire anorexia nervosa or bulimia nervosa and who will not (Fink *et al.*, 2009; Johnson-Sabine *et al.*, 1998). To rectify this situation, research has expanded to conceptualize disordered eating practices through a continuum ranging from unconcerned with weight at one end, to full diagnosis at the other (Crossfield, 2005). Situated in the middle range are maladaptive eating practices (Budd, 2007). Maladaptive eating practices mirror eating disorder definitions as provided by the DSM-IV-TR; the difference lies in severity of presentation.

A broader definition is necessary for maladaptive eating practices because research in this area suggests that subdiagnostic individuals are particularly at risk of developing a clinical eating disorder (Crossfield, 2005), and it is predicted that as many as 40% of these individuals will develop full criteria (Budd, 2007). Although subthreshold individuals may not meet the requirements for formal diagnoses, a significant level of pathology exists within these behaviors (Fox & Leung, 2008). This is important in clinical practice when considering disordered eating behaviors that fall short of traditional clinical guidelines (Perkins *et al.* 2006).

Research by the authors has sought to identify gaps in the subdiagnostic literature and offer a broader perspective than that offered by the current eating disorder frameworks, which would be useful for clients and professionals. Correlates implicated in maladaptive eating disorders were identified and assessed to add to this knowledge. Eating disorder frameworks were used as a guide to understand currently identified maladaptive eating practices and the theories associated with these. Existing frameworks as discussed in current literature include (1) etiologic, (2) psychosocial, (3) multifactor, and (4) single factor.

Eating Disorder Frameworks

The evolution of eating disorder frameworks commenced in the early 19th century and today all of the frameworks remain in practice, to a greater or lesser extent. Of the four frameworks identified none has been wholly discredited and clinical practitioners and researchers over time have expanded upon them. Because of this level of persistence, clarity of these frameworks is essential to this work, and to understanding the need for the new prediagnostic scale.

An early framework that explained the rise in incidence and awareness of maladaptive eating practices and has resulted in substantial research and literature in the field of eating disorders (Evans & le Grange, 2005) is the etiologic framework. Late 19th century etiologic models of disordered eating maintained that family influence was the primary cause of maladaptive eating (le Grange *et al.*, 2009). Etiologic research was grounded in psychoanalytic theory (Lipsitt, 1989). These theories generated a framework which stated that parents were to blame for the development and maintenance of their child's illness (Mazzeo *et al.*, 2005). Etiologic theories in this framework support the theory of blame, which argues that the family system and individuals within that system had an adverse affect upon the identified person (Bjärehed & Lundh, 2008). The dominance of etiologic frameworks prevail as blame theories, which are persistently cited in contemporary literature; this is despite conflicting with the position assumed by relevant eating disorder groups worldwide (Blissett & Haycraft, 2008; Decaluwé *et al.*, 2006; Mott, 1994). Regardless, etiologic theory initiated the psychosomatic movement that attempted to alleviate the void between mind and body (le Grange *et al.*, 2009). Historically the framework addressed theories of blame; today we give emphasis to the family, but through a number of other important frameworks. Another historical framework is the psychosocial framework.

The psychosocial framework was as a result of the paradigm shift away from etiologic theory. This framework added to the awareness of maladaptive eating practices by recognizing that the family has a pathological influence on eating in two conceptual ways. Firstly, the framework considered the parental influence and attitude on the development of food preferences and adoption of eating styles in childhood and adolescence. Baumrind (1971) provided the necessary link between eating disorder research and impact of parental style through research on parental behavior at home and the behavior of the child at school (Davey *et al.*, 2003). Baumrind (1991) uncovered key parenting skills associated with positive outcomes in childhood and used a combination of these skills to codify three behavioral dimensions or parenting styles: *authoritarian, authoritative*, and *permissive*. Parenting styles became critical to the understanding of maladaptive eating practices when it is understood that the authoritarian style, characterized by restrictive feeding practices, was found to be the predominant feeding style adopted by underweight children (Davey *et al.*, 2003). Parents who used an authoritative style showed more supportive involvement and appropriative control over their children's eating. Indulgent and permissive parenting impacted on feeding styles and typically resulted in less use of controlling feeding practices. Uninvolved parents relied on physical punishment rather than more child-centered parenting teaching techniques, when compared with indulgent parents (Enten & Golan, 2008).

Secondly, the framework explored family involvement in the development of control issues central to disordered eating practices in adolescence and early adulthood (Crossfield, 2005). Control is essential as lack of control can lead to a child developing maladaptive eating practices that include the inability to effectively self-regulate with the potential outcomes of overeating or extremely restrictive habits, either of which may lead to the growth and preservation of maladaptive eating practices (Davis *et al.*, 2001). On their own the etiologic and psychosocial frameworks fail to explain all necessary facts, and therefore a multifactor framework was developed.

Unlike the etiologic and psychosocial frameworks, the multifactor framework draws upon multiple determinants as the causes(s) of maladaptive eating behaviors (Enten & Golan, 2008; Latzer *et al.*, 2008). Depression, anxiety, and maladaptive perfectionism (Bardone-Cone *et al.*, 2010) were the variables that united to construct the multicause framework. The etiologic and psychosocial frameworks are single-cause frameworks; however, the impact of family function on eating is only one of the possible factors that may contribute towards the adoption of maladaptive eating practices (Crossfield, 2005; Mott, 1994). The multifactor frameworks, like the etiologic and psychosocial frameworks before it, offer evidence that maladaptive eating practices can occur because children are susceptible to internalizing problems when parents are intrusive and controlling. Other theories, for example, Blatt's (2004) theory of depression and Fleet and colleagues' (2005) theory of perfectionism evolved from the psychosocial framework. These developed into a social expectations factor under the multifactor framework and indicated that linkages occur between the growth of perfectionism and controlling parenting. Currently, etiologic, psychosocial, and multifactor frameworks continue to be important. However, the single-factor framework is today's accepted benchmark, although it has some strengths and weaknesses.

Unlike the multifactor framework, the single-factor family influence framework has as a single focus – *the family* – when seeking to explain the adoption of maladaptive eating practices. This single-focus research at no point took into account how individuals with an eating disorder perceived their own parents' parenting styles. More recently researchers have argued that children's perceptions have psychological reality whether these views are or are not factually correct (Shafran & Robinson, 2004). This is the child's reality and the one that they respond to (Young *et al.*, 2004).

Recent research has started to acknowledge the importance of asking children directly about parenting experiences. Critical gaps remain within this area of knowledge (Crossfield, 2005). A greater understanding of the behavior and growth of children's maladaptive eating practices and the relationship with the child's *perception* of their parents' parenting practices would achieve more clarity with increased information (Enten & Golan, 2008; Renae & Liossis, 2009). The information should provide insight into children's beliefs about their parents' parental behaviors and their subsequent interpretation and assessment of these (Latzer *et al.*, 2008). The views of children are necessary and require further research. This is because their perceptions of their parents' parenting are superior predictors of their own psychosocial development and behavior (Braet *et al.*, 2007; Turner & Cooper, 2002).

This knowledge is the essential missing element in the single-factor family influence framework and its treatment of maladaptive eating practices, an element that this current research sought to address. In order to examine the framework-specific steps were followed. A problem became apparent when seeking to explain the bridge between eating disorders and maladaptive eating practices. This is because the literature defines eating disorders in accordance with the DSM-IV-TR, which relies heavily on occurrence and rating of eating symptomologies for relevance. There were no set diagnostic rules for eating practices, while eating disorders were clearly outlined.

To rectify this shortfall a broader set of causes, or symptomology, was sought which lead to the development and application of a new instrument on eating practices, the Inner Thoughts on Eating Questionnaire (ITEQ). While the role of the individual within the context of the family together with maladaptive eating practices could be explained by each of the above frameworks, the ITEQ was the tool developed for expansion of the most recently developed single-factor family influence framework. Therefore, two distinct stages were adopted to meet this bridge. Firstly, the ITEQ was developed, and secondly, resulting data were used to identify related factors and areas needing further study using the single factor. The remainder of this chapter will report on the authors' research to create a new psychometric measure that would realize domain coverage (cognitive, emotional, behavioral) sufficient to identify maladaptive eating behaviors that fall outside the definition of eating disorders in the DSM-IV-TR (American Psychiatric Association, 2000; Latzer *et al.*, 2008; Wade *et al.*, 2009) and would also demonstrate adequate internal consistency, construct and face validity, and test–retest reliability.

The goal of stage one was to develop and validate the maladaptive eating practices questionnaire. The ITEQ was developed using cognitive, affective, and behavioral statements vetted by 15 subject-matter experts, and trialed in a pilot sample (30 participants) and a university sample (305 participants). To validate the resulting 14-item ITEQ, a clinical sample of 62 participants was recruited from eating disorder clinics across Queensland, Australia. The second stage of the project examined the single-factor family influence framework (which indicates the influence of family on eating habits) to identify how the new scale might add to understanding of the development of eating disorders.

The hypothesis that the new ITEQ scale would have sufficient domain coverage and identify (cognitive, emotional, behavioral) domains reflective of *a priori* definitions derived from eating disorder literature was supported by means of statistical analyses, including a three-factor solution reflecting the three domains of the broader definition of maladaptive eating practices. Table 20.1 shows the 14 items in the ITEQ and indicates the major domain assessed by the item (three items also weighted on another domain, which is indicated in parentheses).

The design of the ITEQ met the researchers' aim to identify maladaptive eating practices and thus enable eating issues to be addressed prior to a potential increase of symptoms that may lead to an eating disorder. Further validation of the ITEQ is ongoing and may lead to improvements, but the initial findings show that the questionnaire can identify prediagnostic criteria (cognitive, affective, and behavioral) that could be precursors to a range of eating disorders.

The subdiagnostics indicators (the three subscales of ITEQ) were used in a series of hypotheses about the single-factor family influence framework, aimed at clarifying the relationships to perceived parenting styles, perfectionism, and internalized psychological distress and identifying

Table 20.1 Orthogonally rotated component loadings of the 14-item ITEQ

	Rotated component matrix		
	Factor 1 Cognitive	Factor 2 Affective/emotional	Factor 3 Behavioral/physical
2. I become nervous when I think people see what I'm really like.	0.778		
11. I lead a double life.	0.770		
1. I feel I have to pretend to be someone better than I really am.	0.755		
14. I often get angry when things don't go the way I want.	0.607		
4. I have personal private rituals that get me through each day.	0.531		0.421
3. I often leave situations because I feel too nervous to stay.	0.670		
8. When things go wrong it's because I deserve to suffer.	0.517	0.424	
5. I am often pleased by my own appearance.		0.679	
9. I regularly feel capable and competent.		0.662	
12. The world is kind to me.		0.631	
7. I believe I can help other people.		0.534	
13. I try not to think of things that upset me.			0.735
10. I try excessively to achieve the perfect body.	0.402		0.485
6. I avoid people who aim to hurt me.			0.466

whether the new subscales might add to the accepted family influence model. Thus an alternate eating disorder framework that included the subdiagnostic indicators was proposed as follows (see Figure 20.1).

In testing the proposed model, data were collected via self-report measures using the ITEQ, Eating Attitudes Test (Garner, 1997), the Parental Authority Questionnaire (Baumrind, 1991; Buri, 1991), the Frost Multidimensional Perfectionism Scale (FMPS; Frost *et al.*, 1990), and the Psychological General Wellbeing Schedule (Bech, 1995). The findings (using appropriate regression analyses) showed relationships between maladaptive eating practices and psychological distress in the prediction of perceived parenting styles (Latzer *et al.*, 2008; Wade *et al.*, 2009). In addition maladaptive perfectionist views were also linked with maladaptive eating behaviors and with perceived parenting styles. The extended (proposed) family influence framework (see Figure 20.1) included the new subdiagnostic indicators of maladaptive eating practices, previously identified variables, and perceived parenting styles and maladaptive perfectionism. Perceived parenting styles and maladaptive perfectionism, while referred to in the literature, are not variables currently included in the single-factor family influence framework (Shafran & Robinson, 2004). However, their inclusion may help inform our understanding of how eating disorders develop. Being able to target maladaptive eating behaviors and thoughts before the development of

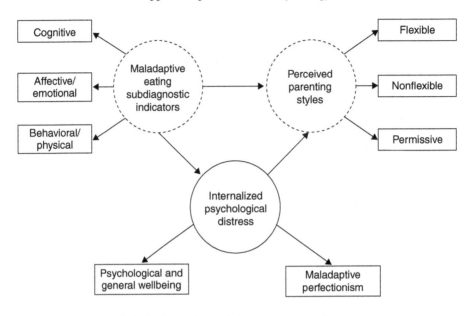

Figure 20.1 **Proposed single-factor family influence framework.**

full-scale eating disorders appears likely to be helped by use of the extended family framework model suggested here. The authors are still working on the extended framework model, including direction of influences and on validation studies, but the model with the ITEQ subscales seems likely to be useful in practice.

Concluding Comments

The identification of maladaptive eating practices that inform the discussion on eating disorders in the formative stages provides the opportunity for a more knowledgeable clinical practitioner. This is because these framework hypotheses clarify the subdiagnostic indicators of maladaptive eating by examining their relationships to perceived parenting styles, perfectionism, and internalized psychological distress. This current reported work by the authors adds to the body of knowledge currently existing in the literature and represented in the single-factor family influence framework. This work adds to the evolution of the eating disorder frameworks, which take us from etiologic, psychosocial, and multifactor frameworks to a single-factor framework. It has been shown that each of these frameworks persist. However, the identification of a single-factor framework that now includes maladaptive eating practices provides clinical practitioners with a new technique to identify individuals at risk at an earlier stage of treatment and because of this many individuals might be helped before full eating disorder symptomology occurs.

Armed with this knowledge the clinical practitioner has the option to be able to assist individuals to identify potentially destructive eating practices, in line with preventative approaches as preferred treatment models (Crossfield, 2005). The DSM-IV-TR classification for eating disorders does not adequately allow for identification of individuals at risk in the *formative stages* of their maladaptive eating practices. The identification of variables at the formative stage of the individual's maladaptive eating practices appears to be related to perceived parenting styles. Harsh and nonflexible parenting styles have been demonstrated through this study to have a probable direct relationship with maladaptive eating practices.

As a method of assessment, the ITEQ helped identify early maladaptive eating practices as a potential precursor to eating disorders as defined by the DSM-IV-TR. The usefulness of a prediagnostic scale for clinical practice has important practical implications, which highlight the need for researchers and clinicians to address a range of eating disorders seen in clinical practice that fall outside the DSM-IV-TR criteria. This is essential if they are to successfully address maladaptive eating in this early and critical stage of development. It enables clinicians to capture significantly wider data and report accordingly. It includes a new definition that moves away from existing traditional eating disorder research. By including this expanded range of disordered eating practices and cross-diagnostic information data may be collected to inform the course and response to treatment and clinically informative subdivisions may be able to be identified (Fairburn & Bohn, 2005).

Maladaptive eating practices are not represented in the literature or in major eating disorder frameworks. The new study conducted by the authors contributes data to the discussion of maladaptive eating practices by adding to existing eating disorder frameworks. This was achieved in two ways. Firstly, the ITEQ on eating practices was developed, tested, and utilized in the data-collection stage of this study. Secondly, the data from the ITEQ on eating practices showed the importance of family attitudes and influences (the single-factor family influence framework model) in affecting disordered outcomes.

References

American Psychiatric Association. (2000). *Diagnostic and Statistical Manual of Mental Disorders* (4th edn, Text revision). Washington DC: American Psychiatric Association.

Bardone-Cone, A. M., Sturm, K., Lawson, M. A., Robinson, P. D., & Smith, R. (2010). Perfectionism across stages of recovery from eating disorders. *International Journal of Eating Disorders, 43*, 139–148.

Baumrind, D. B. (1971). Current patterns of parental authority. *Developmental Psychology, 4*, 91–103.

Baumrind, D. B. (1991). The influence of parenting style on adolescent competence and substance use. *Journal of Early Adolescence, 11*, 56–95.

Bech, P. (1995). Quality of life measurement in the medical setting. *European Psychiatry, 10*(3), 83–85.

Bjärehed, J., & Lundh, L. (2008). Deliberate self-harm in 14-year-old adolescents: How frequent is it, and how is it associated with psychopathology, relationship variables, and styles of emotional regulation? *Cognitive Behaviour Therapy Review, 37*, 26–37.

Blatt, S. J. (2004). *Experiences of Depression: Theoretical, Research and Clinical Perspectives.* Washington DC: American Psychological Association Press.

Blissett, J., & Haycraft, E. (2008). Are parenting style and controlling feeding practices related? *Appetite, 50*, 477–485.

Blodgett, E. H., Gondoli, D. M., Corning, A. F., McEnery, A. M., & Grundy, A. M. (2007). Psychological distress as a mediator of the relation between perceived maternal parenting and normative maladaptive eating among adolescent girls. *Journal of Counseling Psychology, 54*, 434–446.

Braet, C., Soetens, B., Moens, E., Mels, S., Goossens, L., & Van Vlierberghe, L. (2007). Are two informants better than one? Parent–child agreement on the eating styles of children who are overweight. *European Eating Disorders Review, 15*, 410–417.

Budd, G. (2007). Disordered eating: Young women's search for control and connection. *Journal of Child and Adolescent Psychiatric Nursing, 20*, 96–106.

Buri, J. R. (1991). Parental authority questionnaire. *Journal of Personality Assessment, 57*, 110–119.

Crossfield, A. G. (2005). Parental control, low perceived control and perfectionism: An integration of three etiological models of disordered eating. *Science and Engineering, 66*, 2810–2814.

Davey, M., Fish, L. S., Askew, J., & Robila, M. (2003). Parenting practices and the transmission of ethnic identity. *Journal of Marital and Family Therapy, 29*, 195–208.

Davis, C. L., Delameter, A. M., & Shaw, K. H. (2001). Brief report: Parenting styles, regimen adherence, and glycemic control in 4 to 10 year old children with diabetes. *Journal Pediatric Psychology, 26*, 123–129.

Decaluwé, V., Braet, C., Moens, E., & van Vlierberghe, L. (2006). The association of parental characteristics and psychological problems in obese youngsters. *International Journal of Obesity, 30*, 1766–1774.

Enten, R. S., & Golan, M. (2008). Parenting styles and weight-related symptoms and behaviors with recommendations for practice. *Nutrition Reviews, 65*, 10–24.

Evans, J., & le Grange, D. (2005). Body size and parenting in eating disorders: A comparative study of the attitudes of mothers towards their children. *International Journal of Eating Disorders, 37*, 77–79.

Fairburn C. G., & Bohn K. (2005) Eating disorder NOS (EDNOS): An example of the troublesome "not otherwise specified" (NOS) category in DSM-IV. *Behaviour Research and Therapy, 43*, 691–701.

Fink, E. L., Smith, A. R., Gordon, K. H., Holm-Denoma, J. M., & Joiner, T. E. (2009). Psychological correlates of purging disorder as compared with other eating disorders: An exploratory investigation. *International Journal of Eating Disorders, 42*, 31–39.

Fleet, G. L., Hewitt, P. L., Blankstein, K. R., & Koledin, S. (2005). Dimensions of perfectionism and irrational thinking. *Behavioural Science, 9*, 185–201.

Fox, A. P., & Leung, N. (2008). Existential well-being in younger and older people with anorexia nervosa: A preliminary investigation. *European Eating Disorder Review, 4*, 56–59.

Frost, T. O., Marten, P., Lahart, C., & Rosenblate, R. (1990). The dimensions of perfectionism. *Journal of Cognitive Therapy and Research, 14*, 449–468.

Garner, D. M. (1997). *Handbook of Treatment for Eating Disorders.* New York: Guilford Press.

Garner, D. M., Olmsted, M. P., & Polivy, J. (1983). Development and validation of a multidimensional EDI for anorexia nervosa and bulimia. *International Journal of Eating Disorders, 2*, 15–34.

Johnson-Sabine, E. C., Wood, K., Patton, G. C., Mann, A. H., & Wakeling A. (1998). Abnormal eating attitudes in London school girls: A prospective epidemiological study. *Psychosocial Medicine, 18*, 615–622.

Katzman, D.K. (2005). Medical complications in adolescents with anorexia nervosa: a review of the literature. *International Journal of Eating Disorders, 37*, 52–59.

Latzer, Y., Peretz, T., & Kreutzer, S. (2008). Conflict-oriented cognitive behavioral therapy: An integrative approach to the treatment of bulimia nervosa patients. *Clinical Social Work Journal, 36*, 373–383.

le Grange, D., Lock, J., Loeb, K., & Nicholls, D. (2009). Academy for eating disorders position paper: The role of the family in eating disorders. *International Journal of Eating Disorders, 43*, 1–5.

Lipsitt, D. R. (1989) Anorexia nervosa and the associative anamnesis: A psychosomatic kaleidoscope. *Psychosomatic Medicine, 51*, 597–607.

Lock, J., le Grange, D., Agras, W. S., & Dare, C. (2001). *Treatment Manual for Anorexia Nervosa: A Family-Based Approach.* New York: The Guilford Press.

Marcus, M. D., & Wildes, J. E. (2009). Obesity: Is it a mental disorder? *International Journal of Eating Disorders, 42*, 739–753.

Mazzeo, S. E., Zucker, N. L., Gerke, C. K., Mitchell, K. S., & Bulik, C. M. (2005). Parenting concerns of women with histories of eating disorders. *International Journal of Eating Disorders, 37*, 77–79.

McLaughlin, E. F., Karp, S. A., & Herzog, D. B. (2006). Sense of ineffectiveness in women with eating disorders: A clinical study of anorexia nervosa and bulimia. *International Journal of Eating Disorders, 4*, 511–523.

Mintz, L. B., O'Halloran, S. M., Mulholland, A. M., & Schneider, P. A. (1997). Questionnaire for eating disorder diagnoses (Q-EDD): Reliability and validity of operationalizing DSM-IV criteria into a self-report format. *Journal of Counseling Psychology, 44*, 63–79.

Mott, A. (1994) *Understanding Eating Disorders: Anorexia Nervosa, Bulimia Nervosa and Obesity.* London: Taylor & Francis.

Perkins, S. J., Murphy, R., Schmidt, U., & Williams, C. (2006). Self-help and guided self-help for eating disorders. *Cochrane Systematic Reviews, 5*, 191–194.

Pott, W., Ozgur, A., Hebebrand, J., & Pauli-Pott, U. (2009). Treating childhood obesity: Family background variables and the child's success in a weight-control intervention. *International Journal of Eating Disorders, 42*, 284–289.

Renae, E., & Liossis, P. (2009). Australian adolescents' perceptions of their parents: An analysis of parenting styles, communication and feelings towards parents. *Youth Studies Australia, 24,* 265–278.

Shafran, R., & Robinson, P. (2004). Thought-shape fusion in eating disorders. *British Journal of Psychology, 43,* 399–407.

Slane, J. D., Burt, S. A., & Klump, K. L. (2010). The road less travelled: Associations between externalizing behaviors and eating pathology. *International Journal of Eating Disorders, 43,* 149–160.

Stice, E., Telch, C. F., & Rizvi, S. (2000). Development and validation of the eating disorder diagnostic scale: A brief self-report measure of anorexia, bulimia and binge-eating disorder. *Psychological Assessment, 12,* 123–131.

Turner, H., & Cooper, M. (2002). Cognitions and their origins in women with anorexia nervosa, normal dieters and female controls. *Clinical Psychology and Psychotherapy, 9,* 242–252.

Wade, T. D., Treloar, S. A., Heath, A., & Martin, N. (2009). An examination of the overlap between genetic and environmental risk factors for intentional weight loss and overeating. *International Journal of Eating Disorders, 42,* 492–497.

Young, E. A., Clopton, J. R., & Bleckley, M. K. (2004). Perfectionism, low self-esteem, and family factors as predictors of bulimic behavior. *Eating Behaviors, 5,* 273–283.

21

Maternal Obesity Through Pregnancy and the Postpartum

Psychosocial Determinants and the Implications for Childhood Obesity

Helen Skouteris

At the time of the 2007–2008 National Health Survey, 31% of Australian women over the age of 18 years were overweight and 23.6% were obese (Australian Bureau of Statistics, 2009). The importance of childbearing in the development of obesity in women has been recognized for over a decade (Olson, 2007). Pregnancy is a time of significant psychological and physical change for women; consequently, it is a time at which many women are at risk of gaining excessive weight. Although excessive weight gain in pregnancy is a common health-related problem in Western countries, the increased prevalence of overweight and obesity in adult women in developing and non-Western countries (World Health Organization, 2010) suggests that excessive gestational weight gain is an issue that requires global attention. Women who gain excessive weight during pregnancy have an increased risk of postpartum obesity in themselves and their children (Oken et al., 2007; Olsen, 2007). Furthermore, approximately, one in five women retain at least 5 kg of gestational weight gain at 6–18 months postbirth, and this weight retention is a strong predictor of maternal overweight and obesity a decade or more after birth (Amorim et al., 2007). Understanding the antecedents and consequences of maternal obesity through pregnancy and the postpartum is therefore warranted. This chapter begins with an overview of the psychosocial determinants of maternal obesity; the extant literature on gestational and postpartum obesity, published since January 2000, is reviewed. The subsequent section summarizes the findings of research conducted in the last decade focused on the implications of maternal obesity for childhood obesity. The chapter concludes with directions for future research in this area.

Psychosocial Determinants of Maternal Obesity Through Pregnancy and the Postpartum

To the author's knowledge, only 12 studies published in the last decade (2000–2010) have examined the psychosocial determinants of maternal obesity during pregnancy and the postpartum. An overview of psychosocial determinants assessed in each of these studies and the sample size of each study are presented in Table 21.1. One was a qualitative study (Sterling et al., 2009), and of the

Applied Topics in Health Psychology, First Edition. Edited by M. L. Caltabiano and L. Ricciardelli.
© 2013 John Wiley & Sons, Ltd. Published 2013 by John Wiley & Sons, Ltd.

Table 21.1 Psychosocial factors measured in studies focused on maternal obesity through pregnancy and the postpartum

	Depressive symptoms	Anxiety	Social support	Body image/perceived body weight	Locus of control	Self-esteem/ self-efficacy	Belonging	Eating attitudes	Stress	Health behavior/ lifestyle	Restrained behavior
Carter et al. (2000) n = 64	✓	✓	×	×	×	×	×	✓	×	×	×
DiPietro et al. (2003) n = 130	✓	✓	✓	✓	×	×	×	×	✓	×	×
Herring et al. (2008a) n = 1537	×	×	×	✓	×	×	×	×	×	×	×
Herring et al. (2008b) n = 850	✓	×	×	×	×	×	×	×	×	✓	×
Huang et al. (2010) n = 602	✓	×	✓	✓	✓	✓	✓	×	✓	×	×
Krause et al. (2009) n = 491	✓	×	×	×	×	×	×	×	×	×	✓
Mumford et al. (2008) n = 1223	×	×	×	×	×	×	×	✓	×	×	×
Siega-Riz et al. (2010) n = 688	✓	×	×	×	×	×	×	×	×	×	×
Sterling et al. (2009) n = 25	✓	×	×	✓	×	×	×	×	×	×	×
Walker et al. (2002) n = 305	✓	×	×	×	×	×	×	×	×	×	×
Walker & Kim (2002) n = 283	✓	×	×	×	×	×	×	×	×	✓	×
Webb et al. (2008) n = 1605	✓	✓	×	×	✓	✓	×	×	✓	×	×
Total ✓	10	3	2	4	2	2	1	2	3	2	1

✓ = assessed, × = not assessed

others, four were cross-sectional in design (DiPietro *et al.*, 2003; Huang *et al.*, 2010; Krause *et al.*, 2009; Walker & Kim, 2002), and seven studies were longitudinal.

Depression, anxiety, and stress

As noted in Table 21.1, depression has been, by far, the most researched psychological factor. In their cross-sectional studies, Walker and Kim (2002) assessed depressive symptoms in women on the day of delivery, or on the first to third days after delivery, Krause *et al.* (2009) assessed maternal depressive symptoms at 6 weeks postpartum, Huang *et al.* (2010) at 6 months postbirth, and DiPietro *et al.* (2003) at 36 weeks of gestation. None of these studies reported a positive association between depressive symptoms and maternal body mass index (BMI).

Of the seven longitudinal studies, five assessed the prospective associations between depressive symptoms and maternal obesity (Carter *et al.*, 2000; Herring *et al.*, 2008a; Siega-Riz *et al.*, 2010; Walker *et al.*, 2002; Webb *et al.*, 2008). Walker *et al.* (2002) did not report an association between depressive symptoms and maternal obesity; they assessed depressive symptoms after delivery and 6 weeks postpartum. In contrast, Carter *et al.* (2000) assessed depressive symptoms during pregnancy (exact gestation not given) and at 4 and 14 months postpartum and found a significant positive association at both postpartum time points but not during pregnancy. Herring *et al.* (2008a) and Webb *et al.* (2008) also found an association between weight retention/gestational weight gain and depressive symptoms; in their studies women were assessed at 6 and 12 months postpartum (Herring *et al.*, 2008b) and at less than 20 weeks and between 24 and 29 weeks of gestation (Webb *et al.*, 2008).

Interestingly, the findings noted above for Herring *et al.* (2008b) and Webb *et al.* (2008) were for unadjusted models including depression; when they included in their models important covariates, such as weight-related variables (prepregnancy BMI and/or gestational weight gain) as well as parity and maternal sociodemographic factors, and pregnancy/postpartum behaviors, such as physical activity, sleep duration, and dietary intake, there was a modest attenuation in the risk associated with antenatal (Webb *et al.*, 2008) or postnatal (Herring *et al.*, 2008b) depression. Herring *et al.* suggested that the effect of depression postbirth on weight retention of more than 5 kg at 12 months postpartum may be partly explained by a lack of sleep and/or physical activity that are common symptoms of depression. Siega-Riz *et al.* (2010), who assessed depressive symptoms at 3 and 12 months postpartum, argued that Herring *et al.*'s findings mirrored theirs in that bivariate associations for postpartum depressive symptoms and postpartum weight retention no longer remained when more influential factors, such as total energy intake, were included in multivariate models.

Herring *et al.* (2008b) concluded that postnatal depression appears to predict maternal obesity after birth. Their conclusion was based on the fact that prepregnancy BMI and gestational weight gain only slightly attenuated the association found between weight retention at 12 months postbirth and postpartum depression. Gestational weight gain was also shown to be a significant predictor of weight retention at 3 and 12 months postbirth in Siega-Riz *et al.*'s (2010) study. Hence, controlling for these factors in any model of postpartum weight retention is essential. Carter at al. (2000) did not do so, and, as such, their findings that depression and maternal obesity were associated in the postpartum and that BMI at 4 months postbirth predicted depressive symptomatology at 14 months postbirth should be treated with caution. Carter *et al.* did not assess a model of depression predicting maternal BMI; this is not surprising given their small sample size.

Given the paucity of prospective research in this area, further work is needed to better understand the mechanisms underlying the associations between depression and maternal obesity;

such research must necessarily involve multivariate models that include weight-related, sociodemographic, physical, behavioral, and psychosocial variables. A similar recommendation can be made for research on anxiety and stress and maternal obesity because this area of research is even further limited. Only three studies have examined the association between anxiety and maternal obesity during pregnancy and/or the postpartum. Both Carter *et al.* (2000) and Webb *et al.* (2008) assessed anxiety using a longitudinal design across the same time points as noted above for depressive symptoms in each study. Webb *et al.* showed that trait, but not state, anxiety played a modest role in predicting gestational weight gain in uncorrected models ($P<0.007$), whereas Carter *et al.* reported a positive association between state anxiety and maternal obesity during the postpartum only (4 and 14 months postbirth; trait anxiety not measured). In accordance with Carter *et al.*'s findings, DiPietro *et al.* (2003) found that anxiety and maternal BMI were not associated significantly during pregnancy, assessing the relationship between the two variables cross-sectionally at 28 weeks of gestation. DiPietro *et al.* also examined the association between symptoms of stress and maternal weight status at 36 weeks of gestation; no significant association was revealed. This was also the case in Webb *et al.*'s study, with women's stress appraisals assessed prospectively during pregnancy (17–22 and 27–30 weeks of gestation) and in Huang *et al.*'s study (2010) with stress and maternal BMI measured at 6 months postbirth.

Body image/perceived body weight

Four studies measured body image or perceived body weight as a psychosocial determinant of maternal obesity (DiPietro *et al.*, 2003; Herring *et al.*, 2008b; Huang *et al.*, 2010; Walker *et al.*, 2002). In their longitudinal studies, Herring *et al.* (2008b) assessed women at 10 weeks of gestation and delivery, while Walker *et al.* (2002) assessed women immediately following delivery and 6 weeks postpartum. Herring *et al.* found a positive association between misperceived weight status (that is, whether or not a participant perceived they were a normal weight when they were in fact overweight/obese) and excessive gestational weight gain. Walker *et al.* found that maternal weight at 6 weeks postpartum was associated significantly with body image assessed at both postdelivery and 6 weeks postpartum; heavier mothers were more dissatisfied with their body image. In cross-sectional research, DiPietro *et al.* (2003) also reported that heavier women were more likely to report negative body image attitudes and Huang *et al.* (2010) reported that poorer body image was a significant predictor of weight retention 6 months postbirth in both normal weight and obese women.

Clearly, the prevention of high levels of body dissatisfaction and, potentially, obesity during the reproductive phase will only be effective when models of risk factors during these years have been examined systematically and rigorously and the interplay between risk factors is well understood. Given the limited number of studies that have evaluated the association between body image and maternal obesity pre- and postbirth, further research is warranted and needed urgently (Skouteris, 2011).

Other psychosocial factors

Social support (including partner support) and its relationship to maternal overweight/obesity was examined only by DiPietro *et al.* (2003) and Huang *et al.* (2010). Both studies reported that there was no significant association between social support and overweight/obesity or gestational weight gain. Health behaviors/lifestyle has also been assessed in only two studies. Huang *et al.*

showed that nutritional health behavior was associated negatively with maternal obesity, whereas Walker and Kim (2002) found no association between health behaviors, including measurements of self-care and food habits, and BMI or gestational weight gain at the end of the gestational period.

In three studies, the association between eating attitudes or restrained eating and maternal obesity was examined. In Siega-Riz *et al.*'s (2010) longitudinal study, eating attitudes were assessed in relation to weight retention at 3 and 12 months postpartum; a positive association was found at 3 months, but not at 12 months postpartum. Similarly, Carter *et al.* (2000) assessed eating attitudes at two times during the postpartum, but no association was found at either time point. Mumford *et al.* (2008) assessed restrained eating behavior using a longitudinal design. They found restrained eating, which encompassed behaviors such as attitudes towards food, time concerned about food, and concern about weight fluctuations, was related positively to gestational weight gain, with these behaviors assessed at recruitment (mean of 14 weeks of gestation) and at 3 months postpartum.

Sterling *et al.* (2009) conducted a somewhat different study to the aforementioned studies, using a qualitative cross-sectional approach to examine low-income women's experiences of weight changes and depressive symptoms during the late postpartum period. Sterling *et al.* identified that perceived locus of control was a major theme for the 25 women in their focus groups, stating that perceived personal control encompassed feelings of inadequacy surrounding weight changes. In contrast, Webb *et al.* (2008) and Huang *et al.* (2010) did not find a positive association between locus of control and maternal obesity. However, Huang *et al.* reported that low perceived self-efficacy for body weight management and belonging (companionship support) were associated with weight retention among overweight women at 6 months postpartum.

The findings of the studies presented above suggest that psychosocial factors cannot be ignored when considering maternal obesity during pregnancy and/or the postpartum; this is especially the case when considering intervention strategies to prevent excessive gestational weight gain. Indeed, in her review of interventions to manage excessive weight gain during pregnancy, Walker (2007) concluded that interventions to date had limited success possibly because psychosocial factors were not considered. That is, interventions have not included dedicated behavior-change assistance aimed at identifying and addressing behavioral, emotional, cognitive, and situational barriers that might impede behavior change. Instead, interventions to prevent excessive gestational weight gain have focused mostly on dietary intake and physical activity (see Skouteris *et al.*, 2010 for a review of interventions focused on preventing excessive gestational weight gain). The lack of consideration of psychosocial factors was also identified by the American Institute of Medicine (2009). Hence, Skouteris *et al.* (2010) concluded: "Future interventional studies should implement and systematically evaluate alternate strategies to maintain and/or improve women's weight gain management during pregnancy. One such strategy might involve targeting behavioral changes in relation to eating and physical activity *as well as* changes in psychological factors such as mood (depression, anxiety), body image concerns, and motivation and/or confidence to make behavioral changes" (p. 766).

The Implications of Maternal Obesity for Childhood Obesity

Epidemiological studies indicate that childhood overweight is a serious problem in Australia, with an estimated one in four Australian school-aged children and adolescents either overweight or obese (Booth *et al.*, 2007). Alarmingly, recent national data have revealed that 15.3% of preschool children were overweight and a further 5.2% obese (Wake *et al.*, 2007). Overweight and obese children and adolescents are at risk of a range of health problems and have an increased risk of premature death in adulthood; there are both immediate complications and long-term consequences of child and adolescent obesity (Lobstein *et al.*, 2004). Research has shown that obesity can also have psychological consequences among children, such as increased stigmatization, depression, and lower self-concept (Dohnt & Tiggemann, 2004; McCabe & Ricciardelli, 2003). Hence, understanding what modifiable risk factors contribute to patterns of weight gain in young children is essential to effectively address the increase in prevalence of childhood obesity. Strong evidence supports a role of nonmodifiable genetic factors in energy-storage patterns (Rankinen *et al.*, 2006), but these are insufficient to explain the increase in childhood overweight in recent years. The primary social force influencing preschool children is the family; consequently, many of the determinants of risk factors for overweight and obesity in the preschool years are likely to have roots in the family context (Ventura & Birch, 2008). We know that parents are the primary social force influencing child development in the formative preschool years and hence for some time now researchers have been concerned with investigating the parental beliefs and practices known to be associated with overweight or excessive weight gain in children. Parental influences such as feeding styles (pressure to eat, restriction, monitoring, and control of dietary intake), instrumental behaviors (using food as a reward), availability (degree to which parents provide a healthy environment), role modelling (particularly weight-related behaviors), and nutritional knowledge have been shown to be associated with child eating, physical activity habits, and child weight status (see Ventura & Birch, 2008 for a review of this literature). Additionally, when parents model healthy eating themselves and provide children with healthy food options their children are more likely to eat and try new healthy foods (Skouteris *et al.*, 2011). Parenting styles and child weight status have also been found to be associated significantly (see Wake *et al.*, 2007).

Whereas research on the association between parental beliefs/cognitions and practices and child obesity has expanded over the last 10 years, to the author's knowledge only 10 studies have assessed the influence of pre- and postnatal maternal obesity, and maternal psychosocial functioning and behaviors, on children's obesity. Given the small number of studies that have been conducted in this area over the last decade, the details pertaining to the study aim(s), sample, design, and measures, and the findings of each study, are summarized in Table 21.2.

Four studies examined the impact of maternal depressive symptoms on child obesity (Ajslev *et al.*, 2010; Ertel *et al.*, 2010; Grote *et al.*, 2010; Surkan *et al.*, 2008) with two studies reporting a positive association (Ertel *et al.*, 2010; Surkan *et al.*, 2008). Ertel *et al.* (2010) found that antenatal symptoms of depression, but not postnatal symptoms, were associated with child central adiposity at 3 years of age. In contrast, Surkan *et al.* (2008) assessed participants only in the postnatal period (from 6 to 24 months), finding that children of mothers with elevated depressive symptoms had a greater risk of being overweight and an even greater risk of being obese. Given that recent evidence also reveals a positive association between maternal depressive and anxiety symptoms and controlling feeding styles, which are known to be associated with higher child BMI (Blissett & Farrow, 2007; Haycraft & Blissett, 2008; Hurley *et al.*, 2008; Mitchell *et al.*, 2009), prevention of the development of psychopathology may be just as important in the prevention of childhood obesity. Clearly, more research is needed to elucidate the mechanisms by which maternal depressive symptoms (and/or anxiety) contribute to obesity in young children.

The relationship between maternal BMI and/or gestational weight and childhood overweight has been investigated in six studies (Moreira *et al.*, 2007; Oken *et al.*, 2007, 2008; Olson & Strawdermann, 2009; Whitaker, 2004; Wrotniak *et al.*, 2008), with each of these studies reporting a positive association, with the exception of Wrotniak *et al.* (2008). In contrast to the other five studies, they found that children of underweight mothers who gained excessively during pregnancy were at the highest risk of overweight/obesity. As pointed out by Whitaker (2004), there are "many mechanisms by which a mother's obesity in pregnancy might confer risk of obesity to her child, including the child's inheritance of genes that confer susceptibility to obesity, the effects of maternal

Table 21.2 Studies investigating the influence of maternal obesity and psychosocial determinants on childhood obesity

Author, country	Aims	Sample	Design	Psychosocial determinants	BMI measurement and criteria	Findings
Ajslev et al. (2010) Denmark	To investigate the association between maternal obesity and gestational weight gain, postpartum stress (including anxiety and depression), and childhood overweight	n = 21 121 Psychological factors assessed 6 months postpartum Maternal mean age (SD); normal weight: 30.7 (4.1) years, overweight: 30.6 (4.2) years	Longitudinal: data collected twice during pregnancy and when child was 6 and 18 months old Part of a prospective cohort study (Danish National Birth Cohort)	Maternal depressive symptoms, maternal distress, anxiety, and stress Questions assessing psychosocial variables selected from Symptom Distress Checklist and General Health Questionnaire; completed at 6 months postpartum	Children measured for weight status at 5 and 12 months and 7 years old Child BMI determined by international age and sex specific cutoffs; underweight ≤ 18.5 kg/m^2, overweight ≥ 25 kg/m^2, and obese ≥ 30 kg/m^2 if child stays on same growth curve Child BMI measured through parent self-report, maternal weight assessed objectively through interview Maternal BMI classifications according to Institute of Medicine (1990): underweight (<18.5 kg/m^2), normal weight (18.5–24.9 kg/m^2), overweight (25–29.9 kg/m^2), obese (30–34.9 kg/m^2) and severe obesity (≥ 35 kg/m^2)	Depression, anxiety, and stress (postpartum distress) were not associated with childhood obesity at age 7 years Means (SD) of prepregnant BMI in relation to child weight status: 23.1 (3.6) kg/m^2 normal weight, 25.3 (4.7) kg/m^2 overweight, $P < 0.005$ Means (SD) of maternal gestational weight gain for child weight status: 15.2 (5.2) kg/m^2 normal child weight, 15.7 (6.1) kg/m^2 overweight, $P < 0.005$

Study	Aim	Sample	Design	Measures	Findings
Ertel *et al.* (2010) USA	To examine maternal antenatal and postpartum depression, maternal BMI and gestational weight gain, and child outcomes at 3 years old	$n = 838$ Maternal mean age (SD): 32.97 (4.46) years Child mean age (SD): 38.96 (3.23) months	Longitudinal: data collected at five time points: midpregnancy, 6 months, and 1, 2, and 3 years postbirth Child weight assessed at birth, 6 months, and 3 years old Maternal depression assessed midpregnancy and at 6 months postpartum	Maternal depressive symptoms, assessed at midpregnancy (mean 28 weeks gestation) and 6 months postbirth Edinburgh Postnatal Depression Scale	BMI z score according to US national reference data to classify child weight status Child BMI measured with objective measures Child adiposity was assessed measuring subscapular and triceps skinfold thickness Maternal prepregnancy weight was self-reported, subsequent BMI measurements were objectively measured. Weight gain was assessed using the Institute of Medicine (1990) guidelines	Antenatal depression was significantly associated with central adiposity ($p = 0.02$) Postpartum depression associated to higher overall adiposity ($P = 0.14$) Pre-pregnancy weight gain was significantly associated with antenatal depressive symptoms: 26.1% inadequate gains, 33.3% adequate gains and 40.6% inadequate gains, $P = 0.02$ 50% of mothers had excessive weight gain
Grote *et al.* (2010) Germany	To investigate maternal postnatal depression as a risk factor for overweight in later childhood	$n = 929$ Child mean age (SD): 24.2 (0.6) months 39.1% of mothers aged 28–<33 years	Longitudinal: data obtained from a randomized controlled trial conducted in Belgium, Germany, Italy, Poland, and Spain Children were assessed at 3, 6, 12, and 24 months Measurements taken at 2, 3, and 6 months after birth for mothers	Depressive symptoms Edinburgh Postnatal Depression Scale assessed depression at each time point	Child BMI classification based upon WHO growth standards Infant growth assessed using BMI and skinfold thickness Child and maternal BMI measured objectively	No effect was found between maternal postnatal depression and child BMI 20.5% of mothers were overweight, 7.2% were obese Child BMI at 24 months did not differ from normal or high levels of depressive symptoms ($P = 0.64$) Child BMI z scores did not differ significantly between maternal BMI ($P = 0.158$).

(*continued*)

Table 21.2 Studies investigating the influence of maternal obesity and psychosocial determinants on childhood obesity (*Continued*)

Author, country	Aims	Sample	Design	Psychosocial determinants	BMI measurement and criteria	Findings
Moreira *et al.* (2007) Portugal	To assess the association between maternal gestational weight gain and childhood overweight	N = 4845 n = 2445 girls n = 2400 boys Child mean (SD) age: 8.5 (0.92) years in both genders	Cross-sectional Assessed children between 6 and 12 years of age		Child BMI cutoffs were based in the average centiles from a survey by Cole *et al.* (2000). BMI of 25 kg/m² (overweight) and 30 kg/m² (obese) Maternal BMI was assessed using self-report measures Child BMI was measured using objective methods	20.9% of girls and 18.5% of boys were overweight 11.9% of girls and 10.3% of boys were obese Odds ratio (CI) for overweight children with maternal gestational weight gain ≥16.0 kg: 1.53 (1.27–1.48), $p < .001$
Oken *et al.* (2008) USA	To investigate association of maternal gestational weight gain with offspring weight status in adolescence	n = 11 994 Participants part of previous study (Nurses Health Study II) with offspring enrolled in Growing Up Today Study 20.5 and 20.0% of children aged 11 and 10 years old respectively 83.3% of mothers aged 25–34 years	Longitudinal: data taken at prepregnancy (mothers) and at 9–14 years of age (adolescence)		Mother and child BMI was self-reported BMI classification and recommended gestational weight gain in accordance with Institute of Medicine (1990) guidelines Child age and sex-specific BMI z scores were calculated in accordance with the US Centers for Disease Control and Prevention reference data	Maternal: 11.3% overweight and 3.6% obese. Mean gestational weight gain 31.5 (11.2) lb 13.4% of children had a BMI at the 85th to less than 95th percentile, 6.5% had a BMI ≥95th percentile Women with higher excessive weight gain had children with higher odds of obesity (1.42, 95% CI 1.19–1.70) and overweight (1.27, 95% CI 1.12–1.44) compared to women of adequate gain 6.4% of children of mothers that never smoked had a BMI above 95th percentile, compared 8.4% with a mother who smoked during pregnancy

Oken *et al.* (2007) USA	To examine the association between maternal gestational weight gain and child adiposity	$n = 1044$	Longitudinal Children assessed at 6 months and 3 years postpartum	Institute of Medicine (1990) guidelines used to assess gestational weight gain Child weight measured using objective measures Child blood pressure, and tricep and subscapular skinfold thickness were also measured Maternal prepregnancy weight was self-reported; subsequent BMI measurements were objectively measured	Mean (SD) maternal BMI: 24.6 (5.0) kg/m^2. Mean (SD) total gestational weight gain 15.6 (5.4) kg 9% of children were overweight (above 95th percentile) at 3 years of age Gestational weight gain was directly associated with child overweight (OR 1.3, CI, 1.04, 1.62)
Olson *et al.* (2009) USA	To investigate the association between gestational weight gain and BMI in offspring at age 3	$n = 208$ Maternal age not reported Mean age of children not reported	Longitudinal Mothers assessed at first and second trimester of pregnancy, 6 months, 1 and 2 years postpartum	BMI measured objectively BMI and gestational weight gain classified in accordance with Institute of Medicine (1990) guidelines Child BMI classified by US Centers for Disease Control and Prevention growth reference charts Child overweight defined >85th percentile for their sex-specific percentile for age	Predictors of child overweight: maternal BMI (1.109, $P = 0.003$), BMI and gestational weight gain (1.005, $P = 0.05$), and smoking in pregnancy (3.12, $P = 0.02$) 38.5% of mothers were overweight in early pregnancy 47.5% of children of overweight mothers were overweight at 3 years, compared to 23.7% of children of normal or underweight mothers ($P = 0.03$)

(continued)

Table 21.2 Studies investigating the influence of maternal obesity and psychosocial determinants on childhood obesity (*Continued*)

Author, country	Aims	Sample	Design	Psychosocial determinants	BMI measurement and criteria	Findings
Surkan et al. (2008) Brazil	To investigate the association between maternal depressive symptoms and overweight in children	$n = 589$ mothers and children	Cross-sectional Child age of assessment: 27.2% 2–12 months, 31.3% 12–18 months, 41.5% 18–25 months	Maternal depression assessed using Centre for Epidemiological Studies Depression Scale; a score of ≥ 16 defined as presence of depressive symptoms	Child weight assessed using BMI z score Overweight cutoff defined as 85th percentile and obesity cutoff taken at 95th percentile on the WHO Multicentre Growth Reference Study curves Objective measure used to measure BMI	35% of children were overweight and 16% were obese Children of high depressive mothers were up to two times more likely to be in the overweight or obese range Adjusted OR (95% CI) for BMI z score above 85th percentile in association with higher depressive symptoms: 1.7 (1.4–2.2) Adjusted OR (95% CI) for BMI z score above 95th percentile in association with higher depressive symptoms: 2.3 (1.6–3.3) Comparison of child ages indicated that children aged 6–12 years were more likely to be placed in the 85th and 95th compared to children in 12–18 and 18–25 month age groups

Study	Aim	Sample	Design	Measures	Results
Whitaker (2004) USA	To investigate the association between maternal obesity in early pregnancy and obesity in children at 2 and 4 years of age	$n = 8494$ Mean child age at last measurement: 48.2 months	Longitudinal Data for children collected at birth and 2, 3, and 4 years of age Maternal data collected at mean of 9.3 weeks' gestation	Both child and maternal measures of weight status were taken through objective measures	Prevalence of childhood obesity: at 2 years 9.5%, 3 years 12.5%, 4 years 14.8% Mean (SD) maternal BMI: 27.3 (7.2) kg/m² Prevalence of BMI ≥85th percentile among children with obese mothers: at 2 years 28.4%, at 3 years 36.9% and at 4 years 41.2% Prevalence of child obesity was significantly different between maternal BMI categories ($p < 0.001$)
Wrotniak et al. (2008) USA	To examine the association between gestational gain with child overweight	$n = 10\,226$ Median maternal age: 23	Longitudinal Mothers assessed at time of delivery and children assessed at birth and 7 years of age	Maternal BMI categories and recommended gestational weight gain were based on Institute of Medicine (1990) guidelines Maternal gestational weight gain was determined as the difference between self-reported prepregnancy weight and objectively measured weight at time of delivery Child weight was objectively measured	Median prepregnancy maternal BMI was 21.9 kg/m²; 11% of women gained excessive weight 5.7% of children were overweight at 7 years of age Children of mothers with a BMI >29 kg/m² and gained an excessive amount of weight had a 48% greater odds being overweight at 7 years of age Underweight mothers who gained excessively compared to healthy weight gain had an OR of 3.18 (CI 1.38, 7.59)

CI, confidence interval

obesity on intrauterine environment, and the maternal role in shaping the child's postnatal eating and activity environment" (p. e34). Whitaker also argued that the effect of the mother's obesity on the child's obesity was not mediated primarily by the intrauterine influences expressed in higher birth weight, a view shared also by Wrotniak *et al.* Indeed, Wrotniak *et al.* concluded that a causal association between gestational weight gain and overweight in the offspring exists and that, consequently, helping women to prevent excessive gestational weight gain may be an important intervention strategy to prevent childhood obesity.

Future Directions

This chapter has focused on the psychosocial determinants of maternal obesity through pregnancy and the postpartum, and the implications of maternal obesity on childhood obesity. The importance of childbearing in the development of maternal obesity has been recognized for over a decade. Given the distress that many women experience with the change in their bodies during pregnancy and the postpartum, this is a time where interventions to address overweight/obesity in women are likely to be successful. However, the prevention of maternal obesity during the reproductive phase will only be effective when models of risk factors during these years have been examined systematically and rigorously and the interplay between risk factors is well understood. These models must necessarily be multifactorial and include bio-psycho-socio elements; an understanding of the psychological risk factors is critical and highlights the importance of health psychologists in both research and clinical teams. Indeed, health psychologists can and should play an integral role in delivering clinical interventions to promote psychological, social, and physical wellbeing during the perinatal period. Interventions that include a combination of both psychological and behavioral components in addition to patient education are needed urgently to prevent excessive gestational weight gain and postpartum weight retention. There is growing recognition that information/education/advice alone is not sufficient to produce significant changes in health behavior and that adoption of new behaviors is more likely if patients are encouraged to form a behavioral intention at the time of being provided with health information. Health psychologists can contribute significantly to this area of research and practice.

In conclusion, little research has focused on the interplay between maternal obesity, psychosocial factors, practices, beliefs and parenting styles and childhood obesity; research in the area of mother–child interactions and how these might mediate the impact of maternal obesity on child weight gain is also lacking. Observational research is needed to develop a thorough understanding of the complexity of bidirectional interactions in the mother–child dyad during feeding, child eating, and other obesogenic activities, such as child TV viewing, and how these interactions influence child weight gain.

References

Ajslev, T., Anderson, C., Ingstrup, K., Nohr, E., & Sorenson, T. (2010). Maternal postpartum distress and childhood overweight. *PLoS One, 5*, 1–9.

American Institute of Medicine. (2009). *Weight Gain During Pregnancy: Re-examining the Guidelines*. Washington DC: National Academies Press.

Amorim, A. R., Rossner, S., Neovius, M., Lourenco, P. M., & Linne, Y. (2007). Does excess pregnancy weight gain constitute a major risk for increasing long-term BMI? *Obesity, 15*, 1278–1286.

Australian Bureau of Statistics. (2009). *National Health Survey: Summary of Results* 2007–2008. www.abs.gov
.au/ausstats/abs@.nsf/mf/4364.0/.

Blissett, J., & Farrow, C. (2007). Predictors of maternal control of feeding at 1 and 2 years of age. *International Journal of Obesity, 31*, 1520–1526.

Booth, M. L., Dobbins, T., Okely, A. D., Denney-Wilson, E., & Hardy, L. L. (2007). Trends in the prevalence of overweight and obesity among young Australians, 1985, 1997, and 2004. *Obesity (Silver Spring), 15*, 1089–1095.

Carter, A. S., Wood Baker, C., & Brownell, K. D. (2000). Body mass index, eating attitudes, and symptoms of depression and anxiety in pregnancy and the postpartum period. *Psychosomatic Medicine, 62*, 264–270.

Cole, T. J., Bellizzi, M. C., Flegal, K. M., & Dietz, W. H. (2000). Establishing a standard definition for child overweight and obesity worldwide: International survey. *British Medical Journal, 320*, 1–6.

DiPietro, J., Millet, S., Costigan, K., Gurewitsch, E., & Caulfield, L. (2003). Psychosocial influences on weight gain attitudes and behaviours during pregnancy. *Journal of the American Dietetic Association, 103*, 1314–1319.

Dohnt, H. K., & Tiggemann, M. (2004). Development of perceived body size and dieting awareness in young girls. *Perceptual Motor Skills, 99*, 790–792.

Ertel, K. A., Koenen, K. C., Rich-Edwards, J. W., & Gillman, M. W. (2010). Antenatal and postpartum depressive symptoms are differentially associated with early childhood weight and adiposity. *Paediatric and Perinatal Epidemiology, 24*, 179–189.

Grote, V., Vik, T., von Kries, R., Luque, V., Socha, J., & Verduci, E. (2010). Maternal postnatal depression and child growth: A European cohort study. *BMC Pediatrics, 10*, 1471–2431.

Haycraft, E. L., & Blissett, J. M. (2008). Maternal and paternal controlling feeding practices: Reliability and relationships with BMI. *Obesity, 16*, 1552–1558.

Herring, S. J., Oken, E., Haines, J., Rich-Edwards, J. W., Rifas-Shiman, S. L., Kleinman, K. P., & Gillman, M. W. (2008a). Misperceived pre-pregnancy body weight status predicts excessive gestational weight gain: Findings from a US cohort study. *BMC Pregnancy and Child Birth, 8*, 54–54.

Herring, S. J., Rich-Edwards, J. W., Oken, E., Rifas-Shiman, S. L., Kleinman, K. P., & Gillman, M. W. (2008b). Association of postpartum depression with weight retention 1 year after childbirth. *Obesity, 16*, 1296–1301.

Huang, T., Wang, H., & Dai, F. (2010). Effect of pre-pregnancy body size on postpartum weight retention. *Midwifery, 26*, 222–231.

Hurley, K. M., Black, M. M., Papas, M. A., & Caufield, L. E. (2008). Maternal symptoms of stress, depression and anxiety are related to nonresponsive feeding styles in a statewide sample of WIC participants. *Journal of Nutrition, 138*, 799–805.

Institute of Medicine. (1990). *Committee on Nutritional Status during Pregnancy and Lactation. Nutrition during Pregnancy. Part I: Weight Gain. Part II: Nutrient Supplements.* Washington DC: National Academy of Sciences.

Krause, K. M., Ostbye, T., & Swamy, G. K. (2009). Occurrence and correlates of postpartum depression in overweight and obese women: Results from the active mothers postpartum (AMP) study. *Maternal and Child Health Journal, 13*, 832–838.

Lobstein, T., Baur, L., & Uauy, R. (2004). Obesity in children and young people: A crisis in public health. *Obesity Reviews, 5* (Suppl. 1), 4–104.

McCabe, M. P., & Ricciardelli, L. A. (2003). Body image and strategies to lose weight and increase muscle among boys and girls. *Health Psychology, 22*, 39–46.

Mitchell, S., Brennan, L., Hayes, L., & Miles, C. L. (2009). Maternal psychosocial predictors of controlling parental feeding styles and practices. *Appetite, 53*, 384–389.

Moreira, P., Padez, C., Mourao-Carvalhal, I., & Rosado, V. (2007). Maternal weight gain during pregnancy and overweight in Portuguese children. *International Journal of Obesity, 31*, 608–614.

Mumford, S., Siega-Riz, A., Herring, A., & Evenson, K. (2008). Dietary restraint and gestational weight gain. *Journal of the American Dietetic Association, 108*, 1646–1653.

Oken, E., Taveras, E. M., Kleinman, K. P., Rich-Edwards, J. W., & Gillman, M. W. (2007). Gestational weight gain and child adiposity at age 3 years. *American Journal of Obstetrics and Gynecology, 196*, 322 e1–e8.

Oken, E., Rifas-Shiman, S. L., Field, A.E., Frazier, L., & Gillman, M. W. (2008). Maternal gestational weight gain and offspring weight in adolescence. *Obstetrics and Gynecology, 112*, 999–1006.

Olson, C. M. (2007). A call for intervention in pregnancy to prevent maternal and child obesity. *American Journal of Preventive Medicine, 33*, 435–436.

Olson, C. M., & Strawdermann, B. A. (2009). Maternal weight gain during pregnancy and child weight at age 3 years. *Maternal and Child Health, 13*, 839–846.

Rankinen, T., Zuberi, A., Chagnon, Y. C., Weisnagel, S. J., Argyropoulos, G., Walts, B. *et al.* (2006). The human obesity gene map: The 2005 update. *Obesity (Silver Spring), 14*, 529–644.

Siega-Riz, A., Herring, A., Carrier, K., Evenson, K., Dole, N., & Deierlein, A. (2010). Sociodemographic, perinatal, behavioral, and psychosocial predictors of weight retention at 3 and 12 months postpartum. *Obesity, 18*, 1996–2003.

Skouteris, H. (2011). Body image issues in obstetrics and gynecology. In T. Cash & L. Smolak (Eds.), *Body Image: A Handbook of Theory, Research, and Clinical Practice* (pp. 342–349). New York: The Guilford Press.

Skouteris, H., Hartley-Clark, L., McCabe, M., Milgrom, J., Kent, B., Herring, S., & Gale, J. (2010). Preventing excessive gestational weight gain: A systematic review of interventions. *Obesity Reviews, 11*, 757–768.

Skouteris, H., McCabe, M., Swinburn, B., Newgreen, V., Sacher, P., & Chadwick, P. (2011). Parental influence and obesity prevention in preschoolers: A systematic review of interventions. *Obesity Reviews, 12*, 315–328.

Sterling, B., Fowles, E., Gargia, A., Jenkins, S., Wilkinson, S., Kim, M. *et al.* (2009). Altered perceptions of personal control about retained weight and depressive symptoms in low-income postpartum women. *Journal of Community Health Nursing, 26*, 143–157.

Surkan, P. J., Kawachi, I., & Peterson, K. E. (2008). Childhood overweight and maternal depressive symptoms. *Journal of Epidemiology and Community Health, 62*, 1–7.

Ventura, A. K., & Birch, L. L. (2008). Does parenting affect children's eating and weight status? *International Journal of Behavioural Nutrition and Physical Activity, 5*, 15.

Wake, M., Nicholson, J. M., Hardy, P., & Smith, K. (2007). Preschooler obesity and parenting styles of mothers and fathers: Australian national population study. *Pediatrics, 120*, e1520–e1527.

Walker, L. O. (2007). Managing excessive weight gain during pregnancy and the postpartum period. *Journal of Obstetrics, Gynecology & Neonatal Nursing, 36*, 490–500.

Walker, L. O., & Kim, M. (2002). Psychosocial thriving during late pregnancy: Relationship to ethnicity, gestational weight gain and birth weight. *Journal of Obstetrics, Gynaecology & Neonatal Nursing, 31*, 263–274.

Walker, L. O., Timmerman, G. M., Kim, M., & Sterling. (2002). Relationship between body image and depressive symptoms during postpartum in ethnically diverse low income women. *Women & Health, 36*, 101–121.

Webb, J. B., Siega-Riz, A. M., & Dole, N. (2008). Psychosocial determinants of adequacy of gestational weight gain. *Obesity, 17*, 300–309.

Whitaker, R. C. (2004). Predicting pre-schooler obesity at birth: The role if maternal obesity in early pregnancy. *Pediatrics, 114*, e29–e36.

World Health Organization. (2010). *Obesity and Overweight*. www.who.int/dietphysicalactivity/publications/facts/obesity/en/World.

Wrotniak, B. H., Shults, J., Butts, S., & Stettler, N. (2008). Gestational weight gain and risk of overweight in the offspring at age 7 in a multicentre, multiethnic cohort study. *American Journal of Clinical Nutrition, 87*, 1818–1824.

22

The Role of Psychology in Overweight and Obesity Management

Leah Brennan and Kylie Murphy

Obesity is at epidemic proportions in the Western world and is one of the greatest and most complex public health challenges confronting Australia today. Weight maintenance is an important lifelong health goal and even modest weight loss may reduce an individual's risk of developing obesity-related comorbidities (see Wing & Hill, 2001 for a more detailed review). This chapter examines the definition, prevalence, and biopsychosocial consequences of excess weight. It outlines the efficacy of a range of treatment approaches including the key components of behavioral and cognitive-behavioral interventions. Finally, the potential role of other psychological approaches in improving the treatment of obesity is highlighted.

Definitions and Measurement

Body mass index (BMI; kg/m^2) is used internationally to provide a simple and reliable classification system of degrees of overweight [World Health Organization (WHO), 1989, 2000]. Adults with a BMI 25–29.9 kg/m^2 are classified as overweight and those with a BMI $\geq$30 kg/m^2 are classified as obese. These cutoff values indicate the point at which the mortality and morbidity risks of excess weight rise sharply (WHO, 1995). Due to recognized racial and ethnic variations, different BMI cutoff values are used for non-white groups (WHO, 2000). Given the increased disease risk associated with central body fat, waist circumference is also used to classify abdominal obesity (WHO, 1995). Overweight is defined as a waist circumference >94 cm for males (obesity >102 cm) and >80 cm for females (obesity >88 cm). The relationship between waist circumference and central adiposity varies with age and ethnicity; however, separate criteria for specific populations have not yet been developed (WHO, 1995, 2000).

Prevalence

The prevalence of overweight and obesity has increased dramatically in recent years (Australian Institute of Health and Welfare, Dixon, & Waters, 2003). It is estimated that 37% of Australian

Applied Topics in Health Psychology, First Edition. Edited by M. L. Caltabiano and L. Ricciardelli.
© 2013 John Wiley & Sons, Ltd. Published 2013 by John Wiley & Sons, Ltd.

adults are overweight and an additional 24% are obese (Australian Bureau of Statistics, 2009). It is predicted that by 2025 46% of Australian adults will be overweight and 37% will be obese (Haby & Markwick, 2008). The overall rise in the rate of obesity in Australia has corresponded with an increase in sedentary behavior, a decline in physical activity, and easy access to high-energy foods (Cameron *et al.*, 2003). It is these lifestyle changes that are thought to be responsible for the worldwide increase in overweight and obesity (Swinburn & Egger, 2004).

Comorbidities

Excess weight is associated with major physical, psychological, and social comorbidities and economic consequences. The direction of causation is unclear, but available research suggests a bidirectional and perpetuating relationship between obesity and these comorbidities (Australian Institute of Health and Welfare, 2006; Wadden *et al.*, 2002).

Physical comorbidities

The impact of obesity on health and longevity is substantial (Field *et al.*, 2002). A BMI of ≥ 30 kg/m^2 increases risk of premature mortality from diseases such as cardiovascular disease, diabetes mellitus, and a number of cancers by 30%, and at a BMI ≥ 40 kg/m^2 the risk increases by 100% (Wadden *et al.*, 2005a). Other health problems that significantly reduce quality of life such as sleep apnoea, respiratory problems (e.g., asthma), gallstones, osteoarthritis, skin and skeletal disorders, and reproductive problems for women (Field *et al.*, 2002) are also associated with excess weight. Australian data indicate that those with a BMI ≥ 25 kg/m^2 have lower quality of life across all health and psychosocial dimensions tested, and those classified as morbidly obese have significantly reduced mental health and emotional wellbeing (Renzaho *et al.*, 2010).

Social comorbidities

There is substantial research demonstrating the pervasiveness of weight bias and its negative social consequences. Overweight and obese individuals are routinely subjected to weight-based prejudice and discrimination across all areas of life including employment, healthcare, education, the media, and interpersonal relationships (Puhl & Brownell, 2001; Wadden *et al.*, 2002). Stereotypes that obese individuals are emotionally impaired, socially handicapped, unmotivated, lazy, and less competent are widespread and rarely challenged (Andreyeva *et al.*, 2008; Puhl & Brownell, 2001; Roehling, 1999; Teachman *et al.*, 2003). For example, in employment settings, where the evidence for weight bias is the strongest, discrimination occurs in remuneration, job evaluation, hiring, and other employment decisions.

Psychological comorbidities

The negative psychological consequences of excess weight are thought to be largely the result of weight-based prejudice and discrimination. Weight-based teasing across different life stages has been consistently associated with increased body image dissatisfaction (Friedman & Brownell, 2002) and may mediate the relationship between obesity and psychological distress (Puhl & Heuer,

2009). Body image has consistently been shown to be poor in obese adults in both population and clinical samples (Rosen, 2002), and has been proposed as both a mediator and moderator of the relationship between weight and mental health (Markowitz *et al.*, 2008). At a population level, excess weight is weakly associated with poorer psychological wellbeing (Wadden *et al.*, 2002) and obese women are particularly vulnerable to symptoms of depression and low self-esteem (Carpenter *et al.*, 2000).

When compared to normal-weight and obese individuals in the general community, obese treatment-seeking individuals have higher rates of psychopathology, including mood disorders, body image dissatisfaction, binge eating disorder, and night eating syndrome (Colles *et al.*, 2007; Ramacciotti *et al.*, 2010; Wadden *et al.*, 2002), and lower health-related quality of life (Mannucci *et al.*, 2010; Renzaho *et al.*, 2010; Rosen, 2002). The increased prevalence of psychopathology in obese treatment seekers is largely attributed to the prevalence of binge eating disorder, which increases with the degree of obesity and the specificity of the treatment program (Ramacciotti *et al.*, 2010). Obese individuals with binge eating disorder are also more likely to report increased symptoms of depression, lower self-esteem, and a greater lifetime prevalence of any Axis I disorder including substance abuse or dependence (Wadden *et al.*, 2002).

Economic consequences

The healthcare costs associated with obesity are significant. Direct costs of obesity include the running of healthcare services, cost of pharmaceuticals and research, and other direct costs such as health administration. Nondirect costs include productivity losses, carer costs, and equipment, transport, and respite program costs. The "burden of disease," measured in disability-adjusted life years (DALYs), includes the disability, loss of wellbeing, and premature death that results from obesity and its impacts. Taken together, the total cost of obesity in Australia in 2008 was estimated to be AUS$58.2 billion, a substantial increase on the 2005 estimate of $21.0 billion (Access Economics, 2008). This increase in the economic cost of obesity is due to a combination of factors such as cost inflation, population growth, and change in methodology in "value of a statistical life" calculation (Access Economics, 2008).

Treatment of Overweight and Obesity

Long-term weight-loss intervention success is defined as a 10–20% reduction in initial weight, maintained for at least 1 year [National Health and Medical Research Council (NHMRC), 2003]. This loss is deemed clinically significant as it is sufficient to achieve improvements in physical health (Wing & Hill, 2001). Although most approaches are able to achieve short-term improvements in weight, weight is typically regained in the medium to long term. Factors that guide treatment selection include an individual's BMI, health, risk factors, and weight-loss history and preferences, as well as treatment safety, efficacy, and cost (NHMRC, 2003).

Dietary interventions

Dietary interventions typically target overall caloric intake and/or the type or amount of fat and/or carbohydrate consumed. Reviews of dietary interventions demonstrate small weight losses in the short term (i.e., 6 months) (Pirozzo *et al.*, 2002; Thomas *et al.*, 2007), with most weight regained in the medium term (i.e., 12–18 months) (Pirozzo *et al.*, 2002).

A meta-analysis of low-fat diet efficacy demonstrated significant short-term weight loss followed by a return to baseline weight at 18 months with no significant differences between low-fat (mean, $M = -5.08$, -2.3, and 0.1 kg) and comparison diets ($M = -6.5$, -3.4, and -2.3 kg) at 6, 12, and 18 months, respectively. Results regarding the impact of low-fat diets on psychosocial wellbeing were mixed (Pirozzo *et al.*, 2002). A meta-analysis comparing low- and high-glycaemic-index/-load diets demonstrated greater short-term (5 weeks to 6 months) weight loss (weighted mean difference, $WMD = -1.1$ kg) in the low-glycaemic-index/-load diets; longer follow-up is required. Psychosocial outcomes were not reported (Thomas *et al.*, 2007). Very low calorie diets (VLCDs) provide less than 3.4 MJ (300 kcal) and 0.8–1.5 g/day of protein. Meta-analysis indicates that VLCD ($M = 16.1$, 6.3 kg) results in greater short-term weight loss and similar long-term weight loss to low-calorie diets ($M = 9.7$, 5.0 kg). Psychosocial outcomes were not reported (Gilden Tsai & Wadden, 2006).

Exercise interventions

Exercise and physical activity interventions have received relatively little attention in the adult obesity literature. A meta-analysis of exercise for weight loss indicated that the addition of exercise to a dietary intervention improved weight loss ($WMD = -1.0$ kg) and higher-intensity exercise resulted in greater weight loss ($WMD = -1.5$ kg). Psychosocial outcomes were not reported (Shaw *et al.*, 2006). While dieting is more effective than exercise in promoting short-term weight loss, exercise appears to be particularly important for longer-term weight maintenance (Jeffery *et al.*, 2000; Saris, 2002).

Psychological interventions

Behavior therapy and cognitive behavior therapy are the most common psychological weight-loss interventions. Other psychological approaches include cognitive therapy, psychotherapy, psycho-dynamic therapy, humanistic therapy, group therapy, relaxation therapy, and hypnotherapy (Shaw *et al.*, 2005). A meta-analysis of psychological interventions indicated that behavioral therapy alone achieved greater weight loss than placebo at ($WMD = -2.5$ kg) and beyond ($WMD = -2$ kg) 12 months, behavioral therapy combined with diet and exercise achieved greater weight loss than diet and exercise alone, and more intensive behavioral interventions achieved significantly greater weight loss ($WMD = -2.3$ kg) (Shaw *et al.*, 2005). Cognitive behavior therapy resulted in greater weight loss than placebo and cognitive behavior therapy combined with diet and exercise achieved greater weight loss than diet and exercise alone ($WMD = -4.9$ kg). Cognitive behavior therapy resulted in greater weight loss than behavioral therapy. Psychosocial outcomes were not reported (Shaw *et al.*, 2005).

Pharmacotherapy

Orlistat (Xenical) is the only anti-obesity medication approved in Australia (NHMRC, 2003) because sibutramine (Reductal) has recently been withdrawn from the market due to safety concerns (Department of Health and Ageing Therapeutic Goods Association, 2010). A meta-analysis of the effects and safety of orlistat indicated that it resulted in greater weight loss than placebo treatments ($WMD = -2.7$ kg) but it did not result in improved maintenance in those who had already lost weight. Orlistat use was also associated with a variety of adverse gastrointestinal side effects, particularly fatty/oily stool, fecal urgency, fecal incontinence, and oily spotting. Psychosocial outcomes were not reported (Padwal *et al.*, 2003).

Bariatric surgery

Currently, bariatric surgery offers the only method for achieving substantial and sustained weight loss. Laparoscopic adjustable gastric banding, gastric roux-en-Y bypass, biliopancreatic diversion, and tube gastrectomy or gastroplasty bariatric procedures are used in Australia. Each have their own advantages, disadvantages, and risk profile (Colquitt *et al.*, 2005; Fisher & Schauer, 2002). LABG is the method used in 96% of bariatric surgeries in Australia (Favretti *et al.*, 2009). It involves placing a hollow band around the upper stomach, creating a small pouch and narrow tube into the stomach. A small port is placed just below this skin that is used to inflate the band with saline; its tightness can be adjusted as required to promote increased satiety (Fisher & Schauer, 2002).

A systematic review of bariatric surgery outcomes indicated that surgery ($M = -21$ kg) was more effective than conventional treatments (e.g., dietary prescription, VLCD) and resulted in greater improvements in quality of life at 8 year follow-up (Colquitt *et al.*, 2005). A meta-analysis of 12 month weight-loss outcomes following bariatric surgery reported average excess weight loss of 61.2%. Gastric banding (47.5%) resulted in less weight loss at 12-months relative to gastric bypass (61.6%), tube gastrectomy or gastroplasty (68.2%), and biliopancreatic diversion or duodenal switch (70.1%). Psychosocial outcomes were not reported (Buchwald *et al.*, 2004). A meta-analysis of longer-term outcomes following bariatric surgery reported that average excess weight loss was higher for gastric roux-en-Y bypass than laparoscopic adjustable gastric banding at 1 and 2 years postsurgery (67 compared with 42%, 67 compared with 53%, respectively), but the two procedures did not result in different weight loss at 3, 4, 5, 6, or 7 years postsurgery. Psychosocial outcomes were not reported (O'Brien *et al.*, 2006).

Behavioral and Cognitive-Behavioral Intervention Approaches

Behavioral and cognitive-behavioral interventions have been the most extensively evaluated psychological weight-loss interventions (Shaw *et al.*, 2005).

History of behavioral weight-loss interventions

Behavioral therapy was first applied to obesity treatment in the 1960s and 1970s. Early behavioral interventions were based on comprehensive functional analysis whereby the individual underwent comprehensive and ongoing assessment to identify problematic behaviors and the associated antecedents and consequences. Treatment then focused on systematically changing behaviors and restructuring antecedents and consequences to support desired health behaviors. Thus intervention was tailored to target the individual's unique needs and resulted in significant weight loss. The first published study using this approach reported an average weight loss of 17 kg over 12 months (Stuart, 1967). This early, highly successful study sparked extensive research on behavioral weight-loss programs. These programs are almost invariably delivered in a group format (16–26 weeks, 60–90 min sessions, 10–20 participants) and the sessions are primarily educational. While they incorporate many of the strategies used in early research, they do not include comprehensive functional analysis to identify the unique antecedents, behaviors, and consequences to be targeted, and nor do they tailor the intervention to the needs of the individual or ensure mastery of included strategies (Foster *et al.*, 2005; Wadden *et al.*, 2005b; Wing, 2008).

Behavioral and cognitive-behavioral intervention components

Behavioral interventions, informed by classical and operant conditioning principles, aim to modify eating and physical activity behaviors as well as thinking habits influencing these behaviors. This approach uses goal setting and active skills training with the aim of achieving small changes (Wadden *et al.*, 2005b). Behavioral interventions typically include self-monitoring, goal setting, nutrition, physical activity, stimulus control, problem solving, cognitive restructuring, and relapse prevention (Shaw *et al.*, 2005; Wadden *et al.*, 2005b; Wing, 2008). Treatment is generally delivered as a package and the relative contribution of each component has not been systematically evaluated (Foster *et al.*, 2005; Wadden *et al.*, 2005b; Wing, 2008). These treatment components are outlined below (see Brownell, 2004) for a more detailed description.

Self-monitoring involves daily recording of what is eaten and often the amount of physical activity performed. Depending on the program, self-monitoring could include counting calories and/or macronutrients consumed and/or calories expended, and/or information specific to program strategies (e.g., where and with whom they ate, emotional eating triggers, thoughts and emotions during and after eating, etc.). Self-monitoring completion is associated with better weight-loss outcomes (Wadden *et al.*, 2005b; Wing, 2008).

Goal setting involves setting short-term behavioral goals aimed at achieving weight loss. Goals may directly target calories consumed or expended, nutritional content of the diet, or specific behavioral strategies (e.g., eating breakfast, walking to work) (Wadden *et al.*, 2005b; Wing, 2008).

Nutrition components of behavioral interventions typically target knowledge and skills relating to recipe modification, food purchasing, preparation and cooking, label reading, and eating out. Traditionally the nutrition components of behavioral interventions targeted calorie restriction (Wing, 2008).

Physical activity components of behavioral interventions may incorporate structured exercise, lifestyle, or incidental physical activity (e.g., parking further away and walking to your destination, taking the stairs instead of the lift or escalator), and/or reduced sedentary time (e.g., watching less television). Interventions often target planning and preparing for physical activity and managing barriers to being more active. The importance of exercise for long-term maintenance of weight loss is emphasized (Wing, 2008).

Stimulus control involves teaching participants to recognize and manage the physical environment to increase cues for healthy eating and activity behaviors, and reduce cues for unhealthy eating and activity behaviors. This typically includes stimulus-control strategies for food purchasing (e.g., shopping from a list), preparation (e.g., chewing gum while preparing food), service (e.g., keeping serving dishes off the table), and storage (e.g., storing food out of sight), but may also include selecting a single eating location and/or avoiding other activities while eating. Stimulus-control strategies (e.g., keeping exercise clothing and equipment in a prominent location) can also be used to prompt physical activity (Wadden *et al.*, 2005b; Wing, 2008).

Problem solving involves identifying barriers to healthy eating and activity, defining the problem, generating possible solutions, developing a plan for dealing with the problem, evaluating success, and revising the plan as required. It is via problem solving that group behavioral programs attempt to tailor the intervention to meet individuals' needs (Wing, 2008).

Cognitive restructuring involves addressing the cognitive and emotional antecedents and consequences for unhealthy eating and inactivity. Common thinking errors addressed in treatment include all-or-nothing thinking regarding food and activity, rationalizing unhealthy behaviors, impossibility of weight loss, unrealistic behavioral and outcome expectations, and self-criticism in response to behavioral noncompliance or weight gain. Participants are taught to recognize unhelpful thoughts, understand their function, and generate more helpful alternative thoughts. Participants are also taught to recognize the impact of emotions on eating and activity behaviors, to minimize the use of unhealthy eating and inactivity to mange emotions, and to generate alternate coping strategies to better manage emotions (Wadden *et al.*, 2005b; Wing, 2008).

Relapse prevention involves teaching participants to identify and plan to manage high-risk situations and normalizing lapses to avoid them from becoming relapses (Wing, 2008).

Enhancing behavioral weight-loss interventions

In recent times behavioral research has focused on improving weight-loss outcomes by enhancing the dietary, physical activity, and behavioral components of intervention. Dietary and physical activity enhancements have typically targeted increased structure and convenience and reduced time spent in planning and decision-making. Behavioral enhancements have typically targeted increasing support. These approaches and their impact on weight-loss outcomes are summarized below (see Foster *et al.*, 2005; Wadden *et al.*, 2005b; Wing, 2008 for more detailed reviews).

Dietary intervention enhancement efforts have included use of VLCDs, low-fat diets, and increased diet structure. Incorporating VLCDs into behavioral interventions results in greater short-term weight loss but the weight is typically regained such that long-term outcomes are similar to less restrictive dietary approaches. Rather than directly restricting caloric intake, interventions targeting nutritional composition of the diet typically allow participants to consume as much as food as they want, providing it is low fat or low carbohydrate. There is some evidence for improved outcome using this dietary approach. Diet structure has been enhanced by the provision of portion-controlled meals, provision of meal plans and shopping lists, or use of meal replacement shakes, soups, or bars. These approaches result in greater initial weight loss and improved weight maintenance (Foster *et al.*, 2005; Wadden *et al.*, 2005b; Wing, 2008).

Physical activity component enhancement efforts have included the promotion of home-based exercise or short bouts of exercise, the provision of home exercise equipment, personal trainers and financial incentives, and use of resistance training. Encouraging home-based exercise appears to promote better weight maintenance than supervised exercise. Short bursts of exercise (e.g., four lots of 10 min) can be as effective as long bursts (e.g., 40 min) in promoting adherence, weight loss, and maintained fitness improvements. Provision of exercise equipment facilitates increased physical activity and weight-loss maintenance. Provision of personal trainers and financial incentives increases the attendance of exercise sessions but does not increase overall physical activity or weight loss (Wing, 2008).

Behavioral component enhancement approaches have included lengthening treatment, increasing social support and motivation, and using Internet-based interventions. Lengthening treatment by up to 1 year increases weight loss during treatment and delays weight regain following treatment; however, longer treatment is associated with greater attrition. Continued contact with participants after treatment, whether it is face-to-face or via telephone, improves weight-loss maintenance. Involving a spouse in treatment and participating in treatment with friends results in greater weight loss and weight-loss maintenance. Internet and other media-based behavioral interventions provide a way to increase treatment accessibility, reduce treatment costs, and maintain long-term contact with participants. Preliminary research suggests that interactive internet-based interventions incorporating individualized feedback produce similar results to face-to-face interventions (Foster *et al.*, 2005; Wadden *et al.*, 2005b; Wing, 2008; Wing & Hill, 2001; Wing *et al.*, 2008).

Cognitive-behavioral enhancement strategies have been proposed by Cooper and Fairburn (2001), who suggest that weight maintenance outcomes may be improved if cognitive factors, such as unrealistic weight-loss expectations and the underlying reasons for wanting to lose weight, are considered in treatment. Their treatment approach encourages the recognition and appreciation of the weight loss already achieved, promotes the adoption of weight sustainability rather than further weight loss as the key goal, and helps with the acquisition and application of behavioral and cognitive strategies that are required to prevent weight regain. It results in significantly greater improvements in intervention targets; namely, more realistic weight-loss expectations, decreased motivation to lose weight in order to improve self-confidence, increased self-esteem (Ames *et al.*, 2005), and improved body acceptance and psychiatric symptoms (Cooper *et al.*, 2010), but does not result in improved weight or weight regain relative to intensive behavioral weight loss (Ames *et al.*, 2005; Cooper *et al.*, 2010).

Future Directions for Psychology

Supporting pharmacological and surgical interventions

To date, psychological interventions have largely been used to support lifestyle interventions (e.g., diet, exercise). Behavioral and cognitive-behavioral interventions may have a role in improving the efficacy of medical and surgical obesity approaches.

Pharmacological interventions   Weight-loss medications are recommended for use as an adjunct to diet and exercise changes when greater weight loss is required (NHMRC, 2003). There are calls for the integration of pharmacological and behavioral interventions to optimize weight-loss outcomes (Phelan & Wadden, 2002; Sarwer *et al.*, 2009). It is proposed that the behavioral intervention assists with the management of external influences on eating and exercise behavior, while the pharmacotherapy addresses internal influences including hunger, cravings, and nutrient absorption (Phelan & Wadden, 2002). A particularly well-designed trial exploring the effects of pharmacological intervention and behavioral therapy indicated that those receiving sibutramine and intensive behavioral therapy lost the most weight ($M = -12.1$ kg), followed by those receiving sibutramine and brief behavioral therapy ($M = 7.5$ kg), then those receiving intensive behavioral therapy ($M = 6.7$ kg), and finally those receiving sibutramine alone ($M = 5.0$ kg) (Wadden *et al.*, 2005c).

Surgical interventions   While bariatric surgery is the most effective long-term weight-loss intervention currently available, not all patients achieve and/or sustain substantial weight loss. Poor outcomes are rarely attributed to surgical problems; instead they are thought to be due to poor adherence to postsurgical recommendations and/or maladaptive eating (Elkins *et al.*, 2005; Sarwer *et al.*, 2005, 2009). There is surprisingly little research exploring the potential benefits of behavioral and cognitive-behavioral weight-loss interventions following bariatric surgery. Comprehensive behavioral or cognitive-behavioral intervention programs designed to support improved eating behaviors required for weight loss in lifestyle interventions could be adapted to support improved eating behaviors postsurgery with the aim of improving weight loss and complications following surgery (Elkins *et al.*, 2005; Sarwer *et al.*, 2005, 2009).

Integrated treatment for obesity and mental health

Despite the high comorbidity of obesity and mental health issues, the likelihood that obesity and mental health issues perpetuate each other, and that treating one without addressing the other is likely to reduce treatment effectiveness and increase the risk of relapse, to date no studies have evaluated the simultaneous treatment of obesity and mental health issues. There are calls for integrated interventions to address obesity and mental health; for example, treating binge eating disorder and depression simultaneously and synergistically (Markowitz *et al.*, 2008).

Binge eating   Binge eating prevalence is increased in obese, treatment-seeking individuals and is associated with weight gain and poorer outcomes in obesity interventions (Wilfley *et al.*, 2003). Cognitive behavior therapy is recommended as the first-line treatment for binge eating disorder (Hay *et al.*, 2009; Vocks *et al.*, 2010) and results in reductions in binge eating and improvements in other eating disorder and depression symptomatology. Weight loss is not a goal of cognitive behavior therapy for eating disorders; however, intervention typically achieves weight maintenance in obese binge eaters (Hay *et al.*, 2009; Vocks *et al.*, 2010). In contrast, behavioral weight-loss interventions can achieve weight loss in obese binge eaters but eating disorder psychopathology rarely improves (Hay *et al.*, 2009; Vocks *et al.*, 2010). Efficacious treatments are needed for those suffering from both obesity and eating disorders (Hay *et al.*, 2009; Niego *et al.*, 2007). One promising study demonstrated that optimal weight loss and maintenance, and significant improvements in eating disorder psychopathology, were achieved when cognitive behavior therapy was effectively used to treat binge eating disorder prior to commencement of a weight-loss intervention (Agras *et al.*, 1997).

Depression   The prevalence of depression is significantly elevated in obese, treatment-seeking adults (Friedman & Brownell, 2002) and those with both obesity and depression face greater impairment of health and wellbeing and greater loss of function (Markowitz *et al.*, 2008). Longitudinal studies indicate that depression predicts later obesity and obesity predicts later depression (Markowitz *et al.*, 2008). Despite significant comorbidity, obesity and depression have been largely considered as two separate disorders (Hrabosky, 2008; Stunkard *et al.*, 2003). The impact of weight-loss interventions on depressive symptoms has been explored. Weight loss is associated with improvements in depressive symptoms (Brownell & Stunkard, 1981; Chaput *et al.*, 2005; Faulconbridge *et al.*, 2009; Fossati *et al.*, 2004; Painot *et al.*, 2001; Wadden *et al.*, 1988, 1997); however, there is some debate regarding the cause of improved mood following participation in a weight-loss intervention. Some suggest that the improvements in mood are a result of active participation in, and support received from, participation in a weight-loss intervention, rather than weight loss itself (Markowitz *et al.*, 2008). Others report that the improvement in mood following weight-loss intervention is directly related to the degree of weight loss and that surgical obesity interventions, which have the greatest impact on weight, have the greatest impact on mood (Stunkard *et al.*, 2003). There are no intervention studies indicating whether improved mood results in weight loss in obese depressed patients (Markowitz *et al.*, 2008; Stunkard *et al.*, 2003). The treatment of depression, however, can have a negative impact on obesity. Many pharmacotherapeutic agents for depression lead to weight gain, and weight gain is an often cited reason for noncompliance with these medications (Stunkard *et al.*, 2003).

Other promising psychological approaches

There is growing interest in the potential for other psychological approaches to improve the treatment of overweight and obesity. Preliminary research suggests that motivational interviewing, acceptance and mindfulness-based interventions, and the "health at every size" (HAES) approach, may improve obesity intervention outcomes.

Motivational interviewing   Motivational interviewing is an intervention designed to resolve ambivalence and enhance motivation for change (Miller & Rollnick, 2002). This approach was originally developed for the treatment of alcohol dependence and now has demonstrated efficacy in the treatment of a range of health-related behaviors. A recent meta-analysis that identified 41 trials exploring motivational interviewing targeting diet, physical activity, and/or body weight reported a moderate effect on all outcomes ($d = 0.29$), and concluded that motivational interviewing has the potential to be an effective treatment for obesity (DiRosa, 2010). This finding is consistent with the findings of earlier reviews exploring diet, exercise, and/or weight loss (Burke *et al.*, 2003; Dunn *et al.*, 2001; Hettema *et al.*, 2005; Rubak *et al.*, 2005).

Acceptance and mindfulness-based approaches   Acceptance and mindfulness strategies aim to reduce avoidant behaviors and increase psychological flexibility. Experiential avoidance is associated with failure to maintain weight loss (Byrne *et al.*, 2003; Ganley, 1989) and cognitive flexibility is associated with weight-loss maintenance (Westenhoefer *et al.*, 1999). Early research suggests that brief acceptance and mindfulness-based interventions can improve body weight, obesity-related stigma, quality of life, psychological distress, distress tolerance, acceptance, coping, and psychological flexibility (Lillis *et al.*, 2009).

Health at every size (HAES)   The HAES approach was developed in response to concerns that weight-loss interventions fail to result in long-term weight loss and improved health, and may also contribute to body dissatisfaction, weight cycling, reduced self-esteem and emotional wellbeing, eating disorders, weight stigmatization, and discrimination. The HEAS approach focuses on health behaviors and health outcomes rather than weight loss *per se*. It promotes body acceptance rather than weight loss, reliance on hunger and satiety rather than dietary restriction, and enjoyable, lifestyle physical activity rather than structured exercise. Early research indicates that this approach results in better retention and greater improvements in health behaviors (e.g., eating and physical activity), physiological outcomes (e.g., blood pressure, blood lipids), and psychosocial outcomes (e.g., disordered eating, body image, self-esteem, mood) without the potential negative outcomes of weight-focused interventions. Of note, this approach has not resulted in weight gain in any of the 10 published HAES randomized controlled trials (Bacon & Aphramor, 2011).

Summary and Conclusions

The prevalence of obesity is high and increasing and leads to increased negative biopsychosocial consequences for the individual and burgeoning economic costs for society. Lifestyle, behavioral, and pharmacological interventions typically result in small, poorly maintained weight loss. Bariatric surgery results in larger and better-maintained weight losses. There is limited exploration and reporting of outcomes other than weight loss in the literature and more research is required regarding the psychosocial outcomes of these interventions. Behavioral and cognitive-behavioral treatments significantly improve weight-loss outcomes when added to diet and exercise interventions, and may have a role in supporting behavior change in medical and surgical obesity interventions. Psychology also has the potential to further contribute to the treatment of obesity by informing integrated interventions targeting obesity and mental health and via integration of new psychological approaches into obesity-management approaches.

References

Access Economics. (2008). *The Growing Cost of Obesity in 2008: 3 Years On.* Melbourne: Access Economics.

Agras, W. S., Telch, C. E., Arnow, B., Eldredge, K., & Marnell, M. (1997). One-year follow-up of cognitive-behavioral therapy for obese individuals with binge eating disorder. *Journal of Consulting and Clinical Psychology, 65,* 343–347.

Ames, G. E., Perri, M. G., Fox, L. D., Fallon, E. A., De Braganza, N., Murawski, M. E. *et al.* (2005). Changing weight-loss expectations: A randomized pilot study. *Eating Behaviors, 6,* 259–269.

Andreyeva, T., Puhl, R. M., & Brownell, K. D. (2008). Changes in perceived weight discrimination among Americans: 1995–1996 through 2004–2006. *Obesity, 16,* 1129–1134.

Australian Bureau of Statistics. (2009). *National Health Survey: Summary of Results, 2007-2008 (Reissue).* Canberra: Australian Bureau of Statistics.

Australian Institute of Health and Welfare. (2006). *Australia's Health 2006.* Canberra: Australian Institute of Health and Welfare.

Australian Institute of Health and Welfare, Dixon, T., & Waters, A.-M. (2003). *A Growing Problem. Trends and Patterns in Overweight and Obesity Among Adults in Australia, 1980 to 2001,* Bulletin No 8. AIHW cat no. AUS 36. Canberra: Australian Institute of Health and Welfare.

Bacon, L., & Aphramor, L. (2011). Weight science: Evaluating the evidence for a paradigm shift. *Nutrition Journal, 10*(9), 1110–1189.

Brownell, K. D. (2004). *The LEARN Program for Weight Management* (10th edn.). Dallas, TX: American Health Publishing Company.

Brownell, K. D., & Stunkard, A. J. (1981). Couples training, pharmacotherapy, and behavior therapy in the treatment of obesity. *Archives of General Psychiatry, 38,* 1224–1229.

Buchwald, H., Avidor, Y., Braunwald, E., Jensen, M. D., Pories, W., Fahrbach, K., & Schoelles, K. (2004). Bariatric surgery. *JAMA, 292,* 1724–1737.

Burke, L., Arkowitz, H., & Menchola, M. (2003). The efficacy of motivational interviewing: A meta-analysis of controlled clinical trials. *Consulting and Clinical Psychology, 77,* 843–861.

Byrne, S., Cooper, Z., & Fairburn, C. (2003). Weight maintenance and relapse in obesity: A qualitative study. *International Journal of Obesity, 27,* 955–962.

Cameron, A. J., Welborn, T. A., Zimmet, P. Z., Dunstan, D. W., Owen, N., Salmon, J. *et al.* (2003). Overweight and obesity in Australia: The 1999–2000 Australian Diabetes, Obesity and Lifestyle Study (AusDiab). *Medical Journal of Australia, 178,* 427–432.

Carpenter, K. M., Hasin, D. S., Allison, D. B., & Faith, M. S. (2000). Relationships between obesity and DSM-IV, major depressive disorder, suicide ideation, and suicide ideation and suicide attempts: Results from a general population study. *American Journal of Public Health, 90,* 251–257.

Chaput, J. P., Drapeau, V., Hetherington, M., Lemieux, S., Provencher, V., & Tremblay, A. (2005). Psychobiological impact of a progressive weight loss program in obese men. *Physiology and Behavior, 86,* 224–232.

Colles, S., Dixon, J., & O'Brien, P. (2007). Night eating syndrome and nocturnal snacking: association with obesity, binge eating and psychological distress. *International Journal of Obesity, 31,* 1722–1730.

Colquitt, J., Clegg, A., Loveman, E., Royle, P., & Sidhu, M. (2005). Surgery for morbid obesity. *Cochrane Database of Systematic Reviews, 4,* CD003641.

Cooper, Z., & Fairburn, C. G. (2001). A new cognitive behavioural approach to the treatment of obesity. *Behaviour Research and Therapy, 39,* 499–511.

Cooper, Z., Doll, H. A., Hawker, D. M., Byrne, S., Bonner, G., Eeley, E. *et al.* (2010). Testing a new cognitive behavioural treatment for obesity: A randomized controlled trial with three-year follow-up. *Behaviour Research and Therapy*, 48, 706–713.

Department of Health and Ageing Therapeutic Goods Association. (2010). *Sibutramine (Reductil) – Withdrawal in Australia*. www.tga.gov.au/alerts/medicines/reductil-withdrawal.htm.

DiRosa, L. C. (2010). *Motivational Interviewing to Treat Overweight/Obesity: A Meta-Analysis of Relevant Research*. Doctoral dissertation, Wilmington University. http://proquest.umi.com.ezproxy.lib.monash .edu.au/pqdweb?index=0&did=1979792121&SrchMode=2&sid=4&Fmt=6&VInst=PROD&VType=P QD&RQT=309&VName=PQD&TS=1323210358&clientId=.

Dunn, C., Deroo, L., & Rivara, F. P. (2001). The use of brief interventions adapted from motivational interviewing across behavioral domains: A systematic review. *Addiction*, 96, 1725–1742.

Elkins, G., Whitfield, P., Marcus, J., Symmonds, R., Rodriguez, J., & Cook, T. (2005). Noncompliance with behavioral recommendations following bariatric surgery. *Obesity Surgery*, 15, 546–551.

Faulconbridge, L. F., Wadden, T. A., Berkowitz, R. I., Sarwer, D. B., Womble, L. G., Hesson, L. A. *et al.* (2009). Changes in symptoms of depression with weight loss: Results of a randomized trial. *Obesity*, 17, 1009–1016.

Favretti, F., Ashton, D., Busetto, L., Segato, G., & De Luca, M. (2009). The gastric band: First-choice procedure for obesity surgery. *World Journal of Surgery*, 33, 2039–48.

Field, A. E., Barnoya, J., & Colditz, G. A. (2002). Epidemiology and health and economic consequences of obesity. In T. A. Wadden & A. J. Stunkard (Eds.), *Handbook of Obesity Treatment* (pp. 3–18). New York: Guilford Press.

Fisher, B. L., & Schauer, P. (2002). Medical and surgical options in the treatment of severe obesity. *American Journal of Surgery*, 184(Suppl. 2), S9–S16.

Fossati, M., Amati, F., Painot, D., Reiner, M., Haenni, C., & Golay, A. (2004). Cognitive-behavioral therapy with simultaneous nutritional and physical activity education in obese patients with binge eating disorder. *Eating and Weight Disorders*, 9, 134–138.

Foster, G. D., Makris, A. P., & Bailer, B. A. (2005). Behavioral treatment of obesity. *American Journal of Clinical Nutrition*, 82, 230S–235S.

Friedman, M. A., & Brownell, K. D. (2002). Psychological consequences of obesity. In C. G. Fairburn & K. D. Brownell (Eds.), *Eating Disorders and Obesity: A Comprehensive Handbook* (2nd edn., pp. 393–398). New York: Guilford Press.

Ganley, R. M. (1989). Emotion and eating in obesity: A review of the literature. *International Journal of Eating Disorders*, 8, 343–361.

Gilden Tsai, A., & Wadden, T. A. (2006). The evolution of very-low-calorie diets: An update and meta-analysis. *Obesity*, 14, 1283–1293.

Haby, M., & Markwick, A. (2008). *A Future Prevalence of Overweight and Obesity in Australian Children and Adolescents, 2005–2025*. Melbourne: Department of Human Services.

Hay, P., Bacaltchuk, J., Stefano, S., & Kashyap, P. (2009). Psychological treatments for bulimia nervosa and binging. *Cochrane Database of Systematic Reviews*, 4, CD000562.

Hettema, J., Steele, J., & Miller, W.R. (2005). Motivational interviewing. *Annual Review of Clinical Psychology*, 7, 91–111.

Hrabosky, J. (2008). Elucidating the relationship between obesity and depression: Recommendations for future research. *Clinical Psychology Science and Practice*, 15, 28–34.

Jeffery, R. W., Drewnowski, A., Epstein, L. H., Stunkard, A. J., Wilson, G. T., & Wing, R. R. (2000). Long-term maintenance of weight loss: Current status. *Health Psychology*, 19(Suppl.), 5–16.

Lillis, J., Hayes, S. C., Bunting, K., & Masuda, A. (2009). Teaching acceptance and mindfulness to improve the lives of the obese: A preliminary test of a theoretical model. *Annals of Behavioral Medicine*, 37, 58–69.

Mannucci, E., Petroni, M. L., Villanova, N., Rotella, C. M., Apolone, G., & Marchesini, G. (2010). Clinical and psychological correlates of health related quality of life in obese patients. *Health and Quality of Life Outcomes*, 8, 90.

Markowitz, S., Friedman, M. A., & Arent, S. M. (2008). Understanding the relation between obesity and depression: Causal mechanisms and implications for treatment. *Clinical Psychology Science and Practice*, 15, 1–20.

Miller, W. R., & Rollnick, S. (2002). *Motivational Interviewing: Preparing People for Change* (2nd edn.). New York: The Guilford Press.

NHMRC. (2003). *Clinical Practice Guidelines for the Management of Overweight and Obesity in Adults*. Canberra: National Health and Medical Research Council.

Niego, S. H., Kofman, M. D., Weiss, J. J., & Geliebter, A. (2007). Binge eating in the bariatric surgery population: A review of the literature. *International Journal of Eating Disorders, 40*, 349–359.

O'Brien, P. E., McPhail, T., Chaston, T. B., & Dixon, J. B. (2006). Systematic review of medium-term weight loss after bariatric operations. *Obesity Surgery, 16*, 1032–1040.

Padwal, R., Li, S. K., & Lau, D. C. W. (2003). Long-term pharmacotherapy for obesity and overweight. *Cochrane Database of Systematic Reviews, 4*, CD004094.

Painot, D., Jotterand, S., Kammer, A., Fossati, M., & Golay, A. (2001). Simultaneous nutritional cognitive–behavioural therapy in obese patients. *Patient Education and Counselling, 42*, 47–52.

Phelan, S., & Wadden, T. A. (2002). Combining behavioral and pharmacological treatments for obesity. *Obesity, 10*, 560–574.

Pirozzo, S., Summerbell, C. D., Cameron, C., & Glasziou, P. (2002). Advice on low-fat diets for obesity. *Cochrane Database of Systematic Reviews, 2*, CD003640.

Puhl, R., & Brownell, K. D. (2001). Bias, discrimination, and obesity. *Obesity Research, 9*, 788–805.

Puhl, R. M., & Heuer, C. A. (2009). The stigma of obesity: A review and update. *Obesity, 17*, 941–964.

Ramacciotti, C. E., Coli, E., Bondi, E., Burgalassi, A., Massimetti, G., & Dell'Osso, L. (2010). Shared psychopathology in obese subjects with and without binge-eating disorder. *International Journal of Eating Disorders, 41*, 643–649.

Renzaho, A., Wooden, M., & Houng, B. (2010). Associations between body mass index and health-related quality of life among Australian adults. *Quality of Life Research: An International Journal of Quality of Life Aspects of Treatment, Care & Rehabilitation, 19*, 515–520.

Roehling, M. V. (1999). Weight-based discrimination in employment: Psychological and legal aspects. *Personnel Psychology, 52*, 969–1016.

Rosen, J. C. (2002). Obesity and body image. In C. G. Fairburn & K. D. Brownell (Eds.), *Eating Disorders and Obesity. A Comprehensive Handbook* (2nd ed., pp. 399–402). New York: Guilford Press.

Rubak, S., Sandboek, A., Lauritzen, T., & Christensen, B. (2005). Motivational interviewing: A systematic review and meta-analysis. *British Journal of General Practice, 55*, 305–312.

Saris, W. H. M. (2002). Metabolic effects of exercise in overweight individuals. In C. G. Fairburn & K. D. Brownell (Eds.), *Eating Disorders and Obesity. A Comprehensive Handbook* (2nd ed., pp. 495–499). New York: Guilford Press.

Sarwer, D. B., Wadden, T. A., & Fabricatore, A. N. (2005). Psychosocial and Behavioral Aspects of Bariatric Surgery. *Obesity, 13*, 639–648.

Sarwer, D. B., von Sydow Green, A., Vetter, M. L., & Wadden, T. A. (2009). Behavior therapy for obesity: where are we now? *Current Opinion in Endocrinology, Diabetes and Obesity, 16*, 347–352.

Shaw, K., O'Rourke, P., Del Mar, C., & Kenardy, J. (2005). Psychological interventions for overweight or obesity. *Cochrane Database of Systematic Reviews, 2*, CD003818.

Shaw, K., Gennat, H., O'Rourke, P., & Del Mar, C. (2006). Exercise for overweight or obesity. *Cochrane Database of Systematic Reviews, 4*, CD003817.

Stuart, R. B. (1967). Behavioural control of overeating. *Behaviour Research and Therapy, 5*, 357–365.

Stunkard, A. J., Faith, M. S., & Allison, K. C. (2003). Depression and obesity. *Biological Psychiatry, 54*, 330–337.

Swinburn, B. A., & Egger, G. (2004). The runaway weight gain train: Too many accelerators, not enough brakes. *British Medical Journal, 329*, 736–739.

Teachman, B. A., Gapinski, K. D., Brownell, K. D., Rawlins, M., & Jeyaram, S. (2003). Demonstrations of implicit anti-fat bias: The impact of providing causal information and evoking empathy. *Health Psychology, 22*, 68–78.

Thomas, D. E., Elliott, E. J., & Baur, L. (2007). Low glycaemic index or low glycaemic load diets for overweight and obesity. *Cochrane Database of Systematic Reviews, 3*, CD005105.

Vocks, S., Tuschen-Caffier, B., Pietrowsky, R., Rustenbach, S. J., Kersting, A., & Herpertz, S. (2010). Meta-analysis of the effectiveness of psychological and pharmacological treatments for binge eating disorder. *International Journal of Eating Disorders, 43*, 205–217.

Wadden, T. A., Stunkard, A. J., & Liebschutz, J. (1988). Three-year follow-up of the treatment of obesity by very low calorie diet, behavior therapy and their combination. *Journal of Consulting and Clinical Psychology*, *56*, 925–928.

Wadden, T. A., Vogt, R. A., Andersen, R. E., Bartlett, S. J., Foster, G. D., Kuehnel, R. H. *et al.* (1997). Exercise in the treatment of obesity: effects of four interventions on body composition, resting energy expenditure, appetite, and mood. *Journal of Consulting and Clinical Psychology*, *65*, 269–277.

Wadden, T. A., Womble, L. G., Stunkard, A. J., & Anderson, D. A. (2002). Psychosocial consequences of obesity and weight loss. In T. A. Wadden & A. J. Stunkard (Eds.), *Handbook of Obesity Treatment* (pp. 144–169). New York: Guildford Press.

Wadden, T. A., Berkowitz, R. I., Womble, L. G., Sarwer, D. B., Phelan, S., Cato, R. K. *et al.* (2005c). Randomized trial of lifestyle modification and pharmacotherapy for obesity. *New England Journal of Medicine*, *353*, 2111–2120.

Wadden, T. A., Brownell, K. D., & Foster, G. D. (2005a). Obesity: Responding to the global epidemic. *Obesity Reviews*, *6*, 43–65.

Wadden, T. A., Crerand, C. E., & Brock, J. (2005b). Behavioral treatment of obesity. *Psychiatric Clinics of North America*, *28*, 151–170.

Westenhoefer, J., Stunkard, A. J., & Pudel, V. (1999). Validation of the flexible and rigid control dimensions of dietary restraint. *International Journal of Eating Disorders*, *26*, 53–64.

WHO. (1989). MONICA project: Risk factors. *International Journal of Epidemiology*, *18*(Suppl. 1), s46–s55.

WHO. (1995). Physical status: the use and interpretation of anthropometry. Report of a WHO Expert Committee. *World Health Organanization Technical Report Series*, *854*, 1–452.

WHO. (2000). *Obesity: Preventing and Managing the Global Epidemic*. Report of a WHO consultation. Geneva: World Health Organization.

Wilfley, D. E., Wilson, G. T., & Agras, W. S. (2003). The clinical significance of binge eating disorder. *International Journal of Eating Disorders*, *34*(S1), S96–S106.

Wing, R. R. (2008). Behavioural approaches to the treatment of obesity. In G. A. Bray & C. Bouchard (Eds.), *Handbook of Obesity. Clinical Applications* (3rd ed., pp. 227–248). New York: Informa Healthcare.

Wing, R. R., & Hill, J. O. (2001). Successful weight loss maintenance. *Annual Review of Nutrition*, *21*, 323–341.

Wing, R. R., Papandonatos, G., Fava, J. L., Gorin, A. A., Phelan, S., McCaffery, J., & Tate, D. F. (2008). Maintaining large weight losses: The role of behavioral and psychological factors. *Journal of Consulting and Clinical Psychology*, *76*, 1015–1021.

Part 6

Substance Use:
Prevention and Treatment

23

Reducing Harmful Alcohol Consumption in Community Sports Clubs

A Settings-Based Approach to Health Promotion Psychology

Bosco C. Rowland, John W. Toumbourou,
and Felicity C. Allen

In many nations, community sports clubs are associated with high rates of harmful alcohol consumption. The following scenarios are examples of harmful alcohol use that health promotion psychologists may confront in these settings: after the weekend game, players drink into the night and several drive home; posttraining club members enjoy playing competitive drinking games, such as lining spirit drinks up for a public competition in quick consumption; and celebrating success by pouring of alcohol into the premiership cup and emptying it over players. Unfortunately, behaviors such as these are common in many community sports clubs, and for most members they are generally understood to be "normal" or expected practices.

This chapter examines the link between alcohol consumption and community sports clubs. It summarizes evidence for alcohol-related harm in sports clubs. The chapter outlines a settings-based approach to health promotion that sporting clubs and health promotion psychologists can use to plan and implement programs to reduce the link between alcohol and sport. The PRECEDE/PROCEED framework is presented as a comprehensive approach for planning setting-based health promotion programs. The Good Sports program is described as an example of an alcohol health promotion program currently implemented in Australian sports clubs. The framework presented in this chapter can be used by health promotion psychologists to work with organizations to target alcohol and other health behaviors, by modifying environmental factors associated with the particular setting.

Evidence of a Problem

Internationally many people belong to a community sports club. In the UK over 40% of the total population of 60 million people report participating in a moderate-intensity sport (Lifestyle and

Applied Topics in Health Psychology, First Edition. Edited by M. L. Caltabiano and L. Ricciardelli.
© 2013 John Wiley & Sons, Ltd. Published 2013 by John Wiley & Sons, Ltd.

participation, 2009), and in Australia approximately 26% of the total population of 4.5 million are involved with organized community sports clubs, as players, officials, or supporters (Australian Bureau of Statistics, 2010). There is, however, a strong association between excessive alcohol consumption and participation in community sports clubs.

In England, a national household survey indicated that heavier alcohol consumption was associated with playing sport or belonging to a sports club (Poortinga, 2007). In New Zealand, rugby players reported higher levels of harmful alcohol consumption than community members (O'Brien *et al.*, 2005; Quarrie *et al.*, 1996), and American college athletes reported higher levels of harmful consumption than other students (Brenner & Swanik, 2007; Ford, 2007), and that playing sport predicted alcohol misuse. Similar results have been reported in Australia (Duff *et al.*, 2005). The sections that follow examine the concept of risky alcohol use and discuss how it can be reduced in community sports clubs.

Risky Drinking

Recently the Australian National Health and Medical Research Council (NHMRC, 2009) issued a revised set of Australian safe drinking guidelines. Overall, there are four guidelines. The first focuses on long-term risky drinking; another on short-term risky drinking; and the other two focus on children and pregnant women. Table 23.1 depicts the different types of drinking. As outlined above, the amount, type, and patterns of alcohol consumption observed in community sports clubs often exceed the criteria described in these guidelines.

The NHMRC (2009) long- and short-term risky drinking guidelines apply equally to men and women. The long-term risk guideline states that healthy men and women are advised not to drink more than two standard drinks on any one day. According to this guideline, if an individual

Table 23.1   Types of drinking and summary of types of drinking in community sports clubs

Type of drinking	Level of drinking that causes harm	Relevance to community sports clubs
Short-term risky drinking (NHMRC, 2009)	Greater than four standard drinks in one sitting	Higher levels in the community sports clubs compared to the general community
Long-term risky drinking (NHMRC, 2009)	An average of greater than two standard drinks every day	Higher levels in community sports clubs compared to general community
Alcohol dependence (American Psychiatric Association, 1994)	Usually regular and heavy drinking over a prolonged period. When drinking stops, withdrawal symptoms such as tremors, sweating, and inability to sleep are experienced.	No formal studies undertaken with community sports clubs
Alcohol use by young people under 18 and by pregnant women (NHMRC, 2009)	Even low levels of alcohol use are harmful and should be discouraged	Studies indicate that individuals under 18 in sports clubs are introduced and have easy access to alcohol. There are no formal studies on alcohol consumption in community sports clubs and pregnant women.

drinks less than two drinks per day, the "probability" of suffering from long-term alcohol-related disease or injury is substantially reduced, compared to someone who drinks more. Alcohol-related disease or injury includes cirrhosis of the liver, stroke, hypertension, cardiovascular disease, cancers of the mouth, lips, throat, and oesophagus, cancer of the stomach, pancreas, and liver, bowel cancer, and breast cancer (Rehm *et al.*, 2008).

In the last decade there has been a growing concern about acute, episodic drinking; the heavy consumption that often occurs at celebrations or special events. This is sometimes called binge drinking, as it refers to the consumption of large amounts of alcohol in drinking sessions, often on weekends and typically interspersed with days of no alcohol use. Binge drinking patterns are sometimes distinguished from chronic heavy drinking patterns among alcohol-dependent individuals (American Psychiatric Association, 1994).

The second national guideline has been developed to reduce the risk of injury on a single occasion of drinking. It states that, for both men and women, drinking no more than four standard drinks on a single occasion reduces the risk of alcohol-related injury arising from that occasion (Herring *et al.*, 2008). Risk of injury includes physical injury, or road accidents (Rehm *et al.*, 2004). Similar risky drinking guidelines have been implemented around the world (see International Center for Alcohol Policies, 2010). Short-term risky drinking is most often associated with intoxication, and is more common in community sport clubs.

Sporadic binge drinking and even long-term risky drinking are not the same as alcohol dependence. Dependence is characterized by heavy and prolonged drinking, preoccupation with alcohol, loss of control, and withdrawal symptoms such as tremors, sweating, and inability to sleep when the individual stops drinking (American Psychiatric Association, 1994). Table 23.1 depicts the different types of drinking, as applied to community sports clubs. The NHMRC guidelines state that children under the age of 18, and pregnant and breastfeeding women should not consume any alcohol (NHMRC, 2009).

Health Behavior Theory and the Role of the Setting

Many psychological theories used to intervene in health behaviors, such as alcohol consumption, can be broadly described as social cognitive theories. These theories focus on cognitions that individuals use to interpret and respond to the world (Connor & Norman, 2005). The dominant theories include the health belief model, the theory of reasoned action and its companions, the theory of planned behavior, the transtheoretical model/stages of change, and social cognitive theory (Glanz & Bishop, 2010; Glanz *et al.*, 2008).

Behavior in these theories is framed as a product of rational decision-making, a procedure based upon deliberate and systematic processing of information. Sometimes this process is called self-regulation as its focus is on how an individual manages mental processes to achieve an outcome/behavior (Fiske & Taylor, 1991). This way of understanding behavior is a product of the tradition of psychology and medicine which argue that behaviors are principally modified by changing the individual's thoughts or beliefs (Scrambler, 2008).

While all the major theories predict behavior, they generally explain less than 30% of the variation in health behaviors (Godin & Kok, 1996; Harrison *et al.*, 1992; Marcoux & Shope, 1997), leaving plenty of room for improvement. These theories could be improved by giving greater weight to environmental influences (Kasprzyk & Montano, 2007; Kasprzyk *et al.*, 1998; Montano & Kasprzyk, 2008). For example, the dominant health theories rely heavily on intrapersonal constructs (e.g., intention, self-efficacy), while giving little attention to environmental factors which may impede or moderate behavior. These factors may include the salience of the behavior that individuals are trying to change in their current settings: lots of people drinking alcohol makes it harder not to drink or may make people feel that alcohol consumption is expected. The environment could also be the physical setting omitting healthy options, thus while the individual intends to change, he or she maintains existing behavior and habits because alternative options are not readily available. A person will drink full-strength alcohol if there are no low-alcohol drinks or soft drinks available.

A role for the influence of the environment on behavior has been long advocated in the international health promotion movement. One of the first international documents to acknowledge the link between healthy environments and quality of life was the Ottawa Charter for Health Promotion (World Health Organization, 1986). The charter stated that health is determined by the interplay of human biology, healthcare systems, environment/conditions, and lifestyle. Fundamentally the charter stated that health (and therefore quality of life) is a product of how people live, and that individuals and communities do not always have control of surrounding conditions.

As a way forward, the Ottawa charter suggested that the objective of health promoters and program developers is to create conditions/programs that enable people to increase control over their lives and to improve their health. From a sporting club perspective, it is the job of club leaders and health promoters to help create conditions that make healthy choices about alcohol the easier choices. The charter emphasizes that programs can achieve individual behavior change by modifying cultural and collective influences, systems, and rituals, that promote unhealthy individual choices (Frohlich & Potvin, 1999). In the community sports club setting, these cultural practices include celebrating success with excessive consumption. Systemic practices include serving alcohol to intoxicated or underage individuals or permitting intoxicated individuals to leave club premises without ensuring they are not driving home.

An Evidence-Based Framework for Alcohol Management Programs in Sports Clubs

Using the principles that underlie the Ottawa charter, sound interventions can be developed and applied in community sports clubs, or similar settings. Valid setting-based interventions are always based on a critical review of the evidence, thus identifying the most efficient and effective leverage points for behavior change (Bartholomew *et al.*, 2006). Moreover, the most effective setting-based interventions are usually applied simultaneously at several critical leverage points, not just as a single strategy (McLeroy *et al.*, 1988).

Several planning frameworks have been developed to organize multiple levels of influence into a coherent and sound intervention. Frameworks that feature prominently in the health literature include the PRECEDE/PROCEED model (Green & Kreuter, 2005), the capacity building framework (Norton *et al.*, 2002), and RE-AIM (Glasgow *et al.*, 1999). By far the most popular framework is PRECEDE/PROCEED; it has over 900 applied examples in the research literature (Gielen *et al.*, 2008; Green *et al.*, 1996). Programs using this framework include interventions in specific geographic regions, occupational settings, educational settings, and healthcare settings (Green & Kreuter, 2005).

The PRECEDE/PROCEED framework suggests that once evidence of successful leverage points has been identified, these points should be organized into three influential domains: predisposing, reinforcing, and enabling (Green & Kreuter, 2005). Predisposing factors focus on influences that promote individual behavior change. These may pull the individual toward or away from specific behaviors (Green & Kreuter, 2005); these include values, knowledge, and attitudes (Green, *et al.*, 1996).

Enabling factors are environmental elements that facilitate appropriate health behaviors by individuals or groups (Green & Kreuter, 2005). Enabling factors can include social forces and systems, such as making healthy choices/behavior more accessible or more affordable. In the context of a sporting club, enabling factors could include making light-alcohol beer cheaper than full-strength beer and providing safe-transport strategies (e.g., designated-driver services). Other enabling factors would be training bar staff in responsible service of alcohol (RSA) and actively promoting these practices, such as not serving intoxicated individuals. Ensuring there are sufficient and varied enabling factors provides leverage points for behavior change (Green & Kreuter, 2005).

Reinforcing factors are usually social feedback cues that strongly influence whether a behavior is repeated (Green & Kreuter, 2005). They could include recognition, appreciation, or admiration by peers or leaders. In a sports club setting this could be feedback from the local council about the well-behaved members. Environmental feedback could be healthier and more vibrant sporting clubs, now less characterized by drunkenness. Reinforcing factors formalize and validate new behavior and systemic change; they also help initiate and promote new norms of expected behavior (Green & Kreuter, 2005).

Tables 23.2, 23.3, and 23.4 summarize the evidence on factors associated with alcohol-related behavior. This evidence has been gathered from drinking establishments, such as licensed premises. The tables also list how practitioners can use strategies to modify alcohol-related behavior in community sports clubs and similar settings.

The sections that follow use Figure 23.1 to elaborate the PRECEDE/PROCEED model and describe how it can be integrated with dominant health behavior theories; connections with

Table 23.2 Individual predisposing factors associated with alcohol consumption

Factor/ characteristic	Description	Evidence	Relevance to community sports clubs
Knowledge	Provision of information aimed at encouraging healthy behaviors	No evidence for direct link with behavior; knowledge enhancement works best as part of a broader program. Increases health literacy (Loxley *et al.*, 2004).	Clubs can provide information about low-risk drinking levels.
Attitudes	Enduring disposition favoring alcohol use	Evidence suggesting that favorable attitudes to alcohol use in younger years is predictive of alcohol use in later years (Loxley *et al.*, 2004).	Clubs can promote responsible drink messages, such as not tolerating intoxication, and drink-driving.
Values	Guiding principles	No direct link with behavior change, but when included in a broader program can be influential (Loxley *et al.*, 2004).	Clubs can enshrine in their policy values, such as safety, family-friendliness, and responsible alcohol management, as a way of demonstrating what are the guiding principles behind the alcohol-management strategies.

Table 23.3 Environmental enabling factors associated with alcohol consumption (physical, social, economic)

Factor	Description	Evidence	Relevance to community sports clubs
Availability	Restriction in serving practices such as training of bar-staff in RSA	Evidence indicates that availability influences behavior but must be implemented in conjunction with some type of enforcement (Ker & Chinnock, 2010).	Clubs can ensure bar staff are RSA trained. Clubs may set a policy not to serve alcohol to minors.
Accessibility	Defined times for selling alcohol (not selling on particular days/times or to specific groups)	Does not reduce consumption, but linked with a reduction in alcohol-related harms such as violence (APA, 1994; Babor et al, 2010).	Clubs can restrict the sale of alcohol to particular times only and may refuse service to intoxicated patrons.
	Restrictions on discounting, such as happy hours, or alcohol promotions	As part of a broader program can reduce consumption and harmful alcohol-related behaviors, such as drink-driving (Booth et al, 2008).	Clubs can choose not to promote drink promotions, discounting and happy hours.
	Increase in price	Strong evidence linking price with consumption (Gallet, 2007).	Clubs can make low-alcohol drinks cheaper, and provide soft and low-calorie drinks.
Laws	Laws enforcing minimum age of purchase and use	Strong evidence linked with reducing harm in young people (Wagenaar, 2000).	Often poorly implemented; however, most successful when part of a broader community approach (see Community mobilization). Clubs can refuse service to minors and actively enforce the policy.
Community mobilization	Coordinated community approach, involving community members and key stakeholders in the community	Resource intense, but effective in reducing alcohol consumption (Giesbrecht, 2003).	Clubs can work with their local council, police, and licensed venues, to ensure responsible alcohol management and consumption occurs consistently.
Amount of advertising	Specific marketing campaigns explicitly aimed at target groups such as young people	Exposure to media and commercial communications on alcohol is associated with the likelihood that adolescents will start to drink alcohol, and with increased drinking amongst those who already drink (Anderson et al, 2009).	Clubs can choose to ban specific marketing promotions, and not to accept marketing merchandise from the alcohol industry.

Table 23.4   Reinforcing enabling factors associated with alcohol consumption

Factor/behaviors of individuals, groups, or communities	Description	Evidence	Relevance to community sports clubs
Favorable attitudes and behavior of leading individuals	Perceived general consumption levels of alcohol in community	Particularly with young people, perceived consumption in the broader community is linked with personal consumption (Loxley *et al.*, 2004).	Clubs can use high-profile sports celebrities or club members to promote reduced consumption.
Favorable attitudes and behavior of peers	Perceived general consumption levels of peers	Particularly with young people, perceived consumption levels of peers is linked with personal consumption (Loxley *et al.*, 2004).	Clubs can use high-profile sports celebrities or club members to promote a healthy attitude to alcohol consumption.
Favorable attitudes and behaviors of community or group	Licensees code of conduct, such as accords. Accords are negotiated agreements/policy positions between community stakeholders (e.g., police, licensees, and council) covering standards of service and promotion, such as not permitting alcohol promotions.	Evidence suggesting these can be effective when part of a broader community strategy (Hauritz *et al.*, 1998; Homel *et al.*, 2001). Feedback to program implementers increases effectiveness (Oxman *et al.*, 1995).	Clubs can provide feedback to club members from local community members of benefits to the neighbourhood and the increased standing of the club in relation to the way the club manages and consumes alcohol.

learning theories including Skinnerian (Skinner, 1938) operant conditioning, and Pavlovian classical conditioning (Pavlov, 1927) concepts, are also made. To describe the application of the model in an hypothetical setting, consider the following steps:

1. A community sports club attracts a large population of people who like to drink heavily on the weekend (predisposing factors).
2. A club has a dedicated program to reduce risky alcohol consumption, so resources are available in the environment to facilitate this individual to make choices that will promote better health for that individual (enabling factors). These resources could include provision of low-alcohol beer sold more cheaply than full-strength beer, training bar staff not to serve intoxicated individuals, and the provision of food to slow down the metabolism and consumption of alcohol.
3. As the club has implemented a program and is promoting the program, making healthier choices would be followed by some type of reinforcement. This could be satisfaction with the quality of the club and peer group; it could include peers reinforcing healthy choices, which could increase feelings of safety due to reduced drunken behavior in the club.

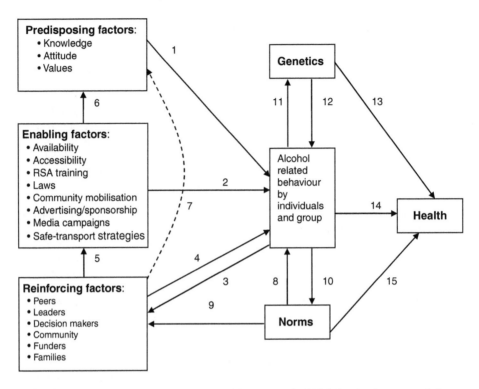

Figure 23.1 A dynamic model of factors influencing alcohol behavior in sports club settings. Predisposing factors focus on influences that impact individual behavior change. These may pull the individual toward or away from specific behaviors. Enabling factors are environmental elements that facilitate health behaviors by individuals or groups. Reinforcing factors are usually social feedback cues that strongly influence whether a behavior is repeated.

4. Behavioral theories (e.g., classical conditioning; Pavlov, 1927) emphasize that once a behavior is reinforced, it is likely that a person will then repeat it.
5. Reinforced behavior results in the seeking of continued resources to support the behavior recurring.
2. These resources also become heightened cues and stimuli for the behavior to recur.
6. Repeated new behaviors inevitably have some impact on the predisposing factors.
7. Reinforcement and positive feedback make it more likely that the same choice will recur. Thus the cycle starts again, and a setting-based program builds up momentum. The reinforcements that promoted a particular behavior now become predisposing factors. These elements now become dominant factors pulling people away from unhealthy alcohol-related choices at their clubs. The club now provides an environment that makes healthier choices around alcohol easier, compared to harmful alcohol-related choices.
8. Over time, as the club continues to support the responsible sale and consumption of alcohol, the club promotes certain norms. These norms also affect individual alcohol consumption.
9 & 10. These norms gradually become the expected behavior, and are promoted overtly (reinforced) by the club.

11, 12, & 13.   While genetics has some influence on individual alcohol-related behavior, this
element is beyond the scope of most health promoters and practitioners.

14 & 15.   Overall, reduction in risky alcohol consumption, and the new norms of behavior,
improve health and quality of life.

When examined closely, several individual health behavior theories can be identified in the different
components of the group-oriented PRECEDE/PROCEED planning model. The theory of planned
behavior, for example, suggests that intention and attitudes predict behavior (Montano & Kasprzyk,
2008; Painter *et al.*, 2008). This can be seen to be part of the model that links predisposing factors
with individual behavior (line 1). Attitudes in the PRECEDE/PROCEED model predict behavior,
but as the model indicates attitude change is not considered sufficient to change or maintain
behavior change.

Similarly the roles ascribed to environmental cues that promote behavior, reinforcement from
peers, and an individual's motivation/attitude/knowledge are comparable to the three components
of influence in Bandura's (1986) social cognitive theory. If reinforcement as described in the
PRECEDE/PROCEED model is to be effective, individuals need to believe the health promotion
message and cues that are being promoted and encouraged, otherwise they may move to another
setting where these messages are not promoted. This notion is in keeping with the health belief
model (Champion & Skinner, 2008). In the PRECEDE/PROCEED planning model it is recognized
that behavior change is not a discrete event, only over time will individuals and groups change
their behaviors. Furthermore, behavior change is seen as contingent on continued cues, and over
time a gradual increase in overt knowledge of expected behavior will develop. These ideas are
consistent with Prochaska *et al.* (2008) transtheoretical theory.

Overall, the PRECEDE/PROCEED planning framing incorporates a number of individual
influencing variables identified in the four major health theories (e.g., attitude and knowledge);
however, consistent with the Ottawa charter, it gives greater emphasis to the role of influences
associated with the environmental setting. Modifying the environment can be an efficient means
of influencing behavior, as it influences the behavior of large numbers of individuals simultaneously
(Rose, 1992). It is also more a sustainable means of intervening with transient populations, such
as community sports clubs where members and spectators may vary from week to week or season
to season (Scribner *et al.*, 2000). Thus, the intervention remains stable and consistent over time,
even though the population moves.

The Good Sports Program: an Alcohol Health Promotion Program for Community Sports Club Settings

In Australia, a program called the Good Sports program has been developed. An initiative of the
Australian Drug Foundation, the primary aim of the Good Sports program is to implement multilevel change within sporting clubs to reduce the incidence of alcohol-related problems. It does this
through a three-level accreditation program (Duff & Munro, 2007) (see box); however, behavior is
principally influenced through modifying the setting. Consistent with the PRECEDE/PROCEED
model, multiple strategies are implemented; strategies focus on modifying the setting. Clubs
progress through the program by gradually implementing agreed alcohol-related strategies;
once clubs have implemented all the strategies they are classified as a Level 3 accredited Good
Sports clubs.

The Accreditation Levels of the Good Sports Program

Level 1

- Clubs comply with state's liquor licensing laws.
- At least one bar staff member on duty is trained in RSA.
- Liquor is only served within specified hours.
- Minors do not serve and are not served alcohol.
- Intoxicated people not served or allowed to enter the premises.

Level 2

- Provision of low-alcohol and nonalcoholic drinks.
- All bar staff members on duty are trained in RSA.
- Bar staff do not consume alcohol on duty.
- Club maintains an incident register.
- Tap water is provided free of charge.
- Substantial food options are available when the bar is open for more than 90 min.
- Clubs implement a safe transport strategy, e.g., a designated-driver program, taxi vouchers, or key register.
- Clubs do not conduct any of the following: happy hours, cheap drink promotions, drinking competitions, drink vouchers, all-you-can-drink functions, and alcohol-only awards or raffle prizes.
- All indoor areas are smoke-free, and club does not sell cigarettes.

Level 3

- Club has a Good Sports written policy which addresses the following: bar management, RSA, underage drinking, alcohol alternatives, food options, safe transport, smoke-free, club trips, noncompliance, promotion of policy, and policy review.

Results from adoption studies of the Good Sports program suggest the program does affect alcohol-related behavior. The evaluation designs are nonrandomized and examine patterns of alcohol use in sports clubs at different accreditation levels. Overall, the findings demonstrated that as clubs progress through the Good Sports program a reduction in risky alcohol use and drink-driving is observed. Using multilevel modelling (Rabe-Hesketh & Skrondal, 2008), findings show that when adjusting for individual demographics the variance explained between clubs was up to 46% for alcohol consumption (Rowland *et al.*, 2011, 2012a), and the variance explained between clubs for drink-driving was up to 73% (Rowland *et al.*, 2012b, 2012c). While the Good Sports program principally focuses on enabling (setting) factors, these findings support the notion that if greater attention were given to predisposing factors and reinforcing factors the program could increase its impact on behavior. Nevertheless, these studies have demonstrated that modifying the setting is associated with a substantial behavior change in this setting.

To extend the program and help create a more health promoting environment for members and spectators, the Good Sports program is also being trialled with additional components that focus on healthy canteens and mental health awareness. These components aim to help clubs to adopt additional health enhancing policies and practices. In respect to healthy eating the program assists clubs to provide healthy options such as fruit and vegetables in club canteens, and encourages these options to be positioned prominently, and promoted through competitive pricing. In respect to mental health, it assists clubs to provide mental health information, and use the sports clubs infrastructure to promote and provide this information. To further enhance the evidence-base for the Good Sports program, a randomized control trial of the program is currently being undertaken.

Conclusion

In this chapter it was shown that risky alcohol consumption is often associated with community sports clubs. It was also argued that the explanatory power of dominant health promotion theories is limited for these behaviors, and they are not particularly useful to develop interventions to modify these behaviors. Using the Ottawa charter as a foundation it was suggested that setting influences should be given greater emphasis in health behavior change interventions. Using community sports clubs as an example the PRECEDE/PROCEED planning framework was used to demonstrate how environmental factors can be used to develop an intervention. It was also shown that the PRECEDE/PROCEED planning model incorporates a number of individual psychological theories, and that more than one theory can be used to explain health behaviors.

Findings to date suggest that using the PRECEDE/PROCEED framework is an effective means of developing and evaluating an alcohol intervention in community sports clubs. Both internationally and at the national and state policy levels sports clubs are being emphasized as a setting that can be targeted to improve population health. Similarly, places such as workplaces, schools, and large organizations are also being highlighted as settings where the behavior of large populations could need changing. It is hoped that the evidence and framework presented in this chapter will enhance the knowledge of health promotion psychologists and sports and program developers to use the environmental setting more effectively to contribute to improving the health and quality of the community, especially when their target group is a large population.

References

Australian Bureau of Statistics. (2010). *Involvement in Organised Sport and Physical Activity*. Canberra: Australian Bureau of Statistics.

Anderson, P., de Bruijn, A., Angus, K., Gordon, R., & Hastings, G. (2009). Impact of alcohol advertising and media exposure on adolescent alcohol use: A systematic review of longitudinal studies. *Alcohol and Alcoholism, 44,* 229–243.

American Psychiatric Association. (1994). *Diagnostic and Statistical Manual of Mental Disorders: DSM-IV* (4th edn.). Washington DC: American Psychiatric Association.

Babor, T. F., Caetano, R., Casswell, S., Edwards, G., Giesbrecht, N., Graham, K. *et al.* (2010). *Alcohol – No Ordinary Commodity: Research and Public Policy* (2nd edn.). Oxford: University Press.

Bandura, A. (1986). *Social Foundations of Thought and Action: A Social Cognitive Theory*. Englewood Cliffs, NJ: Prentice Hall.

Bartholomew, K. L., Parcel, G. S., Kok, G., & Gottlieb, N. H. (2006). *Planning Health Promotion Programs: An Intervention Mapping Approach* (2nd edn.). San Francisco, CA: Jossey-Boss.

Booth, A., Meier, P., Stockwell, T., Sutton, A., Wilkinson, A., & Wong, R. (2008). *Independent Review of the Effects of Alcohol Pricing and Promotion: Systematic Reviews Project Report for the Department of Health.* University of Sheffield, ScHARR, Sheffield. www.sheffield.ac.uk/scharr/sections/ph/research/alpol/research/indreview.

Brenner, J., & Swanik, K. (2007). High-risk drinking characteristics in collegiate athletes. *Journal of American College Health, 56,* 267–272.

Champion, V., & Skinner, C. S. (2008). The health belief model. In K. Glanz, B. K. Rimmer, & K. Viswanath (Eds.), *Health Behavior and Health Education* (pp. 45–65). San Francisco, CA: Jossey-Bass.

Connor, M., & Norman, P. (2005). Prediciting health behaviour: A social cognition approach. In M. Connor & P. Norman (Eds.), *Predicting Health Behaviour* (pp. 1–28). New York: Open University Press.

Duff, C., & Munro, G. (2007). Preventing alcohol-related problems in community sports clubs: The Good Sports program. *Substance Use and Misuse, 42,* 12–13.

Duff, C., Scealy, M., & Rowland, B. (2005). *The Culture and Context of Alcohol Use in Community Sporting Clubs in Australia: Research into Attitudes and Behaviours.* Melbourne: DrugInfo Clearinghouse, Australian Drug Foundation.

Fiske, S. T., & Taylor, S. E. (1991). *Social Cognition* (2nd edn.). New York: McGraw-Hill.

Ford, J. A. (2007). Substance use among college athletes: A comparison based on sport/team affiliation. *Journal of American College Health, 55,* 367–373.

Frohlich, K. L., & Potvin, L. (1999). Health promotion through the lens of population health: Toward a salutogenic setting. *Critical Public Health, 9,* 211–222.

Gallet, C. A. (2007). The demand for alcohol: A meta-analysis of elasticities. *Australian Journal of Agricultural and Resource Economics, 51,* 121–135.

Gielen, A. C., McDonald, E. M., Gary, T. L., & Bone, L. R. (2008). Using the PRECEDE/PROCEED model to apply health behavior theories. In K. Glanz, B. K. Rimmer, & K. Viswanath (Eds.), *Health Behavior and Health Education: Theory, Research, and Practice* (4th edn., pp. 407–435). San Francisco, CA: Jossey-Bass.

Giesbrecht, N. (2003). Alcohol, tobacco and local control: A comparison of several community-based prevention trials. *Nordic Studies of Alcohol an Drugs, 20,* 365–377.

Glanz, K., & Bishop, D. (2010). The role of behavioral science theory in development of public health interventions. *The Annual Review of Public Health, 31,* 399–418.

Glanz, K., Rimmer, B. K., & Viswanath, K. (Eds.). (2008). *Health Behavior and Health Education: Theory, Research and Practice* (4th edn.). San Francisco, CA: Jossey-Bass.

Glasgow, R., Vogt, T., & Boles, S. (1999). Evaluating the public health impact of health promotion in interventions: The RE-AIM framework. *American Journal of Public Health, 89,* 1322–1327.

Godin, G., & Kok, G. (1996). The theory of planned behavior: A review of its applications to health-related behaviors. *American Journal of Health Promotion, 11,* 87–98.

Green, L. W., & Kreuter, M. W. (2005). *Health Program Planning: An Educational and Ecological Approach* (4th edn.). Boston: McGraw Hill.

Green, L. W., Richard, L., & Potvin, L. (1996). Ecological foundations of health promotion. *American Journal of Health Promotion, 10,* 270–281.

Harrison, J. A., Mullen, P. D., & Green, L. W. (1992). A meta-analysis of studies of the health belief model with adults. *Health Education Research, 7,* 107–116.

Hauritz, M., Homel, R., McIlwain, G., Burrows, T., & Townsley, M. (1998). Reducing violence in licensed venues through community safety action projects: The Queensland experience. *Contemporary Drug Problems, 25,* 511–511.

Herring, R., Berridge, V., & Thom, B. (2008). Binge drinking: An exploration of a confused concept. *Journal of Epidemiology and Community Health, 62,* 476–479.

Homel, R., McIlwain, G., & Carvolth, R. (2001). Creating safer drinking environments. In N. Heather, T. J. Peters, & T. Stockwell (Eds.), *International Handbook of Alcohol Dependence and Problems* (pp. 721–740). Chichester: John Wiley and Sons.

International Center for Alcohol Policies. (2010). *International Drinking Guidelines.* www.icap.org/PolicyIssues/DrinkingGuidelines/tabid/102/Default.aspx.

Kasprzyk, D., & Montano, D. E. (2007). Application of an integrated behavioral model to understand HIV prevention behavior of high-risk men in rural Zimbabwe. In I. Azjen, D. Albarracin, & R. Hornik (Eds.), *Prediction and Change of Health Behavior: Applying the Reasoned Action Approach* (pp. 149–172). Mahwah, NJ: Lawrence Erlbaum Associates Publishers.

Kasprzyk, D., Montano, D. E., & Fishbein, M. (1998). Application of an integrated behavioral model to predict condom use: A prospective study among high HIV risk groups. *Journal of Applied Social Psychology, 28,* 1557–1583.

Ker, K., & Chinnock, P. (2010). Interventions in the alcohol server setting for preventing injuries. *Cochrane Database of Systematic Reviews, 8,* 8.

Lifestyle and participation. (2009). *Social Trends 39,* 191–204.

Loxley, W., Toumbourou, J., Stockwell, T., Haines, B., Scott, K., Godfrey, C. *et al.* (2004). *The Prevention of Substance Use, Risk and Harm in Australia: A Review of the Evidence.* Canberra: Commonwealth of Australia.

Marcoux, B. C., & Shope, J. T. (1997). Application of the theory of planned behavior to adolescent use and misuse of alcohol. *Health Education Research, 12,* 323–331.

McLeroy, K. R., Bibeau, D., Steckler, A., & Glanz, K. (1988). An ecological perspective on health promotion programs. *Health Education Quarterly, 15,* 251–377.

Montano, D. E., & Kasprzyk, D. (2008). Theory of reasoned action, theory of planned behavior, and the integrated behavioral model. In K. Glanz, B. K. Rimmer, & K. Viswanath (Eds.), *Health Behavior and Health Education: Theory, Research, and Practice* (4th edn., pp. 67–96). San Francisco, CA: Jossey-Bass.

NHMRC (National Health and Medical Research Council). (2009). *Australian Guidelines to Reduce Health Risks from Drinking Alcohol.* Canberra: National Health and Medical Research Council.

Norton, L. B., Mcleroy, K. L., Burdine, J. N., Felix, M. J. R., & Dorsey, A. M. (2002). Community capacity. In R. J. DiClemente, R. A. Crosby, & M. C. Kegler (Eds.), *Emerging Theories in Health Promotion Practice and Research: Strategies for Improving Public Health* (pp. 194–227). San Francisco, CA: Jossey-Bass.

O'Brien, K., Blackie, J. M., & Hunter, J. (2005). Hazardous drinking in elite New Zealand sports people. *Alcohol and Alcoholism, 40,* 239–241.

Oxman, A., Thomson, M., Davis, D., & Haynes, B. (1995). No magic bullets: A systematic review of 102 trials of interventions to improve professional practice. *Canadian Medical Association Journal, 153,* 1423–1432.

Painter, J. E., Borba, C. P., Hynes, M., Mays, D., & Glanz, K. (2008). The use of theory in health behavior research from 2000 to 2005: A systematic review. *Annals of Behavioral Medicine, 35,* 58–62.

Pavlov, I. (1927). *Conditioned Reflexes.* New York: Oxford University Press.

Poortinga, W. (2007). Associations of physical activity with smoking and alcohol consumption: A sport or occupation effect? *Preventive Medicine, 45,* 66–70.

Prochaska, J. O., Redding, C. A., & Evers, K. E. (2008). The transtheoretical model and stages of change. In K. Glanz, B. K. Rimmer, & K. Viswanath (Eds.), *Health Behavior and Health Education: Theory, Research, and Practice* (4th edn., pp. 97–121). San Francisco, CA: Jossey-Bass.

Quarrie, K. L., Feehan, M., Waller, A. E., Cooke, K. R., Williams, S., & McGee, R. (1996). The New Zealand rugby injury and performance project: Alcohol use patterns within a cohort of rugby players. *Addiction, 91,* 1865–1868.

Rabe-Hesketh, S., & Skrondal, A. (2008). *Multilevel and Longitudinal Modelling using Stata* (2nd edn.). College Station, TX: Stata Press.

Rehm, J., Room, R., Monteiro, M., Gmel, G., Graham, K., Rehn, N. *et al.* (2004). Alcohol use. In M. Ezzati, A. D. Lopez, A. Rodgers, & C. I. J. Murray (Eds.), *Comparative Quantification of Health Risks: Global and Regional Burden of Disease Attributable to Selected Major Risk Factors* (Vol. 1, pp. 959–1108). Geneva: World Health Organization.

Rehm, J., Room, R., & Taylor, B. (2008). Method for moderation: Measuring lifetime risk of alcohol-attributable mortality as a basis for drinking guidelines. *International Journal for Methods in Psychiatric Research, 17,* 141–151.

Rose, G. (1992). *The Strategy of Preventive Medicine.* Oxford: Oxford University Press.

Rowland, B., Allen, F., & Toumbourou, J. W. (2011). Impact of alcohol harm reduction strategies in community sports clubs: a pilot evaluation of the Good Sports program. *Health Psychology. Health Psychology*, doi: 10.1037/a0026397.

Rowland, B., Allen, F., & Toumbourou, J. W. (2012a). Association of risky alcohol consumption and accreditation with the "Good Sports" alcohol management program. *Journal of Epidemiology and Community Health*, doi:10.1136/jech-2011-20033.

Rowland, B., Allen, F., & Toumbourou, J. W. (2012b). Drink-driving in community sports clubs: adopting the Good Sports Alcohol Management Program. *Journal of Studies into Alcohol and Drugs*, *73*, 31–37.

Rowland, B., Toumbourou, J. W., & Allen, F. (2012c). Reducing drink-driving in community sports clubs: testing the Good Sports Program. *Accident Analysis and Prevention*, http://dx.doi.org/10.1016/j.aap.2012.01.024.

Scrambler, G. (Ed.). (2008). *Sociology as Applied to Medicine* (6th edn.). London: Elsevier.

Scribner, R. A., Cohen, D. A., & Fisher, W. (2000). Evidence of a structural effect for alcohol outlet density: A multilevel analysis. *Alcohol Clinical Experimental Research*, *24*, 188–195.

Skinner, B. F. (1938). *The Behavior of Organisms.* New York: Appleton-Century-Crofts.

Wagenaar, A. C. (2000). Alcohol policy: gaps between legislative action and current research. *Contemporary Drug Problems*, *27*, 681–733.

World Health Organization. (1986). Ottawa charter for health promotion. *Health Promotion*, *1*(4), iii–v.

24

Substance-Use Disorders in Young People

Evidence-Based Prevention and Treatment

Adrian B. Kelly, Jason P. Connor, and
John W. Toumbourou

This chapter focuses on the contributions of health psychology to the prevention and treatment of the most prevalent forms of substance use and misuse among Australian young people. The most commonly used substances include alcohol, tobacco, marijuana, and amphetamine-like substances. Alcohol remains the most prevalent form of substance use in our society. About 22.6% of 12–17 year-old high school students report consuming alcohol in the past week, and 18.4% of 17 year-olds have consumed alcohol at risky or high-risk levels in the past week (White & Smith, 2009). Although there have been substantial reductions in the prevalence of tobacco use over the last two decades (AIHW [Australian Institute of Health and Welfare], 2008), 12.1% of 14–19 year olds have used tobacco and 7.3% of people in this age group are daily tobacco smokers (AIHW, 2008). In the same age group, between 18.0 and 22.1% have tried marijuana, between 12.7 and 13.1% have recently used marijuana (in the past year) (variation is related to gender; AIHW, 2008), and 5.6% of 17 year-old high school students have used marijuana in the past week (White & Smith, 2009). Amphetamine-like substance use is relatively uncommon in teenagers, with about 4.3% of 14–19 year-olds reporting use of MDMA (ecstasy), amphetamine, or methamphetamine in the last 12 months. However, use of amphetamine-like substances escalates strongly in the early 20s (Degenhardt, 2007).

The misuse of these substances is associated with considerable individual and societal costs. Alcohol use and misuse in the teen years carries substantial risks, including early sexual debut (Rothman *et al.*, 2009), later alcohol misuse (Buchmann *et al.*, 2009), other drug use (Kelly & Jackson-Carroll, 2007), alcohol-related injury and assault (Kypri *et al.*, 2009), major depression (Fergusson *et al.*, 2009), and adult alcohol abuse/dependence (Palmer *et al.*, 2009). The harmful effects of smoking are well known and include cancer of the lungs, larynx, pharynx, pancreas, oral cavity and stomach, cardiovascular disease, emphysema, and cerebral thrombosis (Department of Health and Human Services, 2004). Regular marijuana use has been associated with chronic impairments of attention and memory, chronic bronchitis and histopathological changes potentially signaling malignant disease, and increased risk of psychosis in vulnerable individuals (Hall & Solowij, 1998). The regular and nonmedical use of amphetamine-like substances (notably speed and meth) is associated with violent and erratic behavior, psychosis, and severe

Applied Topics in Health Psychology, First Edition. Edited by M. L. Caltabiano and L. Ricciardelli.
© 2013 John Wiley & Sons, Ltd. Published 2013 by John Wiley & Sons, Ltd.

withdrawal syndromes characterized by depression, anxiety, extreme fatigue, and strong craving (Hando *et al.*, 1997).

The impact of substance use and misuse on Australian disease and injury burdens is high. The total annual social costs of alcohol abuse in Australia has been estimated at AUS$15.3 billion, which includes tangible costs (e.g., absenteeism, healthcare, criminal costs) and intangible costs (loss of life, pain and suffering) (Collins & Lapsley, 2008). The costs of tobacco use are more than twice as high as for alcohol. The social costs of tobacco use total $31.5 billion per year, including tangible costs associated with premature death (loss of household labor) of $9.2 billion per year (Collins & Lapsley, 2008). The social costs of illicit drug abuse to Australia are estimated at $8.2 billion per year. In the following sections we provide an update on evidence-based prevention and treatment strategies for young people. The focus of the chapter is on alcohol misuse, abuse, and dependence, and nicotine use and dependence, given the prevalence and public health consequences of these drugs in Australia. Throughout the sections we highlight issues and challenges faced by health psychologists working in the area of substance-use disorders (SUDs) prevention and treatment.

Conceptual and Theoretical Bases for the Development, Prevention, and Treatment of SUDs

The overarching conceptual framework for this chapter is ecology of human development theory (EHDT) (Bronfenbrenner, 1989; Brooks-Gunn *et al.*, 1993; Ennett, *et al.*, 2008). From this perspective, individuals are viewed in the context of their environments (families, peers, school, communities), and a key assumption is that health risk behaviors such as SUDs are best addressed with consideration of these multiple nested ecological systems. Health risk behaviors are a consequence of individual differences, their family environments, and peer networks as well as broader macrosystems in which these proximal networks are located, such as institutions (e.g., schools) and communities. Assessment, prevention, and treatment approaches then necessarily need to consider multidimensional strategies that address these nested social influences. An example of EHDT applied to tobacco use is a multidimensional strategy involving treatment at the individual level, prevention programs at the school or family level, and regulations, policy, and marketing strategies at the macrosystem level. The focus of this section is on theoretical frameworks that examine factors that are potentially amenable to change through prevention and intervention strategies.

While EHDT provides an overarching framework, it provides little specification about the theoretical mechanisms that drive health risk behaviors like SUDs. To specify mechanisms related to the development and prevention of substance use, we turn to the social development model (SDM) (Catalano *et al.*, 1996). SDM integrates several earlier models including those that emphasize modelling and vicarious reinforcement of alcohol use (social learning theory, SLT) (Bandura, 1969), and bonding to prosocial institutions such as families, schools, and the community (social control theory, SCT) (Hirschi, 1971). These socially oriented theories have been widely applied to the prevention and treatment of substance use (Ennett *et al.*, 2008; Petraitis *et al.*, 1995).

Social learning theory

A first tenet of SLT is that families, siblings, and peers have key roles in the modelling and vicarious reinforcement of alcohol use. Consistent with SLT, adolescent alcohol and other drug use are significantly correlated with parental alcohol use (Habib *et al.*, 2010; Kelly *et al.*, 2011a; Simons-Morton, 2004; Tildesley & Andrews, 2008), sibling alcohol and other drug use (Fagan & Najman,

2005; Kelly *et al.*, 2011a; Rajan *et al.*, 2003), and peer selection and socialization processes (Abar & Turrisi, 2008; Bahr *et al.*, 2005; Capaldi *et al.*, 2009; Martino *et al.*, 2009).

A second tenet of SLT is that individuals engage in health risk behaviors according to anticipated consequences of that behavior. In the area of substance abuse, this has translated to a focus on alcohol/other drug expectancies and alcohol/drug refusal self-efficacy (or confidence about resisting drug use in particular situations). Substance-use expectations (e.g., "usage makes me more relaxed," "usage helps my ability to be social") develop in early adolescence, initially via vicarious learning process (Leigh & Stacy, 2004). Media, culture, peers, and family of origin play an influential role in the development of these beliefs, subsequently reinforced through actual use. Cross-sectional studies show that elevated alcohol expectancies and low self-efficacy beliefs are associated with problematic use in young adults (Connor *et al.*, 2000; Goldman, 2002; Young *et al.*, 2006) and are indicative of greater severity in treatment-seeking populations (Connor *et al.*, 2007). This "high expectancy, low self-efficacy" model holds over prospective designs that additionally include multiple controls for other factors known to contribute to the development of alcohol abuse and dependence (Connor *et al.*, 2011). Self-efficacy beliefs over the course of alcohol-dependence treatment predict successful outcomes and relapse posttreatment (Blomqvist *et al.*, 2003; Solomon & Annis, 1990). Adolescent alcohol expectancies are strong predictors of adult alcohol misuse (Patrick *et al.*, 2010). Many adolescent and young adult-focused prevention and early intervention programs aim to modify positive substance use expectancies through evidence-based belief challenge processes, and building confidence to resist use (Tobler *et al.*, 2000; Wiers & Kummeling, 2004).

Social control theory

SCT emphasizes the role of connectedness with prosocial institutions like the family, school, and the local community. Through connectedness to such institutions, the likelihood of the development of SUDs is reduced, and long-term outcomes for early intervention and treatment are enhanced. In terms of the early development of substance use, evidence strongly supports the importance of connectedness to social institutions. Emotionally close parent–child relationships predict less alcohol and other drug misuse in young cohorts (Barnes *et al.*, 2000, 2006; Brook *et al.*, 2000; Choquet *et al.*, 2008; Wills & Cleary, 1996) and parent–child closeness predicts positive outcomes for substance-using teenagers receiving intervention (Kelly, 2008). Also consistent with SCT, family conflict predicts adolescent substance use (Kristjansson *et al.*, 2009). Families characterized by low levels of emotional closeness and high conflict may indirectly contribute to the development of substance use by increasing the likelihood of greater connectedness with deviant peer groups (Kelly, 2011; Kelly *et al.*, 2011b, 2011c). In the clinical arena, the importance of connectedness is well established. Moos and Moos (1984) have long demonstrated that in people treated for alcohol problems the risk of recidivism is substantially reduced when there is good family and social support, when connectedness to the intervention program is strong, and when patients continue to stay connected with support programs like Alcoholics Anonymous (Finney & Moos, 1991; McKellar *et al.*, 2006; Moos & Moos, 1984, 2006).

Models of Prevention and Clinical Change

Mental health promotion varies in a continuum from prevention, early intervention, treatment, and continuing care (Haggerty & Mrazek, 1994). *Prevention* refers to strategies or programs that prevent or delay the onset of health and behavior problems. Prevention responses can be classified as "universal" where they apply to the entire population, "selective" where they target groups with elevated average risk, and "indicated" where they target at-risk individuals. *Early intervention* refers to strategies and programs that reduce the progression from health compromising or risky behaviors to health and social consequences. *Treatment* typically refers to the application of programs to address existing SUDs. We acknowledge that public health promotion policies have played a crucial role in reducing the prevalence of drug use, with results most evident in the area of tobacco use. For example, in recent decades significant reductions in tobacco use have been achieved within the Australian school age population (White & Hayman, 2006). These reductions have been the result of deliberate public health strategies aimed at reducing the determinants of adolescent tobacco use including social marketing to ensure attitudes to tobacco are unfavorable, economic taxation interventions to ensure tobacco purchasers face an economic disincentive, and state laws to limit the environments where it is legal to smoke and to ensure minors cannot easily purchase tobacco (e.g., Bernat *et al.*, 2008; Edwards *et al.*, 2008; Hahn *et al.*, 2008; Hamilton *et al.*, 2008; Henriksen *et al.*, 2008; Wakefield *et al.*, 2008; White & Hayman, 2006). A detailed review of these public health strategies is beyond the scope of this chapter (for reviews, see Davis *et al.*, 2007; Willemsen & De Zwart, 1999).

Prevention programs

Prevention programs have typically focused on delaying the onset of substance use as long as possible. This prevention goal is consistent with Australian public health guidelines for alcohol use among adolescents, where recommendations have been tightened to zero alcohol use for adolescents and pregnant women (NHMRC [National Health and Medical Research Council], 2009). However, there have been a very small number of trials that have adopted the goal of harm reduction, where the goal of prevention is to reduce harm associated with substance use, without necessarily reducing or eliminating consumption. This goal is a controversial one, which is at odds with NHMRC guidelines, but does fit with the reality that by the late teens a considerable proportion of adolescents have experimented with various substances (most notably alcohol), and a large proportion of parents choose to supply alcohol to under-age teenagers (Kelly, 2011).

School-based programs Substance-abuse prevention programs have most commonly been delivered in schools, with great variability in program intensity and length, program focus (generic competencies versus drug-specific knowledge and refusal skills), and who delivers the programs (school teachers, police, program specialists). A much smaller body of literature has explored the efficacy of collateral family involvement, and the utility of harm reduction approaches for alcohol use.

We know that short didactic education programs result in little change at the individual level, beyond short-term changes in drug-related attitudes. A good example of this type of program is Drug Abuse and Resistance Education (DARE), which is the single most popular school-based drug and alcohol program in the world (it is currently in use in about 45 countries). DARE is delivered over 17 weekly sessions by police officers in conjunction with peer leaders and role models. Sessions include information about the effects of alcohol and tobacco, assertiveness education, strategies for refusing drugs, and coping with stress without alcohol and tobacco. There is no overall evidence that the DARE program prevents long-term substance abuse (Ennett *et al.*, 1994).

Programs that contain a heavy focus on interactive skills development show better engagement of adolescents and improved drug use outcomes relative to standard (no program) curricula (Kelly, 2011; Tobler *et al.*, 2000). Meta-analyses of school-based prevention programs show that interactive delivery (e.g., role plays, demonstrations, and small group work) results in significant though modest improvements in drug use and increases adolescent engagement (Tobler *et al.*, 2000). We present three examples of such programs. Project ALERT (Ellickson *et al.*, 1993) has an interactive group skills training approach, and is delivered in eight weekly sessions followed by three booster sessions in the year following. Project ALERT was successful at delaying onset of smoking (Ellickson *et al.*, 1993). Life skills training (Botvin *et al.*, 1995a, 1996b, 2001) also focuses on drug refusal skills enhancement and generic social competencies. Compared to project ALERT, life skills training is delivered over a greater period and with greater intensity than project ALERT. Relative to controls, life skills training reduces cigarette use but appears to have small or negligible effects on alcohol use. The School Health and Alcohol Harm Reduction Project (SHAHRP; McBride *et al.*, 2000, 2004) is an interactive program that shows promise in minimising alcohol-related risk and harm. It consists of 29 skills-based activities delivered in two phases over a 2 year period. At 12 month follow-up both intervention and control groups showed increases in alcohol consumption; however, the intervention resulted in significantly smaller increases relative to controls (McBride *et al.*, 2004).

Family-oriented approaches Despite evidence from educational theorists that involvement of parents in student learning is valuable (Chrispeels, 1996), and evidence that families have an important role in protecting adolescents from the development of substance use (Choquet *et al.*, 2008; Edwards *et al.*, 2008; Hahn *et al.*, 2008; Hamilton *et al.*, 2008; Henriksen *et al.*, 2008), there are relatively few evidence-based programs involving families or family–school partnerships. The limited available evidence is that when parent programs exist in parallel with school-focused prevention programs, there are better outcomes for adolescent alcohol and tobacco use (Flay *et al.*, 2004; Spoth *et al.*, 2008). An example of an evidence based universal prevention program is the Strengthening Families Program (SFP), evaluated in the USA, and the Resilient Families program, evaluated in Australia. Other programs have used an early detection and intervention approach, where at-risk families are offered a mixture of family skills training and children receive extended tutoring and support (Conduct Problems Prevention Research Group, 2002a, 2002b, 2004). While such programs are time- and resource-intensive, they are cost-effective ways of reducing the long-term risks of unemployment, criminality, and negative health outcomes.

Community-based approaches In recent years, a new prevention technology has emerged in the USA that has great potential to be adapted to the unique challenges facing Australia. Communities that Care (CtC) is an organizational strategy that matches evidence-based practice to identified needs of communities and empowers communities to manage delivery (Catalano *et al.*, 1996; Hawkins *et al.*, 2002, 2009). The CtC process offers a structured system of training, consulting, and monitoring that enhances local community capacity, and assists communities to identify and then target locally preventable risk and protective factors. At a practical level, the process involves addressing the readiness of communities to address issues, engagement of key leaders within the community, engaging an auspice agency (a local stakeholder organization that commits to the provision of resources and facilitates program delivery), data collection and the profiling of risk and protective factors, and a community resource assessment. The community then develops an action plan with clear and measurable outcomes, and implements programs that have established evidence for their effectiveness. The approach is different from other prevention programs in that programs are not delivered in a prescribed fashion, programs are not limited to specific settings (e.g., schools), the approach is governed by trained coalitions, and it focuses on risk and protective factors rather than exclusively targeting substance misuse.

There is good evidence that the CtC process has worked in the USA. In particular, evaluations of CtC provide good evidence that the process results in communities that develop more effective prevention services, and that the process reduces the level of exposure to risk at a community level (Arthur *et al.*, 2003; Greenberg *et al.*, 2005; Jenson *et al.*, 1997). A community randomized trial of CtC is in its early stages. Early results showing that CtC prevention strategies are implemented with fidelity (Fagan *et al.*, 2008), and result in reductions in alcohol/tobacco initiation and delinquent behavior (Hawkins *et al.*, 2009). There has been some pilot work on CtC in Australia. The Centre for Adolescent Health (CAH) has implemented CtC processes in some local government areas in Victoria (Ballarat, Mornington, Peninsula Shire) and Western Australia (Bunbury). Evaluations show that pilot communities build and maintained strong coalitions, completed assessments of community resources and risks, and developed and implemented their local prevention plans. Repeat administration of large surveys in these communities showed significant reductions in rates of substance use and related behavioral problems. As a consequence of these studies, Australian literature reviews have recommended CtC as a best-practice prevention system (Keleher & Armstrong, 2005; Loxley & Toumbourou, 2004). The approach has great potential utility in Australia given the prevalence of delinquency/ substance abuse in low socioeconomic urban and regional areas.

Integration   School-based prevention programs are effective if they are interactive, sustained, and broad-based in their focus. Australia has led the way in terms of harm-reduction approaches, where a focus of prevention is on the reduction of drug-related harm without necessarily reducing or eliminating substance use. Family-oriented prevention programs are effective for young people, consistent with the role that families have in the early development of substance use. School–family partnerships work well, but are underutilized in Australia. Evidence-based partnerships that target SUDs in young people through consultation, training, ongoing support and monitoring are rare in Australia, though some excellent benchmark programs in this regard are available (e.g., the Gatehouse Project; Bond *et al.*, 2004; Patton *et al.*, 2003). Community-based approaches represent an exciting opportunity for health psychologists to work in teams to facilitate evidence-based program delivery according to the unique needs of Australian communities. There are great opportunities for health psychologists in Australia to develop, implement and advocate for multisystems approaches to the prevention of SUDs.

Treatment programs

For a smaller proportion of the population, substance use increases to a point where it impacts significantly on day-to-day functioning and health (approximately one in 11 individuals) through to substance dependence. It is for this more severe end of problem use that treatment approaches are indicated. There is strong evidence for effective psychology-oriented treatment across high-prevalence substances, notably tobacco, alcohol, and cannabis. More recently, adjunctive use of pharmacological approaches has improved treatment outcomes across some drug classes.

Cognitive behavior therapy (CBT)   CBT represents a cluster of cognitive and behavioral approaches aimed at reducing or ceasing substance use. In the arena of substance abuse one of the dominant cognitive-behavioral paradigms is relapse prevention (Larimer *et al.*, 1999). The relapse prevention model focuses on immediate determinants, including high-risk situations, coping skills, outcome expectancies, and the abstinence violation effect (the tendency for individuals highly committed to abstinence to experience strong guilt when a lapse occurs, leading to the increased chance of a full relapse). The approach involves a range of cognitive-behavioral strategies that target immediate determinants, including challenging myths about the effects of substance abuse, reframing attributions about relapse, and increasing a sense of mastery over high-risk situations. The process of therapy is based on a collaborative and collegial model, where therapists are supportive, practical, and objective observers of the problem and work with the client to develop new skills to combat substance misuse. The relapse prevention model also focuses on covert antecedents, such as lifestyle imbalances, urges, and cravings. Re-engagement of the individual in previously satisfying, nondrinking recreational activities is a key target. Also, relaxation training, stress management, and time management can help reduce exposure to situational risk factors. The great majority of evaluations on relapse prevention have involved adults with SUDs, but several evaluations point to the utility of these approaches for adolescents with SUDs. Adolescents who are high-risk alcohol consumers respond well to interventions based on the relapse prevention model, with several controlled studies showing significant and meaningful reductions in alcohol use and misuse (Becker & Curry, 2008; Wagner *et al.*, 1999; Waldron & Turner, 2008).

However, the realities of treating adolescent substance misuse are that many adolescents are not motivated to attend intensive programs like that offered in CBT/relapse prevention (typically 10–12 sessions). To extend the reach of CBT and to maximize the probability that adolescents stay in therapy once they attend, clinical researchers in the USA have developed a program called Community Reinforcement and Family Training (CRAFT; Waldron *et al.*, 2007). CRAFT involves assisting parents to build the skills necessary to help their adolescent engage in therapy, and improving family relationship quality. Specific strategies include: training to reinforce abstinence or reduced substance use and avoid interfering with natural consequences, communication skills training, planning family activities that interfere and compete with drug use, preventing dangerous situations, and new strategies for approaching the idea of therapy with the adolescent. Small-scale studies on the efficacy of CRAFT are promising. In particular, there are very good rates of engagement of adolescents with a substance-use problem in treatment (71%) (Waldron *et al.*, 2007). This type of program is likely to be helpful in engaging adolescents who otherwise may be resistant to attending time-intensive therapies like CBT.

Motivational interviewing   Originally developed for adult problem drinkers, motivational interviewing (MI) has been more broadly adopted as a frontline therapeutic approach for behavioral change. MI is a client-centered counselling style that aims to assist people to explore and resolve their ambivalence about behavior change, and to enhance confidence about instituting initial changes as well as long term changes (Hettema *et al.*, 2005; Miller & Rollnick, 2002). The motivational interviewer employs Rogerian counselling skills and specific MI techniques such as developing discrepancies between behaviors and values to evoke arguments for change, and ultimately a commitment to change (Miller & Rollnick, 2002). MI has been effectively applied to SUDs (e.g., Kaner *et al.*, 2007; Rubak *et al.*, 2005; Vasilaki *et al.*, 2006), including populations dependent on alcohol (Miller & Wilbourne, 2002) and nicotine (Lai *et al.*, 2010). It is highly regarded as a brief primary treatment for adolescent substance misuse, and produces results equivalent to more intensive programs in young people (Becker & Curry, 2008; Kelly & Lapworth, 2006; Sussman *et al.*, 2006).

Family therapy   With foundations in structural and strategic family systems approaches, family therapy approaches to SUDs in young people are commonly based on the conceptualization that SUDs (and related problems) arise from maladaptive family processes. These include inappropriate family alliances, rigid or permeable family boundaries, and pathologizing a family member (in this case the adolescent) as the root cause of the problem. Family therapy approaches to adolescent substance use have involved "joining" the family around a systemic understanding of the problems, rather than an individual-based understanding, identifying chronic maladaptive interaction patterns, and developing new adaptive structures in the family, often using techniques similar to behaviorally orient communication skills training (Waldron & Turner, 2008). These types of approaches result in significant reductions in substance use and there is evidence of increased engagement of families relative to behaviorally oriented parenting skills training (Friedman, 1989) and supervision of juvenile probation (Henggeler *et al.*, 1991, 1999). The focus of these interventions on family dynamics is consistent with several studies showing that family bonds and family conflict are implicated in cross-sectional and longitudinal prediction of alcohol use and related problems (Kelly, 2011; Kelly *et al.*, 2011b, 2011c; Ryan *et al.*, 2011). However, family-based programs for the treatment of substance use have notoriously low engagement rates and are probably more costly to deliver than other interventions described in this section (notably MI). While many small-scale studies over several decades point to the efficacy of family therapy, there is no evidence that family therapy approaches have any incremental benefit in outcomes when compared to other approaches (Waldron & Turner, 2008).

Pharmacological approaches   The adjunctive use of pharmacological approaches with psychological therapies has gained popularity in the treatment of alcohol-use disorders. Naltrexone (an opiate antagonist) and Acamprosate [a gamma-aminobutyric acid (GABA) receptor agonist] have both independently (Bouza *et al.*, 2004; Feeney *et al.*, 2002) and when used concurrently (Feeney *et al.*, 2006; Kiefer *et al.*, 2003) demonstrated improved treatment outcomes when combined with CBT. In the treatment of nicotine dependence, nicotine-replacement therapy (patch, gum, inhaler, lozenge) (Stead *et al.*, 2008) or bupropion (an antidepressant) (Hughes *et al.*, 2007) have been shown to double the likelihood of a successful quit attempt. Varenicline (a nicotinic receptor partial agonist) has similar outcome rates although current reviews report that the success almost triples due to a proportionally lower success rate in placebo arms (Cahill *et al.*, 2008). Although the precise mechanisms are unknown, these medications are thought to reduce craving and reward, improving the effectiveness of CBT and other active psychological treatments. These medications are typically prescribed for high levels of dependence, and therefore limited research has been undertaken in adolescent populations, although a small but promising study has been published (Niederhofer & Staffen, 2003).

Integration

Health psychologists have available a wide variety of therapeutic approaches that are evidence-based. These approaches vary in their theoretical and philosophical foundations, the intensity of treatment, and the involvement of significant others. There is no clear evidence that one particular type of therapy produces more positive change than others, although the reviewed therapies vary widely in their likely cost-effectiveness and the likelihood that resistant adolescents will engage in therapy. The most widely researched approach for adolescents with SUDs is CBT. There is good evidence that it works, and this is complemented by a broader literature on adults that strongly supports CBT for treatment of alcohol and other drug problems. There is some evidence that "front-end" interventions designed to engage the family in moving the adolescent towards therapy (e.g., CRAFT) are beneficial. An exciting research area is brief MI, which has preliminary evidence of efficacy across drug types. Brief MI is likely to be very cost-effective relative to more intensive interventions. Notably there is some evidence that this type of intervention produces outcomes similar to substantially more time-intensive interventions. Family therapy approaches have attracted some empirical support and may be better at engaging families than other therapies. Studies in this area are generally older (there were a number of studies conducted before the early–mid 90s), and evaluations have attracted criticism because of small sample sizes, the narrowness of samples, and design weaknesses (Waldron & Turner, 2008). Pharmacotherapeutic strategies are often for severe-end dependence, and may not be appropriate for adolescents who fall in the nonalcohol-dependent range.

In general, there is much research needed on which types of interventions might work best for which adolescents. Adolescents commonly present with unique problems associated with substance use. In particular, adolescent substance use may be characterized by harmful use (e.g., occasional heavy drinking episodes), and may by virtue of the truncated longevity of use be less likely to show classical dependence syndromes. Many harms associated with substance use (e.g., smoking- and alcohol-related disease) are outside adolescents' direct experience. This presents unique challenges for engaging adolescents in the idea of therapy. The reviewed approaches seem likely to be most useful at different stages of adolescent engagement in behavior change. Involvement of families in strategies to engage adolescents in therapy are likely to be initially useful. MI may be especially useful for adolescents who are ambivalent about or resistant to the need for change. A blend of MI with traditional cognitive-behavioral strategies and relapse prevention represents an increase in therapeutic intensity, and has positive outcomes for adolescents with more severe substance use issues. Family therapy strategies, as well as more traditional family behavioral skills training, are likely to work for families who have difficulties with anger management and conflict resolution, and who have low levels of rewarding family interactions.

Conclusions

Alcohol, tobacco, and other drug use among Australian young people is a major problem, and it warrants a systematic and evidence-based approach to the prevention, early intervention, and treatment of substance use. There is an abundance of high-quality empirical literature guiding health psychologists on effective universal and indicated prevention. For the treatment of established SUDs in adolescents a generally smaller and more disparate body of empirical literature is available. Strategies that engage adolescents with the idea of therapy, that keep adolescents engaged in therapy, and that involve the family have the strongest empirical support. In Australia, evidence-based approaches to the prevention and treatment of adolescents with SUDs are underutilized. For example, classroom-delivered didactic education programs are widely implemented, despite limited evidence of their effectiveness. Community-based approaches are gaining empirical support internationally, but are only now just starting to be applied in Australia. MI is emerging as an early intervention and therapeutic strategy for adolescents with SUDs, but remains underutilized. Cognitive-behavioral and family interventions have established efficacy, yet it is unclear how widely this type of therapy is used for adolescent SUDs in the Australian context.

Health psychologists have valuable skills in designing, promoting, and implementing programs for adolescent SUDs. Potential roles are diverse, including delivery of programs to consumers, training and capacity building of stakeholders, working within multidisciplinary teams, and bringing expertise to complement other disciplines, such as teachers, nurses, policy makers, and the like.

Training and ongoing professional development of health psychologists in the area of SUDs is crucial, given the suite of approaches that have empirical support, the specialist skills involved in many of these approaches, and the public health costs of SUDs to Australia.

Acknowledgements

Manuscript preparation was supported by NHMRC project 569539 to Adrian Kelly, NHMRC Career Development Fellowship 1031909 to Jason Connor, and a VicHealth Research Fellowship to John Toumbourou. The authors thank Caroline Salom for assistance in the preparation of this chapter.

References

Abar, C., & Turrisi, R. (2008). How important are parents during the college years? A longitudinal perspective of indirect influences parents yield on their college teens' alcohol use. *Addictive Behaviors, 33*, 1360–1368.

AIHW (Australian Institute of Health and Welfare). (2008). *2007 National Drug Strategy Household Survey: Detailed Findings*. Drug statistics series no. 22. Canberra: Australian Institute of Health and Welfare.

Arthur, M. W., Ayers, C. D., Graham, L. A., & Hawkins, J. D. (2003). Mobilizing communities to reduce risks for drug abuse: A comparison of two strategies. In W. J. Bukowski & Z. Sloboda (Eds.), *Handbook of Drug Abuse Prevention: Theory, Science and Practice* (pp. 129–144). New York: Kluwer Academic/Plenum Publishers.

Bahr, S. J., Hoffman, J. P., & Yang, X. (2005). Parental and peer influences on the risk of adolescent drug use. *Journal of Primary Prevention, 26*, 529–551.

Bandura, A. (1969). Social-learning theory of identificatory processes. In D. A. Goslin (Ed.), *Handbook of Socialization Theory and Research* (pp. 213–262). Chicago: Rand McNally.

Barnes, G. M., Reifman, A. S., Farrell, M. P., & Dintcheff, B. A. (2000). The effects of parenting on the development of adolescent alcohol misuse: A six-wave latent growth model. *Journal of Marriage & the Family, 62*, 175–186.

Barnes, G. M., Hoffman, J. H., Welte, J. W., Farrell, M. P., & Dintcheff, B. A. (2006). Effects of parental monitoring and peer deviance on substance use and delinquency. *Journal of Marriage and Family, 68*, 1084–1104.

Becker, S. J., & Curry, J. F. (2008). Outpatient interventions for adolescent substance abuse: a quality of evidence review. *Journal of Consulting and Clinical Psychology, 76*, 531–543.

Bernat, D. H., Erickson, D. J., Widome, R., Perry, C. L., & Forster, J. L. (2008). Adolescent smoking trajectories: Results from a population-based cohort study. *Journal of Adolescent Health, 43*, 334–340.

Blomqvist, O., Hernandez-Avila, C. A., Burleson, J. A., Ashraf, A., & Kranzler, H. R. (2003). Self-efficacy as a predictor of relapse during treatment for alcohol dependence. *Addictive Disorders and their Treatment, 2*, 135–145.

Bond, L., Patton, G., Glover, S., Carlin, J., Butler, H., Thomas, L., & Bowes, G. (2004). The Gatehouse Project: can a multilevel school intervention affect emotional wellbeing and health risk behaviours? *Journal of Epidemiology and Community Health, 58*, 997–1003.

Botvin, G. J., Baker, E., Dusenbury, L., Botvin, E. M., & Diaz, T. (1995a). Long-term follow-up results of a randomized drug abuse prevention trial in a White middle-class population. *Journal of the American Medical Association, 273*, 1106–1112.

Botvin, G. J., Schinke, S. P., Epstein, J. A., Diaz, T., & Botvin, E. M. (1995b). Effectiveness of culturally-focused and generic skills training approaches to alcohol and drug abuse prevention among minority adolescents: Two-Year follow-up results. *Psychology of Addictive Behaviors, 9*, 183–194.

Botvin, G. J., Griffin, K. W., Diaz, T., & Ifill-Williams, M. (2001). Drug abuse prevention among minority adolescents: Posttest and one-year follow-up of a school-based preventive intervention. *Prevention Science, 2,* 1–13.

Bouza, C., Magro, A., Munoz, A., & Amate, J. M. (2004). Efficacy and safety of naltrexone and acamprosate in the treatment of alcohol dependence: A systematic review. *Addiction, 99,* 811–828.

Bronfenbrenner, U. (1989). Ecological systems theory. In R. Vasta (Ed.), *Annals of Child Development – Six Theories of Child Development: Revised Formulations and Current Issues* (pp. 1–103). Greenwich, CT: JAI.

Brook, J. S., Whiteman, M., Finch, S., & Cohen, P. (2000). Longitudinally foretelling drug use in the late twenties: Adolescent personality and social-environmental antecedents. *Journal of Genetic Psychology, 161,* 37–51.

Brooks-Gunn, J., Duncan, G. J., Klebanov, P. K., & Sealand, N. (1993). Do neighborhoods influence child and adolescent development? *American Journal of Sociology, 99,* 353.

Buchmann, A. F., Schmid, B., Blomeyer, D., Becker, K., Treutlein, J., Zimmermann, U. S. *et al.* (2009). Impact of age at first drink on vulnerability to alcohol-related problems: Testing the marker hypothesis in a prospective study of young adults. *Journal of Psychiatric Research, 43,* 1205–1212.

Cahill, K., Stead, L. F., & Lancaster, T. (2008). Nicotine receptor partial agonists for smoking cessation. *Cochrane Database of Systematic Reviews, 3,* CD006103.

Capaldi, D. M., Stoolmiller, M., Kim, H. K., & Yoerger, K. (2009). Growth in alcohol use in at-risk adolescent boys: Two-part random effects prediction models. *Drug and Alcohol Dependence, 105,* 109–117.

Catalano, R. F., Kosterman, R., Hawkins, J. D., & Newcomb, M. D. (1996). Modeling the etiology of adolescent substance use: A test of the social development model. *Journal of Drug Issues, 26,* 429–455.

Choquet, M., Hassler, C., Morin, D., Falissard, B., & Chau, N. (2008). Perceived parenting styles and tobacco, alcohol and cannabis use among French adolescents: Gender and family structure differentials. *Alcohol and Alcoholism, 43,* 73–80.

Chrispeels, J. H. (1996). Effective schools and home-school-community partnership roles: A framework for parent involvement. *School Effectiveness and School Improvement, 7,* 297–323.

Collins, D. J., & Lapsley, H. M. (2008). *The Costs of Tobacco, Alcohol and Illicit Drug Abuse to Australian Society in 2004/05.* Canberra: Commonwealth of Australia.

Conduct Problems Prevention Research Group. (2002a). Evaluation of the first 3 years of the Fast Track prevention trial with children at high risk for adolescent conduct problems. *Journal of Abnormal Child Psychology, 30,* 19–35.

Conduct Problems Prevention Research Group. (2002b). The implementation of the fast track program: An example of a large-scale prevention science efficacy trial. *Journal of Abnormal Child Psychology, 30,* 1–17.

Conduct Problems Prevention Research Group. (2004). The effects of the fast track program on serious problem outcomes at the end of elementary school. *Journal of Clinical Child and Adolescent Psychology, 33,* 650–661.

Connor, J. P., Young, R. M., Williams, R. J., & Ricciardelli, L. A. (2000). Drinking restraint versus alcohol expectancies: Which is the better indicator of alcohol problems? *Journal of Studies on Alcohol, 61,* 352–359.

Connor, J. P., Gudgeon, E. T., Young, R. M., & Saunders, J. B. (2007). The relationship between alcohol expectancies and drinking restraint in treatment seeking alcohol dependent patients. *Addictive Behaviors, 32,* 1461–1469.

Connor, J. P., George, S. M., Gullo, M., Kelly, A. B., & Young, R. M. (2011). A prospective study of alcohol expectancies and self-efficacy as predictors of young adolescent alcohol misuse. *Alcohol and Alcoholism, 46,* 161–169.

Davis, R. M., Wakefield, M., Amos, A., & Gupta, P. C. (2007). The hitchhiker's guide to tobacco control: A global assessment of harms, remedies, and controversies. *Annual Review of Public Health, 28,* 171–194.

Department of Health and Human Services. (2004). *The Health Consequences of Smoking: A Report of the Surgeon General.* Atlanta, GA: Author, Centers for Disease Control and Prevention, National Center for Chronic Disease Prevention and Health Promotion, Office on Smoking and Health.

Edwards, R., Thomson, G., Wilson, N., Waa, A., Bullen, C., O'Dea, D. *et al.* (2008). After the smoke has cleared: Evaluation of the impact of a new national smoke-free law in New Zealand. *Tobacco Control: An International Journal, 17,* e2.

Ellickson, P. L., Bell, R. M., & Harrison, E. R. (1993). Changing adolescent propensities to use drugs: Results from project ALERT. *Health Education and Behavior, 20*, 227–242.

Ennett, S. T., Rosenbaum, D. P., Flewelling, R. L., Bieler, G. S., Ringwalt, C. L., & Bailey, S. L. (1994). Long-term evaluation of drug abuse resistance education. *Addictive Behaviors, 19*, 113–125.

Ennett, S. T., Foshee, V. A., Bauman, K. E., Hussong, A., Cai, L., Luz, H. *et al.* (2008). The social ecology of adolescent alcohol misuse. *Child Development, 79*, 1777–1791.

Fagan, A. A., & Najman, J. M. (2005). The relative contributions of parental and sibling substance use to adolescent tobacco, alcohol and other drug use. *Journal of Drug Issues, 35*, 531–544.

Fagan, A. A., Hanson, K., Hawkins, J. D., & Arthur, M. W. (2008). Bridging science to practice: Achieving prevention program implementation fidelity in the community youth development study. *American Journal of Community Psychology, 41*, 235–249.

Feeney, G. F. X., Young, R. M., Connor, J. P., Tucker, J., & McPherson, A. (2002). Cognitive behavioural therapy combined with the relapse-prevention medication Acamprosate: Are short-term treatment outcomes for alcohol dependence improved? *Australian and New Zealand Journal of Psychiatry, 36*, 622–628.

Feeney, G. F. X., Connor, J. P., Young, R. McD., Tucker, J., & McPherson, A. (2006) Combined acamprosate and naltrexone with cognitive behavioural therapy is superior to either medication alone for alcohol abstinence: A single centres' experience with pharmacotherapy. *Alcohol and Alcoholism, 41*, 321–327.

Fergusson, D. M., Boden, J. M., & Horwood, L. J. (2009). Tests of causal links between alcohol abuse or dependence and major depression. *Archives of General Psychiatry, 66*, 260–266.

Finney, J. W., & Moos, R. H. (1991). The long-term course of treated alcoholism: I. Mortality, relapse and remission rates and comparisons with community controls. *Journal of Studies on Alcohol, 52*, 44–54.

Flay, B. R., Graumlich, S., Segawa, E., Burns, J. L., & Holliday, M. Y. (2004). Effects of 2 prevention programs on high-risk behaviors among African American youth: A randomized trial. *Archives of Pediatrics and Adolescent Medicine, 158*, 377–384.

Friedman, A. S. (1989). Family therapy vs. parent groups: Effects on adolescent drug abusers. *American Journal of Family Therapy, 17*, 335–347.

Goldman, M. S. (2002). Expectancy and risk for alcoholism: The unfortunate exploitation of a fundamental characteristic of neurobehavioral adaptation. *Alcoholism: Clinical and Experimental Research, 26*, 737–746.

Greenberg, M. T., Feinberg, M., Gomez, B. J., & Osgood, D. W. (2005). Testing a community prevention focused model of coalition functioning and sustainability: A comprehensive study of communities that care in Pennsylvania. In T. Stockwell, P. J. Gruenewald, J. W. Toumbourou, & W. Loxley, *Preventing Harmful Substance Use: The Evidence Base for Policy and Practice* (pp. 129–142). Wiley Online Library.

Habib, C., Santoro, J., Kremer, P., Toumbourou, J. W., Evie, L., & Williams, J. (2010). The importance of family management, closeness with father and family structure in early adolescent alcohol use. *Addiction, 105*, 1750–1758.

Haggerty, R., & Mrazek, P. (1994). Can we prevent mental illness? *Bulletin of the New York Academy of Medicine, 71*, 300–306.

Hahn, E. J., Rayens, M. K., Butler, K. M., Zhang, M., Durbin, E., & Steinke, D. (2008). Smoke-free laws and adult smoking prevalence. *Preventive Medicine, 47*, 206–209.

Hall, W., & Solowij, N. (1998). Adverse effects of cannabis. *The Lancet, 352*, 1611–1616.

Hamilton, W. L., Biener, L., & Brennan, R. T. (2008). Do local tobacco regulations influence perceived smoking norms? Evidence from adult and youth surveys in Massachusetts. *Health Education Research, 23*, 709–722.

Hando, J., Topp, L., & Hall, W. (1997). Amphetamine-related harms and treatment preferences of regular amphetamine users in Sydney, Australia. *Drug and Alcohol Dependence, 46*, 105–113.

Hawkins, J. D., Catalano, R. F., & Arthur, M. W. (2002). Promoting science-based prevention in communities. *Addictive Behaviors, 27*, 951–976.

Hawkins, J. D., Oesterle, S., Brown, E. C., Arthur, M. W., Abbott, R. D., Fagan, A. A., & Catalano, R. F. (2009). Results of a Type 2 translational research trial to prevent adolescent drug use and delinquency. *Archives of Pediatrics and Adolescent Medicine, 163*, 789–798.

Henggeler, S. W., Bourduin, C. M., Melton, G. B., Mann, B. J., Smith, L., & Hall, J. A. Cone, L., & Fucci, B. R. (1991). Effects of multisystemic therapy on drug use and abuse in serious offenders: A progress report from two outcome studies. *Family Dynamics of Addiction Quarterly, 1*, 40–51.

Henggeler, S. W., Pickrel, S. G., & Brondino, M. J. (1999). Multisystemic treatment of substance-abusing and dependent delinquents: Outcomes, treatment fidelity, and transportability. *Mental Health Services Research, 1*, 171–184.

Henriksen, L., Feighery, E. C., Schleicher, N. C., Cowling, D. W., Kline, R. S., & Fortmann, S. P. (2008). Is adolescent smoking related to the density and proximity of tobacco outlets and retail cigarette advertising near schools? *Preventive Medicine, 47*, 210–214.

Hettema, J., Steele, J., & Miller, W. R. (2005). Motivational interviewing. *Annual Review of Clinical Psychology, 1*, 91–111.

Hirschi, T. (1971). *Causes of delinquency.* Oxford, England: University of California Press.

Hughes, J. R., Stead, L. F., & Lancaster, T. (2007). Antidepressants for smoking cessation. *Cochrane Database of Systematic Reviews, 1*, CD000031.

Jenson, J. M., Harman, J. C., Smith, J., R, Draayer, D., & Schurtz, R. (1997). *Evaluation of Iowa's juvenile crime prevention community grant fund program.* Iowa City: University of Iowa.

Kaner, E. F. S., Dickinson, H. O., Beyer, F. R., Campbell, F., Schlesinger, C., Heather, N. *et al.* (2007). Effectiveness of brief alcohol interventions in primary care populations. *Cochrane Database of Systematic Reviews, 2*, CD004148.

Keleher, H., & Armstrong, R. (2005). *Evidence-Based Mental Health Promotion Resource: Report for the Department of Human Services and VicHealth.* Melbourne: VicHealth.

Kelly, A. B. (2008). Predictors of response to brief smoking cessation interventions for adolescents who have contravened school smoking policy. *Journal of Substance Use, 13*, 219–224.

Kelly, A. B. (2011). Adolescent alcohol-related harm reduction: Realities, innovations, and challenges. In G. A. Marlatt, M. E. Larimer, & K. Witkiewitz (Eds.), *Harm Reduction: Pragmatic Strategies for Managing High-Risk Behaviors* (2nd edn., pp. 318–338). New York: Guilford Press.

Kelly, A. B. (2012). Perceived father's care protects adolescents from transitions to tobacco use at a highly vulnerable age: A short-term longitudinal study. *Mental Health and Substance Use, 5*(2), 173–181.

Kelly, A. B., & Jackson-Carroll, C. (2007). Equifinality and interactivity of risks for adolescent smoking. *Journal of Child and Adolescent Substance Abuse, 17*, 51–64.

Kelly, A. B., & Lapworth, K. (2006). The HYP program: Targeted motivational interviewing for adolescent violations of school tobacco policy. *Preventive Medicine, 43*, 466–471.

Kelly, A. B., O'Flaherty, M., Connor, J. P., Homel, R., Toumbourou, J. W., Patton, G. C., & Williams, J. (2011a). The influence of parents, siblings, and peers on pre- and early-teen smoking: A multi-level model. *Drug and Alcohol Review, 30*, 381–387.

Kelly, A. B., O'Flaherty, M., Toumbourou, J. W., Connor, J. P., Hemphill, S., & Catalano, R. F. (2011b). Gender differences in the impact of families on alcohol use: A lagged longitudinal study of pre-teens. *Addiction, 106*, 1427–1436.

Kelly, A. B., Toumbourou, J. W., O'Flaherty, M., Patton, G. C., Homel, R., Connor, J. P., & Williams, J. (2011c). Family risks for early alcohol use: Evidence for gender-specific risk processes. *Journal of Studies on Alcohol and Drugs, 72*, 399–407.

Kiefer, F. J., H, Tarnaske, T. H., H, Briken, P., Holzbach, R., Kampf, P., Stracke, R. *et al.* (2003). Comparing and combining Naltrexone and Acamprosate in relapse prevention of alcoholism. *Archives of General Psychiatry, 60*, 92–99.

Kristjansson, A. L., Sigfusdottir, I. D., Allegrante, J. P., & Helgason, A. R. (2009). Parental divorce and adolescent cigarette smoking and alcohol use: Assessing the importance of family conflict. *Acta Paediatrica, 98*, 537–542.

Kypri, K., Paschall, M. J., Langley, J., Baxter, J., Cashell-Smith, M., & Bourdeau, B. (2009). Drinking and alcohol-related harm among New Zealand university students: Findings from a national web-based survey. *Alcoholism: Clinical and Experimental Research, 33*, 307–314.

Lai, D. T. C., Cahill, K., Qin, Y., & Tang, J.-L. (2010). *Motivational interviewing for smoking cessation. Cochrane Database of Systematic Reviews, 1*, CD006936.

Larimer, M. E., Palmer, R. S., & Marlatt, G. A. (1999). Relapse prevention: An overview of Marlatt's cognitive-behavioral model. *Alcohol Research and Health, 23*, 151–160.

Leigh, B. C., & Stacy, A. W. (2004). Alcohol expectancies and drinking in different age groups. *Addiction, 99,* 215–227.

Loxley, W., & Toumbourou, J. W. (2004). *The Prevention of Substance Use, Risk, and Harm in Australia: A Review of the Evidence.* Canberra: Australian Government Department of Health and Ageing.

Martino, S. C., Ellickson, P. L., & McCaffrey, D. F. (2009). Multiple trajectories of peer and parental influence and their association with the development of adolescent heavy drinking. *Addictive Behaviors, 34,* 693–700.

McBride, N., Midford, R., Farringdon, F., & Phillips, M. (2000). Early results from a school alcohol harm minimisation study. *Addiction, 95,* 1021–1042.

McBride, N., Farringdon, F., Midford, R., Meuleners, L., & Philip, M. (2004). Harm minimisation in school drug education: Final results of the school health and alcohol harm reduction project (SHAHRP). *Addiction, 99,* 278–291.

McKellar, J., Harris, A., & Moos, R. (2006). Predictors of outcome for patients with substance-use disorders five years after treatment dropout. *Journal of Studies on Alcohol, 67,* 685–693.

Miller, W. R., & Rollnick, S. (2002). *Motivational Interviewing: Preparing People for Change* (2nd edn.). New York: Guilford Press.

Miller, W. R., & Wilbourne, P. L. (2002). Mesa Grande: A methodological analysis of clinical trials of treatments for alcohol use disorders. *Addiction, 97,* 265–277.

Moos, R. H., & Moos, B. S. (1984). The process of recovery from alcoholism: III. Comparing functioning in families of alcoholics and matched control families. *Journal of Studies on Alcohol, 45,* 111–118.

Moos, R., & Moos, B. (2006). Rates and predictors of relapse after natural and treated remission from alcohol use disorders. *Addiction, 101,* 212–222

NHMRC (National Health and Medical Research Council). (2009). *Australian Guidelines to Reduce Health Risks from Drinking Alcohol.* Canberra: National Health and Medical Research Council.

Niederhofer, H., & Staffen, W. (2003). Acamprosate and its efficacy in treating alcohol dependent adolescents. *European Child and Adolescent Psychiatry, 12,* 144–148.

Palmer, R. H. C., Young, S. E., Hopfer, C. J., Corley, R. P., Stallings, M. C., Crowley, T. J., & Hewitt, J. K. (2009). Developmental epidemiology of drug use and abuse in adolescence and young adulthood: Evidence of generalized risk. *Drug and Alcohol Dependence, 102,* 78–87.

Patrick, M. E., Wray-Lake, L., Finlay, A. K., & Maggs, J. L. (2010). The long arm of expectancies: Adolescent alcohol expectancies predict adult alcohol use. *Alcohol and Alcoholism, 45,* 17–24.

Patton, G., Bond, L., Butler, H., & Glover, S. (2003). Changing schools, changing health? Design and implementation of the Gatehouse project. *Journal of Adolescent Health, 33,* 231–239.

Petraitis, J., Flay, B. R., & Miller, T. Q. (1995). Reviewing theories of adolescent substance use: Organizing pieces in the puzzle. *Psychological Bulletin, 117,* 67–86.

Rajan, K. B., Leroux, B. G., Peterson, A. V., Jr., Bricker, J. B., Andersen, M. R., Kealey, K. A., & Sarason, I. G. (2003). Nine-year prospective association between older siblings' smoking and children's daily smoking. *Journal of Adolescent Health, 33,* 25–30.

Rothman, E. F., Wise, L. A., Bernstein, E., & Bernstein, J. (2009). The timing of alcohol use and sexual initiation among a sample of Black, Hispanic, and White adolescents. *Journal of Ethnicity in Substance Abuse, 8,* 129–145.

Rubak, S., Sandback, A., Lauritzen, T., & Christensen, B. (2005). Motivational interviewing: A systematic review and meta-analysis. *British Journal of General Practice, 55,* 305–312.

Ryan, S. M., Jorm, A. F., Kelly, C. M., Hart, L. M., Morgan, A. J., & Lubman, D. I. (2011). Parent strategies for reducing adolescent alcohol use: A Delphi consensus study. *BMC Public Health Journal, 11,* www.biomedcentral.com/1471-2458/11/13.

Simons-Morton, B. (2004). Prospective association of peer influence, school engagement, drinking expectancies, and parent expectations with drinking initiation among sixth graders. *Addictive Behaviors, 29,* 299–309.

Solomon, K. E., & Annis, H. M. (1990). Outcome and efficacy expectancy in the prediction of post-treatment drinking behaviour. *British Journal of Addiction, 85,* 659–665.

Spoth, R., Randall, G. K., & Shin, C. (2008). Increasing school success through partnership-based family competency training: Experimental study of long-term outcomes. *School Psychology Quarterly, 23,* 70–89.

Stead, L. F., Perera, R., Bullen, C., Mant, D., & Lancaster, T. (2008). Nicotine replacement therapy for smoking cessation. *Cochrane Database of Systematic Reviews, 1*, CD000146.

Sussman, S., Sun, P., & Dent, C. W. (2006). A meta-analysis of teen cigarette smoking cessation. *Health Psychology, 25*, 549–557.

Tildesley, E. A., & Andrews, J. A. (2008). The development of children's intentions to use alcohol: Direct and indirect effects of parent alcohol use and parenting behaviors. *Psychology of Addictive Behaviors, 22*(3), 326–339.

Tobler, N. S., Roona, M. R., Ochshorn, P., Marshall, D. G., Streke, A. V., & Stackpole, K. M. (2000). School-based adolescent drug prevention programs: 1998 meta-analysis. *Journal of Primary Prevention, 20*, 275–336.

Vasilaki, E. I., Hosier, S. G., & Cox, W. M. (2006). The efficacy of motivational interviewing as a brief intervention for excessive drinking: A meta-analytic review. *Alcohol and Alcoholism, 41*, 328–335.

Wagner, E. F., Brown, S. A., Monti, P. M., Myers, M. G., & Waldron, H. B. (1999). Innovations in adolescent substance abuse intervention. *Alcoholism: Clinical and Experimental Research, 23*, 236–249.

Wakefield, M. A., Durkin, S., Spittal, M. J., Siahpush, M., Scollo, M., Simpson, J. A. *et al.* (2008). Impact of tobacco control policies and mass media campaigns on monthly adult smoking prevalence. *American Journal of Public Health, 98*, 1443–1450.

Waldron, H. B., & Turner, C. W. (2008). Evidence-based psychosocial treatments for adolescent substance abuse. *Journal of Clinical Child and Adolescent Psychology, 37*, 238–261.

Waldron, H. B., Kern-Jones, S., Turner, C. W., Peterson, T. R., & Ozechowski, T. J. (2007). Engaging resistant adolescents in drug abuse treatment. *Journal of Substance Abuse Treatment, 32*, 133–142.

White, V., & Hayman, J. (2006). *Smoking behaviours of Australian secondary students in 2005*. Canberra: Australian Government Department of Health and Ageing.

White, V., & Smith, G. (2009). *Australian secondary school students' use of tobacco, alcohol, and over-the-counter and illicit substances in 2008*. Canberra: Australian Government Department of Health and Ageing.

Wiers, R. W., & Kummeling, R. H. C. (2004). An experimental test of an alcohol expectancy challenge in mixed gender groups of young heavy drinkers. *Addictive Behaviors, 29*, 215–220.

Willemsen, M. C., & De Zwart, W. M. (1999). The effectiveness of policy and health education strategies for reducing adolescent smoking: A review of the evidence. *Journal of Adolescence, 22*, 587–599.

Wills, T. A., & Cleary, S. D. (1996). How are social support effects mediated? A test with parental support and adolescent substance use. *Journal of Personality and Social Psychology, 71*, 937–952.

Young, R. M., Connor, J. P., Ricciardelli, L. A., & Saunders, J. B. (2006). The role of alcohol expectancy and drinking refusal self-efficacy beliefs in university student drinking. *Alcohol and Alcoholism, 41*, 70–75.

25

Metacognitive Therapy for Alcohol Abuse and Dependence

Esben Strodl, Dawn Proctor, David Kavanagh, and Lee Beames

Although the consumption of alcohol has been part of the collective psyche of Australians since colonization, the overconsumption of alcohol has been, and continues to be, a significant problem for the Australian community. Currently, motivational interviewing (MI) and cognitive behavior therapy (CBT) are seen as the standard psychological interventions for alcohol-use disorders. Despite these approaches demonstrating significant positive effects in the treatment of these difficulties, they are not without limitations. There is therefore a need to continue exploring the application of novel psychotherapeutic developments to the treatment of problematic drinking behaviors. This chapter highlights the potential for metacognitive therapy (MCT) to be an effective alternative approach in the treatment of alcohol-use disorders. Firstly, the history and significance of problematic drinking behaviors in Australia are briefly outlined, and the literature regarding MI and CBT is summarized. A metacognitive conceptual model for alcohol use is outlined and discussed. Two brief case studies are put forward to illustrate the application of MCT for the treatment of alcohol abuse and dependence. From this discussion we propose that the combination of MI and MCT is a promising new approach that has theoretical underpinnings and could provide positive benefits in the treatment of alcohol-use disorders.

History and Significance of Problematic Drinking Behaviors

From the beginning of European settlement in Australia, drinking has been an important part of its social and cultural history. As noted in Fitzgerald and Jordan's recent history of alcohol in Australia (2009), it was used to toast the end of the first day when Captain Arthur Phillip's crew came ashore, and it became a drunken revelry when the final ship of the first fleet landed. There were convict ditties about drinking, Henry Kendall wrote poems about it, and the national 19th century magazine *The Bulletin* caricatured a nation of "boozers" or "wowsers." From the infamous rum rebellion in the 19th century, the Eureka Stockade and the 1918 Beer Boycott in the Northern Territory, through to the more recent concerns about its impact on indigenous communities, alcohol has significantly shaped our culture (Fitzgerald & Jordan, 2009).

Applied Topics in Health Psychology, First Edition. Edited by M. L. Caltabiano and L. Ricciardelli.
© 2013 John Wiley & Sons, Ltd. Published 2013 by John Wiley & Sons, Ltd.

Throughout this history there has been a consistent concern that alcohol consumption can be harmful. Its use has been linked to moral degeneration, criminality, medical disease, psychopathology, and other socially aberrant behavior (Fitzgerald & Jordan, 2009). This harm from excessive use (e.g., injury, physical illness, crime, unemployment, and relationship deterioration) can be devastating. In Australia, it has been estimated that physical harm from alcohol accounts for 3.8% of the burden of disease for males and 0.7% for females. The tangible costs attributed to alcohol consumption through lost productivity, and costs of healthcare, road accidents, and crime were estimated at AUS$10.8 billion (AIHW [Australian Institute of Health and Welfare], 2008).

In recent years there has been significant concern about this negative impact and a perception that many Australians are now in a "drunken culture" rather than a drinking culture (Ministerial Council on Drug Strategy, 2006). We are in fact quite diverse in our drinking. While Australians have a relatively high per-capita consumption of alcohol (9.8 litres per year on average and 34th out of 185 countries) this figure declined steadily from the late 1980s until the early 1990s. However, the proportion of the population aged 14 years and older that report drinking alcohol in the previous year increased from 77.9% in 1993 to 82.9% in 2007 (AIHW, 2008). Despite less than 50% of the Australian population drinking on a daily or weekly basis, approximately 1.46 million Australians consume alcohol daily, and 600 000 of those are 60 or over (AIHW, 2008).

Some patterns of drinking are especially concerning. For example, 16% of Australians aged 20–29 report drinking at levels that are considered risky for long-term harm, and 20% have at least one episode a year that puts them at risk of short-term harm (AIHW, 2008). Levels of harmful consumption have been relatively stable since 2001 (Ministerial Council on Drug Strategy, 2006). People living in remote or very remote areas are more likely to drink at risky or high-risk levels, and while Aboriginal and Torres Strait islanders are more likely to abstain from alcohol, those who do drink are more likely to drink at risky levels for short-term harm (AIHW, 2008). These high levels of alcohol misuse within indigenous groups have been associated with particularly high levels of social disruption, family violence and breakdown, child abuse and neglect, diversion of income, and incarceration (Wilson *et al.*, 2010).

The 2006–11 National Alcohol Strategy in Australia emphasizes harm minimization, recommending a comprehensive approach to achieving it, including an intersectoral partnership with all relevant agencies and community sectors, and a balance between preventing risky and high-risk drinking and facilitating access to treatment. A key aim of the strategy is to improve health outcomes among all who are affected by alcohol consumption, and an integral part of achieving this aim has been the use and development of psychosocial treatment strategies.

Psychological Treatments for Problematic Drinking Behaviors

Although there has been a long-standing recognition of approaches such as Alcoholics Anonymous (AA) and rehabilitation centres for drinking problems, it was only in the 1950s that psychotherapy for alcohol problems became a significant focus within treatment (Heather, 2007). Treatment approaches based on learning theory have had a particularly strong influence over the content of interventions and that has continued to the present day.

With the routine availability of community-wide surveys from the 1970s onwards in many Western countries there has been a shift to considering the broad spectrum of alcohol problems, rather than only focusing on the most severely affected people (Heather, 2007; Office of National Statistics, 2007). This has reflected an increasing recognition that most people who experience problems from alcohol do not have severe dependence, and are typically not seeking treatment. Currently, approaches with the greatest empirical support for broad application to individuals are brief interventions, including MI. Among the more expensive treatments, pharmacotherapies (primarily naltrexone and acamprosate) and CBTs, including coping skills training, relapse prevention, and behavioral couples therapy, have greatest support (Miller & Wilbourne, 2002; Proude *et al.*, 2009).

MI

MI (Miller & Rollnick, 2002) is a brief intervention that is empathic and client-centered, but which has an agenda. MI encourages clients to discuss potential behavior change, by (for example) discussing the benefits and costs of both current and alternative behavior, and accentuating the ambivalence they express. It boosts self-efficacy, by eliciting recollections of past success, but supports the person's own decisions about change, avoiding confrontation.

A meta-analysis by Hettema *et al.* (2005) reviewed 72 clinical trials, 31 of which focused on alcohol. MI generally showed small to medium effects on outcomes across providers, settings, and target groups. MI was effective on its own, when compared with no treatment or education. It also improved outcomes when used with other treatment approaches, increasing the duration of response to them.

In the largest randomized treatment trial of psychosocial interventions for alcohol use, Project MATCH (Project MATCH Research Group, 1997), compared motivational enhancement therapy (or MET, a four-session version of MI) with 12 sessions of either CBT or 12-step facilitation. There were no significant differences between the three conditions at the 3 year follow-up. The Alcohol Treatment Trial (UK Alcohol Treatment Trial Research Team, 2005) compared three sessions of motivational enhancement therapy with eight sessions of social behavior and network therapy (which integrated successful interpersonal approaches) and, once again, both interventions were equally effective. Proude *et al.* (2009) concluded that the evidence base for MI remains "strong" as both a stand-alone approach and in combination with other therapies.

As impressive as the results are for MI, it does not always show differential improvements above control treatments, with effect sizes ranging from -0.08 to 3.07, and a mean of 0.41 after treatment (Hettema *et al.*, 2005). There is room for combination treatments that may accentuate the benefits from MI.

CBT

CBT for alcohol-use disorders typically consists of a functional analysis of drinking behavior, plus some form of coping skills training and relapse prevention. Strategies focusing on behavioral self-control (Hester, 1995), behavioral contracting (Keane *et al.*, 1984), social skills training (Monti *et al.*, 1995), and behavioral marital therapy (O'Farrell, 1993) are effective (Heather, 2007). Additional treatment targets include problem solving, self-monitoring, and relaxation training (Heather, 2007).

A large-scale review of alcohol treatments, the Mesa Grande project (Miller & Wilbourne, 2002), found that the CBTs with strongest evidence were social skills training, behavior contracting, and behavior marital therapy. Evidence for behavioral self-control appears strongest for those clients with low physical dependence (Proude *et al.*, 2009). Coping skills training contributes to impact, but has greatest effect when combined with other approaches. While cue exposure has moderately good results, it is no more effective than other CBTs (Dawe *et al.*, 2002; Kavanagh *et al.*, 2006).

However, as already noted above, CBTs typically do not have a greater average impact than MI alone, while being longer and therefore more expensive. The case for improving treatment impact is even stronger for CBTs than it is for MI.

The Metacognitive Model

Metacognition refers to the knowledge of one's cognitive processes and the efficient use of strategies to regulate, control, modify, and interpret these (Flavell, 1979). The metacognitive model was developed by Wells (2000) and draws on information processing theory. In contrast with cognitive theory that focuses on content, the model emphasizes the importance of the *processes* that generate, monitor, and maintain cognitions. Metacognitive factors proposed to contribute towards the development and maintenance of psychological disorders are outlined in the self-regulatory executive function model (S-REF; Wells & Matthews, 1994). The model describes how an individual's choice of coping strategy and focus of attention may be directly influenced by their metacognitive beliefs. These metacognitions may focus attention towards disorder-congruent information or lead the individual to choose unhelpful styles of coping that fail to challenge their negative beliefs.

The S-REF model consists of three levels (Wells & Matthews, 1994, 1996). Initially stimuli undergo some automatic and stimulus-driven "lower-level" processing. This functions outside of conscious awareness, although occasionally experiences may occur in consciousness (e.g., intrusions). The next level is involved in the controlled and conscious processing of actions and thoughts. Level three incorporates the declarative and procedural beliefs that form our individual plans for processing information, including metacognitive beliefs. This store of self-knowledge (beliefs) directs selective attention, memory retrieval, appraisal, and metacognitive processing (Wells, 2009).

The S-REF model offers a transdiagnostic explanation for the development and maintenance of various psychological disorders (Wells, 2009). Metacognitive beliefs concerning the utility of particular processing styles guide the selection and utilization of online strategies that can be maladaptive and perpetuate the individual's emotional distress. The perseverative pattern of processing that becomes established consists of worry/rumination, threat monitoring, and unhelpful coping behaviors (e.g., thought suppression and avoidance), and is called the cognitive attentional syndrome (CAS). The establishment of the CAS may prevent the conceptually driven processing that could otherwise proceed naturally (Kindt *et al.*, 2008).

Understanding Substance-Use Disorders: a Metacognitive Perspective

Previous research suggests that substance-use disorders can develop in response to difficulties with emotional regulation (Toneatto, 1995). Similarly, according to the metacognitive model the individual may experience an intrusion such as a memory, image, or thought. This cognitive stimulus triggers an emotional response which for some individuals may simultaneously elicit a craving or desire for a particular substance. This strong affective response could be positive or negative (e.g., excitement, anxiety, happiness, anger). The emotional response activates positive metacognitive beliefs guiding the selection of strategies to manage and "contain" the affect, due to concerns about the potential consequences if the internal state were to persist; e.g., "I must stop thinking in this way or my anxiety will get worse and I could lose control."

Metacognitive beliefs concern the perceived value of particular thought control and behavioral strategies for coping. However, the selection of maladaptive strategies may involve attentional focus upon substance-related cues (e.g., reminders in the environment), worry/rumination and monitoring for danger, or threat-related signals such as physical shakes. For example, based on the belief detailed above, the individual may initiate thought-control strategies such as suppression, which paradoxically increase the frequency and intensity of alcohol-related intrusions. The individual may have simultaneously focused their attention internally to monitor for a decrease in arousal levels but this typically heightens their awareness and increases distress.

Applying unhelpful strategies could therefore increase the emotional response and the perceived uncontrollability of cognition. This activates a second set of metacognitive appraisals regarding the perceived danger related to the individual's current state. Negative emotional and physiological responses may be exacerbated and the person may continue to apply their unhelpful "blueprint" or maladaptive processing style. Being locked within a perseverative cycle of trying to suppress or control their cognitive state by utilizing unhelpful strategies may serve to maintain distress.

Substance use fits within this information-processing model as a behavioral strategy with the primary aim of maintaining cognitive and emotional control. If problematic patterns of substance use become established, the person may increasingly use maladaptive strategies to increase their perceived control over levels of consumption. The selection of these processing styles may be driven by positive metacognitive beliefs regarding their potential usefulness. Metacognitive beliefs may develop relatively early and become salient when the individual attributes success to the application of particular processing styles in other areas or domains of their life. For example, a person may develop a positive metacognition such as "thinking a lot about a problem will help me to find a solution." This may result in times where the person works towards an appropriate solution and puts this down to their analytical cognitive style, rather than a logical problem solving approach. This metacognition may then generalize to other areas of the person's life so that he or she tries to master other problems by applying this perseverative style of processing (e.g., "thinking a lot about my drinking will help me to control the amount I drink"). Rather than concluding that continued distress or the persistence of aversive states is the result of the application of unhelpful strategies, the individual believes the strategy has not been applied consistently or sufficiently and the maladaptive program is repeatedly applied. The person is maintained within a continual cycle of distress without reevaluating the blueprint or program applied to cognitive regulation.

MCT for Substance-Use Disorders

Increasingly, research evidence supports the use of MCT for treatment of a range of anxiety and mood disorders (Fisher & Wells, 2008; Wells & King, 2006; Wells & Sembi, 2004; Wells *et al.*, 2009). However, few studies have applied the metacognitive model to substance-use disorders, and currently there are no published interventions using MCT with substance-use disorders. This is complicated by the fact that consumption represents a maladaptive behavior, rather than reflecting a cognitive processing style. In applying the metacognitive model to substance-use disorders it is therefore necessary to propose the mechanism by which the behavior may be driven by metacognitive beliefs.

Researchers suggest that substances can be used by individuals to manage cognitive or emotional experiences that are perceived to be undesirable and/or aversive (Toneatto, 1999). The substance may induce relaxation, facilitate escape from painful or fear-related cognition, reduce awareness, or indirectly modify negative metacognitive beliefs about the aversive nature of the internal cognitive or emotional state. Toneatto (1999) suggests that applying the metacognitive approach to understanding substance use differs from motivational or expectancy analyses. The metacognitive model focuses upon the beliefs about cognitive states as precursors and consequences of drug or alcohol use. In contrast to focusing upon the positive beliefs about alcohol, a metacognitive analysis involves exploring the cognitive effect that is desired when engaging in substance use. This can be explored by asking what would happen to the person's cognitive state if the person were unable to drink alcohol (Toneatto, 1999). This helps the clinician to map out the substance-relevant positive (driving the selection of maladaptive thought control and behavioral control strategies) and negative metacognitive beliefs (appraisals relating to the negative effects of the cognitive state persisting). Importantly, when clinicians adopt this approach it enables the reframe of negative craving statements into normalized coping statements (e.g., "You drink to cope with your boredom;" Toneatto, 1999).

Spada and Wells (2006) conducted semi-structured interviews to examine the link between metacognition and substance use in greater depth. Across 10 interviews with adults with problematic drinking behaviors, all respondents endorsed positive metacognitions concerning the usefulness of alcohol as an emotional, cognitive, and image self-regulatory tool (e.g., "drinking helps me control my thoughts"). Negative metacognitive beliefs concerning uncontrollability and harm were also endorsed ("alcohol will damage my mind"). The majority reported that during a drinking episode negative emotions subsided and alcohol helped to reduce feelings of self-consciousness. The authors suggest that problem drinking becomes maintained by the impact of alcohol use upon reduced metacognitive monitoring and control.

Building on the transdiagnostic application of the metacognitive model, similar relationships have been observed across other substances. Spada *et al.* (2007) identified metacognition as a mediator of the relationship between emotion and nicotine dependence. Positive correlations were identified between smoking and three dimensions of metacognition (positive beliefs about worry, negative beliefs about worry concerning uncontrollability and danger, and beliefs about cognitive confidence).

More recently, Spada and Wells (2009) examined the metacognitive model of problem drinking across a larger sample ($n = 174$). As predicted, positive beliefs about alcohol use and negative affect resulted in alcohol use as a means of affect regulation. Positive metacognitive beliefs about alcohol use were also found to be associated with a reduction in metacognitive monitoring, which contributed towards further drinking. Spada and Wells (2009) suggest that alcohol initiation brings a disruption in metacognitive monitoring leading to a continuation of drinking. Following a drinking episode, alcohol use is appraised as uncontrollable and dangerous. This strengthens negative metacognitive beliefs about the persistence of aversive cognitive or emotional states. These beliefs are associated with an escalation of negative affect, which acts as a trigger for further drinking and the re-activation of the "blueprint" guiding the selection of maladaptive strategies in an attempt to establish control.

The majority of research to date has examined the metacognitive model applied to drinking behavior. This research has supported key components of MCT targeting problematic drinking behavior:

- metacognitive awareness, monitoring and control,
- attentional flexibility towards internal and external cues,
- cognitive coping strategies to aversive cognitive states,
- positive and negative metacognitions.

MCT: Problem Drinking Behavior

The present authors recently undertook a yet-to-be-published study to explore the effectiveness of MCT for excessive alcohol use. Based on principles of the metacognitive model (Wells, 2009), a manualized treatment protocol was devised. Assessment involved identifying the nature and appraisals of cognitive experience. Rather than enquiring about the cognitive content, the emphasis was placed upon the process. Clients were asked about the perceived discomfort associated with persistence of the cognitive state if they were unable to engage in drinking. The core aspects of treatment involved the removal of the maladaptive processing style and attentional retraining to

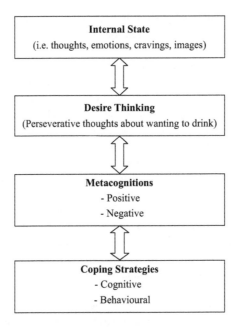

Figure 25.1 **Metacognitive model used for therapy.**

remove the salience of substance-related cues. Verbal and behavioral reattribution techniques were used to challenge the metacognitive beliefs guiding the selection of unhelpful coping strategies and linking the metacognitive appraisal of danger and uncontrollability. Postponement and detached mindfulness increased meta-awareness by encouraging the individual to notice intrusions and be able to step back from these cognitive events, rather than engaging in excessive cognitive processing. Attentional retraining aimed to increase the flexibility of attentional control and reduce the negative impact of excessive monitoring of internal or external substance-related cues. A simplified model, shown in Figure 25.1, was used to socialize the participants to the metacognitive model.

The pilot randomized controlled trial aimed to examine the relative impact of MCT in reducing problematic drinking behavior in adults with alcohol abuse or dependence. An additive research design was used. All participants initially received two face-to-face sessions of MI. After the second MI session, participants were randomly allocated to one of two groups: a further two phone sessions of MI, or six sessions of MCT plus two MI phone sessions.

The following two cases were selected from the sample of MCT participants as they were deemed to illustrate important aspects of the application of MCT to the treatment of problematic drinking behaviors. They are not intended to give a comprehensive illustration of every aspect of MCT. These participants were monitored over 10 weeks. They attended two sessions of MI, were randomized to the MCT arm of the study and subsequently received six weekly sessions of MCT with telephone MI during weeks 5 and 8.

Applying the model in practice: case study 1

AB was a 31 year-old male who worked as an engineer. While he grew up in a rural area, he had lived in the metropolitan area for the past 15 years. He described himself as someone who did not socialize much. AB stated that his father, uncles, and grandfather were all "alcoholics." The structured clinical interview identified no current or past history of any mental disorder but he did meet criteria for alcohol dependence. AB's responses to the Alcohol Use Disorders Identification Test (AUDIT; Saunders *et al.*, 1993) put him in the "high-risk" category for long-term harm. AB disclosed that he drank an average of 40–50 standard drinks each week, drinking mainly bourbon with coke and white wine daily, with no alcohol-free days.

The first two sessions with AB involved standard MI strategies. These included encouraging AB to engage in change talk, rolling with resistance, developing discrepancy between his current behavior and his goals. The therapist helped AB to explore the advantages and disadvantages of behavior change, with the aim of resolving ambivalence. As AB rated his level of importance to change as 9 out of 10 and his confidence to change as 4 out of 10, time was also spent brainstorming ideas that would strengthen his confidence to change.

In the first two MCT sessions, AB was presented with the MCT model which he stated he understood intellectually; however, he had great difficulty initially identifying any internal state associated with drinking (i.e., specific emotional response or experience of cravings). However, AB became visibly agitated and restless in his chair when discussing the possibility of these internal responses, indicating that this topic of discussion created some discomfort. Through guided discussion it became clear that while AB was not initially able to articulate the relationship between his emotions, his desires, and his drinking behavior, feelings of anger, frustration, and anticipation did appear to be associated with his drinking behavior. AB possessed both negative metacognitions about his internal state (e.g., "anger is not good as it will lead me to lose control," "if there is no way out of frustration, I will have a breakdown"), and positive metacognitions about managing his internal state (e.g., "drinking will relax me when I am angry and stop me from losing control"). As such, AB's coping strategy for anger, frustration, and anticipation involved the use of alcohol to mitigate these feelings, as they were seen as dangerous with the potential of a loss of control.

In addition to helping AB recognize these processes within himself, the first two sessions also helped AB understand his use of thought suppression. The therapist hypothesized that one of the reasons that AB was initially unaware of the relationships between his emotions and drinking behavior was that he used thought suppression whenever he experienced negative affect. While there were initial signs of alexithymia, these were representative of his common approach to use avoidant strategies to deal with negative affect (i.e., thought suppression and drinking alcohol). AB was therefore actively encouraged to explore the usefulness of thought suppression by first attempting to suppress thoughts of a blue rabbit followed by engaging in a detached mindfulness exercise. AB responded well to these activities and was set the homework task of using detached mindfulness to just observe his negative internal state rather than reacting to any intrusive images, feelings, or thoughts associated with anger, frustration, or anticipation. Figure 25.2 illustrates the success of these first two MCT sessions with a significant reduction in drinking behavior following these two sessions.

Subsequent MCT sessions involved (1) challenging AB's negative and positive metacognitions and (2) helping him to direct his attention away from his negative internal state. AB's negative metacognitions were challenged using Socratic questioning as well as in-session behavioral experiments, where he was asked to experience his negative automatic thoughts and aversive affect while actively applying detached mindfulness. These experiential techniques showed AB that he could experience these cognitions without active interpretation or analysis leading to negative emotions. He was able to just observe his internal world, developing an enhanced meta-awareness without any loss of control.

Part of the process of challenging his positive metacognitions was to help AB realize that he held a thought–action fusion metabelief and then to challenge this belief. That is, AB believed that if he experienced thoughts about needing to drink in order to manage his negative internal state then he had to act on these thoughts. AB was assisted in realizing that thoughts are just thoughts

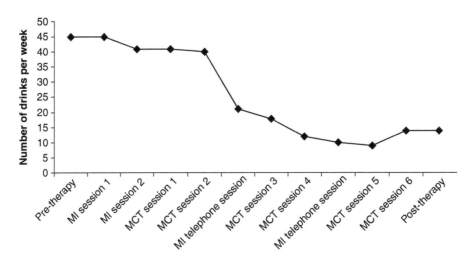

Figure 25.2 Average frequency of standard drinks consumed per week by AB.

and that he did not have to act upon these thoughts and that they could just come and go without the need for any action.

Another strategy that was useful for AB was worry postponement. Anticipation or worry was a trigger for AB's drinking behavior. If AB experienced an unpleasant internal conflict, on the one hand AB believed that worry or anticipation was useful to him in that it would prevent him from succumbing to old habits of abandoning responsibility, while on the other hand too much worry or anticipation would build his emotional distress leading to the activation of his negative metacognitive belief around "losing control." Drinking was seen as a useful strategy in managing his worry. By encouraging AB to set aside designated times to worry each day and then to postpone his worry until these times, AB realized that his worry was something that was not harmful and did not require him to drink in order to manage it.

The final MCT session involved relapse prevention, where the therapist summarized AB's case formulation and provided a brief blueprint reviewing the content of sessions. AB and the therapist collaboratively discussed the metacognitive processes that were driving his drinking behavior and the strategies that had been applied in therapy, checking that he was clear on how to apply these in low- and high-risk future situations. As can be seen from Figure 25.2, AB was able to progressively build upon the success he experienced after the first two sessions of MCT and was able to effectively apply the strategies he learned. At the start of therapy AB had no alcohol-free days a week, but by the end of therapy he had 4 or 5 alcohol-free days each week.

Applying the model in practice: case study 2

CD was a 53-year-old male who was unemployed at baseline due to arthritis, and reported marital conflict. He reported 70 standard drinks a week and scored within the harmful range on the AUDIT (Saunders *et al.*, 1993). CD had experienced chronic pain linked to his arthritis for the past 5–6 years and described drinking for self-medication purposes. As with other participants in the study, the therapist initially conducted two sessions of MI. CD stated that his perception of importance to change was 7.5 out of 10, while his confidence to change was 6.5 out of 10. CD reported that he tried to use a range of strategies in the past (e.g., alternating alcoholic with non-alcoholic drinks), but found them of limited assistance.

During the first two sessions of MCT, a formulation was developed and discussed with CD. Metacognitive beliefs were elicited and maintenance processes explored. Negative metacognitions involved the beliefs that "if I don't have control of my thoughts then life will be a mess," "I can't stand this pain and it will be overwhelming." CD's positive metacognitions included the following beliefs: "drinking relaxes me and helps me forget the pain," "drinking is good as it helps slow down the thoughts so that I can plan better and so will have my life back in control," and "worry is good as it helps me to make plans and to be on top of things." In the first MCT session, therapy focused on the metacognitions relating to the use of alcohol to manage his pain. When CD returned to the second session, he expressed awareness that he used alcohol not only to manage pain, but also worry. Subsequent sessions therefore involved helping CD to apply MCT strategies to not only his pain-related metacognitions but also to worry-related metacognitions.

Therapy was initially a little challenging, because although CD seemed to have an intellectual understanding of MCT principles and strategies, he did not appear to properly apply the strategies, either within or between sessions. The therapist became more directive, giving real-time feedback about how CD continued to ruminate about his worries during sessions rather than applying the strategies. His therapist also helped him recognize the difference between worry and mindful awareness. Attentional retraining exercises appeared to help CD better shift his attention from his ruminating thoughts to external stimuli and break up his rigid attentional focus on ruminations. These attentional strategies included in-session exercises asking CD to shift attention between physical sensations and various environmental auditory stimuli. (These exercises are described in more detail in Wells, 2000.) CD reported that therapist assistance with the detached mindfulness exercise, while listening to paired associate words of drinking and pain-related cues (e.g., relaxed – wine), was also useful. This paired associates task was used in sessions with the aim of generating substance-related intrusions. These strategies were supplemented with Socratic questioning and verbal reattribution targeting his negative and positive metacognitions.

In spite of a number of experiences that could have set CD back during the course of therapy (a friend dying, running out of his anti-inflammatory medication with resultant increased pain, and exacerbated pain after increased activity), CD had a significant reduction in the frequency of his drinking over the course of his therapy, from 70 to 20 standard drinks a week.

This case illustrates the advantage of a more directive and comprehensive approach of MCT over conventional therapeutic models that might use similar strategies such as mindfulness, but in a more passive application. Detached mindfulness also differs in several important ways to these other mindfulness conceptualizations: it does not require regular and lengthy training, it involves meta-awareness and introspection on cognitive process, rather than awareness in its broadest sense, and it does not focus on physiological grounding techniques that could be hypothesized to exacerbate distress in some cases within this cohort.

Discussion

Alcohol abuse and dependence are clearly significant problems internationally, with unacceptably large percentages of adults and adolescents consuming harmful levels of alcohol. While the standard interventions of MI and CBTs have provided a sound basis for intervening in problematic drinking behaviors, their limited impact leaves a continuing need to explore alternative therapeutic options. MCT has been successfully applied to the treatment of anxiety and depressive disorders, and holds promise in the treatment of alcohol abuse and dependence. This chapter described some of the principles and strategies of MCT for alcohol misuse, and illustrated their application in two case studies.

While there is an overlap between MCT and other approaches (e.g., Socratic questioning in CBT, or some mindfulness-based interventions), we see one of the strengths of MCT as its more direct targeting of higher-order cognitive processes that are associated with the maintenance of problematic drinking. Explicitly targeting both metacognitions and attentional focus on alcohol-related cues — hypothesized to be important underlying mechanisms maintaining problematic drinking — allows the person to initiate change in their drinking. Alcohol-related cognitions are targeted in traditional CBT interventions, but in the metacognitive model it is not important to apply verbal and behavioral reattribution strategies to these cognitions, as this content-oriented approach is unnecessary. Rather, therapists focus on metacognitive beliefs or blueprints that drive the process-generating negative automatic thoughts. This allows those seeking treatment to more successfully access and change causal cognitive mechanisms that are more proximal to the target behavior than can be achieved using other treatment paradigms.

The case studies included in this chapter highlight different aspects of the application of MCT to problematic drinking behaviors. One is that many problematic drinkers are initially unaware of the association between their negative internal states and drinking (see Case study 1). This may come across as a form of alexithymia, but it is possible that much of this represents a common theme of cognitive avoidance as a coping strategy for dealing with their negative internal state. While an explicit understanding of the relationship between one's internal state and drinking is certainly helpful in the application of MCT to problematic drinking, we have found that it is not always necessary and that a number of our clients have still made significant progress in spite of not being fully aware of their own internal states. This may be partially explained by the fact that MCT therapists encourage clients to build self-efficacy and self-management through the application of alternative and more helpful coping strategies.

The other important consideration highlighted by the first case is the importance of identifying and targeting the negative and positive metacognitions associated with drinking. These beliefs differ from most outcome expectancies in that they focus purely on the negative consequences of an internal state and how best to manage this internal state. This is in contrast to other broader expectancy beliefs about drinking (e.g., drinking will help me become more confident socially and will help me to better interact with others).

The second case study illustrates briefly the importance of attentional strategies. These are often omitted from traditional CBT approaches, but we believe are an important component of therapy, as problematic drinkers often have very automated and rigid rules directing their attentional resources to internal and external drinking-related cues (e.g., environmental alcohol cues). Helping clients rewrite these metacognitive processes allows the client to become more flexible in directing their attention to neutral aspects of their surroundings, thereby decreasing the salience of internal and external drinking cues.

The two case studies in this chapter illustrate the potential application and effectiveness of MCT over MI. MI helps to foster the will to change one's drinking behavior, while MCT helps provide an effective way to do so, for those who need this further assistance. Apart from confirming whether this is the case, future research may elucidate whether the process-oriented focus of MCT offers potential to generate more positive long-term outcomes. The marriage of MI and MCT offers exciting prospects for more effective alcohol treatment.

References

AIHW (Australian Institute of Health and Welfare). (2008). *2007 National Drug Strategy Household Survey: Detailed Findings*. Canberra: Australian Institute of Health and Welfare.

Dawe, S., Rees, V. W., Mattick, R., Sitharthan, T., & Heather, N. (2002). Efficacy of moderation-oriented cue exposure for problem drinkers: A randomized controlled trial. *Journal of Consulting & Clinical Psychology*, *70*, 1045–1050.

Fisher, P., & Wells, A. (2008). Metacognitive therapy for obsessive-compulsive disorder: A case series. *Journal of Behavior Therapy and Experimental Psychiatry*, *39*, 117–132.

Fitzgerald, R., & Jordan, T. (2009). *Under the Influence: A History of Alcohol in Australia*. Sydney: ABC Books.

Flavell, J. H. (1979). Metacognition and cognitive monitoring: A new area of cognitive-developmental inquiry. *American Psychologist*, *34*, 906– 911.

Heather, N. (2007). Alcohol problems. In C. Freeman & M. Power (Eds.), *Handbook of Evidence Based Psychotherapies: A Guide for Research and Practice* (pp. 251–268). London: Wiley.

Hester, R. K. (1995). Behavioural self control training. In R. K. Hester & W. R. Miller (Eds.), *Handbook of Alcoholism Treatment Approaches: Effective Alternatives* (2nd edn., pp. 148–159). Boston, MA: Allyn & Bacon.

Hettema, J., Steele, J., & Miller, W. (2005). Motivational interviewing. *Annual Review of Clinical Psychology*, *1*, 91–111.

Kavanagh, D. J., Sitharthan, G., Young, R. McD., Sitharthan, T., Saunders, J. B., Shockley, N., & Giannopoulos, V. (2006). Addition of cue exposure to cognitive-behaviour therapy for alcohol misuse: A randomized controlled trial with dysphoric drinkers. *Addiction*, *101*, 1106–1116.

Keane, T. M., Foy, D. W. Nunn, B., & Rychtarik, R. G. (1984). Spouse contracting to increase antabuse compliance in alcoholic veterans. *Journal of Clinical Psychology*, *40*, 340–344.

Kindt, M., van den Hout, M., Arntz, A., & Drost, J. (2008). The influence of data-driven versus conceptually-driven processing on the development of PTSD-like symptoms. *Journal of Behavior Therapy and Experimental Psychiatry*, *39*, 546–557.

Miller, W. R., & Rollnick, S. (Eds.). (2002). *Motivational Interviewing: Preparing People for Change* (2nd edn.). New York: Guilford.

Miller, W. R., & Wilbourne, P. L. (2002). Mesa Grande: A methodological analysis of clinical trials for alcohol use disorders. *Addiction*, *97*, 265–277.

Ministerial Council on Drug Strategy. (2006). *National Alcohol Strategy 2006–2011*. Canberra: Australian Government Department of Health and Ageing.

Monti, P. M., Rohsenovw, D. J., Colby, S. M., & Abrams, D. (1995). Coping and social skills training. In R. K. Hester & W. R. Miller (Eds.), *Handbook of Alcoholism Treatment Approaches: Effective Alternatives* (2nd edn., pp. 221–241). Boston, MA: Allyn & Bacon.

O'Farrell, T. J. (Ed.) (1993). *Treating Alcohol Problems: Marital & Family Interventions*. New York: Guilford Press.

Office of National Statistics. (2007). *Estimating Alcohol Consumption From Survey Data: An Updated Method of Converting Volumes to Units*. National Statistics Methodological Series no. 37 (Dec). Newport: Office of National Statistics.

Project MATCH Research Group (1997). Matching alcoholism treatment to client heterogeneity: Project MATCH post treatment drinking outcomes. *Journal of the Studies in Alcohol*, *58*, 7–29.

Proude, E., Lopatko, O., Lintzeris, N., & Haber, P. (2009). *The Treatment of Alcohol Problems: A Review of the Evidence*. Canberra: Australian Government Department of Health and Ageing.

Saunders, J. B., Aasland, O. G., Babor, T. F., de la Fuente, J. R., & Grant, M. (1993). Development of the Alcohol Use Disorders Identification Test (AUDIT): WHO collaborative project on early detection of persons with harmful alcohol consumption II. *Addiction*, *88*, 791–804.

Spada, M. M., & Wells, A. (2006). Metacognitions about alcohol use in problem drinkers. *Clinical Psychology and Psychotherapy*, *13*, 138–143.

Spada, M. M., & Wells, A. (2009). A metacognitive model of problem drinking. *Clinical Psychology and Psychotherapy*, *16*, 383–393.

Spada, M. M., Nikcevic, A. V., Moneta, G. B., &Wells, A. (2007). Metacognition as a mediator of the relationship between emotion and smoking dependence. *Addictive Behaviors*, *32*, 2120–2129.

Toneatto, T. (1995). The regulation of cognitive states: A cognitive model of psychoactive substance abuse. *Journal of Cognitive Psychotherapy: An International Quarterly*, *9*, 93–104.

Toneatto, T. (1999). A metacognitive analysis of craving: Implications for treatment. *Journal of Clinical Psychology, 55,* 527–537.

UK Alcohol Treatment Trial Research Team (2005). Effectiveness of treatment of alcohol problems: Findings of the randomized UK Alcohol Treatment Trial (UKATT). *British Medical Journal, 351,* 541–544.

Wells, A. (2000). *Emotional Disorders and Metacognition: Innovative Cognitive Therapy.* Chichester: Wiley.

Wells, A. (2009). *Metacognitive Therapy for Anxiety and Depression.* London: Guilford Press.

Wells, A., & Matthews, G. (1994). *Attention and Emotion: A Clinical Perspective.* Hove: Erlbaum.

Wells, A., & Matthews, G. (1996). Modelling cognition in emotional disorder: The S-REF model. *Behaviour Research and Therapy, 34,* 881–888.

Wells, A., & Sembi, S. (2004). Metacognitive-focused therapy for PTSD: A preliminary investigation of a new brief treatment. *Journal of Behaviour Therapy and Experimental Psychiatry, 35,* 307–318.

Wells, A., & King, P. (2006). Metacognitive therapy for generalized anxiety disorder: An open trial. *Journal of Behavior Therapy & Experimental Psychiatry, 37,* 206–212.

Wells, A., Fisher, P., Myers, S., Wheatley, J., Patel, T., & Brewin, C.R. (2009). Metacognitive therapy in persistent depression: A multiple baseline study of a new treatment. *Cognitive Therapy and Research, 33,* 291–300.

Wilson, M., Stearne A., Gray, D., & Saggers, S. (2010). *The Harmful use of Alcohol Amongst Indigenous Australians.* www.healthinfonet.ecu.edu.au/alcoholuse_review.

Part 7

Chronic Illness: Facilitating Adjustment

26

Psycho-oncology

The Role of Psychology in Cancer Care

Sue Burney and Jane Fletcher

Cancer is Australia's leading cause of disease burden (19% of the total), followed by cardiovascular disease (16%) and mental disorders (13%) (Begg *et al.*, 2007). In 2004–5, approximately 2% of the population (about 390 000 people) were diagnosed with cancer. With the current incidence rates, one in three men and one in four women in Australia will develop cancer by the age of 75 years, with the risk increasing further with advanced age. Unfortunately, some sections of the Australian population have poorer cancer outcomes than others. These groups include people from an Aboriginal or Torres Strait Islander, or culturally and linguistically diverse, backgrounds; people living in rural and remote areas; and individuals who are socially and economically disadvantaged (Australian Institute of Health and Welfare, 2010).

While cancer accounts for most of the premature deaths around the world, more than half are successfully treated, and survival rates for some common cancers have increased by more than 20% in the past two decades (Thun *et al.*, 2010; World Health Organization, 2007). For example, the 5-year survival rates for the most common cancers affecting men (prostate) and women (breast) are now more than 80% (National Institutes of Health, 2010). Given this substantial increase in survival, cancer is now considered a chronic disease (Phillips & Currow, 2010). As a result cancer survivorship has gained much research and clinical attention in recent times (Gusani *et al.*, 2009).

While the knowledge, skills, and experience required by psychologists to provide high-level supportive care to cancer patients and their families are, in the main, the same as those required in other health settings, there are several aspects that are unique to the cancer experience (Epstein & Street, 2007). For example, there are few other illnesses that are both potentially life-threatening and potentially curable. Furthermore, there are often major treatment decisions to be made that are not only complex but must be undertaken in a short period of time with a range of specialists providing detailed information. Furthermore, the treatment period is frequently very long and there can be an extended period of uncertainty after treatment, as there is often a possibility that the cancer will return.

Given the uniqueness of the cancer experience it is important that psychologists working in this area have extensive knowledge of the disease and its treatment, as well as the key supportive care

Applied Topics in Health Psychology, First Edition. Edited by M. L. Caltabiano and L. Ricciardelli.
© 2013 John Wiley & Sons, Ltd. Published 2013 by John Wiley & Sons, Ltd.

issues that patients and their families face. It is also vitally important that psychologists who are planning to work in oncology develop high-level knowledge of, and experience with, the evidence-based psychological strategies that are known to be effective in this patient group. The aim of this chapter therefore is to provide psychologists who are preparing to work in oncology settings in either research or practice with a basic background knowledge of cancer and the specialist area known as psycho-oncology.

What is Cancer?

Cancer is a term used for diseases in which abnormal cells divide without control and are able to invade other tissues (Sekeres, 2004). Cancer is not one disease, as there are more than 100 different types [NCI (US National Cancer Institute), 2010a]. The main categories of cancer are carcinoma, which begins in the skin or in tissues that cover or line internal organs; leukaemia, which starts in blood-forming tissue such as the bone marrow and enters the bloodstream; lymphoma and myeloma, which begin in the cells of the immune system; central nervous system cancers, which begin in the tissues of the brain and spinal cord; and sarcoma, which start in bone, cartilage, fat, muscle, blood vessels, or other connective or supportive tissue (NCI, 2010a).

It is essential that psychologists working in oncology settings not only learn about the various types of cancer but understand the staging and grading systems of these cancers so that they are able to converse confidently with medical professionals, cancer patients, and their families. Staging describes the severity of a person's cancer based on the extent of the original (primary) tumor and whether or not the cancer has spread in the body (metastasis) (NCI, 2010b). The TNM system, which refers to tumor (T), node (N), metastasis (M), is one of the most widely used staging systems (American Joint Committee on Cancer, 2010). Based on the microscopic appearance of cancer cells, pathologists commonly describe tumor grade by four degrees of severity: Grades 1, 2, 3, and 4. The NCI's website provides an excellent summary of both cancer staging and grading (NCI, 2010b).

Cancer Treatments and Side Effects

Cancer treatments vary according to the type of cancer and the stage of the tumor (NCI, 2010b). The main treatment options include surgery, chemotherapy, and radiation treatment. If a surgical procedure has been undertaken to remove the cancer, chemotherapy and/or radiation treatments will often follow once the cancer patient has recovered sufficiently to withstand the effects of these treatments. The aim of radiation and/or chemotherapy is to treat any local or distant spread of cancer cells.

Chemotherapy is a treatment in which large doses of strong anticancer drugs are used to kill cancer cells (Ho, 2004). These drugs prevent the growth of tumor cells by interfering with the processes required for cell division. In most cases, chemotherapy drugs are administered intravenously but some are taken orally. Most chemotherapy is given periodically in cycles that vary in length. The time intervals between treatments are required to allow the patient to recover their strength and for blood counts to return to normal levels, but not so much time that the cancer has time to grow. Loss of hair (alopecia) is a common side effect of chemotherapy, as are nausea, vomiting, and diarrhoea. However, there are now many drugs that can control these latter symptoms but most cancer patients will generally experience a loss of appetite and associated weight loss (NCI, 2010a). Infertility after chemotherapy is another major concern. While not all chemotherapy drugs cause infertility, the risk varies with the dose and the recipient's age (Lenz & Valley, 1996).

Radiation treatment uses intense beams of X-rays that are targeted directly and precisely at the tumor to kill cancer cells (Chon, 2004). Radiation therapy can be administered either internally or externally. In external-beam radiation, a linear accelerator directs high-energy rays at the cancer and a small margin of surrounding normal tissue. Internal radiation (brachytherapy) is when a small amount of radioactive material is placed directly into the affected tissue, organ, or body cavity. Some burning of the skin often occurs with external-beam radiation and this causes some discomfort. Patients also frequently report fatigue during the usual 5–6 week period of this treatment.

A range of nonchemotherapy agents to treat cancer has recently become available. These agents, often referred to as targeted cancer therapies, interfere with specific molecules involved in tumor growth and progression, and therefore stop the growth and spread of some cancers (NCI, 2010c). These treatments are often used in conjunction with chemotherapy and or radiotherapy but can be used as stand-alone treatments.

Cognitive impairment is often associated with all the major cancer treatments. This impairment is often the result of medications that cause malaise, sedation and fatigue that then lead to problems with attention and concentration (Tannock *et al.*, 2004).

At the present time approximately 10% of cancers are known to be inherited [NBCC (National Breast Cancer Centre), 2006; NBCC & NCCI (National Cancer Control Initiative), 2003; NCI, 2010d]. Those individuals with a strong family history of cancer may face difficult decisions in relation to the management of their increased cancer risk. Such patients may undergo extensive genetic counselling at a specialist Family Cancer Centre and some will be referred for specialist psychological assessment and intervention.

Psycho-Oncology

Psycho-oncology (sometimes referred to as psychosocial oncology) is a professional subspecialty in oncology. It incorporates the formal study, understanding, and treatment of the social, psychological, emotional, spiritual, quality-of-life, and functional aspects of cancer as applied across the cancer trajectory from prevention through to bereavement. It seeks to develop and integrate new knowledge and techniques of the psychosocial and biomedical sciences as they relate to cancer care (Canadian Association of Psychosocial Oncology, 1999). In particular, psycho-oncology addresses the two major psychological dimensions of cancer. These are the psychological responses of patients, their families, and carers to cancer at all stages of the disease, and the psychological, behavioral, and social factors that may influence the disease process (Holland & Weiss, 2010). Furthermore, the role of the family, carers, and social networks in all stages of the cancer continuum is an important aspect of this specialist discipline (Folkman, 1997).

Psycho-oncology is an area of multi-disciplinary interest and the major specialities in oncology are therefore involved (Department of Health, Western Australia, 2008). The development of psycho-oncology as a specialist area in oncology began in the 1970s and was spearheaded by Professor Jimmie Holland, MD (Holland & Weiss, 2010). In 1977 with two colleagues, Professor Holland started the Psychiatry Service at New York's Memorial Sloan-Kettering Cancer Centre. She developed the methods for diagnosing and treating psychiatric illness in people with cancer. Professor Holland also conducted some of the first epidemiologic studies of the psychological impact of cancer on individuals, their families, and caregivers, and how psychological and behavioral factors affect risk of cancer and survival.

Issues Facing Cancer Patients and Their Families

To provide optimal care to cancer patients and their families it is important that members of the treatment team have a detailed understanding of the issues that they face as well as their reactions at all stages of the cancer "journey" (NBCC & NCCI, 2003). The major concerns faced by cancer patients are described below.

Physical issues

These are many and varied and are dependent on the type, site, stage, and grade of the cancer. They include side effects from treatment such as nausea and vomiting, impaired libido and sexual function, fatigue, pain, fertility issues, scarring and disfigurement, urinary and fecal incontinence, bowel problems, lack of appetite, nutritional deficiencies, swallowing difficulties, respiratory symptoms, comorbid medical conditions, poor general health, and disability (NBCC & NCCI, 2003). Some cancer patients may have to live part of, or the rest of, their life with the side effects of treatment. These might include a stoma, which is an opening connecting an internal organ to the surface of the body that is formed by surgery (NCI, 2010e). Others may develop lymphoedema (swelling of the soft tissues caused by a buildup of lymph fluid, which can occur when lymph vessels or lymph nodes are removed or damaged) after treatment (The Lymphoedema Association of Australia, 2010).

Social and practical concerns

Separation from family is a major social issue for many cancer patients and can lead to separation anxiety, particularly when the patient is a child or young person (NBCC & NCCI, 2003). New dependencies leading to a change in social roles are often formed after a cancer diagnosis, as the patient is unable to engage in their normal activities of daily living (Morris *et al.*, 2010). Financial difficulties may also negatively impact on relationships that may have been strained before the cancer diagnosis. This can lead to relationship breakdowns, causing additional distress for the patient, their family, and friends. Social isolation can result when treatment at a distance from home leads to lack of opportunity for family and friends to visit, and an inability to work can result in lack of interaction and support from work colleagues. Communication problems are common in cancer populations and can lead to strained relationships. For example, family and friends often want the patient to leave the cancer experience behind, as they may have difficulty understanding that the cancer experience is now part of the person's identity. Furthermore, the partners of cancer patients often experience similar levels of distress over the course of illness to that of the person with cancer (Coyne & Smith, 1991; Northouse & Peters- Golden, 1993; Wootten *et al.*, 2007). For cancer patients entering a new relationship there may be additional difficulties. For instance, the patient may not be comfortable telling a new partner about their cancer diagnosis and their associated physical (e.g., stoma, scarring, disfigurement) and emotional (e.g., depression and anxiety; see section below) problems. As a result, intimacy may be compromised by poor body image, self-concept, and impaired sexual function.

Emotional and psychological issues

While a negative reaction to a diagnosis of cancer is considered normal, 35–45% of all cancer patients will experience psychological distress at some stage of their cancer journey (Carlson & Bultz, 2003; Carlson *et al.*, 2004; Kissane *et al.*, 2004; Zabora *et al.*, 2001). Some patients will become depressed and anxious and a small group will be diagnosed with posttraumatic stress disorder (NBCC & NCCI, 2003). Furthermore, although accurate figures are difficult to obtain, results from two Swedish studies suggest that the incidence of suicide is higher in cancer populations compared to the general population (Allebeck & Bolund, 1991; Allebeck *et al.*, 1989). Common negative emotional and psychological reactions are associated with a change in self-concept and body image, and reduced libido and sexual functioning (Krychman *et al.*, 2004; NCI, 2011). Many will experience anger at the time of diagnosis and some will feel guilt and self-blame if their lifestyle contributed to their cancer (e.g., smoking and lung cancer) (Faller *et al.*, 1995). Grief and sadness at the anticipatory and actual loss of their future and a fear of recurrence of the cancer are also common reactions. Loss of control and the realization that bodies are fallible are experienced by many cancer patients, as is the likelihood that they will possibly be labelled as a cancer patient for the rest of their lives (NBCC & NCCI, 2003).

Another significant issue in the clinical care of cancer patients is the overlap between depression and treatment side effects. Alteration in mood, fatigue, low energy, loss of appetite, loss of sleep, and psychomotor retardation are all symptomatic of depression but these are also the main side effects of cancer treatment (Miller & Massie, 2010; NBCC & NCCI, 2003). It therefore requires a great deal of experience to diagnose depression in cancer patients who are undergoing treatment (see Screening for distress, below).

Spiritual and existential issues

Many patients and their families will engage in a search for meaning when diagnosed with cancer (Breitbart, 2002; NBCC & NCCI, 2003). Confrontation with mortality, a search for meaning and consolation, philosophical explanations for illness, and loss of hope are common concerns. However, cancer is not universally a negative experience. For example, studies have revealed that some patients who survive their cancer experience have reported that it has had a positive impact on their lives (Schroevers *et al.*, 2011). Cordova *et al.* (2001) found that many cancer patients reported improvements in relating to others, appreciation of life, and spiritual change. This phenomenon is known as posttraumatic growth (Calhoun & Tedeschi, 2006).

Issues with the healthcare system

The healthcare system itself is associated with distress for many cancer patients. In fact, anecdotal evidence suggests that lack of parking or the high costs associated with it can often be more distressing than the cancer treatment for some patients. The fact that medical clinics and hospitals are impersonal places, where complex treatment decisions have to be made and invasive and often painful treatments have to be endured, can also be stressful for many patients with cancer and their families. Other concerns in the healthcare system include the lack of information, the use of medical jargon by health professionals, the lack of intimacy, the cost, lack of access to services, and the distance from treatment services (Jong *et al.*, 2005; NBCC & NCCI, 2003).

The Supportive Care of Patients with Cancer and Their Families

According to the NCI (2010a) supportive care encompasses all activities that lead to an improvement in the quality of life of individuals who have a serious or life-threatening illness. It includes the prevention or treatment of the symptoms of the disease and the side effects of treatment as early as possible, and the psychological, social, and spiritual issues associated with the disease or its treatment. Supportive care includes self-help and support, information, psychological support, symptom control, social support, rehabilitation, spiritual support, palliative care, and bereavement support (Victorian Government, 2010).

While a diagnosis of cancer can have a devastating effect on the person with cancer and their family and friends, not all patients require psychological intervention. In fact, supportive care agencies in many parts of Australia have adopted the tiered approach, described by Fitch (2000) (see Figure 26.1), to conceptualize service delivery. This approach recognizes that effective, efficient allocation of resources is required to respond to the diversity of needs of the cancer population.

In this model, screening for supportive care needs and the provision of information is considered mandatory for all cancer patients, family, and friends, with some patients requiring further assessment and early intervention. According to Fitch (2000), referral to a specialist in psycho-oncology clinical practice (i.e., a psychologist or psychiatrist) should only be considered for those patients or family members presenting with complex needs, such as those with a pre-existing psychological disorder.

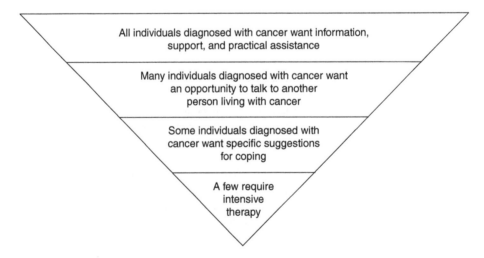

All individuals diagnosed with cancer want information, support, and practical assistance

Many individuals diagnosed with cancer want an opportunity to talk to another person living with cancer

Some individuals diagnosed with cancer want specific suggestions for coping

A few require intensive therapy

Figure 26.1 Tiered approach to supportive care.

Psychological Strategies in the Care of Cancer Patients and Their Families

Screening for distress

Depression, anxiety, and broadly defined distress are common emotional complications of cancer that deserve the attention of oncology professionals (Mitchell, 2010). These issues are frequently underrecognized and underreported by both patients and health professionals (NBCC & NCCI, 2003). In recent years there has been a plethora of research into screening for distress in oncology settings, resulting in the acknowledgment of emotional distress as the sixth vital sign, following pulse rate, temperature, blood pressure, respiration, and pain (Bultz & Carlson, 2006).

The process of screening for distress is complex. While there is considerable evidence highlighting the utility of screening (Bultz & Carlson, 2006) there is little evidence regarding optimal timing and frequency, and there is a lack of consensus about the tools and processes to be utilized (NBCC & NCCI, 2003). It is important to keep in mind that screening is the start of a more extensive process. For instance, once a distressed patient is identified, it is essential that they are adequately assessed and that an appropriate referral is made. This referral may not always be psychological in nature, as many of the issues causing emotional distress will be practical (e.g., financial hardship, child care), medical (e.g., pain, fatigue, weight loss, or other treatment-/disease-related side effects), or social (e.g., relationship stress).

Psychological interventions

There is now considerable evidence to support the role of psychological interventions in cancer care (NBCC & NCCI, 2003). Although there is no consistent evidence that psychological interventions extend patient survival (Moorey & Greer, 2002), improvements in emotional adjustment and social functioning and reductions in distress associated with treatment and the cancer itself have been reported (NBCC & NCCI, 2003). Meta-analysis has established the effectiveness of supportive and cognitive-behavioral interventions for the treatment of depressive disorders in patients with cancer (Devine & Westlake, 1995; Sheard & Maguire, 1996) and the efficacy of both individual and group therapy (Sheard & Maguire, 1996).

With the utility of these interventions established, the choice of individual or group therapy will depend on a range of factors including the patient's/carer's or family member's preference, the presenting issues, and the skill of the therapist delivering the intervention (NBCC & NCCI, 2003). As previously stated, Fitch (2000), in her model of supportive care, highlighted the importance of information provision for all cancer patients and those who support them. Given this, psycho-educational interventions that provide evidence-based information for patients and caregivers are an essential aspect of care. These interventions may be incorporated into a formal psychotherapeutic relationship or provided in group settings at key time points along the cancer continuum (e.g., before chemotherapy, end of treatment). As psychologists know, communication, rapport, and empathy are essential components of any therapeutic relationship.

It is important to remember that psychological interventions are often combined with pharmacological agents to manage more severe issues such as anxiety, depression, agitation, and confusion [APOS (American Psychosocial Oncology Society), 2006]. Psychiatric assessment is essential for those whose symptomatology meets criteria for major disorder or for whom psychological interventions are not appropriate (e.g., those with significant cognitive impairment). Suicidality should be adequately assessed in all patients', and action plans developed and psychiatric or medical referrals made as needed. All referrals should be made to a health professional with adequate experience in oncology and the intervention(s) in question (NBCC & NCCI, 2003). Following is a summary of the evidence-based interventions that psychologists frequently use with oncology patients.

Supportive psychotherapy There is high-level evidence (i.e., meta-analysis of randomised controlled trials) for the utility of supportive psychotherapy in an oncology setting (Mullan, 1992; Spiegel & Spira, 1991). This therapeutic approach incorporates empathetic listening, encouragement, and information provision and promotes the expression of emotions and the validation of the individual's experiences. Supportive psychotherapy reflects on the individual's strengths and adaptive coping strategies and has been found to improve mood, coping, and both physical and functional adjustment (Seiegel, 1995).

Cognitive and behavioral interventions   Cognitive-behavioral interventions encapsulate a variety of techniques to attend to emotional, behavioral, and social concerns and reduce anxiety, depression, and distress (APOS, 2006). Cognitive-behavioral strategies enhance sense of personal control and self-efficacy and are appropriate for issues related to living with uncertainty, emotional distress, coping, anxiety, depression, and a range of physical issues such as nausea, vomiting, and insomnia (NBCC & NCCI, 2003). Behavioral techniques, such as systematic desensitization (graduated exposure therapy), have been useful in the treatment of phobic responses associated with the cancer experience, such as needle phobia (Kettwich *et al.*, 2007).

A range of cognitive techniques such as focused problem solving and cognitive reframing and modification are used to challenge or reduce the impact of thoughts, images, and attitudes (APOS, 2006). A cognitive-behavioral approach incorporates a range of stress-reduction and relaxation exercises including guided imagery, passive and progressive muscle relaxation, and meditation including mindfulness meditation, biofeedback, and hypnosis (APOS, 2006).

Moorey and Greer (2002) have developed adjuvant psychological therapy (or APT), a model of cognitive-behavioral therapy specific to oncology. The aim of adjuvant psychological therapy is to reduce emotional distress, improve mental adjustment, develop a sense of personal control and effective coping strategies, improve communication, and encourage open expression of feelings. Based on Beck (1970), the patient is taught the cognitive model of adjustment to cancer and the impact of thoughts on distress over 6–12 weekly sessions.

Other approaches include mindfulness-based stress reduction (MBSR) and mindfulness-based cognitive therapy (MBCT). These mindfulness-based approaches are nonjudgmental, focus attention in the present moment, and increase awareness (Kabat-Zinn, 1994). MBSR is a manualized program for the reduction of stress and other issues such as pain and there is considerable evidence of the effectiveness of this approach in oncology (Ledesma & Kumano, 2009). MBCT adds to MBSR by integrating elements of cognitive therapy that promote distancing an individual from their thoughts (Sharplin *et al.*, 2010). The results from a series of randomized controlled trials have indicated MBCT's effectiveness as an intervention for a range of issues facing oncology patients including depression and anxiety (Foley *et al.*, 2010; Sharplin *et al.*, 2010).

Acceptance and commitment therapy (ACT) is a mindfulness-based behavioral therapy (Harris, 2006) considered to be a "new generation" or "third-wave" cognitive-behavioral therapy (Hofmann *et al.*, 2010). ACT uses acceptance and mindfulness, and commitment and behavioral change processes, to produce psychological flexibility. The process also encourages acceptance of what is out of the individual's personal control, while committing to do whatever is in their personal control. ACT practitioners teach psychological mindfulness skills to deal effectively with painful thoughts and feelings. The aim of therapy is to clarify what is truly important and meaningful (i.e., values) then use that knowledge to guide, inspire, and motivate the patient to change their life for the better. At present, there is limited evidence of the effectiveness of ACT with oncology patients. There are, however, a number of randomized controlled trials currently underway and anecdotal evidence and results from small trials are promising (Branstetter *et al.*, 2004; Karekla & Constantinou, 2010; Montesinos & Luciano, 2005).

Existential therapy   A range of therapeutic approaches have been developed to address the existential challenges faced by cancer patients. The focus of existential therapy is the search for meaning in the face of suffering. Many of the existential or meaning based therapies have developed from Frankl's (1963) logotherapy, where the patient's task is accepting responsibility for finding the meaning of life that is unique to them at a particular moment. These approaches are useful for patients with advanced cancer and those nearing end of life (Spira, 2000). These strategies include meaning-centered group therapy (Breitbart & Applebaum, 2010; Greenstein & Breitbart, 2000), "meaning and purpose" (or MaP) therapy (Lethborg, 2010), and dignity-conserving therapy (Chochinov *et al.*, 2005). Meaning-centered group therapy is a group-based 8 week intervention to enhance meaning and purpose at end of life. Results from a pilot randomized controlled trial indicate that the intervention is of benefit to the spiritual and emotional wellbeing of patients (Lethborg, 2010). MaP therapy is a shorter, four-session intervention used to chart a description of the meaning and purpose in the life of individuals with advanced cancer. Lethborg (2010) found that this strategy reduced psychological distress and increased meaning for individuals with advanced disease. Dignity-conserving therapy is a therapeutic process developed to help those at the end of life experience "death with dignity." The therapy helps patients to develop a narrative of their life story, which can be used as a legacy or may help clarify meaning and purpose for the dying person. The therapy is conducted over two or three sessions. During the first session, the patient is asked a series of questions and the interview is recorded, transcribed, edited, and honed into a narrative that is reviewed by the patient during the second session. Evidence suggests that this therapy can reduce psychological distress at end of life (Hall *et al.*, 2009).

Additional psychological strategies   A range of additional strategies have been shown to benefit cancer patients. These include the role of physical exercise and expressive therapies. The extensive benefits of exercise include increased energy, improved sleep, reduced fatigue, pain, depression, and anxiety (Galvao & Newton, 2005). There is mounting evidence to support the utility of expressive psychotherapies such as keeping a journal or expressive writing, art therapy, music, and dance therapy in an oncology setting (APOS, 2006; Classen *et al.*, 2001).

In summary, although there has been a great deal of progress in the recent past much still needs to be done to ensure that "gold-standard" supportive care is available to all cancer patients, their families, and carers. To ensure that this occurs psychologists can and should play a vital role in oncology settings by educating health professionals about the psychosocial impact of a diagnosis of cancer and subsequent treatment. They can also engage doctors, nurses, and allied health personnel in research into the physical and psychosocial impact of various types of cancer at all stages of the cancer continuum on patients and families. Finally, psychologists who are practicing in oncology settings should be encouraged to work together to further refine and develop evidence-based strategies to ensure that psychological distress is reduced and quality of life enhanced in this patient group.

Resources for Health Professionals

Books

APOS (American Psychosocial Oncology Society). (2006). *Quick Reference for Oncology Clinicians: The Psychiatric and Psychological Dimensions of Cancer Symptom Management*. Charlottesville, VA: IPOS Press.

Holland, J. C., & Lewis, S. (2000). *The Human Side of Cancer: Living with Hope, Coping with Uncertainty*. New York: Harper Collins.

Holland, J. C., Breitbart, W. S., Jacobsen, P. B., Lederberg, M. S., Loscalzo, M. J., & McCorkle, R. (2010). *Psycho-oncology* (2nd edn.). New York: Oxford University Press.

Moorey, S., & Greer, S. (2002). *Cognitive Behavioural Therapy for People with Cancer.* Oxford: Oxford University Press.

Stern, T. A., & Sekeres, M. A. (Eds.). (2004). *Facing Cancer: A Complete Guide for People with Cancer, their Families, and Caregivers.* New York: McGraw-Hill.

Reports

National Breast Cancer Centre and National Cancer Control Initiative. (2003). *Clinical Practice Guidelines for the Psychosocial Care of Adults with Cancer.* Camperdown, NSW: National Breast Cancer Centre and National Cancer Control Initiative. www.nhmrc.gov.au/publications/synopses/cp90syn.htm.

Websites

Australian Institute of Health and Welfare (AIHW), www.aihw.gov.au/cancer/

Cancer Australia, www.canceraustralia.gov.au/

International Psycho-Oncology Society, http://ipos-society.org/

International Union against Cancer, www.iuac.org

Medbioworld, www.medbioworld.com

National Breast and Ovarian Cancer Centre, www.nbocc.org.au/

National Comprehensive Cancer Network, www.nccn.org/index.asp

National Health and Medical Research Council, www.nhmrc.gov.au/guidelines/publications/subject/Cancer

Psycho-oncology Journal, www.apos-society.org/about/journal.asp

The Psycho-Oncology Co-operative Research Group, www.pocog.org.au

US National Cancer Institute (NCI), www.cancer.gov

World Health Organization (WHO), http://search.who.int/search?q=cancer&ie=utf8&site=default_collection &client=_en&proxystylesheet=_en&output=xml_no_dtd&oe=utf8

World Oncology Network, www.worldoncology.net/psycho.htm

References

Australian Institute of Health and Welfare. (2010). *Australia's Health.* Cat. no. AUS 122. Canberra: Australian Institute of Health and Welfare.

Allebeck, P., & Bolund, C. (1991). Suicide and suicide attempts in cancer patients. *Psychological Medicine, 21,* 979–984.

Allebeck, P., Bolund, C., & Ringback, G. (1989). Increased suicide rate in cancer patients: A cohort study based on the Swedish Cancer-Environment Register. *Journal of Clinical Epidemiology, 42,* 611–616.

American Joint Committee on Cancer. (2010). *What is Cancer Staging?* www.cancerstaging.org/mission/whatis.html.

APOS (American Psychosocial Oncology Society). (2006). *Quick Reference for Oncology Clinicians: The Psychiatric and Psychological Dimensions of Cancer Symptom Management.* Charlottesville, VA: International Psycho-Oncology Society Press.

Beck, A. (1970). Cognitive therapy: Nature and relation to behavior therapy. *Behavior Therapy, 1,* 184–200.

Begg, S., Vos, T., Barker, B., Stevenson, C., Stanley, L., & Lopez, A. (2007). *The Burden of Disease and Injury in Australia, 2003.* Canberra: Australian Institute of Health and Welfare. www.aihw.gov.au/publications/index.cfm/title/10317.

Branstetter, A. D., Wilson, K. G., Hildebrandt, M., & Mutch, D. (2004). *Improving Psychological Adjustment Among Cancer Patients: ACT and CBT.* Paper presented at the 38th Annual Association for Advancement of Behavior Therapy, New Orleans.

Breitbart, W. (2002). Spirituality and meaning in supportive care: Spirituality- and meaning-centered group psychotherapy interventions in advanced cancer. *Supportive Care in Cancer 10,* 272–280.

Brietbart, W., & Applebaum, A. (2010). Meaning-centred group therapy. In M. Watson & D. Kissane (Eds.), *Handbook of Psychotherapy* (pp. 137–148). West Sussex: Wiley Blackwell.

Bultz, B. D., & Carlson, L. E. (2006). Emotional distress: The sixth vital sign. Future directions in cancer care. *Psycho-Oncology, 15*, 93–95.

Calhoun, L. G., & Tedeschi, R. G. (Eds.). (2006). *The Handbook of Posttraumatic Growth: Research and Practice.* Mahwah, NJ: Lawrence Erlbaum.

Canadian Association of Psychosocial Oncology. (1999). *National Psychosocial Standards for Canada.* www.capo.ca/eng/finalstandards.asp#S2.

Carlson, L. E., & Bultz, B. D. (2003). Cancer distress screening: Needs, methods and models. *Journal of Psychosomatic Research, 55*, 403–409.

Carlson, L. E., Angen, M., Cullum, J., Goodey, E., Koopmans, J., Lamont, L., *et al.* (2004). High levels of untreated distress and fatigue in cancer patients. *British Journal of Cancer, 90*, 2297–2304.

Chochinov, H. M., Hack, T., Hassard, T., Kristjanson, L., J., McClement, S., & Harlos, M. (2005). Dignity therapy: A novel psychotherapeutic intervention for patients near the end of life. *CA: A Cancer Journal for Clinicians, 56*, 84–103.

Chon, B. (2004). Radiation therapy. In T. A. Stern & M. A. Sekeres. (2004). *Facing Cancer: A Complete Guide for People with Cancer, their Families, and Caregivers* (pp. 191–202). New York: McGraw-Hill.

Classen C., Butler, L. D., Koopman, C., Miller, E., DiMiceli, S., Giese-David, J. *et al.* (2001). Supportive-expressive group therapy and distress in patients with metastatic breast cancer: A randomized clinical intervention trial. *Archives of General Psychiatry, 58*(5), 494–501.

Cordova, M. J., Cunningham, L. L., Carlson, C. R., & Andrykowski, M. A. (2001). Posttraumatic growth following breast cancer: A controlled comparison study. *Health Psychology, 20*, 176–185.

Coyne, J. C., & Smith, D. A. F. (1991). Couples coping with a myocardial infarction: A contextual perspective on wives' distress. *Journal of Personality and Psychology, 61*, 404–412.

Department of Health, Western Australia. (2008). *Psycho-oncology Model of Care.* Perth, WA: Cancer and Palliative Care Network.

Devine, E. C., & Westlake, S. K. (1995). The effects of psychoeducational care provide to adults with cancer: Meta analysis of 116 studies. *Oncology Nursing Forum, 22*, 1369–1381.

Epstein, R. M., & Street, R. L. Jr. (2007). *Patient-Centered Communication in Cancer Care: Promoting Healing and Reducing Suffering.* Bethesda, MD: National Cancer Institute.

Faller, H., Schilling, S., & Lang, H. (1995). Causal attribution and adaptation among lung cancer patients. *Journal of Psychosomatic Research, 39*, 619–627.

Fitch, M. (2000). Supportive care for cancer patients. *Hospital Quarterly, 3*, 39–46.

Foley, E., Baillie, A., Huxter, M., Price, M., & Sinclair, E. (2010). Mindfulness-based cognitive therapy for individuals whose lives have been affected by cancer: A randomized controlled trial. *Journal of Consulting and Clinical Psychology, 78*, 72–9.

Folkman, S. (1997). Positive psychological states and coping with severe stress. *Social Science and Medicine, 45*, 1207–1221.

Frankl, V. E. (1963). *Man's Search for Meaning. An Introduction to Logotherapy.* Boston, MA: Beacon Press.

Galvao, D. A., & Newton, R. U. (2005). Review of exercise intervention studies in cancer patients. *Journal of Clinical Oncology, 23*, 899–909.

Greenstein, M., & Breitbart, W. (2000). Cancer and the experience of meaning: A group psychotherapy program for people with cancer. *American Journal of Psychotherapy, 54*, 486–500.

Gusani, N. J., Schubart, J. R., Wise, J., Farace, E., Green, M. J., Jiang, X. *et al.* (2009). Cancer survivorship: A new challenge for surgical and medical oncologists. *Journal of Internal Medicine, 24*, 456–458.

Hall, S., Chochinov, H., Harding, R., Murray, S., Richardson, A., & Higginson, I. J. (2009). A Phase II randomised controlled trial assessing the feasibility, acceptability and potential effectiveness of dignity therapy for older people in care homes: Study protocol. *BMC Geriatrics, 9*, 9.

Harris, R. (2006). Embracing your demons: An overview of Acceptance and Commitment Therapy. *Psychotherapy in Australia, 12*(4), 2–8.

Ho, V. T. (2004). Chemotherapy. In T. A. Stern, & M. A. Sekeres. (2004). *Facing Cancer: A Complete Guide for People with Cancer, their Families, and Caregivers* (pp. 169–178). New York: McGraw-Hill.

Hofmann, S. G., Sawyer, A. T., & Fang A., (2010). The empirical status of the 'new wave' of cognitive behavioral therapy. *Psychiatry Clinic of North America, 33,* 701–10.

Holland, J. C., & Weiss, T. A. (2010). History of psycho-oncology. In J. C. Holland., W. S. Breitbart., P. B. Jacobsen., M. S. Lederberg., M. J. Loscalzo., & R. McCorkle (Eds.), *Psycho-oncology* (2nd edn., pp. 3–12). New York: Oxford University Press.

Jong, K. E., Vale, P. J., & Armstrong, B. K. (2005). Rural inequalities in cancer care and outcome. *Medical Journal of Australia, 182,* 13–14.

Kabat-Zinn, J. (1994). *Wherever You Go There You Are: Mindfulness Meditation for Everyday Life.* New York: Hyperion.

Karekla, M., & Constantinou, M. (2010). Religious coping and cancer: Proposing an acceptance and commitment therapy approach. *Cognitive and Behavioral Practice, 17,* 371–381.

Kettwich, S. C., Sibbit, W. L Jr., Brandt, J. R., Johnson, C. R., Wong, C. S., & Bankhurst A. D. (2007). Needle phobia and stress–reducing medical devices in pediatric and adult chemotherapy patients. *Journal of Pediatric Oncology Nursing, 24,* 20–28.

Kissane, D. W., Grabsch, B., Love, A., Clarke, D. M., Bloch, S., & Smith, G. G. (2004). Psychiatric disease in women with early stage and advanced breast cancer: A comparative analysis. *Australian and New Zealand Journal of Psychiatry, 38,* 320–326.

Krychman, M. L., Amsterdam, A., & Carter, J. (2004). Sexual medicine and the female cancer patient. *Current Sexual Health Reports, 1,* 145–150.

Ledesma, D., & Kumano, H. (2009). Mindfulness-based stress reduction and cancer: A meta-analysis. *Psycho-Oncology, 18*(6), 571–579.

Lenz, K. L., & Valley, A. W. (1996). Infertility after chemotherapy: A review of the risks and strategies for prevention. *Journal of Oncology Pharmacy Practice, 2,* 75–100.

Lethborg, C. (2010). Meaning and purpose: A pilot study of 'MaP' therapy in an advanced cancer cohort. *Psycho-Oncology, 19*(Suppl. 2), S1–S313.

Miller, K., & Massie, M. J. (2010). Depressive disorders. In J. C. Holland., W. S. Breitbart, P. B. Jacobsen., M. S. Lederberg., M. J. Loscalzo., & R. McCorkle (Eds.), *Psycho-oncology* (2nd edn., pp. 311–318). New York: Oxford University Press.

Mitchell, A. J. (2010). Screening procedures for psychosocial distress. In J. C. Holland., W. S. Breitbart., P. B. Jacobsen., M. S. Lederberg., M. J. Loscalzo., & R. McCorkle (Eds.), *Psycho-Oncology* (2nd edn., pp. 389–396). New York: Oxford University Press.

Montesinos, F., & Luciano, M. C. (2005). *Treatment of Relapse Fear in Breast Cancer Patients Through an ACT-Based Protocol.* Paper presented at the 9th European Congress of Psychology, Granada.

Moorey, S., & Greer, S. (2002). *Cognitive Behavioural Therapy for People with Cancer.* Oxford: Oxford University Press.

Morris, B. A., Campbell, M., Dwyer, M., Dunn, J., & Chambers S. K. (2011). Survivor identity and post-traumatic growth after participating in challenge-based peer-support programmes. *British Journal of Health Psychology, 16*(3), 660–674.

Mullan, H. (1992). Existential therapists and their group therapy practices. *International Journal of Group Psychotherapy, 42,* 453–468.

National Institutes of Health. (2010). *Cancer.* www.nih.gov/about/researchresultsforthepublic/Cancer.pdf.

NBCC (National Breast Cancer Centre). (2006). *Advice About Familial Aspects of Breast Cancer and Ovarian Cancer: A Guide for Health Professionals.* Camperdown, NSW: National Breast Cancer Centre.

NBCC, & NCCI. (National Cancer Control Initiative). (2003). *Clinical Practice Guidelines for the Psychosocial Care of Adults with Cancer.* Camperdown, NSW: National Breast Cancer Centre and National Cancer Control Initiative.

NCI. (US National Cancer Institute). (2010a). *What is Cancer?* www.cancer.gov/cancertopics/cancerlibrary/what-is-cancer.

NCI. (2010b). *Cancer Staging.* www.cancer.gov/cancertopics/factsheet/detection/staging.

NCI. (2010c). *Targeted Cancer Therapies.* www.cancer.gov/cancertopics/factsheet/Therapy/targeted.

NCI. (2010d). *Cancer Genetics Overview.* www.cancer.gov/cancertopics/pdq/genetics/overview/healthprofessional/page1.

NCI. (2010e). *Colon and Anal Cancer.* www.cancer.gov/cancertopics/types/colon-and-rectal.

NCI. (2011). *Sexuality and Reproductive Issues.* www.cancer.gov/cancertopics.

Northouse, L. L., & Peters-Golden, H. (1993). Cancer and the family: Strategies to assist spouses. *Seminars in Oncology Nursing, 9,* 74–82.

Phillips, J. L., & Currow, D. C. (2010). Cancer as a chronic disease. *Collegian: Journal of the Royal College of Nursing Australia, 17,* 47–50.

Schroevers, M. J., Kraaij, V., & Garnefski, N. (2011). Cancer patients' experience of positive and negative changes due to the illness: Relationships with psychological well-being, coping, and goal reengagement. *Psycho-Oncology, 20,* 165–172.

Seiegel, D. (1995). Essentials for psychotherapeutic interventions for cancer patients. *Supportive Care in Cancer, 3,* 252–256.

Sekeres, M. A. (2004). What is cancer? In T. A. Stern & M. A. Sekeres. (2004). *Facing Cancer: A Complete Guide for People with Cancer, their Families, and Caregivers* (pp. 1–12). New York: McGraw-Hill.

Sharplin, G., Jones, S., Hancock, B., Knott, V., Bowden, J., & Whitford, H. (2010). Mindfulness-based cognitive therapy: An efficacious community-based group intervention for depression and anxiety in a sample of cancer patients. *Medical Journal of Australia, 193,* S79-S82.

Sheard, T., & Maguire, P. (1996). The effect of psychological interventions on anxiety and depression in oncology: Results of two meta-analyses. *Third World Congress of Psycho-oncology,* 3–6.

Spiegel, D., & Spira, J. (1991). *Supportive-Expressive Group Therapy: A Treatment Manual of Psychosocial Intervention for Women with Recurrent Breast Cancer. A Summary of the Literature 1976–1996.* Woolloomooloo, NSW: National Breast Cancer Centre.

Spira, J. L. (2000). Existential psychotherapy in palliative care. In H. M. Chochinov & W. Breitbart (Eds.), *Handbook of Psychiatry in Palliative Medicine* (pp. 197–214). New York: Oxford University Press.

Tannock, I. F., Ahles, T. A., Ganz, P. A., & van Dam, F. S. (2004). Cognitive impairment associated with chemotherapy for cancer: Report of a workshop. *American Society of Clinical Oncology, 22,* 233–2239.

The Lymphoedema Association of Australia. (2010). *What is Lymphoedema?* http://lymphoedema.org.au/lymphoed.html.

Thun, M. J., DeLancey, J. O., Center, M. M., Jemal, A., & Ward, E. M. (2010). The global burden of cancer: Priorities for prevention. *Carcinogenesis, 31,* 100–110.

Victorian Government (2010) *Cancer Services in Victoria.* www.health.vic.gov.au/cancer/framework/supportive.htm.

World Health Organization. (2007). *Cancer Control: Knowledge into Action. WHO Guide for Effective Programs.* Geneva: World Health Organization.

Wootten, A. C., Burney, S., Foroudi, F., Frydenberg, M., Coleman, C., & Ng, K. T. (2007). Psychological adjustment of survivors of localised prostate cancer: Investigating the role of dyadic adjustment, cognitive appraisal and coping style. *Psycho-Oncology, 16,* 1–9.

Zabora, J., Brintzenhofe-Szoc, K., Curbow, B., Hooker, C., & Piantadosi, S. (2001). The prevalence of psychological distress by cancer site. *Psycho-Oncology, 10,* 19–28.

27

Psychological Approaches to Assisting Individuals Diagnosed with Cancer

Lisa Beatty and Melissa Oxlad

Cancer diagnosis and treatment elicit higher levels of distress and psychopathology than normally observed in the community. This chapter first provides an overview of the potential psychosocial concerns and problems with which an individual with a cancer diagnosis may present, then provides guidelines for conducting assessments. The third, and major, focus for this chapter is to summarize the range of evidence-based interventions that can be applied, and professional issues to be aware of that may impact upon clinicians. Clinical case tasks are provided to enable the application of learning to a case scenario.

Cancer in Australia

One in two men and one in three women will be diagnosed with cancer by the age of 85 (Australian Institute of Health and Welfare & Australasian Association of Cancer Registries, 2008). Cancer is the leading cause of disease burden in Australia, accounting for 19% of the total burden on the healthcare system, and is the most common cause of death for men and the second most common cause of death for women behind cardiovascular disease (AIHW, 2010). Over the past decades medical treatment (typically comprised of surgery, chemotherapy, radiotherapy, biologic, and hormonal therapies) and survival rates have substantially improved, resulting in a corresponding increase in the number of individuals living with or beyond cancer. However, the adverse psychological impact of cancer remains problematic, with the literature consistently showing that 30–40% of cancer patients and survivors experience distress (Carlson et al., 2004a; Zabora et al., 2001).

Prevalent Psychosocial Concerns

A recent Australian study showed that 20% of individuals with cancer meet diagnostic criteria for anxiety and depression (Sharpley et al., 2010), an issue that is often underrecognized and undertreated (Fann et al., 2008). Other common psychological issues include maladaptive coping

Applied Topics in Health Psychology, First Edition. Edited by M. L. Caltabiano and L. Ricciardelli.
© 2013 John Wiley & Sons, Ltd. Published 2013 by John Wiley & Sons, Ltd.

strategies, grief and loss concerns, body image, sexuality and fertility difficulties, interpersonal problems, making treatment-related decisions, managing medical phobias, and coping with cancer symptoms, treatment side effects, and end-of-life challenges. While the majority of long-term survivors recover psychologically, a recent study of Australian survivors showed that a small subset continue to experience clinically significant anxiety and depression (Boyes *et al.*, 2009). It should also be noted that the prevalence and nature of presenting problems may differ depending on the type of cancer, with lung and brain cancer patients typically experiencing higher levels of distress than other cancer populations (Zabora *et al.*, 2001). Psychologists clearly can have a prominent role in oncology, not only in a supportive care context, but also in reducing the burden on the healthcare system via the promotion of treatment adherence (Carlson & Bultz, 2004).

Assessment

To appropriately assess and develop psychological interventions clinicians need to be aware of the typical range of treatment-related side effects. There can be considerable overlap in the reported side effects of cancer treatment and the somatic symptoms of commonly diagnosed psychological disorders such as impaired concentration and memory, fatigue, decreased motivation/lethargy, nausea, dizziness, and insomnia. Therefore, careful assessment, with an increased emphasis on cognitive and emotional symptoms rather than the somatic, is required when screening new referrals.

Who is assessed and by whom?

One important issue when working in oncology is how to identify those in need of psychological treatment. While many services rely solely on referrals from medical consultants, momentum has been building for universal screening for distress, with distress being endorsed as the sixth vital sign of oncology (Bultz & Carlson, 2006). Implementing a universal distress screening program would overcome current issues relating to the misidentification of those in need of services, with research suggesting that medical staff are not well trained in identifying distressed patients (National Breast Cancer Centre [NBCC] & National Cancer Control Initiative [NCCI], 2003). This can occur when (1) a generally well-functioning patient who happens to be emotional in one consultation with a doctor *is* referred when there is no perceived need by the patient and (2) when a patient is *not* referred by clinicians as they do not display symptoms of distress, despite internal turmoil. Thus, part of the role for psychologists in oncology settings is to educate staff regarding methods for assessing distress, or to provide simple distress checklists/tools that can be routinely utilized, such as the Distress Thermometer (National Comprehensive Cancer Network, 2003; Roth *et al.*, 1998). Demographic risk factors for distress include female gender, younger age, single/dwelling alone, having young or adolescent children, economic disadvantage, low social support, poor marital functioning, and having a psychiatric history (including substance abuse). Medical risk factors include having more treatment side effects, greater functional impairment, and having chronic pain and fatigue (NBCC & NCCI, 2003).

When to assess?

Should assessments be conducted as a once-off at diagnosis or repeatedly? Current clinical practice guidelines state that assessments and distress screening should be conducted regularly by medical practitioners throughout the treatment trajectory (NBCC & NCCI, 2003), as early detection of distress leads to better outcomes. It is recommended to assess at the major treatment milestones as a minimum: at diagnosis, commencing treatment, completing treatment, anniversaries and checkups, at cancer recurrence or advanced cancer diagnosis, and during palliation.

What to assess?

The typical intake assessment will cover a range of domains, including: the patient's perspective of their cancer history, presenting problem(s), current coping strategies (emotional, cognitive, and behavioral responses), current psychosocial, occupational, and social functioning, social and psychiatric history, and goals for treatment. This can be supplemented with standardized self-report measures, which may include an *appraisal* measure such as the Illness Perception Questionnaire (Moss-Morris *et al.*, 2002), a *coping* measure such as the Mental Adjustment to Cancer Scale Short-Form (Watson *et al.*, 1994), a brief *quality-of-life* (QOL) measure such as the Medical Outcomes Study Short Form-36 (Ware *et al.*, 2000), and a *distress measure* such as the Depression, Anxiety, Stress Scale (Lovibond & Lovibond, 1995). These measures are a useful assessment adjunct, in providing a quantitative baseline level from which to track changes over time, thus providing an objective indicator of progress.

Assessment as an intervention?

The importance of conducting a thorough assessment cannot be overstated. Assessment provides an opportunity to provide psycho-education, normalize and validate symptoms, begin gently challenging the clients' unhelpful beliefs about their illness and coping responses, and develop a strong therapeutic alliance and inspire hope that change is possible. It may also represent the first opportunity for the client to openly discuss their full range of concerns that they do not wish to burden family members with, such as existential concerns.

Case Formulation

A number of health psychology models are used in psycho-oncology research and practice for case-formulations. Among the most widely used is stress and coping theory (Lazarus & Folkman, 1984; Folkman & Greer, 2000), which states that an individual's emotional response to a stressor (e.g., cancer diagnosis) is dependent on whether the demands of that situation are *appraised* as exceeding their perceived coping resources. See Figure 27.1 for a simplistic version of the model.

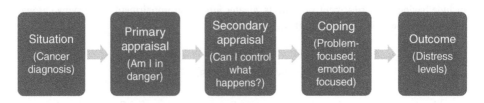

Figure 27.1 Stress and coping theory.

The appraisal process consists of an initial *primary appraisal* of the situation in terms of the level of threat (i.e., "Am I in trouble/danger?"), after which an individual will make a *secondary appraisal* in terms of how controllable or alterable the situation is (i.e., "Are there any methods of overcoming the threat or improving future prospects?"). Distress is more likely when an event is appraised as highly threatening, as carrying little potential benefit, and as uncontrollable. After the appraisal is concluded, the *coping* process commences, defined as an individual's cognitive and behavioral efforts to manage the specific internal or external demands of the situation (Lazarus & Folkman, 1984). Coping serves three major functions. The first is to address the problem causing the distress (problem-focused coping), the second is to regulate emotions (emotion-focused coping), and the third is to find some meaning from the experience (benefit-finding coping). Research has shown that coping directed at disengagement, such as behavioral and cognitive avoidance, is associated with increased distress, while coping that promotes continued engagement with, and positive orientation towards, the stressor is associated with reduced distress (Carver *et al.*, 1989; Stanton & Snider, 1993). After the appraisal and coping processes have occurred, an individual then makes a judgment regarding whether the situation has been resolved successfully. It should be noted that the actual stressor (e.g., cancer) does not need to be resolved, as long as the individual believes that the demands of the situation were met as well as could be expected.

Therefore, in clinical practice an assessment of an individual's *illness perceptions* (how threatened they are by the cancer, how much control they have, their perceptions of the cause and likely duration of their illness) is important, and can often uncover erroneous thinking patterns and associated feelings such as self-blame and guilt. An assessment of the individual's current *coping strategies* is also a logical target for intervention.

Case example

Jane is a single 53 year-old woman who had been living overseas but returned home 2 years ago to care for her elderly father. She is on a centrelink benefits, works as a retail assistant one day a week, and has a small group of close girlfriends. Six months after returning home, Jane noticed a lump in her left breast and after undergoing a mammogram, ultrasound, and fine-needle aspiration biopsy she received a diagnosis of Grade II early-stage breast cancer. Her treatment consisted of a mastectomy, six cycles of chemotherapy, and 6 weeks of daily radiotherapy. She is referred to you 2 months after completing treatment by her practice nurse and medical oncologist, for "difficulty coping." Upon assessment she informs you that she had been "coping really well during treatment," and although she doesn't understand why she has felt very anxious and worried since completing treatment. Symptoms include crying more frequently, feeling tense and shaky, sleep onset and maintenance insomnia, loss of interest and motivation to do activities, social withdrawal, and constant racing thoughts which are exacerbated when alone. Cognitions relate to her: (1) *health*, with thoughts that she should be better and back to normal by now, and that her cancer will come back; (2) *family*, with thoughts she is a bad daughter as she had to place her father in residential care during her treatment; (3) *occupational status*, worrying she's unemployable now with a cancer history; (4) *financial circumstances*, worrying she will no longer be eligible for centrelink benefits but not feeling emotionally or physically ready to seek employment; (5) *intimate relationships*, feeling she will never be able to have a close sexual relationship in the future, as "who will want to be with someone so disfigured;" and (6) *anxiety*, with Jane sure that she is "going nuts" and that the anxiety will bring on a recurrence.

Clinical Case Tasks

(1) Write up a potential case formulation for Jane based on Lazarus and Folkman's (1984) model. (2) Write down your hypotheses of the illness perceptions and assumptions that may be initiating and maintaining Jane's anxiety. How would you go about challenging these?

Treatment

A range of therapy options have been empirically evaluated for people with cancer. It should be noted that the empirical evidence base draws heavily from the breast cancer population, due to this population being typically utilized as pilot samples for establishing efficacy, prior to implementing interventions across other cancer types. However, all interventions described below have subsequently also been examined in heterogeneous cancer populations. Meta-analyses have demonstrated that all psychosocial interventions are efficacious and enduring (Meyer & Mark, 1995; Zimmermann *et al.*, 2007), with small effect sizes ($d = 0.26$).

Cognitive behavior therapy

Cognitive behavior therapy (CBT) currently has the widest evidence base for its effectiveness in cancer settings. It is typically offered in a group format, due to cost-effectiveness, but provides the additional benefit of social support, and yields equivalency in outcomes to individual interventions (Fawzy, 1999). CBT is structured in nature, usually comprised of between six and 10 weekly sessions of 90 min, and generally consists of three major components (Fawzy, 1999). First, *psychoeducation* is provided about the presenting psychological problem, normalizing symptoms in the health context, how current cognitive and behavioral responses maintain the problem, and identifying targets for intervention. Second, *cognitive procedures* are implemented, such as cognitive restructuring, distraction, problem solving, behavioral experiments to test key cognitions, communication training, and coping skills training. Third, *behavioral procedures*, including behavior activation, exposure, guided imagery/relaxation, and goal setting are established (Antoni *et al.*, 2001, 2009; Cohen & Fried, 2007; Zimmermann *et al.*, 2007). More recently, programs have been designed specifically for cancer patients (Antoni *et al.*, 2001; Cunningham *et al.*, 1998), such as the 10 week cognitive behavior stress-management (CBSM) group program implemented among breast (Antoni *et al.*, 2009; Beatty & Koczwara, 2010) and prostate (Penedo *et al.*, 2006) cancer patients. Numerous studies have demonstrated the efficacy of CBT (Manne & Andrykowski, 2006), particularly in decreasing emotional distress (Beatty & Koczwara, 2010; Jacobsen & Jim, 2008), and increasing benefit finding (McGregor *et al.*, 2004), QOL (Antoni *et al.*, 2006), and immune function (Antoni *et al.*, 2009). Several moderating variables have been identified in terms of efficacy. First, CBT has higher effect sizes when offered earlier, such as during medical treatment rather than after treatment completion (Vos *et al.*, 2006; Zimmermann *et al.*, 2007). Second, greater benefits have been reported when CBT is led by a psychologist rather than nonpsychologist (Zimmermann *et al.*, 2007). Third, individuals with higher levels of psychological distress have been shown to experience greater reductions in distress after CBT (Manne & Andrykowski, 2006).

CBT in the cancer context

Therapists new to working in psycho-oncology will often ask "but how is CBT relevant given that the thoughts are true? These people *could* have died, and *may* die in the future." This is particularly evident for working with advanced cancer, where individuals are facing a shortened life expectancy. Yet a number of studies have demonstrated the utility of CBT for advanced cancer (Edelman & Kidman, 2000). While some cognitions are realistic, most clients will have a number of unhelpful beliefs about their illness, current symptoms, and the future which are amenable to challenging through CBT. All-or-nothing thinking, such as "I may as well stop working now, I'm only going to die anyway" or "If I can't do everything I used to be able to do, I'm a failure," is clearly challengeable. Clients have often decreased their level of activity due to the physical fatigue, pain, and nausea associated with medical treatment and depression. Thus, education, gentle behavior activation, and introduction of activity-pacing is helpful for rebuilding physical functioning.

Clinical Case Tasks

For the case example, Jane, (1) identify the unhelpful cognitions that would be amenable to cognitive restructuring. (2) What questions would you ask, or exposure tasks would you set, to challenge these? (3) What behaviors is she engaging in that are potential targets for modification?

Mindfulness-based interventions

Mindfulness is defined as moment-to-moment purposeful and nonjudgmental attention or aware-ness (Kabat-Zinn, 1982). It originated as part of Buddhist teachings more than 2500 years ago, and is a fundamental part of Buddhist meditative practice (Matchim & Armer, 2007). Introduced into the Western world in the 1960s, two particular forms of mindfulness have been trialled in psycho-oncology: mindfulness-based stress reduction (MBSR; Kabat-Zinn, 1982) and mindfulness-based cognitive therapy (MBCT; Segal *et al.*, 2002). MBSR was developed first, in 1979 by Kabat-Zinn (1982), to provide some relief in the suffering associated with numerous medical conditions such as chronic pain, HIV, anxiety, and cancer. Largely based on MBSR, MBCT was subsequently developed to specifically address the ruminative thought processes present in chronic recurrent depression (Teasdale *et al.*, 1995). Both programs are offered as an 8–10-session group program, for the reasons outlined for group CBT above; are offered weekly for 2.5 h; have experiential meditation practice, including mindful body scanning, sitting meditation, walking meditation, and basic yoga; contain an education and discussion component; and require participants to in-corporate mindfulness into everyday life through daily homework, including listening to a 45 min CD (Smith *et al.*, 2005). The programs differ in that MBSR does not explicitly examine thinking processes, while MBCT incorporates elements of cognitive therapy by encouraging participants to take a detached or decentered view of one's thoughts, such as "thoughts are not facts" (Kenny & Williams, 2007).

While these interventions are becoming increasingly popular and gaining credibility for use in oncology (Ott *et al.*, 2006), empirical studies of MBSR in oncology have only started to appear since 2000 (Brown & Ryan, 2003; Carlson & Garland, 2005; Carlson *et al.*, 2003, 2004b; Shapiro *et al.*, 2003; Speca *et al.*, 2000), and only one study to date has reported the efficacy of MBCT in cancer populations (Foley *et al.*, 2010). Findings suggest MBSR may be effective in reducing cancer stress and anxiety (Tacon *et al.*, 2004), and in improving mood, sleep disturbance, fatigue (Carlson & Garland, 2005; Speca *et al.*, 2000), sleep quality (Carlson & Garland, 2005; Shapiro *et al.*, 2003), QOL (Carlson *et al.*, 2003, 2004b), and coping and health locus of control (Witek-Janusek *et al.*, 2008). The recent MBCT study also showed benefits for depression, anxiety, distress, and QOL (Foley *et al.*, 2010). While these studies show promise, mindfulness research is still in its infancy with the majority of research being uncontrolled; thus, recent meta-analyses and reviews recommend that more basic efficacy research is warranted prior to implementation as part of standard clinical practice (Matchim & Armer, 2007; Smith *et al.*, 2005; Zimmermann *et al.*, 2007).

Clinical Case Tasks

(1) In what ways do you think mindfulness may benefit Jane? (2) What particular aspects of her case presentation would make you think MBSR/MBCT is an appropriate therapeutic framework? (3) How do you think mindfulness may complement CBT?

Clinical hypnosis

Clinical hypnosis, has been defined as "a procedure during which a health professional or researcher suggests that a client, patient, or subject experience changes in sensations, perceptions, thoughts or behaviors" (Kirsch, 1994, p. 143). It is an intervention that in various forms has been used for thousands of years with fluctuating levels of acceptability. Indications and contraindications for the use of hypnosis have been revised over time but a solid rule of thumb is that a therapist should never treat anything in hypnosis that they are not qualified to treat out of hypnosis. With regards to cancer, hypnosis can be used in all phases of treatment and recovery to assist with medical phobias (Cyna *et al.*, 2007; Morgan 2001), procedure-related pain (Liossi *et al.*, 2006, 2009; Richardson *et al.*, 2006), treatment-related side effects such as anticipatory nausea and vomiting (Richardson *et al.*, 2007), fatigue (Montgomery *et al.*, 2009), sleep (Ng & Lee, 2008), pain (Butler *et al.*, 2009), anxiety (Hammond, 2010; Lynn & Kirsch, 2006), depression (Shih *et al.*, 2009; Yapko, 2001, 2006), and smoking cessation (Carmody *et al.*, 2008).

In recent years, vast literature has been generated in relation to the efficacy of hypnosis among many varying populations and in relation to CBT. For example, in meta-analysis, CBT interventions that include hypnosis have been found to be significantly more effective than CBT interventions alone (Kirsch *et al.*, 1995). Among cancer patients, hypnosis, used alone or in conjunction with CBT or supportive expressive therapy, has resulted in decreased nausea, fatigue, pain, and emotional distress following breast cancer surgery (Beatty & Koczwara, 2010; Jacobsen & Jim, 2008; Montgomery *et al.*, 2007), significant decreases in daily and weekly hot flashes and decreased impact of the flashes on daily activities and QOL (Elkins *et al.*, 2007), fatigue levels remaining stable over the course of radiotherapy (Montgomery *et al.*, 2009), reductions in negative affect and increases in positive affect in breast cancer patients undergoing radiotherapy (Schnur *et al.*, 2009), and less increase in the intensity of pain and suffering over time among women with metastatic breast cancer (Butler *et al.*, 2009). Also, in a recent meta-analytic study, hypnosis was found to be more effective for managing anticipatory and chemotherapy induced nausea and vomiting than treatment as usual or CBT (Richardson *et al.*, 2007). Among pediatric cancer patients, self-hypnosis in combination with local anesthetic has been found to result in less anticipatory anxiety, and less procedure-related anxiety, pain, and distress during venepuncture blood sampling than those who received local anesthetic alone or in combination with attention from a professional (Liossi *et al.*, 2009). Parents of children in the self-hypnosis group also reported less than anxiety than parents whose children received either of the other two treatments (Liossi *et al.*, 2009).

Hypnosis can be used individually or in a group format, but should not be used without a specific purpose. An assessment is therefore needed to determine the client's goals, the new resources the client will need to build to achieve their goals, the current resources the client may need assistance with in employing, and how required resources will be made available in the context in which they are needed (Yapko, 2003). The therapist should also be able to crystallize in 25 words or fewer the message they wish to convey to the client before commencing hypnosis (Yapko, 2003). As a generic structure hypnosis interventions generally consist of 11 sections. First, *psycho-education and orientation* is provided to address some of the myths and misconceptions about hypnosis, and orientates the client to hypnosis. Second, *induction procedures* are utilized, which can be formal traditional methods such as eye fixation or counting, or conversational indirect methods such as building an internal focus or using past hypnotic experiences. Third, *deepening methods* are employed, such as stairs, verbal or manual compounding, or silence. Fourth, a *response set* is built to increase the momentum of responsiveness. Fifth, *themes are introduced*, which match the identified goals from assessment. Sixth, *suggestions* are provided to resolve the problem/achieve the goal, by eliciting and utilizing appropriate hypnotic phenomena, such as age regression, age progression, amnesia, analgesia, anaesthesia, catalepsy, hallucinations and sensory alterations, and time distortion. Seventh, therapists then *check in with the client*, to ensure they received the message as intended, and eighth *steps five to seven* are repeated until all planned themes for the session have been delivered. *Post-hypnotic suggestions* are then delivered as a ninth step, so that the client can utilize what they have learned in hypnosis in other everyday contexts. A *closure procedure* is then implemented to allow the client to process the experience before suggesting closure, and finally *disengagement/reorientation of the client* occurs to encourage the client to reorient to the current day, time, and place. It is beneficial to record the sessions on a digital recorder so a copy can be given to the client to listen to on other occasions. Where possible, clients should also be taught self-hypnosis.

Clinical Case Tasks

(1) What aspects of Jane's case presentation make you think hypnosis may be appropriate? (2) Try to identify goals for Jane, the resources she will need to achieve her goals, whether she already has the resources and needs help to employ them or needs assistance to build them, and identify how the required resources will be made available in the context in which they are needed. (3) What message in 25 words or fewer would you want to convey to Jane in the first hypnosis session?

Self-help interventions

Self-help interventions are an established therapeutic modality in many mental health populations such as panic disorder and social anxiety (Griffiths & Christensen, 2006), but to date few studies have examined them in the cancer context. Self-help interventions address both practical and personal access barriers by providing a convenient and private method of processing psychological concerns. Two modalities of delivering self-help have been investigated recently: print self-help workbook resources and Internet-based self-help programs.

Print self-help

Two print self-help programs have been reported in cancer. Angell *et al.* (2003) developed the first complete package of interactive self-help with their workbook journal, based on supportive-expressive group therapy principles. This resource provided women with comprehensive psychosocial information, therapeutic suggestions, and opportunities for journal writing to facilitate emotional release. It was specifically targeted for women who resided in rural areas of the USA or who could not afford to attend support groups, and were either within 3 months of (1) diagnosis or (2) ending treatment. Women who had completed treatment experienced fewer posttraumatic stress symptoms if they received the workbook compared to the control group, and private rural practice patients reported a decreased fighting spirit and increased emotional venting if they did not receive the workbook. The authors argued that the workbook journal could be particularly beneficial to women in rural communities, and for those nearing treatment completion, as this is a time during which resources and support become limited. It was noteworthy that Angell and collegues found a stronger effect of their workbook in women completing treatment, as this contrasts with results from CBT interventions that found higher effect sizes when interventions are offered closer to diagnosis (Vos *et al.*, 2006; Zimmermann *et al.*, 2007). This workbook has subsequently been successfully trialled in conjunction with videoconferencing for women in rural settings (Collie *et al.*, 2007), and as a basis for a professionally facilitated Internet support group (Winzelberg *et al.*, 2003).

The second print self-help program was developed for the Australian breast cancer population, and based on cognitive behavior principles (Beatty *et al.*, 2010a, 2010b). Two separate workbooks were developed and evaluated using randomized controlled trials: one for breast cancer survivors after completion of medical treatment (Beatty *et al.*, 2010b), and one for women recently diagnosed and commencing cancer treatment (Beatty *et al.*, 2010a). Both books were developed in consultation with consumers, and consisted of psychosocial information, ranging from physical side effects, to body image and identity, to survivorship; suggestions and worksheets; and survivor quotes and stories. In contrast to Angell *et al.* (2003), the *survivor* workbook was not efficacious, as no significant changes between groups over time occurred (Beatty *et al.*, 2010b). However, the *patient* workbook was efficacious in reducing posttraumatic stress symptoms and levels of helplessness/hopelessness and cognitive avoidance 3 months after diagnosis (Beatty *et al.*, 2010a), particularly among women with higher baseline distress. These findings were consistent with the CBT literature for cancer which suggest that targeting diagnosis is more effective (Zimmermann *et al.*, 2007), and demonstrates the feasibility of delivering therapy via a self-help format.

Clinical Case Tasks

(1) What factors should you consider in terms of whether to offer a client face-to-face or self-help therapy? (2) What would you recommend for Jane if she were (i) living in an urban setting or (ii) living in a rural or regional setting? What would be the benefits and disadvantages of each option for her?

Internet-based self-help

Two online self-help programs have been reported to date, but these programs have not been "pure" self-help, as they have often contained social networking features or have been facilitated by an online therapist. Gustafson *et al.* (2001) were the first to report on an interactive self-help web program: the Comprehensive Health Enhancement Support System (CHESS) program. The CHESS program provides *information* including a question and answer section, a library of breast cancer articles, a consumer guide, and a list of web links; *communication* including a facilitated discussion board and ask-the-expert feature; and *decision-support* tools, such as decision aids, health charts, and action plans. Early studies compared CHESS with an information control group and found greater benefits for the intervention in terms of social support, but no differences in QOL or wellbeing (Gustafson *et al.*, 2001); however, later studies found that CHESS was superior to general Internet use and no-Internet control in providing social support, QOL, and healthcare competence benefits (Gustafson *et al.*, 2005, 2008). While promising, it appears that this website has a social and decision-support function, rather than having psychological therapy as its framework.

In contrast, Owen and colleagues developed a structured therapeutic self-guided online coping group which provided 12 weeks of coping skills training exercises presented through a series of web pages, an online discussion board, and education on symptom management (Owen *et al.*, 2004, 2005). A randomized controlled trial then compared this group with a wait-list control (Owen *et al.*, 2005), and while no main effects for treatment were found a significant interaction showed that women with poorer self-perceived health status at baseline experienced greater improvements in perceived health over time when assigned to the online group. Subanalyses showed that improvements in QOL were associated with greater expression of negative emotions (Owen *et al.*, 2005).

Given the recent surge in online self-help therapy programs in other clinical populations, including depression, anxiety, stress, insomnia, and headaches (Griffiths & Christensen, 2006), all of which are common presenting problems for cancer, it is likely that this format for delivering psychological interventions will continue to grow in popularity.

Clinical Case Tasks

(1) What do you think are some of the benefits of the Internet over print self-help? (2) How do you think Internet self-help may be of assistance for Jane? (3) Compare the Gustafson and Owen options and list the advantages and disadvantages of each if Jane were to use them.

Therapist Self-Care

Working with patients diagnosed with cancer and their families can be very satisfying and rewarding, yet the process can also be very distressing and exhausting. Although it is beyond the scope of this chapter to provide detailed information about the professional and personal issues that can arise when working in oncology settings, therapists must be aware that working with such clients facing their mortality and reminding therapists about the fragility of life can take its toll in the form of secondary stress, compassion fatigue, job satisfaction, and burnout (Sherman *et al.*, 2006; Simon *et al.*, 2005). Over time, the presence of secondary stress can also compromise a therapist's empathy towards their clients (Simon *et al.*, 2005). It has been argued that therapists should view the need to employ strategies to minimise compassion fatigue as normal, rather than as a weakness (Najjar *et al.*, 2009). Therapists can implement a number of personal and professional strategies to minimize possible adverse effects. *Personal* strategies include having a good work–life balance, and regular contact with members of one's personal support network. *Professional* strategies could include balancing direct client contact with nonclient contact activities, developing and maintaining a support network of other oncology professionals, obtaining regular supervision to discuss clients and the therapist's responses to clients, and allowing time to grieve for lost patients. It is also important to have an organizational structure that enables workers to feel supported.

Clinical Case Tasks

(1) How do you maintain a good work–life balance? (2) What self-care behaviors do you engage in and how do you ensure that you use them regularly? (3) Make a list of clinicians with whom you could form a regular support network.

Conclusion

In summary, cancer elicits greater distress than any other medical diagnosis, irrespective of prognosis (Shapiro *et al.*, 2001). Given the high prevalence rates of depression and anxiety disorders in the Australian cancer population, appropriate and timely assessment and intervention by psychologists is likely to benefit the patient and the health system via the reduction of the burden of disease. Innovative and accessible alternatives to face-to-face therapy may need to be considered in the Australian context, where personal and geographic barriers to attendance occur; however, the recent growth in print and online self-help interventions provide potential solutions. Practitioners working in this area need to have an adequate self-care program established, which includes regular supervision, debriefing, ongoing professional development, and social support to prevent the potential for therapist burnout. While challenging, most clinicians who work in oncology find this to be a rewarding field.

References

Angell, K. L., Kreshka, M. A., McCoy, R., Donnelly, P., Turner-Cobb, J. M., Graddy, K. *et al.* (2003). Psychosocial intervention for rural women with breast cancer: The Sierra Stanford partnership. *Journal of General Internal Medicine, 18*, 499–507.

Antoni, M. H., Lehman, J. M., Kilbourn, K. M., Boyers, A. E., Culver, J. L., Alferi, S. M. *et al.* (2001). Cognitive-behavioral stress management intervention decreases the prevalence of depression and enhances benefit finding among women under treatment for early-stage breast cancer. *Health Psychology, 20*, 20–32.

Antoni, M. H., Lechner, S. C., Kazi, A., Wimberly, S. R., Sifre, T., Urcuyo, K. R. *et al.* (2006). How stress management improves quality of life after treatment for breast cancer. *Journal of Consulting & Clinical Psychology, 74*, 1143–1152.

Antoni, M. H., Lechner, S., Diaz, A., Vargas, S., Holley, H., Phillips, K. *et al.* (2009). Cognitive behavioral stress management effects on psychosocial and physiological adaptation in women undergoing treatment for breast cancer. *Brain, Behavior, and Immunity, 23*, 580–591.

Australian Institute of Health and Welfare. (2010). *Australia's Health 2010*. Australia's health series no 12. Cat. no. AUS 122. Canberra: Australian Institute of Health and Welfare.

Australian Institute of Health and Welfare & Australasian Association of Cancer Registries. (2008). *Cancer in Australia: An Overview, 2008*. Canberra: Australian Institute of Health and Welfare.

Beatty, L., & Koczwara, B. (2010). An effectiveness study of a CBT group program for women with breast cancer. *Clinical Psychologist, 14*, 45–53.

Beatty, L., Koczwara, B., Rice, J., & Wade, T. (2010a). A randomised controlled trial to evaluate the effects of a self-help workbook intervention on distress, coping and QOL after breast cancer diagnosis. *Medical Journal of Australia, 193*, S68–S73.

Beatty, L., Oxlad, M., Koczwara, B., & Wade, T. (2010b). A randomised pilot of a self-help workbook intervention for breast cancer survivors. *Supportive Care in Cancer, 18*, 1597–603.

Boyes, A. W., Girgis, A., Zucca, A. C., & Lecathelinais, C. (2009). Anxiety and depression among long-term survivors of cancer in Australia: Results of a population-based survey. *Medical Journal of Australia, 190*, S94–S98.

Brown, K. W., & Ryan, R. M. (2003). The benefits of being present: Mindfulness and its role in psychological wellbeing. *Journal of Personality and Social Psychology, 84*, 822–848.

Bultz, B. D., & Carlson, L. E. (2006). Emotional distress: The sixth vital sign – future directions in cancer care. *Psycho-Oncology, 15*, 93–95.

Butler, L. D., Koopman, C., Neri, E., Giese-Davis, J., Palesh, O., Thorne-Yocam, K. A. *et al.* (2009). Effects of supportive-expressive group therapy on pain in women with metastatic breast cancer. *Health Psychology, 28*, 579–587.

Carlson, L. E., & Bultz, B. D. (2004). Efficacy and medical cost offset of psychosocial interventions in cancer care: Making the case for economic analysis. *Psycho-Oncology, 13*, 837–849.

Carlson, L. E., & Garland, S. N. (2005). Impact of mindfulness-based stress reduction (MBSR) on sleep, mood, stress and fatigue symptoms in cancer outpatients. *International Journal of Behavioural Medicine, 12*, 278–285.

Carlson, L. E., Speca, M., Patel, K. D., & Goodey, E. (2003). Mindfulness-based stress reduction in relation to quality of life, mood, symptoms of stress, and immune parameters in breast and prostate cancer outpatients. *Psychosomatic Medicine, 65*, 571–581.

Carlson, L. E., Angen, M., Cullum, J., Goodey, E., Koopmans, J., Lamont, L. *et al.* (2004a). High levels of untreated distress and fatigue in cancer patients. *British Journal of Cancer, 90*, 2297–2304.

Carlson, L. E., Speca, M., Patel, K. D., & Goodey, E. (2004b). Mindfulness-based stress reduction in relation to quality of life, mood, symptoms of stress and levels of cortisol, dehydroepiandrosterone sulfate (DHEAS) and melatonin in breast and prostate cancer outpatients. *Psychoneuroendocrinology, 29*, 448–474.

Carmody, T. P., Duncan, C., Simon, J. A., Solkowitz, S., Huggins, J., Lee, S., & Delucchi, K. (2008). Hypnosis for smoking cessation: A randomized trial. *Nicotine & Tobacco Research, 10*, 811–818.

Carver, C. S., Scheier, M. F., & Weintraub, J. K. (1989). Assessing coping strategies: A theoretically based approach. *Journal of Personality and Social Psychology, 56*, 267–283.

Cohen, M., & Fried, G. (2007). Comparing relaxation training and cognitive-behavioral group therapy for women with breast cancer. *Research on Social Work Practice, 17*, 313–323.

Collie, K., Kreshka, M. A., Ferrier, S., Parsons, R., Graddy, K., Avram, S. *et al.* (2007). Videoconferencing for delivery of breast cancer support groups to women living in rural communities: A pilot study. *Psycho-Oncology, 16*, 778–782.

Cunningham, A. J., Edmonds, C. V. I., Jenkins, G. P., Pollack, H., Lockwood, G. A., & Warr, D. (1998). A randomized controlled trial of the effects of group psychological therapy on survival in women with metastatic breast cancer. *Psycho-Oncology, 7*, 508–517.

Cyna, A., Tomkins, D., Maddock, T., & Barker, D. (2007). Brief hypnosis for severe needle phobia using switch-wire imagery in a 5 year old. *Paediatric Anaesthesia, 17*, 800–804.

Edelman, S., & Kidman, A. D. (2000). Application of cognitive behaviour therapy to patients who have advanced cancer. [application/description of techniques]. *Behaviour Change, 17*, 103–110.

Elkins, G., Marcus, J., Stearns, V., & Rajab, M. H. (2007). Pilot evaluation of hypnosis for the treatment of hot flashes in breast cancer survivors. *Psycho-Oncology, 16*, 487–492.

Fann, J. R., Thomas-Rich, A. M., Katon, W. J., Cowley, D., Pepping, M., McGregor, B. A., & Gralow, J. (2008). Major depression after breast cancer: A review of epidemiology and treatment. *General Hospital Psychiatry, 30,* 112–126.

Fawzy, F. I. (1999). Psychosocial interventions for patients with cancer: What works and what doesn't. *European Journal of Cancer, 35,* 1559–1564.

Foley, E., Baillie, A., Huxter, M., Price, M., & Sinclair, E. (2010). Mindfulness-based cognitive therapy for individuals whose lives have been affected by cancer: A randomised controlled trial. *Journal of Consulting and Clinical Psychology, 78,* 72–79.

Folkman S, & Greer S. (2000). Promoting psychological well-being in the face of serious illness: When theory, research and practice inform each other. *Psycho-Oncology, 9,* 11–9.

Griffiths, K. M., & Christensen, H. (2006). Review of randomized controlled trials of internet interventions for mental conditions and related disorders. *Clinical Psychologist, 10,* 16–29.

Gustafson, D. H., Hawkins, R., Pingree, S., McTavish, F., & Arora, N. (2001). Effect of computer support on younger women with breast cancer. *Journal of General Internal Medicine, 16,* 435–445.

Gustafson, D. H., McTavish, F. M., Stengle, W., Ballard, D., Jones, E., Julesberg, K. *et al.* (2005). Reducing the digital divide for low-income women with breast cancer: A feasibility study of a population-based intervention. *Journal of Health Communication, 10,* 173–193.

Gustafson, D. H., Hawkins, R., McTavish, F., Pingree, S., Chen, W. C., Volrathongchai, K. *et al.* (2008). Internet-based interactive support for cancer patients: Are integrated systems better? *Journal of Communication, 58,* 238–257.

Hammond, D.C. (2010). Hypnosis in the treatment of anxiety- and stress-related disorders. *Expert Review of Neurotherapeutics, 10,* 263–273.

Jacobsen, P. B., & Jim, H. S. (2008). Psychosocial interventions for anxiety and depression in adult cancer patients: Achievements and challenges. *CA A Cancer Journal for Clinicians, 58,* 214–230.

Kabat-Zinn, J. (1982). An outpatient program in behavioral medicine for chronic pain patients based on the practice of mindfulness meditation: Theoretical considerations and preliminary results. *General Hospital Psychiatry, 4,* 33–42.

Kenny, M. A., & Williams, J. M. (2007). Treatment-resistant depressed patients show a good response to mindfulness-based cognitive therapy. *Behavior Research and Therapy., 45,* 617–625.

Kirsch, I. (1994). APA definition and description of hypnosis: Defining hypnosis for the public. *Contemporary Hypnosis, 11,* 142–143.

Kirsch, I., Montgomery, G., & Sapirstein, G. (1995). Hypnosis as an adjunct to cognitive-behavioral psychotherapy: A meta-analysis. *Journal of Consulting and Clinical Psychology, 63,* 214–220.

Lazarus, R. S., & Folkman, S. (1984). *Stress, Appraisal and Coping.* New York: Springer.

Liossi, C., White, P., & Hatira, P. (2006). Randomized clinical trial of local anesthetic versus a combination of local anesthetic with self-hypnosis in the management of pediatric procedure-related pain. *Health Psychology, 25,* 307–315.

Liossi, C., White, P., & Hatira, P. (2009). A randomized clinical trial of a brief hypnosis intervention to control venepuncture-related pain of pediatric cancer patients. *Pain, 142,* 255–263.

Lovibond, S. H., & Lovibond, P. H. (1995). *Manual for the Depression Anxiety Stress Scales (DASS).* Sydney: University of New South Wales.

Lynn, S.J., & Kirsch, I. (2006). Anxiety disorders. In S. J. Lynn & I. Kirsch (Eds.), *Essentials of Clinical Hypnosis: An Evidence-Based Approach* (pp. 135–157). Washington DC: American Psychological Association.

Manne, S. L., & Andrykowski, M. A. (2006). Are psychological interventions effective and accepted cancer patients? II. Using empirically supported therapy guidelines to decide. *Annals of Behavioral Medicine, 32,* 98–103.

Matchim, Y., & Armer, J. M. (2007). Measuring the psychological impact of mindfulness meditation on health among patients with cancer: A literature review. *Oncology Nursing Forum, 34,* 1059–1066.

McGregor, B. A., Antoni, M. H., Boyers, A. E., Alferi, S. M., Blomberg, B. B., & Carver, C. S. (2004). Cognitive-behavioral stress management increases benefit finding and immune function among women with early-stage breast cancer. *Journal of Psychosomatic Research, 56,* 1–8.

Meyer, T. J., & Mark, M. M. (1995). Effects of psychosocial interventions with adult cancer patients: A meta-analysis of randomized experiments. *Health Psychology, 14*, 101–108.

Montgomery, G. H., Bovbjerg, D. H., Schnur, J. B., David, D., Goldfarb, A., Weltz, C. R. *et al.* (2007). A randomized clinical trial of a brief hypnosis intervention to control side effects in breast surgery patients. *Journal of the National Cancer Institute, 99*, 1304–1312.

Montgomery, G. H., Kangas, M., David, D., Hallquist, M. N., Green, S., Bovbjerg, D. H. *et al.* (2009). Fatigue during breast cancer radiotherapy: An initial randomized study of cognitive-behavioral therapy plus hypnosis. *Health Psychology, 28*, 317–322.

Morgan, S. (2001). Brief hypnosis for needle phobia. *Australian Journal of Clinical & Experimental Hypnosis, 29*, 107–115.

Moss-Morris, R., Weinman, J., Petrie, K. J., Horne, R., Cameron, L. D., & Buick, D. (2002). The revised illness perception questionnaire (IPQ-R). *Psychology and Health, 17*, 1–16.

Najjar, N., Davis, L. W., Beck-Coon, K., & Carney Doebbeling, C. (2009). Compassion fatigue: A review of the research to date and relevance to cancer-care providers. *Journal of Health Psychology, 14*, 267–277.

NBCC (National Breast Cancer Centre), & NCCI (National Cancer Control Initiative). (2003). *Clinical Practice Guidelines for the Psychosocial Care of Adults with Cancer*. Camperdown, NSW: National Breast Cancer Centre.

National Comprehensive Cancer Network. (2003). Distress management clinical practice guidelines. *Journal of the National Comprehensive Cancer Network, 1*, 344–374.

Ng, B.Y., & Lee, T.S. (2008). Hypnotherapy for sleep disorders. *Annals Academy of Medicine Singapore, 37*, 693–688.

Ott, M. J., Norris, R. L., & Bauer-Wu, S. M. (2006). Mindfulness meditation for oncology patients: A discussion and critical review. *Integrative Cancer Therapies, 5*, 98–108.

Owen, J. E., Klapow, J. C., Roth, D. L., Nabell, L., & Tucker, D. C. (2004). Improving effectiveness of adjuvant psychological treatment for women with breast cancer: The feasibility of providing online support. *Psycho-Oncology, 13*, 281–292.

Owen, J. E., Klapow, J. C., Roth, D. L., Shuster Jr, J. L., Bellis, J., Meredith, R., & Tucker, D. C. (2005). Randomized pilot of a self-guided internet coping group for women with early-stage breast cancer. *Annals of Behavioral Medicine, 30*, 54–64.

Penedo, F. J., Molton, I., Dahn, J. R., Shen, B.-J., Kinsinger, D., Traeger, L. *et al.* (2006). A randomized clinical trial of group-based cognitive-behavioral stress management in localized prostate cancer: Development of stress management skills improves quality of life and benefit finding. *Annals of Behavioral Medicine, 31*, 261–270.

Richardson, J., Smith, J.E., Mccall, G., & Pilkington, K. (2006). Hypnosis for procedure-related pain and distress in pediatric cancer patients: A systematic review of effectiveness and methodology related to hypnosis interventions. *Journal of Pain and Symptom Management, 31*, 70–84.

Richardson, J., Smith, J.E., Mccall, G., Richardson, A., Pilkington, K., & Kirsch, I. (2007). Hypnosis for nausea and vomiting in cancer chemotherapy: A systematic review of the research evidence. *European Journal of Cancer Care, 16*, 402–412.

Roth, A. J., Kornblith, A. B., Batel-Copel, L., Peabody, E., Scher, H. I., & Holland, J. C. (1998). Rapid screening for psychologic distress in men with prostate carcinoma: A pilot study. *Cancer, 82*, 1904–1908.

Schnur, J. B., David, D., Kangas, M., Green, S., Bovbjerg, D. H., & Montgomery, G. H. (2009). A randomized trial of a cognitive-behavioral therapy and hypnosis intervention on positive and negative affect during breast cancer radiotherapy. *Journal of Clinical Psychology, 65*, 443–455.

Segal, Z. V., Williams, J. M. G., & Teasdale, J. D. (2002). *Mindfulness-based cognitive therapy for depression: A new approach to preventing relapse*. New York: Guilford Press.

Shapiro, S. L., Lopez, A. M., Schwartz, G. E., Bootzin, R., Figueredo, A. J., Braden, C. J., & Kurker, S. F. (2001). Quality of life and breast cancer: Relationship to psychosocial variables. *Journal of Clinical Psychology, 57*, 501–519.

Shapiro, S. L., Bootzin, R. R., Figueredo, A. J., Lopez, A. M., & Schwartz, G. E. (2003). The efficacy of mindfulness-based stress reduction in the treatment of sleep disturbance in women with breast cancer: An exploratory study. *Journal of Psychosomatic Research, 54*, 85–91.

Sharpley, C. F., Bitsika, V., & Christie, D. R. H. (2010). Incidence and nature of anxiety-depression comorbidity in prostate cancer patients. *Journal of Men's Health, 7,* 125–134.

Sherman, A. C., Edwards, D., Simonton, S., & Mehta, P. (2006). Caregiver stress and burnout in an oncology unit. *Palliative & Support Care, 4,* 65–80.

Shih, M., Yang, Y.H., & Koo, M. (2009). A meta-analysis of hypnosis in the treatment of depressive symptoms: A brief communication. *International Journal of Clincial & Experimental Hypnosis, 57,* 431–442.

Simon, C., Pryce, J., Roff, L., & Klemmack, D. (2005). Secondary traumatic stress and oncology social work: Protecting compassion from fatigue and compromising the worker's worldview. *Journal of Psychosocial Oncology, 23,* 1–14.

Smith, J. E., Richardson, J., Hoffman, C., & Pilkington, K. (2005). Mindfulness-based stress reduction as supportive therapy in cancer care: A systematic review. *Journal of Advanced Nursing, 52,* 315–327.

Speca, M., Carlson, L. E., Goodey, E., & Angen, M. (2000). A randomized, wait-list controlled clinical trial: The effect of a mindfulness meditation-based stress reduction program on mood and symptoms of stress in cancer outpatients. *Psychosomatic Medicine, 62,* 613–622.

Stanton, A. L., & Snider, P. R. (1993). Coping with breast cancer diagnosis: A prospective study. *Health Psychology, 12,* 16–23.

Tacon, A. M., Caldera, Y. M., & Ronaghan, C. (2004). Mindfulness-based stress reduction in women with breast cancer. *Families, Systems & Health, 22,* 193–203.

Teasdale, J. D., Segal, Z., & Williams, M. G. (1995). How does cognitive therapy prevent relapse and why should attentional control (mindfulness) training help? *Behaviour Research and Therapy, 33,* 25–39.

Vos, P. J., Visser, A. P., Garssen, B., Duivenvoorden, H. J., & de Haes, H. C. J. M. (2006). Effects of delayed psychosocial interventions versus early psychosocial interventions for women with early stage breast cancer. *Patient Education and Counseling, 60,* 212–219.

Ware, J. E., Snow, K. K., & Kosinski, M. (2000). *SF-36 Health Survey: Manual and interpretation guide.* Lincoln, RI: Quality Metric.

Watson, M., Law, M., dos Santos, M., Greer, S., Baruch, J., & Bliss, J. (1994). The Mini-MAC: Further development of the Mental Adjustment to Cancer scale. *Journal of Psychosocial Oncology, 12,* 33–46.

Winzelberg, A. J., Classen, C., Alpers, G. W., Roberts, H., Koopman, C., Adams, R. E. *et al.* (2003). Evaluation of an internet support group for women with primary breast cancer. *Cancer, 97,* 1164–1173.

Witek-Janusek, L., Albuquerque, K., Chroniak, K. R., Chroniak, C., Durazo-Arvizu, R., & Mathews, H. L. (2008). Effect of mindfulness based stress reduction on immune function, quality of life and coping in women newly diagnosed with early stage breast cancer. *Brain,* Behavior, and Immunity, 22, 969–981.

Yapko, M. (2001). *Treating Depression with Hypnosis: Integrating Cognitve Behavioral and Strategic Approaches.* Philadelphia: Brunner Routledge.

Yapko, M. (2003). *Trancework: An Introduction to the Practice of Hypnosis* (3rd edn.). New York: Brunner-Routledge.

Yapko, M. (2006). *Hypnosis and Treating Depression: Applications in Clinical Practice* (1st edn.). New York: Routledge.

Zabora, J., Brintzenhofeszoc, K., Curbow, B., Hooker, C., & Piantadosi, S. (2001). The prevalence of psychological distress by cancer site. *Psycho-Oncology, 10,* 19–28.

Zimmermann, T., Heinrichs, N., & Baucom, D. H. (2007). " Does one size fit all?" Moderators in psychosocial interventions for breast cancer patients: A meta-analysis. *Annals of Behavioral Medicine, 34,* 225–239.

28

Major Musculoskeletal Disorders and their Management

Felicity C. Allen

Disorders of the musculoskeletal system hinder people in their performance of activities of daily living and can prevent employment outside the home. As they are typically more common in older people, they are becoming an increasing concern as the population ages. Despite the challenges that these disorders pose, a great deal can be done to assist patients to cope with them and to maintain their health and independence. This chapter will consider what health psychologists have to offer in the management of the "arthritis" group of disorders and then fibromyalgia (FM). These diseases are all painful and disabling, with chronic muscle and joint disorders having a devastating effect on the employment potential and quality of life of the patients and their families. Musculoskeletal disorders typically have major comorbidity with depression, possibly as a reaction to severe pain and loss of independence. In addition to pain and disability, FM sufferers often have to contend with a climate of disbelief as the cause of their disorder remains unknown. Health psychologists may need to support these patients in dealing with the self-doubt and distress that these reactions can cause.

Arthritis: Diagnosis and Prognosis

The term arthritis describes a group of several distinct, chronic, and progressive joint disorders that vary in their frequency, prognosis, and demographics. Osteoarthritis (OA) is the most common of these and typically affects the knees, hands, feet, and neck. One or several joints may be affected. Symptoms usually begin gradually and slowly worsen. The other types of arthritis, except for rheumatoid arthritis (RA), are all very rare. Even RA affects only about 1% of the population. Given the rarity of the others, only OA and RA will be considered further. OA is one of the most common chronic conditions in developed societies and is the major form of arthritis in Australia, with almost 1.2 million people having symptoms (Grainger & Cicuttini, 2004). RA is the second most common form of arthritis.

The different forms of arthritis have diverse etiologies. While there is an acknowledged genetic component, OA is largely due to damage to the joint itself, from trauma, infection, or accumulated

Applied Topics in Health Psychology, First Edition. Edited by M. L. Caltabiano and L. Ricciardelli.
© 2013 John Wiley & Sons, Ltd. Published 2013 by John Wiley & Sons, Ltd.

exposures of increasing age (Kramer, 2006). OA can result from one or two major events, but usually arises from the repeated microtrauma of heavy physical work. While OA sufferers experience pain, they do not suffer the malaise typical of RA patients.

OA causes loss of joint cartilage, and narrows the spaces between the bones. Obesity, joint injury, and repetitive use of the joints are risk factors [Australian Institute of Health and Welfare (AIHW), 2007]. OA causes joint pain, typically worse with weight-bearing and activity, and stiffness after inactivity, especially in the morning. Behavioral reactions to the pain can worsen the disease. Joints are normally supported by muscles and ligaments. If people use a joint less because it is painful to do so, the surrounding muscles and ligaments then weaken, so the joint has less support, setting up a vicious cycle of increasing disability. Depression may appear as a response to increasing disability, but does not appear to be an intrinsic part of the disease itself.

RA is an inflammatory autoimmune disease (Klarenbeek *et al.*, 2011) characterized by inflamed synovial tissue in the joints, causing swelling, pain, and stiffness, particularly of the joints of the hands, feet, and wrists, leading to functional limitations. Blood tests may show the auto-antibodies believed to cause the main damage of RA, but not all RA sufferers have them. Genetic susceptibility is important but is not sufficient to cause RA. A further trigger, such as infection, starts the disease in susceptible people.

There is no single test for diagnosing RA and early diagnosis can be difficult because the symptoms are nonspecific. Diagnosis is based on a combination of X-rays, laboratory tests, and clinical assessment. The need for a specific test has become urgent, now that early treatment in RA is so important. Without one, many patients present late after serious and irreversible joint damage has occurred (Deighton & Scott, 2011).

The clinical course of RA varies greatly, although there are three main pathways (AIHW, 2009), called monocyclic, polycyclic, and progressive. Monocyclic patients experience complete remission within 2 years of disease onset (about one-third of patients). The condition of polycyclic patients slowly worsens and the progress of their disease is marked by acute flare-ups and remissions (about 40% of patients). Progressive patients suffer an aggressive disease process in which joint destruction is continual and life expectancy is markedly reduced (20% of patients).

The experience of RA is marked by pain, malaise, and depression. Patients often report general symptoms including morning stiffness, fatigue, fever, sweats, and weight loss (Klarenbeek *et al.*, 2011). As with OA, pain usually reduces physical activity, causing loss of muscle tone and bulk, but RA has an additional destructive effect on muscle tissue. Erosive joint destruction with consequent deformity, loss of mobility, and pain are common characteristics. Patients may develop a fear of moving because of increased pain following activity. As well as joint and inflammatory symptoms, about half of RA patients suffer depression. RA may affect other organs, including the skin, nervous system, eyes, and mouth. Nerve compression as a result of inflammation is the main impact on the nervous system. It can lead to pins-and-needles-type sensations and further weakness (AIHW, 2009). Unlike OA, RA reduces life expectancy by 3–18 years, although the mechanism for this is not clear.

Women are more likely to develop both OA and RA than men, and are typically affected more severely and at more joints (AIHW, 2007; Klarenbeek *et al.*, 2011). The incidence of both diseases peaks among people in their fifties and early sixties, but after that age RA becomes rare, probably because it reduces patients' life expectancy.

Obesity also contributes to OA risk, especially of the knee joint, by increasing mechanical stress on cartilages and ligaments. Mechanical stress is not the only factor involved because obesity further increases the likelihood of OA of the hands, suggesting that general physiological aspects of the disease are affected by obesity. Even very minor weight loss (approximately 5 kg over 10 years) has a marked effect on the progress of OA. It decreases the chance of developing knee OA by 50% (Rejeski *et al.*, 2002). Obesity and OA, frequently occurring in the same patient, can lead to an especially vicious cycle in which the patient engages in less activity because of the pain of OA, gaining more weight, and becoming more vulnerable to OA as a result.

Depression is common in OA. In one study almost half (40.7%) of the 54 patients (Axford *et al.*, 2010) had symptoms of depression. Pain and disability scores are positively correlated. Higher pain and disability scores from OA are associated with declines in mental health, and particularly with the development of depression. Depression predicts disability rather than disease, although it is unclear exactly how pain, functional impairment, and depression are related. Depressive symptoms are also a common presentation in RA and appear to be part of the disease process (Klarenbeek *et al.*, 2011).

As far as is known, Aboriginal and Torres Strait Islander people are no more likely to suffer from OA than other Australians. RA is relatively rare in Aboriginal and Torres Strait Islander people, possibly because they typically lack the genetic factors that predispose people to this disease (AIHW, 2009).

Managing and treating OA and RA

Recent innovations in drug treatment have led to a divergence of the management strategies for OA and RA, so they will be discussed separately. The objectives of treatment in OA are to maintain patients' independence, promote their physical health and improve the quality of their lives and to enable them to cope with disease as effectively as possible. To meet these objectives, the goals of treatment include controlling pain, maintaining the integrity of the affected joints and limiting functional impairment (Grainger & Cicuttini, 2004).

Although OA is a chronic condition, treatment and self-management activities can prevent decline in, and even improve, functional status (Kaptein *et al.*, 2010). Treatment currently consists of medications and surgical or other interventions to reduce the pain and retain or improve the function of the joint. Maintaining or increasing the strength of the supporting muscles, and controlling weight gain, is important to protect the joint. Optimal management for an OA patient ideally involves a multidisciplinary team of the patient, family, carers, general practitioner, specialists, health psychologists, and allied health professionals, since a wide range of strategies is required, particularly when the patient has comorbid depression. These are shown in Table 28.1.

Education improves patients' and carers' understanding of the disease so that they can seek appropriate help and plan for the future. A variety of courses is offered by Arthritis Australia (see Useful Websites, below). Education to promote self-management is optimally developed in small groups (6–8 people) led by a health practitioner. In addition to basic knowledge about the disease process these interventions can teach strategies for pain management and the importance of exercise and relaxation. Although educational interventions are believed to be useful in helping patients manage their illness, they have rarely been evaluated.

Recent advances in drug treatment for RA now mean that the ultimate goal of treatment for newly diagnosed patients is sustained remission (Klarenbeek *et al.*, 2011). This can occur if treatment is begun early so that the disease activity is suppressed as soon as possible. There are various definitions of clinical remission. The European League Against Rheumatism (EULAR; www.eular.org/) has proposed the following criteria: no more than one swollen or painful joint, the patient's self-assessment of no more than 10 on a visual analog scale of pain going from 0 to 100, and normal concentrations of serum antibodies.

The first line of drug treatment for RA is still methotrexate, often accompanied by corticosteroids such as prednisolone. Administering the combination of these two drugs early in the disease

Table 28.1 Management strategies for OA

Broad strategy	Detailed description
Education/self-management	Optimize quality of life, promote adherence to treatment and physical therapies
Medications	Typically include paracetamol for pain and NSAIDs (e.g., diclofenac, celecoxib, and naproxen) to reduce swelling and pain
Dietary supplements	Micro- or macronutrients or herbs (e.g., glucosamine, vitamin D, chondroitin)
Psychosocial interventions	CBT, biofeedback training, stress management, emotional disclosure, hypnosis and psychodynamic interventions
Physical therapy	Targeted exercise, resistance training, water therapy or massage
Diet and weight loss	By dietary restraint or exercise
Mechanical aids	Modifications to the home or workplace (e.g., grips on taps, ergonomic cutlery) and aids for the patient, such as knee braces
Joint replacement/repair	Arthroplasty: total joint replacement; arthrodesis: joint fusion; osteotomy: reshaping of bone

NSAID, nonsteroidal anti-inflammatory drug.

rapidly reduces inflammation and thus prevents joint damage. The side effects of corticosteroids mean that their use should be tapered off once symptoms are under control. "Disease-modifying antirheumatic drugs" (DMARDs) slow down disease progression (e.g., penicillinamine). One of these is typically combined with methotrexate to reduce clinical symptoms and retard the onset of joint damage. If treatment with DMARDs is delayed more than 3 months after symptoms begin then joint inflammation is perpetuated. Ongoing inflammation damages the joints, causing disability and loss of independence (Deighton & Scott, 2011). For patients with long-standing RA, or those who present late, new drugs known as "biologicals" can be effective. These typically inhibit the production of tumor necrosis factor-α (TNF-α) by the patient's immune system.

The medication regime should be tailored to the patient's individual needs, including medications taken for other conditions. Paracetamol is the oral analgesic of first choice and, if successful, can be continued in the long term (Pisetsky, 2007). Opioid medication may be needed if the pain is unrelieved by nonsteroidal anti-inflammatory drugs. Glucosamine gives moderate pain relief in mild knee arthritis (Grainger & Cicuttini, 2004).

Where patients with OA or RA are insufficiently active, muscle bulk around the arthritic joints is lost so that they become more painful (Grainger & Cicuttini, 2004). The need for exercise is well understood and acted on in the Australian community; about 20% of people with OA exercise most days to help maintain flexibility and strength (AIHW, 2007). Hydrotherapy is widely used in both main forms of arthritis. Patients often enjoy it and it can be a gentle introduction to a lifestyle incorporating more exercise.

Obesity is a serious management problem, particularly if the knee joint is affected. Although weight loss would reduce the impact load on knee and hip joints and consequent pain, only 5–6% of people with OA had tried to lose weight to manage their condition (AIHW, 2007). Pain and disability make it difficult for people to exercise enough to lose weight, but weight loss can be achieved by reducing caloric intake. Rejeski *et al.* (2002) randomly assigned 316 older patients to four weight-loss interventions and found that participants in the diet-only group lost 5.7% of their body weight over 18 months. This improved their health-related quality-of-life scores. Given the relatively high proportions (about one-third) of OA patients who are obese, this option needs greater emphasis and clinical attention.

Psychological interventions have particular appeal in the treatment of arthritis because they target pain and associated debility, assist in the management of disability, and lack the toxicity of drug interventions. Psychosocial interventions have been shown to be effective in reducing arthritic pain in experimental settings, but are almost never prescribed outside them (Pisetsky, 2007). Further studies on their effectiveness in the community are needed to assess their usefulness.

The importance of early treatment in RA has led to campaigns promoting public knowledge about the importance of seeking treatment if stiffness, swelling, and squeezing of joints causing pain are experienced (Deighton & Scott, 2011). The effectiveness of this is unknown thus far.

Psychological factors can hamper management of disability resulting from arthritis. Axford and colleagues' (2008) randomized controlled trial of a primary care-based education package for 170 English patients with knee OA found progressive decreases in mental health among all patients over 1 year. Greater arthritic pain reduced coping, increased depression, and reduced physical ability. Depressed patients were less able to profit from arthritis self-management education programs than those with normal mood. Axford *et al.* (2008) suggested individually targeted analgesics and antidepressants to treat knee OA. Kaptein *et al.*'s (2010) longitudinal study of 241 Dutch OA patients suggested that illness perceptions influence self-reported functional status. Patients who viewed their illness as beyond their control reported lower functional status. This suggested that interventions to change these beliefs may improve functional status.

In line with the findings above on depression, self-efficacy – the belief that a patient can perform a specific behavior to achieve an outcome – predicts functional status in OA (McKnight *et al.*, 2010). OA patients with high self-efficacy show more physical activity and report less pain than those without. Self-efficacy is more strongly related to self-reported physical status than objective test results. By contrast, catastrophizing – focusing on pain and magnifying negative consequences – is associated with higher levels of self-reported pain and disability. Reduced physical functioning increases patients' risk of cardiovascular disease. McKnight *et al.* recommended boosting self-efficacy and decreasing catastrophizing to reduce a sense of helplessness and reduce disability.

Pain has been the main focus of psychological interventions in OA. Dixon *et al.* (2007) conducted a meta-analysis of 27 randomized controlled trials of psychosocial interventions for arthritic pain in which self-reported pain intensity ratings were the primary outcome variable. The typical intervention was cognitive behavior therapy (CBT) for pain management or pain coping skills (23 studies), then stress management (five studies), and psychodynamic intervention (two studies). The visual analog scale was the most frequently used pain measure.

There was a strong emphasis in the research on psychosocial interventions for pain (15 studies) and these had a significant, but small, effect on pain. Psychosocial interventions had their strongest effect on measures of coping (effect size = 0.72), with medium effect sizes on measures of anxiety (effect size = 0.28) and joint swelling (effect size = 0.35).

Participants in OA psychosocial intervention trials have been largely female, white, and middle-aged. Dixon *et al.* (2007) commented that the effects of psychosocial interventions on males and people of other cultures remained largely unexplored. They recommended that patients be advised that psychosocial interventions are most likely to improve coping, anxiety, depression, and joint swelling. These improvements might increase patients' quality of life.

Arthritis is second only to coronary heart disease in contributing to unemployment (Dixon *et al.*, 2007). In both OA and RA, job loss impoverishes workers and their families and contributes to demoralization and depression. Absenteeism from OA alone cost Australia over AUS$4.1 billion in 2007 (Reavley *et al.*, 2010). Until recently, employment-related research has focused on RA patients because they are typically younger (Gobelet *et al.*, 2007). The Australian WorkHealth program–Arthritis is developing an education program for the workplace to minimize disease-onset risk and prevent or reduce OA-related absenteeism.

RA causes significant work disability. In a study of 497 RA patients in Adelaide (Australia) it was found that only 25.8% worked full time, but another 24.6% worked part time, giving an overall workforce participation rate of 51%; compared with the Australian rate of 64% (Shanahan *et al.*, 2008). Although 82% of RA patients were in the paid workforce at diagnosis, half had ceased paid work within 4 years. Most (82%) of those stated that their RA had contributed to their decision, with pain (38%) being the main reason, but other important contributors to the decision were the workload (16%) or fatigue (12%). Patients in paid work were younger, with higher education levels and less severe disease.

Early management of RA should be accompanied by vocational assessment and rehabilitation. Doctors in rheumatology clinics rarely ask their patients work-related questions and members of a multidisciplinary team should ensure that rehabilitation and disease management extends to paid work where appropriate.

FM: Diagnosis and Prognosis

FM is a musculoskeletal disorder at the extreme end of the spectrum of chronic widespread pain syndromes, usually accompanied by other symptoms (notably fatigue), suggesting that "fibromyalgia syndrome" might be a better name. The cause is unknown, but often follows trauma (e.g., car accident) or viral infection (Bond & Simpson, 2006). It is associated with abnormalities in central nervous system processing of painful stimuli. Severe pain, after trauma or injury, may start the process of sensitization in susceptible people (Arnold, 2010), either by the production of proinflammatory cytokines or by disrupting the descending pain inhibitory pathways in the brain and spinal cord that normally diminish pain.

As with RA, there are no objective diagnostic tests but nor are there physical abnormalities on examination, making FM a controversial diagnosis with some medical practitioners disputing its status as a disease. These critics argue that a disease label legitimizes patients' illness behavior and may slow their recovery. FM patients encountering these arguments usually become more distressed and may come to distrust the medical profession.

The American College of Rheumatology diagnostic criteria (as cited in McLean & Clauw, 2005) are the most widely accepted. They are chronic widespread pain, and intense pain on gentle palpation of at least 11 out of 18 defined tender point sites without detectable tissue damage. The diagnosis of chronic widespread pain requires that pain must have been present in at least two contralateral (right and left) quadrants of the body, above and below the waist, for at least 3 months. Intense pain when one of these points is palpated with 4 kg of pressure is considered a positive tender point (McLean & Clauw, 2005), but the amount of pressure cannot be standardized. Tender points are defined via nine paired regions in the body. Higher numbers of tender points are associated with higher levels of distress. The number of tender points "active" varies over time. Diagnostic difficulties arise when a patient presents with the other features of FM but has fewer than 11 tender points. Only about 50% of patients meet the tender points criterion and it is unclear how the other patients should be managed (Amris *et al.*, 2010).

FM patients usually fit one of three profiles (Turk *et al.*, 2004). These profiles include dysfunctional, interpersonally distressed, and adaptive copers. Dysfunctional patients typically have high pain levels, emotional distress and perceived interference with activities by the pain, low levels of activity, and low perceived control over their lives. Interpersonally distressed patients usually have intermediate levels of pain and interference with activities, but relatively high levels of punishing responses from significant others with low levels of caring responses or social support. Adaptive copers typically report relatively low levels of pain, emotional distress or perceived interference,

Table 28.2 Common comorbid conditions in FM

Associated disorder	Frequency
Cognitive dysfunction	Common
Dizziness	Common
Chronic fatigue syndrome	Common
Anxiety	72%
Nonrestorative sleep	75%
Headache	75%
Irritable bowel syndrome	60%
Irritable bladder syndrome	50%
Multiple chemical sensitivities	50%
Depression	37%
Paraesthesia	36%
Restless legs syndrome	30%
Cold intolerance	30%
Neurally mediated hypotension	15%

and relatively high levels of activity and perceived control. Onset after injury is common, so that FM patients are often involved in the validation of their symptoms, particularly where medicolegal, compensation, or safety-net issues are involved.

FM overlaps with other "systemic" conditions such as chronic fatigue syndrome and with regional syndromes, notably irritable bowel syndrome and chronic fatigue syndrome (McLean *et al.*, 2005). Sufferers usually experience several symptoms. Comorbidity with major psychiatric disorders such as anxiety and depression is typical. The observation that other regional syndromes are commonly present in the same patient has given rise to the term chronic multisymptom illness to describe the experience. Pain and other symptoms may vary in severity in response to weather change (particularly high winds), emotional distress, or physical activity. The consequent unpredictability makes the disorder harder to cope with. Common comorbid medical conditions are shown in Table 28.2.

Reported cognitive deficits include impaired memory and concentration (Glass, 2010). Patients describe these in colorful terms such as "brain mud" or "fibro fog" and find them highly disruptive. Although studies using validated psychological tests of cognitive function remain rare, there is evidence for reduced working memory, and executive control of attention; dealing with distraction is very difficult. Long-term verbal memory may also be disrupted. Preliminary work suggested that the most important contributor to cognitive dysfunction in FM is pain. Chronic headaches are very common among FM patients (Marcus *et al.*, 2005) and almost half (48%) have migraine. Marcus *et al.* (2005) reported that headaches usually predated the FM and may be a risk factor for the disease. Surprisingly, given their multiple problems and chronic pain, affected individuals often look well (Cunningham & Jillings, 2006), which may mean that clinicians find patients' descriptions of their level of distress difficult to accept.

The causes of FM are not fully understood, but disruption of the central nervous system pain-processing mechanisms and abnormal sensitivity of the pain receptors contribute to the problem (Arnold, 2010; McLean & Clauw, 2005). While FM patients have normal *detection* thresholds for electrical, pressure, or thermal stimuli, their *pain* thresholds for these stimuli are abnormally low. Functional magnetic resonance imaging studies of the brain have corroborated patients' self-reports. The nature of the changes in pain perception remains unclear.

Approximately 50% of patients state that their pain began after a traumatic event (Peterson, 2007). The first step in establishing causation is to discover events which precede the condition. Environmental factors satisfying this requirement for FM include physical trauma, some infections (e.g., hepatitis C, Epstein–Barr virus), emotional stress, other regional pain conditions, and autoimmune disorders (McLean & Clauw, 2005). A common major triggering event in FM is a car accident, but although there are many case histories of patients whose FM first appeared shortly after a car accident these observations cannot establish cause (McLean *et al.*, 2005). FM may also occur in a context of multiple adverse life experiences, including childhood abuse or neglect, drug abuse, or eating disorders (Gupta *et al.*, 2007).

Patients' experiences following a potential triggering event influence their likelihood of developing chronic symptoms. If the event was experienced while driving or at work, patients may sue for compensation and some clinicians argue that the condition is "chosen" by patients to win a legal case. Liberal compensation systems can act as permissive environments which may increase the apparent prevalence of chronic diseases but, on the other hand, adversarial systems may increase patients' distress and disability by forcing them to continue to prove their illness.

McLean *et al.* (2005) tested the evidence for a causal relationship between car accidents and FM against Hill's (1965) criteria for causation. The progression from acute regional pain to widespread pain and fatigue occurs within weeks after the accident. In terms of biological plausibility, McLean *et al.* argued that spinal and superspinal mechanisms controlling pain perception might be disrupted by a car accident. The context of stress may influence the physiological impact. Stressors perceived as unavoidable and unpredictable reliably evoke strong adverse biological consequences. Hence, victims of motor vehicle accidents get FM more often than those responsible for them.

The lack of a positive diagnostic test makes epidemiological studies of FM difficult. No Australian epidemiological work could be located. The community prevalence of FM in Europe, South Africa, and Canada varies between 0.7 and 4.5% (Arnold, 2010). Among patients presenting to rheumatologists, 15–20% have FM, making it a common diagnosis in clinical practice.

The prevalence of FM apparently increases with age and predominantly affects women. Community studies show a gender ratio of 1.6:1 in favor of women (McBeth & Jones, 2007). Women are three times more likely than men to report fatigue and sleep disturbance and typically experience greater pain and more tender points (Arnold, 2010).

No studies of the prevalence or incidence of FM among Aboriginal and Torres Strait Islander people were located. Given its association with traumatic physical incidents and childhood abuse, it might be expected to be more common than among other Australians.

Family members have an 8-fold risk for developing FM as well as for the common overlapping conditions, classified as central sensitivity syndrome (Arnold, 2010; McLean & Clauw, 2005). The mode of inheritance is unknown but almost certainly polygenetic.

Longitudinal studies have shown that people with depressive symptoms, but no musculoskeletal problems are more likely to develop FM within the next 8 years than nondepressed people (McBeth & Jones, 2007). Psychosocial factors, including stressful negative life events, also predict the development of FM in people free of it at baseline. Gupta *et al.* (2007) followed up an English community sample of 4201 people aged between 25 and 65 years. Of the 3171 people who did not have FM at baseline, 10.2% reported it 15 months later. People with some pain at baseline were at greater risk of it becoming widespread at follow-up (odds ratio of 6:1) than those originally without pain. Three other factors were predictive. These included illness behavior, multiple physical symptoms, and sleep problems. Physical abuse in adult life, more likely to occur among women, has a strong, specific relationship with FM (Arnold, 2010).

The association between FM, abuse, and stressful life events suggested a disturbed stress-response system in these patients (Arnold, 2010). There is evidence that the magnitude of their stress response is abnormally low. A chronic decrease in stress response, leading to abnormally low secretion of corticosteroids would reduce physiological and behavioral arousal and cause lower production of endogenous opioids. The autonomic nervous system in FM patients is less responsive to physical stressors such as cold and noise and they show a reduced heart rate response to exercise compared to controls (Arnold, 2010). It is unclear whether these autonomic nervous system changes cause FM (primary) or whether they are a response to the condition (secondary).

No Australian data could be found on the economic and social burden of FM. Silverman *et al.* (2009) compared American FM and RA patients, finding that the burden of illness in FM is comparable to RA, costing just under US$11 000 on average per patient per year and that FM patients had more consultations than RA patients. Mean costs for absence from work were similar in the two groups and a slightly greater proportion of FM patients had short-term disability days than RA patients (20% versus 15%).

Relatively few long-term studies of the course of FM have been done, but they suggested that the symptoms persist unchanged over several years (Arnold, 2010). Uncertainty is rife in FM, not only with respect to its cause or prognosis but in terms of daily living. Cunningham and Jillings (2006) conducted a qualitative study of eight informants (seven female and one male) recruited through a faculty newsletter. One linked the unpredictability of the condition with adverse impacts on her mental health:

> One minute you're fine, the next minute you can't walk. FM is one of the most irrational illnesses I ever dealt with. I'm not a depressed type of personality, but I do get depressed because when you wake up in the morning, you can't get up. Doesn't make sense, you know, so FM does affect the mental health and wellbeing. (p. 262)

FM patients may become afraid to move, especially to take vigorous exercise (Turk *et al.*, 2004). As in RA patients, fear of movement produces a vicious circle of poor lifestyle, worsening health, and greater pain, with many patients showing severe muscle deconditioning and obesity. Turk *et al.*'s (2004) study of 233 women entering a rehabilitation program showed that over a third (38.6%) feared movement. Patients with high levels of fear showed reduced levels of physical activity when tested and reported greater disability than those with low levels of fear. Turk *et al.* suggested that these patients be offered specific treatment to target the phobia. Persuading patients to increase their exercise levels and improve fitness is an important aspect of treatment.

Lack of information about the causes and long-term prognosis of FM is stressful in itself (Reich *et al.*, 2006), sensitizing patients to the negative effects of illness and predicting poor adjustment to illness are important factors. Reich *et al.* (2006) compared community samples of 51 female patients with FM and 32 patients with OA, assessing health status, relationship satisfaction, and partner support. Lack of a clear explanation for FM influences partners' attitudes and reduces the level of support they provide. Where perceived caregiver burden was greater, partners of women with FM provided less support; no such reaction was observed among partners of women with OA.

Management and treatment of FM

The two main aims of treating FM are to decrease pain and increase function by means of a multimodal strategy, which usually includes both drug and nondrug treatments and is targeted to the needs of individual patients (Arnold, 2010; Sarzi-Puttini *et al.*, 2008; Spaeth, 2010; Turk *et al.*, 2008). The complexity of the disease, high prevalence of depression and wide range of other comorbidities mean that a multidisciplinary team is an essential approach to treatment.

Practitioners focus on symptom management and alleviation rather than removal of symptoms. The multidisciplinary approach to treatment is guided by three assumptions: patients need to learn skills to manage their symptoms on a day-to-day basis, they can then learn to self-manage their symptoms, and the effective practice of healthy behavior will lead to positive changes in symptoms and health status.

In Australia, FM is usually managed in primary care settings where the doctor knows the patients' typical stressors, although this type of setting does not preclude a multimodal approach. Health psychologists could play an important role in devising means to target the fear of movement and using the transtheoretical model to implement a 'stages of change' approach to improving quality of life. Patients usually find it empowering to learn the diagnosis provided that they understand that they have a pain sensitization problem which is not due to tissue damage or injury. Providing the diagnosis in this form focuses on the fact that the problem will not cause further tissue injury and stresses the need for appropriate self- management. It provides a basis for improving health and wellness rather than focusing on illness.

Sarzi-Puttini *et al.* (2008) recommended a four-step approach to treatment, beginning with education, including pharmacology and nonpharmacological approaches and possible additional modalities (e.g., acupuncture) chosen by the patient. Education is an important part of management and validates the patients' symptoms and acknowledges the suffering involved, but stresses that patients must become actively involved in their own rehabilitation. Spaeth (2010) found that education could reduce pain and improve function as well as improving compliance with other treatments. Clear treatment goals can be set during education sessions for both patient and family. Specific functional goals may include reduced medication use, increased ability to perform household work or tasks, or improved mood (Turk *et al.*, 2008).

Many therapies have been used for FM though evidence for their effectiveness is lacking (Sarzi-Puttini *et al.*, 2008). Symptoms typically fluctuate between acute exacerbations to daily functioning with minimal treatment. Therefore all forms of treatment must be seen as an ongoing process rather than the management of a single episode.

FM has been treated with a wide range of drugs including antidepressants, opioids, nonsteroidal anti-inflammatory drugs, sedatives, muscle relaxants, and antiepileptic agents, but few of these have been shown to help patients in randomized controlled trials (Sarzi-Puttini *et al.*, 2008; Spaeth, 2010). Tramadol is the only opioid shown in placebo-controlled trials to be effective for the pain of FM (Spaeth, 2010). Pregbalin, an anxiolytic as well as an analgesic, is more effective against pain and also improves sleep and health-related quality of life.

Most research in this condition has been done on the usefulness of antidepressants and they are the primary pharmacological therapy for FM (Arnold, 2010; Turk *et al.*, 2008), despite findings of varying degrees of efficacy. There are three reasons for using antidepressants to treat FM; they are effective in other chronic pain conditions, they are effective in treating the common comorbid depression, and they might improve the action of the inhibitory pain pathways, thus reducing the amount of pain perceived. Tricyclic antidepressants block the reuptake of noradrenaline (norepinephrine) and serotonin, which can help treat sleep disturbances and associated pain, although they are not useful for 60–70% of patients. In about one-third of FM patients low doses of amitriptyline produce moderate short-term improvement in pain, disturbed sleep, and physical and psychological status. Selective serotonin reuptake inhibitors (SSRIs) are not effective against the pain but can counter the depression which amplifies the pain (Arnold, 2010; Spaeth, 2010).

In practice most FM patients use between three and seven medications (Hooten *et al.*, 2007) over a 6 month period, but only about 50% of them comply with a medication regime. In addition to prescription medications, these patients also use vitamins, minerals, and dietary supplements.

CBT and education programs are effective (Sarzi-Puttini *et al.*, 2008; Spaeth, 2010). CBT programs can teach patients to reduce their symptoms, increase their use of coping strategies, and identify and eliminate maladaptive illness behavior. CBT increases patients' sense of control over the disease, but the improvement in self-efficacy declines after 1 year. This technique is best used in conjunction with an exercise regime, where it can improve patients' self-efficacy to participate in exercise. Among patients who attended six CBT sessions focused on improving physical function over a 4 week period, significantly more attained meaningful improvement in physical function compared to a control group receiving standard medical care. Nevertheless, adherence to CBT was low with only 15% of patients consistently achieving their stated monthly cognitive goals (Arnold, 2010).

CBT interventions typically target behavioral and psychological processes that maintain and worsen chronic pain and disability. Fear of pain contributes to chronic pain through avoidance of activities, catastrophizing, and hypervigilance. Long-term avoidance can lead to physical deconditioning or "disuse syndrome." These behavior patterns could be risk factors for the development of chronic pain. Van Koulil *et al.* (2008) pointed out that there is also a group of pain-persistent patients who ignore pain sensations and persist with activities despite pain. Their study of 359 adult FM patients recruited from the Netherlands FM support association found that over half (59.6%) showed pain persistence, while only 40.4% had a pain-avoidance pattern. Pain-avoidant patients were far more disabled than the pain-persistent. Van Koulil *et al.* recommended screening patients for pain-avoidance behaviors and offering them CBT tailored to their specific dysfunctional mechanisms in order to reduce drop-out rates and improve treatment effectiveness.

Exercise is the most highly recommended physical treatment but the best type of exercise remains controversial. Many FM patients limit their physical activity because of comorbid depression, and because some develop a fear of movement due to the pain that often results (Turk *et al.*, 2004). Physical rehabilitation programs are needed but persuading patients to start the program (because of fatigue) and to maintain it (because of pain on exertion) is challenging. If this can be done, benefits in mood and physical function are well established and patients with FM have the same ability to improve fitness with exercise as healthy people (Peterson, 2007). A Cochrane review of exercise in the treatment of FM showed that a moderate-intensity 12 week aerobic training program improved overall wellbeing and physical function, but made little difference to pain levels (Busch *et al.*, 2007).

Patients' fear increased pain, so muscle-strengthening regimes which avoid pain flare-ups should be used (Sarzi-Puttini *et al.*, 2008). Graded aerobic exercise, particularly water aerobics and walking, are recommended. Slow graduation of exercise programs is crucial to prevent dropping out and effective pain control should be established before an exercise program starts (Turk *et al.*, 2008). Stretching exercises can relieve regionalized tightness around spinal areas and reduce pain generation. A general rule is to recommend to patients that they do less than they think they can manage and then slowly build endurance (Arnold, 2010).

While many patients turn to complementary medicine, only acupuncture has convincing evidence of effectiveness (Sarzi-Puttini *et al.*, 2008). Although many patients will experience both drug and nondrug approaches to treatment there has been no experimental work testing the relative effectiveness of various combinations of these two main modalities (Sarzi-Puttini *et al.*, 2008).

Summary

OA is the leading cause of disability and chronic pain in Australia; nevertheless, because it usually affects only one or two of the larger joints, surgical joint replacement or remodelling may be curative. Most OA patients learn to manage their disability without needing surgery by undertaking regular exercise and using analgesics. RA is a chronic inflammatory condition, usually affecting several joints, impairing work capacity and reducing life expectancy. Management of this condition has been revolutionized by recent advances in pharmacotherapy. The aging of the Australian population will pressurize employers into adjusting to the needs of people with either OA or RA. Comparatively little research has been carried out on the needs of people with OA, but employment can often be maintained in less physically demanding jobs.

In contrast to arthritis, FM is a poorly understood syndrome of unknown etiology with limited treatment options. Characterized by severe, fluctuating pain and overlapping with other unexplained medical conditions, the very existence of the diagnosis as a separate entity has been challenged. Pain researchers have argued that it represents a disruption of the usual systems which inhibit pain perception, possibly due to a malfunction of physiological stress responses. The impact of this condition on patients' lives is great and these patients are often described as "very distressed." Treatment focuses on symptom management rather than cure, although recently an antiepileptic drug has been accepted as an appropriate pharmacological treatment by the US Food and Drug Administration. CBT interventions can be useful in helping patients manage the condition. The most highly recommended treatment is exercise but it is difficult to persuade patients to begin and to adhere to an exercise program.

Useful Websites

Arthritis Australia, www.arthritisaustralia.com.au
Arthritis Self Efficacy Scale, http://patienteducation.stanford.edu/research/searthritis.pdf
Australian Canadian Osteoarthritis Hand Index, www.auscan.org/
Australian Rheumatology Association, www.rheumatology.org.au
European League Against Rheumatism (EULAR), www.eular.org/
ME/CFS Society of NSW, www.me-cfs.org.au/node/22

References

AIHW (Australian Institute of Health and Welfare). (2007). *A Picture of Osteoarthritis in Australia*. AIHW cat. no. PHE 93. Canberra: Australian Institute of Health and Welfare.

AIHW. (2009). *A Picture of Rheumatoid Arthritis in Australia*. AIHW Arthritis Series no. 9. Canberra: Australian Institute of Health and Welfare.

Amris, K., Jespersen, A., & Bliddal, H. (2010). Self reported somatosensory symptoms of neuropathic pain in fibromyalgia and chronic widespread pain correlate with tender point count and pressure-pain thresholds. *Pain, 151*, 664–669.

Arnold, L. M. (2010). The pathophysiology, diagnosis and treatment of FM. *Psychiatric Clinics of North America, 33*, 375–408.

Axford, J., Heron, C., Ross, F., & Victor, C. R. (2008). Management of knee osteoarthritis in primary care: Pain and depression are the major obstacles. *Journal of Psychosomatic Research, 64*, 461–467.

Axford, J., Butt, A., Heron, C., Hammond, J., Morgan, J., Alavi *et al.* (2010). Prevalence of anxiety and depression in osteoarthritis: Use of the Hospital Anxiety and Depression Scale as a screening tool. *Clinical Rheumatology, 29*, 1277–1283.

Bond, M. R., & Simpson, K. H. (2006). *Pain: Its Nature and Treatment*. London: Churchill Livingstone.

Busch, A. J., Barber, K. A., & Overend, T. J. (2007). Exercise for treating fibromyalgia syndrome. *Cochrane Database Systematic Review, 4*, CD003786.

Cunningham, M. M., & Jillings, C. (2006). Individuals' descriptions of living with fibromyalgia. *Clinical Nursing Research, 15*, 258–273.

Deighton, C., & Scott, D. L. (2011). Treating inflammatory arthritis early. *British Medical Journal, 342*, 63–64.

Dixon, K. E., Keefe, F. J., Scipio, C. D., Perri, L., & Abernethy, A. (2007). Psychological interventions for arthritis pain management in adults: A meta-analysis. *Health Psychology, 26*, 241–250.

Glass, J. M. (2010). Cognitive dysfunction in fibromyalgia syndrome. *Journal of Musculoskeletal Pain, 18*, 367–372.

Gobelet, C., Luthi, F., Al-Khodairy, A. T., & Chamberlain, M. A. (2007). Work in inflammatory and degenerative joint diseases. *Disability & Rehabilitation, 20*, 1331–1339.

Grainger, R., & Cicuttini, F. M. (2004). Medical management of osteoarthritis of the knee and hip joints. *Medical Journal of Australia, 180*, 232–236.

Gupta, A., Silman, A. J., Ray, D., Morriss, R., Dickens, C., MacFarlane, G. J. et al. (2007). The role of psychosocial factors in predicting the onset of chronic widespread pain: Results from a prospective population-based study. *Rheumatology, 46*, 666–671.

Hill, A. B. (1965). The environment and disease: Association or causation? *Proceedings of the Royal Society of Medicine, 58*, 295–300.

Hooten, W. M., Townsend, C. O., Sletten, C. D., Bruce, B. K., & Rome, J. (2007). Treatment outcomes after multidisciplinary pain rehabilitation with analgesic medication withdrawal for patients with fibromyalgia. *Pain Medicine, 8*, 8–16.

Kaptein, A., Bjisterbosh, J., Scharloo, M., Hampson, S. E., Kroon, H. M., & Kloppenburg, M. (2010). Using the commonsense model of illness perceptions to examine osteoarthritis change: A 6 year longitudinal study. *Health Psychology, 29*, 56–64.

Klarenbeek, N. B., Kerstens, P. J., Huizinga, T., Dijkmans, B. A., & Allart, C. F. (2011). Recent advances in the management of rheumatoid arthritis. *British Medical Journal, 342*, 39–44.

Kramer, P. A. (2006). Prevalence and distribution of spinal osteoarthritis in women. *Spine, 31*, 2843–2848.

Marcus, D. A., Bernstein, C., & Rudy, T. E. (2005). Fibromyalgia and headache: An epidemiological study supporting migraine as part of the fibromyalgia syndrome. *Clinical Rheumatology, 24*, 595–601.

McBeth, J., & Jones, K. (2007). Epidemiology of chronic musculoskeletal pain. *Best Practice & Research, Clinical Rheumatology, 21*, 403–425.

McKnight, P. E., Afram, A., Kashdan, T. B., Kasle, S., & Zautra, A. (2010). Coping self-efficacy as a mediator between catastrophising and physical functioning: treatment target selection in an osteoarthritis sample. *Journal of Behavioral Medicine, 33*, 239–249.

McLean, S. A., & Clauw, D. J. (2005). Biomedical models of fibromyalgia. *Disability and Rehabilitation, 27*, 659–665.

McLean, S. A., Williams, D. A., & Clauw, D. J. (2005). Fibromyalgia after motor vehicle collision: Evidence and implications. *Traffic Injury Prevention, 6*, 97–104.

Pisetsky, D. S. (2007). Clinician's comment on the management of pain in arthritis. *Health Psychology, 26*, 657–659.

Plasqui, G. (2008). The role of physical activity in rheumatoid arthritis. *Physiology and Behaviour, 94*, 270–275.

Reavley, N., Livingston, J., Buchbinder, R., Bennell, K., Stecki, C., & Osborne, H. (2010). A systematic grounded approach to the development of complex interventions: The Australian WorkHealth Program – Arthritis as a case study. *Social Science and Medicine, 70*, 342–350.

Reich, J. W., Olmsted, M. E., & Puymbroeck, C. M. (2006). Illness uncertainty, partner caregiver burden and support, and relationship satisfaction in fibromyalgia and osteoarthritis patients. *Arthritis and Rheumatism, 55*, 86–93.

Rejeski, W. J., Focht, B. C., Messier, S. P., Morgan, T., Pahor, M., & Penninx, B. (2002). Obese, older adults with knee osteoarthritis: Weight loss, exercise and quality of life. *Health Psychology, 21*, 419–426.

Sarzi-Puttini, P., Buskila, D., Carrabba, M., Doria, A., & Atzeni, F. (2008). Treatment strategy in fibromyalgia syndrome: Where are we now? *Seminars in Arthritis and Rheumatology, 37*, 353–365.

Shanahan, E. M., Smith, M., Roberts-Thomson, L., Esterman, A., & Ahern, M. (2008). Influence of rheumatoid arthritis on work participation in Australia. *Internal Medicine Journal, 38*, 166–173.

Silverman, S., Dukes, E. M, Johnston, S. S., Brandenburg, N. A., Sadosky, A., & Huse, D. M. (2009). The economic burden of fibromyalgia: Comparative analysis with rheumatoid arthritis. *Current Medical Research and Opinions, 25*, 829–840.

Spaeth, M. (2010). Fibromyalgia syndrome treatment from a multidimensional perspective. *Journal of Musculoskeletal Pain, 18,* 373–379.

Turk, D. C., Robinson, J. P., & Burwinkle, T. (2004). Prevalence of fear of pain and activity in patients with fibromyalgia syndrome. *The Journal of Pain, 5,* 483–490.

Turk, D. C., Vierck, C. J., Scarbrough, E., Crofford, L. J., & Rudin, N. J. (2008). Fibromyalgia: Combining pharmacological and nonpharmacological approaches to treating the person, not just the pain. *The Journal of Pain, 9,* 99–104.

Van Koulil, S., Kraaimaat, F. W., van Lankveld, W., van Helmond, T., Vedder, A., van Hoorn, H. *et al.* (2008). Screening for pain persistence and pain-avoidance patterns in fibromyalgia. *International Journal of Behavioral Medicine, 15,* 211–220.

29

Rumination as a Cognitive Process in Chronic Illness

Heather Soo and Kerry Sherman

Cognitive models of coping in illness have traditionally highlighted the role of maladaptive cognitive *content*, yet increasingly attention is turning towards the role of cognitive *style*. Rumination, a repetitive style of thinking, has been demonstrated to be a key predictor of depression and, to a lesser extent, anxiety, in nonclinical populations. Current research on rumination in illness suggests that rumination may be important in physical, affective, and behavioral outcomes. Extending cognitive models to incorporate cognitive style will provide an additional mechanism to identify individuals at particular risk of developing psychological distress and will also facilitate the development of appropriately targeted interventions. The quotations used throughout the chapter are drawn from the first author's clinical experience.

Thinking about Illness

"The night I received my diagnosis, my mind was in turmoil. I couldn't stop thinking about what had been said, turning every single sentence over and over in my head, almost as if, in doing so, the world would suddenly shift and make complete sense once again . . . ." (Jayne, 43, diagnosed with systemic lupus erythematosus)

The diagnosis of a chronic illness, such as diabetes or cardiovascular disease, presents a fundamental threat to the individual. Beyond concerns about potential health outcomes, the diagnosis forces consideration of how this change of health status sits with the individual's current self-concept. Diagnosis may lead to contemplation of life plans and goals, and, when there's a disparity between the ideal self as "healthy" and the real self (as affected by illness), the individual will engage in a sense-making process to try to understand their illness and its effect on them personally. Thinking about illness in this way entails processing of both cognitive and emotional context

---

Applied Topics in Health Psychology, First Edition. Edited by M. L. Caltabiano and L. Ricciardelli.
© 2013 John Wiley & Sons, Ltd. Published 2013 by John Wiley & Sons, Ltd.

(Leventhal *et al.*, 1980) and has been found to result in increased levels of psychological distress, particularly anxiety and depression (Moldin *et al.*, 1993). However, not all outcomes are necessarily negative, with reports of positive psychological change, posttraumatic growth, which results from finding increased meaning in day-to-day life and increased value in close relationships (Calhoun *et al.*, 2000).

Until recently, focus has been on cognitive content and the role of maladaptive cognitive patterns when considering psychological outcomes in illness (Beck, 1967, 1976). The formation of illness schema, with elements relating to risk encodings, and beliefs about such aspects as symptoms associated with the condition (identity), reasons for the condition (causality), anticipated duration (timeline), ability to cure or treat the condition (controllability), and the consequences of the illness, are regarded as key determinants of responses to health threats in numerous models of health and illness including the common-sense model (CSM; Leventhal *et al.*, 1980), the cognitive-social health information processing model (C-SHIP; Miller, 1980), and self-regulation theory (SRT; Carver & Scheier, 1981). Focus on these concerns potentially provides substantial negative cognitive material (Crane & Martin, 2003).

Less attention has been given to the *emotional* processing of the health threat posed by the diagnosis of chronic illness, even though the mutual relationship of cognition and affect is widely acknowledged (Bargh & Williams, 2007). Increasing attention is being given to the role of rumination, "the cognitive process of actively thinking about a stressor, the thoughts and feelings it evokes and the implications for one's life and future," in an effort to understand the role of emotional responses to illness (Watkins, 2008, p. 164). Characterized by self-focus and a repetitive and passive deliberation on thoughts, there is no consensus as to the function and outcomes of rumination; it is regarded as potentially an adaptive, positive coping mechanism, and an integral part of the problem solving process, but it can also be a maladaptive process that increases the likelihood of psychological disorders (Joorman *et al.*, 2006).

Rumination, a Maladaptive Process?

"I believed that thinking about my illness would help me work out how best to manage the diabetes and to find alternative ways to achieve what I want in life . . . ." (Erica, 31, diagnosed with Type 1 diabetes)

Given that rumination is not universally adaptive, what purpose does it serve for an individual to engage in this process? Rumination is a common reaction to stressful circumstances, such as diagnosis of illness, experience of natural disasters, or loss of a loved one (Nolen-Hoeksema *et al.*, 1997; Nolen-Hoeksema & Morrow, 1991). Its use may be a conscious choice, adopted as a self-regulatory process to minimize emotional distress arising from a threatening or traumatic event (Tedeschi & Calhoun, 2004), or an unconscious process, invariably experienced in a negative manner as intrusive or uncontrollable: "I can't seem to stop thinking about my illness" or "I think about my illness when I least expect it."

Where rumination is consciously chosen as a coping strategy, it is typically based on the belief that it is a means of "working through" difficulties. Hence, in this instance, rumination is an instrumental behavior, whereby there is a focus on understanding the illness experience and initiation of adaptive behaviors to help resolve perceived disparity between real, or "unhealthy," versus ideal, or "healthy," states (Martin & Tesser, 1989, 1996). Thinking about illness in this way entails a concrete approach aimed at finding solutions to problems that arise out of the illness experience. It is a form of reflection, "a purposeful turning inwards to engage in cognitive problem solving" (Treynor *et al.*, 2003, p. 256). Therefore, rumination in this sense relates to developing coping strategies to meet the demands of the illness, "Thinking about my diabetes helps me work out what to do to manage it," or to finding new approaches so that life goals remain achievable, "I am thinking about how I can get to where I want to be in life."

Although the process of rumination can have a facilitatory effect on coping processes, it may also prove maladaptive if the inherent self-focus is more abstract and evaluative rather than experiential, or brooding, characterized by anxious or melancholic thought, as opposed to reflective and contemplative in nature (Treynor *et al.*, 2003; Watkins & Teasdale, 2004). If rumination causes an individual to focus their thinking on the causes, symptoms, and consequences of an illness diagnosis, any associated negative affect may be amplified and more extensive and detailed risk representations developed, with the potential to further increase psychological distress (Lyubomirsky *et al.*, 1998). Additionally, the individual may find him or herself making negative comparisons of self: "What's wrong with me that I got sick?," or of current self and past self, "Why can't I do everything I used to do?"

> "There are times when I get lost in thought about HIV . . . I find myself focusing on the negative aspects. This worries me as I notice my mood spiralling downwards when I think like this . . . . It can be so hard to stop even when I want to . . . ." (Jonathan, 47, diagnosed with HIV)

The debate about whether rumination is an adaptive or maladaptive process may reflect differences of opinion on its precise definition. There is evidence that ruminative processes are useful for solving problems and resolving difficult emotions (Watkins & Baracaia, 2001). Conversely, evidence exists that rumination is negatively related to problem solving through its interference with attention and ability to generate alternatives (Lyubomirsky *et al.*, 2003b). It may be that rumination is an emotional regulation strategy that masquerades as a problem solving strategy: rumination prevents more complex emotional engagement and, paradoxically, acts as an avoidance strategy (Nolen-Hoeksema, 1996). When a failure to generate solutions is further compounded by negative beliefs about rumination, in terms of lack of controllability, "I can't stop thinking about my illness," or the perceived harmful effects of rumination, "Thinking about my illness will make me sicker," psychological outcomes are likely to be poor.

These contradictory views underline the reality that rumination is a complex and multifaceted concept, with both adaptive and maladaptive elements duly reflected in the differential outcomes reported for rumination in the literature. The distinction between subtypes, reflection and experiential versus brooding and evaluative, has important implications, with the latter considered more critical in the development of adverse psychological outcomes (Watkins & Teasdale, 2001). Ruminative content may remain important, as shown by the volume of research focusing on rumination in response to the experience of depressed mood (Nolen-Hoeksema, 1991, 2000; Nolen-Hoeksema & Morrow, 1991; Spasojevic & Alloy, 2001), but psychological outcomes are also likely to be a function of individual metacognitive beliefs about rumination. While positive beliefs may explain why people initiate and maintain the ruminative process ("Thinking about my illness helps me understand its cause"), negative beliefs ("I exhaust myself thinking about my illness") may provide a connection to psychopathology (Michael *et al.*, 2007). As there is likely to be a complex interplay of these elements, any examination of rumination in response to illness must carefully consider the influence of all these various subcomponents of rumination.

Rumination and Health Outcomes

"While thinking about chronic fatigue is useful, I can't help but feel the sadness and anxiety all over again." (John, 24, diagnosed with chronic fatigue syndrome)

Much of what we understand about the role of rumination and psychological outcomes is based on the general population; very little is currently known about how rumination influences the physical and psychological outcomes of individuals with chronic illness. In general, rumination has been linked to poorer health consequences including the experience of heightened levels of pain (Sullivan & Neish, 1998), primary insomnia and poor quality of sleep (Guastella & Moulds, 2007; Thomsen *et al.*, 2003), and activation of the immune system with increased levels of leukocytes and other immune system measures (Thomsen *et al.*, 2004b).

In line with the view that rumination is adaptive, some argue that it reduces stress, but the majority of evidence suggests the contrary that it helps to prolong bodily responses associated with emotion (Brosschot *et al.*, 2006). Rumination has been shown to delay heart rate and blood pressure recovery following the experience of stressful events (Glynn *et al.*, 2002; Roger & Jamieson, 1988). In individuals who find hard to regulate emotional response, rumination is thought to reactivate the cardiovascular system by mentally recreating an earlier stress reaction, even though the originating stressor may no longer exist (Melamed, 1986). A study among undergraduate students who were asked to recall exposure to a prior stressor found an association between increased blood pressure and higher emotional component of the stressor (Glynn *et al.*, 2002). Similarly, Roger and Najarian (1998) linked rumination to increased levels of cortisol, the stress hormone, which reflects an index of activation of the hypothalamic-pituitary-adrenal axis, a neuroendocrine system that regulates many bodily processes. While the research is largely correlational, it is, nonetheless, suggestive that ruminative tendencies may have a detrimental impact on physiological health through increased experience of stress.

Along with the evidence supporting negative physiological states, rumination has been linked to poorer levels of self-reported health, including increased levels of stress, number of health complaints reported, and healthcare use (Lok & Bishop, 1999; Thomsen *et al.*, 2004a). In examining the impact of rumination on self-reported health and healthcare use, Thomsen *et al.* (2004a, 2004b) examined both young and older groups. Rumination was found to be of greater significance to the health of older adults. While similar associations existed in the younger group, these were much weaker and of limited significance, suggesting that rumination is likely to be a more significant concern for vulnerable groups. These findings were limited by the use of self-report measures and a failure to differentiate outcomes on the basis of specific health concerns (Thomsen *et al.*, 2004a, 2004b). Rumination has also been implicated in delays in seeking medical assistance, which may have important implications in terms of health outcomes (Lyubomirsky *et al.*, 2003a). Lyubomirsky *et al.* (2003a) studied help-seeking behavior in two groups: women were asked to imagine they had discovered a breast lump and actual breast cancer survivors. In both groups, the women who delayed seeking help the longest tended to be ruminators. Lyubormirsky *et al.* (2003a) ascribed the delay to the consequences of the negative bias inherent in rumination and the associated impairment of concentration, impeding instrumental behaviors such as seeking a medical opinion. This reinforces research that shows individuals who are more likely to ruminate require more time to solve a problem (Ward *et al.*, 2003).

Research on rumination in illness is in its infancy. While there has been some investigation of physiological and behavioral outcomes as described previously, the research on psychological outcomes remains limited, although initial studies echo similar patterns of influence on depression and anxiety as in studies undertaken in the clinically well and suggest that content valence of rumination may be important (Bower *et al.*, 1998; Chan *et al.*, 2010; Soo *et al.*, 2007). While positive outcomes of rumination have been demonstrated (Chan *et al.*), the majority of the available evidence suggests a negative effect for rumination in illness (Brosschot *et al.*, 2006, Lyubomirsky *et al.*, 2003a; Soo *et al.*, 2007). However, the findings of many of the studies are restricted by their correlational nature, small sample sizes, and limitations in the physiological data collected (Suchday *et al.*, 2004). As such, further work is needed to explore the precise influence of rumination on outcomes in the context of illness.

Breaking the Ruminative Cycle

"I find it hard to stop thinking about my illness. I try and keep busy, try and distract myself but, more often than not, thoughts break through . . . ." (Rebecca, 42, diagnosed with multiple sclerosis)

Given the demonstrated associations between rumination and psychological outcomes in clinically well populations (Nolen-Hoeksema, 2000; Spasojevic & Alloy, 2001), therapeutic responses have largely been concerned with approaches to minimize rumination. Cognitive behavior therapy (CBT) has been used extensively in the setting of illness, not only in treatment of psychological distress but also in relation to health maintenance, including disease management (Turk & Salovey, 1993). While CBT is considered to be an extremely effective treatment approach, it appears to be less effective in managing ruminative processes, suggesting that a sole focus on cognitive *content* may be insufficient. Addressing the cognitive *process*, in particular by interrupting the stream of ruminative thoughts, is considered to be critical (Ciesla & Roberts, 2007).

At the most basic level, distraction has been used to break the ruminative cycle. This might involve being more social or undertaking pleasurable activities. Research, however, suggests that distraction has only limited use in rumination, with distraction criticized as extending the cognitive avoidance inherent in rumination and prompting recurrence rather than remediation of negative affect (Watkins & Teasdale, 2004). Watkins (2010) linked the ineffectiveness of distraction to the chaining of thoughts seen in rumination, where one negative thought is followed by another; for example, "This illness leaves me no energy for anything," "I'll never be able to achieve what I wanted to," and "I'll never do anything worthwhile again." Watkins argued, therefore, that distraction would only be successful if it caught the initial thought in a ruminative chain.

This has led to the development of a "third wave" of CBT, as exemplified by mindfulness-based cognitive therapy (MBCT; Segal *et al.*, 2002) and acceptance and commitment therapy (ACT; Hayes *et al.*, 1999). Both share the combination of present-focused cognitive-behavioral techniques with the use of mindfulness practices, an emphasis on direct intuitive experience and acceptance, whereby thoughts and feelings are observed without judgment, elaboration, or reaction (Kabat-Zinn, 2003).

Interventions such as MBCT focus on "changing awareness of, and relationship to, thoughts, feelings and bodily sensations" (Segal *et al.*, 2002, p. 54), as opposed to attempting to change content of thoughts about illness. Mindfulness facilitates decentering or defusion, detachment from the meaning of thoughts about illness, so they are experienced as naturally occurring internal events. For example, in chronic illness, individuals learn to recognize the different sensations of their illness and, in doing so, may notice that sometimes no sensations exist or that sensations experienced are neutral, thereby promoting acceptance. Thoughts such as "I can't take any more of this" are simply noted and let go without further processing. In this way, the pitfalls associated with rumination are averted (Bishop *et al.*, 2004).

Segal *et al.* (2002) claim that repeated mindfulness meditation allows for the recognition and interruption of recurrent thinking patterns, facilitating the self-regulation of emotional states and resulting in enhanced psychological wellbeing. In this manner, mindfulness addresses the rumination problem by shifting the individual from the maladaptive evaluative self-focus to the experiential approach outlined by Watkins and Teasdale (2004), from the brooding ruminative style outlined by Treynor *et al.* (2003) associated with psychological distress to a more reflective style.

> "Mindfulness has helped me to let go of some of future concerns I had in relation to my illness, to allow me to focus on what is important for me right now . . . ." (John, 35, diagnosed with hepatitis C)

Both MBCT (Segal *et al.*, 2002) and ACT (Hayes *et al.*, 1999) promote cognitive distancing in conjunction with the acceptance of experiences for what they are. MBCT is based on the mindfulness-based stress reduction (MBSR; Kabat-Zinn, 1990) program used extensively in health settings with demonstrated benefits in patients with a broad range of chronic disorders including chronic pain, fibromyalgia, cancer, and cardiovascular disease (Grossman *et al.*, 2004). Reported benefits include reductions in rumination, psychological distress, and reported medical symptoms (Bishop *et al.*, 2004; Carmody *et al.*, 2008). Similarly, MBCT has been shown to reduce symptoms and relapse rates in individuals with a history of depression and anxiety (Kenny & Williams, 2007), with some initial evidence to suggest that MBCT can be beneficial in the treatment of psychological stress secondary to health issues such as chronic fatigue and cancer (Foley *et al.*, 2010; Surawy *et al.*, 2005). Equally, ACT has also proven effective with a diverse range of medical conditions including chronic pain and diabetes (Dahl & Lundgren, 2006; Gregg *et al.*, 2007).

The research on MBCT and ACT is in its early days and it is premature to make conclusions about effectiveness in the management of rumination in illness. While studies are suggestive of benefits of mindfulness practice, findings are weakened by a number of methodological issues including a lack of randomized controlled studies, sample size considerations, concomitant use of additional program elements, and concerns about actual compliance to mindfulness practice (Baer & Krietemeyer, 2006; Bishop *et al.*, 2004). Additionally, the situation is complicated by a lack of distinction between rumination and associated constructs such as worry and the fact that rumination is often considered as a single entity, with subcomponents of brooding and reflection overlooked. This is reflected in inconsistent findings with Ramel *et al.* (2004) demonstrating that mindfulness produced a significant reduction in reflection but not in brooding. This is not surprising given that brooding represents a more analytical rather than experiential form of rumination, which would align more closely with the "here and now" that forms the core of mindfulness techniques.

Thinking about Thinking

An alternative approach, metacognitive therapy (MCT; Wells, 2000), considers rumination as one of several repetitive thinking styles related to cognitive attentional syndrome (CAS), in which attention is focused on internal and external sources of threat and negative information as a coping strategy (Wells & Papageorgiou, 2004). CAS is linked to metacognitions that determine thinking processes. Negative beliefs about rumination, such as "I can't seem to control my thinking about my illness" or "I find myself thinking about my illness when I least expect it," highlight rumination as problematic. Positive beliefs, such as "Thinking about my illness helps me work out how to manage it," make it difficult for individuals to abandon rumination. MCT introduces the idea of rumination as a problem and facilitates abandonment of the cognitive process, increases cognitive control through attentional training treatment (ATT; Wells, 1990), challenges metacognitive beliefs, and modifies negative beliefs about emotion that lead to self-focus (Wells & Papageorgiou, 2004). Preliminary studies have demonstrated the efficacy of MCT in depression and anxiety (Wells *et al.*, 2007) but research has not, as yet, been extended to the setting of chronic illness.

Ruminating on the Future

Rumination has been demonstrated to be important in the development of depression and anxiety in clinically well populations. Early research on rumination in health contexts suggests that rumination may play an important role in determining health outcomes. First, rumination has been linked to the activation of cardiovascular, immune, and hypothalamus-pituitary-adrenal systems and it will be important to clarify any association and to determine the possible duration of the rumination effect. Second, rumination has a documented role in psychological disorders in clinically well populations. Initial research suggests that these findings are likely to be equally significant within the context of illness. The presence of increased levels of psychological distress in the setting of illness can have considerable ramifications, not only in respect of adding to the total burden of the illness, but also in respect of adherence to treatment regimens, decreased quality of life, and increased healthcare utilization. If the association between rumination and psychological outcomes is replicated in the context of illness, this will provide an additional mechanism for identifying individuals at particular risk and facilitate the provision of an early and appropriate intervention.

While the existent research provides initial steps towards the development of a conceptualization of the relationship between rumination and illness, this area is largely underdeveloped. It will be of primary importance to learn more about the exact nature of any association between rumination and physiological, psychological, and behavioral outcomes in illness. In doing so, it will be important to account for the differential effects of the particular components of rumination, such as brooding and reflection. It will also be useful to explore how any relationship might vary according to specific health conditions. Such research will require the issues of earlier studies to be addressed with a greater focus on randomized controlled studies, larger sample sizes, and longitudinal research.

Rumination is rapidly developing as a key area of interest in current research. Whereas there has been a significant amount of work done in the area of the role of rumination in psychological disorders in clinically well populations, this work has yet to be extended to any great extent in the setting of illness. Early studies provided results hinting at the importance of this area, but many opportunities for research, with an initial emphasis on defining the precise role of rumination in illness, remain. When this has been achieved, identification of risk factors for rumination specific to illness will become clearer and further exploration of intervention strategies, specific to this unique setting, will be possible.

References

Baer, R. A., & Krietemeyer, J. (2006). Overview of mindfulness and acceptance-based treatment approaches. In R. A. Baer (Ed.), *Mindfulness-Based Treatment Approaches* (pp. 3–27). San Diego, CA: Academic Press.

Bargh, J. A., & Williams, L. E. (2007). The non-conscious of emotion regulation. In J. Gross (Ed.), *Handbook of Emotion Regulation* (pp. 429–445). New York: Guilford Press.

Beck, A. T. (1967). *Depression: Clinical, Experimental, and Theoretical Aspects.* New York: Harper & Row.

Beck, A. T. (1976). *Cognitive Therapy and the Emotional Disorders.* New York: International Universities Press.

Bishop, S. R., Lau, M., Shapiro, S., Carlson, L., Anderson, N. D., Carmody, J. *et al.* (2004). Mindfulness: A proposed operational definition. *Clinical Psychology: Science and Practice, 11,* 230–241.

Bower, J. E., Kemeny, M. E., Taylor, S. E., & Fahey, J. L. (1998). Cognitive processing, discovery of meaning, CD4 decline, and AIDS-related mortality among bereaved HIV-seropositive men. *Journal of Consulting and Clinical Psychology, 66,* 979–986.

Brosschot, J. F., Gerin, W., & Thayer, J. (2006). The perseverative cognition hypothesis: A review of worry, prolonged stress-related physiological activation and health. *Journal of Psychosomatic Research, 60,* 113–124.

Calhoun, L. G., Cann, A., Tedeschi, R. G., & McMillan, J. (2000). A correlational test of the relationship between posttraumatic growth, religion and cognitive processing. *Journal of Traumatic Stress, 13,* 521–527.

Carmody, J., Reed, G., Kristeller, J., & Merriam, P. (2008). Mindfulness, spirituality and health-related symptoms. *Journal of Psychosomatic Research, 64,* 393–403.

Carver, C. S., & Scheier, M. F. (1981). *Attention and Self-Regulation: A Control Theory Approach to Human Behavior.* New York: Springer.

Chan, M. W. C., Ho, S., M. Y., Tedeschi, R. G., & Leung, C. W. L. (2010). The valence of attentional bias and cancer-related rumination in posttraumatic stress and posttraumatic growth among women with breast cancer. *Psycho-Oncology, 20,* 544–552.

Ciesla, J. A., & Roberts, J. E. (2007). Rumination, negative cognition and their interactive effects on depressed mood. *Emotion, 7,* 555–565.

Crane, C., & Martin, M. (2003). Illness schema and level of reported gastrointestinal symptoms in irritable bowel syndrome. *Cognitive Therapy and Research, 27,* 185–203.

Dahl, J., & Lundgren, T. (2006). Acceptance and commitment therapy (ACT) in the treatment of chronic pain. In R. A. Baer (Ed.), *Mindfulness-Based Treatment Approaches: Clinician's Guide to Evidence Base and Applications* (pp. 285–305). Burlington, MA: Academic Press.

Foley, E., Baillie, A., Huxter, M., Price, M., & Sinclair, E. (2010). Mindfulness-based cognitive therapy for individuals whose lives have been affected by cancer: A randomised controlled trial. *Journal of Consulting and Clinical Psychology, 78,* 72–79.

Glynn, L. M., Christenfeld, N., & Gerin, W. (2002). The role of rumination in recovery from reactivity: Cardiovascular consequences of emotional states. *Psychosomatic Medicine, 64,* 714–726.

Gregg, J. A., Callaghan, G. M., Hayes, S. C., & Glenn-Lawson, J. L. (2007). Improving diabetes self-management through acceptance, mindfulness and values: A randomised controlled trial. *Journal of Consulting and Clinical Psychology, 75,* 336–343.

Grossman, P., Niemann, L., Schmidt, S., & Walach, H. (2004). Mindfulness-based stress reduction and health benefits: A meta-analysis. *Journal of Psychosomatic Research, 57,* 35–43.

Guastella, A. J., & Moulds, M. L. (2007). The impact of rumination on sleep quality following a stressful life event. *Personality and Individual Differences, 42,* 1151–1162.

Hayes, S. C., Strosahl, K. D., & Wilson, K. G. (1999). *Acceptance and commitment therapy: An experiential approach to behavior change.* New York: Guilford Press.

Joorman, J., Dkane, M., & Gotlib, I. H. (2006). Adaptive and maladaptive components of rumination? Diagnostic specificity and relation to depressive biases. *Behavior Therapy, 37,* 269–280.

Kabat-Zinn, J. (1990). *Full Catastrophe Living: Using the Wisdom of your Body and Mind to Face Stress, Pain, and Illness.* New York: Delacorte.

Kabat-Zinn, J. (2003). Mindfulness-based interventions in context: Past, present and future. *Clinical Psychology: Science and Practice, 10,* 144–156.

Kenny, M. A., & Williams, J. M. G. (2007). Treatment-resistant depressed patients show a good response to Mindfulness-based cognitive therapy. *Behaviour Research and Therapy, 45,* 617–625.

Leventhal, H., Meyer, D., & Nerenz, D. (1980). The common-sense representation of illness danger. In S. Rachman (Ed.), *Contributions to medical psychology,* vol. 2 (pp. 7–30). New York: Guilford Press.

Lok, C.-F., & Bishop, G. D. (1999). Emotion control, stress and health. *Psychology and Health, 14,* 813–827.

Lyubomirsky, S., Caldwell, N. D., & Nolen-Hoeksema, S. (1998). Effects of ruminative and distracting responses to depressed mood on retrieval of autobiographical memories. *Journal of Personality and Social Psychology, 75,* 166–177.

Lyubomirsky, S., Kasri, F., Chang, O., & Chung, I. (2003a). *Ruminative Response Styles and Delay of Seeking Diagnosis for Breast Cancer Symptoms.* www.faculty.ucr.edu/~sonja/papers/LKCCinpress.pdf.

Lyubomirsky, S., Kasri, F., & Zehm, K. (2003b). Dysphoric rumination impairs concentration on academic tasks. *Cognitive Therapy and Research, 27,* 309–330.

Martin, L., & Tesser, A. (1989). Toward a motivational and structural theory of ruminative thought. In J. S. Uleman & J. A. Bargh (Eds.), *Unintended Thought* (pp. 306–326). New York: The Guilford Press.

Martin, L. L., & Tesser, A. (1996). Some ruminative thoughts . In R. S. Wyer (Ed.), *Advances in Social Cognition:* Vol. 9. *Ruminative Thoughts.* (pp. 1–47). Mahwah, NJ: Lawrence Erlbaum Associates.

Melamed, S. (1986). Emotional reactivity and elevated blood pressure. *Psychosomatic Medicine, 49,* 217–225.

Michael, T., Halligan, S. L., Clark, D. M., & Ehlers, A. (2007). Rumination in post-traumatic stress disorder. *Depression and Anxiety, 24,* 307–317.

Miller, S. M. (1980). When is a little information a dangerous thing? Coping with stressful life events by monitoring versus blunting. In S. Levine & H. Ursin (Eds.), *Health and Coping* (pp. 145–169). New York: Plenum.

Moldin, S. O., Scheftner, W. A., Rice, J. P., Nelson, E., Knesevich, M. A., & Akiskal, H. (1993). Association between major depressive disorder and physical illness. *Psychological Medicine, 23,* 755–761.

Nolen-Hoeksema, S. (1991). Responses to depression and their effects on the duration of depressive episodes. *Journal of Abnormal Psychology, 100,* 569–582.

Nolen-Hoeksema, S. (1996). Chewing the cud and other ruminations. In R. S. Wyer (Ed.), *Advances in Social Cognition: Ruminative Thoughts,* vol. IX (pp. 135–144). Mahwah, NJ: Lawrence Erlbaum Associates.

Nolen-Hoeksema, S. (2000). The role of rumination in depressive disorders and mixed anxiety/depressive symptoms. *Journal of Abnormal Psychology, 109,* 504–511.

Nolen-Hoeksema, S., & Morrow, J. (1991). A prospective study of depression and posttraumatic stress symptoms after a natural disaster: The 1989 Loma Prieta earthquake. *Journal of Personality and Social Psychology, 61,* 115–121.

Nolen-Hoeksema, S., McBride, A., & Larson, J. (1997). Rumination and psychological distress among bereaved partners. *Journal of Personality and Social Psychology, 72,* 855–862.

Ramel, W., Goldin, P. R., Carmona, P. E., & McQuaid, J. R. (2004). The effects of mindfulness meditation on cognitive processes and affect in patients with past depression. *Cognitive Therapy and Research, 28,* 435–455.

Roger, D., & Jamieson, J. (1988). Individual differences in delayed heart-rate recovery following stress: The role of extroversion, neuroticism and emotional control. *Personality and Individual Differences, 9,* 721–726.

Roger, D., & Najarian, B. (1998). The relationship between emotional rumination and cortisol secretion under stress. *Personality and Individual Differences, 24,* 531–538.

Segal, Z. W., Williams, J. M. G., & Teasdale, J. D. (2002). *Mindfulness Based Cognitive Therapy for Depression: A New Approach for Preventing Relapse.* New York: Guilford Press.

Soo, H., Burney, S., & Basten, C. (2007). The impact of rumination in depression and anxiety among patients with Type 2 diabetes. Unpublished manuscript, Monash University, Melbourne, Victoria.

Spasojevic, J., & Alloy, L. B. (2001). Rumination as a common mechanism relating depressive risk factors to depression. *Emotion, 1,* 25–37.

Suchday, S., Carter, M. M., Ewart, C. K., Larkin, K. T., & Desiderato, O. (2004). Anger cognitions and cardiovascular recovery following provocation. *Journal of Behavioral Medicine, 27,* 319–341.

Sullivan, M. J. L., & Neish, N. R. (1998). Catastrophising, anxiety and pain during dental hygiene treatment. *Community Dentistry and Oral Epidemiology, 26,* 344–349.

Surawy, C., Roberts, J., & Silver, A. (2005). The effect of mindfulness training on mood and measures of fatigue, activity and quality of life in patients with chronic fatigue syndrome on a hospital waiting list: A series of exploratory studies. *Behavioural and Cognitive Psychotherapy, 33,* 103–109.

Tedeschi, R. G., & Calhoun, L. G. (2004). Posttraumatic growth: Conceptual foundations and empirical evidence. *Psychological Inquiry, 15,* 1–18.

Thomsen, D. K., Mehlsen, M. Y., Christensen, S., & Zachariae, R. (2003). Rumination: Relationship with negative mood and sleep quality. *Personality and Individual Differences, 34,* 1293–1301.

Thomsen, D. K., Mehlsen, M. Y., Olesen, F., Hokland, F., Viidik, A., Avlund, K., & Zachariae, R. (2004a). Is there an association between rumination and self-reported health? *Journal of Behavioral Medicine, 27,* 215–231.

Thomsen, D. K., Mehlsen, M. Y., Hokland, F., Viidik, A., Olesen, F., Avlund, K. *et al.* (2004b). Negative thoughts and health: Associations among rumination, immunity, and health care utilization in a young and elderly sample. *Psychosomatic Medicine, 66,* 363–371.

Treynor, W., Gonzalez, R., & Nolen-Hoeksema, S. (2003). Rumination reconsidered: A psychometric analysis. *Cognitive Therapy and Research, 27,* 247–259.

Turk, D. C., & Salovey, P. (1995). Cognitive-behavioral treatment of illness behaviour. In P. M. Nicassio & T. W. Smith (Eds.), *Managing Chronic Illness: A Biopsychosocial Perspective* (pp. 245–284). Washington DC: American Psychological Association.

Ward, A., Lyubomirsky, L., Sousa, L., & Nolen-Hoeksema, S. (2003). Can't quite commit: Rumination and uncertainty. *Personality and Social Psychology Bulletin, 29,* 96–107.

Watkins, E. R. (2008). Constructive and unconstructive repetitive thought. *Psychological Bulletin, 134,* 163–206.

Watkins, E. R. (2010). Cognitive-behaviour therapy for depressive rumination. Unpublished manuscript, University of Exeter, Exeter.

Watkins, E., & Baracaia, S. (2001). Why do people ruminate in dysphoric moods? *Personality and Individual Differences, 30,* 723–734.

Watkins, E., & Teasdale, J. D. (2001). Rumination and overgeneral memory in depression: Effects of self-focus and analytic thinking. *Journal of Abnormal Psychology, 110,* 353–357.

Watkins, E., & Teasdale, J. D. (2004). Adaptive and maladaptive self-focus in depression. *Journal of Affective Disorders, 82,* 1–8.

Wells, A. (1990). Panic disorder in association with relaxation induced anxiety. An attentional training approach to treatment. *Behavior Therapy, 21,* 273–280.

Wells, A. (2000). *Emotional Disorders and Metacognition: Innovative Cognitive Therapy.* Chichester: Wiley.

Wells, A., & Papageorgiou, C. (2004). Metacognitive therapy for depressive rumination. In C. Papageorgiou & A. Wells (Eds.), *Depressive Rumination: Nature, Theory and Treatment* (pp. 259–273). Chichester: Wiley.

Wells, A., Fisher, P., Myers, S., Wheatley, J., Patel, T., & Brewin, C. R. (2007). Metacognitive therapy in recurrent and persistent depression: A multiple-baseline study of a new treatment. *Cognitive Therapy and Research, 33,* 291–300.

30

Illness Cognition, Coping, and Emotion in the Management of Diabetes

Evidence-Based Interventions for Self-Regulation

Marie L. Caltabiano

The increased prevalence rates for diabetes worldwide attest to the important role health psychologists can play in helping those afflicted with insulin-dependent diabetes mellitus (IDDM) to manage the condition, and in the prevention and management of noninsulin-dependent diabetes mellitus (NIDDM) through health promotion efforts to reduce obesity and increase physical activity. Self-regulation theory provides a useful guide for understanding motivational factors influencing health-related behaviors, in addition to the interplay of cognition, emotion, and coping in the management of health conditions. This chapter reviews the existing evidence for the role of cognition, coping, and emotion in the management of both Type 1 and Type 2 diabetes. It provides an in-depth coverage of the evidence-based efficacy (as measured by diabetes self-management, lifestyle changes, metabolic control, and psychological adjustment) of selected psychological interventions such as cognitive behavior therapy (CBT) methods to address negative attitudes towards diabetes, psycho-education to change incorrect illness perceptions, stress-management training, and the enhancement of coping and problem solving skills to improve self-efficacy expectations and quality of life.

Diabetes mellitus refers to a group of metabolic diseases where the pancreas does not produce sufficient insulin or the body does not respond effectively to the insulin produced [World Health Organization (WHO), 2011]. Insulin is the hormone responsible for blood sugar regulation. There are three types of diabetes (Ratner, 1998; WHO, 2011). Type 1 diabetes or IDDM is a chronic condition which is usually diagnosed in childhood or adolescence and requires the administration of insulin each day to compensate for low insulin production. Type 2 diabetes or NIDDM is typically diagnosed in adulthood, although age of onset is becoming earlier. This type of diabetes is associated with an ineffective response of the body to insulin. Type 2 diabetes is linked to excess body weight and inactivity. As such it is often referred to as a lifestyle disease which can be prevented through attention to diet and physical activity. The third type of diabetes, which is not covered in this chapter, is gestational diabetes, where high blood glucose is diagnosed during pregnancy. The symptoms of gestational diabetes resemble those of Type 2 diabetes. Although gestational diabetes is usually short term, the likelihood of the woman developing Type 2 diabetes

Applied Topics in Health Psychology, First Edition. Edited by M. L. Caltabiano and L. Ricciardelli.
© 2013 John Wiley & Sons, Ltd. Published 2013 by John Wiley & Sons, Ltd.

at a later time is increased if attention is not given to diet and physical activity [Australian Bureau of Statistics (ABS), 2011; Ratner, 1998; WHO, 2011].

High levels of blood glucose, otherwise known as hyperglycemia, result from the body's inability to convert glucose from foods into energy. Hypoglycemia is the term for low blood sugar. Symptoms of diabetes include frequent urination (polyuria), constant thirst (polydipsia), and constant hunger (polyphagia). Nerve damage (diabetic neuropathy) and damage to the blood vessels results from uncontrolled diabetes, putting the person at risk of later complications such as limb amputation, blindness, kidney failure, heart disease, or stroke (WHO, 2011). A severe complication, predominantly in Type 1 diabetes though not restricted to it, is diabetic ketoacidosis which results from a shortage of insulin and is characterized by rapid deep breathing, nausea, vomiting, abdominal pain, and altered consciousness (WHO, 2011). Diabetes complications have been linked to reduced quality of life (Bradley & Speight, 2002).

The number of persons with diagnosed diabetes is increasing around the world. It has been estimated that 346 million people have diabetes worldwide (WHO, 2011). In 2007–8 in Australia 721 000 persons reported having Type 2 diabetes, while 82 000 had Type 1 diabetes (ABS, 2011). More Australian males than females have diabetes, with prevalence rates peaking around the age of 45 years (ABS, 2011). Obesity is the risk factor which distinguishes both males and females with Type 2 diabetes from those who do not have the condition, with obese people being twice as likely to have Type 2 diabetes. Males who are inactive are more likely to have Type 2 diabetes, although women do not seem to be affected in the same way (ABS, 2011). Socioeconomic disadvantage is associated with a 2-fold likelihood of Type 2 diabetes in Australia, after adjusting for age (ABS, 2011). The prevalence of diabetes is highest for Indigenous Australians, and persons born in southern and central Asia (ABS, 2008).

Management of the different types of diabetes to maintain normal blood glucose levels and thus prevent the likelihood of long-term complications necessitates differing regimens (Drotar, 2000; Ratner, 1998). In Type 1 diabetes this involves daily insulin administration either by injection or pump, daily blood glucose monitoring, eating prescribed food, regular physical activity, and problem solving strategies to minimize blood glucose fluctuations, notably hypoglycemia. In Type 2 diabetes the regimen involves blood glucose monitoring, oral hypoglycemic agents or insulin in the later stages if metabolic control has not been achieved, dietary changes, and exercise. Adherence to the diabetes management tasks tends to be higher in Type 1 diabetes, especially for insulin administration and blood glucose monitoring, although diet and exercise are not adhered to rigorously in persons with either type of diabetes, with this being more pronounced in people with Type 2 diabetes (Donnelly *et al.*, 2007; Pereira *et al.*, 2008). Self-monitoring of blood glucose is also lower in those with Type 2 diabetes (Monnier *et al.*, 2004).

The standard measure of metabolic control is glycosylated hemoglobin (HbA1c, HbA1, or A1C), also referred to as glycated hemoglobin (Goldstein *et al.*, 2004), which gives the average level of glucose in the blood for the preceding 8–12 weeks, with a recommended level below 7% (where 4–6% is the normal range). Glycemic or metabolic control and psychological adjustment are the outcomes typically measured by psychologists evaluating the efficacy of interventions for persons with diabetes, although a number of other indicators of good management of the condition would include optimal cardiovascular functioning, low blood lipid levels, normal body mass index, visual acuity, wound healing, and the absence of skin infections. Since persons with either Type 1 or Type 2 diabetes have responsibility for the self-management of their condition within the supportive context of their healthcare team (general practitioner, dietician, health psychologist), the next section gives consideration to theories of self-regulation and how they may be applied to diabetes management.

Self-Regulation, Self-Determination, and Self-Management

A definition of self-regulation which accords with both general theories of self-regulation such as that of Deci and Ryan (2000), or self-regulation models specific to health (Leventhal *et al.*, 1998), is that proposed by Maes and Karoly (2005): "Self-regulation can be defined as a goal-guidance process aimed at the attainment and maintenance of personal goals" (p. 267). Self-regulation models assume that humans engage in purposeful behavior in pursuit of goals. This involves problem solving in the selection of a goal, evaluating one's current state in relation to the goal, selecting strategies to achieve the goal, enacting these strategies, evaluating the outcome of such action, and revising strategies and goals from the feedback obtained. The feedback mechanism which governs self-regulatory behavior is test, operate, test, exit (or TOTE) (Miller *et al.*, 1960). In Carver and Scheier's (1998) control systems model, the goal or "reference value" is the standard by which an input function (perceived current status) is appraised via a comparator and any discrepancy is corrected by an output function. Feedback, motivation, and goal pursuit are central to self-regulation (Cameron & Leventhal, 2003).

Maes and Karoly (2005) identify three phases in self-regulation, these being (1) goal selection, construal/representation, (2) active goal pursuit, and (3) goal attainment, maintenance, or disengagement. Their conceptual framework unifies many of the theoretical ideas in health behavior change which are covered in more detail in Chapters 1 and 2 of this volume. At the goal-selection stage, Maes and Karoly (2005) acknowledge the importance of cognitive determinants of health behavior intentions as proposed by subjective utility models, these being risk perception and outcome expectancies (health belief model: Becker, 1974), social influence (theory of reasoned action/planned behavior: Fishbein & Ajzen, 1975; Ajzen, 1985), and self-efficacy expectancies (Bandura, 1997). The importance of illness representations (Leventhal *et al.*, 1992) and autonomous motivation (self-determination theory, SDT: Deci & Ryan, 2000) in influencing goal selection is also acknowledged. At the active goal pursuit stage, implementation intentions (Gollwitzer, 1993), feedback (control systems model: Carver & Scheier, 1998) and feedforward (self-efficacy expectations and outcome expectancies) (Bandura, 1997), and attention/emotional control (health action process approach: Schwarzer, 1992) are incorporated. The third phase of attainment, maintenance, or disengagement takes into account the theoretical ideas of stage models of change (Prochaska & DiClemente, 1986).

SDT as proposed by Deci and Ryan (2000) is an organismic-dialectical meta theory: "humans are . . . active, growth-oriented organisms who are naturally inclined toward the development of an organized coherence among the elements of their psychological makeup and between themselves and the social world" (p. 262). According to the theory, three innate psychological needs – the needs for competence, relatedness, and autonomy – are necessary for psychological growth, integrity, and wellbeing. Self-determined behavior is intrinsically motivated autonomous behavior; i.e., behavior in which the individual freely chooses to engage, and provides feelings of competence. An internal perceived locus of causality (I-PLOC) is associated with intrinsic motivation. Nondetermined behavior, or amotivation, is a state characterized by a lack of intention to act and reflects an impersonal causality in the regulation of behavior. Extrinsically motivated behavior is generally controlled behavior; i.e., behavior done because the person feels pressure to do so. There are four regulatory styles: external regulation, introjected regulation, identified regulation, and integrated regulation. The first two styles, external regulation and introjected regulation, typify extrinsic motivation; that is, behavior regulated on the basis of reward by others, or self-approval (introjection) and reflect an external locus of causality. It is only when the value of a behavior is acknowledged and accepted by the person (identified regulation) and integrated with other aspects of the self that extrinsic motivations become internalized as part of self-determined behavior. SDT (Deci & Ryan, 2000) also holds that there are individual differences in the general tendencies to behave in an autonomous (intrinsically motivated), controlled (externally motivated), or impersonal (amotivated) manner. These causality orientations are respectively autonomy-oriented, control-oriented, and impersonally oriented.

In relation to goal-directed health behavior, two of the psychological needs proposed by SDT (Deci & Ryan, 2000) – the needs for autonomy and competence – are important for understanding self-regulatory behavior. Those individuals with autonomous motivation as opposed to controlled motivation are more likely to engage in health behaviors. The person with diabetes who chooses to eat foods with a low glycemic index in order to maintain metabolic control is demonstrating autonomous motivation. Controlled motivation is shown by someone who adheres to a dietary plan because of pressure from their doctor or dietician. In relation to the second psychological need, those individuals who perceive themselves as having the competence to manage their diabetes would be expected to be more successful compared to those who do not feel competent. SDT can thus be used to understand what motivates some diabetic persons and not others to engage in effective self-management of the condition and thus prevent diabetic complications.

Perceived competence in SDT is closely related to the self-efficacy construct from social cognitive theory (Bandura, 1997), which relates to the person's belief that they can be effective in achieving desired goals. Feelings of competence serve to foster autonomous motivation. Senecal *et al.* (2000) found support for both self-efficacy and autonomous motivation to independently predict dietary self-care in their cross-sectional study of persons with diabetes. Longitudinal research by Sweet *et al.* (2009) further supports the sequencing of motivational constructs (efficacy/competence and autonomous motivation) in understanding maintenance of physical activity in persons with Type 2 diabetes. Their research indicated that 12 month maintenance of physical activity was predicted by autonomous motivation at 6 months. While perceived efficacy to overcome barriers at 3 months was linked to maintained physical activity, this relationship was mediated by autonomous motivation.

Autonomous motivation can be facilitated by supportive healthcare providers. In a study by Williams *et al.* (1998) of 128 patients with diabetes (having either Type 1 or Type 2 diabetes), those patients who perceived their healthcare providers as autonomy-supportive became more autonomous in their regulation of diet and exercise, reported increased competence to manage their diabetes, and showed an improvement in HbA1c levels over a 12 month period. In an extension of this study, Williams *et al.* (2004) used a randomized trial of patient activation versus passive education to facilitate care provider autonomy support and monitor effects on glycemic control, autonomous motivation, perceptions of competence, and self-management behaviors. There was no intervention effect of patient activation on HbA1c levels over 12 months. However, there was further confirmation of SDT in that autonomy support impacted on long-term glycemic control through increased autonomous motivation, perceived competence, and diabetes self-care behaviors. Perceived competence mediated the effect of autonomous motivation on glycemic control. Self-care behaviors and glycemic control were predicted by perceived competence from 6 to 12 months.

Central to the commonsense model (CSM) of self-regulation (Leventhal *et al.*, 1992, 1998, 2003) is the concept of illness representations. Representations of an illness threat guide health behavior and treatment adherence. These representations comprise concrete somatic experiences (symptoms) and abstract knowledge (semantic illness label). Illness representations are characterized by five content attributes: (1) identity (illness label and symptoms), (2) timeline (acute, chronic, cyclical nature of the illness), (3) consequences (physical, social, and economic), (4) causes (injury, infection, genetics), and (5) cure/control (whether the illness is perceived as preventable or able to be controlled or cured). The CSM invokes a symmetry rule whereby concrete symptoms are linked to the abstract illness label and vice versa. Illness representations do not only have *content* but also *structure* based on symptom patterns, illness schemata, and syndromes. The specific attributes of an illness representation determine coping responses and appraisal of coping efforts. For example, if an individual diagnosed with Type 2 diabetes is not experiencing symptoms and views this condition as acute rather than chronic, the likelihood of engaging in appropriate self-management of the illness is greatly reduced. The self-regulatory system involves parallel processing of two independent systems. One system is the objective representation of the health threat, with its associated coping strategies (treatment) and evaluation of treatment outcomes. The other system is the subjective or emotional processing system with its unique coping procedures and appraisal of efforts to manage emotion. The CSM allows for interaction between the cognitive and emotional systems. Self-regulatory processes (illness representation, coping, and appraisal) are determined by the sociocultural context. The meaning given to symptoms, the associated disease label, expectations about treatment and outcomes are shared by families, practitioners, and the wider social group. When this occurs, there is coherence of the self-regulation system at the interpersonal level. The CSM (Leventhal *et al.*, 1992) also maintains that coherence occurs when there is a match between coping appraisal, coping procedures, and outcome expectations based on attributes of the illness representation. Within the individual, coherence between personal attributes and illness cognition is desirable for self-regulatory behavior.

Self-management is the term which is often used interchangeably with self-regulation and is used to refer to the disease-specific tasks undertaken by the ill person to control or minimize the impact and progression of a disease. Barlow (2001) defines self-management as:

> the individual's ability to manage the symptoms, treatment, physical and psychosocial consequences and life style changes inherent in living with a chronic condition. Efficacious self-management encompasses ability to monitor one's condition and to affect the cognitive, behavioural and emotional responses necessary to maintain a satisfactory quality of life. Thus, a dynamic and continuous process of self-regulation is established. (p. 546)

In a review of self-management approaches for people with chronic illness, Barlow *et al.* (2002) concluded that both group and individual approaches were effective in increasing knowledge, symptom management, self-management behaviors, self-efficacy, and psychological wellbeing. Across the self-management interventions a range of components were represented including supplementary material in booklet or manual forms, audiotapes, Internet information, skill demonstration by a health professional, individual counselling, telephone counselling, and telephone follow-up. Specific to diabetes, the review found that self-management approaches were effective in increasing blood glucose monitoring by participants. The long-term effectiveness of self-management approaches requires study because most of the intervention studies in Barlow *et al.*'s (2002) review did not assess outcomes beyond 3 or 6 months.

Cognitive Processes, Emotion, and Coping in Diabetes

Since cognition, emotion, and behavior are central to self-regulation (Cameron & Leventhal, 2003), this section examines some of the research on these concepts in relation to the lived experience of diabetes. Where gender and sociocultural differences have been studied, the effects of these variables on beliefs about the disease, emotions related to the disease, and the use of different coping strategies are considered. Studies generally have examined an age group in depth rather than examining cross-sectional age differences on these variables.

Sociocultural differences in diabetes-related illness perceptions can influence diabetes management and treatment adherence. Barnes *et al.* (2004) found cultural differences between Tongan and New Zealand patients of European descent in the illness beliefs related to cause, timeline, and cure/control dimensions for diabetes which influenced management of the condition. Tongan patients were more likely to view diabetes as an acute, cyclical, uncontrollable illness caused by spiritual factors and as a consequence were less likely to adhere to a prescribed diabetic diet or to take medication. Qualitative research on Chinese immigrants with poorly controlled Type 2 diabetes (Jayne & Rankin, 2001) confirmed the importance of illness perceptions for the effective management of the condition. These immigrants were uncertain about the cause and timeline for the condition and viewed the diabetes as stigmatizing. Coping strategies used were wishful thinking, belief in powerful others, keeping diabetes a secret and avoiding social activities. There was little indication of appraisal of coping efforts.

There has been mixed evidence for the impact of illness representations on self-management of diabetes in adolescents. Illness beliefs of Type 1 adolescents as measured by the Illness Perception Questionnaire-Revised (IPQ-R) were not found to be related to self-management behaviors of diet, exercise, blood glucose control, or insulin injecting (Law *et al.*, 2002). Illness beliefs, however, were related to psychological wellbeing. Diabetes was viewed by both male and female youth as chronic, able to be personally controlled, cyclical, with treatment being moderately effective in controlling the disease. Adolescents in this study generally had positive emotions in regard to their diabetes. Other research on adolescents with Type 1 diabetes has been able to distinguish between cognitions which predict treatment adherence and metabolic control (Griva *et al.*, 2000). Self-reported overall adherence was predicted by IPQ perceived control over the disease. Generalized self-efficacy expectancies and control beliefs were associated with adherence to diet and exercise requirements, while diabetes-specific self-efficacy predicted blood glucose monitoring. Metabolic control was predicted by generalized and specific self-efficacy beliefs and the consequences and identity attributes of illness representations.

Illness perceptions have also been linked to care seeking in persons with Type 1 diabetes (Lawson *et al.*, 2007). Those with positive models of diabetes in relation to symptoms, cause, control, course, and consequences engaged in more problem-focused coping which involved seeking instrumental social support and were more likely to attend the diabetes clinic for specialist care. Nonattenders at the diabetes clinic tended to have more negative views about their diabetes and coped with avoidance, behavioral disengagement, and emotion-focused strategies such as alcohol.

Research by Paddison *et al.* (2008) provides some indication that illness perceptions are as important as clinical variables (hemoglobin levels, treatment regimen and comorbidities) in explaining variability in quality of life of people with Type 2 diabetes. All illness perceptions predicted quality of life and HbA1c levels with the exception of treatment control. High levels of glycosylated hemoglobin were associated with illness representations of diabetes as a temporary condition. Quality of life was lower in those who had negative emotional representations of diabetes and who perceived the consequences as more severe, while a perception of being able to exert personal control over diabetes was associated with better quality of life.

Illness beliefs of those who do not currently have a diagnosis of diabetes could be of potential significance for health promotion programs in the prevention of Type 2 diabetes. Arcury *et al.* (2004) investigated the explanatory models of immigrant Latinos in a rural community. They found that diabetes meanings could be accounted for by two explanatory models. One model reflected a lack of knowledge about the causes, symptoms, treatment, or consequences of diabetes, and little experience with the illness. Another explanatory model held by these immigrants identified heredity as the primary cause, with behavior/lifestyle (eating too much sugar, not taking care of health) and intense emotion leading to damage of the blood or organs. Both genders and different age groups held these explanatory models. Older males and older females were more aware of the long-term consequences of diabetes and that diabetes was controlled rather than cured.

Karlsen and Bru (2002) sought to identify components of diabetes-related coping and any overlap with general coping styles among 534 adults with Type 1 or Type 2 diabetes. A general measure of coping, the COPE scale by Carver *et al.* (1989), the Self-Blame subscale of the Ways of Coping Questionnaire (Folkman & Lazarus, 1988), Welch's (1994) Diabetes Coping Measure (DCM), and a Seeking Knowledge subscale developed by Karlsen and Bru (2002) were administered to the sample. Factor analysis found seeking social support for instrumental and emotional reasons to be loaded on the same factor. Denial and mental disengagement seemed to share similar functions for patients with diabetes. Other subscales which were conceptually similar in coping with diabetes included passive resignation and avoidance coping. Two subscales from the DCM emerged as distinct factors: Tackling spirit and Diabetes integration. It is interesting to note though that many of the diabetic patients in Karlsen and Bru's study did not use active/task-oriented coping and this form of coping was not linked to diabetes integration as would be expected. Further analysis of the Norwegian data by Karlsen *et al.* (2004b) indicated that diabetes-related coping is linked to perceptions of support from the family, with coping mediating the relationship between perceptions of support and psychological wellbeing of adults with Type 1 and Type 2 diabetes. Those who reported supportive family behavior tended to engage in more problem-focused coping such as active planning of diabetes regimen and seeking knowledge and assistance. Nonsupportive family behavior was linked to more emotion-focused coping and self-blame, especially among those with Type 2 diabetes.

Research which has used a grounded theory approach to study the coping methods used by persons with Type 2 diabetes identified 136 strategies, which could be collapsed into 40 distinct coping methods (Decoster & Cummings, 2004). Of these 13 could be classified as problem-focused and 27 as emotion-focused. The most frequently reported ways of coping with the emotional aspects of diabetes were *prayer*, *faith in God*, and *preoccupy mind*. Problem-focused strategies with the highest usage were determination, seeking diabetes education, and self-discipline. Sociocultural differences in coping emerged, with African-Americans more likely to use prayer and faith in God, and other Americans using determination, self-discipline, or the seeking of diabetes education. Males engaged in fewer coping strategies, but when they did so their coping strategies were more problem-focused compared to the emotion-focused coping of females. Problem-focused coping was associated with better glycemic control.

Other evidence exists for emotion-focused coping to be associated with good diabetic control. In a longitudinal study of coping in diabetes (Sultan *et al.*, 2008) it was found that emotion-focused coping had benefits for glycemic control in adults with Type 1 diabetes if these persons were high on trait anxiety at baseline. State anxiety, however, was reduced by use of task-oriented coping such as planning and problem solving. These findings are significant as they demonstrate interactions between coping and emotion in the management of Type 1 diabetes.

One type of coping which appears to exacerbate diabetes-related distress and lead to metabolic dysregulation is anger coping. In a longitudinal study of 100 patients (Yi *et al.*, 2008) with either Type 1 or Type 2 diabetes, those who coped with their disease using anger at baseline reported more emotional distress at 6 months and had higher levels of HbA1c at 12 months, even after controlling for baseline HbA1c. Although there was participant attrition over the year, and the relationship between anger coping and glycemic control was higher for those who remained in the study, the suggestion by Yi *et al.* (2008) that anger management be incorporated in interventions for those who cope with diabetes using anger seems valid.

Smari and Valtysdottir (1997) found that males cope with IDDM differently than females, and that this has implications for metabolic control. Males who engaged in task-oriented coping had better self-reported glycosylated hemoglobin and less anxiety. For females task-oriented coping was not related to disease-control variables, but was related to less anxiety and depression. Emotion-oriented coping was related to higher anxiety and depression in both genders, as well as higher levels of HbA1. It should be noted, however, that all the outcome measures, including glycosylated hemoglobin, were based on self-report and that the study was cross-sectional so we do not know whether coping changes over time or whether there are gender differences in coping over time.

In adolescents with Type 1 diabetes, gender did not moderate the relationship between coping and glycemic control (Skocic *et al.*, 2010); nor were there gender differences in psychopathological dimensions and diabetic control. The psychopathological dimensions measured were internalizing behaviors (withdrawn, somatic complaints, anxious/depressed) and externalizing behaviors (conflict with others). Coping, emotional reactivity, internalizing, and externalizing behaviors all had independent influences on HbA1c levels. Optimal glycemic control was evident in adolescents who used cognitive restructuring and problem solving coping strategies. This study used averaged HbA1c scores taken over 12 months to take into account the effects of psychological variables on a physiological parameter which may not be evident in the short time frame, typically assessed by glycemic measures (3 months).

Meta-analytic results on the relationship between coping and overall adjustment in diabetes generally support the above findings from selected studies. Duangdao and Roesch (2008) conducted a meta-analysis of 21 studies of 3381 persons with diabetes (comprising more people with Type 1 diabetes) and found that problem-focused, approach coping was associated with less depression and anxiety and better glycemic control. Neither avoidance or emotion-focused coping were significantly associated with overall adjustment, although emotion-focused coping was negatively associated with depression and anxiety.

While coping with diabetes has received much research attention, less research has focused exclusively on emotions experienced in diabetes. Where emotion has been studied this has been in relation to other variables which may impact on diabetic control. Depression and anxiety have been studied either as outcomes of poor metabolic control or as precursors to ineffective self-management (Fisher *et al.*, 2007; Harris, 2003; Lustman & Clouse, 2005). Research by Cherrington *et al.* (2010) indicated a relationship between depression and poor glycemic control in males but not in females with Type 2 diabetes. Diabetes self-efficacy – i.e., confidence in one's ability to manage diabetes – lessened the impact of depression on glycemic control in these males. Other research on adolescents with Type 1 diabetes has found similar results with related constructs. Fortenberry *et al.* (2009) used a 2 week daily diary method to assess positive and negative affect and daily monitoring of blood glucose and perceived task competence. They found that perceived task competence in these adolescents mediated the effect of positive and negative affect on daily blood glucose. Positive affect enhanced self-management through perceived task competence, whereas negative affect served to diminish self-regulation.

The emotional experiences of persons with diabetes and those of family members have also been considered by researchers. In a study by Decoster (2003), who interviewed 34 persons with Type 2 diabetes specifically in relation to the emotions experienced while living with diabetes, 76 emotions arising from 38 different sources were identified. The three most common emotions were fear, irritation, and sadness, with the sources for these emotions being initial diagnosis, treatment, and complications. Since individuals experience diabetes in a social context, this mostly being within the family, some research has examined the effect of expressed emotions by family members. Koenigsberg *et al.* (1993) found family-expressed emotion, in particular critical comments by family members, to explain 19% of the variance in HbA1c levels in their sample of IDDM persons. Emotional overinvolvement did not have the same effect on glucose control. One of the shortcomings of the study was the small sample size.

Some research has looked at interactions between thoughts, emotion, and coping in diabetes. In a study by Sultan and Heurtier-Hartmann (2001) on persons with IDDM, problem-focused coping impacted on glycemic control through self-care behaviors, while neither emotion-focused coping nor avoidance were related to self-care behaviors. Diabetes-related distress was found to predict poor glycemic control, with women being more susceptible compared to men. Emotion-focused coping has been found to have a partial mediating effect on depression in a group of adults with diabetes who engaged in negative rumination (Clarke & Goosen, 2009). The negative thought patterns of these people could be explained to some extent by use of emotion-focused coping such as self-blame and wishful thinking. Clarke and Goosen (2009) assessed general coping rather than coping specific to diabetes, such that we do not know whether these findings would be replicated with a measure of diabetes-related coping.

Diabetes-Specific Psychological Assessment

There are a number of diabetes-specific assessments developed for use with either children/adolescents or adults. These instruments measure a range of psychosocial outcomes such as quality of life, coping, adjustment to diabetes, stress, satisfaction with diabetes treatment, or diabetes self-efficacy. In relation to self-regulation theory, scales have been developed to measure specific components such as illness perceptions, or autonomous versus controlled motivation. Some instruments have also been developed to specifically measure problem solving in diabetes self-management. Internal consistency and validity of these scales is generally high within the development samples, although more psychometric study of the applicability of each instrument to persons of different ages, gender, and sociocultural background would enhance the generalizability of the scales. Diabetes-specific instruments tend to have better predictive ability than generic measures (e.g., diabetes self-efficacy versus generalized self-efficacy; diabetes-specific problem solving measures) (Hill-Briggs & Gemmell, 2007). A useful compendium of scales for health psychologists working in the area of diabetes is Bradley's (2003) *Handbook of Psychology and Diabetes: A Guide to Psychological Measurement in Diabetes Research*. A brief description follows of some of the assessment instruments in the field and particularly those that focus on constructs emphasized in this chapter.

In relation to the assessment of self-regulation components, autonomous motivation and controlled motivation, constructs central to SDT can be measured using the Treatment Self-Regulation Questionnaire (TSRQ) which is based on an approach for assessing self-regulation by Ryan and Connell (1989). Both the TSRQ (Diet) and TSRQ (Exercise) contain 15 items. The format of the questions involves a stem "The reason I would eat a healthy diet is..." and "The reason I would exercise regularly is..." followed by reasons which reflect autonomous or controlled motivation. An example of an autonomous motivational response is "because I feel that I want to take responsibility for my own health". A response reflecting controlled motivation would be "because I want others to approve of me." A seven-point Likert scale (where 1 is not at all true and 7 is very true) is used to rate agreement with the reason for following the recommended diet and exercise. In respect to autonomous motivation, Williams *et al.* (2004) reported internal consistency reliabilities of 0.88 for TSRQ (Diet) and 0.87 for TSRQ (Exercise). Reliabilities for controlled motivation for the TSRQ (Diet) and TSRQ (Exercise) were 0.73 and 0.67 respectively. Evidence of concurrent validity was reported by Levesque, *et al.* (2007) for the TSRQ subscales and positive health behaviors of diet, exercise, and not smoking.

The IPQ-R developed by Moss-Morris *et al.* (2002) measures the components of illness representations specified by the CSM (Leventhal *et al.*, 1992, 1998). These components and their respective subscales include identity, consequences, timeline (chronic, cyclical), control/cure (treatment/personal control), and illness coherence. The IPQ-R also includes a subscale to measure emotional representations. Diabetes-specific illness representations can be assessed by answering the items in relation to diabetes. Paddison *et al.* (2008) reported acceptable internal consistency reliability of above 0.65 for all scales in their diabetes-specific version of the IPQ-R with the exception of the treatment control subscale ($\alpha = 0.52$). Evidence for the predictive validity of the subscales Consequences, Emotional representations, and Personal control for quality of life in people with diabetes was modest (β values of around 0.20).

Knowledge of the strategies people use to cope with diabetes can inform coping training interventions. The DCM developed by Welch (1994) is a 21-item instrument which assesses cognitive and behavioral coping specific to diabetes. It uses a five-point Likert scale of item agreement. The items fall into one of four subscales, these being Tackling spirit, Avoidance, Passive resignation, and Diabetes integration. The DCM has good internal reliability (α value of around 0.70). Factor analyses support the construct validity of the DCM. Associations with glycemic control and quality of life support the external validity of the DCM.

Health psychologists wishing to assess patients' perceptions of self-efficacy of diabetes self-management behaviors can use the Perceived Diabetes Self-Management Scale (PDSMS) developed by Wallston *et al.* (2007). The scale consists of eight items which are answered using a five-point scale where high scores reflect more confidence in managing aspects of the diabetes. The PDSMS has high internal reliability ($\alpha = 0.85$). Support for the external validity of the PDSMS comes from significant associations with self-care activity, body mass index, and glycemic control.

Adjustment to diabetes in adolescents can be measured using the Teen Adjustment to Diabetes Scale (TADS) developed by Wysocki (1993). This scale contains 21 items which are answered using a five-point Likert scale to measure treatment adherence. It assesses behavioral, affective, and attitudinal adjustment to IDDM. There are parallel forms for parents and adolescent. Cronbach alpha values for adolescents (0.81) and parents (0.89, 0.92) are high, indicating good reliability. Validation of the TADS is ongoing.

The Diabetes Stress Questionnaire (DSQ) developed by Delamater *et al.* (1988) is a 65-item measure of everyday stress and hassles experienced by adolescents in relation to diabetes. The degree of perceived stress is rated on a four-point scale ranging from not at all to very much, with high scores indicating greater perceived stress. Two sample items include "Not being able to eat foods that my friends can eat" and "Testing my blood when friends are with me." The DSQ has good concurrent validity. Internal consistency for the DSQ is 0.97.

The Diabetes Quality of Life Measure (DQOL) was originally developed to measure wellbeing of patients in the Diabetes Control and Complications Trial (DCCT Research Group, 1988). The scale contains 46 items: 15 items assess satisfaction with various aspects of life (five-item scale from very satisfied to very dissatisfied), 20 items measure the impact of diabetes (five-item scale measuring frequency from never to all the time), and 11 items measure social worry or diabetes worry (scale endpoints never to all the time). The DQOL can be used for persons with either Type 1 or Type 2 diabetes, and there are 13 items which are specific to adolescents. Internal consistency for the DQOL is 0.92 for both adults and adolescents with IDDM and 0.70 for adults with NIDDM. Test–retest reliability coefficients for the subscales ranges from 0.78 to 0.92 for adults and from 0.88 to 0.92 for adolescents with NIDDM (Jacobson & DCCT, 2003). The DQOL demonstrates external validity in its discrimination between patients with varying diabetic complications.

A measure of problem solving in diabetes self-management is the Diabetes Problem Solving Scale (DPSS) which consists of 30 items rated on a five-point Likert scale from not at all true for me (rating of 0) to extremely true for me (rating of 4). The DPSS contains seven subscales: Effective problem solving, Past experience/learning, Negative transfer of past experience/learning, Positive motivational factors, Negative motivational factors, Impulsive problem solving, and Avoidant problem solving. High subscale scores and high total scale scores indicate better diabetes-related problem solving. There is evidence of acceptable reliability (α range of 0.73–0.78) and predictive validity of the DPSS in relation to medication adherence, blood glucose self-monitoring, and hemoglobin HbA1c level (Hill-Briggs *et al.*, 2007).

Psychological Interventions for Persons with Diabetes

Educational and self-management interventions

Diabetes educational interventions provide instruction on the importance of medication, diet, and exercise for metabolic control, as well as the importance of foot and eye care, and provide training in blood and urine testing. Specific to IDDM is training in insulin injections. Both IDDM and NIDDM educational interventions cover causes, symptoms, and complications in diabetes. Educational interventions are designed to increase self-care adherence through the provision of information, enhance metabolic control, and reduce diabetes complications. Self-management interventions have educational and skill-based training components, but may also address attitudes and beliefs (e.g., self-efficacy), and emotional responses (stress, anxiety, depression) which impact on self-care, metabolic control, and quality of life (Norris *et al.*, 2001; Steed *et al.*, 2003).

In an earlier Australian randomized study by Campbell *et al.* (1996) which compared the effects of minimal education, individual education, group education, and a behavioral program, improvements were found for HbA1c and body mass index across all treatments. There were no between-group differences on total or high-density liporotein cholesterol, systolic blood pressure, or number of patients consulting an ophthalmologist for eye health. Those in the behavioral program were more likely to remain in the study, and to have lower diastolic blood pressure over 12 months. The behavioral program used techniques of goal setting, contracting, self-monitoring, problem solving, and goal renegotiation in relation to eating, exercise, and smoking.

In a review paper by Steed *et al.* (2003) which assessed psychosocial outcomes as a result of educational, self-management, or psychological interventions, the overwhelming majority of studies reported beneficial effects. Wellbeing, quality of life, depression, and – to a lesser extent – anxiety all showed improvements that were maintained in the long term (12 months). Self-management interventions which provide skills-based training enhance self-efficacy and are associated with better glycemic control than didactic education interventions. When glycemic control was the outcome measure, both education and self-management interventions did not demonstrate sustained long-term effects. A meta-analysis by Gary *et al.* (2003) comparing educational and behavioral interventions on glycemic control in Type 2 diabetes, of 18 studies and 2720 participants, indicated only modest improvement in glycemic control (mean reduction of 0.43%), substantiating Steed *et al.*'s (2003) systematic review. The efficacy of self-management training in Type 2 diabetes across 72 randomized controlled trials was assessed by Norris *et al.* (2001). Their review indicated that self-management training had short-term beneficial effects for blood glucose self-monitoring, dietary lifestyle changes, and glycemic control. Diabetes education increased knowledge but this did not always translate into better glycemic control. Similarly, some studies reviewed by Norris *et al.* (2001) did not show improvements in glycemic control even though glucose self-monitoring increased or physical activity increased. Collaborative approaches to self-management (e.g., goal setting by client) rather than didactic education were more effective for weight and glycemic control, and in improving lipid levels. In regard to outcomes other then glycemic control, one study by Trento *et al.* (2004) was able to demonstrate effects lasting over 5 years for a group-based education intervention compared to standard care on diabetes knowledge, problem solving ability, and quality of life.

Some self-management interventions have gone beyond self-care skill development to focus on training in problem solving. Cook *et al.* (2002) in their Choices Diabetes Program taught adolescents with Type 1 diabetes skills in dealing with problem situations of insulin adjustment, dietary control, monitoring blood glucose, dealing with glycemic fluctuations, and psychosocial issues. Those in the problem solving diabetes education program showed improved problem solving skills and better glycemic control from baseline to 6 months. The only outcome which differentiated the treatment from the control group receiving usual care was increased blood glucose monitoring for those receiving training in problem solving.

A systematic review by Hill-Briggs and Gemmell (2007) of intervention studies on problem solving in diabetes self-management identified 52 studies since 1990 of which 16 were qualitative or conceptual. Examples of aspects of problem solving in self-management considered in these studies included how to adjust insulin dose according to self-monitored blood glucose to prevent hypoglycemia, or how to modify carbohydrate dietary intake to insulin dose. Improvements in glycemic control were found in a quarter of the studies on children/adolescents, and in 50% of the intervention studies on adults. Problem solving interventions demonstrated reduced depression, better problem solving, and improvements in self-management behaviors of diet, exercise, and blood glucose self-monitoring for adults.

Counselling and psychotherapeutic approaches

Both individual and group counselling approaches have been studied for their potential to change hemoglobin levels, self-management behaviors, or psychological outcomes. Di Loreto *et al.* (2003) studied the usefulness of a counselling strategy which focused on motivation and self-efficacy to increase physical activity in adults with Type 2 diabetes. While self-regulation theory (Deci & Ryan, 2000) and implementation intentions (Gollwitzer, 1993) are relevant to some of the components in Di Loreto *et al.*'s (2003) counselling strategy, the design of the intervention did not seem to be based on a sound application of theory apart from Bandura's (1997) social cognitive concept of self-efficacy. Nevertheless, compared to a control group who received standard care, the group who received counselling maintained their increased physical activity up to 2 years following the intervention, and showed improvements in body mass index and HbA1c levels. The effects of group-based counselling on stress, coping, psychological wellbeing, and metabolic control for people with both Type 1 and Type 2 diabetes was studied by Karlsen *et al.* (2004a). They used a stratified randomization procedure to allocate participants to either a nine session group-based counselling programme or a wait-list control. The group-based counselling sought to enhance skills in cognitive restructuring, problem solving, and decision making. Acceptable levels of metabolic control were maintained for the treatment group who received the group counselling, with this group reporting less stress, less self-blame, more optimism, and more problem-focused coping both at 6 and 12 month follow-up. Group-based counselling did not affect psychological wellbeing, although this is probably due to the way that wellbeing was measured in the study as a combination of scales including the Short Zung Symptoms of Depression Rating Scale, the Hopkins Symptom Checklist (anxiety), and the WHO Wellbeing Index.

Behavioral family systems therapy has been used for adolescents with IDDM to increase treatment adherence and facilitate adjustment to the condition. In a large-scale randomized controlled trial by Wysocki *et al.* (2000), 119 families of adolescents with IDDM received either 10 sessions of behavioral family systems therapy (BFST), 10 sessions of education and support (ES), or current medical treatment. BFST targets family communication, family problem solving, problematic beliefs about family members which may cause conflict, and structural aspects of the family environment. Behavior therapy techniques of instruction, modeling, rehearsal, and feedback underlie BFST. Social validation of BFST against ES at 3 month follow-up using the Treatment Evaluation Questionnaire indicated that, compared to ES, family members viewed BFST as more acceptable, applicable, and effective for improving family relations specific to diabetes (Wysocki *et al.*, 1997). Outcomes assessed by Wysocki *et al.* (2000) after 3 months of treatment included glycated hemoglobin, adjustment to IDDM, parent–adolescent relationships, and treatment adherence. Boys and younger girls receiving BFST seemed to benefit somewhat in respect to metabolic control and adjustment to IDDM. Treatment adherence did not change as a result of BFST. Compared to education/support and usual medical treatment, BFST was associated with improvement in parent–adolescent relations and diabetes-specific conflict. Although randomization to the three groups was stratified by adolescent gender and treatment center, it should be noted that there were differences between the groups at baseline which limits the results. Follow-up at 6 and 12 months supported the findings in relation to parent–adolescent relations (fewer extreme beliefs and less conflict over diabetes tasks), though gender–age interactions on metabolic control and adjustment observed at 3 months were no longer observed (Wysocki *et al.*, 2001). Evidence for the usefulness of BFST with economically disadvantaged youth from single-parent families and different cultures is lacking. Harris *et al.* (2005) did not indicate initial improvements in diabetes-related conflict or behavior problems to be sustained at 6 months posttreatment, and metabolic control showed no change from baseline to posttreatment follow-up.

Stress-management training using behavioral methods such as biofeedback and relaxation has had some glycemic control benefits for people with Type 2 diabetes. Activation of the hypothalamic-pituitary-adrenal axis during stress can impede glycemic control through the release of counterregulatory stress hormones, but also indirectly by affecting self-care behaviors. McGrady *et al.* (1996) found blood glucose to be lower in NIDDM patients treated with biofeedback-assisted relaxation compared to a control group receiving usual treatment. Surwit *et al.* (2002) found a reduction of 0.5% in HbA1c at 12 month follow-up in Type 2 diabetes patients receiving group-based instruction in progressive muscle relaxation compared to a control group who received diabetes education only.

Treatment approaches based on CBT have been used for both adults and adolescents with either type of diabetes to enhance psychosocial and metabolic outcomes. In a randomized controlled study by Lustman *et al.* (1998) persons with Type 2 diabetes and depression received either 10 weeks of individual CBT with diabetes education or education alone. Following treatment the CBT group had less depression compared to the control group who received only education. At 6 months follow-up only the treatment group demonstrated reductions in HbA1c levels. Hains *et al.* (2000) used a CBT stress-management approach which focused on cognitive restructuring and problem solving for NIDDM youth with poorly controlled diabetes. Within the treatment group improvements were observed for anxiety, diabetes-related stress, and negative coping but not metabolic control. No differences between the treatment and control group were found on any of the measured outcomes. Hains *et al.* (2001) used a multiple baseline design for six adolescents with Type 1 diabetes who had elevated stress, anxiety, and anger. As part of the CBT intervention the youth were taught to identify and monitor negative thoughts, and were then trained in cognitive-restructuring and problem solving techniques. Improvement in stress, anxiety, and anger were found for four of the six youths. Coping skills training for adolescents which used identification of problematic situations, role playing, feedback, problem solving, social skills training, and conflict resolution was found to have enduring effects at 12 months posttreatment for glycosylated hemoglobin, diabetes self-efficacy, medical self-efficacy, and quality of life compared to intensive diabetes management alone (Grey *et al.*, 2000).

Both systematic reviews and meta-analyses of interventions using CBT report mixed results depending on the type of diabetes, age group, presence of psychological problems, and outcome variables assessed. Snoek and Skinner (2002) identified 11 randomized controlled trials which assessed the effects of psychotherapy for diabetic persons with comorbid psychological problems of depression, anxiety, eating disorders, interpersonal and family conflict, or self-destructive behaviors leading to ketoacidosis or hypoglycemia. In Type 2 diabetes, CBT in the treatment of depression was associated with better glycemic control and showed potential in treating binge eating. In the area of anxiety, stress management was found to reduce distress but did not decrease glycosylated hemoglobin levels. The treatment of self-destructive behaviors in IDDM was found to respond to CBT of even short duration. Snoek and Skinner (2002) reported benefits of individual, group, and family psychotherapy for children and adolescents with poorly controlled Type 1 diabetes. Better glycemic control, fewer diabetic complications, and fewer hospitalizations were associated with therapy. Winkley *et al.*'s (2006) meta-analysis of randomized controlled trials with a focus on glycemic control in Type 1 diabetes concluded that most of the psychological interventions which used variants of CBT evidenced improvements in diabetic control for children (reduction of 0.5% in glycated hemoglobin), but not for adults. For Type 2 diabetes, CBT was found to be effective for long-term glycemic control and in improving psychological distress, but not for weight control (Ismail *et al.*, 2004).

Other therapeutic treatments with potential efficacy, and which are receiving increased consideration, include acceptance and commitment therapy (ACT) and multisystemic therapy (MST). In ACT the person is taught to accept thoughts and feelings about diabetes and to focus mindfully on achieving valued goals such as attaining metabolic control or avoiding diabetes complications. Unlike CBT, which is concerned with altering negative thoughts and feelings, ACT emphasizes "experiencing" emotions and thoughts. In a randomized controlled trial of 81 persons with Type 2 diabetes (Gregg *et al.*, 2007) receiving either a 1 day educational workshop or a combination of ACT and education, those in the ACT condition engaged in better self-management (in relation to diet, exercise, and glucose monitoring), used more acceptance coping, and had better metabolic control at 3 months postintervention. Those who received education alone showed improvement in self-care behaviors but not in diabetic control. MST is a family- and community-based treatment ideally suited for adolescents with poorly controlled diabetes and behavioral problems (Henggeler *et al.*, 1998). It uses a multisystemic assessment of the family environment, peer network, school, and wider community to tailor treatment to the adolescent. MST adopts techniques from CBT and BFST. In relation to diabetes management these techniques would include monitoring the adolescent's self-care behaviors, providing reinforcement for appropriate self-management, improving family communication, avoiding family conflict, and creating structured family routines facilitative of diabetes management. In a randomized controlled trial comparing the effect of MST against standard care for 127 adolescents with Type 1 diabetes (Ellis *et al.*, 2005), those in the MST condition had less diabetes-related stress and better metabolic control following the 6 month intervention. Most of the effect of MST on diabetic control, however, was due to increased regimen adherence rather than reduced stress.

Self-regulation interventions for diabetes management

Maes and Karoly (2005) outlined a set of "orienting intervention principles" as a guideline for psychologists designing interventions based on self-regulatory models. These principles include assessment of the individual's risk perception and representation of the health problem, goal setting, self-monitoring of problematic health behaviors, developing an action plan, building self-efficacy, monitoring emotions, engaging in anticipatory coping, deriving support from the social environment, identification of competing goals, administering self-incentives, coping with relapse, and goal reformulation. Similarly, McAndrew *et al.* (2008) offer guidelines for the development of diabetes interventions based on the CSM. They advocate either a cognitive (top-down) or a behavioral (bottom-up) approach depending on whether flawed diabetes representations need addressing or behavior needs to be modified to facilitate coping. Although many diabetes interventions incorporate some components which reflect these principles (e.g., goal setting, goal ownership, self-efficacy, illness representations), interventions which have included all the orienting principles or which have been based exclusively on self-regulation theories (Deci & Ryan, 2000; Leventhal *et al.*, 2003) have not been substantial.

One randomized controlled trial by Huisman *et al.* (2009b), comparing the effect of a self-regulation intervention for overweight Type 2 diabetes patients against standard care and standard care with a manual, found no differences between groups on primary outcomes of weight, body mass index, and HbA1c, or on secondary outcomes of diabetes quality of life, exercise, and nutrition behavior. However, patients' self-regulation skills as measured by the Self-regulation Skills Battery were associated with lowered HbA1c at both 6 and 18 months, suggesting that skill development would benefit those patients with poor metabolic control. The findings were interpreted by Huisman *et al.* (2009b) as indicating the importance of assessing patients for self-regulation skills such as goal planning, help-seeking, self-monitoring, self-efficacy enhancement, attention control, and emotion control in order to match patients to interventions.

Adoption of a self-regulation framework in weight reduction interventions for Type 2 diabetes appears to be efficacious. A meta-analysis by Huisman *et al.* (2009a) indicated that interventions which included some component of self-regulation such as goal efficacy, emotion control, relapse prevention, or control over competing goals demonstrated better effects on weight control and HbA1c hemoglobin than those interventions which did not have self-regulation components. Effect sizes were higher for glycemic control compared to weight and remained stable beyond 6 months' assessment. Of the self-regulation principles, goal reformulation moderated weight control, while emotion control was a significant moderator of HbA1c levels. These aspects of the intervention were even more important than other features such as number of sessions, or individual versus group treatment, in affecting metabolic control.

Conclusion

This chapter has considered the important role of cognition, emotion, and behavior in the management of Type 1 and Type 2 diabetes. A self-regulation framework based on the theoretical formulations of Deci and Ryan (2000) and Leventhal and associates (Leventhal *et al.*, 1992, 1998, 2003) appears useful in understanding how individuals perceive their illness, adjust emotionally, and manage their diabetes to reduce future complications. The evidence-based efficacy of diabetes interventions including educational and self-management approaches, problem solving training, biofeedback-assisted relaxation, coping skills training, CBT, BFST, ACT, and MST has been demonstrated in a number of randomized controlled trials. Measured outcomes of self-care (blood glucose self-monitoring) and medication adherence, psychosocial adjustment, and dietary and physical behavior change have all demonstrated positive response to psychological interventions. Glycemic control has shown improvement in response to a number of the interventions reviewed, although reductions in HbA1c levels have been modest and not always sustained in the long term. Intervention research has responded to calls to study the long-term benefits of diabetes interventions and to increase sample sizes to enhance the power and generalizability of results. The last 20 years have seen an impressive array of studies on all aspects of coping with diabetes, the evidence-based efficacy of diabetes interventions, the development of diabetes-specific assessment, and both systematic reviews and meta-analyses on the efficacy of different types of interventions. The dynamic synergy represented in diabetes research thus far can only inspire health psychologists working in the area to help people with diabetes achieve optimal self-regulation.

References

ABS. (2008). *Year Book Australia, 2008. Feature Article 2: Diabetes Mellitus.* Cat. no. 1301.0. www.abs.gov.au/ausstats/abs@.nsf/7d12b0f6763c78caca257061001cc588/3e1940d483190ad3ca2573d2001076c6!OpenDocument.

ABS. (2011). *Diabetes in Australia: A Snapshot, 2007–08.* Cat. no. 4820.0.55.001. www.abs.gov.au/ausstats/abs@.nsf/mf/4820.0.55.001.

Ajzen, I. (1985). From intentions to actions: A theory of planned behaviour. In J. Kuhl & J. Beckman (Eds.), *Action-Control: From Cognition to Behaviour* (pp. 11–39). Heidelberg: Springer-Verlag.

Arcury, T. A., Skelly, A. H., Gesler, W. M., & Dougherty, M. C. (2004). Diabetes meanings among those without diabetes: Explanatory models of immigrant Latinos in rural North Carolina. *Social Science & Medicine, 59*, 2183–2193.

Bandura, A. (1997). *Self-efficacy: The exercise of control.* New York: W.H. Freeman.

Barlow, J. H. (2001). How to use education as an intervention in osteoarthritis. In M. Doherty & M. Dougados (Eds.), *Osteoarthritis. Balliere's Best Practice and Research* (pp. 545–558). London: Harcourt.

Barlow, J., Wright, C., Sheasby, J., Turner, A., & Hainsworth, J. (2002). Self-management approaches for people with chronic conditions: A review. *Patient Education and Counseling, 48*, 177–187.

Barnes, L., Moss-Morris, R., & Kaufusi, M. (2004). Illness beliefs and adherence in diabetes mellitus: A comparison between Tongan and European patients. *The New Zealand Medical Journal, 117*(1188).

Becker, M. H. (1974). The health belief model and personal health behaviours. *Health Education Monographs, 2*, 376–423.

Bradley, C. (Ed.). (2003). *Handbook of Psychology and Diabetes: A Guide to Psychological Measurement in Diabetes Research.* New York: Psychology Press.

Bradley, C., & Speight, J. (2002). Patient perceptions of diabetes and diabetes therapy: Assessing quality of life. *Diabetes Metabolism Research and Reviews, 18* (Suppl. 3), S64–S69.

Cameron, L. D., & Leventhal, H. (2003). Self-regulation, health, and illness: An overview. In L. D. Cameron & H. Leventhal (Eds.), *The Self-Regulation of Health and Illness Behaviour* (pp. 1–13). London: Routledge.

Campbell, E. M., Redman, S., Moffitt, P. S., & Sanson-Fisher, R. W., (1996). The relative effectiveness of educational and behavioural instruction programs for patients with NIDDM: A randomized trial. *The Diabetes Educator, 22*, 379–386.

Carver, C. S., & Scheier, M. F. (1998). *On the Self-Regulation of Behavior.* New York: Cambridge University Press.

Carver, C. S., Scheier, M. F., & Weintraub, J. K. (1989). Assessing coping strategies: A theoretically based approach. *Journal of Personality and Social Psychology, 56*, 267–283.

Cherrington, A., Wallston, K. A., & Rothman, R. L. (2010). Exploring the relationship between diabetes self-efficacy, depressive symptoms, and glycaemic control among men and women with Type 2 diabetes. *Journal of Behavioral Medicine, 33*, 81–89.

Clarke, D., & Goosen, T. (2009). The mediating effects of coping strategies in the relationship between automatic negative thoughts and depression in a clinical sample of diabetes patients. *Personality and Individual Differences, 46*, 460–464.

Cook, S., Herold, K., Edidin, D. V., & Briars, R. (2002). Increasing problem solving in adolescents with Type 1 diabetes: The Choices Diabetes Program. *The Diabetes Educator, 28*, 115–124.

DCCT Research Group (1988). Reliability and validity of a Diabetes Quality of Life Measure for the Diabetes Control and Complication Trial (DCCT). *Diabetes Care, 11,* 725–732.

Deci, E. L., & Ryan, R. M. (2000). The "what" and "why" of goal pursuits: Human needs and the self-determination of behavior. *Psychological Inquiry, 11,* 227–268.

Decoster, V. A. (2003). The emotions of adults with diabetes. *Social Work in Health Care, 36*(4), 79–99.

Decoster, V. A., & Cummings, S. (2004). Coping with Type 2 diabetes. *Social Work in Health Care, 40*(2), 37–53.

Delamater, A. M., Smith, J. A., Lankester, L., & Santiago, J. V. (1988). *Stress and Metabolic Control in Diabetic Adolescents.* Paper presented at the 9th annual meeting of Behavioral Medicine, Boston.

Di Loreto, C., Fanelli, C., Lucidi, P., Murdolo, G., De Cicco, A., Parlanti, N., De Feo, P. (2003). Validation of a counselling strategy to promote the adoption and the maintenance of physical activity by Type 2 diabetic subjects. *Diabetes Care, 26,* 404–408.

Donnelly, L. A., Morris, A. D., & Evans, J. M. (2007). Adherence to insulin and its association with glycaemic control in patients with Type 2 diabetes. *Quarterly Journal of Medicine, 100,* 345–350.

Drotar, D. (2000). *Promoting Adherence to Medical Treatment in Chronic Childhood Illness: Concepts, Methods, and Interventions.* Mahwah, NJ: Lawrence Erlbaum Associates Publishers.

Duangdao, K. M., & Roesch, S. C. (2008). Coping with diabetes in adulthood: A meta-analysis. *Journal of Behavioral Medicine, 31,* 291–300.

Ellis, D. A., Frey, M. A., Naar-King, S., Templin, T., Cunningham, P. B., & Cakan, N. (2005). The effects of multisystemic therapy on diabetes stress among adolescents with chronically poorly controlled Type 1 diabetes: Findings from a randomized, controlled trial. *Pediatrics, 116,* 826–832.

Fishbein, M., & Ajzen, I. (1975). *Belief, Attitude, Intention, and Behaviour: An Introduction to Theory and Research.* Reading, MA: Addison-Wesley.

Fisher, E. B., Thorpe, C. T., Devellis, B. M., & Devellis, R. F. (2007). Healthy coping, negative emotions, and diabetes management: A systematic review and appraisal. *Diabetes Educator, 33,* 1080–1103.

Folkman, S., & Lazarus, R.S. (1988). *Manual for the Ways of Coping Questionnaire.* Palo Alto, CA: Consulting Psychologist Press.

Fortenberry, K. T., Butler, J. M., Butner, J., Berg, C. A., Upchurch, R., & Wiebe, D. J. (2009). Perceived diabetes task competence mediates the relationship of both negative and positive affect with blood glucose in adolescents with Type 1 diabetes. *Annals of Behavioral Medicine, 37,* 1–9.

Gary, T. L., Genkinger, J. M., Guallar, E., Peyrot, M., & Brancati, F. L. (2003). Meta-analysis of randomized educational and behavioural interventions in Type 2 diabetes. *The Diabetes Educator, 29,* 488–501.

Goldstein, D. E., Little, R. R., Lorenz, R. A., Malone, J. I., Nathan, D., Peterson, C. M., & Sacks, D. B. (2004). Tests of glycemia in diabetes. *Diabetes Care, 27,* 1761–1773.

Gollwitzer, P. M. (1993). Goal achievement: The role of intentions. In W. Stroebe & M. Hewstone (Eds.), *European Review of Social Psychology,* vol. 4 (pp. 141–185). Chichester: Wiley.

Gregg, J. A., Callaghan, G. M., Hayes, S. C., & Glenn-Lawson, J. L. (2007). Improving diabetes self-management through acceptance, mindfulness and values: A randomized controlled trial. *Journal of Consulting and Clinical Psychology, 75,* 336–343.

Grey, M., Boland, E. A., Davidson, M., Li, J., & Tamborlane, W. V. (2000). Coping skills training for youth with diabetes mellitus has long-lasting effects on metabolic control and quality of life. *Journal of Pediatrics, 137,* 107–113.

Griva, K., Myers, L. B., & Newman, S. (2000). Illness perceptions and self efficacy beliefs in adolescents and young adults with insulin dependent diabetes mellitus. *Psychology and Health, 15,* 733–750.

Hains, A. A., Davies, W. H., Parton, E., Totka, J., & Amoroso-Camarata, J. (2000). A stress management intervention for adolescents with Type 1 diabetes. *The Diabetes Educator, 26,* 417–424.

Hains, A. A., Davies, W. H., Parton, E., & Silverman, A. H. (2001). Brief report: A cognitive behavioural intervention for distressed adolescents with Type 1 diabetes. *Journal of Pediatric Psychology, 26,* 61–66.

Harris, M. (2003). Psychosocial aspects of diabetes with an emphasis on depression. *Current Diabetes Reports, 3,* 49–55.

Harris, M. A., Harris, B. S., & Mertlich, D. (2005). Brief report: In-home family therapy for adolescents with poorly controlled diabetes: Failure to maintain benefits at 6-month follow-up. *Journal of Pediatric Psychology, 30,* 683–688.

Henggeler, S. W., Schoenwald, S. K., Borduin, C. M., Rowland, M. D., & Cunningham, P. B. (1998). *Multisystemic treatment of antisocial behavior in children and adolescents.* New York: Guilford Press.

Hill-Briggs, F., & Gemmell, L. (2007). Problem solving in diabetes self-management and control: A systematic review of the literature. *The Diabetes Educator, 33,* 1032–1050.

Hill-Briggs, F., Yeh, H.-C., Gary, T. L., Batts-Turner, M., D'Zurilla, T., & Brancati, F. L. (2007). Diabetes Problem-Solving Scale development in an adult, African American sample. *The Diabetes Educator, 33,* 291–299.

Huisman, S. D., de Gucht, V., Dusseldorp, E., & Maes, S. (2009a). The effect of weight reduction interventions for persons with Type 2 diabetes: A meta-analysis from a self-regulation perspective. *The Diabetes Educator, 35,* 818–835.

Huisman, S., de Gucht, V., Maes, S. Schroevers, M., Chatrou, M., & Haak, H. (2009b). Self-regulation and weight reduction in patients with Type 2 diabetes: A pilot intervention study. *Patient Education and Counseling, 75,* 84–90.

Ismail, K., Winkley, K., & Rabe-Hesketh, S. (2004). Systematic review and meta-analysis of randomized controlled trials of psychological interventions to improve glycaemic control in patients with Type 2 diabetes. *The Lancet, 363,* 1589–1597.

Jacobson, A. M., & DCCT. (2003). The Diabetes Quality of Life Measure. In C. Bradley (Ed.), *Handbook of Psychology and Diabetes: A Guide to Psychological Measurement in Diabetes Research* (pp. 65–87). New York: Psychology Press.

Jayne, R. L., & Rankin, S. H. (2001). Application of Leventhal's self-regulation model to Chinese immigrants with Type 2 diabetes. *Journal of Nursing Scholarship, 33,* 53–59.

Karlsen, B., & Bru, E. (2002). Coping styles among adults with Type 1 and Type 2 diabetes. *Psychology, Health & Medicine, 7,* 245–259.

Karlsen, B., Idsoe, T., Dirdal, I., Hanestad, B. R., & Bru, E. (2004a). Effects of a group-based counselling programme on diabetes-related stress, coping, psychological well-being and metabolic control in adults with Type 1 or Type 2 diabetes. *Patient Education and Counseling, 53,* 299–308.

Karlsen, B., Idsoe, T., Hanestad, B. R., Murberg, T., & Bru, E. (2004b). Perceptions of support, diabetes-related coping and psychological well-being in adults with Type 1 and Type 2 diabetes. *Psychology, Health & Medicine, 9,* 53–70.

Koenigsberg, H. W., Klausner, E., Pelino, D., Rosnick, P., & Campbell, R. (1993). Expressed emotion and glucose control in insulin-dependent diabetes mellitus. *American Journal of Psychiatry, 150,* 1114–1115.

Law, G. U., Kelly, T. P., Huey, D., & Summerbell, C. (2002). Self-management and well-being in adolescents with diabetes mellitus: Do illness representations play a regulatory role? *Journal of Adolescent Health, 31,* 381–385.

Lawson, V. L., Lyne, P. A., Bundy, C., & Harvey, J. N. (2007). The role of illness perceptions, coping and evaluation in care-seeking among people with type 1 diabetes. *Psychology and Health, 22,* 175–191.

Leventhal, H., Diefenbach, M., & Leventhal, E. A. (1992). Illness cognition: Using common sense to understand treatment adherence and affect cognition interactions. *Cognitive Therapy and Research, 16,* 143–163.

Leventhal, H., Leventhal, E. A., & Contrada, R. J. (1998). Self-regulation, health, and behavior: A perceptual-cognitive approach. *Psychology and Health, 13,* 717–733.

Leventhal, H., Brissette, I., & Leventhal, E. A. (2003). The common-sense model of self-regulation of health and illness. In L. D. Cameron & H. Leventhal (Eds.), *The Self-Regulation of Health and Illness Behaviour* (pp. 42–65). London: Routledge.

Levesque, C. S., Williams, G. C., Elliot, D., Pickering, M. A., Bodenhamer, B., & Finley, P. J. (2007). Validating the theoretical structure of the Treatment Self-Regulation Questionnaire (TSRQ) across three different health behaviors. *Health Education Research, 22,* 691–702.

Lustman, P., & Clouse, R. (2005). Depression in diabetic patients: The relationship between mood and glycaemic control. *Journal of Diabetes Complications, 19,* 113–122.

Lustman, P. J., Griffith, L. S., Freedland, K. E., Kissel, S. S., & Clouse, R. E. (1998). Cognitive behaviour therapy for depression in Type 2 diabetes mellitus. A randomized controlled trial. *Annals of International Medicine, 129,* 613–621.

Maes, S., & Karoly, P. (2005). Self-regulation assessment and intervention in physical health and illness: A review. *Applied Psychology: An International Review, 54*, 267–299.

McAndrew, L. M., Musumeci-Szabo, T. J. Mora, P. A., Vileikyte, L., Burns, E., Halm, E. A., Leventhal, H. (2008). Using the common sense model to design interventions for the prevention and management of chronic illness threats: From description to process. *British Journal of Health Psychology, 13*, 195–204.

McGrady, A. V., Graham, G., & Bailey, B. (1996). Biofeedback assisted relaxation in insulin dependent diabetes: A replication and extension study. *Annals of Behavioral Medicine, 18*, 185–189.

Miller, G., Galanter, E., & Pribram, K. (1960). *Plans and the stucture of behavior.* New York: Henry Holt & Co.

Monnier, L., Colette, C., Lapinski, H., & Boniface, H. (2004). Self-monitoring of blood glucose in diabetic patients: From the least common denominator to the greatest common multiple. *Diabetes Metabolism, 30*, 113–119.

Moss-Morris, R., Weinman, J., Petrie, K. J., Horne, R., Cameron, L. D., & Buick, D. (2002). The Revised Illness Perception Questionnaire (IPQ-R). *Psychology and Health, 17*, 1–16.

Norris, S. L., Engelgau, M. M., & Narayan, K. M. V. (2001). Effectiveness of self-management training in Type 2 diabetes. *Diabetes Care, 24*, 561–587.

Paddison, C. A., Alpass, F. M., & Stephens, C. V. (2008). Psychological factors account for variation in metabolic control and perceived quality of life among people with Type 2 diabetes in New Zealand. *International Journal of Behavioral Medicine, 15*, 180–186.

Pereira, M. G., Berg-Cross, L., Almeida, P., & Machado, J. C. (2008). Impact of family environment and support on adherence, metabolic control, and quality of life in adolescents with diabetes. *International Journal of Behavioral Medicine, 15*, 187–193.

Prochaska, J. O., & DiClemente, C. C. (1986). Toward a comprehensive model of change. In W. R. Miller & N. Heather (Eds.), *Treating Addictive Behaviors* (pp. 3–27). New York: Plenum.

Ratner, R. E. (1998). Type 2 diabetes mellitus: The grand overview. *Diabetic Medicine, 15*, S4–S7.

Ryan, R. M., & Connell, J. P. (1989). Perceived locus of causality and internalisation: Examining reasons for acting in two domains. *Journal of Personality and Social Psychology, 57*, 749–761.

Schwarzer, R. (1992). Self-efficacy in the adoption and maintenance of health behaviours: Theoretical approaches and a new model. In R. Schwarzer (Ed.), *Self-Efficacy: Thought Control and Action* (pp. 217–242). Washington DC: Hemisphere.

Senecal, C., Nouwen, A., & White, D. (2000). Motivation and dietary self-care in adults with diabetes: Are self-efficacy and autonomous self-regulation complementary or competing constructs? *Health Psychology, 19*, 452–457.

Skocic, M., Rudan, V., Brajkovic, L., & Marcinko, D. (2010). Relationship among psychopathological dimensions, coping mechanisms, and glycaemic control in a Croatian sample of adolescents with diabetes mellitus Type 1. *European Child and Adolescence Psychiatry, 19*, 525–533.

Smari, J., & Valtysdottir, H. (1997). Dispositional coping, psychological distress and disease-control in diabetes. *Personality and Individual Differences, 22*, 151–156.

Snoek, F. J., & Skinner, T. C. (2002). Psychological counselling in problematic diabetes: Does it help? *Diabetic Medicine, 19*, 265–273.

Steed, L., Cooke, D., & Newman, S. (2003). A systematic review of psychosocial outcomes following education, self-management and psychological interventions in diabetes mellitus. *Patient Education and Counseling, 51*, 5–15.

Sultan, S., & Heurtier-Hartemann, A. (2001). Coping and distress as predictors of glycaemic control in diabetes. *Journal of Health Psychology, 6*, 731–739.

Sultan, S., Epel, E., Sachon, C., Vaillant, G., & Hartemann-Heurtier, A. (2008). A longitudinal study of coping, anxiety and glycaemic control in adults with Type 1 diabetes. *Psychology and Health, 23*, 73–89.

Surwit, R. S., van Tilburg, M. A., Zucker, N., McCaskill, C. C., Parekh, P., Feinglos, M. N. *et al.* (2002). Stress management improves long-term glycaemic control in Type 2 diabetes. *Diabetes Care, 25*, 30–34.

Sweet, S. N., Fortier, M. S., Guerin, E., Tulloch, H., Sigal, R. J., Kenny, G. P., & Reid, R. D. (2009). Understanding physical activity in adults with Type 2 diabetes after completing an exercise intervention trial: A mediation model of self-efficacy and autonomous motivation. *Psychology, Health & Medicine, 14*, 419–429.

Trento, M., Passera, P., Borgo, E., Tomalino, M., Bajardi, M., Cavallo, F., & Porta, M. (2004). A 5-year randomized controlled study of learning, problem solving ability, and quality of life modifications in people with Type 2 diabetes managed by group care. *Diabetes Care, 27,* 670–675.

Wallston, K., Rothman, R., & Cherrington, A. (2007). Psychometric properties of the perceived diabetes self-management scale (PDSMS). *Journal of Behavioral Medicine, 30,* 395–401.

Welch, G. W. (1994). The Diabetes Coping Measure: A measure of cognitive and behavioural coping specific to diabetes. In C. Bradley (Ed.), *Handbook of Psychology and Diabetes: A Guide to Psychological Measurement in Diabetes Research and Practice* (pp. 391–404). London: Harwood Academic.

WHO. (2011). *Diabetes Fact Sheet No. 312.* www.who.int/mediacentre/factsheets/fs312/en/.

Williams, G. C., Freedman, Z. R., & Deci, E. L. (1998). Supporting autonomy to motivate patients with diabetes for glucose control. *Diabetes Care, 21,* 1644–1651.

Williams, G. C., McGregor, H. A., Zeldman, A., Freedman, Z. R., & Deci, E. L. (2004). Testing a self-determination theory process model for promoting glycaemic control through diabetes self-management. *Health Psychology, 23,* 58–66.

Winkley, K., Landau, S., Eisler, I., & Ismail, K. (2006). Psychological interventions to improve glycaemic control in patients with Type 1 diabetes: Systematic review and meta-analysis of randomized controlled trials. *British Medical Journal, 333,* 65–68.

Wysocki, T. (1993). Associations among teen-parent relationships, metabolic control and adjustment to diabetes in adolescents. *Journal of Pediatric Psychology, 18,* 441–452.

Wysocki, T., Harris, M. A., Greco, P., Harvey, L. M., McDonell, K., Elder Danda, C. L. *et al.* (1997). Social validity of support group and behavior therpy interventions for families of adolescents with insulin-dependent diabetes mellitus. *Journal of Pediatric Psychology, 22,* 635–649.

Wysocki, T., Harris, M. A., Greco, P., Bubb, J., Elder Danda, C., Harvey, L. M. *et al.* (2000). Randomized, controlled trial of behavior therapy for families of adolescents with insulin-dependent diabetes mellitus. *Journal of Pediatric Psychology, 25,* 23–33.

Wysocki, T., Greco, P., Harris, M. A., Bubb, J., & White, N. H. (2001). Behavior therapy for families of adolescents with diabetes. *Diabetes Care, 24,* 441–446.

Yi, J. P., Yi, J. C., Vitaliano, P. P., & Weinger, K. (2008). How does anger coping style affect glycaemic control in diabetes patients? *International Journal of Behavioral Medicine, 15,* 167–172.

31

The Experience and Management of Asthma

Felicity C. Allen

Asthma is a common chronic respiratory disease, marked by recurring episodes of wheezing, chest tightness, and shortness of breath due to widespread narrowing of the airways (bronchioles) and airflow obstruction (Horne *et al.*, 2007). The amount of airway obstruction caused by asthma may be fixed or increasing. Increasing airway obstruction causes ongoing decline in lung function. There is evidence that it is a multifactorial disease with environmental, psychological, infectious, genetic, and allergic elements all contributing to the end state. Common psychological comorbidities with asthma include anxiety, panic attacks, depression, and negative affectivity. Any of these may impair patients' asthma management.

Psychological aspects of the disease are extremely important to the successful, long-term management of asthma. Patients' beliefs (notably that asthma is "cured" when the attack has stopped) and unmet expectations of therapy often contribute to poor control of the condition (Horne *et al.*, 2007). A subgroup of asthmatics who experience regular exacerbations and repeated hospitalization are at high risk of dying from the disease, but there is evidence that psychological interventions can help stabilize these patients and motivate them to manage their condition effectively (Horne *et al.*, 2007).

In the normal lung, the airways (bronchioles and bronchi) are open to allow healthy respiration. Relaxed muscles allow air to flow freely and the passages are free of mucus and not narrowed by chronic inflammation. Among asthmatic patients, the bronchial tubes are markedly narrowed (Horne *et al.*, 2007). They are often also inflamed, clogged with mucus, and virtually closed because of the spasm of the surrounding bronchial muscles. Air flows through them only with difficulty.

What changes the lungs of people with asthma? Typically, chronic inflammation of the air passages and overproduction of mucus combines with hyperreactivity to a wide range of triggering substances. Common environmental triggers for acute attacks include vigorous exercise (particularly in cold air), viral antigens, allergens, tobacco smoke, food chemicals, and medications such as aspirin (Horne *et al.*, 2007). Behaviors elicited by strong emotions, including laughter and weeping, can lead to an asthma attack if they produce hyperventilation, a pattern of deep, rapid breathing, which is also the main cause of exercise-induced asthma.

Applied Topics in Health Psychology, First Edition. Edited by M. L. Caltabiano and L. Ricciardelli.
© 2013 John Wiley & Sons, Ltd. Published 2013 by John Wiley & Sons, Ltd.

When the airways within the lungs narrow in reaction to a trigger, wheezing and breathlessness occur, due to reduced air flow in the lungs. Hospital treatment may be necessary. In 2007–8 hospitalizations for asthma in Australia represented almost 1 in 200 of all hospitalizations during that year [Australian Institute of Health and Welfare (AIHW), 2010]. Asthma can be fatal when the airways become so narrowed that the patient cannot get enough air to survive. Preventing these episodes is the main target of asthma management.

Diagnosis is difficult, with no single objective diagnostic test, but is usually based on the presence of wheezing and bronchial hyperresponsiveness. Many people suffer asthma, and its negative health consequences and risks, without being aware of it. By comparison approximately one-third of all physician-diagnosed patients do not have asthma (McLeish & Zvolensky, 2010).

Asthma cannot be cured, but can be controlled by effective treatment and by educating patients to manage their condition. Ongoing treatment with inhaled corticosteroids (ICS) reduces airway inflammation. Recovery from an attack is defined as return to the normal range of airflow, although this is not always possible. Nevertheless small improvements in air flow can be clinically important. The chronic nature of the condition, combined with significant side effects from the medication, means that patient adherence to medication and monitoring is vital to adequate treatment (Horne et al., 2007). The demography of asthma will now be discussed.

Asthma affects 10–12% of the population. It is a common chronic condition among Australians, (AIHW, 2010). Death rates are high compared with other developed countries, probably due to suboptimal management (Smith et al., 2007). Asthma incidence, in Australia and worldwide, increased up until the 1990s, but the incidence has now begun to decrease (AIHW, 2010), so that the prevalence of asthma is falling. Asthma deaths have fallen by 50% since the 1990s. The reasons for these recent changes in prevalence and mortality rates are unclear. Despite the falling incidence rates, asthma ranks 10th as a contributor to the overall burden of disease in Australia.

Clinical asthma is more common among children under 15 (14–16%) than among adults (10–12%) and is the most common chronic childhood illness (Drotar, 2006). Adult urbanized Aboriginal and Torres Strait Islander people have a higher prevalence of asthma and higher rates of hospitalization for the disease than other Australian adults (AIHW, 2010). Even after adjusting for differences in age structure between the two populations, Aboriginal and Torres Strait Islander people were 1.5 times more likely to report having asthma than other Australians (AIHW, 2010). Risk factors for asthma will now be considered.

Cigarette smoking is more common among people with asthma than those without (McLeish & Zvolensky, 2010), although it is not clear whether cigarette smoking alone can cause the disease. Asthmatics should not smoke cigarettes for three important reasons: smoking reduces lung capacity and increases mucus production; it is associated with decreased asthma control and increased risk of mortality, asthma attacks, and exacerbations; and it reduces the anti-inflammatory action of the steroids used in asthma management.

Forced expiratory volume (FEV_1) measures the amount of air that a person can exhale within 1 min and is an indicator of lung capacity. FEV_1 normally declines with age, but this age-related decline is significantly greater among both asthmatics and smokers. James et al. (2005) tested the combined effects of asthma and smoking on lung capacity.

At age 60, nonsmoking nonasthmatics retained the highest average lung capacity, followed by nonsmoking asthmatics and then by smokers who were not asthmatic. Smokers with asthma had the lowest mean lung capacities. Number of pack years of smoking and heavier smoking were associated with decreasing levels of asthma control (McLeish & Zvolensky, 2010). Those who had smoked more than 20 pack years were six times more likely to die from asthma than nonsmokers. Recommending smoking cessation is likely to be a useful clinical strategy.

Obesity has recently been identified as a risk factor for the development of asthma. Burgess *et al.* (2007) conducted a 25 year longitudinal study of a birth cohort of 8583 Tasmanians (Australia) and found that overweight girls who were asthma-free at 7 years of age were three times more likely to have developed asthma at 32 years of age than women who had been normal weight as girls. Overweight people breathe deeply less often than normal people. If deep in-breaths occur too rarely, bronchial hyperresponsiveness and ultimately asthma may result. Once asthma has developed, higher body mass index values also worsen baseline asthma control (Warrier & Hershey, 2008).

Housing quality has been linked with morbidity from several infectious and chronic illnesses. Living in a damp and moldy home can increase the risk of developing asthma-related symptoms, such as coughing, wheezing, and irritation of the upper respiratory tract, by 30–50% (AIHW 2010). This factor may explain the greater prevalence of asthma among Aboriginal and Torres Strait Islander people (see above) who frequently live in substandard dwellings.

Psychological Factors in the Etiology and Management of Asthma

The idea that negative emotions or acute stress may cause or worsen asthma is widespread among sufferers and even professionals. This belief is contrary to clear physiological evidence that the human stress response (fight/flight reaction) *improves* respiratory function. Healthy people show decreased airway resistance under stress, but asthmatics do not (Aboussafy *et al.*, 2005). Strong emotions, either positive or negative, cause sobbing, shouting, or laughing. All of those behaviors can cause hyperventilation, a trigger for an asthma attack. Hyperventilation alone will not cause the underlying condition of asthma.

Earlier perspectives (e.g., Alexander, 1950, 1962) suggested that psychological factors were the major, if not the sole, cause of the disease. Evidence for this view is limited to case histories. Nevertheless, psychological factors may contribute to the development of childhood asthma (e.g., Kozyrskyj *et al.*, 2008).

Psychological factors may predispose adults with existing asthma to serious exacerbations, although evidence is limited (e.g., Alvarez & Fitzgerald, 2007). On the basis of a meta-analysis of 423 articles, Alvarez and Fitzgerald (2007) explored the arguments that psychological factors such as anxiety and depressive disorders, coping mechanisms, and abnormal family dynamics may be associated with near-fatal asthma or fatal asthma. Four hypotheses might explain associations between dysphoric mood states, coping mechanisms, and asthma. The first hypothesis is that emotional factors may aggravate or maintain asthma. The second hypothesis states that psychological factors may be confused with worsening asthma, leading to a vicious circle in which the patient inhales β-agonist medication which in turn increases the anxiety. Thirdly, psychological risk factors may impair disease management; for example, denial may mean that action plans are ignored. The fourth hypothesis maintains that the unremitting tensions of living with an unpredictable, potentially fatal disease may increase the risk of developing an anxiety disorder.

Alvarez and Fitzgerald (2007) found that only seven articles were case-controlled studies. Even among these, some authors assessed psychological factors by examining medical records rather than interviewing the patients or using validated psychological tests. Such an interview should ideally occur before the patient's discharge from hospital. The controls were usually matched to the patients for age and gender, but only one study attempted to match cases and controls for the severity of the disease. Given the poor quality of the research, Alvarez and Fitzgerald could not definitively conclude that psychological disorders increased the risk of either near-fatal asthma or fatal asthma and recommended that a large-scale case-controlled study should be carried out.

Comorbid psychological conditions are common among asthmatic patients and their prevalence and impact on asthma management will now be discussed. Approximately one asthma patient in 10 has a panic disorder, a far higher proportion than in the general population. Panic attacks may trigger an asthma attack through hyperventilation (Cooper *et al.*, 2007). Lehrer *et al.* (2004) commented that chronic anxiety might impair the complex self-care behavior required to manage asthma. The frightening nature of a life-threatening asthma attack might evoke panic by classical conditioning. Among patients with both disorders, the asthmatic condition usually occurred first, supporting the argument that the high prevalence of panic disorder among asthmatics arises from conditioning of the extreme fear evoked by inability to breathe (Lehrer *et al.*, 2004).

Lifetime rates of major depressive disorder between 31 to 47% are found in adults with asthma, almost twice as high reported for the general population (Brown *et al.*, 2008). When depression and asthma co-occur, medication adherence is impaired so that hospitalizations and asthma-related deaths increase. These observations underline the need for well-controlled research into the possibility that existing psychological or psychiatric disorders predispose asthmatics to fatal or near fatal attacks.

Watching a sad film can produce sadness and bronchoconstriction among asthmatics, showing that negative emotion can produce adverse physical changes (Lehrer *et al.*, 2004). At the same time, some common effects of asthma (fatigue, disability) can contribute to depression, so that adverse physical effects can cause negative emotional states. Negative affectivity – the tendency to experience negative emotions – is positively related to higher rates of symptoms generally, but also to specific respiratory symptoms (Janssens *et al.*, 2009). Negative affectivity is associated with bronchoconstriction and facilitates learning to associate an environmental cue with an expectation of symptoms.

The high frequency of both severe anxiety and depression among asthmatics strongly suggests that practitioners should routinely enquire about their presence during the intake interview. Taking appropriate steps to deal with anxiety and depression will almost certainly assist patients maintain good asthma management. Other aspects of asthma management will now be discussed.

Asthma Management

Asthma is a chronic disease which can only be managed, although patients may not understand or believe this and their beliefs are very important contributors to how well they manage their condition. The four goals of asthma therapy are minimizing symptoms, normalizing lung function, eradicating exacerbations, and improving quality of life (Horne *et al.*, 2007). Controlled asthma is characterized by the following symptoms and signs: minimal or no symptoms either day or night, no acute attacks, no emergency visits to hospitals, minimal need for reliever medications, no limitations on physical activities, nearly normal lung function, and minimal side effects from medication.

Currently available medical treatments can achieve this goal for most asthmatics in a clinical setting. In the community, where patients make their own choices, control of asthma is often poor. Ideally, an asthma attack (showing poor control) would motivate health professionals to revise their treatment programme and patients to adhere more closely to it. Unfortunately this reaction, even to life-threatening attacks, is found only in a minority of patients and treating professionals may not even be consulted.

Airway inflammation is a key causative feature of asthma so reducing inflammation is a critical factor in asthma therapy. Less inflammation eases bronchoconstriction and patients can breathe more easily. The mainstay of management of severe asthma is drug treatment, usually inhaled from a small portable inhaler, but sometimes injected. Current asthma medications are broadly divided into two groups: anti-inflammatory medications (e.g., ICS, long-acting bronchodilators) and "rescue" medications (e.g., short-acting bronchodilators).

ICS are powerful anti-inflammatory drugs; unfortunately they have serious long-term side effects including osteoporosis. Current guidelines recommend the use of ICS as first-line treatment in persistent asthma of all severities with add-on therapies such as long-acting inhaled β2 agonists in severe disease. Most patients (90–95%) respond well to ICS, but the minority who do not account for nearly half of the healthcare dollars spent on asthma (Warrier & Hershey, 2008).

Despite advances in treatment, management often remains suboptimal, with many patients relying on rescue medication because they do not use enough ICS consistently to control symptoms on an ongoing basis (Horne *et al.*, 2007). Horne *et al.* (2007) found that over half (56%) of respondents in a large, population-based study reported daytime symptoms in the 4 weeks before the interview and about one-third of them had symptoms which disrupted their sleep at least once a week.

Promoting Treatment Adherence Among Asthmatics

Nonadherence to treatment regimens occurs in about 30% of patients with any chronic disease and non-adherence increases when treatment regimens are complex and demanding (Horne *et al.*, 2007). Treatment in asthma is challenging; some regimens use several medications at different times to achieve different outcomes (e.g., control of inflammation versus bronchodilation). Teaching patients how to adhere to these programs requires considerable time and patience (Lehrer *et al.*, 2004). Treating severe asthma is particularly difficult as patients must avoid common triggers including pollens, pets, foods, and air pollutants. Following a regimen to control severe asthma requires commitment, planning, and behavioral organization.

Any psychological factor, such as depression, which reduces behavioral organization, will in turn reduce asthma control and lead to increased attacks. Tobacco addiction has been shown to reduce the effectiveness of steroid medications and increase asthma mortality. Poor patient–physician communication has been found repeatedly in asthma management studies, and patients' beliefs about the nature of the disease and the need for medication influences adherence to drug treatment and recommendations for monitoring their airways.

To investigate barriers to effective management, a comparative study of the beliefs of 100 treating physicians and 100 adults with asthma was undertaken (Heiner, 2007). From the physicians' perspective ICS were the gold standard of treatment for asthma, although they were concerned about the short-term side effects (e.g., oral thrush). Almost all the patients (95%) had either taken or currently took ICS and were satisfied with their efficacy (97%), ease of use (93%), and rapid onset, but concerned about their long-term side effects (e.g., osteoporosis or cataracts). Safety concern was an important reason for patients changing medications and a common cause of skipping or reducing doses.

Patients and physicians differed markedly in assessing treatment adherence. While 50% of patients reported full adherence with their asthma medication, only 1% of physicians thought that their patients were fully adherent (Heiner, 2007). Both groups thought that symptom cessation, forgetfulness, and concerns about the side effects of treatment were important reasons for poor adherence. Physicians emphasized "difficulty understanding the instructions" more than patients. Almost all (91%) patients who did not take their medication as instructed reported worsening asthma symptoms and used rescue medications.

There was a marked discrepancy in reported discussion of side effects by physicians and patients. No physician admitted "never" discussing short-term side effects while only 2% said that they did not discuss long-term side effects. By contrast, 52% of patients reported that they had "never" discussed short-term side effects with their doctors and 59% of patients said that they had "never" discussed long-term side effects. As a result, physicians believed that patients were far more aware of the potential for side effects than they were. Physicians believed that 92% of their patients knew of the long-term side effects of ICS therapy, but only 51% of the patients said that they did.

Horne *et al.* (2007) remarked that there are many reasons for poor control of asthma, including the type of asthma and comorbidities, but that behavior of patients and clinicians was also an important determinant of the level of control. They found that many patients had very low expectations of treatment and believed that frequent symptoms and lifestyle disruptions were inevitable consequences of having asthma.

A vital component of the management of asthma is detecting changes in the condition of the airways. Under-estimators may not take medications and/or may delay seeking medical attention, which can be fatal, overestimators may take too much medication, experience side effects, and overuse medical resources (Lehrer *et al.*, 2004). Smokers (see above) are particularly likely to underestimate the severity of the symptoms. Certainly there is a subgroup of asthma sufferers who will not respond appropriately even to severe and frightening symptoms. The reasons for this are unclear and various explanations including denial and defensiveness have been proposed. Lehrer *et al.* (2004) reported that clinical levels of anxiety or depression impair the accuracy of asthma symptom perception. Both under- and overperceivers of airflow have higher rates of psychological disorders than accurate perceivers.

Janssens *et al.* (2009) reported considerable within-person variation in reported symptoms. Several psychological variables and expectations influenced symptom reporting, including expecting to have symptoms after being confronted with a cue associated with a previous episode, high levels of negative affectivity, defensiveness, and transient emotional states.

Asthma patients are more likely to report symptoms when they expect to have them, irrespective of their pulmonary state. High levels of negative affectivity are associated with high levels of reported symptoms. Defensiveness is associated both with high levels of symptoms and poor therapeutic compliance. If a positive emotional state can be induced, asthmatics tend to experience fewer symptoms.

Physicians' view of asthma as a chronic disease requiring consistent management differs from the typical patients' view that they only suffer the disease when symptoms are intrusive (Horne *et al.*, 2007). It is unclear whether physicians are unaware of this discrepancy in viewpoints, or believe that patients' views of asthma cannot be changed in the consulting room. Certainly, patients report receiving far less discussion and education in the consultation room than physicians report providing.

An Australian qualitative study of 25 adult asthmatics suggested that part of the communication problem may lie in the way patients and doctors use terms (Vincent *et al.*, 2006). Doctors use the term "exacerbation" to describe a sudden worsening of the condition, but 12 of the asthma patients had never heard the word. Of the 13 patients who had, only 11 understood it. A number of patients understandably substituted the term "exasperation." The participants usually talked about an "attack," usually to describe a situation requiring medical attention.

Widespread lack of knowledge of basic terms like "exacerbation" supports patients' reports about the low level of discussion about their disease that they receive, but communication between patient and healthcare provider about educational material and asthma plans depends on readily understood and unambiguous terms. Vincent *et al.* (2006) suggested that it might be easier to construct action plans if healthcare workers used the same terms as the patients.

An American study of 73 patients hospitalized for an asthma exacerbation found little data about the effects of inadequate health literacy in patients with asthma and no validated measures of patients' understanding of asthma medications (Paasche-Orlow *et al.*, 2005). Almost one-quarter (22%) of participants had inadequate health literacy and this subgroup were more likely to have been hospitalized for asthma in the preceding 12 months. Only just over two-thirds (69%) of the participants used their inhalers correctly and poor inhaler technique was associated with a history of near-fatal asthma. Both findings suggested that the proper use of effective therapies was not reaching this high-risk population. Paasche-Orlow *et al.* (2005) organized an educational intervention to teach inhaler technique and knowledge of asthma and the medication regime and found that inadequate health literacy was not associated with difficulty learning or retaining instructions. They concluded that the high prevalence of poor inhaler technique and poor understanding of the discharge regimen showed that patients' comprehension should be evaluated before discharge.

Written asthma action plans (AAPs) are well known to prevent emergency department attendances and hospitalizations (Fardy, 2003), yet only about 40% of asthmatics have one. Qualitative research has shown that doctors are unenthusiastic about standardized plans, preferring to manage patients individually. Similarly patients believe that others might benefit from action plans, but not them personally. It is unclear which asthma patients would benefit most from an AAP, but certainly people with more severe disease would benefit from responding appropriately to a deterioration in lung function. Evidence on the effectiveness and acceptability of AAP is largely limited to severe cases, but research into their usefulness in milder cases might mean that this useful strategy could be offered to a larger proportion of people with asthma.

An Australian community-based study of 1205 adults found that use of AAPs had declined since the 1990s, despite their proven effectiveness (Marks *et al.*, 2007). Only about one-third of adults with daily symptoms were taking inhaled steroids (36.5%) or had a written action plan (31.1%). Marks *et al.* (2007) called for strategies to improve doctors' and patients' perceptions of AAP and research into factors contributing to the low rate of steroid prescription in Australia.

Asthma control is measured by achievement of goals relevant to healthcare professionals (e.g., lung function) that may not be relevant to the patients. Horne *et al.* (2007) reported that most patients can set goals (e.g., improving activity) and that they responded well to efforts directed to help them achieve these.

As well as the relevance of goals for management, patients' beliefs about the nature of asthma may influence their degree of adherence to treatment. Before following advice, patients evaluate how reasonable it seems to them in the light of their beliefs about, and understanding of, their illness. If patients believe that their illness is episodic, they may also believe that their asthma has gone when the symptoms are absent and cease medication. Patients who believed that asthma was episodic were less adherent to treatment regimens than those who accepted that they had a chronic illness (Horne *et al.*, 2007).

Mancuso *et al.* (2003) interviewed 230 New York asthma patients about their expectations from treatment. While some expectations were realistic (e.g., symptom relief), others (e.g., a cure for the condition) were not. Over one-third (36%) of their sample expected to be cured. Although patient expectations are important determinants for their requests for treatment and adherence to it, there have been few studies of expectations in chronic conditions. Mancuso *et al.* (2003) found that those expecting a cure had worse quality of life. They advocated that patients should receive appropriate education to encourage realistic expectations.

Patients' beliefs about the nature of asthma are important determinants of how well they will manage the disease. Where beliefs are inaccurate, they can lead to poor management with adverse outcomes. These beliefs can, and should, be changed through education and discussion with a treating practitioner. Psychological interventions for asthma will now be discussed.

The clear evidence that intense emotion leading to hyperventilation can induce asthmatic exacerbations combined with findings of high comorbidity rates of depression, anxiety, and panic with asthma have led many clinicians to argue that psychological interventions may be useful, especially for adults with asthma. Although the available medications are effective for most patients, given their side effects it would be desirable to reduce dependence on them so far as possible. The aim of holistic asthma management, including psychological interventions, is not only to improve physical health, but to facilitate the patient's adjustment to the illness, which should include coping and measures of the patients' quality of life. This being the case, a wide range of outcomes might be appropriate targets for intervention in addition to measure of lung function and health services utilization. Choosing an objective endpoint (e.g., FEV_1) to combine with self-reports on quality of life is an important methodological consideration.

There are at least five recognized groups of psychological interventions for adult asthma patients and these include relaxation therapies, behavioral therapies, cognitive therapies, cognitive behavior therapy (CBT), and psychodynamic psychotherapies. Unfortunately systematic reviews of research on several of these intervention groups have consistently reported finding small numbers of poorly designed studies which have failed to show evidence for the efficacy of the wide range of therapies attempted. The available evidence on their efficacy will now be described.

Anxiety both precipitates asthma attacks and results from them. Acute psychological stress increases airway resistance in asthmatic subjects. Therefore, it might be expected that relaxation therapies would assist patients to deal with their symptoms more effectively or even improve physical functioning. A wide range of relaxation therapies are used in the treatment of asthmatic adults including Jacobsonian progressive relaxation, hypnotherapy, autogenic training, biofeedback training, and transcendental meditation. There is a lack of evidence that relaxation therapies assist in the management of asthma, though finding an appropriate control technique for relaxation is difficult (Lahmann *et al.*, 2009).

Huntley *et al.* (2002) conducted a meta-analysis of 15 randomized controlled trials (RCT) of the effectiveness of these techniques for both children and adults. Only nine of these RCTs included statistical tests of the outcomes of treatment between control and intervention groups. Huntley *et al.* (2002) commented that the general standard of research methodology in these trials was poor. Data from some studies suggested that muscular relaxation may improve lung function, but there was no evidence to support the use of hypnosis, autogenic training, or biofeedback.

Yorke *et al.* (2007) reviewed 14 RCTs including 617 adults. Those using relaxation therapy as the intervention ($n = 7$ studies) reported that the use of "as needed" medications was reduced in the intervention group. Three of the relaxation studies also used a measure of lung function (FEV_1) as the outcome measure but no significant difference between the intervention groups was found on this measure.

In response to the lack of evidence of efficacy, Lahmann *et al.* (2009) reported an RCT of 64 patients with allergic asthma assigned to functional relaxation (FR), guided imagery (GI), both modalities (FR/GI), and a placebo relaxation technique in a single blind design. The study was designed to detect differences in specific airway resistance. FR is a somato-psychotherapeutic intervention believed to deliver therapeutic effects by positive stimulation of the autonomic nervous system as well as by facilitating proprioceptive awareness. Minute movements of small joints are performed during relaxed expiration, accompanied by focus on the perceived differences of body feelings triggered by these movements. The GI intervention consisted of a series of standardized guided images targeting the airways. These included positive visualization of a situation, imagining the mast cells (part of the immune system) helping their hypersensitive lungs, and imagining a better physical condition in future. The placebo relaxation technique involved performing isotonic exercises. Each group had a 1 hour weekly session for 4 weeks and they were followed up for 4 months. The FR group showed a significant improvement in lung function which remained stable at 4 months. The underlying mechanism of the improvement is not as yet understood.

Few studies of CBT in asthma have been conducted. Yorke *et al.* (2007) combined two studies to give a sample of 48 patients treated with CBT. They reported that quality of life improved after CBT, but not measures of physical functioning such as FEV_1. This is an important outcome of therapy even if physical functioning is not improved. The two studies reviewed are now old and should be replicated with a larger sample.

There are many different forms of biofeedback intervention, few of which have been evaluated in the treatment of asthma. Lehrer *et al.* (2004) randomized 94 adults to four groups: (group 1) a full protocol with heart rate variability (HRV) biofeedback and abdominal breathing through pursed lips and prolonged exhalation, (group 2) HRV biofeedback alone, (group 3) placebo electroencephalogram (EEG) feedback, and (group 4) a wait-list control. All participants had 1 hour weekly sessions. Spirometry (a measure of lung function) was performed weekly for all groups. The participants in the two biofeedback groups both improved relative to the two control groups on the measure of lung function and required less medication.

Biofeedback was also found to improve measures of lung function according to Yorke *et al.*'s (2007) meta-analysis. Their biofeedback conclusion was based on a combined total of 51 patients, whose peak expiratory flow was found to improve after biofeedback interventions.

Summary

Transient strong emotions can bring on an asthma attack due to the impact of hyperventilation on over-reactive bronchial tubes. Asthmatics are more likely to suffer from anxiety, panic attacks, depression, and negative affectivity than healthy people, but it remains unclear whether these negative emotions are results or causes of the asthma. Depression and anxiety symptoms are markedly more common among asthmatic adults than healthy adults. Panic attacks may arise from the experience of asthma attacks.

Although they often do, asthmatics should not smoke cigarettes, partly because tobacco smoke can trigger an attack and partly because smoking reduces lung volume and makes anti-inflammatory medication less effective. Targeting smoking and encouraging asthmatics to quit is an important clinical intervention.

Asthma cannot be cured, only managed, but a substantial proportion of patients do not understand this, believing that they suffer the disease only when symptoms are present. Asthma management could be considerably improved with a great improvement in quality of life for patients and saving of health costs to the community. The use of written AAPs, a well-established intervention, is declining in frequency. At present asthma education is the primary psychological intervention among adults, but the quality and effectiveness of the education provided is variable.

Psychological interventions are always used alongside drug therapy in asthma. Given the clear evidence that intense emotion triggers attacks, and a need for support in coping with a difficult chronic illness, it would seem reasonable that psychological interventions would be both widespread and helpful. This is not the case at present because there is limited, if any, convincing evidence for the effectiveness of psychological interventions in asthma. Poor methodology including small groups, lack of baseline measures, failure to randomize participants, and the use of nonstandardized psychological tests is commonly found in research in this area. Recent meta-analyses of the effectiveness of a wide range of psychological interventions for both adults and children have shown an urgent need for large-scale, properly controlled trials of well-described psychological interventions.

Useful Websites

Asthma Management Handbook, www.nationalasthma.org.au/cms/index.php
National Asthma Council of Australia, www.nationalasthma.org.au
Provides access to information about the global burden of asthma, www.ginasthma.com

References

Aboussafy, D., Campbell, T., Lavole, F., Aboud, F., & Ditto, B. (2005). Airflow and autonomic responses to stress and relaxation in asthma: The impact of stressor type. *International Journal of Psychophysiology, 57,* 195–201.

AIHW. (2010). *Australia's Health 2010.* Cat. no. AUS 122. Canberra: Australian Institute of Health and Welfare.

Alexander, F. (1950). *Psychosomatic Medicine.* New York: Norton.

Alexander, F. (1962). The development of psychosomatic medicine. *Journal of Psychosomatic Medicine, 23,* 13–24.

Alvarez, G. G., & Fitzgerald, J. M. (2007). A systematic review of the psychological risk factors associated with near fatal asthma or fatal asthma. *Respiration, 74,* 228–236.

Brown, E. S., Murray, M., Carmody, T. J., Kennard, B. D., Hughes, C. W. *et al.* (2008). The Quick Inventory of Depressive Symptomatology-Self-report: a psychometric evaluation in patients with asthma and major depressive disorder. *Annals of Allergy, Asthma, & Immunology, 100*(5), 433–438.

Burgess, J. A., Walters, E. H., Byrnes, G. B., Giles, G. G. Jenkins, M. A., Abramson, M. J. *et al.* (2007). Childhood adiposity predicts adult onset current asthma in females: A 25 year prospective study. *European Respiratory Journal, 29,* 668–675.

Cooper, C. L., Parry, G. D., Saul, C., Morice, A. H., Hutchcroft, B. J., Moore, J., & Esmonde, L. (2007). Anxiety and panic fear in adults with asthma: prevalence in primary care. *BMC Family Practice, 8,* 62–68.

Drotar, D. (2006). Psychological interventions in childhood chronic illness. In *Psychological Intervention: Asthma* (pp. 123–138). Washington DC: American Psychological Association.

Fardy, H. J. (2003). Asthma action plans. *Australian Family Physician, 32,* 469.

Heiner, M. M. (2007). Key barriers to optimal management of adult asthma in Australia: Physician and patient perspectives. *Current Medical Research and Opinion, 23,* 1799–1898.

Horne, R., Price, D., Cleland, J., Costa, R., Covey, D., Gruffydd-Jones, K. *et al.* (2007). Can asthma control be improved by understanding the patient's perspective? *BMC, 7.* www.biomedcentral.com.ezproxy.lib .monash.edu.au/1471-2466/7/8.

Huntley, A., White, A. R., & Ernst, E. (2002). Relaxation therapies for asthma: A systematic review. *Thorax, 57,* 127–131.

James, A. L., Palmer, L. J., Kicic, E., Maxwell, P. S., Lagain, S. E., Ryan, G. F., & Musk, A. W. (2005). Decline in lung function in the Busselton health study: The effects of asthma and cigarette smoking. *American Journal of Respiratory Critical Care Medicine, 171,* 109–114.

Janssens, T., Verleden, G., de Peuter, S., van Diest, I., & van den Bergh, O. (2009). Inaccurate perception of asthma symptoms: A cognitive affective framework and implications for asthma treatment. *Clinical Psychology Review, 29,* 317–327.

Kozyrskyj, A. L., Mai, X. M., McGrath, P., Hayglass, K. T., Becker, A. B., & MacNeil, B. (2008). Continued exposure to maternal distress in early life is associated with an increased risk of childhood asthma. *American Journal of Respiratory & Critical Care Medicine, 177,* 142–147.

Lahmann. C., Nickel, M., Schuster, T., Sauer, N., Ronel, J., Noll-Hussong, M. *et al.* (2009). Functional relaxation and guided imagery as complementary therapy in asthma: a randomized controlled clinical trial. *Psychotherapy and Psychosomatics, 78,* 233–239.

Lehrer, P., Vaschillo, E., Vaschillo, B., Lu, S., Scardella, A., Siddique, M., & Habib, R. (2004). Biofeedback treatment for asthma. *Chest, 126*, 352–361.

Mancuso, C. A., Rincon, M., Robbins, L., & Charlson, M. E. (2003). Patients' expectations of asthma treatment. *Journal of Asthma, 40*, 873–881.

Marks, G. B., Abramson, M. J., Jenkins, C. R., Kenny, P., Mellis, C. M., Ruffin *et al.* (2007). Asthma management and outcomes in Australia: a nationwide telephone survey. *Respirology, 12*, 212–219.

McLeish, A. C., & Zvolensky, M. J. (2010). Asthma and cigarette smoking: A review of the empirical literature. *Journal of Asthma, 47*, 345–361.

Paasche-Orlow, M., Riekert, K., Bilderback, A., & Chanmugam, A. (2005). Tailored education may reduce health literacy disparities in asthma self management. *American Journal of Respiratory and Critical Care Medicine 172*, 980–987.

Smith, L., Bosnic-Anticevich, S. Z., Mitchell, B., Saini, B., Krass, I., & Armour, C. (2007). Treating asthma with a self-management model of illness behaviour in an Australian community pharmacy setting. *Social Science and Medicine, 64*, 1501–1511.

Vincent, S. D., Toelle, B. G., Aroni, R. A., Jenkins C. R., & Reddel, H. K. (2006). 'Exasperations' of asthma: A qualitative study of patient language about worsening asthma. *Medical Journal of Australia, 184*(9), 451–455.

Warrier M. R., & Hershey, G. K. (2008). Asthma genetics: Personalizing medicine. *Journal of Asthma, 45*, 257–264.

Yorke, J., Fleming, S. L., &, Shuldham, C. (2007). Psychological interventions for adults with asthma: A systematic review. *Respiratory Medicine, 101*, 1–14.

32

Enhancing Adherence to Medications

Mitchell K. Byrne

Keep a watch also on the faults of the patients, which often make them lie about the taking of things prescribed.

(Hippocrates of Cos, *c*.400 BC)

Medication is an essential tool in the clinician's armamentarium yet it is estimated that 50% of patients with a chronic health condition fail to adhere to prescribed treatments. This chapter outlines what we mean by adherence and the implications of nonadherence in chronic health conditions. Difficulties in measuring adherence are discussed, followed by a brief review of theoretical models used to explain nonadherence. The chapter concludes with a discussion of the major practical issues that affect patient adherence and strategies for clinical intervention.

Defining Adherence

Adherence to treatment has been defined as "the extent to which patients follow the instructions they are given for prescribed treatments" (Haynes *et al.*, 2005, p. 2). Within this definition it is possible to recognize four types of adherence behavior: adoption, consistency, amount, and cessation (Martin *et al.*, 2000). Adoption reflects the number of prescriptions filled for the patient. Consistency relates to how reliably the patient takes their medication on a day-to-day basis over a specified period of time and picks up on fluctuations in medication-taking behavior. Amount refers to medication taken over a cumulative period. "Amount" of adherence can reflect great variations in behavior in that the patient may accumulate a near normal dose of medication, while varying widely (both over and under dose) on a daily basis. Finally, cessation of medication or "dropout" can reflect permanently or temporarily stopping the medication.

Adherence and nonadherence are not seen as polar phenomena. Rather, adherence exists on a continuum from completely adherent, through levels of partial adherence, to not taking medication at all (Aslani & du Pasquier, 2002). In addition, both the *form* and *intentionality* of nonadherence

Applied Topics in Health Psychology, First Edition. Edited by M. L. Caltabiano and L. Ricciardelli.
© 2013 John Wiley & Sons, Ltd. Published 2013 by John Wiley & Sons, Ltd.

may vary. For example, exceeding recommended doses or consuming medications in a single dose rather than spread across the day may be seen as nonadherence. Further, patients may vary on the degree of intentionality with respect to nonadherence, with some patients *intending* to take their medication as prescribed but failing to do so (due, for example, to forgetting) and others *intending* (consciously deciding) not to take their medication as prescribed (Aslani & du Pasquier, 2002).

Nonadherence in Chronic Illness

Within conventional medicine, the use of pharmacotherapy remains an essential feature of clinical practice. However, medications are only effective if they are appropriately used by patients. High rates of nonadherence have been observed in conditions as diverse as glaucoma (Kowing *et al.*, 2010), hypertension (Pladevall *et al.*, 2010), and asthma (Park *et al.*, 2010) and is as much a problem for children and adolescents as it is for adults (Dean *et al.*, 2010). Across chronic medical conditions, nonadherence to prescribed medicines accounts for a significant proportion of treatment failure (Balkrishnan, 2005) and is associated with increased emergency department visits and hospitalizations (Patel & Zed, 2002; Sokol *et al.*, 2005). Poor adherence is found in preventative medicine as well as acute and chronic healthcare regimens (Dunbar-Jacob, 1993) and remains a key predictor of relapse in major mental health disorders (Ascher-Svanum *et al.*, 2006). Generally, adherence rates for prescribed medicines average 50% (Cutler & Everett, 2010; World Health Organization, 2003) and may cost as much as US$300 billion annually (Balkrishnan & Jayawant, 2007).

Difficulties with adherence are pronounced in older patients who are more likely to experience chronic health problems, with between 70 and 80% of persons over the age of 65 taking at least one prescription medicine (Kaufman *et al.*, 2002). Older patients often have additional impediments to their adherence, such as physical and cognitive changes, which necessitate individually designed or tailored treatment programs (Ruppar *et al.*, 2008). The success of efforts to promote self-management of chronic health conditions needs to also consider to whom the patient attributes responsibility for their healthcare, which may not always be "the self" (Audulv *et al.*, 2010).

Measuring Adherence

The measurement of adherence, particularly in clinical, ecologically valid studies, remains a major challenge in adherence research. It is generally agreed that there is no recognized "best method" for assessing adherence (Byerly *et al.*, 2007). Estimates of adherence by prescribing physicians have been found to be inaccurate (Roth & Caron, 1978) as have pill counts (Morisky *et al.*, 1989). Physiological measures often reflect only recent medication-taking behavior (Urquhart, 1994). The most advanced method of medication monitoring to date – the Medication Events Monitoring System (MEMS®; Apex Corporation, Fremont, CA, USA) – involves an electronic record of each occasion the top of a medicine container is opened. However, this does not provide information about whether the medication is actually taken (Svarstad *et al.*, 1999).

The measurement of adherence can be broadly ascribed to two categories of activity: objective measures of medication-taking, such as pill counts and electronic monitoring; and subjective measures of medication use, such as clinician ratings or patient questionnaire (Sajatovic *et al.*, 2010). Adherence may also be predicted by patient attitudes and beliefs as they relate to treatment (Byrne *et al.*, 2008) or from their level of insight into their need for treatment (Byrne &

Deane, 2011). While there appears to be no superior method to gain an exact measurement of medication adherence, self-report measures, particularly questionnaires, are the most efficient and cost-effective method of assessing medication adherence (Thompson *et al.*, 2000). Given that one of the goals of adherence measurement is to identify opportunities for the enhancement of adherence behavior, self-report measures which include attitude and belief dimensions, such as the Beliefs about Medicines Questionnaire (BMQ; Horne *et al.*, 1999), may be particularly useful (Sajatovic *et al.*, 2010).

In addition to measures which identify current adherence behavior, several recent measures have emerged which seek to predict which patients are likely to experience difficulties with adherence to treatment. For example, the ASK-20 Adherence Barrier Survey (Hahn *et al.*, 2008; Matza *et al.*, 2008) has proven useful in identifying barriers to adherence across a range of chronic health conditions, including asthma, depression, diabetes, and congestive heart failure. Similarly, McHorney (2009) has developed the Adherence Estimator, a three-item screening instrument which enables healthcare providers to identify the propensity to adhere to medication among patients with chronic illness. Finally, Byrne and his colleagues have developed a behavioral rating scale which can be used to predict inpatient engagement with medications among psychiatric patients (Byrne *et al.*, 2009).

Ultimately, the choice of the measure of adherence should be based not only on its psychometric properties, but also on its utility with respect to the researcher or clinicians goals (Farmer, 1999). In general, it is best that measures of adherence employ a continuous scale so that variations in levels of adherence can be assessed (Balkrishnan & Jayawant, 2007). Given that self-report as a single measure of adherence has unacceptably low sensitivity (Stewart, 1987), when using self-report measures it is preferable to combine them with other sources of data or related domains such as clinician reports or patient attitudes (Svarstad *et al.*, 1999). This might include not only multiple patient-based measures, but also the ratings of clinicians, which have been shown to broadly concur with patient ratings (Kampman *et al.*, 2001).

Explaining Nonadherence

The causes of nonadherence are multifaceted, but most explanatory models of adherence behavior focus on the individual patient (Dunbar-Jacob, 1993). It has been observed that there is no consequence of nonadherence that is severe enough to ensure that all patients will adhere to treatment (Cramer & Rosenheck, 1998). Patient behavior sometimes defies logic and common sense, but the field of health psychology has provided a range of models that can be used to explain adherence behavior. Among these, three specific models, collectively referred to as social cognition models, seem pre-eminent: the health belief model (HBM; Strecher *et al.*, 1997), the theory of planned behavior (TpB; Ajzen & Fishbein, 2005), and the self-regulation model (SRM; Leventhal *et al.*, 1998).

Health belief model (HBM)

The HBM proposes that adherence is the result of an individual's cost-benefit analysis of adherence behavior. Further, the HBM suggests that four beliefs contribute to a person's adherence behavior: what benefits they see arising from adherence (benefits, such as reduced symptoms), what barriers they anticipate to adherence (costs; for example, side effects), perceived vulnerability to the illness (susceptibility, such as the extent to which they believe that they might relapse), and perceived severity of the outcome (severity; i.e., how bad they appraise an illness incident would be). Higher adherence is expected when the person sees themselves as more susceptible to illness, the more severe they appraise the consequences of the illness, the greater the expected treatment benefits, and the lower the assessed barriers to adherence (relative to benefit). These beliefs are influenced by other variables such as the individual's personality, the opinion of others, and their previous experiences.

Theory of planned behavior (TpB)

The fundamental premise of the TpB is that an individual's behavior may be predicted by their intentions. The intention to perform a behavior is a function of the person's attitude toward the behavior (expected value), his/her subjective norm in relation to the behavior, and the individual's perceived ability to perform the behavior, termed behavioral control. While the TpB assumes that an individual's intention to behave in a given fashion is directly related to their beliefs about engaging in the behavior, there is no assumption that beliefs are *accurate*: they may be biased or irrational. Once beliefs have been formed, behavior-specific attitudes are developed in relation to the specific behavior, appraisals of social norms about the behavior, and perceptions regarding control or ability to perform the behavior. Intentions to engage in the behavior are seen to follow on from these attitudes in a consistent manner.

Self-regulation model (SRM)

According to the SRM, patients' responses to illness are a function of their evaluation of the illness based on their own knowledge and perceptions. Central to the process of responding is the recognition that *illness* (the experience of being unwell) is different to *disease* (a condition involving diagnosed pathology). Illness is a subjective experience that may or may not be associated with physical pathology (disease). When faced with a health threat (being told that one has an illness), the individual must construct a personal representation of the illness. Illness representations consist of the patient's own "common sense" beliefs about their illness. This "cognitive" level of illness representation is paralleled by the generation and processing of concomitant emotional responses.

In seeking to understand nonadherence (and therefore intervene to enhance adherence), social cognition models have identified a range of variables that relate to the individual. These variables, and the implications for intervention, are detailed in Table 32.1.

Causes of Nonadherence

Patient factors alone do not fully explain why an individual does or does not adhere to treatment. Generally, four categories are used to capture the variables contributing to treatment adherence. These include factors associated with the treatment (such as complexity), factors associated with the clinician (such as skill), factors associated with the patient (such as insight), and factors associated with the relationship between clinician and therapist (McDonald *et al.*, 2002). These variables usually overlap (Meichenbaum & Turk, 1987), but their influences will be reviewed separately.

Table 32.1 Variables affecting adherence derived from social cognition models*

Variable	Implications	Model
Perceived benefit	Psycho-education, motivational strategies, strategies to enhance "insight" (e.g., cognitive therapy)	HBM
Perceived costs	Motivational strategies, problem solving skills	HBM
Perceived vulnerability	Strategies to enhance insight, psycho-education	HBM
Perceived severity	Psycho-education, motivational strategies	HBM
Beliefs and attitudes	Psycho-education, strategies to enhance "insight" or challenge irrational beliefs (such as cognitive therapy)	TpB
Normative appraisal of others' beliefs	Enhancement of alignment with pro-adherence others (therapeutic alliance with clinician), involvement of carers, destigmatizing mental ill health (normalizing strategies)	TpB
Behavioral control/ self-efficacy	Problem solving strategies, motivational strategies, behavioral strategies (such as "behavioral tailoring")	TpB
Recognition and representation of illness	Psycho-education, strategies to enhance "insight," motivational strategies	SRM

*The interventions listed under Implications are described in the text.

Treatment factors

Treatment factors incorporate a broad range of variables from characteristics of the treatment setting through to the clarity of the prescriber's instructions (Meichenbaum & Turk, 1987). More than 35 years ago, Kasl (1975) asserted that knowledge of the treatment regime can, in and of itself, provide information about the likelihood of adherence. For example, the more complex the medication regimen, the more likely it is that the patient will not adhere. Polypharmacy has been cited as an issue in adherence across chronic health conditions (DiMatteo, 2004). Simplifying medication regimens has proven effective in enhancing adherence in a range of chronic health disorders, such as glaucoma (Robin *et al.*, 2007) and AIDS (Battaglioli-DeNero, 2007). It has been suggested that increasing from as few as one to two doses per day is enough to affect adherence (MacKean & Elkington, 1983).

There is also substantial research on the influence of side effects on adherence. Side effects are generally considered an issue across chronic health conditions (e.g., heart failure, Wu *et al.*, 2008; blood pressure, Elliott, 2008; and cancer, Faiman, 2007) and have received considerable attention in the management of severe mental illness (Hamer & Haddad, 2007). While it is generally accepted that negative side effects can reduce patient adherence and should be managed by the clinician (Weinmann *et al.*, 2005), clinicians often overestimate the extent to which side effects influence individual adherence decisions. Side effects are a relatively uncommon reason reported by patients for nonadherence (Cooper *et al.*, 2007) and are not a consistent predictor of adherence in research studies (Lacro *et al.*, 2002).

Other "treatment"-related issues that influence adherence include accessibility, which refers to how easy it is to get the medications. Issues such as difficulty travelling to the pharmacy or doctor and not having sufficient funds to purchase the medications are examples of accessibility barriers to adherence. Finally, a commonly reported finding in chronic illness is that when patients are asymptomatic, they waiver in their adherence to treatment. This is often explained in terms of the difficulty relating treatment to illness when no symptoms are apparent or where symptoms are not ego-dystonic. Cardiovascular disease is a good example of chronic illnesses where symptoms may not be detected by patients and where nonadherence to medications is a major challenge (Munger *et al.*, 2007).

Patient factors

There is a substantial literature on patient-related factors associated with adherence. This is in part due to the tendency of health researchers to focus on patient-centered reasons for nonadherence (Dunbar-Jacob, 1993), and because the models of health-related behavior, such as those reviewed above, focus on aspects of the individual. A consistent finding in the literature is an association between poor medication adherence and comorbid substance abuse (Janssen *et al.*, 2006). This is particularly a problem in severe mental health disorders, where up to 50% of patients diagnosed with schizophrenia meet criteria for a comorbid diagnosis of substance-abuse disorder (Hunt *et al.*, 2002).

Another patient-related factor associated with poor adherence has been lack of insight into illness (McEvoy, 1998). Insight is a term associated with various meanings, both medical and nonmedical. However, most definitions relate to an individual's understanding of a given situation. While much of the research into insight has focused on mental health (Amador *et al.*, 1994), lack of insight into the need to maintain treatment in order to maintain health is not confined to patients with psychotic illnesses. For example, Shaw (2005) observes that glaucoma patients often need to be convinced that there is something wrong with them before they will adhere to preventative treatments.

Poor insight has been associated with reduced help seeking behavior, dangerousness to self and others, reduced treatment adherence, and a generally poorer prognosis (Yen *et al.*, 2002). Most frequently, it is the patient's absence of an understanding that there is a need for treatment that predicts nonadherence in chronic illness (Buckley *et al.*, 2007). Insight problems are likely to influence attitudes to treatment and the interplay of attitude and insight is important given the association between attitudes toward medication and medication adherence.

Attitude to medication

Attitude to health behaviors have been central in social cognition models (see above) and thus are salient patient factors in relation to adherence behavior. Patients' cognitions (beliefs and attitudes) can have a profound affect on treatment outcomes – directly through placebo (expectation that a substance or treatment will help when in fact it is inert) and nocebo (expectation that a substance or treatment will cause harm when in fact it is inert) effects and indirectly through their influence on patient behavior (Horne, 2006). Clinicians should not assume that they share similar beliefs about medications with their patients (Ramström *et al.*, 2006). Patients hold complex beliefs about medicines and their failure to take medications may be the result of "misguided" beliefs (Grunfeld *et al.*, 2005).

Cognitive skills

Cognitive skills refer to a range of memory and executive functions that allow humans to undertake complex behaviors. This includes planning a sequence of tasks, overcoming unanticipated obstacles, and remembering to do things. Cognitive functioning can be affected by dementia, intellectual disability, substance misuse, or the aspects of mental disorders, such as concentration and memory in depression or schizophrenia (Neufeld, 2007). Cognitive skills deficits enhance the likelihood of nonadherence to treatment (Wallace *et al.*, 2006) and such deficits have been attributed to nonadherence in a range of samples and disorders (for example, older adults, Mackin & Arean, 2007; patients with chronic heart failure, Callegari *et al.*, 2002; and patients with HIV, Waldrop-Valverde *et al.*, 2006).

Motivation

A frequently cited factor in health behavior change is the importance of "patient motivation" (Rollnick *et al.*, 2000) with motivation being found to be directly related to treatment adherence (Brondolo & Mas, 2001). Motivation has often mistakenly been seen as a trait feature of a person. However, it is generally accepted that motivation is more accurately construed as a state or situational disposition, affected by interpersonal processes and amenable to change (Miller & Rollnick, 2002). The improvement of motivation, through specific motivational enhancement techniques such as motivational interviewing (MI), has contributed to enhanced treatment adherence in a range of studies (Bisonó *et al.*, 2006), supporting the contention that motivation is an influential factor in treatment adherence.

Clinician factors

While patient adherence to prescribed treatments may be influenced by clinician interventions (Petrilla *et al.*, 2005), not all clinicians actively try to enhance patient adherence using research-driven methodologies (Faris & Schopflocher, 1999; Ramström *et al.*, 2006; Weinmann *et al.*, 2005; Stern *et al.*, 1999). Given that medication remains an essential component of treatment of chronic health disorders, it could be asserted that effective implementation of "adherence therapies" would be a core activity of health clinicians. Why this is not so may be due to a multitude of clinician-based factors, including the clinician's own competencies, attitudes, and resources (Byrne *et al.*, 2005). For example, positive or at least non-stigmatizing attitudes toward patients are essential for the development of effective clinician–patient relationships (Buchanan *et al.*, 2007). However, there is no guarantee that clinicians in training hold appropriate attitudes toward patients, nor that they develop them as a consequence of their training relationships (Buchanan *et al.*, 2007). If the clinician's attitudes to medication are negative, it is likely that their ability to work effectively with patients to facilitate medication adherence would be compromised.

Clinicians' beliefs about their own adequacy have also been shown to influence intended engagement in specific professional behaviors. For example, mental health clinicians' engagement in adherence interventions (Byrne *et al.*, 2008), pharmacists' delivery of medication advice and support (Farris & Schopflocher, 1999), pediatric providers' (pediatricians and nurse practitioners) screening of risky adolescent behaviors (Ozer *et al.*, 2004), and the response by healthcare providers to domestic violence victims (Gadomski *et al.*, 2001) are diverse examples of where efficacy beliefs either increase or decrease the given behavior.

Brawley and Culos-Reed (2000) observe that self-efficacy beliefs are not traits of the individual but are sets of beliefs about specific areas of functioning. Self-efficacy does not relate to a quantum of skills but rather utility of possessed skills in a given situation. Self-efficacy can be enhanced through mastery experiences, but in the absence of adequate knowledge and skills training experiences, self-efficacy for a given behavior can be expected to be low, reducing the likelihood of the clinician engaging in the desired behavior. Thus, attention to the needs of the clinician may be as important as the focus on the patient when seeking to improve engagement in treatment.

Relationship factors

Collaborative therapeutic relationships are essential in enhancing adherence (Sajatovic *et al.*, 2005) and there is broad acceptance that the nature of the therapeutic relationship between the treating clinician and the patient has an important impact upon the outcomes of treatment (Ackerman & Hilsenroth, 2001, 2003; Horvath & Bedi, 2002) and may even serve as a predictor of treatment outcome (Howgego *et al.*, 2003). The therapeutic relationship between clinician and patient has been referred to as the "therapeutic alliance." Both the behavior of the clinician in session (Binder & Strupp, 1997) and the clinician's attitudes and expectations influence the development and maintenance of the therapeutic alliance (Brossart *et al.*, 1998). This perspective emphasizes the importance of nonspecific features of therapy (i.e., those unrelated to technique) as well as the need to facilitate clinician behaviors that promote the alliance and clinician attitudes that sustain it.

Skilled use of specific activities within the therapy session may enhance the likelihood of developing a strong therapeutic alliance. For example, significant correlations have been found between poor alliance and the clinician's failure to structure the session (such as through the use of an agenda), address patient resistance (for example by using techniques derived from MI), adopting an inflexible stance (lacking a collaborative framework for intervention), and using destructive interventions (based on coercion) (Eaton *et al.*, 1993). Clinicians' attributes and behaviors that *positively* affect the alliance include the ability to convey to the patient an adequate level of competence (with demonstrable self-confidence), to be responsive and empathic, and to be flexible (Ackerman & Hilsenroth, 2003). Furthermore, clinicians' behaviors such as exploration, reflection, and attending to the patient's past experiences also supported the establishment of the alliance. Overall, collaborative clinician activities are usually associated with the deepening of the therapeutic alliance (Ackerman & Hilsenroth, 2003).

Strategies for the Enhancement of Adherence

The range of adherence interventions that have been reported in the literature fall broadly into three classes or approaches: psycho-educational approaches, behavioral strategies, and cognitive-behavioral interventions.

Psycho-educational approaches

There is good reason to believe that enhanced patient knowledge about medications can play an important role in adherence, especially where the patient holds negative beliefs about treatment (Fernandez *et al.*, 2006). Knowledge can enhance insight, the patient's appreciation of the relationship between symptoms and illness, treatment, and recovery and thus improve motivation to adhere to treatment.

The most successful psycho-educational interventions are those that target both behavioral and attitudinal change. This has been demonstrated by the failure of numerous studies to effect significant changes in adherence or clinical functioning using psycho-education alone (for example,

Mundt *et al.*, 2001). One domain that has recognized the importance of behavioral and attitudinal variables in the success of psycho-educational strategies is that of "health literacy." Health literacy refers to the extent to which individuals have the capacity to obtain, process, and understand health information and services such that they are able to make appropriate health decisions (Rawson *et al.*, 2009). Lower rates of health literacy are associated with generally poorer health status, lower use of preventative and screening health services, increased hospitalization, lower adherence to treatment, and reduced self-management of chronic illness (DeWalt *et al.*, 2004). According to Jorm and colleagues (1997) mental health literacy comprises six facets:

1. recognition of disorder,
2. knowledge and beliefs about causes,
3. knowledge and beliefs about self-help,
4. knowledge and beliefs about professional help,
5. attitudes that facilitate recognition and help-seeking, and
6. knowledge of how to seek information.

Clearly in this model, attitudinal variables play an important role. Furthermore, both recognition of disorder and knowledge and beliefs about causes seem associated with insight, for which perhaps additional (cognitive-behavioral) interventions may be necessary to maximize the benefits of psycho-educational strategies.

Behavioral interventions

Treatment complexity has long been identified as a source of patient nonadherence (Haynes, 1976). It is well known that patients with problems in "executive function," principally due to deficits in the frontal structures, particularly the prefrontal cortex, experience difficulties with attention, memory, abstraction, and planning (Falloon *et al.*, 2007). Executive function deficits may be apparent in patients who are elderly, intellectually disabled, or who have chronic and severe mental health problems (such as depression and psychotic disorders). Given that different patients will have different levels of cognitive functioning (and therefore capacity to tolerate complex treatment regimes), a range of behavioral strategies have emerged to assist patients to overcome their "functional" barriers to adherence. Unlike psycho-educational interventions, behavioral interventions are often tailored specifically to the needs of the individual patient, thus increasing treatment specificity.

One of the core strategies in behavioral self-management is the use of problem solving techniques (Chang & D'Zurilla, 1996). Problem solving training has proven useful and effective for both the treatment and prevention of a wide variety of clinical problems (Falloon *et al.*, 2007). Problem solving interventions aim to change both the individual's "problem orientation" as well as the individual's skills at solving problems. Problem orientation refers to the extent to which the individual perceives everyday life problems as "solvable" and how capable they feel at initiating problem solving strategies (self-efficacy). A particular strength of a problem solving approach is that it is amenable to the use of worksheets and templates, enabling the individual to experience self-efficacy and empowerment in the implementation of problem solving strategies.

Across chronic health conditions, problem solving strategies hold additional benefits relevant to the enhancement of adherence, such as improving readiness to recognize problems (motivation), the normalization of the experience of "problems" in life, and the development of skills in attributing causes of problems accurately (Chang *et al.*, 2004). The process of problem solving also enhances the perception of problems as challenges to be met, as opposed to catastrophes or situations to avoid, and offers the patient an opportunity to improve self-efficacy.

Cognitive-behavioral interventions

Many aspects of cognitive behavior therapies (CBTs) have been incorporated into adherence interventions. Cognitive therapy (Beck, 1964, 1995) is based on the precept that all psychological disorders involve the generation of dysfunctional or distorted thoughts and it is these thoughts which influence mood and behavior. Cognitive-behavioral interventions to improve adherence aim to get patients actively involved in their treatment and seek to work with patients to investigate the range of factors that might influence medication-taking behavior (Gray *et al.*, 2002). Given the apparent benefits of CBT, cognitive and behavioral approaches have formed the basis of most contemporary adherence programs such as compliance therapy (Kemp *et al.*, 1996, 1998), medication management (Gray *et al.*, 2004), and more recently, medication alliance (Byrne *et al.*, 2004; Byrne & Deane, 2011).

MI (Miller & Rollnick, 2002), which has been incorporated into most CBT-based interventions, is a directive counselling style that is patient-centered and collaborative. The core strategy in MI is to assist the patient to understand their reasons for and against a change in behavior, and to make decisions about change that are intrinsically motivated. It is patient-centered as the focus is the concerns and perspectives of the patient, rather than the clinician. While the "therapy" may be directive, the term interviewing is used to capture the process of listening and strategic questioning rather than "teaching" the patient.

MI emphasizes a partnership relationship between the clinician and the patient and seeks to elicit behavior change within the patient by assisting them to explore and resolve ambivalence. Furthermore, MI stresses the importance of supporting the patient to generate arguments for change rather than reliance upon the clinician to generate such information. Essentially, MI draws upon the idea that if a person can talk themselves out of change they may also talk themselves into change.

The process of MI involves the identification of the patient's goals and values and an awareness in the patient of the discrepancies between current behavior (such as nonadherence) and personally relevant goals. From this awareness, the patient, rather than the clinician, generates reasons for behavior change (Burke *et al.*, 2003). Ultimately, the patient's readiness for change is thought to stem from two main factors: the importance of change from the patient's perspective and the patient's confidence in their ability to engage in the change process. MI emphasizes that the clinician must assess both importance and confidence and target intervention to improve both. Confidence relates directly to the patient's self-efficacy and is a good predictor of treatment outcome (Burke *et al.*, 2003).

Summary and Conclusions

The enhancement of adherence to treatment should be a core activity for all health and allied health professionals. There are many interventions which aim to enhance patient adherence and which intervention to choose should be determined from the individual adherence *behaviors* of the patient. Detailed assessment of the factors which predict nonadherence, with recognition of the motivational contingencies influencing the patient's behaviors, is the best strategy to use to determine how to support improved adherence. However, this can be time-consuming and there are brief strategies that the clinician can use which will enhance adherence among a significant proportion of patients, outlined below as "quick tips."

Quick tips

- Provide education about the illness and *how* treatment can assist: encourage the patient to ask questions.
- Listen to the patient's fears and beliefs about treatment and correct false beliefs or irrational fears.
- Check that the patient understands what has been said about the illness and treatment by asking *them* to explain *their* understanding of the situation.
- Make sure all your recommendations are simple, personalized, and built into the patient's daily rituals. Write down in simplified terms what you want the patient to do, when, where, and how often; if possible, show the patient what you want.
- Keep the treatment as simple as possible.
- Use as little jargon as possible and as much reflective listening to the patient as you can: *be a team.*
- Send reminders and follow-up notes (including appointment reminders); for example, using SMS text messaging.
- Communicate with other members of the health team what your treatment plan is so that the patient receives a consistent message.
- Reward any improvement in adherence, not just complete "compliance."

References

Ackerman, S. J., & Hilsenroth, M. J. (2001). A review of therapist characteristics and techniques negatively impacting the therapeutic alliance. *Psychotherapy, 38*, 171–185.

Ackerman, S.J., & Hilsenroth, M.J. (2003). A review of therapist characteristics and techniques positively impacting the therapeutic alliance. *Clinical Psychology Review, 23*, 1–33.

Ajzen, I., & Fishbein, M. (2005). The influence of attitudes on behaviour. In D. Albarracin, B. T. Johnson, & M. P. Zanna (Eds.) *The Handbook of Attitudes* (pp. 173–221). Mahwah, NJ: Lawrence Erlbaum Associates.

Amador, X. F., Flaum, M., Andreasen, N. C., Strauss, D. H., Yale, S. A., Clark, S. C., & Gorman, J. M. (1994). Awareness of illness in schizophrenia and schizoaffective mood disorders. *Archives of General Psychiatry, 51*, 826–836.

Ascher-Svanum, H., Faries, D. E., Zhu, B., Ernst, F. R., Swartz, M. S., & Swanson, J. W. (2006). Medication adherence and long-term functional outcome in the treatment of schizophrenia in usual care. *Journal of Clinical Psychiatry, 67*(3), 453–460.

Aslani, P., & du Pasquier, S. (2002). Compliance, adherence or concordance? *Australian Pharmasicist, 12*, 170–174.

Audulv, A., Asplund, K., & Norbergh, K. (2010). Who's in charge? The role of responsibility attribution in self-management among people with chronic illness. *Patient Education and Counseling, 81*, 94–100.

Balkrishnan, R. (2005). The importance of medication adherence in improving chronic-disease related outcomes: What we know and what we need to further know. *Medical Care, 43*, 517–520.

Balkrishnan, R., & Jayawant, S. S. (2007). Medication adherence research in populations: Measurement issues and other challenges. *Clinical Therapeutics, 29*, 1180–1183.

Battaglioli-DeNero, A. M. (2007) Strategies for improving patient adherence to therapy and long-term patient outcomes. *Journal of the Association of Nurses in AIDS Care, 18*, S17–S22.

Beck, A. T. (1964). Thinking and depression II: Theory and therapy. *Archives of general Psychiatry, 10*, 561–571.

Beck, J. S. (1995). Cognitive therapy: Basics and beyond. New York: Guilford Press.

Binder, J. L., & Strupp, H. H. (1997). " Negative process": A recently discovered and underestimated facet of therapeutic process and outcome in the individual psychotherapy of adults. *Clinical Psychology Science and Practice, 4*, 121–139.

Bisonó, A. M., Manuel, J. K., & Forcehimes, A. A. (2006). Promoting treatment adherence through motivational interviewing. In W. T. O'Donohue & E. R. Levensky (Eds.), *Promoting Treatment Adherence: A Practical Handbook for Health Care Providers* (pp. 71–84). *Thousand Oaks, CA*: Sage.

Brawley, L. R., & Culos-Reed, N. (2000). Studying adherence to therapeutic regimens: Overview, theories, recommendations. *Controlled Clinical Trials, 21*, 156S-163S.

Brondolo, E., & Mas, F. (2001). Cognitive-behavioral strategies for improving medication adherence in patients with bipolar disorder. *Cognitive and Behavioral Practice, 8*, 137–147.

Brossart, D. F., Willson, V. L., Patton, M. J., Kivlighan, D. M., & Multon, K. D. (1998). A time series model of the working alliance: A key process in short-term psychoanalytic counselling. *Psychotherapy, 35*, 197–205.

Buchanan, D., Rohr, L., Stevak, L., & Sai, T. (2007). Documenting attitude changes towards homeless people: Comparing two standardised surveys. *Medical Education, 41*, 346–348.

Buckley, P. F., Wirshing, D. A., Bhushan, P., Pierre, J. M., & Wirshing, W. C. (2007). Lack of insight in schizophrenia: Impact on treatment adherence. *CNS Drugs, 21*, 129–141.

Burke, B. L., Arkowitz, H., & Menchola, M. (2003). The efficacy of motivational interviewing: A meta-analysis of controlled clinical trials. *Journal of Consulting and Clinical Psychology, 71*, 843–861.

Byerly, M. J., Thompson, A., Carmody, T., Bugno, R., Erwin, T., Kashner, M., & Rush, A.J. (2007). Validity of electronically monitored medication adherence and conventional adherence measures in schizophrenia. *Psychiatric Services, 58*, 844–847.

Byrne, M. K., & Deane, F. P. (2011). Enhancing patient adherence: Outcomes of medication alliance training on therapeutic alliance, insight, adherence and psychopathology with mental health patients. *International Journal of Mental Health Nursing, 20*, 284–295.

Byrne, M. K., Deane, F. D., Lambert, G., & Coombs, T. (2004). Enhancing medication adherence: Clinician outcomes from the 'Medication Alliance' training program. *Australian & New Zealand Journal of Psychiatry, 36*, 246–253.

Byrne, M. K., Deane, F. P., & Coombs, T. (2005). Nurse's beliefs and knowledge about medications are associated with their difficulties when using patient adherence strategies. *Journal of Mental Health, 14*, 513–521.

Byrne, M. K., Deane, F. P., & Caputi, P. (2008). Mental health clinicians' beliefs about medicines, attitudes and expectations of improved medication adherence in patients. *Evaluation and the Health Professions, 31*, 390–403.

Byrne, M. K., Deane, F. P., Willis, A., Hawkins, B., & Quinn, R. (2009). Preliminary reliability of an observer rating scale for assessing medication adherence on psychiatric wards. *Journal of Evaluation in Clinical Practice, 15*, 246–251.

Callegari, S., Majani, G., Giardini, A., Pierobon, A., Opasich, C., Cobelli, F., & Tavazzi, L. (2002). Relationship between cognitive impairment and clinical status in chronic heart failure patients. *Monaldi Archives for Chest Disease, 58*, 19–25.

Chang, E. C., & D'Zurilla, T. J. (1996) Relations between problem orientation and optimism, pessimism, and trait affectivity: A construct validation study. *Behaviour Research and Therapy, 34*, 185–194.

Chang, E. C., Downey, C. A., & Salata, J. L. (2004). Social problem solving and positive psychological functioning: Looking at the positive side of problem solving. In E. C. Chang, T. J. D'Zurilla, & L. J. Sanna (Eds.), Social Problem Solving: Theory, Research, and Training (pp. 99–116). Washington DC: American Psychological Association.

Cooper, C., Bebbington, P., King, M., Brugha, T., Meltzer, H., Bhugra, D., & Jenkins, R. (2007). Why people do not take their psychotropic drugs as prescribed: Results of the 2000 National Psychiatric Morbidity Survey. *Acta Psychiatrica Scandinavica, 116*, 47–53.

Cramer, J. A., & Rosenheck, M. D. (1998). Compliance with medication regimes for mental and physical disorders. *Psychiatric Services, 49*, 196–201.

Cutler, D. M., & Everett, W. (2010). Thinking outside the pillbox: Medication adherence as a priority for health care reform. *New England Journal of Medicine, 362*, 1553–1555.

Dean, A. J., Walters, J., & Hall, A. (2010). A systematic review of interventions to enhance medication adherence in children and adolescents with chronic illness. *Archives of Disease in Childhood, 95*, 717–723.

DeWalt, D. A., Berkman, N. D., Sheridan, S., Lohr, K. N., & Pignone, M. P. (2004). Literacy and health outcomes: A systematic review of the literature. *Journal of General Internal Medicine, 19*, 1228–1239.

DiMatteo, M. R. (2004). Variations in patients' adherence to medical recommendations: A quantitative review of 50 years of research. *Medical Care, 42*, 200–209.

Dunbar-Jacob, J. (1993). Contributions to patient adherence: Is it time to share the blame? *Health Psychology, 12*, 91–92.

Eaton, T. T., Abeles, N., & Gutfreund, M. J. (1993). Negative indicators, therapeutic alliance, and therapy outcome. *Psychotherapy Research, 3*, 115–123.

Elliott, W. J. (2008). What factors contribute to inadequate control of elevated blood pressure? *Journal of Clinical Hypertension, 10*(S1), 20–26.

Faiman, B. (2007). Clinical updates and nursing considerations for patients with multiple myeloma. *Clinical Journal of Oncology Nursing, 11*, 831–840.

Falloon, I. R. H., Barbieri, L., Boggian, I., & Lamonaca, D. (2007). Problem solving for schizophrenia: Rationale and review. *Journal of Mental Health, 16*, 553–568.

Farmer, K. C. (1999). Methods for measuring and monitoring medication regimen adherence in clinical trials and clinical practice. *Clinical Therapeutics, 21*, 1074–1090.

Farris, K. B., & Schopflocher, D. P. (1999). Between intention and behavior: An application of community pharmacists' assessment of pharmaceutical care. *Social Science & Medicine, 49*, 55–66.

Fernandez, R. S., Evans, V., Griffiths, R. D., & Mostacchi, M. S. (2006). Educational interventions for mental health consumers receiving psychotropic medication: A review of the evidence. *International Journal of Mental Health Nursing, 15*, 70–80.

Gadomski, A. M., Wolff, D., Tripp, M., Lewis, C., & Short, L. M. (2001). Changes in health care providers' knowledge, attitudes, beliefs, and behaviors regarding domestic violence, following a multifaceted intervention. *Academic Medicine, 76*, 1045–1052.

Gray, R., Wykes, T., & Gournay, K. (2002). From compliance to concordance: A review of the literature on interventions to enhance compliance with antipsychotic medication. *Journal of Psychiatric Mental Health Nursing, 9*, 277–284.

Gray, R., Wykes, T., Edmonds, M., Leese, M., & Gournay, K. (2004). Effect of a medication management training package for nurses on clinical outcomes for patients with schizophrenia: Cluster randomised controlled trial. *British Journal of Psychiatry, 185*, 157–162.

Grunfeld, E. A., Hunter, M. S., Sikka, P., & Mittal S. (2005). Adherence beliefs among breast cancer patients taking tamoxifen. *Patient Education and Counselling, 59*, 97–102.

Hahn, S. R., Park, J., Skinner, E. P., Yu-Isenberg, K. S., Weaver, M. B., Crawford, B., & Flowers, P. W. (2008). Development of the ASK-20 Adherence Barrier Survey. *Current Medical Research and Opinion, 24*, 2127–2138.

Hamer, S., & Haddad, P. M. (2007). Adverse effects of antipsychotics as outcome measures. *British Journal of Psychiatry, 50*, S64–S70.

Haynes, R. B. (1976). A critical review of the 'determinant' of patients' compliance with therapeutic regimens. In R. B. Haynes, & D. L. Sackett (Eds.), *Compliance with Therapeutic Regimens* (pp. 27–39). Baltimore, MD: John Hopkins University Press.

Haynes, R. B., Yao, X., Degani, A., Kripalani, S., Garg, A., & McDonald, H. P. (2005). Interventions for enhancing medication adherence. *Cochrane Database of Systematic Reviews, 4*, CD000011.

Horne, R. (2006). Beliefs and adherence to treatment: The challenge for research and clinical practice. In: P. W. Halligan and M. Aylward (Eds.), *The Power of Beliefs: Psychosocial Influence on Illness, Disability and Medicine* (pp. 115–136). Oxford: Oxford University Press.

Horne, R., Weinman, J., & Hankins, M. (1999). The Beliefs about Medicines Questionnaire: The development and evaluation of a new method for assessing the cognitive representation of medication. *Psychology and Health, 14*, 1–24.

Horvath, A. O., & Bedi, R. P. (2002). The alliance. In J. C. Norcross (Ed.), *Psychotherapy Relationships that Work: Therapist Contributions and Responsiveness to Patients* (pp. 37–69). New York: Oxford University Press.

Howgego, I. M., Yellowlees, P., Owen, C., Meldrum, L., & Dark, F. (2003). The therapeutic alliance: The key to effective patient outcome? A descriptive review of the evidence in community mental health case management. *Australian and New Zealand Journal of Psychiatry, 37,* 169–183.

Hunt, G. E., Bergen, J., & Bashir, M. (2002). Medication compliance and comorbid substance abuse in schizophrenia: Impact on community survival 4 years after relapse. *Schizophrenia Research, 54,* 253–264.

Janssen, B., Gaebel, W., Haerter, M., Komaharadi, F., Lindel, B., & Weinmann, S. (2006). Evaluation of factors influencing medication compliance in inpatient treatment of psychotic disorders. *Psychopharmacology, 187,* 229–236.

Jorm, A. F., Korten, A. E., Jacomb, P. A., Christensen, H., Rodgers, B., & Pollitt, P. (1997). 'Mental health literacy': A survey of the public's ability to recognise mental disorders and their beliefs about the effectiveness of treatment. *Medical Journal of Australia, 166,* 182–186.

Kampman, O., Lehtinen, K., & Lassila, V. (2001). The reliability of compliance assessments performed by doctors and patients during neuroleptic treatment: a comparison of compliance ratings. *Acta Psychiatrica Scandinavica, 104,* 299–304.

Kasl, S. V. (1975). Issues in patient adherence to health care regimens. *Journal of Human Stress, 1,* 5–18.

Kaufman, D. W., Kelly, J. P., Rosenberg, L., Anderson, T. E., & Mitchell, A. A. (2002). Recent patterns of medication use in the ambulatory adult population of the United States: The Slone survey. *Journal of the American Medical Association, 287,* 337–344.

Kemp, R., Hayward, P., Applewhaite, G., Everitt, B., & David, A. (1996). Compliance therapy in psychotic patients: Randomised controlled trial. *British Medical Journal, 312,* 345–349.

Kemp, R., Kirov, G., Everitt, B., Hayward, P., & David, A. (1998). A randomised controlled trial of compliance therapy: 18-month follow-up. *British Journal of Psychiatry, 172,* 413–419.

Kowing, D., Messer, D., Slagle, S., & Wasik, A. (2010). Programs to optimize adherence in glaucoma. *Optometry, 81,* 339–350.

Lacro, J. P., Dunn, L. B., Dolder, C. R., Leckband, S. G., & Jeste, D. V. (2002). Prevalence of and risk factors for medication nonadherence in patients with schizophrenia: A comprehensive review of recent literature. *Journal of Clinical Psychiatry, 63,* 892–909.

Leventhal, H., Leventhal, E. A., & Contrada, R. J. (1998). Self-regulation, health and behaviour: A perceptual-cognitive approach. *Psychology and Health, 13,* 717–733.

MacKean, J. M., & Elkington, A. R. (1983). Compliance with treatment of patients with chronic open-angle glaucoma. *British Journal of Ophthalmology, 67,* 46–49.

Mackin, R. S., & Arean, P. A. (2007). Cognitive and psychiatric predictors of medical treatment adherence among older adults in primary care clinics. *International Journal of Geriatric Psychiatry, 22,* 55–60.

Martin, K. A., Bowen, D. J., Dunbar-Jacob, J., & Perri, M. G. (2000). Who will adhere? Key issues in the study and prediction of adherence in randomized controlled trials. *Controlled Clinical Trials, 21,* 195S–199S.

Matza, L. S., Yu-Isenberg, K. S., Coyne, K. S., Park, J., Wakefield, J., Skinner, E. P., & Wolever, R. Q. (2008). Further testing of the reliability and validity of the ASK-20 adherence barrier questionnaire in a medical center outpatient population. *Current Medical Research and Opinion, 24,* 3197–3206.

McDonald, H. P., Garg, A. X., & Haynes, R. B. (2002). Interventions to enhance patient adherence to medication prescriptions. *Journal of the American Medical Association, 288,* 2868–2879.

McEvoy, J. P. (1998). The relationship between insight in psychosis and compliance with medications. In X. F. Amador & A. S. Anthony (Eds.), *Insight and Psychosis* (pp. 289–306). New York: Oxford University Press.

McHorney, C. (2009). The Adherence Estimator: A brief, proximal screener for patient propensity to adhere to prescription medications for chronic disease. *Current Medical Research and Opinion, 25,* 215–238.

Meichenbaum, D., & Turk, D. C. (1987). Treatment adherence: Terminology, incidence and conceptualisation. In M. Meichenbaum & D. Turk (Eds.), *Facilitating Treatment Adherence* (pp. 19–39). New York: Plenum Press.

Miller, W. R., & Rollnick, S. (2002). *Motivational Interviewing: Preparing People for Change* (2nd edn.). New York: The Guilford Press.

Morisky, D. E., Green, L. W., & Levine, D. M. (1989). Concurrent and predictive validity of a self-reported measure of medication adherence. *Medical Care, 24,* 67–73.

Mundt, J. C., Clarke, G. N., Burroughs, D., Brennman, D. O., & Griest, J. H. (2001). Effectiveness of antidepressant pharmacotherapy: The impact of medication compliance and patient education. *Depression and Anxiety, 13*, 1–10.

Munger, M. A., Van Tassell, B. W., & LaFleur, J. (2007). Medication nonadherence: An unrecognized cardiovascular risk. *Medscape General Medicine, 9*, 58.

Neufeld, R. W. (2007). *Advances in Clinical Cognitive Science: Formal Modeling of Process and Symptoms.* Washington DC: American Psychological Association.

Ozer, E. M., Adams, S. H., Gardner, L. R., Mailloux, D. E., Wibbelsman, C. J., & Irwin, C. E., Jr. (2004) Provider self-efficacy and the screening of adolescents for risky health behaviors. *Journal of Adolescent Health, 35*, 101–107.

Park, J., Jackson, J., Skinner, E., Ranghell, K., Saiers, J., & Cherney, B. (2010). Impact of an adherence intervention program on medication adherence barriers, asthma control, and productivity/daily activities in patients with asthma. *Journal of Asthma, 47*, 1072–1077.

Patel, P., & Zed, P. J. (2002). Drug-related visits to emergency department: How big is the problem? *Pharmacotherapy, 22*, 915–923.

Petrilla, A. A., Benner, J. S., Battleman, D. S., Tierce, J. C., & Hazard, E. H. (2005). Evidence-based interventions to improve patient compliance with antihypertensive and lipid-lowering medications. *International Journal of Clinical Practice, 59*, 1441–1451.

Pladevall, M., Brotons, C., Gabriel, R., Arnau, A., Suarez, C., de la Figuera, M. *et al.* (2010). Multicenter cluster-randomized trial of a multifactorial intervention to improve antihypertensive medication adherence and blood pressure control among patients at high cardiovascular risk. *Circulation, 122*, 1183–1191.

Ramström, H., Afandi, S., Elofsson, K., & Petersson, S. (2006). Differences in beliefs between patients and pharmaceutical specialists regarding medication. *Patient Education and Counseling, 62*, 244–249.

Rawson, K. A., Gunstad, J., Hughes, J., Spitznagel, M. B., Potter, V., Waechter, D., & Rosneck, J. (2009). The METER: A brief, self-administered measure of health literacy. *Journal of General Internal Medicine, 25*, 67–71.

Robin, A. L., Novack, G. D., Covert, D. W., Crockett, R. S., & Marcic, T. S. (2007). Adherence in glaucoma: Objective measurements of once-daily and adjunctive medication use. *American Journal of Opthalmology, 144*, 533–540.

Rollnick, S., Mason, P., & Butler, C. (2000). *Health behavior change: A guide for practitioners.* London: Churchill Livingstone.

Roth, H. P., & Caron, H. S. (1978). Accuracy of doctors' estimates and patients' statements on adherence to a drug regimen. *Clinical Pharmacological Therapy, 23*, 361–370.

Ruppar, T. M., Conn, V. S., & Russell, C. L. (2008). Medication adherence interventions for older adults: Literature review. *Research and Theory for Nursing Practice: An International Journal, 22*, 114–147.

Sajatovic, M., Davies, M., Bauer, M., McBride, L., Hays, R. A., Safavi, R., & Jenkins, J. (2005). Attitudes regarding the collaborative practice model and treatment adherence among individuals with bipolar disorder. *Comprehensive Psychiatry, 46*, 272–277.

Sajatovic, M., Velligan, D. I., Weiden, P. J., Valenstein, M. A., & Ogedegbe, G. (2010). Measurement of psychiatric treatment adherence. *Journal of Psychosomatic Research, 69*, 591–599.

Shaw, M. E. (2005). Increasing compliance with glaucoma therapy: "So, convince me I have something wrong with my eyes." *Insight: The Journal of the American Society of Ophthalmic Registered Nurses, 30*, 7–9.

Sokol, M. C., Kimberly, M. S., McGuigan, A., Verbrugge, R. R., & Epstein, R. S. (2005). Impact of medication adherence on hospitalization risk and healthcare cost. *Medical Care, 43*, 521–530.

Stern, S. L., Williams, T., Dixon, S. L., Clement, J.A., Butt, Z. A., Schwartzbaum, J. A., & Busch, K. (1999). Do health professional's attitudes interfere with the treatment of depression? *Depression and Anxiety, 9*, 151–155.

Stewart, M. S. (1987). The validity of an interview to assess a patient's drug taking behaviour. *American Journal of Preventive Medicine, 3*, 95–100.

Strecher, V. J., Champion, V. L., & Rosenstock, I. M. (1997). The health belief model and health behaviour. In D. S. Gochman (Ed.), *Handbook of Health Behaviour Research 1: Personal and Social Determinants* (pp. 71–91). New York: Plenum.

Svarstad, B. L., Chewning, B. A., Sleath, B. L., & Claesson, C. (1999). The brief medication questionnaire: A tool for screening patient adherence and barriers to adherence. *Patient Education and Counseling, 37,* 113–124.

Thompson, K., Kulkarni, J., & Sergejew, A. A. (2000). Reliability and validity of a new medication adherence rating scales (MARS) for the psychoses. *Schizophrenia Research, 42,* 241–247.

Urquhart, J. (1994). Role of patient compliance in clinical pharmacokinetics: A review of recent research. *Clinical Pharmacokinetics, 27,* 202–215.

Waldrop-Valverde, D., Ownby, R. L., Wilkie, F. L., Mack, A., Kumar, M., & Metsch, L. (2006). Neurocognitive aspects of medication adherence in HIV-positive injecting drug users. *AIDS & Behavior, 10*(3), 287–297.

Wallace, M. D., Dyer, E. J., & Penrod, B. (2006). Treatment adherence in developmental disabilities/cognitively impaired patients. In W. T. O'Donohue & E. R. Levensky (Eds.), *Promoting Treatment Adherence: A practical Handbook for Health Care Providers* (pp. 415–420). Thousand Oaks, CA: Sage.

Weinmann, S., Janssen, B., & Gaebel, W. (2005). Guideline adherence in medication management of psychotic disorders: An observational multi-site hospital study. *Acta Psychiatrica Scandinavica, 112,* 18–25.

World Health Organization. (2003). *Adherence to Long-Term Therapies – Evidence for Action.* www.who.int/chp/knowledge/publications/adherence_report/en/.

Wu, J. R., Moser, D. K., Lennie, T. A., & Burkhart, P. V. (2008). Medication adherence in patients who have heart failure: A review of the literature. *Nursing Clinics of North America, 43,* 133–153.

Yen, C. F., Yeh, M. L., Chen, C. S., & Chung, H. H. (2002). Predictive value of insight for suicide, violence, hospitalization and social adjustment for outpatients with schizophrenia: A prospective study. *Comprehensive Psychiatry, 43,* 443–447.

33

Psychological Management of the Common Primary Headaches

Paul R. Martin

Almost everyone experiences a headache at one time or another, as evidenced by epidemiological studies that typically report lifetime prevalences of headache in excess of 90% for both males and females (e.g., Boardman *et al.*, 2003; Rasmussen *et al.*, 1991). However, from the perspective of individuals who present for treatment of their headache/migraine, this fact can be one of their biggest problems because it means that everyone thinks they know what it is like to have a headache. At one level this is true but most people have no idea what it is like to have headaches of the severity that lead people to seek help: headaches that can involve pain of unbearable intensity, headaches that are frequent and long-lasting or even continuous, and headaches associated with a range of debilitating symptoms that occur prior to or during the headache (e.g., nausea, vertigo, photophobia). This combination of ignorance and assumed knowledge can result in headache sufferers not getting the support they need from health professionals on the one hand and family, friends, and work colleagues on the other.

There is a long tradition of headache/migraine sufferers expressing their pain experience and the consequences of their disorder through art and poetry, and this material is readily accessible via the Internet. It is a good strategy for health professionals who assess and treat individuals with headaches to look at headache/migraine art and poems as a start towards understanding the experience of their patients.

It has been estimated that globally the percentages of the adult population with an active headache disorder are 46% for headache in general, 11% for migraine, 42% for tension-type headache, and 3% for chronic daily headache (Stovner *et al.*, 2007). These authors calculated that on the ranking of causes of disability of the World Health Organization, this would bring headache disorders into the 10 most disabling conditions for the two genders, and into the five most disabling conditions for women. Solomon *et al.* (1993) concluded that patients with chronic headache have a level of functioning worse than that of patients with such chronic conditions as arthritis, diabetes, and back problems. The only chronic conditions that had similar levels of functional impairment to chronic headache were myocardial infarction and congestive heart failure, and the only disorder with worse levels of patient wellbeing and functioning was symptomatic HIV infection. In attempts to rank the severity of different diseases, migraine has been ranked among those causing the greatest

Applied Topics in Health Psychology, First Edition. Edited by M. L. Caltabiano and L. Ricciardelli.
© 2013 John Wiley & Sons, Ltd. Published 2013 by John Wiley & Sons, Ltd.

degree of handicap, together with conditions such as quadriplegia, dementia, and active psychosis (Dahlof & Solomon, 2006).

The Headache Classification System and Diagnosing Headaches

The current headache classification system is the *International Classification of Headache Disorders*, 2nd edition (ICHD-IIR1), described in a 160-page supplement to *Cephalalgia* (Headache Classification SubCommittee, 2004), plus revisions in two journal articles (Headache Classification SubCommittee, 2005; Headache Classification Committee, 2006). ICHD-IIR1 is divided into three parts: (1) primary headaches, (2) secondary headaches, and (3) cranial neuralgias, central and primary facial pain and other headaches. Primary headaches are headaches for which no underlying secondary cause can be identified and are divided into: (1) migraine, (2) tension-type headache, (3) cluster headache, and (4) other primary headaches. Tension-type headache and migraine are the most common types of headaches and the ones for which there is most evidence for the efficacy of psychological interventions. Other types of primary headache, such as cluster headache and new daily-persistent headache, may also be amenable to psychological interventions. Secondary headaches are rarely the target of psychological intervention, but psychologists should be aware of "headache attributed to a substance or its withdrawal" as medication-overuse headache (MOH) is the third most common type of headache and often unidentified.

In ICHD-IIR1, migraine is divided into seven types and 19 subtypes. The main types are migraine without aura (previously referred to as common migraine) and migraine with aura (previously referred to as classic migraine). Notable subtypes are typical aura with migraine headache and chronic migraine. Migraine without aura is a "recurrent headache disorder manifesting in attacks lasting 4–72 hours (untreated or unsuccessfully treated)" that tends to have the following characteristics: (1) unilateral location, (2) pulsating quality, (3) moderate or severe pain intensity, (4) aggravated by or causing avoidance of routine physical activity (e.g., walking or climbing stairs), (5) associated with nausea and/or vomiting, and (6) associated with photophobia and phonophobia. Auras are reversible focal neurological symptoms (e.g., flickering lights, loss of vision, numbness) that usually develop gradually over 5–20 min and last for less than 60 min, occurring just before or at onset of migraine headache. Chronic migraine is migraine headache occurring on 15 or more days per month for more than 3 months in the absence of medication overuse.

Tension-type headache (previously referred to as tension headache) is divided into four types and nine subtypes, of which the main types are infrequent episodic tension-type headache, frequent episodic tension-type headache, and chronic tension-type headache. The former type is rarely enough of a problem to constitute a clinical disorder. Episodic tension-type headache consists of "episodes of headache lasting 30 minutes to 7 days," and the pain typically has the following features:(1) bilateral location, (2) pressing/tightening (nonpulsatile) in quality, (3) mild or moderate intensity, (4) not aggravated by routine physical activity such as walking or climbing stairs, (5) no nausea or vomiting, and (6) no more than one of photophobia or phonophobia. Chronic tension-type headache is a disorder evolving from episodic tension-type headache, with headache occurring on 15 or more days per month for more than 3 months, lasting minutes to days. The criteria for chronic tension-type headache therefore parallel the criteria for chronic migraine in terms of frequency of headaches.

MOH is caused by using headache medications too frequently. Medications known to lead to headaches with overuse include the migraine-abortive medications (ergotamine and the triptans), analgesics, and opioids. MOH can be caused by taking any of these medications individually in too large a quantity, or by taking too many acute medications in combination. The diagnosis of MOH is based on (1) headaches present on more than 15 days per month, (2) medication intake on 10 or more days per month ($\geq$15 days per month for analgesic-overuse headache) on a regular basis for 3 months or more, (3) headache that has developed or markedly worsened during medication overuse, and (4) headache that resolves or reverts to its previous pattern within 2 months of discontinuation of use.

Genetic and Environmental Influences in Primary Headaches

Migraine with aura and migraine without aura carry a substantial genetic liability. Genetic/epidemiologic studies have shown a 2-fold increased risk of migraine without aura among first-degree relatives and a 4-fold increase in migraine with aura (Russell & Olesen, 1995). Nevertheless, monozygotic twins with migraine were only concordant in 20–50% of cases. Therefore 50% or more of those with a genetic predisposition to migraine never experience migraine attacks. Also, those with a genetic predisposition only experience migraine during some of their life as migraine increases up to age 40 and decreases in old age (Lipton *et al.*, 2001). Bille (1997) reported a longitudinal cohort study of children with migraine which showed that the children often became migraine-free for years or decades, but many later had a recurrence of migraine attacks. In a study of almost 30 000 twin pairs, Mulder *et al.* (2003) estimated that the genetic variance associated with migraine was between 37 and 57%. One form of migraine – "familial hemiplegic migraine" – has a much stronger genetic component, and is considered to be a rare autosomal dominantly inherited subtype of migraine with aura (Ferrari *et al.*, 2006).

Little research has been done on the genetics of tension-type headache (Montagna, 2008). In a twin study, Ulrich *et al.* (2004) concluded that for episodic tension-type headache the environmental influence is of major importance and that, if a genetic factor exists, it is of minor importance. They concluded that for chronic tension-type headache the genetic factor may be more important. Ostergaard *et al.* (1997) calculated that first-degree relatives had a 3-fold increased risk of chronic tension-type headache. A review by Russell (2007) argued that frequent episodic and chronic tension-type headache are caused by a combination of genetic and environmental factors, but infrequent episodic tension-type headache is caused primarily by environmental factors.

Peripheral and Central Mechanisms of Migraine and Tension-Type Headache

For many years, migraine was considered to be a vascular disorder, as illustrated by the fact that in the headache classification system that preceded the current system migraine was classified under Vascular headaches of the migraine type (Ad Hoc Committee, 1962). The predominant theory was proposed by one of the pioneers of headache research, Harold Wolff, who argued for a two-stage model: (1) intracranial spasm (vasoconstriction) caused cortical spreading depression (a wave of electrophysiological hyperactivity followed by a wave of inhibition) and (2) extracranial vasodilation caused the pain of migraine (Shevel, 2011a). This theory is of considerable significance as it underpins the use of vasoctonstrictors (ergotamine and the triptans) as the main abortive medications for migraine. Over the years, however, there has been much controversy with respect to this theory with researchers making statements about their positions in the title of their articles, such as "The vascular theory of migraine: a great story wrecked by the facts" (Goadsby, 2009) versus "The extracranial vascular theory of migraine: a great story confirmed by the facts" (Shevel, 2011b). Some have moved on to neuronal theories of migraine (e.g., Tajti *et al.*, 2011).

In recent years, the focus of headache research has moved away from peripheral mechanisms to central mechanisms, a shift that has been facilitated by all the technological advances that have been made in neuroimaging (May, 2006). The complexity of the situation currently is well illustrated by the fact that in *The Headaches*, the "bible" of the field, 16 chapters are devoted to the mechanisms of migraine (Olesen *et al.*, 2006). Space limits allow only the briefest introduction to this voluminous and complex literature.

Cortical spreading depression is considered the probable cause of migraine aura (Olesen & Goadsby, 2006). Patients without eyes or who are totally blind have reported typical visual auras, emphasizing that auras originate in the cerebral cortex and not in the eyes. It has also been suggested that cortical spreading depression can excite trigeminovascular afferents and thereby the pain of migraine as well (Lauritzen & Kraig, 2006).

Central neuronal hyperexcitability has been proposed as a mechanism of migraine attacks (Bussone, 2004; Hargreaves & Shepheard, 1999; Welch, 2004). Specifically, it is argued that the level of neuronal excitability in the occipital (visual) cortex is elevated in migraine sufferers and it is this level that determines the threshold for triggering attacks. It is further argued that sensitivity to triggers is genetically determined (e.g., Bussone, 2004; Nedeltchev *et al.*, 2004).

Much less research has been reported on tension-type headache than migraine but again the situation is complicated: there are nine chapters in *The Headaches* on the mechanisms of tension-type headache (Olesen *et al.*, 2006). Just as early theories of migraine focused on peripheral mechanisms, early theories of tension-type headache focused on peripheral mechanisms. The mechanism of tension-type headache was considered to be tension in muscles around the head, and in fact this type of headache was referred to as a "muscle-contraction headache" in the early headache classification system (Ad Hoc Committee, 1962). Much research has demonstrated that muscle tension does not play an important role in headaches (e.g., Martin & Mathews, 1978). However, there is evidence that pericranial myofacial tissues are more tender in patients with tension-type headache than nonheadache controls, and that the tenderness is positively correlated with both the intensity and frequency of tension-type headaches. These findings apply to both episodic and chronic tension-type headache, and to both during and between headaches (Jensen, 1999; Lipchik *et al.*, 2000). The increased sensitivity could be caused by release of inflammatory mediators resulting in sensitization of peripheral sensory afferents (Bendtsen, 2000) but firm evidence is lacking. In ICHD-IIR1, presence or absence of associated pericranial tenderness is used to define subtypes.

In addition to the possibility of peripheral sensitization, there is evidence of central sensitization for chronic tension-type headache but not for episodic tension-type headache. Pressure-pain detection and tolerance thresholds are reduced in patients with chronic tension-type headache (Bendtsen, 2000). These patients are also hypersensitive to electrical and thermal stimuli, and the sensitivity is increased both at cephalic and extracephalic locations (Langemark *et al.*, 1993; Schoenen *et al.*, 1991). The sensitization is believed to occur at both the spinal and supraspinal levels. Bendtsen and Schoenen (2006) have argued that sensitization of pain pathways in the central nervous system, resulting from prolonged nociceptive stimuli from pericranial myofascial tissues, is responsible for conversion of episodic to chronic tension-type headache.

The literature on mechanisms of headaches is difficult to summarize for many reasons. Even when statements are made in this literature as though there is a solid evidence base, critical review of the research findings often undermines the conclusions. For example, many of the recent studies have had small samples (typically 12 or less), probably reflecting the high costs associated with neuroimaging. Samples have often been limited to migraine with aura, which is experienced by a minority of migraine sufferers, but the results have been generalized to migraine without aura. With these caveats, current thinking is that migraine is a neurovascular disorder which originates in the brain. Tension-type headaches are associated with pericranial tenderness and the chronic form of tension-type headache is also associated with central sensitization.

Migraine and Tension-Type Headache: Distinct Types or on a Continuum?

The headache classification system plays a central role in headache research and the practice of headache specialists, but there has been a long-running debate as to whether migraine and tension-type headache are distinct types, as suggested by the classification system, or are better conceptualized as lying on a continuum. A number of researchers have proposed a continuum theory in which migraine and tension-type headache exist at opposite ends of a spectrum of headache activity (e.g., Featherstone, 1985; Raskin & Appenzeller, 1980). More recently, Cady *et al.* (2002) have proposed a convergence hypothesis for which they note that "similarities between these two types of primary headaches outweigh the differences, and so hypothesize that these headaches share a common pathophysiology" (p. 204). These authors suggest that "successive symptoms experienced clinically reflect an escalating pathophysiological process, beginning with the pre-monitory period and progressing into tension-type headache and, if uninterrupted, finally into migraine" (p. 204).

The rationale for a headache classification system is that it differentiates headaches with different mechanisms and therefore requiring different treatments. With respect to migraine and tension-type headache, however, these assumptions are debateable. For example, peripheral and central sensitization have mainly been discussed in the context of the mechanisms of tension-type headache but it has been suggested that these mechanisms are also operative in migraine (e.g., Bendtsen, 2002). A recent systematic review and meta-analysis concluded that antidepressant medication is effective in preventing both migraine and tension-type headache (Jackson *et al.*, 2010). Sumatriptan is the main abortive medication for migraine but has been shown to have a significant effect with chronic tension-type headache (Brennum *et al.*, 1992) if not episodic tension-type headache (Brennum, Brinck *et al.*, 1996). Cady *et al.* (1997) reported a positive response to sumatriptan in 96% of migraine cases and 97% of tension-type headache cases. We have compared the response of migraine and tension-type headache to psychological treatments and found no significant differences (Martin *et al.*, 2007).

The Functional Model of Primary Headaches

For headaches, particularly those of recent onset or ones that have changed recently, the critical first clinical step is diagnosis, because the headache may be a secondary headache, with the cause of the headache requiring management. Once the diagnostic decision has been made that the headaches are migraine or tension-type headache, however, there is limited value in focusing assessment on the differential diagnosis, let alone the type or subtype of migraine or tension-type headache. At least from a psychologist's perspective, the more useful questions with respect to management are the "why" questions: (1) why does the patient get headaches at certain times rather than other times?, (2) why is the patient getting headaches at this time in her/his life rather than at other times?, (3) why did the headache disorder begin when it did or become significantly worse when it did?, and (4) why is this person vulnerable to getting headaches?

Psychologists have typically tried to answer this type of question via functional analysis; that is, by investigating the antecedents and consequences of the problem. A functional model of primary headaches has been developed by Martin and colleagues (Martin *et al.*, 1993; Martin, 1993), and an adaptation of this model is presented as Figure 33.1.

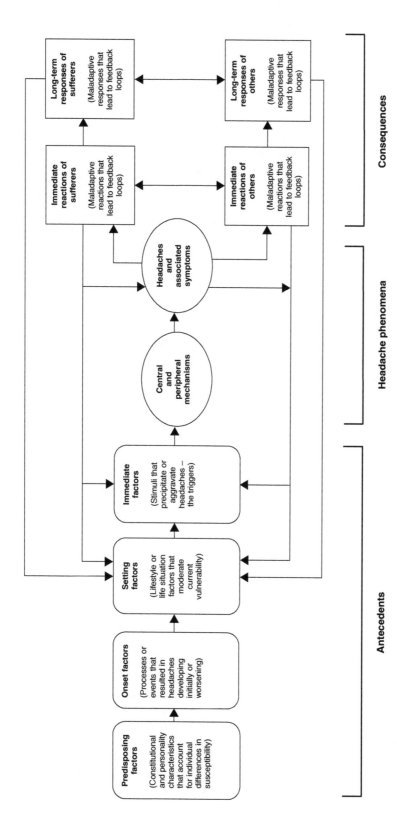

Figure 33.1 The functional model of primary headaches. Adapted from *Psychological Management of Chronic Headaches* by P. R. Martin (1993), Copyright Guilford Press. Reprinted with permission of The Guilford Press.

In the center of the model are headaches and associated symptoms, and the central and peripheral mechanisms that underlie the headaches. The immediate antecedents of headaches are the triggers that precipitate or aggravate the headaches. In a large study of the triggers of migraine attacks, Kelman (2007) reported that the mean number of triggers per patient was 6.7, with almost two-thirds having four to nine triggers. The most commonly listed triggers in the headache literature are (1) stress and negative emotions, (2) sensory triggers, (3) hunger, (4) lack of sleep or excess of sleep, (5) food and drink, (6) alcohol, (7) menstruation, and (8) weather (e.g., Andress-Rothrock *et al.*, 2010; Kelman, 2007; Leone *et al.*, 2010). Empirical evidence relating to many of these triggers is limited to self-reporting but some triggers have been experimentally validated, including stress (Martin & Seneviratne, 1997), visual disturbance (flicker, glare, and eyestrain; Martin & Teoh, 1999), noise (Martin *et al.*, 2005), and hunger (Martin & Seneviratne, 1997).

The setting antecedents are the psychosocial context in which the headaches occur. For example, if stress triggers headaches, important questions pertain to the main sources of stress (e.g., work pressures, marital disharmony), and the mediators/moderators of stress; that is, coping style and social support. Negative emotions are a common trigger of headaches and so mood disorders are potential setting factors for headaches. Research has shown that chronic headaches are associated with anxiety disorders (particularly panic and phobia) and major depression (Radat & Swendsen, 2004; Sheftell & Atlas, 2002).

The most common onset antecedent is periods of high stress (e.g., Henryk-Gutt & Rees, 1973). Physical and sexual abuse in women can be associated with the onset of headaches (Domino & Haber, 1987). Also for women, events associated with hormonal factors are often linked to headache onset such as menarche, use of oral contraceptives, and pregnancy (e.g., Hering & Rose, 1992).

With respect to predisposing antecedents, headaches tend to run in families and there is a genetic component as discussed previously. Personality has both genetic and environmental determinants and there is a long tradition of describing the "migraine personality" or "headache personality" using terms such as tense, sensitive, obsessional, perfectionistic, and inflexible. Many studies have failed to find support for such personality types, however, particularly the better-controlled studies that have investigated the relationship in community rather than clinical samples (e.g., Philips, 1976). Nevertheless, personality traits or combinations of traits often seem significant in understanding headaches. Martin *et al.* (1987) reported, for example, that 68–90% of sufferers of chronic headaches may be classified as Type A.

The other side of the model focuses on the consequences of headaches which are divided into responses of the headache sufferer and their significant others, in the short and long term. The responses are included in the model because they often are maladaptive as they lead to negative feedback cycles. For example, anxiety exacerbates pain perception so if the response to a headache is to worry about the headache or consequences of having a headache, the pain of the headache will feel worse. The feedback loops may go back to the antecedents rather than the headaches themselves. For example, if stress triggers a headache and the headache results in the stress levels of the sufferer increasing, then a loop is created of stress → headache → stress. If the main source of stress is a dysfunctional marriage, and if a headache results in the sufferer feeling irritable, then this can lead to arguments with the spouse and further deterioration in the marriage. Hence this is a loop going back to the setting factor of a dysfunctional marriage. Excessive consumption of medication in response to headaches can result in MOH.

Significant others can react in a number of ways that can contribute to the headache disorder becoming worse. If the complaint of headache is consistently followed by positive reinforcement (e.g., attention, sympathy) or negative reinforcement (e.g., avoiding nonpreferred activities), the frequency of headache complaints may increase. Alternatively, if significant others respond in ways that are experienced as aversive by the headache sufferer (e.g., communicating to them that they are making too big a fuss), then this can complete a loop whereby stress leads to headaches and the reactions cause more stress.

Long-term consequences that can be maladaptive include withdrawing from leisure activities after such activities have been spoiled on a number of occasions by the development of headaches. This can have various adverse effects such as a reduction in the size of a person's social network, thus resulting in less social support as a buffer against stress. This is an example of a long-term response feeding back to the setting factor of inadequate social support. Withdrawal can lead to reduced positive reinforcement, which increases the likelihood of depressed mood, a potential trigger for headaches.

Psychological Assessment of Primary Headaches

The starting point for headache assessment should be a diagnosis and medical practitioners, particularly neurologists, are uniquely qualified to carry out this task. Psychologists can differentiate between migraine and tension-type headache and this can be useful in communicating with medical practitioners, but it is argued here that it will not be very helpful in guiding psychological treatment. Functional analysis will provide more useful management information and is viewed as complementary to diagnosis. Functional assessment of primary headaches utilizes interviewing, self-monitoring, and questionnaires/inventories (Martin, 1993).

Interviewing

The information to be collected at interview falls into two categories, the first of which is personal and social history, as this provides the context in which the headache problem is evaluated. The second category relates to the headaches themselves. The best way to begin an assessment of headaches is to ask whether the person can identify more than one type of headache, as a high proportion of patients can. Not asking this question can result in a confused headache history as there is a danger that some questions are answered on the basis of one type of headache and other questions are answered on the basis of another type of headache.

The headache assessment needs to include the phenomenology of headaches, as this is the basis for diagnosis. It also should include documenting the history of the assessment and treatment of the headaches, particularly with a view to evaluating the degree to which appropriate medical specialists have investigated the headaches. A functional analysis should follow that assesses the antecedents and consequences of headaches. Inquiry can begin with open-ended questions but checklists are often helpful. Patients recall more headache triggers when they are shown a list of potential triggers, for example, than without such a list (Kelman, 2007). A list of common stressful events can assist people recall onset factors, which is particularly important for headaches that began many years previously. The reactions of the headache sufferer and significant others in the short- and long-term should also be assessed with the objective of identifying maladaptive responses. Psychological assessment usually takes two sessions but varies according to factors such as whether there are one or two types of headaches, and the length and complexity of the headache history.

Self-monitoring

Self-monitoring of headaches provides information that contributes to the assessment of the headache problem and measures of treatment outcome (Andrasik *et al.*, 2005; Martin, 1993).

The most common type of headache diary uses time-sampling to record headaches at regular intervals (usually hourly) throughout the waking day. Patients are provided with graphs and are requested to record their level of pain by rating it on a scale and placing a cross on the graph at the intersection of the time of day and the selected rating. Traditionally the graphs have been printed on cards/paper but recently systems have been developed for recording using the Internet or apps for mobile phones. The diaries are also used for recording medication consumed, whether taken for headaches or other problems. Other types of information can be recorded in the diaries such as pain location, associated symptoms, and the triggers of headaches.

Headache diaries provide information on the frequency, duration, and intensity of headaches, as well as patterns in headache activity such as whether the headaches are worse at some times of the day than others, worse some days of the week than others, and worse at certain times of the month. They also enable assessment of the effect of medication on headaches.

An alternative to time-sampling is event-sampling, whereby recording follows an "event" occurring rather than a time interval. Martin (1993), for example, advocated completing "change" cards whenever a headache begins or gets worse, or ends or improves. These cards involve recording thoughts, feelings, and activities, before and after the change has occurred. Hence, they have the advantage of focusing on the time of most interest to assessment.

Questionnaires and inventories

Questionnaires can contribute to assessment, particularly for investigating setting antecedents. Headaches are often associated with anxiety and depression and hence the routine administration of inventories such as the Beck Depression Inventory (BDI II) (Beck & Steer, 1987) and State-Trait Anxiety Inventory (Spielberger *et al.*, 1970) has advantages. Measures of stress such as the Perceived Stress Scale (Cohen *et al.*, 1983) can help determine the level of stress and sources of stress. If inadequate social support is suspected as a setting factor, administration of scales measuring support such as the Interpersonal Support Evaluation List (Cohen *et al.*, 1985) will reveal what type of support is lacking. Questionnaires can also be useful for assessing potential predisposing antecedents such as the personality characteristics of low self-esteem and the Type A behavior pattern.

A number of questionnaires have been developed for measuring disability and quality of life in headache sufferers such as the Migraine Disability Assessment (MIDAS) questionnaire (Stewart *et al.*, 2001), Headache Impact Test (HIT) (Garber, *et al.*, 2001), and Headache Disability Inventory (HDI) (Jacobson *et al.*, 1994). The MIDAS is a five-item questionnaire that sums the number of productive days lost over the previous 3 months in the workplace and the home. It also assesses disability in family, social, and leisure activities. The HIT asks questions about six areas of functioning that headaches might affect including pain, daily/social activities, and energy/fatigue. The HDI is a 25-item questionnaire that measures the functional and emotional impact of headache on everyday life.

Psychological Treatment of Primary Headaches

Psychological treatment approaches for primary headaches include biofeedback training, relaxation training, cognitive behavior therapy (CBT), transcendental meditation, hypnosis, and operant approaches. Treatment has been administered individually and in group settings, as well as via the Internet. The focus here will be on biofeedback, relaxation, and CBT, as these are the only approaches that have been evaluated extensively. Each of these approaches has a number of variations and the approaches overlap. Some researchers have advocated using all of these approaches together (e.g., Holroyd *et al.*, 2010; Lipchik *et al.*, 2002). Only a brief overview can be provided here and a more detailed account can be found in Borkum (2007).

Biofeedback training

Biofeedback training involves helping patients learn to control biological processes by providing feedback with respect to the process. This is achieved by attaching electrodes or transducers to patients to monitor the process, and providing feedback to the patient in an auditory (e.g., tone varying in frequency) or visual form (e.g., line varying in length). Patients are sometimes provided with home trainers to enable practice between office visits.

The rationale for the various forms of biofeedback training were based on the understanding of headache mechanisms in the 1960s and 1970s; that is, migraines were vascular and tension-type headaches were muscular, as discussed previously. Hence the most common forms of biofeedback are thermal biofeedback training for migraine in which patients are trained to warm their hands on the basis that this results in diverting blood flow from distended extracranial arteries to the hands, and electromyographic (EMG) biofeedback training in which patients are trained to reduce the tension in muscles around the head (Nestoriuc *et al.*, 2008). Other forms of biofeedback training have been used such as feedback of temporal pulse amplitude, electroencephalographic (EEG) biofeedback, and skin-conductance biofeedback, but they have been evaluated less fully. Biofeedback training is usually combined with relaxation training, including instructions to practice at home.

Relaxation training

The rationale for relaxation training with headache patients has varied and includes combating the stress and negative emotions that precipitate and aggravate headaches, and targeting the (outdated) peripheral mechanisms of headaches, such as muscle tension. The most commonly used forms of relaxation training with headache patients are progressive relaxation and autogenic training, particularly the former (Martin, 1993). All forms of relaxation training include instructions to practice at home, usually assisted by a cassette/CD.

Cognitive behavior therapy

CBT typically involves a number of techniques including challenging thoughts and beliefs that are dysfunctional from a headache perspective, patient education, pain management strategies (e.g., imagery, attention-diversion), and relapse prevention training. Some authors advocate a "standard package" of cognitive and behavioral techniques (e.g., Holroyd, 2002), and others advocate a broader, more individualized approach based on the results of a functional analysis (Martin, 1993). The defining technique of this approach is identifying and challenging maladaptive thoughts and beliefs related to headaches, and these thoughts and beliefs pertain to the antecedents and consequences of headaches. As stress and negative affect are the most common triggers of headaches, for example, cognitive techniques can be used to modify the thoughts that give rise to stress and negative emotions, and the beliefs that underlie the thoughts. Also, headaches are perceived as stressful and give rise to negative emotions that feed back to aggravate the headaches, and therefore cognitive techniques can be used to break this vicious cycle.

The results of a functional analysis suggest a variety of ways of intervening. One level is to consider behavioral management of triggers. The traditional wisdom is to advise that the best way to prevent headaches is to avoid the triggers (e.g., World Health Organization, 2006), but we have argued that avoidance can result in sensitization to triggers in the same way that avoidance of situations that elicit anxiety can result in an increased capacity for those situations to elicit anxiety in the future (Martin & MacLeod, 2009; Martin, 2010a, 2010b). We have provided some evidence to support this proposition (e.g., Martin, 2001), and that repeated, prolonged exposure to triggers can desensitize patients to triggers (Martin, 2000). Hence, we advocate "learning to cope with triggers" (LCT) (Martin, 2010a, 2010b), which involves avoidance of triggers that are inconsistent with a healthy lifestyle (e.g., too little sleep, dehydration), and the use of exposure to desensitize to other triggers. LCT uses exposure to triggers in three ways: (1) exposure as a behavioral experiment to test whether a perceived trigger really does precipitate headaches, (2) exposure as an opportunity for practicing new skills (e.g., inducing low levels of stress and practicing stress coping techniques), and (3) exposure to triggers as a method of developing adaptation/habituation to the trigger. Early data from a randomized controlled trial evaluating LCT suggests that it is three times as effective in reducing headaches as encouraging avoidance of all triggers.

Other types of intervention suggested by a functional analysis include targeting and setting antecedents, for example, the main source of stress such as marital dysfunction, or inadequate social support. Predisposing factors such as Type A behavior pattern can be part of a treatment plan. Maladaptive reactions to headaches are potential targets. For example, some headache sufferers respond to a headache beginning by rushing to complete activities that they would not be able to do when a headache has fully developed, thus guaranteeing that the headache will be worse than if they had adopted a strategy designed to minimize headache development. Partners who respond to headaches with reinforcement need to be trained to maintain the level of reinforcement but to reduce the link between reporting headaches and receiving reinforcement.

Effectiveness of Psychological Treatment for Primary Headaches

Rains *et al.* (2005) summarized the results of four meta-analytic reviews for psychological treatment of tension-type headache (using EMG biofeedback, relaxation training, and CBT) published between 1980 and 2001, and concluded that average improvements ranged between 35 and 55%, compared with 2% for no-treatment controls. These authors also summarized the results of five meta-analytic reviews for psychological treatment of migraine (with thermal biofeedback, EMG biofeedback, relaxation training, and CBT) published between 1980 and 1999, and concluded that average improvement ranged from 33 to 55%, compared with 5% for no-treatment controls.

Individual studies have reported superior results. For example, Martin *et al.* (2007) evaluated CBT using an individualized approach based on the results of functional analysis on a mixed sample of migraine and tension-type headache, and reported an average decrease in headaches of 68% posttreatment, which had extended to 77% at 12 month follow-up. Medication consumption decreased by 70% posttreatment. These results were achieved in a group of patients who had experienced headaches for an average of 24.4 years.

In addition to reducing headaches, psychological treatment leads to many other positive changes (Martin, 1993). Treatment is associated with decreases in negative moods such as depression and anxiety, and various cognitive changes including a shift toward a more internal locus of control, enhanced self-efficacy to cope with headaches, and alterations in cognitive reactions to stress, such as changes in appraisal and coping processes. Enhanced quality of life has been reported in a number of treatment studies.

Conclusions

The primary headaches of migraine and tension-type headache are common and associated with significant functional impairment. Genetic predisposition plays a role in most primary headaches but environmental factors are also highly significant. The mechanisms of migraine and tension-type headache are not well understood, and it is not clear whether they are better conceptualized as distinct types of headache or on a continuum. Functional analysis has much to contribute to the psychological management of the primary headaches as it provides a model that assists treatment planning. A range of psychological treatments have been shown to be effective in reducing headaches and the associated medications.

References

Ad Hoc Committee. (1962). Classification of headache. *Journal of American Medical Association, 179,* 717–718.

Andrasik, F., Lipchik, G. L., McCrory, D. C., & Wittrock, D. A. (2005). Outcome parameters in behavioral headache research: Headache parameters and psychosocial outcomes. *Headache, 45,* 429–437.

Andress-Rothrock, D., King, W., & Rothrock, J. (2010). An analysis of migraine triggers in a clinic-based population. *Headache, 50,* 1366–1370.

Beck, A. T., & Steer, R. A. (1987). *Manual for the Revised BDI.* San Antonio, TX: The Psychological Corporation.

Bendtsen, L. (2000). Central sensitisation in tension-type headache – possible pathophysiological mechanisms. *Cephalalgia, 20,* 486–508.

Bendtsen, L. (2002). Sensitization: Its role in primary headache. *Current Opinions in Investigational Drugs, 3,* 449–453.

Bendtsen, L., & Schoenen, J. (2006). Synthesis of tension-type headache mechanisms. In J. Olesen, P. J. Goadsby, N. M. Ramadan, P. Tfelt-Hansen, & K. M. A. Welch (Eds.), *The Headaches* (3rd edn., pp. 679–683). Philadelphia: Lippincott Williams & Wilkins.

Bille, B. (1997). A 40-year follow-up of school children with migraine. *Cephalalgia, 17,* 488–491.

Boardman, H. F., Thomas, E., Croft, P. R., & Milson, D. S. (2003). Epidemiology of headache in an English district. *Cephalalgia, 23,* 129–137.

Borkum, J. M. (2007). *Chronic Headaches: Biology, Psychology and Behavioral Treatment.* Mahwah, NJ: Lawrence Erlbaum Associates.

Brennum, J., Kjeldsen, M., & Olesen, J. (1992). The $5-HT^1$-like agonist sumatriptan has a significant effect in chronic tension-type headache. *Cephalalgia, 12,* 375–379.

Brennum, J., Brinck, T., Schriver, L., Wanscher, B., Soelberg Sorensen, P., Tfelt-Hansen, P., & Olesen, J. (1996). Sumatriptan has no clinically relevant effect in the treatment of episodic tension-type headache. *European Journal of Neurology, 3,* 23–28.

Bussone, G. (2004). Pathophysiology of migraine. *Neurological Sciences. 25,*s239.

Cady, R. K., Gutterman, D., Saiers, J. A., & Beach, M. E. (1997). Responsiveness of non-IHS migraine and tension-type headache to sumatriptan. *Cephalalgia, 17,* 588–590.

Cady, R. K., Schreiber, C., Farmer, K., & Sheftell, F. (2002). Primary headaches: A convergence hypothesis. *Headache, 42,* 204–216.

Cohen, S., Kamark, T., & Mermelstein, R. (1983). A global measure of perceived stress. *Journal of Health and Social Medicine, 24,* 385–396.

Cohen, S., Mermelstein, R., Kamark, T., & Hoberman, H. M. (1985). Measuring the functional components of social support. In I. G. Sarason & B. R. Sarason (Eds.), *Social Support: Theory, Research and Application* (pp. 73–94). The Hague: Martinus Nijhoff.

Dahlof, C. G. H., & Solomon, G. D. (2006). Impact of the headache on the individual and the family. In J. Olesen, P. J. Goadsby, N. M. Ramadan, P. Tfelt-Hansen, & K. M. A. Welch (Eds.), *The Headaches* (3rd edn., pp. 27–34). Philadelphia: Lippincott Williams & Wilkins.

Domino, J. V., & Haber, J. D. (1987). Prior physical and sexual abuse in women with chronic headache: Clinical correlates. *Headache, 27,* 310–314.

Featherstone, H. J. (1985). Migraine and muscle contraction headaches: A continuum. *Headache, 25,* 194–198.

Ferrari, M. D., Hann, J., & Palotie, A. (2006). Genetics of migraine. In J. Olesen, P. J. Goadsby, N. M. Ramadan, P. Tfelt-Hansen, & K. M. A. Welch (Eds.), *The Headaches* (3rd edn., pp. 251–267). Philadelphia: Lippincott Williams & Wilkins.

Garber, W. H., Kosinski, M., Dahlof, C., Tepper, S., Kujawski, S.C., Ware J., & Batenhorst A. (2001). HIT-6 reliably measures the impact of headaches. *Cephalalgia, 21,* 333.

Goadsby, P. J. (2009). The vascular theory of migraine: A great story wrecked by the facts. *Brain, 132,* 6–7.

Hargreaves, R. J., & Shepheard, S. L. (1999). Pathophysiology of migraine: New insights. *Canadian Journal Neurological Science, 26,* S12–S19.

Headache Classification Committee, Olesen, J., Bousser, M. G. *et al.* (2006). New appendix criteria open for a broader concept of chronic migraine. *Cephalalgia, 26,* 742–746.

Headache Classification Subcommittee of the International Headache Society. (2004). The International Classification of Headache Disorders (2nd edn.). *Cephalalgia, 24* (Suppl. 1), 1–151.

Headache Classification Subcommittee of the International Headache Society. (2005). Revision of criteria for 8.2 Medication-overuse headache. *Cephalalgia, 25,* 460–465.

Henryk-Gutt, R., & Rees, W. L. (1973). Psychological aspects of migraine. *Journal of Psychosomatic Research, 17,* 141–153.

Hering, R., & Rose, F. C. (1992). Menstrual migraine. *Headache Quarterly, 3,* 27–31.

Holroyd, K. A. (2002). Assessment and psychological treatment of recurrent headache disorders. *Journal of Consulting and Clinical Psychology, 70,* 656–677.

Holroyd, K. A., Cottrell, C. K., O'Donnell, F. J., Cordingley, G. E., Drew, J. B., Carlson, B. W., & Himawan, L. (2010). Effect of preventive (β blocker) treatment, behavioural migraine management, or their combination on outcomes of optimised acute treatment in frequent migraine: Randomised controlled trial. *British Medical Journal, 341,* c4871.

Jackson, J. L., Shimeall, W., Sessums, L., DeZee, K. J., Becher, D., Diemer, M. *et al.* (2010). Tricyclic antidepressants and headaches: Systematic review and meta-analysis. *British Medical Journal, 341,* c5222.

Jacobson, G. P., Ramadan, N. M., Aggarwal, S. K., & Newman, C.W. (1994). The Henry Ford Hospital Headache Disability Inventory (HDI). *Neurology, 44,* 837–842.

Jensen, R. (1999). Pathophysiological mechanisms of tension-type headache: A review of epidemiological and experimental studies. *Cephalalgia, 19,* 602–621.

Kelman, L. (2007). The triggers or precipitants of the acute migraine attack. *Cephalalgia, 27,* 394–402.

Langemark, M., Bach, F. W., Jensen, T. S., & Olesen, J. (1993). Decreased nociceptive flexion reflex threshold in chronic tension-type headache. *Archives of Neurology, 50,* 1061–1064.

Lauritzen, M., & Kraig, R. P. (2006). Spreading depression. In J. Olesen, P. J. Goadsby, N. M. Ramadan, P. Tfelt-Hansen, & K. M. A. Welch (Eds.), *The Headaches* (3rd edn., pp. 269–274). Philadelphia: Lippincott Williams & Wilkins.

Leone, M., Vila, C., & McGown, C. (2010). Influence of trigger factors on the efficacy of almotriptan as early intervention for the treatment of acute migraine in a primary care setting: The START study. *Expert Review of Neurotherapeutics, 10,* 1399–1408.

Lipchik, G. L., Holroyd, K. A., O'Donnell, F. J., Cordingley, G. E., Waller, S., Labus, J. *et al.* (2000). Extereoceptive suppression periods and pericranial muscle tenderness in chronic tension-type headache: Effects of psychopathology, chronicity and disability. *Cephalalgia, 20,* 638–646.

Lipchik, G. L., Holroyd, K. A., & Nash, J. M. (2002). Cognitive-behavioral management of recurrent headache disorders: A minimal-therapist-contact approach. In D. C. Turk & R. J. Gatchel (Eds.), *Psychological Approaches to Pain Management* (2nd edn.). New York: Guilford Press.

Lipton, R. B., Stewart, W. F., Diamond, S., Diamond, M. L., & Reed, M. (2001). Prevalence and burden of migraine in the United States: Data from the American Migraine Study II. *Headache, 41,* 646–657.

Martin, P. R. (1993). *Psychological Management of Chronic Headaches.* New York: Guilford Press.

Martin, P. R. (2000). Headache triggers: To avoid or not to avoid, that is the question. *Psychology and Health, 15,* 801–809.

Martin, P. R. (2001). How do trigger factors acquire the capacity to precipitate headaches? *Behaviour Research and Therapy, 39,* 545–554.

Martin, P. R. (2010a). Managing headache triggers: Think 'coping' not 'avoidance'. *Cephalalgia, 30,* 634–637.

Martin P. R. (2010b). Behavioral management of migraine headache triggers: Learning to cope with triggers. *Current Pain and Headache Reports, 14,* 221–227.

Martin, P. R., & Mathews, A. M. (1978). Tension headaches: Psychophysiological investigation and treatment. *Journal of Psychosomatic Research, 22,* 389–399.

Martin, P. R., & Seneviratne, H. M. (1997). Effects of food deprivation and a stressor on head pain. *Health Psychology, 16,* 1–9.

Martin, P. R., & Teoh, H.-J. (1999). Effects of visual stimuli and a stressor on head pain. *Headache, 39,* 705–715.

Martin, P. R., & MacLeod, C. (2009). Behavioral management of headache triggers: Avoidance of triggers is an inadequate strategy. *Clinical Psychology Review, 29,* 483–495.

Martin, P. R., Nathan, P. R., & Milech, D. (1987). The type A behaviour pattern and chronic headaches. *Behaviour Change, 4,* 33–39.

Martin, P. R., Milech, D., & Nathan, P. R. (1993). Towards a functional model of chronic headaches: Investigation of antecedents and consequences. *Headache, 33,* 461–470.

Martin, P. R., Todd J., & Reece, J. (2005). Effects of noise and a stressor on head pain. *Headache, 45,* 1353–1364.

Martin, P. R., Forsyth, M. R., & Reece, J. (2007). Cognitive-behavioral therapy versus temporal pulse amplitude biofeedback training for recurrent headache. *Behavior Therapy, 38,* 350–363.

May, A. (2006). A review of diagnostic and functional imaging in headache. *Journal of Headache Pain, 7,* 174–184.

Montagna, P. (2008). The primary headaches: Genetics, epigenetics and a behavioural genetic model. *Journal of Headache Pain, 9,* 57–69.

Mulder, E. J., van Baal, C., Gaist, D., Kallela, M., Kaprio, J., Svensson, D. A. *et al.* (2003). Genetic and environmental influences on migraine: A twin study across six countries. *Twin Research, 6,* 422–431.

Nedeltchev, K., Arnold, M., Schwerzmann, M., Nirkko, A., Lagger, F., Mattle, H. P., & Sturzenegger, M. (2004). Cerebrovascular response to repetitive visual stimulation in interictal migraine with aura. *Cephalalgia, 24,* 700–706.

Nestoriuc, Y., Martin, A., Rief, W., & Andrasik, F. (2008). Biofeedback treatment for headache disorders: A comprehensive efficacy review. *Applied Psychophysiology and Biofeedback, 33,* 125–140.

Olesen, J., & Goadsby, P. J. (2006). Synthesis of migraine mechanisms. In J. Olesen, P. J. Goadsby, N. M. Ramadan, P. Tfelt-Hansen, & K. M. A. Welch (Eds.), *The Headaches* (3rd edn., pp. 393–398). Philadelphia: Lippincott Williams & Wilkins.

Olesen, J., Goadsby, P. J., Ramadan, N. M., Tfelt-Hansen, P., & Welch K. M. A. (Eds.). (2006). *The headaches* (3rd edn.). Philadelphia: Lippincott Williams & Wilkins.

Ostergaard, S., Russell, M. B., Bendtsen, L., & Olesen, J. (1997). Comparison of first degree relatives and spouses of people with chronic tension-type headache. *British Medical Journal, 314,* 1092–1093.

Philips, H. C. (1976). Headache and personality. *Journal of Psychosomatic Research, 20,* 535–542.

Radat, F., & Swendsen, J. (2004). Psychiatric comorbidity in migraine: A review. *Cephalalgia, 25,* 165–178.

Rains, J. C., Penzien, D. B., McCrory, D. C., & Gray, R. N. (2005). Behavioral headache treatment: History, review of empirical literature, and methodological critique. *Headache, 45* (Suppl. 2), S92–S109.

Raskin, N. H., & Appenzeller, O. (1980). Headache. In L. H. Smith (Ed.), *Major Problems in Internal Medicine,* vol. 19 (pp. 131–141). Philadelphia: WB Saunders.

Rasmussen, B. C., Jensen, R., Schroll, M., & Olesen, J. (1991). Epidemiology of headache in a general population: A prevalence study. *Journal of Clinical Epidemiology, 44,* 1147–1157.

Russell, M. B. (2007). Genetics of tension-type headache. *Journal of Headache Pain, 8,* 71–76.

Russell, M. B., & Olesen, J. (1995). Increased familial risk and evidence of genetic factor in migraine. *British Medical Journal, 311,* 541–544.

Schoenen, J., Bottin, D., Hardy, F., & Gerard, P. (1991). Cephalic and extracephalic pressure pain thresholds in chronic tension-type headache. *Pain, 47,* 145–149.

Sheftell, F. D., & Atlas, S. J. (2002). Migraine and psychiatric comorbidity: From theory and hypothesis to clinical application. *Headache, 42,* 934–944.

Shevel, E. (2011a). The extracranial vascular theory of migraine: An artificial controversy. *Journal of Neural Transmission, 118,* 525–530.

Shevel, E. (2011b). The extracranial vascular theory of migraine: A great story confirmed by the facts. *Headache, 51,* 409–417.

Solomon, G. D., Skobieranda, F. G., & Gragg, L. A. (1993). Quality of life and well-being of headache patients: Measurement by the Medical Outcomes Study Instrument. *Headache, 33,* 351–358.

Spielberger, C. D., Gorusch, R. L., & Lushene, R. G. (1970). *The State-Trait Anxiety Inventory.* Palo Alto, CA: Consulting Psychologists Press.

Stewart, W. F., Lipton, R. B., Dawson, A. J., & Sawyer, J. (2001). Development and testing of the Migraine Disability Assessment (MIDAS) Questionnaire to assess headache-related disability. *Neurology, 56* (suppl. 6), S20–S28.

Stovner, L. J., Hagen, K., Jensen, R., Katsarava, Z., Lipton, R. B., Scher, A. I. *et al.* (2007). The global burden of headache: A documentation of headache prevalence and disability worldwide. *Cephalalgia, 27,* 193–210.

Tajti, J., Pardutz, A., Vamos, E., Tuka, B., Kuris, A., Bohar, Zs. *et al.* (2011). Migraine is a neuronal disease. *Journal of Neural Transmission, 118,* 511–524.

Ulrich, V., Gervil, M., & Olesen, J. (2004). The relative influence of environment and genes in episodic tension-type headache. *Neurology, 62,* 2065–2069.

Welch, K. M. A. (2004). Research developments in the physiopathology of primary headaches. *Neurological Sciences, 25,* S97–S103.

World Health Organization. (2006). *Neurological Disorders: Public Health Challenges.* Geneva: World Health Organization.

34

Interdisciplinary Pain Management

The Role of the Psychologist

Jacqui Stanford and Lester E. Jones

The person with persistent pain is best managed by health professionals from a range of disciplines. While the pain literature supports the role of multidisciplinary treatment, in which each discipline brings their own perspective to the client, interdisciplinary treatment goes a step further and is an integration of the different aspects into one. From our understanding of pain and from experience with clients, people with persistent pain do not present with separate "physical" and "psychological" issues. Therefore, the integrated, interdisciplinary approach to management is more appropriate. For psychologists to effectively work in pain management, they need to adopt this interdisciplinary approach and expand their knowledge of other health disciplines, as well as understand the complexities and impact of the human pain experience.

The Human Pain Experience

Pain is commonly considered a simple pathophysiological process. Tissue is damaged and pain is felt. However, many clinical health examples, and increasing evidence from clinical and laboratory-based research, demonstrate that pain is complex. Indeed, pain can exist without tissue damage, and tissue damage can be present without pain.

Nociception

A common misconception is that pain arises from tissues. Specialized sensory nerves known as nociceptors do indeed respond to high-threshold stimuli often associated with tissue damage, and can trigger pain. However, nociceptors, like other nerves, are transmitting electrical signals, not pain. The signal transmitted once a nociceptor has been activated undergoes a series of modulations before it triggers a brain response. These modulations can augment or dampen the

Applied Topics in Health Psychology, First Edition. Edited by M. L. Caltabiano and L. Ricciardelli.
© 2013 John Wiley & Sons, Ltd. Published 2013 by John Wiley & Sons, Ltd.

signal and occur in the affected tissues, at the dorsal root ganglion, the spinal cord, and within the cortex itself (Anand *et al.*, 2007; Noguchi, 2006; Tracey *et al.*, 2007; Woolf, 2011; Yilmaz *et al.*, 2010). Nociception may be a common trigger for pain, but it is not pain.

Neuromatrix theory of pain

The complexity of human pain is represented in the neuromatrix theory of pain (Melzack, 2005). A neuromatrix is defined as the "anatomical substrate of the body self" (p. 86), consisting of a "large, widespread network of neurons" (p. 86) and involving the cortex, thalamus, and limbic system (Melzack, 2005). Essentially the theory attempts to explain how, despite the multitude of inputs to the brain, a person perceives a unified experience, albeit a constantly changing one. The neuromatrix is the template for the whole body and can, through processing of neural activity, establish characteristic patterns of response and activation (a neurosignature) (Melzack, 2005). The so-called body-neuromatrix incorporates the body's stress-response system responsible for homeostasis (Melzack, 2005). Important to this theory is recognizing that pain is essentially part of the stress-response system.

Inputs to the body-self neuromatrix include cognition-related factors such as recalled memory, meaning, and attention, sensory factors including nociception, and emotion-related factors associated with homeostatic and stress mechanisms (Melzack, 2005). Outputs include pain perception (cognitive, sensory, and emotion dimensions), action programs, and stress-regulation programs (Melzack, 2005). Therefore, pain can be thought of as an output of the brain, resulting from complex processing of inputs from multiple sources. Pain is of the brain and not of the tissues.

Imaging studies

A recent article reinforces the notion that pain is part of the body's stress-response system. In a review of activity in the anterior cingulate cortex, Shackman and colleagues contest previously held beliefs about the functional segregation of pain, negative affect, and cognitive control (Shackman *et al.*, 2011). From their meta-analysis, they identified that the anterior mid-cingulate cortex was activated by all three domains. Studies have shown that when one domain is manipulated the other two would be affected. That is, when cognitive control is challenged, pain sensitivity and negative affect are increased (Buhle & Wager, 2010; Wiech *et al.*, 2008; van Dillen *et al.*, 2009).

Pain, Disability, and Function

International Classification of Functioning, Disability and Health

Pain can impact greatly on a person's ability to function. In children and adolescents there is potential to impact on participation at school and social interactions (Hooten, 2010; Miró, 2009; Miró *et al.*, 2009), in adults it is common for pain to impact on vocational activities (Phillips *et al.*, 2008) and the parental role (White *et al.*, 2009), and in older adults pain can interfere with a person's ability to live independently (Koltyn *et al.*, 2009; Peat & Thomas, 2009).

An appropriate framework for modeling the impact of pain on function is the International Classification of Functioning, Disability and Health (ICF; for further introduction see La Trobe University Library, 2009). The ICF was developed as a framework for exploring the impact of

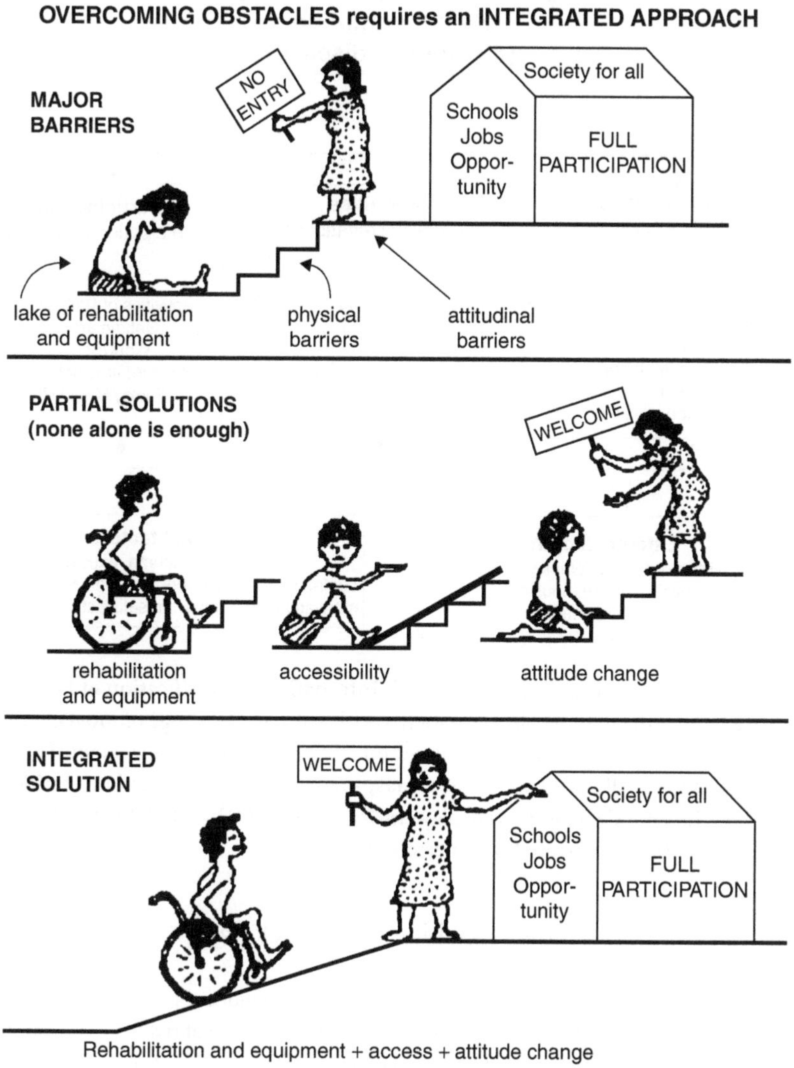

OVERCOMING OBSTACLES requires an INTEGRATED APPROACH

Figure 34.1 Overcoming obstacles requires an integrated approach. From *Label Us Able: A Pro-active Evaluation of Finnish Development Co-operation from the Disability Perspective,* by THL (Terveyden ja hyvinvoinnin laitos [former STAKES], 2003). Drawing by David Warner. Reprinted with permission. Retrieved from http://formin.finland.fi/Public/default.aspx?contentid=50655&nodeid=15454&contentlan=2&culture=en-US.

health conditions on human function and reflects the multiple factors and influences on human function by incorporating body structure and body function, abilities of an individual, and societal influences. The interplay of these factors is well reflected in the cartoon in Figure 34.1. Persistent pain is an appropriate health condition to explore using the ICF and is advocated by the International Association for the Study of Pain (IASP; Wittink & Carr, 2008) as a tool to improve understanding of pain, the assessment of pain, and its management, as shown in Figure 34.2.

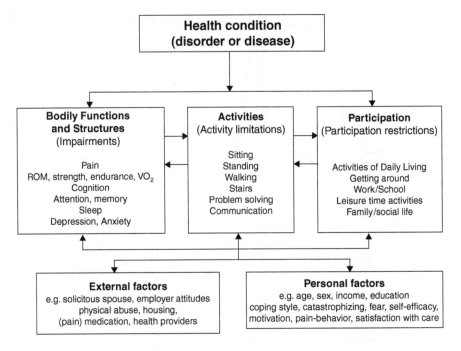

Figure 34.2 The World Health Organization's International Classification of Functioning, Disability and Health (ICF) model for patients with pain. ROM, range of movement. From Wittink, H., & Carr, D. B. (2008). *Outcomes and Effective Pain Management*. IASP Clinical Updates, *XVI*(1). Retrieved from www.iasp-pain.org/AM/AMTemplate.cfm?Section= Home&TEMPLATE=/CM/ContentDisplay.cfm&CONTENTID=12087&SECTION=Home (accessed 5 May 2012). Reprinted with permission.

Yellow flags, blue flags, black flags

In an attempt to contain the level of pain-related disability, guidelines have been developed to assist clinicians to identify risk factors. Similar to the established use of red flags to communicate the need to be alert for sinister pathologies (Greenhalgh & Selfe, 2006), yellow, black, and blue flags can be used for risks associated with pain-related disability. While these systems of flags are used in assessment processes, it is useful to discuss them here to further appreciate the association of pain, disability, and function.

Yellow flags refer to a collection of psychosocial factors that are proposed to predict future disability (Kendall *et al.*, 1998; Watson & Kendall, 2000). These include attitudes and beliefs of the person about pain behaviors that reinforce a passive approach to recovery, involvement in a compensation claim, an uncertain or unclear diagnosis, evidence of negative emotions especially pain-related fear, nonexistent or unhelpful social support, and barriers to continuing, or return to, work.

Recent discussions have challenged the process of assessing yellow flags. Criticisms include that it may not be necessary to target all of the identified psychosocial factors (Chou & Shekelle, 2010). Also, the use of standardized questionnaires to identify yellow flags may oversimplify the complex presentations and interactions seen in individuals (Stewart *et al.*, 2011). As such, the assessment of psychosocial risk factors for long-term disability is still being refined.

Blue and black flags refer to occupational factors that may provide barriers to the person returning to work. Specifically, blue flags refer to the person's belief about how he or she might be prevented from getting back to work. An example would be where the person perceives that attitudes in the workplace are antagonistic to his or her return. Black flags refer to occupational processes that affect all workers, but are not conducive to getting an injured worker back to work. For example, a business might not have the capacity to offer a graduated return-to-work program. Return to work has been shown to have significant mental and physical health benefits (Franche *et al.*, 2005), so it is important to identify and overcome any barriers.

Physical rehabilitation

Persistent pain has impact on multiple facets of a person's life. The physical rehabilitation approach needs to reflect this by considering a whole body approach (Frost *et al.*, 1998), and not just focus on the painful part. This can include strengthening, exercises to improve range of movement at joints, and endurance tasks. Activities that have been avoided can be reintroduced in a supportive environment in conjunction with education that targets and challenges unhelpful beliefs about function. This often includes giving the person responsibility for setting the goals for an exercise with regard to repetitions or level of difficulty (Moseley, 2003; Nicholas *et al.*, 2002). As such, the physical management is not simply an approach that improves physical attributes (e.g., strength), it offers behavioral tasks that confirm or disconfirm the person's current function despite pain.

Role for psychological intervention

Despite an exponential growth in the scientific understanding of pain there is evidence that pain remains poorly managed (Blyth *et al.*, 2001; Sawyer *et al.*, 2010). When pain is poorly managed a multitude of additional problems can develop. Physical functioning is affected with the resultant impact on work and family life and social pursuits. The disability that can affect those with persistent pain is often far beyond what would be expected from the original problem. In such cases, clinical studies have shown that while there may be some benefit from physical rehabilitation, improvement in psychological functioning can lead to substantial change in physical functioning and quality of life (Nicholas & George, 2011). Involving psychological interventions in physical rehabilitation has explicit benefits beyond those achieved by simply addressing mental health issues. In other words, the role of the psychologist is to promote optimal functioning, even in cases where there are no mental health issues.

Assessment

Due to the complexity of pain the assessment process needs to be multidimensional if it is to be comprehensive (Turk & Melzack, 2001). The goal of the assessment process is to gather information related to the client and his/her presenting problem in order to develop a clinical formulation, which in turn shapes the treatment plan. The literature supports assessing a range of factors related to the person's pain, including pain history (see box), pain intensity, management strategies, and treatment approaches (Loggia *et al.*, 2008; Searle & Bennett, 2008). It is important to gain an understanding about the client's beliefs about his/her pain, the impact of the pain on function, and the context surrounding the onset of the pain.

Pain History

The history of the person's pain will inform the clinician of the onset and duration of pain, the site(s) of the body involved, and the behavior of the pain; i.e., constant, fluctuating, or contextual. The intensity of the pain is commonly measured by a verbal numerical rating where the person is asked to give the intensity of pain a value. Common end values which the person is asked to consider are that 0 equals no pain and 10 equals worst imaginable pain. It is argued that better measures of pain intensity are visual analog scales, as the ratings on numerical scales are more likely to be remembered from one test to the next (for further comment on pain intensity and memory, see Marty *et al.*, 2009). In any case, the validity of the measurement of pain intensity alone has been questioned (Williams *et al.*, 2000) and commonly two scales are presented, one for intensity and one for pain unpleasantness.

A comprehensive assessment should include the colored flag systems already mentioned and also an evaluation of other factors that have been found to be influenced by pain, or to influence the pain experience. Factors that have been shown in the literature to be important and therefore need to be assessed include depression (Boettger *et al.*, 2010; Loggia *et al.*, 2008), anxiety (Keogh *et al.*, 2010; Vassend *et al.*, 2011), trauma and torture (Beck & Coffey, 2007; Williams & Amris, 2007), acceptance (McCracken, 2005), self-efficacy (Costa *et al.*, 2011), pain beliefs (Roelofs *et al.*, 2004; Vlaeyen & Linton, 2000), catastrophizing (Campbell *et al.*, 2010; Crombez *et al.*, 1998; Keogh *et al.*, 2010), sleep (Lavigne, 2010), prescribed medication and recreational drugs (Gardell *et al.*, 2006), and social support (Gil *et al.*, 1987; McCracken, 2005). Case studies 1 and 2 at the end of this chapter provide clinical examples of some of these issues.

Outcome measures

To facilitate the assessment process a range of outcome measures have been developed. These include the importance of pain beliefs (Roelofs *et al.*, 2004; Roland & Morris, 1983; Waddell *et al.*, 1993), catastrophizing (Sullivan *et al.*, 1995), self-efficacy (Nicholas, 2007), and acceptance (McCracken & Eccleston, 2005).

Jensen and colleagues (2000) developed two versions of the Survey of Pain Attitudes (SOPA57 and SOPA35) to assess a range of key pain beliefs, categorized as Pain control, Disability, Harm, Emotions, Medication, Solicitude, and Cure. The long version (SOPA57) is the most reliable but the short version (SOPA35) allows for quicker completion and provides a representation of the broader aspects of the domains measured. The data collected for the SOPA can assist in understanding what the pain means to a person and the beliefs about pain that create a barrier to normal function.

Catastrophizing is a variable that has received considerable attention in the literature as a predictor for disability associated with pain (Haythornwaite, 2009; Keogh *et al.*, 2010). Catastophizing about pain is also integral to the well-accepted fear-avoidance model (Leeuw *et al.*, 2007). The Pain Catastrophizing Scale (PCS; Sullivan *et al.*, 1995) was developed to measure three aspects of catastrophic thinking about pain: rumination about pain, magnification of the impact of pain on health and function, and helplessness about self-managing pain. Using the PCS, researchers have linked catastrophizing to pain severity, avoidance of activity, and disability in a number of contexts (Flink *et al.*, 2009; Mitchell *et al.*, 2009; Vervoort *et al.*, 2006; Williams *et al.*, 2009).

Self-efficacy is another variable that has been associated with disability related to pain/ability to make functional gains. Nicholas (2007) developed the pain self-efficacy scale which assesses the client's belief in their ability to manage their pain and change their situation. Clients with high self-efficacy for pain self-management have less disability, require less analgesic medication, and are more likely to manage flare-ups of pain than clients with low self-efficacy (Asghari & Nicholas, 2001).

The Chronic Pain Acceptance Questionnaire provides a valuable indication of whether a client is ready to engage in rehabilitation (McCracken & Eccleston, 2005). That is not to say that acceptance cannot be enabled by rehabilitation; however, rate of progress is often limited by the client's acceptance of the presence of pain and its impact on function. Case study 1 below provides an example of someone who is having difficulty accepting pain.

The inclusion of the above measures reflects the authors' preference based on clinical utility. Often a battery of psychometric tests are presented to the person with persistent pain in the attempt for comprehensive assessment but this can be a burden to complete, which in turn may affect the quality of the data collected. Being selective or using short versions of measures may reduce the assessment burden.

Treatment/Management

Setting treatment goals

Following a multidimensional assessment a clinical formulation is developed to provide an overview of the client's presenting problem and associated factors (Tarrier & Calam, 2002). Clients with persistent pain often have a range of difficulties, all of which could be conceptualized as the presenting problem, but it is important to determine the focus for the client, considering the situation they are in.

The purpose of the formulation is to account for all relevant factors. Once the presenting problem is defined, the formulation identifies the predisposing, precipitating, perpetuating, and protective factors for the client. Some aspects of the client's story can be relevant to more than one of these factors. For example, conflict with the employer may have precipitated an injury, but the ongoing conflict may be a perpetuating factor. The predisposing and precipitating factors cannot be changed in and of themselves. The perpetuating and protective factors are the focus of therapy as they are modifiable (Jackson, 1993). In sum, the focus of therapy is to reduce the impact of the factors perpetuating the presenting problem and to enhance or create new factors that are protective.

Goals and treatment plan

By identifying the perpetuating and protective factors the goals and the treatment plan can be developed. Goals are ideally functional and tap into what is important to the client. Clients are assisted to develop goals that are specific, measurable, assignable, realistic, and time-related (SMART; Doran, 1981). The process of setting goals actually serves both a motivational and a therapeutic process. In order to set goals appropriately the person must reflect on the real-life, day-to-day context – which may be challenging – and also take responsibility for future action (Bailey *et al.*, 2010).

Cognitive behavior therapy

Cognitive behavior therapy (CBT) is the framework that has the most empirical support as a treatment approach for clients with persistent pain (Airaksinen *et al.*, 2006; Dixon *et al.*, 2007; Hoffman *et al.*, 2007; McCracken & Turk, 2002; Nicholas & Tonkin, 2004). Some of the strategies include education about pain, pacing, thought reframing, addressing core beliefs, relaxation, and engagement in pleasant activities. It is important that the intervention is client-centered and takes into account the factors identified in the formulation. The presenting problems that are considered in the formulation often coexist and can be managed collectively through a CBT framework.

If a client has experienced trauma, this needs to be addressed early. The evidence supports the use of trauma-focused CBT that accounts for the hyperarousal, avoidance, and reexperiencing that can occur in response to a trauma (Beck & Coffey, 2007; Ehlers & Clark, 2008; Kar, 2011; Smeeding *et al.*, 2010; Williams & Amris, 2007). Issues around grief and acceptance also need to be addressed. The grief that many of these clients experience is not often acknowledged or accepted by society or some health professionals. Hence, this type of grief has been termed disenfranchized grief (Doka, 1989). Normalization and processing of this grief is important to enable clients to move forward.

Clients frequently present with a combination of pain and mood issues. Persistent pain conditions and conditions of mood disorder are often associated with a similar range of symptoms and associated factors, such as poor sleep. Clients will often believe the pain or the mood need to change before they can engage in activity, yet for both persistent pain and depression activity engagement is an important part of treatment (Airaksinen *et al.*, 2006; Cuijpers *et al.*, 2007; Lewinsohn & Libet, 1972).

Sleep is an area that many clients report as problematic, whether it is onset, maintaining sleep, early morning waking, or unrefreshed sleep. Clients often report it is their pain that causes the sleep problems. Interestingly, poor sleep is a better predictor of level of pain the next day than level of pain is of poor sleep (Miaskowski *et al.*, 2004). Strategies to improve sleep include education about sleep waves and good sleep hygiene strategies (Dworkin *et al.*, 2007). Due to the relationship between pain and sleep, as the sleep improves the level of pain may improve, and as pain management improves so sleep may improve (Miaskowski & Lee, 1999).

Core beliefs about pain and mood require psycho-education, and it is important to relate the intervention back to the client's own experience. Providing education about the interaction between mood and pain is often a core component of challenging and reframing the client's beliefs about his/her pain. For example, in Case study 2 the client requires education about pain not equalling ongoing damage before further progress can be made. In addition to psycho-education, thought monitoring and reframing through challenging the thoughts is often incorporated into CBT approaches. It is not just the superficial language that needs to be challenged, rather the underlying thoughts and beliefs that are the basis for the language (Stroud *et al.*, 2000).

Relaxation is a core component to many pain-management programs and has also been found to be effective as a single treatment with chronic headache (Eccleston *et al.*, 2009). Relaxation is a skill that is developed and can include a range of strategies including mindfulness, breathing techniques, muscle relaxation, and visualization. Clients may benefit from developing a range of strategies that can be used in different contexts, such as during a flare up, as a prevention strategy, or during a conflict (Nicholas *et al.*, 2002).

As mentioned above clients may believe that they need their pain and their mood to improve before they are able to engage in particular activities, be they social, domestic, or occupational. Yet engagement in activity is an important strategy in the management of depression (Cuijpers *et al.*, 2007) and in the management of pain (Nicholas *et al.*, 2002; Nicholas & Tonkin, 2004). Therefore, facilitation of engagement in activity should be part of the therapeutic process and forms the basis for many interdisciplinary programs designed to restore physical function.

While engagement in activity is important, clients with persistent pain may have a low tolerance to an increase in activity and this results in an increase in pain. Despite an understanding that an increase in pain does not generally mean damage has occurred, it is unpleasant and may increase the client's avoidance of this activity. If it continually results in increased pain it may further sensitize the pain system due to ongoing flare-ups (Butler & Moseley, 2003; Nicholas *et al.*, 2002; Nicholas & Tonkin, 2004; Woolf, 2011).

Pacing is about reducing the so-called boom-and-bust cycle which is a repetitive pattern of "overdoing" activity one day followed by prolonged rest due to a flare-up of symptoms. Instead, the aim is to develop a more consistent and sustainable level of activity within the person's capacity (Butler & Moseley, 2003; Nicholas *et al.*, 2002; Nicholas & Tonkin, 2004). In relation to pain, a client's physical tolerances to an activity are determined by identifying the point before the pain system is activated. In other words, this involves determining how much of an activity a person can complete without a significant increase in pain, at that time or later, i.e., flare up. Pain can have a latent response to activity in people with persistent pain (Butler & Moseley, 2003; Nicholas *et al.*, 2002; Nicholas & Tonkin, 2004). As such, activity needs to remain within this level regardless of how the person is feeling. People will have different tolerances for each activity; e.g., sitting, standing, walking, lifting. Pacing is initially used to reduce flare-ups and can then be used to increase a desired activity (pacing up) or decrease an undesired activity (pacing down) (Moseley, 2003). See Case study 2 for an example of this.

The graded exposure and upgrade that is critical in pacing assists the desensitization process from a physical perspective by allowing the body to normalize – get used to – the movement experience and it also allows the mind to get used to an activity by addressing fear and anxiety. Fear of tissue damage or fear of pain leads to avoidance of activity and therefore can be extremely disabling (Vlaeyen & Linton, 2000). The literature supports systematic desensitization to address anxiety and phobias, and these principles are used in addressing fear-avoidant behaviors for clients with persistent pain (Bailey *et al.*, 2010; Boersma *et al.*, 2004; de Jong *et al.*, 2005; Crombez *et al.*, 2002; Vlaeyen & Linton, 2000).

Relationships can be problematic for people with persistent pain. As they try to learn to manage their own expectations, pain, and function they also need to learn to work with the expectations of others. Relationships with family and friends, and relationships with work colleagues, are all likely to be affected, especially where the person's role has changed (Smith, 1998). The role of the psychologist can be to facilitate healthy relationships by helping the client to build communication and conflict-resolution skills (Blanchard *et al.*, 2009; Overall *et al.*, 2009; Smith *et al.*, 2008). Assisting clients in the development of assertive communication skills promotes respect of their own needs and the needs of those with whom they share relationships.

Interdisciplinary

The role of any health professional who is a member of an interdisciplinary team is to bring discipline-specific skills and knowledge to the team, and also to develop an understanding – and in some cases the knowledge and skills – of the other disciplines that make up the team. Ideally, clients should experience a unified and cohesive approach to care where concepts and strategies are reinforced across treatment sessions.

An interdisciplinary approach is illustrated in the following brief example. A client had difficulty putting on her shoes and socks. It was considered that from a physical perspective stretches and developing appropriate movement techniques might be helpful, yet the client's fear of provoking her back pain was restricting her mobility. By having the psychologist assist with relaxation strategies, while the physiotherapist assisted with muscle stretching, the client was successful in completing the physical activity required. This led to her independence with dressing which may not have been achieved if the physiotherapist, working alone with the client, had been unable to achieve an effective stretch to achieve the required movement.

The interdisciplinary role of the psychologist requires a basic understanding of the physical and functional strategies used by physiotherapists and occupational therapists. These include aerobic, strengthening, and range-of-movement exercises, addressing body mechanics, and pacing of activities. With this understanding, the psychologist can best address with the client the beliefs that may limit implementation. Such beliefs include that an activity always has to be completed in one attempt (e.g., vacuuming the entire house or mowing all the lawn) and cannot be split into achievable parts. Psychologists can also address problem solving and motivational factors that limit the use of strategies, such as the compliance with a home stretching exercise program.

Some practical strategies can facilitate interdisciplinary treatment. Providing a combined assessment that seeks to understand the whole person, including the physical and psychological factors, is important. This not only allows a greater understanding of the person, it also validates the client's experience. An opportunity to freely communicate and discuss the assessment findings at a meeting, where all disciplines are represented, promotes interdisciplinary decision making about treatment options. For this to be effective, however, the team of health professionals needs to understand each discipline's involvement in the process, and have a mutual respect for the interpretation of assessment findings and clinical reasoning process.

Interdisciplinary management presents its own challenges. Where team members lack understanding (or respect) of the role and approach of another discipline, the decision-making process can become skewed to emphasize one aspect of the client's issues. This is unlikely to provide the best outcome for the client, particularly if this leads to an inconsistency in the message the client receives about the nature or severity of his or her pain, or the prognosis regarding pain relief.

Case Studies

Case study 1: Persistent arm pain and difficulty returning to work

Mary is a 52 year-old woman who tripped over a box at work and injured her shoulder 18 months ago. Pain persists in her right shoulder and arm, and down into her back. Mary's mood has deteriorated and now meets the criteria for adjustment disorder with anxiety and depression. Mary currently is attending physiotherapy and psychology sessions. She also sees her general practitioner frequently, who provides work capacity certificates, and a psychiatrist for review of mood medication.

Mary has very limited function. She has had two failed attempts at returning to work as a receptionist and has recently commenced a third plan. While Mary reports wanting to return to work she continues to identify barriers to increasing her hours. She also is very influenced by clinicians' opinions and when there are discrepant opinions Mary has been noted to change her own response to what she feels able to do.

Mary presents with very flat affect, continues to focus on how she is different to the "old me," and is still seeking a cure for her pain.

Psychological treatment is focused on increasing her acceptance of her pain and current function. In order to increase acceptance of pain a client's beliefs about cure need to be challenged, without shattering hope. This is done through education and understanding about pain, as well as exploring treatment history and outcome. It is accepting the current reality without knowledge of the future. Acceptance is developed through developing a mindful, nonjudgmental awareness, and through engaging in meaningful activities. As such, treatment also focuses on increasing functional behaviors within her domestic, social, and occupational roles by setting small and meaningful goals.

Outcome   Frequent team communication about the management plan to ensure consistency of message was important in assisting Mary to achieve her goals of returning to part time work. She continues to experience symptoms of depression and has ongoing pain but is able to function at work. While her affect is often quite flat, when she has made functional gains, including increasing work hours, her affect brightens.

Case study 2: Persistent back pain and shifting beliefs and expectations

Jane is a 34 year-old nurse with chronic back pain. She has had a discectomy which provided some short-term relief. Jane manages her pain with medication and rest. Her goals are to cease taking OxyContin (oxycodone, a slow-release strong opioid). Jane has no psychiatric diagnoses. She does report feeling frustrated by the pain and has low mood at times.

Jane attends physiotherapy and psychology sessions for pain management. Earlier sessions provided Jane with the insight that an increase in pain did not mean further damage but can be explained as a flaring-up or sensitivity in her pain system. Jane realized she was caught in the "boom/bust" cycle of activity, where on low-pain days her activity is high and this results in subsequent flaring-up of her pain and very low activity.

Jane is being provided with education on strategies for pacing activities. Both the physiotherapist and psychologist are assisting her to challenge thoughts and beliefs that promote pushing through the pain in order to get a task done, and the psychologist is helping Jane to identify ways of reframing thoughts and beliefs to be more helpful. For example, Jane has been avoiding the long drive to visit family but she is now challenging her expectation that this drive needs to be done without rest stops. Jane is also learning to use relaxation strategies when in a flare-up and also to assist in the management of both stress and pain.

Through the use of the strategies Jane's pain stabilized significantly and she was able to function at a higher level than previously. Once her pain stabilized she gradually reduced her medication. She was able to do this under the guidance of her treating doctor, and by adopting active self-management strategies supported by the therapeutic alliance with the physiotherapist and psychologist. These strategies contributed to enhanced self-efficacy, less frequent flare-ups, and management of flare-ups through nonpharmacological strategies, including pacing, challenging her thinking, and using relaxation strategies.

Outcome   Jane realized her anxiety about the long drive to visit her family was leading to avoidance but with the new strategies she felt that with a few stops she would be able to manage the drive. Through exploring her motivations Jane changed her initial social and exercise goals to something that was meaningful to her, resulting in greater compliance and, as such, attainment.

Future Developments

Over recent years acceptance and commitment therapy (ACT) has gained recognition in psychology and is considered to be the third wave of behavior therapy. The components of ACT are designed to create psychological flexibility, and include acceptance and mindfulness processes (acceptance, defusion, mindfulness, and the observing self) and commitment and behavioral change processes (values, committed action, mindfulness, and observing self) (Ciarrochi *et al.*, 2010). ACT is now often being used in the treatment of many conditions, including chronic pain. The literature provides strong support for the role of ACT, in particular the role of mindfulness, acceptance, and values-based action (Vowles *et al.*, 2009)

The first time many clients receive effective, evidence-based pain management can be many months and more often many years after pain onset. The Örebro Musculoskeletal Pain Screening tool is increasingly used in order to identify those who may need early implementation of interdisciplinary pain management. The tool is designed to screen people with recent injuries to determine risk of developing chronic pain and disability (e.g., not working 6 months following injury) based on psychosocial factors (Westman *et al.*, 2008). The tool is designed for use at 4 weeks but more recently a modified version has been used as early as 48 hours. When intervention aims at addressing the physical and psychological factors in the early stage there is some evidence that the complexity of the pain experience may be able to be prevented. As such, it is important that screening and interdisciplinary treatment are provided earlier.

Concluding Comments

This chapter has emphasized three key points about the role of the psychologist in interdisciplinary pain management. The first point is that psychology professionals need to recognize their potential to assist people with conditions, other than mental illness. Second, constructing a formulation is a valuable adjunct to clinical decision making, and is most important where complexity is a feature of the client's presentation, as is usually the case with people who have persistent pain. Finally, an interdisciplinary approach to care is needed to address multidimensional problems such as persistent pain.

References

Airaksinen, O., Brox, J. I., Cedraschi, C., Hildebrandt, J., Klaber-Moffett, J., Kovacs, F. *et al.* (2006). Chapter 4. European guidelines for the management of chronic nonspecific low back pain. *European Spine Journal, 15*(Suppl. 2), S192–S300.

Anand, P., Aziz, Q., Willert, R., & van Oudenhove, L. (2007). Peripheral and central mechanisms of visceral sensitization in man. *Neurogastroenterology and Motility, 19*(1 Suppl), 29–46.

Asghari, A., & Nicholas, M. K. (2001). Pain self-efficacy beliefs and pain behaviour: A prospective study. *Pain, 94*, 85–100.

Bailey, K. M., Carleton, R. N., Vlaeyen, J. W. S., & Asmundson, G. J. G. (2010). Treatments addressing pain-related fear and anxiety in patients with chronic musculoskeletal pain: a preliminary review. *Cognitive Behaviour Therapy, 39*, 46–63.

Beck, J. G., & Coffey, S. F. (2007). Assessment and treatment of PTSD after a motor vehicle collision: Empirical findings and clinical observations. *Professional Psychology, Research and Practice, 38*, 629–639.

Blanchard, V. L., Hawkins, A. J., Baldwin, S. A., & Fawcett, E. B. (2009). Investigating the effects of marriage and relationship education on couples' communication skills: A meta-analytic study. *Journal of Family Psychology, 23*, 203–214.

Blyth, F. M., March, L. M. *et al.* (2001). Chronic pain in Australia: a prevalence study. *Pain, 89*(2), 127–134.

Boersma, K., Linton, S., Overmeer, T., Jansson, M., Vlaeyen, J., & de Jong, J. (2004). Lowering fear-avoidance and enhancing function through exposure in vivo: A multiple baseline study across six patients with back pain. *Pain, 108*, 8–16.

Boettger, M. K., Greiner, W., Rachow, T., Brühl, C., & Bär, K.-J. (2010). Sympathetic skin response following painful electrical stimulation is increased in major depression. *Pain, 149*, 130–134.

Buhle, J., & Wager, T. D. (2010). Performance-dependent inhibition of pain by an executive working memory task. *Pain, 149*(1), 19–26.

Butler, D., & Moseley, G. L. (2003). *Explain Pain.* Adelaide, SA: NOI Group Publishing.

Campbell, C. M., Witmer, K., Simango, M., Carteret, A., Loggia, M. L., Campbell, J. N. *et al.* (2010). Catastrophizing delays the analgesic effect of distraction. *Pain, 149*, 202–207.

Chou, R., & Shekelle, P. (2010). Will this patient develop persistent disabling low back pain? *Journal of the American Medical Association, 303*, 1295–1302.

Ciarrochi, J., Bilich, L., & Godsell, C. (2010). Psychological flexibility as a mechanism of change in acceptance and commitment therapy. In R.A. Baer (Ed.), *Assessing Mindfulness and Acceptance: Illuminating the Theory and Practice of Change* (pp. 51–76). Oakland, CA: New Harbinger Publications.

Costa, L. D. C. M., Maher, C. G., McAuley, J. H., Hancock, M. J., & Smeets, R. J. E. M. (2011). Self-efficacy is more important than fear of movement in mediating the relationship between pain and disability in chronic low back pain. *European Journal of Pain, 15*, 213–219.

Crombez, G., Eccleston, C., Baeyens, F., & Eelen, P. (1998). When somatic information threatens, catastrophic thinking enhances attentional interference. *Pain, 75*, 187–198.

Crombez, G., Eccleston, C., Vlaeyen, J. W. S., Vansteenwegen, D., Lysens, R., & Eelen, P. (2002). Exposure to physical movements in low back pain patients: Restricted effects of generalization. *Health Psychology, 21*, 573–578.

Cuijpers, P., Van Straten, A., & Warmerdam, L. (2007). Behavioral activation treatments of depression: A meta-analysis. *Clinical Psychology Review, 27*, 318–326.

de Jong, J. R., Vlaeyen, J. W. S., Onghena, P., Cuypers, C., Hollander, M., & Ruijgrok, J. (2005). Reduction of pain-related fear in complex regional pain syndrome type I: The application of graded exposure in vivo. *Pain, 116*, 264–275.

Dixon, K. E., Keefe, F. J., Scipio, C. D., Perri, L. C. M., & Abernethy, A. P. (2007). Psychological interventions for arthritis pain management in adults: A meta-analysis. *Health Psychology, 26*, 241.

Doka, K. J. (1989). *Disenfranchised Grief.* Lexington, MA: Lexington Books.

Doran, G. T. (1981). There'sa SMART way to write management's goals and objectives. *Management Review, 70*(11), 35–36.

Dworkin, R. H., O'Connor, A. B., Backonja, M., Farrar, J. T., Finnerup, N. B., Jensen, T. S. *et al.* (2007). Pharmacologic management of neuropathic pain: Evidence-based recommendations. *Pain, 132*, 237–251.

Eccleston, C., Palermo, T., Williams, A. C., Lewandowski, A., & Morley, S. (2009). Psychological therapies for the management of chronic and recurrent pain in children and adolescents. *Cochrane Database of Systematic Reviews, 2*, CD003968.

Ehlers, A., & Clark, D. M. (2008). Post-traumatic stress disorder: The development of effective psychological treatments. *Nordic Journal of Psychiatry, 62*, 11–18.

Flink, I. K., Mroczek, M. Z., Sullivan, M. J. L., & Linton, S. J. (2009). Pain in childbirth and postpartum recovery: The role of catastrophizing. *European Journal of Pain, 13*, 312–316.

Franche, R.-L., Cullen, K., Clarke, J., Irvin, E., Sinclair, S., Frank, J. *et al.* and Health Workplace-Based RTWILRRT. (2005). Workplace-based return-to-work interventions: A systematic review of the quantitative literature. *Journal of Occupational Rehabilitation, 15*, 607–31.

Frost, H., Lamb, S. E., Klaber Moffett, J. A., Fairbank, J. C., & Moser, J. S. (1998). A fitness programme for patients with chronic low back pain: 2-year follow-up of a randomised controlled trial. *Pain, 75*, 273–279.

Gardell, L. R., King, T., Ossipov, M. H., Rice, K. C., Lai, J., Vanderah, T. W., & Porreca, F. (2006). Opioid receptor-mediated hyperalgesia and antinociceptive tolerance induced by sustained opiate delivery. *Neuroscience Letters, 396*, 44–49.

Gil, K. M., Keefe, F. J., Crisson, J. E., & Van Dalfsen, P. J. (1987). Social support and pain behavior. *Pain, 29*, 209–217.

Greenhalgh, S., & Selfe, J. (2006). *Red Flags. A Guide to Identifying Serious Pathology of the Spine.* Oxford: Churchill Livingstone Elsevier.

Haythornwaite, J. A. (2009). It's a belief. It's an appraisal. It's coping. No, it's catastrophising. In J. Castro-Lopes (Ed.), *Current Topics in Pain: 12th World Congress on Pain* (pp. 271–287). Seattle: IASP Press.

Hoffman, B. M., Papas, R. K., Chatkoff, D. K., & Kerns, R. D. (2007). Meta-analysis of psychological interventions for chronic low back pain. *Health Psychology, 26,* 1–9.

Hooten, W. M. (2010). Chronic pain in adolescents. *Pain Medicine, 11,* 911–911.

Jensen, M. P., Turner, J. A., & Romano, J. M. (2000). Pain belief assessment: A comparison of the short and long versions of the survey of pain attitudes. *The Journal of Pain, 1,* 138–150.

Kar, N. (2011). Cognitive behavioral therapy for the treatment of post-traumatic stress disorder: A review. *Neuropsychiatric Disease and Treatment, 7,* 167–181.

Kendall, N. A. S., Linton, S. J., & Main, C. (1998). Psychosocial yellow flags for acute low back pain: 'yellow flags' as an analogue to 'red flags'. *European Journal of Pain, 2,* 87–89.

Keogh, E., Book, K., Thomas, J., Giddins, G., & Eccleston, C. (2010). Predicting pain and disability in patients with hand fractures: Comparing pain anxiety, anxiety sensitivity and pain catastrophizing. *European Journal of Pain, 14,* 446–451.

Koltyn, K., Colbert, L., & Trentham-Dietz, A. (2009). Pain and function in older, long-term colorectal cancer survivors. *The Journal of Pain, 10,* S7.

La Trobe University Library (2009, 10 May 2009). *WHO ICF Resource.* http://latrobe.libguides.com/who_icf.

Lavigne, G. J. (2010). Effect of sleep restriction on pain perception: Towards greater attention! *Pain, 148,* 6–7.

Leeuw, M., Goossens, M. E. J. B., Linton, S. J., Crombez, G., Boersma, K., & Vlaeyen, J. W. S. (2007). The fear-avoidance model of musculoskeletal pain: Current state of scientific evidence. *Journal of Behavioral Medicine, 30,* 77–94.

Lewinsohn, P. M., & Libet, J. (1972). Pleasant events, activity schedules, and depressions. *Journal of Abnormal Psychology, 79,* 291.

Loggia, M. L., Schweinhardt, P., Villemure, C., & Bushnell, M. C. (2008). Effects of psychological state on pain perception in the dental environment. *Journal of the Canadian Dental Association, 74,* 651–656.

Marty, M., Rozenberg, S., Legout, V., Durand-Zaleski, I., Moyse, D., Henrotin, Y., & Perrot, S. (2009). Influence of time, activities, and memory on the assessment of chronic low back pain intensity. *Spine (Phila Pa 1976), 34,* 1604–1609.

McCracken, L. M. (2005). Social context and acceptance of chronic pain: The role of solicitous and punishing responses. *Pain, 113,* 155–159.

McCracken, L. M., & Turk, D. C. (2002). Behavioral and cognitive-behavioral treatment for chronic pain: Outcome, predictors of outcome, and treatment process. *Spine, 27,* 2564–2573.

McCracken, L. M., & Eccleston, C. (2005). A prospective study of acceptance of pain and patient functioning with chronic pain. *Pain, 118,* 164–169.

Melzack, R. (2005). Evolution of the neuromatrix theory of pain. The Prithvi Raj lecture: Presented at the third world congress of world institute of pain, Barcelona 2004. *Pain Practice, 5,* 85–94.

Miaskowski, C., & Lee, K. A. (1999). Pain, fatigue, and sleep disturbances in oncology outpatients receiving radiation therapy for bone metastasis: A pilot study. *Journal of Pain and Symptom Management, 17,* 320–332.

Miaskowski, C., Dodd, M., & Lee, K. (2004). Symptom clusters: The new frontier in symptom management research. *JNCI Monographs, 2004,* 17–21.

Miró, J. (2009). A one-year longitudinal study of chronic pain in children and adolescents. *The Journal of Pain, 10,* S5.

Miró, J., Olivé, R., & Huguet, A. (2009). Pain, disability, and quality of life in children following surgery. *The Journal of Pain, 10,* S7.

Mitchell, T., O'Sullivan, P. B., Smith, A., Burnett, A. F., Straker, L., Thornton, J., & Rudd, C. J. (2009). Biopsychosocial factors are associated with low back pain in female nursing students: A cross-sectional study. *International Journal of Nursing Studies, 46,* 678–688.

Moseley, G. (2003). A pain neuromatrix approach to patients with chronic pain. *Manual Therapy, 8,* 130–140.

Nicholas, M. K. (2007). The pain self-efficacy questionnaire: Taking pain into account. *European Journal of Pain, 11*, 153–163.

Nicholas, M. K., & Tonkin, L. (2004). Application of cognitive-behavioural principles to activity-based pain management programs. In K. Refshauge & E. Gaff (Eds.), *Musculoskeletal Physiotherapy: Clinical Science and Evidence Based Practice* (pp. 277–293). Oxford: Elsevier.

Nicholas, M. K., & George, S. Z. (2011). Psychologically informed interventions for low back pain: an update for physical therapists. *Physical Therapy, 91*(5), 765–776.

Nicholas, M. K., Siddal, P., Tonkin, L., & Beeston, L. (2002). *Manage Your Pain.* Sydney: ABC Books.

Noguchi, K. (2006). Pain and neuroplastic changes in the dorsal root ganglia. In H. Flor, E. Kalso, & J. O. Dostrovsky (Eds.), *Proceedings of the 11th World Congress on Pain* (pp. 93–108). Seattle: IASP Press.

Overall, N. C., Fletcher, G. J. O., Simpson, J. A., & Sibley, C. G. (2009). Regulating partners in intimate relationships: The costs and benefits of different communication strategies. *Journal of Personality and Social Psychology, 96*, 620–639.

Peat, G., & Thomas, E. (2009). When knee pain becomes severe: A nested case-control analysis in community-dwelling older adults. *The Journal of Pain, 10*, 798–808.

Phillips, C., Main, C., Buck, R., Aylward, M., Wynne-Jones, G., & Farr, A. (2008). Prioritising pain in policy making: The need for a whole systems perspective. *Health Policy, 88*, 166–175.

Roelofs, J., Goubert, L., Peters, M. L., Vlaeyen, J. W. S., & Crombez, G. (2004). The Tampa Scale for Kinesiophobia: Further examination of psychometric properties in patients with chronic low back pain and fibromyalgia. *European Journal of Pain, 8*, 495–502.

Roland, M., & Morris, R. (1983). A study of the natural history of back pain. Part I: Development of a reliable and sensitive measure of disability in low-back pain. *Spine, 8*, 141–144.

Sawyer, J., Haslam, L., Daines, P., & Stilos, K. (2010). Pain prevalence study in a large Canadian teaching hospital. Round 2: Lessons learned? *Pain Management Nursing, 11*, 45–55

Searle, R. D., & Bennett, M. I. (2008). Pain assessment. *Anaesthesia & Intensive Care Medicine, 9*, 13–15.

Shackman, A. J., Salomons, T. V., Slagter, H. A., Fox, A. S., Winter, J. J., & Davidson, R. J. (2011). The integration of negative affect, pain and cognitive control in the cingulate cortex. *Nature Reviews Neuroscience, 12*, 154–167.

Smeeding, S. J. W., Bradshaw, D. H., Kumpfer, K., Trevithick, S., & Stoddard, G. J. (2010). Outcome evaluation of the Veterans Affairs Salt Lake City Integrative Health Clinic for chronic pain and stress-related depression, anxiety, and post-traumatic stress disorder. *Journal of Alternative and Complementary Medicine, 16*, 823–835.

Smith, L., Ciarrochi, J., & Heaven, P. C. L. (2008). The stability and change of trait emotional intelligence, conflict communication patterns, and relationship satisfaction: A one-year longitudinal study. *Personality and Individual Differences, 45*, 738–743.

Smith, R. (1998). Impact of migraine on the family. *Headache: The Journal of Head and Face Pain, 38*, 423–426.

Stewart, J., Kempenaar, L., & Lauchlan, D. (2011). Rethinking yellow flags. *Manual Therapy, 16*, 196–198.

Stroud, M. W., Thorn, B. E., Jensen, M. P., & Boothby, J. L. (2000). The relation between pain beliefs, negative thoughts, and psychosocial functioning in chronic pain patients. *Pain, 84*, 347–352.

Sullivan, M. J. L., Bishop, S. R., & Pivik, J. (1995). The Pain catastrophizing scale: Development and validation. *Psychological Assessment, 7*, 524–532.

Tarrier, N., & Calam, R. (2002). New developments in cognitive-behavioural case formulation. Epidemiological, systemic and social context: An integrative approach. *Behavioural and Cognitive Psychotherapy, 30*, 311–328.

Tracey, I., Schweinhardt, P., McQuay, H., & Wartolowska, K. (2007). Functional MRI as a tool for diagnosis in neuropathic pain. *European Journal of Pain, 11*(1, Suppl. 1), 24–24.

Turk, D. C., & Melzack, R. (Eds.). (2001). *Handbook of Pain Assessment* (2nd edn.). New York: Guildford Press.

van Dillen, L. R., Maluf, K. S. *et al.* (2009). Further examination of modifying patient-preferred movement and alignment strategies in patients with low back pain during symptomatic tests. *Manual Therapy, 14*(1), 52–60.

Vassend, O., Røysamb, E., & Nielsen, C. S. (2011). Dental anxiety in relation to neuroticism and pain sensitivity: A twin study. *Journal of Anxiety Disorders, 25*, 302–308.

Vervoort, T., Goubert, L., Eccleston, C., Bijttebier, P., & Crombez, G. (2006). Catastrophic thinking about pain is independently associated with pain severity, disability, and somatic complaints in school children and children with chronic pain. *Journal of Pediatric Psychology, 31*, 674–683.

Vlaeyen, J. W., & Linton, S. J. (2000). Fear-avoidance and its consequences in chronic musculoskeletal pain: A state of the art. *Pain, 85*, 317–332.

Vowles, K. E., Wetherell, J. L., & Sorrell, J. T. (2009). Targeting acceptance, mindfulness, and values-based action in chronic pain: Findings of two preliminary trials of an outpatient group-based intervention. *Cognitive and Behavioral Practice, 16*, 49–58.

Waddell, G., Newton, M., Henderson, I., Somerville, D., & Main, C. J. (1993). A Fear-Avoidance Beliefs Questionnaire (FABQ) and the role of fear-avoidance beliefs in chronic low back pain and disability. *Pain, 52*, 157–168.

Watson, P., & Kendall, N. A. S. (2000). Assessing psychosocial yellow flags. In L. Gifford (Ed.), *Topical Issues in Pain*, vol. 2 (pp. 111–129). Falmouth: CNS Press.

Westman, A., Linton, S., Öhrvik, J., Wahlen, P., & Leppert, J. (2008). Do psychosocial factors predict disability and health at a 3-year follow-up for patients with non-acute musculoskeletal pain? A validation of the Örebro Musculoskeletal Pain Screening Questionnaire. *European Journal of Pain, 12*, 641–649.

White, C. P., Mendoza, J., White, M. B., & Bond, C. (2009). Chronically ill mothers experiencing pain: Relational coping strategies used while parenting young children. *Chronic Illness, 5*, 33–45.

Wiech, K., Ploner, M. *et al.* (2008). Neurocognitive aspects of pain perception. *Trends in Cognitive Sciences, 12*(8), 306–313.

Williams, A. C., & Amris, K. (2007). Pain from torture. *Pain, 133*, 5–8.

Williams, A. C. C., Davies, H. T. O., & Chadury, Y. (2000). Simple pain rating scales hide complex idiosyncratic meanings. *Pain, 85*, 457–463.

Williams, S. E., Smith, C. A., Bruehl, S. P., Gigante, J., & Walker, L. S. (2009). Medical evaluation of children with chronic abdominal pain: impact of diagnosis, physician practice orientation, and maternal trait anxiety on mothers' responses to the evaluation. *Pain, 146*, 283–292.

Wittink, H., & Carr, D. B. (2008). Outcomes and effective pain management. *IASP Clinical Updates, XVI*(1). www.iasp-pain.org/AM/AMTemplate.cfm?Section=Home&TEMPLATE=/CM/ContentDisplay.cfm&CONTENTID=12087&SECTION=Home.

Woolf, C. J. (2011). Central sensitization: Implications for the diagnosis and treatment of pain. *Pain, 152*(3, Suppl. 1), S2–S15.

Yilmaz, P., Diers, M., Diener, S., Rance, M., Wessa, M., & Flor, H. (2010). Brain correlates of stress-induced analgesia. *Pain, 151*, 522–529.

Part 8

Multidisciplinary Approaches

35

Working in Healthcare Teams

A Nursing Perspective

Ann Bonner and Julie Pryor

Introduction

This chapter aims to provide a comprehensive review of the role of nurses in the multidisciplinary healthcare team. Nurses are the principal group of all health professionals and they practice in a wide variety of settings to provide healthcare to individuals and families across the lifespan regardless of where along the health–illness continuum healthcare is required. Nurses provide physical, psychosocial, developmental, cultural, and spiritual nursing care to assist individuals and families to attain their highest possible level of health and recovery or to achieve a dignified death. Fundamentally nurses establish and maintain links between individuals, families, communities, and the rest of the healthcare system. As part of the multidisciplinary team, the nurse is often in a leadership position and coordinating the activities of other team members. Finally this chapter will illustrate cases that include nurse-led support teams, particularly for individuals with chronic health conditions.

The Nursing Profession in Australia

The Australian health workforce consists of three main groups, namely medical practitioners, nurses, and allied health professionals. Of these, nurses are the largest component, comprising approximately 40% of the health workforce [Australian Institute of Health and Welfare (AIHW), 2010]. Even today nursing remains a female-dominated workforce (9.4% of nurses are male) encompassing two levels of nurse (AIHW, 2010); both of which are regulated by national, state, and territory legislation and are licensed to practice by the national Nursing and Midwifery Board of Australia. In addition the Australian Nursing and Midwifery Council oversee the national competency standards and codes of professional conduct.

In Australia, a registered nurse [RN or division 1 RN (Victoria)] undertakes a minimum of a 3 year Bachelor's degree and is responsible for the provision of all nursing care, the supervision

Applied Topics in Health Psychology, First Edition. Edited by M. L. Caltabiano and L. Ricciardelli.
© 2013 John Wiley & Sons, Ltd. Published 2013 by John Wiley & Sons, Ltd.

of enrolled nurses (ENs) and other unregulated carers (such as assistants in nursing), and for delegation of nursing decisions. The second level of nurse is the EN or division 2 RN (Victoria) who has undertaken formal training at diploma or advanced diploma level within the Tertiary and Further Education sector. An EN practices under the direct or indirect supervision of a RN and provides direct patient care. The assistant in nursing (AIN) is an unregulated worker who carries out some nursing duties under the direct supervision of a RN. These duties are mostly associated with activities of daily living such as hygiene, feeding, and personal care. Increasingly, undergraduate nursing students are being employed as AINs (Chow *et al.*, 2010; New South Wales Department of Health, 2010).

Nurses work in a variety of healthcare places, settings and specialty areas of practice providing primary, secondary, and tertiary healthcare. Box 1 identifies the common clinical practice settings of nurses. Regardless of the level of nurse, registered and enrolled nurses practice in metropolitan, regional, rural, and remote public and private health facilities across Australia (AIHW, 2010). Very few nurses are self-employed, although this is possible.

Box 1: Clinical Practice Settings

- Acute hospitals
- Aged care service/residential care facilities
- Mental health services and facilities
- Community health centers
- Multipurpose services[a]
- General practitioner centers
- Day procedure centers
- Schools
- Industries (occupational health)
- Justice health (remand centers, prisons, and juvenile justice settings)
- Developmental disability service
- Hospice/respite services
- Private home care

[a]Multipurpose services are an integration of a Commonwealth-funded aged care facility with at least one other state-funded health service (typically a hospital and/or ambulance service) in small, rural Australian communities (Anderson *et al.*, 2009).

Nursing has a wide and varied career path in clinical practice, education, management, and research. The career path for an EN is less well structured than for RNs, but some ENs upgrade their qualification to that of a RN. Following registration and a graduate year, RNs tend to continue with professional education at various postgraduate levels of study. For many RNs this will be in a specialized field of practice, and, depending on the state or territory, these nurses will be identified as clinical nurse specialists or clinical nurse consultants. The highest level for clinical practice in nursing in Australia is the nurse practitioner (NP), a role that was introduced over 10 years ago (Gardner *et al.*, 2009). The role is specifically endorsed to practice with an extended scope of practice and authorized to order diagnostic tests, make patient referrals to other health professionals, and prescribe medications (Gardner *et al.*, 2007). NPs can work in all healthcare settings although, at present, they largely work in emergency departments, specialized chronic healthcare settings (e.g., heart failure, diabetes, chronic kidney disease, mental health), and in rural and remote areas. To become a NP further postgraduate education at Master's level is required (i.e., Master of Nurse Practitioner course).

Another growing group of nurses are practice nurses, which should not be confused with NPs. These nurses are either a registered or enrolled nurse who is employed to work within a general medical practice setting (Patterson *et al.*, 2007). Medicare reimbursement for an episode of care is provided. In some situations a practice nurse may also be qualified and licensed to practice as a NP. Community nurses, another type of nurse, are employed by various state, federal, and nongovernmental organizations, and provide nursing care in community health centers and in people's homes (Cioffi *et al.*, 2007). Both practice and community nurses have the opportunity to provide continuous and ongoing care of individuals, particularly for those with chronic conditions outside of acute hospitals. With the Federal Government moving towards establishing Medicare Local (local, independent, multidisciplinary health services designed to integrate primary healthcare, hospital, and aged care services), there will be a greater integration and blurring of the roles for community and practice nurses, with most of these nurses working within interprofessional teams made up of general practitioners and other health professionals (Williams & Kralik, 2008).

What is Nursing?

RNs are autonomous practitioners as they have the responsibility, accountability, and authority to make nursing decisions and perform nursing actions. They also have the ability to delegate some tasks to others (e.g., to AINs or ENs) but retain the responsibility for the actions of others. The International Council of Nurses' definition of nursing (see Box 2) captures the notion of what nurses do (International Council of Nurses, 2010). Among the critical tasks carried out by nurses are (1) ongoing monitoring and assessment of patients and, as necessary, initiating interventions to address complications or reduce risk; (2) coordinating care delivered by other providers; and (3) educating patients and family members (Needleman & Hassmiller, 2009).

Box 2: International Council of Nurses' Definition of Nursing

Nursing encompasses autonomous and collaborative care of individuals of all ages, families, groups, and communities, sick or well, and in all settings. Nursing includes the promotion of health, prevention of illness, and the care of ill, disabled, and dying people. Advocacy, promotion of a safe environment, research, participation in shaping health policy and in patient and health systems management, and education are also key nursing roles. (International Council of Nurses, 2010)

What nurses do changes and develops as needs in society change and health technology advances. As such, nurses are not limited to specific tasks, functions, or responsibilities. Nurses are required to be flexible and adaptable, to expect the unexpected, and to provide patient-centered care in a changing and expanding healthcare environment. To support nurses in responding to and coping with the dynamic and complex healthcare environment, the discipline of nursing draws upon a number of other health disciplines such as medicine, psychology, sociology, and pharmacology as well as nursing-specific knowledge generated by nursing research. Nurses are also taught and expected to engage in continuous professional development (mandated through annual practicing registration), critical thinking, critical reflection, and evidence-based practice.

Nurses provide nursing care according to varying degrees of control and independence (Doran *et al.*, 2006). The independent nursing role focuses on the functions and responsibilities that nurses are held accountable for in the care environment. The interdependent nursing role is concerned with the functions that are partially or totally dependent on other healthcare providers and vice versa. The dependent nursing role is concerned with the functions and responsibilities associated with implementing medical orders and treatments.

Over the years nursing knowledge and practice has become more specialized and has followed the lead of medicine; however, the fundamentals of nursing care remain directed towards providing assistance with physical, psychosocial, developmental, cultural, and spiritual needs. This is traditionally viewed as the caregiver role; however, nurses also assume a number of other roles such as communicator, teacher, advocate, counsellor, change agent, leader, manager, and case manager (Berman *et al.*, 2010). Depending on the needs of the patient and/or the context of practice, nurses often perform these roles concurrently rather than exclusively.

Nursing practice involves four areas: promoting health, preventing illness, restoring health and function, and caring for the dying (Berman *et al.*, 2010). Promoting health and wellness may involve activities such as improving nutrition and physical fitness, preventing drug and alcohol misuse, and preventing accidents and injury in the workplace. Nursing activities directed toward preventing illness include providing immunizations, child and family healthcare, sexual healthcare, and health education. Restoring health focuses on the person who is ill and includes providing care to support activities of daily living, performing assessment and diagnostic procedures, teaching, coaching, and rehabilitating patients. Nursing practice also involves providing care to the person who is dying, to help them to live as comfortably as possible until death, and to support family members and friends to cope with death.

Among all of the health professions that contribute to a healthcare team, only nurses are required to attend to the patient's needs 24 h a day. Nurses are therefore an integral part of the healthcare team and in many respects it can be argued that they are the glue that holds everything together by being the link between the patient or client and various members of the healthcare team.

Multidisciplinary Healthcare

Multidisciplinary service delivery is common in healthcare, making teamwork a core skill for all health professionals. Basically, a team is a group organized to work together, and teamwork is the cooperative effort by the members of a group or team to achieve a common goal (Macquarie Dictionary, 2011). However, while it is widely recognized that multiple disciplines bring a broader range of expertise to the treatment of individual patients, the processes of effective teamwork are less well understood. The following warning from Forbes and Fitzsimons (1993) remains relevant in healthcare today (see Box 3).

Box 3: Teamwork: a Warning

"It is naive to bring diverse, skilled professionals together and assume that by simply calling this group a team the members will act like a team." (Forbes & Fitzsimons, 1993, p. 2)

In the healthcare context the commonly used terms for the various types of teamwork are multi-, inter-, and transdisciplinary. More recently, the word professional has been used instead of discipline, particularly in the *Journal of Interprofessional Care*. Mumma and Nelson (2002) explain the differences as follows: multidisciplinary teams have clear boundaries with limited communication between the many professions, each of which has discipline-specific goals; interdisciplinary teams work more collaboratively towards patient goals; and, in trans-disciplinary teams, there is a blurring of professional boundaries and cross-training to minimise duplication of effort. The three types of team sit on a continuum. Multidisciplinary teams, where disciplines work more or less alone, are on one end of the continuum and trans-disciplinary teams, where disciplines work together sharing their expertise, are on the other. Interdisciplinary teams sit between these two positions. There is evidence in the literature that all three types of teamwork are used in heathcare, with trans-disciplinary being the least common (Petri, 2010). According to Zwarenstein *et al.* (2009), research in the area of healthcare teams is complicated by the use of varied terms such as collaboration, communication, coordination, and teamwork, as well as the overlap of the field with other fields of study which also examine how healthcare is organized and delivered.

Most importantly, effective healthcare teamwork is about "collective capability," i.e., "what professionals know and what they do collectively" (Soubhi *et al.*, 2009, p. 52) with a patient and the patient's supporters to meet the patients' needs. Typically, however, the roles and contributions of the patient and their supporters are overlooked in discussions of teamwork. For example, Embling (1995) lists the key attributes and process for healthcare team effectiveness as including shared goals, interdependence, cooperation, coordination of activities, task specialization, division of effort, and mutual respect. To this, Bakheit (1996) adds a competent leader, operational guidelines that outline the process of team activity, a mechanism for decision making, clear lines of communication and clearly defined roles, and responsibilities and accountability for team members. In the healthcare team literature the uniqueness of the patient and their illness experience is frequently overshadowed by emphasis on standardized processes. More recently, the role of nonhealthcare professionals has been acknowledged. For example, following a review of the literature by Nijhuis *et al.* (2007) in contexts involving children, parental involvement is suggested as the sixth dimension of team collaboration as it is relevant to all the defining elements, namely communication, decision making, goal setting, organization, and team processes.

Because the goal of teamwork is achievement of a common goal, interpersonal relationships within the team are critical. For instance, Fonouni *et al.* (2010) found that a multidisciplinary transplant team, consisting of a transplant nurse, a transplant surgeon, a nephrologist, a pediatrician, a radiologist, a psychologist, and a transplant coordinator, working together in a structured team achieved an increase in the living kidney donation rate, and thereby reduced the waiting time for people with end-stage kidney disease to receive a kidney transplant. However, this study confusingly uses both multi- and interdisciplinary terms to describe the team. While systematic structures and processes can enhance the effectiveness of teamwork, the centrality of the interpersonal nature of teamwork cannot be overemphasized. Some, for example Pryor (2005) and Burton *et al.* (2009), have found that personal relationships can positively influence cross-disciplinary working between nursing and allied health. However, sole reliance on the goodwill of individuals does not create a strong foundation for team effectiveness.

In addition to technical expertise and cognitive intelligence, McCallin and Bamford (2007) argue that emotional intelligence is required for team effectiveness. Similarly, Koch *et al.* (2009) suggest that, beyond therapeutic and clinical empathy, interdisciplinary empathy is required. Most importantly, emotional intelligence and empathy are important between individuals and between disciplines. Through informal dialogue teams can deconstruct traditional ways of working and reconstruct new approaches to interdisciplinary work (McCallin, 2004). In a study of teams in practice, McCallin (2004) found that by breaking with stereotypical images and grappling with different mindsets, healthcare teams can rethink their professional responsibilities. By negotiating service provision (with a focus on problem solving for the client) and engaging in a dialogic culture, individual and professional responsibilities can be reframed to meet the patient's needs. The outcome of consciously focusing on a team approach is suggestive of trans-disciplinary teamwork as described by Shaw *et al.* (2005), namely professional synergy.

Peck and Norman (1999) provide an easy to follow example of how dialogue to explore team roles was established within an adult community mental health service. Each professional group was asked to:

- generate an account of their roles and responsibilities and, more generally, the professional identity of the members of the discipline, and
- delineate the origins and the means of maintenance of that professional identity, through facilitated discussion (Peck & Norman, 1999, p. 232).

Each story explored core skills as well as skill overlap, and relationships between professions. This research provides a way to demystify and value different professional groups within a multidisciplinary team. The telling, hearing and responding to each professional group is a process that could form the basis for assisting other teams to move to work within interprofessional teams. It could also improve the quality of the relationships between the team and the consumers of their services (Peck & Norman, 1999).

Formal and informal interprofessional learning are widely advocated as a means for enhancing cross-disciplinary working (Petri, 2010). Formal interprofessional education can provide a safe place to explore the values, beliefs, attitudes, customs, and behaviors that contribute to each discipline's unique culture and hence uncover how professional cultures can act as barriers to effective teamwork (Hall, 2005). Increasingly in Australia and elsewhere interprofessional education between nursing and other health discipline students has become a feature of undergraduate (or pre-licensure) courses. Courses which actively use interprofessional learning in both classroom and workplaces provide opportunities for socialization, and understanding and valuing of other disciplines, to occur.

In the practice setting, without systematic processes in place informal dialogue relies mostly on opportunistic encounters. Such encounters can be hindered or facilitated by structural features of healthcare environments. For example, Pryor (2008) found that discipline-specific use of the built environment kept nursing and allied health apart, while Clarke (2010) found that colocating team members and joint working between disciplines enhanced cross-disciplinary teamwork between nurses and allied health. Furthermore, regular and repeated "thinking and talking out loud" about practice fosters "team identity and develops team thinking" (Clarke, 2008, p. 111). Nurses are ideally situated to drive such team- and practice-development initiatives and as a consequence enhance the collective capability of healthcare teams.

Nurses Enhancing the Collective Capability of Healthcare Teams

In a context of increasing specialization and hence healthcare team size, the importance of nursing's role in "maintaining a holistic overview of patient care" (Jinks & Hope, 2000, p. 273) cannot be overemphasized. This is especially true in inpatient settings where nursing provides the glue that holds the patient, healthcare, and the system together. It can also be the case in non-inpatient settings, for example in a study by Booth and Waters (1995) the nurse was described as "the lynchpin of day hospital activity" (p. 700). In these roles nurses may be compensating for what nurses have described as a fragmented approach to patient care (Long *et al.*, 2003) or care system deficiencies (Burton, 2000).

Due to their holistic overview of patient care, nurses can enhance the collective capability of healthcare teams in a number of ways. All nurses can extend the contribution of other disciplines in two ways: by fulfilling a "carry on" role and by facilitating "carry over." Carry on involves nurses supporting other disciplines by continuing the work of other healthcare professionals in their absence or supervising support staff in this role. Carry over, however, involves nurses facilitating patients and their supporters to integrate what they have been taught by other disciplines into their everyday life. In so doing, nurses rely heavily on their own disciplinary expertise as skilled therapeutic companions of patients on illness journeys (Pearson *et al.*, 1997). Through extended day-to-day interactions with patients, nurses develop "an understanding of what it means to be ill and an understanding of the illness experience" (Pearson *et al.*, 1997, p. 51). In addition to being therapeutic in their own right, these relationships are an ideal mechanism for carry on and carry over.

For example, inpatient brain injury rehabilitation relies heavily on effective teamwork between nursing and psychology. In this setting, psychology expertise in relation to behavior support is channelled to patients through their everyday interactions with nurses. Regular cross-disciplinary meetings provide a forum for problem identification and treatment planning. Nurses collect and present data to assist in problem identification. Treatment plans are developed collaboratively. Psychology scripted interventions are implemented by nurses and evaluated collaboratively.

In addition to carry on and carry over, nurses enhance the collective capability of healthcare teams by fulfilling a more central role in the coordination and leadership of health teams and services. They do this in a wide variety of ways and across all healthcare settings. Coordination of patient care is critical to team effectiveness. Typically nurses are case managers for patients and coordinate the (multidisciplinary) healthcare team to ensure that care is coordinated, planned, and monitored for outcomes for patients. For example, primary roles of palliative care clinical nurse consultants in one Australian study were described as "the internal link" between disciplines in the inpatient setting and as the lynchpin between hospital and community services (O'Connor & Chapman, 2008). In Australia, the importance of coordination in stroke care is also recognized (National Stroke Foundation, 2010). One UK study (Burton, 1999) identifies the centrality of (multidisciplinary) healthcare team work and the facilitation of clinical processes by nurses in stroke coordination roles.

In Australia, practice nurses who work with general practitioners are in an ideal position to coordinate healthcare teams, particularly for chronic conditions. These nurses coordinate, implement, and monitor chronic illness multidisciplinary care plans. For instance, a proactive collaboration between nursing and psychology professionals is one in which the healthy aging model, as explained by Potempa *et al.* (2010), could involve practice nurses acting in the role of coaches using a goal-driven approach developed by psychologists that taps into supports in the patient's personal health system. This type of collaboration could be effective in assisting older Australians to maintain health and wellbeing in their own home.

Nurses frequently provide leadership in the development of multidisciplinary clinical service delivery. Such nursing leadership is evident in the description of an initiative to improve the management of bariatric patients in one Australian acute care hospital. The commitment of Nowicki *et al.* (2009) to healthcare team practice development is evidenced in statements such as "one of our greatest achievements has been to involve and empower expert staff from a myriad of specialities" (p. 173).

Nurse-led clinical programs and services can also enhance the collective capability of healthcare teams in a wide variety of contexts. Examples of such programs and services include nurse-led mental health clinics (e.g., Wand & White, 2007; Wand *et al.*, 2008), nurse-led follow-up for cancer patients (see Lewis *et al.*, 2009, for a review of the literature), and nurse-led case management for peritoneal dialysis patients (Chow & Wong, 2010).

In Australia, emergence of the NP role illustrates nursing's ability to provide clinical leadership. As NPs are able to function in an extended clinical role particularly in "unpredictable and complex situations" (Australian Nursing and Midwifery Council, 2006, p. 2), they are ideally situated to identify aspects of patient care that other disciplines can contribute. Their ability to undertake comprehensive patient assessment and to refer to other health professionals (Carryer *et al.*, 2007) means that they are ideally suited to lead healthcare teams into the future.

Conclusion

Given the increasing burden of chronic conditions and the aging population on healthcare systems, it is imperative that interprofessional collaboration through cohesive healthcare teams be implemented to improve health outcomes and service delivery, and to control the escalating financial burden of healthcare on society. Nurses have, and will continue to be, the backbone in the delivery of healthcare regardless of the patient's age, location, or need. Better understanding of the different levels, responsibilities, and roles of nurses within the healthcare team will reduce fragmentation and duplication of services, and will enable better integration of healthcare and more effective support for the individual and their family.

References

AIHW. (2010). *Nursing and Midwifery Labour Force 2008.* Bulletin no. 81. Cat. no. AUS 130. Canberra: Australian Institute of Health and Welfare.

Anderson, J., Grootjens, J., & Bonner, A. (2009). The impact of rhetoric and reality on community anticipation of risk in the development of multi-purpose services (MPS): A grounded theory study. *Proceedings of the 10th National Rural Health Conference*, G. Gregory (Ed.), Cairns, QLD, 17–20 May 2009. Canberra: National Rural Health Alliance.

Australian Nursing and Midwifery Council. (2006). *National Competency Standards for the Nurse Practitioner.* Canberra: Australian Nursing and Midwifery Council.

Bakheit, A. (1996). Effective teamwork in rehabilitation. *International Journal of Rehabilitation Research, 19,* 301–306.

Berman, A., Snyder, S., Kozier, B., & Erb, G. (2010). *Kozier and Erb's Fundamentals of Nursing.* Frenchs Forest: Pearson.

Booth, J., & Waters, K. R. (1995). The multifaceted role of the nurse in the day hospital. *Journal of Advanced Nursing, 22,* 700–706.

Burton, C. R. (1999). An exploration of the stroke co-ordinator role. *Journal of Clinical Nursing, 8,* 535–541.

Burton, C. R. (2000). A description of the nursing role in stroke rehabilitation. *Journal of Advanced Nursing, 32*(1), 174–181.

Burton, C. R., Fisher, A., & Green, T. L. (2009). The organisational context of nursing care in stroke units: A case study approach. *International Journal of Nursing Studies, 46,* 86–95.

Carryer, J., Gardner, G., Dunn, S., & Gardner, A. (2007). The core role of the nurse practitioner: practice, professionalism and clinical leadership. *Journal of Clinical Nursing, 16,* 1818–1825.

Chow, J., San Miguel, S., LiDonni, M., & Isbister, J. (2010). The introduction of assistants in nursing in an Australian haemodialysis service. *Renal Society of Australasia Journal, 6,* 81–87.

Chow, S. K. Y., & Wong, F. K. Y. (2010). Health-related quality of life in patients undergoing peritoneal dialysis: effects of a nurse-led case management programme. *Journal of Advanced Nursing, 66,* 1780–1792.

Cioffi, J., Wilkes, L., Warne, B., Harrison, K., & Vonu-Boriceanu, O. (2007). Community nursing care for clients with chronic and complex conditions. *Collegian, 14,* 21–25.

Clarke, D. J. (2008). Talking about stroke rehabilitation can improve team processes. *International Journal of Therapy and Rehabilitation, 15,* 110–111.

Clarke, D. (2010). Achieving teamwork in stroke units: The contribution of opportunistic dialogue. *Journal of Interprofessional Care, 24,* 285–297.

Doran, D., Harrison, M., Laschinger, H., Hirdes, J., Rukholm, E., Sidani, S. *et al.* (2006). Relation between nursing interventions and outcome achievement in acute care settings. *Research in Nursing & Health, 29,* 61–70.

Embling, S. (1995). Exploring multidisciplinary teamwork. *British Journal of Therapy and Rehabilitation, 2,* 142–144.

Fonouni, H., Golriz, M., Mehrabi, A., Oweira, H., Schmied, B. M., Müller, S. A. *et al.* (2010). The role of an interdisciplinary transplant team on living donation kidney transplantation program. *Transplantation Proceedings, 42,* 137–140.

Forbes, E. J., & Fitzsimons, V. (1993). Education: The key for holistic interdisciplinary collaboration. *Holistic Nurse Practice, 7,* 1–10.

Gardner, A., Gardner, G .E., Middleton, S., & Della. P. R. (2009). The status of Australian nurse practitioners: The first national census. *Australian Health Review, 33,* 679–689.

Gardner, G., Chang, A., & Duffield, C. (2007). Making nursing work: breaking through the role confusion of advanced practice nursing. *Journal of Advanced Nursing, 57,* 382–391.

Hall, P. (2005). Interprofessional teamwork: Professional cultures as barriers. *Journal of Interprofessional Care,* Suppl. *1,* 188–196.

International Council of Nurses. (2010). *Definition of Nursing.* www.icn.ch/about-icn/icn-definition-of-nursing/.

Jinks, A. M., & Hope, P. (2000). What do nurses do? An observational survey of the activities of nurses on acute surgical and rehabilitation wards. *Journal of Nursing Management, 8,* 273–279.

Koch, L., Gitchel, D., & Higgins, K. (2009). Preparing students to be empathetic interdisciplinary rehabilitation team members. *Rehabilitation Education, 23,* 119–126.

Lewis, R., Neal, R. D., Williams, N. H., France, B., Wilkinson, C., Hendry *et al.* (2009). Nurse-led vs. conventional physician-led follow-up for patients with cancer: Systematic review. *Journal of Advanced Nursing, 65,* 706–723.

Long, A. F., Kneafsey, R., & Ryan, J. (2003). Rehabilitation practice: Challenges to effective team working. *International Journal of Nursing Studies, 40,* 663–673.

Macquarie Dictionary. (2011). *The Macquarie Dictionary Online.* www.macquariedictionary.com.au/anonymous@9c9FF842487876/-/p/dict/index.html.

McCallin A. (2004). Pluralistic dialoguing: A theory of interprofessional teamworking. The *Grounded Theory Review, 4,* 25–42.

McCallin, A., & Bamford, A. (2007). Interdisciplinary teamwork: Is the influence of emotional intelligence fully appreciated? *Journal of Nursing Management, 15,* 386–391.

Mumma, C. M., & Nelson, A. (2002). Models for theory-based practice of rehabilitation nursing. In S. Hoeman (Ed.), *Rehabilitation Nursing: Process, Application and Outcome* (pp. 21–33). St Louis, MO: Mosby.

National Stroke Foundation. (2010). *Clinical Guidelines for Stroke Management 2010.* Melbourne: National Stroke Foundation.

Needleman, J., & Hassmiller, S. (2009). The role of nurses in improving hospital quality and efficiency: Real-world results. *Health Affairs, 28*(4), w625–w633.

New South Wales Department of Health. (2009). *Assistants in Nursing Working in the Acute Care Environment: An Implementation Package.* www.health.nsw.gov.au/pubs/2010/pdf/ain_acute_care.pdf.

Nijhuis, B. J. G., Reinders-Messelink, H. A., de Blecourt, A. C. E., Olijve, W. G., Groothoff, J. W., Nakken, H., & Postema, K. (2007). A review of salient elements defining team collaboration in paediatric rehabilitation. *Clinical Rehabilitation, 21,* 195–211.

Nowicki, T., Burns, C., Fulbrook, P., & Jones, J. (2009). Changing the mindset: An interdisciplinary approach to management of the bariatric patient. *Collegian, 16,* 171–175.

O'Connor, M., & Chapman, Y. (2008). The palliative care clinical nurse consultant: An essential link. *Collegian, 15,* 151–157.

Patterson, E., Muenchberger, H., & Kendall, E. (2007). The role of practice nurses in coordinated care of people with chronic and complex conditions. *Australian Health Review, 31,* 231–238.

Pearson, A., Borbasi, S., & Walsh, K. (1997). Practising nursing therapeutically through acting as a skilled companion on the illness journey. *Advanced Nursing Quarterly, 3,* 46–52.

Peck, E., & Norman, I. J. (1999). Working together in adult community mental health services: Exploring inter-professional role relations. *Journal of Mental Health, 8,* 231–242.

Petri L. (2010). Concept analysis of interdisciplinary collaboration. *Nursing Forum, 45,* 73–82.

Potempa, K. M., Butterworth, S. W., Flaherty-Robb, M. K., & Gaynor, W. L. (2010). The healthy ageing model: Health behaviour change for older adults. *Collegian, 17,* 51–55.

Pryor, J. (2005). A grounded theory of nursing's contribution to inpatient rehabilitation. Unpublished PhD thesis, Deakin University, Melbourne. http://adt.caul.edu.au/deakin.html.

Pryor, J. (2008). A nursing perspective on the relationship between nursing and allied health in inpatient rehabilitation. *Disability and Rehabilitation, 30,* 314–322.

Shaw, L., Walker, R., & Hogue, A. (2007). The art and science of teamwork: Enacting a transdisciplinary approach to work rehabilitation. *Work, 20,* 297–306.

Soubhi, H., Rege Colet, N., Gilbert, J. H. V., Lebel, P., Thivierge, R. L., Hudson, & C., Fortin, M. (2009). Interprofessional learning in the trenches: Fostering collective capability. *Journal of Interprofessional Care, 23,* 52–57.

Wand, T., & White, K. (2007). Progression of the mental health nurse practitioner role in Australia. *Journal of Psychiatric and Mental Health Nursing, 14,* 644–651.

Wand, T., White, K., & Patching, J. (2008). Refining the model for an emergency department-based mental health nurse practitioner outpatient service. *Nursing Inquiry, 15,* 231–241.

Williams, A., & Kralik, D. (2008). Working with people with chronic conditions. In D. Kralik & A. van Loon (Eds.), *Community Nursing in Australia.* Carlton: Blackwell Publishing.

Zwarenstein, M., Goldman, J., & Reeves, S. (2009). Interprofessional collaboration: Effects of practice-based interventions on professional practice and healthcare outcomes. *Cochrane Database of Systematic Reviews, 3,* CD000072.

36

The General Practice Team and Allied Health Professionals

Jennifer Chamberlain-Salaun, Jane Mills,
and Nichola Davis

Australian general practice has undergone a transformation since the early 2000s that has largely been contingent on the establishment of funding streams for health professionals other than medical practitioners. This chapter provides an overview of general practice in Australia that includes a description of common models of primary healthcare provision. Various roles are discussed, including general practitioners, practice nurses, mental health nurses, psychologists and allied health professionals. The provision of primary care services in rural and remote Australia is outlined, with contextual differences between urban, rural, and remote areas discussed using a four-point framework: access, a stronger multidisciplinary approach, privacy and confidentiality, and cultural safety. A commentary on the future of primary healthcare in Australia concludes the chapter.

Introduction to General Practice in Australia

General practice in Australia is defined as "the component of the healthcare system which provides primary, subsequent and continuing medical care and coordinates services to individuals, families and communities" together with the integration of "current biomedical, psychological and social understandings of health issues" (Commonwealth Department of Health and Aged Care, 2000, p. 160). Australia's primary healthcare sector, in which general practice plays a key role, comprises various diverse and assorted public and private services and commonwealth and state government-funded programs (Commonwealth Department of Health and Aged Care, 2000). The Australian Government has major responsibility for general practice through the Medicare fee-for-service payment system and state and territories governments have major responsibility for hospitals and publicly funded community health services (McDonald *et al.*, 2006).

Models of general practice in Australia primarily operate as a small business and include solo practitioner practices (38%), multi general practitioner practices (44% of practices have between two and five general practitioners), and large frequently corporately owned entrepreneurial businesses (18% of practices have more than six more general practitioners) (Primary Health Care

Applied Topics in Health Psychology, First Edition. Edited by M. L. Caltabiano and L. Ricciardelli.
© 2013 John Wiley & Sons, Ltd. Published 2013 by John Wiley & Sons, Ltd.

Research and Information Service, 2010), often incorporating a variety of health services, such as allied health, dentistry, and pharmacy, in a one-stop-shop location. Most general practitioners are remunerated under the Medicare fee-for-service system either directly or indirectly along with payments from consumers. In most instances, nurses and some allied health professionals are salaried (Southern *et al.*, 2002).

General practice is often a consumer's first point of contact with the healthcare system, and in 2009–10 83% of the population consulted a general practitioner at least once (Britt *et al.*, 2010). As consumers' health requirements and treatment options become more complex and varied, general practitioners are increasingly required to integrate and coordinate a diverse selection of inputs across the health continuum. A multidisciplinary approach to healthcare is an integral part of the current healthcare environment (Australian Institute of Health and Welfare, 2008; Propp *et al.*, 2010).

There is no one model for team practice; however, in the literature a multidisciplinary approach to healthcare is defined as health professionals from different disciplines working parallel to one another assessing and treating clients and sharing information with each other (Kvarnstrom, 2008; McCallin, 2005; Sheehan *et al.*, 2007; Sorrell-Jones, 1997). The development of multidisciplinary healthcare teams can be traced to Engel's 1977 biopsychosocial model of health, which generated a shift in focus from disease to health (Black, 2005; Connor *et al.*, 2002). Although Engel (1989) acknowledged that a more holistic approach to medicine was not a new concept, he highlighted the inadequacies of the traditional biomedical model of care that considered the disease and not the client as a whole. As an alternative, Engel (1989) presented a biopsychosocial model of health and illness that incorporated "the social, psychological and behavioral dimensions of illness" (p. 37). With a shift in focus from disease to health and the gradual transition in Australia from doctor-centric service delivery to multidisciplinary service delivery the role of psychologists and other allied health professionals has never been more important.

Roles Within a Multidisciplinary Team

As part of a multidisciplinary approach to healthcare, allied health professionals communicate and interact with general practitioners and practice nurses in varying degrees. Understanding the roles of other health professionals and effective communication are important factors in establishing professional relationships that support client care.

General practitioners

The key elements of a general practitioner's role include direct provision of primary care and acting as conduits, linking consumers to the broader health system. In the literature the terminology "gatekeeper" is often used to define the latter (Davies *et al.*, 2009; Phillips *et al.*, 2004; Proude *et al.*, 2006; Russell & Mitchell, 2002). We believe that the term gatekeeper conjures negative images of general practitioners scrutinizing clients access to the broader health system, while the use of "conduit" more positively connotes general practitioners as facilitators and coordinators of client flow between general practice and the broader health system.

The role of general practitioners as a primary care provider may include prescribing and advising on medication and/or providing nonpharmacological treatments. Linking consumers to the wider health system can include ordering investigative tests and referring clients to medical specialists, allied health professionals, and support services (Australian Medical Workforce Advisory

Committee, 2005). General medical conditions, particularly chronic disease, may also be accompanied by mental problems and illnesses (Katon, 2003); therefore, during most client encounters general practitioners also routinely assess client's mental health. This assessment may be done informally through general questioning for mental health "red flags," such as unusual tiredness, insomnia, or loss of libido, or through the use of formal screening tools such as the Kessler 10 (K10) standardized questionnaire (Slade *et al.*, 2009) and the Edinburgh post-natal depression questionnaire (Sharp & Lipsky, 2002). Formal screening tools do not diagnose depression, but they provide general practitioners with an indication of the severity of symptoms during a given period of time, which can be used to guide further care.

If a client is assessed as having mental health problems they may be treated within the general practitioner's scope of practice or referred to an allied mental health professional. General practitioners may elect not to refer a client for a range of reasons. This may be due to a client's lack of personal insight, clients' refusal to seek help, or clients not wishing to seek help as diagnosed mental illness may have implications for disability or other insurance claims. General practitioners may also elect to treat clients through prescribed medication and, depending on their experience and interests, may decide to conduct behavioral therapies, counselling, and focused psychological strategies themselves. General practitioners who have successfully completed the requisite training and have registered as a provider of focused psychological strategies can access additional Medicare Benefit Schedule item numbers (Royal Australian College of General Practitioners, 2010). A 2005 report on the general practice workforce in Australia (Australian Medical Workforce Advisory Committee, 2005) highlighted an increase in the counselling role of general practitioners, especially among female practitioners who are more likely to deal with what is commonly referred to as the "tears and smears" of general practice (Australian Medical Workforce Advisory Committee, 2005). Tears and smears refers to women's health consultations which provide an opportunity to discuss other issues that may be concerning female clients and may involve a counselling element.

In instances of general practitioners referring clients to allied mental health and other allied professionals the client's age and circumstances, including their financial situation, will influence referral patterns and the types of professionals involved in a multidisciplinary approach to care. In the case of children, general practitioners may coordinate referrals to psychologists through the education system, through public health pediatricians, or may refer directly to a private psychologist. Elderly clients may be referred for an aged care community psychiatry assessment, which may provide them with access to a range of state, or commonwealth funded programs. High-risk clients across all client groups may be referred to medical health crisis teams through the public health system, while lower-risk clients may be referred to an allied mental health professional with or without an accompanying GP Mental Health Care Plan which can be completed using the Medicare item number 2710 [Australian Government Department of Health and Ageing (DoHA), 2010a].

Practice nurses

Since 2000 the role of practice nurses in Australia has broadened, due mainly to the recognition of general practice nursing as a specialist area of nursing practice, the introduction of government-driven initiatives that reward general practices for employing practice nurses, and the introduction of Medicare item numbers that provide rebates for specific services provided by practice nurses on behalf of a general practitioner (Mills & Fitzgerald, 2008). In a recent study of practice nurse roles researchers identified six roles of nurses in general practice: patient carer, quality controller, organizer, problem solver, educator, and agent of connectivity (Phillips *et al.*, 2009). In their role

Table 36.1   Examples of organizational tasks undertaken by practice nurses

Organizational element	Activities
Clinical care	Actioning recall and reminders
	Setting up for procedures
	Undertaking telephone and face-to-face triage
	Monitoring the waiting room
	Managing daily pathology results
	Following-up specialist appointments and other care for patients
	Conducting Pap smears
	Conducting health assessments
	Administering and management of immunizations
	Wound dressing
Practice management	Managing and ordering stock
	Instrument sterilization
	Developing policies and procedures
	Clearing contaminated waste
	Maintaining a safe working environment

Adapted from Phillips, C., Pearce, C., Dwan, K., Hall, S., Porritt, J., Yates, R., Kljakovis, M., & Sibbald, B. (2008). *Charting New Roles for Australian General Practice Nurses: Abridged Report of the Australian General Practice Nurses Study*. Canberra: Australian Primary Health Care Institute.

as patient carer, nurses undertake clinical and practice management activities, some of which are presented in Table 36.1.

The introduction of Medicare item number 10997, which provides for monitoring and support to people with a chronic disease, offers a formal framework for the recognition of practice nurses and registered Aboriginal health workers in the management of chronic illness. Under this Medicare item number general practices are remunerated for nurses and the Aboriginal health workers role in the provision of self-management advice, monitoring of medication compliance, and clinical progress checks within the scope of a general practitioner care plan (DoHA, 2007).

Although practice nurses are reportedly involved in 9% of all general practice encounters (Britt, *et al.*, 2010) their role extends beyond prescribed activities. Research has identified that undertaking clinical tasks provides nurses with an opportunity to encourage clients to "chat" about themselves in more informal ways than general practitioner–client interactions (Phillips *et al.*, 2007). For example, practice nurses are perfectly placed to assess the presence of mental health symptoms in mothers during routine 4 year-old health checks or baby and child immunizations.

Mental health nurses

Mental health nurses also play an important role in general practice. Since the inception of the Mental Health Nurse Incentive Program in 2007 community general practices, private psychiatric services, and other appropriate organizations, such as divisions of general practice, have been able to engage nationally credentialed mental health nurses (Australian Government Department of Human Services, 2011). The role of mental health nurses includes conducting comprehensive mental health assessments, assisting in the development of GP Mental Health Care Plans, providing counselling and psychological therapies and coordinating referrals to allied mental health and other allied health professionals (Australian Government Department of Human Services, 2011; Chamberlain-Salaun *et al.*, 2011).

Psychologists

Psychologists are included in multidisciplinary teams either via direct employment in general practice or in divisions of general practice, or via referrals from general practitioners, psychiatrists, pediatricians, or other healthcare providers. In all instances Medicare provides funding mechanisms to support a multidisciplinary approach to healthcare.

Eligible general practices, Aboriginal medical services, and Aboriginal community controlled health services who elect to directly employ psychologists are supported with some of the employment costs. Additionally, funded government programs enable divisions of general practice to employ psychologists to support the delivery of allied healthcare.

Registered psychologists who have a Medicare provider number are able to use a range of Medicare item numbers to obtain rebates for a limited number of services provided on referral from a general practitioner. Medicare rebates are available for psychologists' services when a general practitioner refers eligible clients under a management plan. Management plans may include general practitioner mental healthcare plans for clients with mental health issues, general practitioner management plans and team care arrangements for clients with chronic and complex illness, and multidisciplinary care plans for residents of aged care facilities where the plan is prepared by the facility, with input from a general practitioner. Of course, clients may be referred to psychologists beyond the scope of these mechanisms; however, clients will be required to pay the full consultation fee set by the individual psychologist or claim, where applicable, on their private health insurer's ancillary benefits.

Psychologists are experts in human behavior. Their role includes treating clients with mental health issues and providing assistance to those with chronic or complex illness. Psychologists are specialists who assess clients mental health and provide therapies such as counselling for a range of mental health issues including depression, addictive behaviors, serious and enduring mental illness, and childhood behavior disorders.

Psychologists, however, are not interested in mental health alone. Clinical health psychology applies psychological knowledge to the "promotion and maintenance of health, the prevention and treatment of illness, and the identification of etiologic and diagnostic correlates of health, illness, and related dysfunction" (Matarazzo, 1980, p. 215).

As agents of behavioral change, clinical health psychologists support clients with chronic and complex illness to adopt and manage lifestyle changes including, but not limited to diet, physical activity, alcohol intake, and smoking habits. Being confronted with the diagnosis of a chronic or complex illness and associated lifestyle changes can be an emotional time for clients. Health psychologists may use cognitive-behavioral approaches to assist clients in the management of stress, feelings, and pain associated with individual conditions. Health psychologists also use cognitive behavior therapy to enable clients to change their maladaptive ways of thinking about their illness and achieving goals. Psychologists empower clients to better manage their illness (Gatchel & Oordt, 2003).

Useful Multidisciplinary Approaches for Psychologists and Other Allied Health Professionals

It must be remembered that a multidisciplinary approach involves more than a client referral to an allied health professional. Establishing strategies for communicating and sharing information between health professionals on an ongoing basis supports client care.

In recent research that explored how people living with mental illness are supported in the Australian general practice setting (Chamberlain-Salaun *et al.*, 2011), general practitioners identified that they are more likely to refer to psychologists and other allied mental health professionals with whom they have established professional relationships, and who provide timely reports back to them following referral. In addition, general practitioners highlight the importance of psychologists maintaining referral management and communication systems that record when referrals are received and allow for prompt communication with the referring practitioner if there are likely to be delays between a referral being received and an allied health professional being able to see a client. Psychologists and other allied mental health professionals also have medicolegal responsibilities (Psychology Board of Australia, 2011; Australian Psychological Society, 2011) for informing referring practitioners of concerns for a client's welfare, a client's sudden failure to attend appointments, and deterioration of a client's condition.

In some primary healthcare models psychologists may work in the general practice setting, allowing for the sharing of client files with other colocated health practitioners. Consideration of privacy and confidentiality of client information is a legislative requirement under the Australian Privacy Act 1988, and is especially important when clients' files are shared between practitioners. In all situations where practitioners are accessing a single client file, sharing independent client files, or making client files available for research the client's informed consent is required.

Rural and Remote Healthcare

Delivering health services in rural and remote areas presents challenges different to urban settings. There is an expectation that health professionals considering or embarking on healthcare practice in rural and remote areas gain an understanding of the rural and remote context and adapt their practice style as necessary (Bourke *et al.*, 2004; Wakerman, 2004). Some of the distinguishing characteristics of rural and remote health relate to the following aspects of healthcare service delivery:

- access,
- a stronger multidisciplinary approach,
- privacy and confidentiality,
- cultural safety.

Access

Access to health services in rural and remote areas presents unique issues that are not encountered in urban areas. Firstly, in rural and remote areas there are fewer numbers and types of services. For example, medical specialists are generally located in larger metropolitan areas. Some rural communities may have access to specialist services through scheduled specialist visits; however, in remote areas clients are generally required to travel greater distances to access services, which requires more time and additional travel expenses and which may impact on loss of wages. Access to health services in rural and remote areas are also associated with higher costs than comparable services in metropolitan areas (Australian Medical Workforce Advisory Committee, 2005; Bourke, *et al.*, 2004).

A stronger multidisciplinary approach

Participants in a 2005 study identified that a lack of resources means that stronger cooperation between health professionals is essential in remote areas if clients' needs are to be met (Australian

Medical Workforce Advisory Committee, 2005). However, there is no one template for a multi-disciplinary approach to healthcare. In rural and remote areas health services may be provided by practitioners who are locally based, by teams of visiting health professionals or via remote access. Collaboration, communication, and the establishment of partnerships between health professionals gains significance when considered in rural and remote contexts (Mills *et al.*, 2010). Practitioners' understanding of each other's roles is often cited as a key strength of collaborative teamwork (Carpenter *et al.*, 2003; Kvarnstrom, 2008; Mills *et al.*, 2010).

Privacy and confidentiality

Privacy and confidentiality of client information is a high priority in any healthcare setting. In rural and remote communities, however, the family and close social and personal relationships of smaller communities impacts on the anonymity of residents. As Bourke *et al.* (2004) highlight, "privacy is more difficult to maintain as the receptionist, patient, [and health professional] may have relationships prior to and separate from any healthcare consultation" (p. 182). In an environment where anonymity may be compromised, psychologists may find clients more reluctant to engage in group therapy and support groups.

Cultural safety

An understanding of cross-cultural issues is important in any health service setting, but even more so for practitioners in rural and remote health areas where culturally specific services are less accessible than in metropolitan areas. Cultural safety was a term first coined by Maori nurses (Williams, 1999). It encompasses more than an awareness of other cultures and is defined as "an environment which is safe for people; where there is no assault, challenge or denial of their identity, of who they are and what they need. It is about shared respect, shared meaning, shared knowledge and experience, of learning together with dignity, and truly listening" (Williams, 1999, p. 213).

Polaschek (1998) states that "no healthcare interaction is ever simply objective" (p. 453). The concept of cultural safety acknowledges that individuals have cultural views, which are influenced by societal structures. In a health service context these views influence how health professionals practice and how consumers use health services. It is the interrelationship between the personal and the social dimensions to which cultural safety refers. To deliver culturally safe services, health practitioners need to understand and recognize their own culture and their hegemonic position of power in provider–consumer interactions and adapt their practice accordingly to provide an environment that is culturally safe for clients (Bourke *et al.*, 2004).

Models of Primary Healthcare in Rural and Remote Australia

Wakerman *et al.* (2008) conducted a systematic review of the literature, which resulted in five categories of rural and remote primary healthcare models: discrete services, integrated services, comprehensive primary healthcare services, outreach services, and virtual outreach services, also known as IT/telehealth. Table 36.2 outlines the typology of each category.

In this schema, the different categories of models relate to a geographical continuum from discrete services located in the community being served to virtual outreach services that provide services using telecommunications technology. Discrete services are located in rural and remote

Table 36.2 Typology of rural and remote PHC models

Category	Health service models	Rationale/sentinel issue	Measures of success
Discrete services	Walk-in, walk-out Viable models/sustainable models University clinics	*Sustainable* medical *workforce* (getting GPs into rural services)	• Increased number of doctors recruited
Integrated services	Shared care Co-ordinated Care Trials (CCTs mainstream) Multi-Purpose Services Program	*Coordination* between *access* to services otherwise not available locally or not sufficient	• Decreased suicide rate; decreased GP isolation and increased confidence • Decreased waiting times, reduced after-hours call-outs; enhanced continuity of care; reduced inappropriate emergency department attendance • Increased service access; reduced residential care; increased home-based service
Comprehensive primary healthcare services	Aboriginal Controlled Community Health Services (including Aboriginal CCTs)	Primary focus on improved *access* to services	• Some improved processes of care; increased community participation; enhanced funding, improved community participation, improved governance, increased staff numbers, increased utilization, new population health programs
Outreach services	Hub-and-spoke Visiting/periodic services Fly-in, fly-out	*Access* to services for communities too small to support discrete rural service; a secondary driver relates to sustainable workforce.	• Increased occasions of service; increased workforce length of stay; increased referrals; improved cost-effectiveness
Virtual outreach services (IT/telehealth)	Virtual amalgamation Virtual clinics: video pharmacy/assessment and monitoring Telehealth/telemedicine	Use of IT to increase *access* to and *sustain* service for communities too small to support discrete rural services	• Improved access to records; reduced GP on call; increased consultation hours

Reproduced from Wakerman, J., Humphreys, J. S., Wells, R., Kuipers, P., Entwistle, P., & Jones, J. (2008). Primary health care delivery models in rural and remote Australia: A systematic review. *BMC Health Services Research*, 8, doi:27610.1186/1472-6963-8-276.

communities and are generally owned by entities such as local councils, universities, or other incorporated bodies. The focus of this category of service is on sustaining general practitioner services in communities experiencing recruitment and retention difficulties.

Integrated services are also located in the community being served and provide consumers with a single entry point to a range of integrated primary healthcare services that may not otherwise be available locally. This category of service allows colocation and common administration of services to maximize economies of scale.

Comprehensive primary healthcare services are typified by Aboriginal community controlled health services. Community controlled heath services "aim to improve health outcomes through better access to services and by addressing underlying social determinants of health" (Wakerman *et al.*, 2008). This model enables community control of health services and provides a broader scope than integrated services. The scope of community controlled health services encompasses primary clinical care, health promotion activities, and community and workforce capacity building through education and training.

Outreach services are not located in the community being served. This category of service-delivery model enables widely dispersed and isolated populations to access health services. Services may be provided through a "hub-and-spoke" arrangement where a central service provides visiting health services to satellite communities or services are provided on a fly-in, fly-out basis.

Virtual outreach services use telecommunications technology to augment other service-delivery models. This category of primary healthcare model addresses issues related to health professional workforce shortages in rural and remote locations and is widely used in Australia.

Despite many descriptive accounts, a comprehensive evaluation of primary healthcare service models is lacking in the published literature (Wakerman *et al.*, 2008). "This paucity of evaluations is hardly surprising given a policy environment that has been characterized by a notable absence of a national PHC [primary health care] policy" (Wakerman *et al.*, 2008). The introduction of Australia's first primary healthcare strategy (DoHA, 2010b) may provide a framework for addressing the lack of comprehensive evaluations of primary healthcare models.

Future of Primary Healthcare in Australia

Current Australian Government health reforms aim to provide a stronger primary healthcare system so that healthcare can be delivered when and where individuals and communities need it. These reforms include the establishment of Medicare Locals, investment in GP Super Clinics, and infrastructure grants to expand and improve general practice services (DoHA, 2011).

Medicare Locals are independent legal entities with strong links to local hospital networks, health services, and health professionals. These entities play a key role in coordinating health service planning, coordinating and integrating primary healthcare with other sectors of the healthcare system, and working with health providers to improve client access to after-hours health services in their region (DoHA, 2011). While general practitioners will maintain a pivotal role in individual patient's primary healthcare, Medicare Locals will take a lead role in identifying the population healthcare needs of their regional community to provide more integrated care.

The GP Super Clinics national program includes the establishment of clinics, primarily in regional and rural areas. GP Super Clinics and expanded general practices will support the provision of primary healthcare and allied healthcare services in "one-stop-shop" locales (DoHA, 2011). The aim of these clinics is to bring together general practitioners, nurses, allied health professionals, and other healthcare providers to deliver multidisciplinary patient-centered primary healthcare. There is no one model for GP Super Clinics; rather, the program is about "Clinics offer[ing] the right services for their particular local needs" (Roxon, 2011). GP Super Clinics may be privately owned or may be located in state, territory, or local government owned and operated facilities, such as public hospitals (DoHA, 2010c). As of mid 2011 27 clinics were "operational, providing early services or under construction" (Roxon, 2011).

Conclusion

Changing landscapes in urban, rural, and remote primary care service provision are resulting in new roles for a range of healthcare professionals based in the community. The work of multidisciplinary teams in providing primary care and primary healthcare is reliant on clear communication and the development of supportive infrastructure. Australian Government initiatives and policy developments are resulting in a new wave of models of healthcare provision that promise greater access to services and a more integrated approach to care.

References

Australian Government. (2011). *National Health Reform: Improving Primary Health Care for all Australians.* Canberra: Australian Government.

Australian Government Department of Human Services. (2011). *Medicare Australia: Mental Health Nurse Incentive Program.* www.medicareaustralia.gov.au/provider/incentives/mental-health.jsp.

Australian Institute of Health and Welfare. (2008). *Australia's Health 2008.* Cat. no. AUS 99. Canberra: Australian Institute of Health and Welfare.

Australian Medical Workforce Advisory Committee. (2005). The *General Practice Workforce in Australia: Supply and Requirements to 2013.* AMWAC Report 2005.2. Sydney: Australian Medical Workforce Advisory Committee.

Australian Psychological Society. (2011). *Ethics.* www.psychology.org.au/about/ethics.

Black, K. (2005). Advance directive communication practices: Social workers' contributions to the interdisciplinary health care team. *Social Work in Health Care, 40,* 39–55.

Bourke, L., Sheridan, C., Russell, U., Jones, G., DeWitt, D., & Liaw, S.-T. (2004). Developing a conceptual understanding of rural health practice. *Australian Journal of Rural Health, 12,* 181–186.

Britt, H., Miller, G. C., Charles, J., Henderson, J., Bayram, C., Pan, Y., Valenti, L., Harrison, C., O'Halloran, J., & Fahridin, S. (2010). *General Practice Activity in Australia 2009–10.* Canberra: Australian Institute of Health and Welfare.

Carpenter, J., Schneider, J., Brandon, T., & Wooff, D. (2003). Working in multidisciplinary community mental health teams: The impact on social workers and health professionals of integrated mental health care. *British Journal of Social Work, 33,* 1081–1103.

Chamberlain-Salaun, J., Mills, J., & Park, T. (2011). Mental health nurses employed in Australian general practice: Dimensions of time and space. *International Journal of Mental Health Nursing, 20,* 112–118.

Commonwealth Department of Health and Aged Care. (2000). *General Practice in Australia: 2000.* Canberra: Author.

Connor, S. R., Egan, K. A., Kwilosz, D. M., Larson, D. G., & Reese, D. J. (2002). Interdisciplinary approaches to assisting with end-of-life care and decision making. *American Behavioural Scientist, 46,* 340–356.

Davies, G., Perkins, D., McDonald, J., & Williams, A. (2009). Integrated primary health care in Australia. *International Journal of Integrated Care, 9,* e95.

DoHA. (2007). *MBS Item 10997 for the Provision of Monitoring and Support to People with a Chronic Disease by a Practice Nurse or Registered Aboriginal Health Worker on Behalf of a GP.* Canberra: Department of Health and Ageing.

DoHA. (2010a). *MBS Primary Care Items: Allied Health MBS Item Numbers by Profession.* www.health.gov.au/internet/main/publishing.nsf/Content/health-programs-amhpm-pdf-mbsitemtable.

DoHA. (2010b). *Building a 21st Century Primary Health Care System: Australia's First National Primary Health Care Strategy.* Canberra: Department of Health and Ageing.

DoHA. (2010c). *GP Super Clinics: National Program Guide.* www.health.gov.au/internet/main/publishing.nsf/Content/pacd-gpsuperclinics-ProgramGuide2010.

DoHA. (2011). *National Health Reform: Medicare Locals Discussion Paper on Governance and Functions.* www.yourhealth.gov.au/internet/yourhealth/publishing.nsf/Content/medicare-locals-dp-toc~what.

Engel, G. L. (1989). The need for a new medical model: A challenge for biomedicine. *Journal of Interprofessional Care, 4,* 37–53.

Gatchel, R. J., & Oordt, M. S. (2003). *Clinical Health Psychology and Primary Care: Practical Advice and Clinical Guidance for Successful Collaboration.* Washington DC: American Psychological Association.

Katon, W. J. (2003). Clinical and health services relationships between major depression, depressive symptoms and general medical illness. *Biological Psychiatry, 54,* 216–226.

Kvarnstrom, S. (2008). Difficulties in collaboration: A critical incident study of interprofessional healthcare teamwork. *Journal of Interprofessional Care, 22,* 191–203.

Matarazzo, J. D. (1980). Behavioural health and behavioural medicine. *American Psychologist, 35,* 801–815.

McCallin, A. (2005). Interprofessional practice: Learning how to collaborate. *Contemporary Nurse, 20,* 28–37.

McDonald, J., Cumming, J., Harris, M. F., Powell Davies, G., & Burns, P. (2006). *Systematic Review of System-Wide Models of Comprehensive Primary Health Care.* Sydney: Research Centre for Health Care and Equity, School of Public Health and Community Medicine, UNSW.

Mills, J., & Fitzgerald, M. (2008). The changing role of practice nurses in Australia: An action research study. *Australian Journal of Advanced Nursing, 26,* 16–20.

Mills, J. E., Francis, K., Birks, M., Coyle, M., Henderson, S., & Jones, J. (2010). Registered nurses as members of interprofessional primary health care teams in remote or isolated areas of Queensland: Collaboration, communication and partnerships in practice. *Journal of Interprofessional Care, 24,* 587–596.

Phillips, C., Dwan, K., Pearce, C., Hall, S., Porrit, J., Yates, R., & Siebold, C. (2007). Time to talk, time to see: Changing microeconomies of professional practice among nurses and doctors in Australian general practice. *Contemporary Nurse, 26,* 136–144.

Phillips, C., Pearce, C., Dwan, K., Hall, S., Porritt, J., Yates, R., Kljakovis, M., & Sibbald, B. (2008). *Charting New Roles for Australian General Practice Nurses: Abridged Report of the Australian General Practice Nurses Study.* Canberra: Australian Primary Health Care Institute.

Phillips, C. B., Pearce, C., Hall, S., Kljakovic, M., Sibbald, B., Dwan, K., Porritt, J., & Yates, R. (2009). Enhancing care, improving quality: The six roles of the general practice nurse. *Medical Journal of Australia, 191,* 92–97.

Phillips, K. A., Haas, J. S., Liang, S.-Y., Baker, L. C., Tye, S., Kerlikowsle, K. *et al.* (2004). Are gatekeeper requirements associated with cancer screening utilization? *Health Services Research, 39,* 153–178.

Polaschek, N. R. (1998). Cultural safety: A new concept in nursing people of different ethnicities. *Journal of Advanced Nursing, 27,* 452–457.

Primary Health Care Research and Information Service. (2010). *Fast Facts: General Practice Size in Australia 2005–06 to 2007–08.* www.phcris.org.au/fastfacts/fact.php?id=4970&search=solo+practices.

Propp, K. M., Apker, J., Ford, W. S. Z., Wallace, N., Serbenski, M., & Hofmeister, N. (2010). Meeting the complex needs of the health care team: Identification of nurse-team communication practices perceived to enhance patient outcomes. *Qualitative Health Research, 20,* 15–28.

Proude, E., Britt, H., & Conigrave, K. M. (2006). The relationship between self-reported alcohol intake and the morbidities managed by GPs in Australia. *BMC Family Practice, 7,* 17.

Psychology Board of Australia. (2011). *Registration Standards.* www.psychologuboard.gov.au/Registration-Standards.aspx.

Roxon, N. (2011). *Community Input Sought for New GP Super Clinics.* www.health.gov.au/internet/ministers/publishing.nsf/Content/re-yr11-nr008.htm.

Royal Australian College of General Practitioners. (2010). *All About Providing Focussed Psychological Strategies.* www.racgp.org.au/gpmhsc/fps.

Russell, G., & Mitchell, G. (2002). Primary care reform: View from Australia. *Canadian Family Physician, 48,* 440–443.

Sharp, L. K., & Lipsky, M. S. (2002). Screening for depression across the lifespan: A review of measures for use in primary care settings. *American Family Physician, 66,* 1001–1008.

Sheehan, D., Robertson, L., & Ormond, T. (2007). Comparison of language used and patterns of communication in interprofessional and multidisciplinary teams. *Journal of Interprofessional Care, 21,* 17–30.

Slade, T., Johnston, A., Teesson, M., Whiteford, H., Burgess, P., Pirkis, J., & Saw, S. (2009). *The Mental Health of Australians 2. Report on the 2007 National Survey of Mental Health and Wellbeing.* Canberra: Department of Health and Ageing.

Sorrell-Jones, J. (1997). The challenge of making it real: Interdisciplinary practice in a "seamless" organization. *Nurse Administration Quarterly, 21,* 20–30.

Southern, D. M., Young, D., Dunt, D., Appleby, N. J., & Batterham, R. W. (2002). Integration of primary health care services: Perceptions of Australian general practitioners, non-general practitioner health service providers and consumers at the general practice – primary care interface. *Evaluation and Program Planning, 25,* 47–59.

Wakerman, J. (2004). Defining remote health. *Australian Journal of Rural Health, 12,* 210–214.

Wakerman, J., Humphreys, J. S., Wells, R., Kuipers, P., Entwistle, P., & Jones, J. (2008). Primary health care delivery models in rural and remote Australia: *A systematic review. BMC Health Services Research, 8,* doi:27610.1186/1472-6963-8-276.

Williams, R. (1999). Cultural safety: What does it mean for our work practice? *Australian and New Zealand Journal of Public Health, 23,* 213–214.

Index

Applied Topics in Health Psychology, First Edition. Edited by M. L. Caltabiano and L. Ricciardelli.
© 2013 John Wiley & Sons, Ltd. Published 2013 by John Wiley & Sons, Ltd.

Lightning Source UK Ltd.
Milton Keynes UK
UKHW03f1301131018
330485UK00001B/2/P